249 AT WAR

249

AT WAR

Brian Cull

GRUB STREET · LONDON

Published by
Grub Street
The Basement
10 Chivalry Road
London SW11 1HT

British Library Cataloguing in Publication Data

Cull, Brian
    249: with fists and heels: the authorised history of the RAF's top scoring squadron of WWII
    1. Great Britain. Royal Air Force. Squadron, No.249 — History.
    2. World War, 1939-1945 — Aerial operations, British.
    3. Great Britain — History, Military — 20th century.
    I. Title. II. Galea, Frederick. III. Two four nine. IV. Two hundred and forty nine.
    358.4'00941

ISBN 1 898697 49 3

Typeset by Pearl Graphics, Hemel Hempstead
Printed and bound by Biddles Ltd, Guildford and King's Lynn

Brian Cull is the author of the following Grub Street titles:

AIR WAR FOR YUGOSLAVIA, GREECE AND CRETE, 1940-41 with Christopher Shores
    and Nicola Malizia

MALTA: THE HURRICANE YEARS, 1940-41 with Christopher Shores and Nicola Malizia

MALTA: THE SPITFIRE YEAR, 1942 with Christopher Shores and Nicola Malizia

BLOODY SHAMBLES Volume 1 with Christopher Shores and Yasuho Izawa

BLOODY SHAMBLES Volume 2 with Christopher Shores and Yasuho Izawa

SPITFIRES OVER ISRAEL with Shlomo Aloni and David Nicolle

TWELVE DAYS IN MAY with Bruce Lander and Heinrich Weiss

WINGS OVER SUEZ with David Nicolle and Shlomo Aloni

Contents

Acknowledgements

This book could not have been compiled without the generous assistance of many former 249ers, including a number of veterans of World War II. I am particularly indebted to Marshal of the Royal Air Force Sir John Grandy GCB GCVO KBE DSO who, despite ill health, insisted on reading the draft and has kindly provided a Foreword; Wg Cdr Laddie Lucas CBE DSO DFC, also in poor health, who has nevertheless written a splendid Malta Introduction; Wg Cdr Tom Neil DFC AFC for permitting use of many extracts from his excellent books relating to his 249 experiences; to Sqn Ldr Mac McCaig MBE AFC, Leighton Fletcher, Terry Gladwell, and Brian Cooper for permission to quote from their respective unpublished manuscripts/journals; Mac, as Hon Sec of the Squadron Association, was instrumental in advising members of the impending history and subsequently provided many leads. Thanks are also due to Spy Boulton for permission to use his version of the Squadron's 1944/45 history as the basis for Chapters Eleven and Twelve of this book.

Among those who have kindly provided recollections, anecdotes, copies of logbooks, photographs etc which have enriched and enhanced this history of 249, of one of the Royal Air Force's most illustrious squadrons, are Sqn Ldr John Alton, Sqn Ldr Doug Barfoot, Wg Cdr Butch Barton OBE DFC, Bill Bones, Alf Branch, Ken Browne, Bob Byrne, Joe Chilton, Ray Crompton, John Dickerson, Wg Cdr Barry Dove AFC, Sqn Ldr Charles Edmondson DSO, the late Fred Etchells, Dave Ferraby, John Gardner, Eric Geddes, Tony Gronert, Cyril Hampshire, Grp Capt Alan Hastings OBE, Roy Jones, Sqn Ldr Tom Lecky-Thompson, the late Sqn Ldr Gerald Lewis DFC, Sqn Ldr Jock Maitland DFC(US), Bill Monkman DFM, Bryan Montgomery, Sqn Ldr Harry Moon, Denis Moyes, Don Nicholson DFC, Sqn Ldr Charles Palliser DFC, Sqn Ldr Bob Sergeant, Grp Capt Charlie Slade, Wg Cdr Peter Steib OBE DFC, George Stroud, Air Marshal Sir John Sutton KCB, Sqn Ldr Tam Syme DFC, Sqn Ldr Jack te Kloot DSO, ARF Tommy Thompson DFC, Jerry Turner, Dave Welch, Sqn Ldr Pat Wells DSO, Sqn Ldr David Williams MBE, and Wg Cdr John Young AFC. Should I have unwittingly omitted any contributor, please accept my apology.

My gratitude is also extended to the following friends and fellow aviation writers for their contributions, in particular Frederick Galea, Hon Sec of Malta's National War Museum Association, who supplied many of the photographs used in the book, and to his associate Fred Coldman; Chris Shores and Nicola Malizia, with whom I co-authored two books which covered 249's exploits at Malta during the siege years of 1941-42, on which Chapters Five through to Nine of this book are largely based. Flt Lt Andy Thomas was, as ever, most generous with the loan of photographs. Jack Foreman, Russell Guest, Dennis Newton, Dr Alfred Price, Tony Rodgers, Mike Schoeman, Paul Sortehaug, Andrew Stamatopoulos, Michael Payne, and Trevor Williams, all contributed in one way or another; and special thanks to Mr Jack Lee. Similarly, the staff of AHB3 of the Ministry of Defence, the Public Record Office and the Bury St Edmunds Public Library are to be thanked for their assistance. Last but by no means least, my wife Val must be thanked for her untiring dedication to this study, for she spent many lonely hours at the Public Record Office extracting details from the Squadron records. Finally, I thank Mr John Davies of Grub Street for yet another excellent production.

Foreword

by

Marshal of The Royal Air Force Sir John Grandy GCB GCVO KBE DSO

Commanding Officer of 249 Squadron, May – December 1940

Brian Cull is to be congratulated on the painstaking and far-reaching research which has enabled him to put this book together.

The early chapters record the day-to-day lives of those members of 249 Squadron who were actively engaged in the Royal Air Force's two biggest turning point air defence battles of World War II — the defence of the United Kingdom and the defence of Malta. Repetitive maybe, but this is nevertheless a true reflection of the relentless, tiring and continuous pressures under which both contestants operated in those historic times.

The remaining chapters reflect how 249 Squadron demonstrated its ability to continue to fly with its well-known and well-proven disciplined and aggressive spirit in the ground-attack role.

John Grandy

John Grandy MRAF

Windsor, May 1997

Malta Introduction

by

Wg Cdr P.B. 'Laddie' Lucas CBE DSO DFC

Commanding Officer of 249 Squadron, June – July 1942

One evening, long after the end of World War II, my good German friend, Eduard Neumann, came to dine with me in London. He was then staying for a day or two with his country's representative at the Court of St James.

Neumann had been an exceptionally able and popular Luftwaffe commander in wartime. He had fought with his Messerschmitt wing during the break-through in the West in 1940 and throughout the Battle of Britain. Thereafter promotion followed rapidly and soon he was posted to be the Kommodore of Jagdgeschwader 27, the Luftwaffe group supporting General Erwin Rommel and his Afrika Korps in Libya — a tough assignment. In that capacity, he soon became familiar with the fluctuating fortunes of the Desert War.

"Edu," I said, "you were in the thick of the fighting in Libya and saw everything at first hand, tell me — what impact did Malta really make upon the outcome of the North African campaign?" Neumann put his knife and fork down on his plate and held up a cautionary finger for emphasis. "Malta," he said, "was the key. You must read Kesselring."

I did indeed read Kesselring — Field Marshal, genial Bavarian aristocrat, commander of Fliegerkorps II in Sicily and C-in-C South throughout most of the Malta Siege, and the Mediterranean and North African battles. As I read on I found the quote that Neumann had in mind:

> "To guarantee supplies [to the Afrika Korps in Libya] the capture of Malta was necessary . . . The abandonment of this project was the first deathblow to the whole undertaking in North Africa . . . The one fatal blunder was the abandoning [by Hitler] of the plan to invade Malta. When this happened the subsequent course of events [the loss of North Africa] was almost inevitable."

Prime Minister Churchill saw probably more clearly than anyone on the Allied side the strategic importance of the Island as a base for our strike aircraft and the Royal Navy's submarines, delivering their devastating assault on Rommel's convoys as they fought their hazardous passage southwards, across the Mediterranean from southern European ports, to Libya. His repetitive signals to General Aucklineck, commanding the Allied forces in the Middle East, sent with the full support of the War Cabinet in London, left no possible doubt about this understanding:

> "We are determined that Malta shall not be allowed to fall without a battle being fought by your whole army for its retention."

But to hold the beleaguered base, and offer some limited chance for vital convoys to be run through, the Royal Air Force had, first, to wrest control of the daylight air over it in the face of massive odds represented by the Luftwaffe's front-line strength on the Sicilian airfields, little more than 60 miles away.

It was against this daunting background that 249 Squadron, with its Battle of Britain honours still thick upon it, flew into Malta in May 1941 from the carrier

Ark Royal, there to play, first, with the Hurricanes and, later, with the Spitfires, its considerable part in what was to become a decisive battle of World War II.

In the chapters which now follow, Brian Cull, with the historian's enviable flair for picking out detail and fact — enemy as well as Allied — leaves us with a proud picture of the extent of the Squadron's contribution to a famous Mediterranean victory. It makes a compelling period in the Squadron's imperishable story.

Read on and savour the triumph to the full.

South Kensington, March 1997   Laddie Lucas

Dedication

As the history was about to go to print, a letter was received from one of the original members of the re-formed 249 Squadron, Bill Bones, extracts from which follow:

> "I was one of the original 249 Squadron when they formed at Church Fenton under Sqn Ldr Grandy. I was appointed to 249 Ops so got to know all the pilots and groundcrews; indeed, made some very good friends. I often think of the good and the bad times we all shared. I did manage to contact 20 of us after the war; sadly there are only four of us left alive now. However, I have managed to contact Pat Wells and, through him, Tom Neil and John Beazley, to whom I wrote and had wonderful letters back from them. So, after 57 years, us four originals were back in touch again. I am now 83-years-old, deaf as a beetle, and not too clever on my legs these days, but still here to tell the tale."

This book is dedicated to Bill and all past members of 249 Squadron, aircrew and ground personnel; to those who survived "to tell the tale", and to those who paid the supreme sacrifice.

Comparative Ranks of the RAF, Luftwaffe and Regia Aeronautica

RAF	LUFTWAFFE	REGIA AERONAUTICA
Group Captain (Grp Capt)	Oberst (Obst)	Colonello (Col)
Wing Commander (Wg Cdr)	Oberstleutnant (Obstlt)	Tenente Colonello (Ten Col)
Squadron Leader (Sqn Ldr)	Major (Maj)	Maggiore (Magg)
Flight Lieutenant (Flt Lt)	Hauptmann (Hptm)	Capitano (Cap)
Flying Officer (Flg Off)	Oberleutnant (Oblt)	Tenente (Ten)
Pilot Officer (Plt Off)	Leutnant (Lt)	Sottotenente (Sottoten)
Warrant Officer (Wt Off)	Fahnenjunker (Fhj)	Maresciallo (Mar)
Flight Sergeant (Flt Sgt)	Oberfeldwebel (Obfw)	Sergente Maggiore (Serg Magg)
Sergeant (Sgt)	Feldwebel (Fw)	Sergente (Serg)
Corporal (Cpl)	Unteroffizier (Uffz)	Aviere Scelto (AvSc)
Leading Aircraftsman (LAC)	Obergefreiter (Obgfr)	1° Aviere (1°Av)
Aircraftsman 1 (AC 1)	Gefreiter (Gfr)	Aviere (Av)

Glossary

Luftwaffe

Stab	= Staff Flight
Staffel	= RAF Squadron (although a Staffel comprised only nine aircraft)
Gruppe	= RAF Wing (a Gruppe comprised three Staffeln)
Geschwader	= RAF Group (a Geschwader comprised three Gruppen)
JG	= Jagdgeschwader (short-range fighter group)
ZG	= Zerstörergeschwader (long-range fighter group)
KG	= Kampfgeschwader (bomber group)
LG	= Lehrgeschwader (instructional/operational development group)
StG	= Stukageschwader (dive-bomber group)
NJG	= Nachtjagdgeschwader (night fighter group)
Aufkl	= Aufklärungsgruppe (reconnaissance wing)
KüFlGr	= Küstenfliegergruppe (coastal reconnaissance wing)
ErproGr	= Erprobungsgruppe (experimental test wing)
Seenot	= Seenotflugkommando (Air-Sea Rescue service)

Regia Aeronautica

Squadriglia	= RAF Squadron (a squadriglia comprised nine aircraft)
Gruppo	= RAF Wing (a gruppo comprised three squadriglie)
Stormo	= RAF Group (a stormo comprised two gruppi)
CT	= Caccia Terrestre (fighters, land based)
BT	= Bombardamento Terrestre (bombers, land based)
RM	= Ricognizione Marittima (reconnaissance, water based)

In the beginning . . .

On 18 August 1918, 249 Squadron was formed by an amalgamation of 400, 401 and 450 Seaplane Flights at Dundee, on the east coast of Scotland, where a RNAS seaplane station had been established in 1914. Initially under the command of Maj E.V.S. Wilberforce and equipped with a variety of seaplanes including Short S184s, Fairey Hamble Babies and Sopwith Babies, the Squadron flew coastal patrol and anti-submarine duties over the North Sea as part of 78 Wing. It remained at Dundee until April 1919 when, without its aircraft, it moved to the RNAS station at Killinghome in Lincolnshire. A new Commanding Officer, Maj J.E.B. MacLean, arrived in August but the Squadron was disbanded on 8 October 1919. It was to be almost 21 years before its resurrection.

Chapter One

THE SQUADRON IS REBORN

May – August 1940

"Flt Lt Nicolson remained in his cockpit in order to get a burst at a ME110 which appeared in front of him. He was then forced to abandon his aircraft owing to the heat."

249 Squadron Record Book, 16 August 1940

On 10 May 1940, German forces launched their invasion of the Low Countries, sweeping all before them in a matter of weeks. In support of the invasion, the Luftwaffe was able to call upon almost 3,700 operational aircraft, most of which were bombers and front-line fighters. Facing this armada was the paper-powerful French Armée de l'Air, together with the much smaller Belgian Aeronautique Militaire and Dutch Militaire Luchtvaart, supported by half a dozen RAF fighter squadrons, plus a similar number of RAF light bomber and reconnaissance units with the British Expeditionary Force. Within days, RAF reinforcements and replacements were being rushed to France at the expense of Home Command. In just twelve days of severe fighting the RAF lost almost 400 Hurricanes in France and Belgium, many abandoned on the airfields as unserviceable as the retreat got under way. 56 RAF fighter pilots were killed during this brief period, 18 taken prisoner and 36 wounded. The Phoney War was well and truly over.

To help replace these losses, the Air Ministry authorised the formation of a number of new fighter squadrons. One of these was 249 Squadron, which was officially re-formed at RAF Church Fenton, about 15 miles east of Leeds, on 16 May, at the height of the German invasion of the Low Countries. To command the new squadron came Sqn Ldr John Grandy from 13 FTS at RAF Drem, where he had been Chief Flying Instructor since May 1939*:

"My orders were to get 249 Squadron formed and trained up to a standard acceptable to day-fighter operations in the shortest possible time. One of my first moves was to fly to Cranwell. At that time I had had some experience of our University Air squadrons and had formed a high opinion of the calibre of undergraduates who chose to learn to fly in those splendid volunteer units. I knew that a number of these stalwarts were by then continuing their training at Cranwell and it was quite clear to me that if my Squadron was to be as good as I wanted it to be, some of them would be a great asset and, furthermore, make my operational training task that much easier and quicker of achievement."

To assist in the day-to-day running of the Squadron came Flg Off Ewart Lohmeyer DFC as Adjutant, of whom Sqn Ldr Grandy noted:

"He was known to us all as 'Loh', was much older than me and a veteran of the First War where he served in the Royal Flying Corps as an observer (he wore a Flying Badge carrying an 'O') and that was where he won his DFC. He was a tremendous support to me on the admin side of running the Squadron."

However, the first pilots to arrive were Flt Lt R.G. Kellett from 616 Squadron and Flg Off J.R.C. Young, a QFI posted from 603 Squadron, who was to assist with training the new pilots. They arrived at Church Fenton in a Battle light-bomber (N2027) flown by Kellett, and were followed

---

* Sqn Ldr Grandy had served with 54 Squadron (1932-35) and 604 Squadron (1935-36). The following year he was posted to the London University Air Squadron, which flew from Northolt, as Adjutant and Flying Instructor.

next day by Flg Off R.A. Barton from 41 Squadron who was promoted to Flight Lieutenant on arrival; Flg Off J.B. Nicolson was transferred from 72 Squadron, but other pilots posted to the Squadron were less experienced. A signal from HQ 13 Group arrived on 16 May informing the Squadron that eight Hurricanes had been allocated as initial equipment from 41 Group, and two of these (P2767 and P2769) were collected the same day from 19 MU at RAF St Athan by Flt Lt Kellett and Flg Off Young. However, next day a further signal cancelled the Hurricane allocation and advised that the Squadron was to receive Spitfires instead, and that the Squadron was to move to RAF Leconfield, 30 miles to the east. The move was made next day. The two Hurricanes from St Athan were left behind and were re-allocated to 242 Squadron.

18 May, therefore, found the Squadron in transit to Leconfield; two pilots had travelled to 27 MU at RAF Shawbury to collect the first two of 20 Spitfires allocated to the Squadron. Two Miles Masters were also delivered to the Squadron for pilot training, while Sqn Ldr D.F.W. Atcherley of the Air Ministry arrived by air from London to assist in its establishment. Atcherley had authority to circumvent normal channels to ensure that all the Squadron's equipment was obtained as rapidly as possible — thus, the Squadron had 16 fully operational Spitfires, together with all maintenance equipment, within four days of forming! At 1730, the Squadron was visited by Air Vice-Marshal R.E. Saul DFC, AOC 13 Group, who advised that Air Chief Marshal Sir Hugh Dowding GCB GCVO CMG ADC, the AOC-in-C Fighter Command, had ordered that the Squadron was to become operationally trained in the shortest possible time.

Over the next few days more pilots arrived, including Plt Off J.R.B. Meaker from 46 Squadron via 263 Squadron and Sgt J.M. Bentley Beard from 609 Squadron. Bryan Meaker, although born in County Cork was brought up and educated in Sussex and had been a reporter on the *Chichester Observer*. The remainder of the Squadron's complement of pilots arrived directly from Flying Training Schools, sufficient in numbers to form two Flights:

A Flight	**B Flight**
Flt Lt R.G. Kellett	Flt Lt R.A. Barton
Flg Off J.R.C. Young	Flg Off J.B. Nicolson
Plt Off T.F. Neil (8 FTS)	Plt Off J.R.B. Meaker
Sgt J.M. Bentley Beard	Plt Off J.H.S. Beazley (Cranwell)
Sgt E.A. Fletcher (11 FTS)	Plt Off P.A. Loweth (11 FTS)
Sgt R. Smithson (10 FTS)	Sgt D.J. Pether (8 FTS)
	Sgt P.A. Rowell (14 FTS)

Flt Lt Kellett (known as Boozy to his friends) from County Durham had joined the Auxiliary Air Force in 1933, while Flt Lt Barton, a Canadian known as Butch to his contemporaries, hailed from Kamloops, British Columbia, and had joined the RAF in 1936. Both had many hours in their logbooks. Posted to the Squadron were Flg Off W. Smith as Engineer Officer and Plt Off G.D. Gibson as Intelligence Officer; however, the latter's stay was brief and he was re-posted four days later, being replaced by Flg Off H. Young from the Air Ministry, while Smith also soon departed to be replaced as Engineer Officer by Plt Off H.R. Tucker.

Flying training began with all haste. Plt Off Neil soloed in P9506 on 22 May and was allocated P9332 as his personal aircraft, which was soon to bear the markings GN-D. By the end of May, air-to-air and air-to-ground practices had been undertaken by all pilots, using towed targets at RAF Acklington and a marker dropped in Filey Bay. On arrival at Acklington, Flg Off Nicolson forgot to lower his undercarriage and consequently damaged his aircraft. More pilots arrived, these direct from 5 OTU at RAF Aston Down: Plt Off I.N. Bayles and Sgt M.C.B. Boddington joined A Flight, while Flg Off D.G. Parnall and Sgt A.D.W. Main went to B Flight; Parnall had been commissioned in the RAFO in 1936 before transferring to the RAFVR two years later. However, within two weeks, Bayles and Boddington were re-posted to 152 and 234 Squadrons respectively. Next day (10 June) four more pilots arrived from 5 OTU: Plt Off M.A. King and Sgt F.W.G. Killingback joined A Flight and Plt Off J.T. Crossey, a South African from Johannesburg, and Sgt H.J. Davidson went to B Flight. The same day a further signal arrived from 13 Group HQ advising that the Spitfires were being withdrawn and were to be replaced by Hurricanes, and the first two, P2910 — which became the CO's aircraft, coded GN-J — and P3576 (both ex-234 Squadron aircraft), arrived on 11 June. More arrived over the next two days. On 13 June the Squadron received a signal from Air Vice-Marshal Saul, which read:

> "I note with much satisfaction that 249 Squadron have carried out 329 hours 20 minutes flying during the week ending 8 June. Please convey my congratulations to all ranks on their most creditable performance."

Four new pilots arrived on 15 June, Flg Off P.H.V. Wells, a South African, Plt Off P.R.F. Burton (also a South African, the son of a former Union Minister of Finance and Railways), Plt Off R.G.A. Barclay and Plt Off R.D.S. Fleming — all of whom had attended FTS at RAF Cranwell, as had Plt Off Beazley:

> "Like a number of others in the Squadron, I came direct from Cranwell FTS and the University Air Squadron. We were a very happy bunch, and the thing that impressed us was the complete absence of bullshit and the friendly reception given to us by the regulars, and the Flight Commanders."

These were the men Sqn Ldr Grandy had specifically earmarked for his Squadron. The four latest arrivals were immediately sent to 5 OTU for seven days further training. At the same time two NCO pilots departed, having been considered insufficiently trained, Sgt Fletcher being transferred to 7 Bombing and Gunnery School and Sgt Pether to 12 OTU. However, Sgt P.H. Waghorn was posted to the Squadron about this time.

Excitement came to Leconfield on the night of 18/19 June, when the airfield was attacked by a lone Heinkel, apparently a straggler from the main force of 70 aircraft of KG4 and KG27 raiding targets in the Midlands and East Anglia. The intruder arrived as three Squadron pilots were undergoing night flying training. The flare-path and all lights at Leconfield were immediately extinguished and, at the same time, the three pilots were told to switch off their navigation lights and to remain airborne until the flare-path was re-lit; this occurred some 40 minutes later. No casualties were suffered during the attack and damage was negligible, all bombs — except a single small one — dropped outside the precincts of the Station. Flying training continued but not without the occasional mishap: Plt Off Meaker crashed on landing at Leconfield on 27 June when his aircraft's undercarriage failed to function; however, he was not hurt. Two days later the Squadron was considered operational, although selected pilots were sent to RAF Prestwick for further night training.

First action for the Squadron came during the afternoon of 4 July when Flg Off Young, Plt Off Neil and Sgt Smithson were vectored onto a Do17 at about 1700, as Young recalled:

> "I was stalking him from up sun, when Neil saw him and waggled his wings so that we were seen. I ordered line astern No1 Attack as the best way of intercepting, so as not to collide with No3, as the Hun dived down and to our left . . ."

Neil wrote:

> "I saw the bogey immediately, about three miles away, a slim, dark shape cruising as calm as you like between scattered white dumplings of cloud . . . A German! A Dornier 'Flying Pencil'. Going through the nonsensical No1 Attack routine, we reared up like startled pheasant chicks, dropped into line astern, then plummeted down on the Dornier . . . We shot into cloud after him and out the other side . . . He must be somewhere. Absolutely nothing! The Hun had disappeared."

Four days later, on the morning of 8 July, the Squadron opened its account as a result of an engagement between two Spitfires of 41 Squadron from RAF Catterick and a Ju88 of 9/KG4 near Scarborough. The intruder, returning from a sortie to Sunderland, although damaged, managed to evade the Spitfires only to run into three Hurricanes of B Flight's Green Section led by Flg Off Parnall off Flamborough Head. Flying at 17,000 feet, it was immediately engaged. Parnall recorded:

"I observed a Ju88 proceeding south at same height. I formed section into line astern and was about to commence No1 Attack when Spitfire observed attacking. The Spitfire fired for about three seconds then broke away, with slight smoke issuing from port engine — no evasive tactics taken by Ju88. Then commenced No1 Attack and Ju88 immediately started evasive tactics of stall turns and slow flying. I fired a nine-seconds burst, commencing 350 yards, breaking away at 40 yards. Return fire not observed."

Plt Off Beazley (Green 2) followed his leader into the attack:

"I attacked enemy after No1 had broken away. After a two-second burst, enemy stall-turned to right and I had to go into firm pitch to pull up and follow him round. Enemy entered cloud but I caught him coming out the other side and got in a burst before he again turned sharply to the left, diving slightly. I again opened fire as he straightened out. I observed white streaks coming past the starboard wing. I ceased firing as he dived into cloud again. There was a strong smell of burning metal as I went into the cloud. Enemy not seen again."

Flying No3 was Sgt Main, who reported:

"I gave a short burst before No2 broke away. Following e/a through cloud I came out to find myself on his tail, gave a burst of three to four seconds. By this time both engines appeared to be on fire. I then broke away and regained section."

The bomber (5J+AT) crashed in flames at Aldbrough near Darlington, killing the pilot, Staffel-kapitän Hptm Rohloff, although his crew — Uffz Abel, Uffz Kuhnapfel and Uffz Öchler — managed to bale out. One landed at Aldbrough close to the Caldwell farm, where one of the workers saw the German airman land and hurried to the farmhouse to warn the farmer's wife, Mrs Nora Caldwell. She tried, unsuccessfully, to telephone her husband at the Local Defence Volunteer office, and then sent the farm worker to fetch the police. When the limping German approached the farmhouse, she unwaveringly walked to the airman and gestured him to raise his hands and then relieved him of his pistol. The police arrived shortly afterwards and took him into custody. Mrs Caldwell was later awarded the OBE for her bravery and initiative. Of these initial encounters, Sqn Ldr Grandy recalled:

"Although putting myself on the readiness state during the period of these early engagements, I, much to my chagrin, invariably missed out, being fully engaged with the Master aircraft in formation training, conversion from Spitfire to Hurricane, formation and instrument flying, and what were to become the rapidly outdated attack routines. Little did I know then that I would be able to make up for this in later months."

The Squadron moved back to Church Fenton on 9 July, from where six pilots of A Flight were sent to Acklington on 15 July to carry out air firing training on the nearby ranges. Sgt Davidson crashed on landing, damaging his aircraft (L1715) although he was uninjured. The Squadron suffered its first fatality that night when a number of Hurricanes were sent off, just after midnight, to search for bombers involved in an attack on Leeds. Sgt Alistair Main, a 22-year-old Scot from Dundee, who had shared the Squadron's first victory, was killed following engine failure shortly after take-off and his Hurricane (P2995) burst into flames when it crashed into Copmanthorpe Wood, eight miles north of Church Fenton. Another Hurricane, P3057 flown by Plt Off Meaker, was damaged in a take-off accident when it struck an obstacle; Meaker subse-quently carried out a successful belly-landing on return and, although the aircraft was badly damaged, he was unhurt. None of the raiders were engaged although Flt Lt Barton caught sight of a Do17 behind him, but it was soon lost in the darkness.

A further Hurricane was lost four days later (20 July) when Flg Off Young force-landed P3154 GN-H at Wellburn Hall following engine failure; although the Hurricane collided with heavy obstruction cables, the pilot was not hurt nor was the aircraft seriously damaged:

"The Hurricane had no armour for bullet proofing of the saddle tank (forward of the instrument panel), which contained 28 gallons. It seemed worth a try to see if the tank could be emptied before switching to the wing tanks or, put another way, was the use of the gravity tank a fossil of an earlier aircraft age? It was calculated that at the engine's maximum consumption of one gallon a minute the tank would last 25-plus minutes. I taxied out on it, primed the lines of the wing tanks after take-off but switched back to centre tank and climbed away, in cloud, in a cloud formation exercise. Alas, at about 13,000 feet the engine fuel light came on — there was no power and inspite of all efforts to restore fuel flow it did not come back. I broke cloud at about 3,000 feet, saw Wellburn Hall and shaped for it. Wheels and flaps came down and when committed I saw the wires. I hopped over one, landed three points and struck the next. The prop was broken.

Why did the engine cut when the gravity tank was still almost half full? We never did find the trick. Of course, nobody was pleased with the loss of an aircraft, temporary though indeed it was. Unfortunately, it was one of the first fully modified Hurricanes with Rotol prop (wood), proofed tanks, deflector armour, pilot seat armour, metal wings and ailerons. No wonder no one was pleased, least of all myself."

Shortly after this incident Young was affected by a major sinus problem while flying at about 17,000 feet when still suffering from the after effects of a head cold:

"I really don't remember much about the flight except that it was an abortive interception of a very cunning recce aircraft, and on beginning descent I was in severe trouble. I told No2 and No3 to return and commenced a slow and painful descent. I landed covered in snot and blood and was immediately flown by an Anson to York Hospital where I was treated with cocaine (up my nose) and stainless steel tubing by an Australian ENT specialist. He succeeded in clearing me completely and I was returned to Church Fenton, sternly forbidden to fly above 2,000 feet. However, my eardrums had become infected and after such duties for about ten days, I was not improving and was ordered on sick leave to swim in the sea. The nearest unobstructed and unmined beach I knew of was at Buckie in Aberdeenshire and to my surprise I was immediately given petrol coupons to go with my wife and little boy. I remember being briefed by Grp Capt Horsley [the Station Commander] to report to the police but not to return if the invasion took place; I was to await orders under police authority. The weather was pretty good. I swam twice a day in the harbour. With no invasion I returned at the end of the week."

However, on his return to Church Fenton, Young was not allowed to fly above 2,000 feet until his condition improved and was consequently employed testing Squadron aircraft then being fitted with the new Rotol propeller*.

The Squadron lost the services of Flt Lt Kellett on 19 July when he was posted to Northolt to form and command 303 Squadron, a unit comprised mainly of Polish pilots who had escaped from Europe to continue the fight. Flg Off Nicolson was promoted to command B Flight in his place. 12 Group was obviously pleased with the way Squadron training was progressing, as the AOC sent the following message:

"I do not remember a case where a squadron has ever passed the 1,000 hour mark in a month, and this intensive effort to become operational at the earliest moment reflects the greatest effort to all concerned."

Plt Off R.E.N. Wynn joined the Squadron from 6 OTU on 4 August, followed next day by Sgt

---

* In the event, Flg Off Young did not return to operational flying duties with 249 but was later posted as an instructor to 306 Squadron, the third Polish fighter squadron to be formed within the RAF.

W.L. Davis, also from 6 OTU, and Sqn Ldr E.B. King, who was attached to the Squadron as a supernumerary to gain experience prior to taking command of his own squadron. He had flown in this capacity with 253 Squadron at RAF Turnhouse during the previous two weeks. On 6 August the Squadron diarist noted:

> "There seems to be very little activity in the north now, but things are boiling up in the south
> of England and attacks are being carried out by large numbers of enemy aircraft on convoys
> and south coast ports. We are all hoping to get a move south."

And, in fact, the Squadron was about to move to RAF Boscombe Down in Wiltshire. The new location was in the RAF Middle Wallop Sector of 10 Group, where its main priority was to be the defence of Portsmouth and Southampton. Before the move, however, there occurred a near fatal incident at Church Fenton when an armourer, working on a 73 Squadron Hurricane, inadvertently fired two rounds of .303 ammuntion, one bullet striking 249's Cpl Parry Jones who was attending a pay parade. He was rushed to York Military Hospital by ambulance.

On 14 August, the Squadron made its move to Boscombe Down. Two transport aircraft, a Bombay and a HP42 Hannibal, arrived at Church Fenton at 0930 to take key airmen and their equipment. These departed at 1035 and 1115 respectively and the remaining 34 airmen travelled by road in Squadron vehicles, followed by the Adjutant and Intelligence Officer in the CO's Hillman, while Sqn Ldr Grandy led 20 Hurricanes into the air at midday, as he recalled:

> "My wife told me that this was a very emotional occasion for wives, sweethearts and girlfriends
> gathered on the ground, watching this large formation of fighters led by me flying south on
> their way to the 'war', followed by two large transports carrying the airmen."

On arrival at Boscombe Down they were greeted by the Station Commander, Grp Capt R.S. Sorley OBE DSC DFC, with the news that:

> "The Squadron will be required to operate from dawn to dusk and provide an available section
> for night state. This section will only be called upon in an emergency."

The Squadron was soon in action. At about 1700 next day (15 August), radar stations on the Sussex and Hampshire coasts reported the approach of two large formations of aircraft and, 20 minutes later, 27 Ju87s of 1/StG1 and 20 more from II/StG2 headed for Portland, while a dozen Ju88s of I/LG1 and 15 more from II Gruppe, escorted by Bf109s of JG27 and JG53, and Bf110s of V(Z)/LG1, II and III/ZG76, were sighted by patrolling Hurricanes and Spitfires south-east of the Isle of Wight. Interceptions were made by a number of squadrons over Southampton and the Solent, but the mass of bombers forced its way inland, half making for the airfield at RNAS Worthy Down, the remainder targeting the RAF airfields at Middle Wallop and Odiham, although one attacked RAF Tangmere:

> ". . . the Station air-raid siren sounded and three of 249's Hurricanes were soon airborne.
> They were circling the airfield in an anti-clockwise direction at approximately 1,000 feet and,
> as they turned along the western leg of the circuit, three Ju87s dived out of clouds directly
> astern of them. The Stukas dived straight down one behind the other, delivered their bombs
> and pulled back into the clouds. Meanwhile, the three Hurricanes sailed serenely on,
> completely unaware of the attack." *

LAC Bill Baguley had been detailed for dispersal guard and was patrolling an area adjacent to 249's dispersal. He recalled:

> "My most vivid memory is of a Flight Lieutenant leaping on to the port mainplane of the
> nearest Hurricane, snatching his flying helmet from the control column and bellowing into the

---

* See *Action Stations 4* by Bruce Barrymore Halpenny.

microphone, 'Behind you! Behind you! For Christsake turn the bloody things round!' The whole episode was over in seconds and the only damage was three cows killed in a nearby field." *

Meanwhile, the Squadron had been ordered to patrol RAF Warmwell at 15,000 feet and during the patrol, B Flight encountered 11 Ju88s escorted by an estimated 50 Bf110s near Middle Wallop. The six Hurricanes of B Flight engaged the escort, which also came under attack by Spitfires of 609 Squadron from Warmwell. Flt Lt Barton and Plt Off Meaker of Blue Section each claimed a Messerschmitt shot down, while Flg Off Parnall, Plt Off Beazley and Sgt Davidson of Green Section jointly claimed a third in the Ringwood area. In addition to his claim for one destroyed, Barton claimed a second as damaged, and reported:

> "Blue Section was ordered to patrol Ringwood area . . . I observed 30-50 e/a and ordered No1 Attack on rearmost section. E/a turned and attacked Blue Section. Fired two-seconds burst, 30° deflection on ME110 and observed smoke from engine; then attacked another ME110 and fired two bursts with full deflection. Saw my bullets entering fuselage behind pilot; smoke poured from starboard engine. I followed e/a down and it crashed about four miles NW of Romsey."

The Bf110 claimed by Flt Lt Barton was apparently shared with two pilots of 609 Squadron and was probably a Stab II/ZG76 machine which crashed at Broadlands near Romsey at 1755, in which Uffz Karl-Rudolf Röhrich and Uffz Theodor Neymeyer were killed.

Of his victory, Plt Off Meaker wrote:

> "I was Blue 2 and followed Blue Leader (Flt Lt Barton) in No1 Attack but got into a spin. On coming out of the spin I saw four ME110 circling and picked out one, giving full deflection burst on beam. He took violent evasive action, but I gave him further bursts and saw streams of white vapour from both engines. I followed him to 500 feet and saw him crash about ten miles north of Southampton."

Apparently the same Messerschmitt was also under attack by a Spitfire of 609 Squadron. Their victim was M8+WP of 6/ZG76 in which Fw Franz Wagner and Uffz Fritz Sporl were killed when it crashed and exploded at West Willow near Romsey at 1745. Plt Off Crossey (Blue 3) reported engaging a Bf110 which was following Meaker. He then attacked another formation but broke away when engaged by three fighters which he believed were He113s (*sic*). His assailants were probably Spitfires since no Luftwaffe single-seaters participated in this action. Meanwhile Green Leader, Flg Off Parnall, reported:

> "Large numbers of e/a were sighted at about 15,000 feet, which began to circle. Ordered line astern No1 Attack on straggler ME110 at 350 yards. I opened fire with two-seconds burst, then six-seconds burst. Observed grey smoke from starboard engine, which increased in density. Continuous return fire encountered from top of fuselage. Broke away at 100 yards and re-formed section after Green 2 and 3 had fired. My aircraft had six bullet holes in wings and tail. Port spar broken."

Plt Off Beazley added:

> "I was Green 2 and followed Green Leader into attack and observed tracer fire by enemy aircraft, which suddenly ceased. Greyish smoke from starboard engine after No1 broke away and it increased after my four-seconds burst. I broke away at 150 yards and noticed that the enemy aircraft dropped behind. No damage to my aircraft. I did attacks on two other aircraft circling in line astern, about 15 in number, but was unable to observe effects."

---

* See *Action Stations 4* by Bruce Barrymore Halpenny.

A Messerschmitt from 5 Staffel flown by Oblt Gerhard Bremer which exploded alongside the Farley Road at Slackstead may have also been a victim of one of 249's pilots; the remains of Bremer and his gunner, Uffz Leo Pauli, were buried in the nearby village churchyard at Hursley, as two Unknown Airmen. Meanwhile, Sqn Ldr King, flying on his own, attacked a formation of Ju88s:

> "Sighted 12 Ju88s in three loose formations of three with one in the box south of Middle Wallop. Attacked outside e/a on port side of formation; gave two deflection shots from beam and fired rest of ammunition from dead astern. Closed from 400 to 200 yards. E/a glided out of formation with slight smoke from port engine but still under control."

A Flight did not make contact. Despite the attacks by 249 and 609 Squadrons, and other units, the raiders were able to reach Middle Wallop where two hangars were hit: two Blenheims were destroyed and five damaged, although little damage was inflicted on Worthy Down and Odiham. II and III/ZG76 lost a dozen Bf110s in this action, while eight Ju88s of LG1 were also shot down; additionally, a pilot of 609 Squadron attacked a Blenheim in mistake for a Ju88, the damaged aircraft crash-landing at Middle Wallop.

Next day (16 August) a dozen Ju88s escorted by 18 Bf110s (possibly from II/ZG2) carried out a sharp raid on Gosport, causing some damage and killing six servicemen. Spitfires of 234 Squadron were scrambled but failed to make contact. A dozen Hurricanes led by Flt Lt Barton were sent off at 1305 to patrol between Poole and Southampton, where a formation of Bf109Es was sighted. Red Section led by Flt Lt Nicolson (P3576 GN-A) was sent to investigate but the three Hurricanes were bounced from above and astern. Nicolson's aircraft was hit and set afire. Of the ensuing few minutes, the Squadron's diarist wrote:

> "Flt Lt Nicolson remained in his cockpit in order to get a burst at a ME110 which appeared in front of him. He was then forced to abandon his aircraft owing to the heat."

Plt Off Martyn King's aircraft, P3616 GN-F, was also badly damaged by a cannon shell and he, too, baled out. As they floated down on their parachutes, barely a quarter of a mile apart, both Nicolson and King were fired at by soldiers of a local artillery detachment, who were joined by some Local Defence Volunteers, in the mistaken belief that they were German paratroopers. Whether King was hit is not known, but his parachute canopy collapsed and he crashed through a tall tree before falling onto the lawn of a house in Clifton Road, Shirley, a suburb of Southampton, where he died in the arms of Mr Fred Poole, who lived nearby. Meanwhile Nicolson, in great pain from his burns, was further wounded by shotgun pellets:

> ". . . a Home Guard [sic] Sergeant opened up on Nicolson with a shotgun, the pellets hitting him on his right side . . . a butcher's delivery boy ran over to him as he landed and, looking down at the severely burned and bleeding airman, shouted at the Sergeant: 'Did you do this?' When the NCO replied that he had, the lad hit out; a fight started and it was only the arrival of a policeman and an ambulance that saved the Sergeant from being lynched. Although the vehicle was intended for Nicolson, it was used instead to evacuate the severely-beaten Sergeant!" *

Nicolson was eventually taken to the Royal Southampton Hospital. His Hurricane is believed to have crashed on the playing field at Rownham's School on the outskirts of Southampton, while King's aircraft fell in a field beside the A3057 near the village of Ashfield. The third Hurricane of Red Section, P3870 flown by Sqn Ldr King, was hit in several places but he was able to reach base safely. When news of the action reached Boscombe Down, Sqn Ldr Grandy immediately scrambled with four more Hurricanes but by the time they reached the area the enemy fighters had departed.

A few days later Nicolson, from his hospital bed, sent a report of the action to Sqn Ldr Grandy:

---

* See *The Blitz: Then and Now*, Volume One, edited by Winston Ramsey.

"I was proceeding with Red Section . . . when I noticed three enemy aircraft some distance away to the left. I informed Butch [Flt Lt Barton], who told me to go and investigate. As however the three unfortunates ran into 12 Spitfires long before I got in range, I turned round to rejoin Butch, climbing from 15,000 feet to 17,500 feet so that I could catch him when I saw him. As I approached Southampton I heard Yellow Leader shout 'Tally-ho, one mile to port' and immediately turned off to join the scrap, at the same time reaching for my map. As I was opening my map, I was struck in the cockpit by four successive cannon shells; the first of which burst on the hood; the second in the reserve petrol tanks, which immediately fired; the third on my left foot.

On hearing the first bang, I had stuffed my nose down and turned hard right and, as the flames came back, pulled my feet up on the seat. I noticed, to my astonishment, during the course of this dive a ME110 diving at approximately the same angle and converging with my course — I opened fire at approximately 200 yards and fired until I could bear the heat no more. I am not prepared to swear whether my trigger button was at 'safe' or 'fire' but I do know the sight was switched on . . . four separate eyewitnesses from the ground however confirm this as a victory. The 110 zig-zagged as soon as I opened fire, although this may have been due to the rear gunner sighting me, and shortly afterwards ceased zig-zagging and steepened its angle of dive. I see no reason to believe, however, that this was in any way out of control, and I jumped at this point, striking my head on the roof! I tore the hood open and jumped again only to be brought back by the straps! I pulled the pin and jumped a third time, kicking the stick with my left foot as I did so, leaving the plane like a cork from a champagne bottle." *

From available records it is not clear whether the Hurricanes were shot down by Bf110s or Bf109Es. Certainly both types were active in the area, Hptm Heinz Bretnütz of 6/JG53 alone claiming two Hurricanes in quick succession at about this time. With the loss of Flt Lt Nicolson to the Squadron, command of A Flight passed to Flg Off Parnall, who was promoted to Acting Flight Lieutenant.

Although the tempo of German attacks was on the increase, the Squadron was not heavily committed at this stage. However, patrols were maintained and Red Section was ordered to intercept a Ju88 during the morning of 21 August but no contact was made. Sqn Ldr Grandy and Plt Off Neil were then sent off to intercept another but it escaped into cloud. During the day Sgt Waghorn was posted to 111 Squadron at Debden, while Sqn Ldr King left the Squadron to take command of 151 Squadron at Stapleford Tawney; he was killed in action nine days later.

The next success came when B Flight had a brief encounter with a small number of Bf109Es on the afternoon of 24 August, while the Squadron patrolled over the Isle of Wight. The Messerschmitts were part of the escort for a Ju88 raid on Portsmouth which killed in excess of 100 civilians and injured almost 300, including 50 Royal Navy personnel.

Spitfires from Middle Wallop had initially been scrambled to counter the raid, 249 meeting part of the indirect escort. One of the Messerschmitts was engaged at 1720 by Flt Lt Barton:

"Blue Section sighted e/a at 19,000 feet proceeding south. [I] fired a head-on attack on a ME109 which was firing at [me], then turned away to attack others. A few seconds later saw e/a diving towards sea, emitting white vapour. The e/a were much too far above for us to make an effective attack."

Plt Off Wynn (Blue 3) added:

". . . fired on a ME109 (which attacked from beam) giving e/a a half-second burst with deflection as it passed diagonally. Almost immediately after saw a ME109 diving towards sea and half on its back off south coast of Isle of Wight, emitting white smoke."

---

* Flt Lt Nicolson was transferred to the RAF Hospital at Halton for specialised treatment; then to Palace Hotel Torquay which had been requisitioned by the RAF as a convalescent home. On 15 November, the award of the Victoria Cross was announced.

Plt Off Meaker (Blue 2) observed a Messerschmitt fall into the sea although it seems unlikely that this was 249's victim. The aircraft attacked by Barton and Wynn was probably that flown by Fw Otto Werner of 6/JG2 who crash-landed his damaged Messerschmitt near Le Havre following combat off the Isle of Wight.

The Squadron lost the temporary services of Hurricanes P2910 and P3660 following an uneventful patrol on the afternoon of 26 August; the former, due to a frozen radiator, was force-landed by Sqn Ldr Grandy at Tangmere, where Plt Off Burton landed the latter with a broken tailwheel. Plt Off Wynn made news again on the last day of the month when he force-landed L2067 near Whitchurch, after engine failure during a routine patrol; he was unhurt. On the same day the Squadron received instructions from Group HQ to move 14 aircraft, all pilots and 36 airmen for maintenance duties to RAF North Weald in Essex (about 20 miles west of Chelmsford), where they were to relieve 56 Squadron. The transfer was to take place next day, 1 September.

Chapter Two

THE THIN BLUE LINE

September 1940

"Foolishly, I had not noticed what must have been a 109 behind me at this time. There was a loud bang, I was hit in the face and there were flames on the cockpit floor. I decided to bale out . . ."

Sqn Ldr John Grandy, Commanding Officer 249 Squadron

At daybreak on 1 September, 249 was therefore released from its operational state to allow the transfer of aircraft and personnel to RAF North Weald. Two Flamingos and a DH87 of 24 Squadron arrived in the morning to convey the Squadron's airmen and their small kit. The transports departed at 1130 but, shortly afterwards, North Weald's Commanding Officer, Wg Cdr F.V. Beamish DSO AFC, telephoned Sqn Ldr Grandy to say the transfer of ground personnel was unnecessary since the idea of the move was to relieve the battle-fatigued pilots of 56 Squadron. It was agreed that (a) 249 maintenance personnel should return to Boscombe Down and (b) 249 pilots should fly to North Weald in their Hurricanes, although these aircraft would be flown back to Boscombe Down by 56 Squadron pilots. The change of pilots and not aircraft was necessary due to 56 Squadron's aircraft operating with VHF radio while 249 had the old TR9 HF radio which was not suitable for 11 Group operations.

Fourteen Hurricanes eventually took off and headed eastwards in formation, the CO in the lead in P2910 GN-J. On arrival at North Weald the Squadron was welcomed by Wg Cdr Beamish and the Sector Ops officer, Sqn Ldr John Cherry (Sqn Ldr Grandy's brother-in-law) who gave a short lecture to all pilots on the code words in use in the Sector, and on the use of VHF radio. 56 Squadron left shortly afterwards. There was no time to repaint the inherited Hurricanes with 249's GN code letters and they were subsequently operated in the US codes of 56 Squadron until time could be found to repaint them. The CO selected as his personal aircraft R4229, which bore the code US-J. Initial impressions of 249's pilots by the groundcrews of 56 Squadron were none too flattering, as Cpl Eric Clayton recalled:

"We were sad to see our pilots go, having shared so much of the battle together, and not being keen to take on a new bunch. Indeed, we started by being suspicious and rather critical of them. The first few days reinforced this attitude. 249 Squadron were immediately involved in this intense activity. However, the groundcrew were dismayed to witness the nonchalant attitude of 249 Squadron pilots when ordered to scramble for combat sorties. They strolled casually out to the aircraft whilst groundcrews stood by them, engines running, waiting with disbelief. They seemed unaware of the critical need for urgency. Over the months, 56 Squadron had perfected a rapid response when the alarm bell rang to scramble. However, within days of intense activity the lesson had been learned, prejudices forgotten and an efficient team spirit established."

The Squadron was brought to readiness at dawn on 2 September. At 0650 instructions were received to prepare for take-off and at 0720 ten Hurricanes were scrambled on the approach of a large formation of Do17s of III/KG3, which crossed the Kent coast at Deal just after 0730. The bombers were escorted by an estimated 100 Bf109Es and Bf110s. Their targets were RAF airfields. In all, six squadrons of Spitfires and Hurricanes were scrambled to meet the threat, although only 249 and the Spitfires of 72 Squadron from Croydon made contact owing to controllers maintaining standing patrols of sector airfields. Led by Sqn Ldr Grandy, the

Squadron was ordered to patrol Rochester at 15,000 feet where, at about 0800, the bombers were sighted, in close vics of three. Plt Off Meaker noted:

"Was still slightly dopey when at 15,000 feet we sighted a large lump of blitz. Solid block of 20 Dorniers with a large fighter escort."

The CO reported:

"I was leading the Squadron on a patrol over Eastchurch when we were ordered to intercept large forces of e/a to the south. We sighted them flying NW from Dover direction, we being at about their height. I ordered line astern and we carried out a beam attack on a formation of mixed bombers and fighters — approximately 30-40. These were supported to the rear by over 100 ME110s. At approximately 300 yards I fired one two or three-seconds burst and then broke away underneath the formation."

Sgt Bentley Beard also caused a Dornier to smoke heavily and saw pieces fall off, the bomber then dropping out of the formation. He claimed this as probably destroyed although this may have been the same aircraft as that attacked by the CO. Flt Lt Barton's Blue Section engaged Oblt Rohr's 9/KG3 aircraft near Chatham, as Barton reported:

"I selected a Dornier which had broken formation after our first attack and was flying eastwards on its own. I carried out an astern attack, firing about ten bursts at both engines and cockpit. No evasive tactics were adopted but there was a lot of return fire, some of which hit my aircraft. Pieces flew off the e/a and I noticed what appeared to be a weight on a piece of wire ejected from the aircraft, but this did not hit me. E/a gradually lost height. Plt Off Meaker also attacked this aircraft which crash-landed on Rochford aerodrome, having just caught fire. One occupant baled out at 100 feet and his parachute failed to open in time."

In his diary, Meaker wrote a graphic description of the action:

"Attacked *en masse*, then dived away as fighters came down. Joined Butch again after a frantic tail-watching breakaway, and started after bombers again. Suddenly we see a Dornier coming towards us — running for home. We jump on it — Butch sits on its tail, pumping lead at it. I do quarter attacks. He doesn't like this, lumps fall off and smoke pours out. I am awake now and feeling hungry. Butch says, 'Don't waste any more ammunition on him; this guy's finished.' I say, 'OK Bud,' and formate on the Dornier as he heads for Rochford. He is a wreck — rudders in ribbons and pieces falling off all the time. One guy comes out at 100 feet. Parachute streams as he hits the ground — bounces. Butch and I are very cocky, go home and shoot a line."

The stricken bomber (5K+BT) belly-landed on Rochford airfield, where it slid to a halt. As the Station MO assisted the wounded pilot from the aircraft, he noticed the rear machine-gun was pointed in his direction, with the gunner behind it. He approached cautiously and found the gunner (Uffz Hilbrecht) was dead with his finger still on the trigger. The other two crew members, Uffz Seidel and Fw Sprink survived, although both had suffered wounds or injuries. Presumably one of these two had baled out just before the aircraft crash-landed, as noted by Barton and Meaker.

A probable was claimed by Plt Off Burton (Yellow 2) who was bringing up the rear of the Squadron:

"I turned to look at my tail and lost Yellow 1 [Flt Lt Parnall]. I singled out a straggler. I got on his tail and fired at his port engine from 300-250 yards, giving him several short bursts. He turned to port and I aimed at his cockpit, using deflection, and I could see my ammunition hitting him. I broke off as I was attacked by some ME110s from behind and above. I evaded them and fired at one which overshot me, but without visible result.

I returned to the attack on the Dornier, firing again at his port engine from astern 300-250 yards with two four-seconds bursts. Thick, black smoke came from his port engine and he started going down slowly — by this time he was well out of formation. I do not think he could have got home. During the whole engagement I experienced intense return fire from the Dornier, coming apparently from four machine-guns simultaneously from the top rear of the cockpit. I was hit and glycol fumes filled the cockpit, followed by glycol fluid. As a result my engine cut at 10,000 feet and I had to force-land at Meopham, Kent, in a field with my undercarriage up. I do not think my aircraft was very seriously damaged."

In addition to the claims made by 249, the Spitfire pilots of 72 Squadron reported shooting down two of the raiders plus several others damaged. Records indicate that an aircraft of 8/KG3 returned to St Trond in a damaged condition and with a wounded pilot, while 5K+MT of 9/KG3 crashed on landing at St Trond with one dead and three wounded on board; a third Dornier, 5K+GT of 9 Staffel, belly-landed at St Omer.

Meanwhile, Yellow Section engaged the escorting Bf110s of II/ZG26, as reported by Flt Lt Parnall, who was credited with damaging one near Rochester at 0755:

"I attacked ME110 almost straight above me, flying on same course, range 300 yards. Fired three bursts of three-seconds each while climbing until at same level as ME110, which then went into gentle dive. Aircraft flew like this for 2,000 feet during which I gave another two-seconds burst and saw bullets hit fuselage, range 200 yards. No return fire encountered. Was forced to break away by pressure of other aircraft."

Plt Off Beazley (Green 1) claimed one of the twin-engine fighters probably destroyed in an action near Canterbury:

"I fired broadside on two Dorniers but without effect. I then wheeled and, as I was chasing the bombers, I saw a Hurricane being attacked from astern on my right by a ME110. I gave the ME110 a quarter deflection shot from about 250 yards. He did a slow turn to the right exposing a full underneath plan view, and I gave him a three-seconds burst. He dived and straightened out and I got astern of him, giving him another two or three-seconds burst from 300/250 yards range. He then flicked completely over onto his back and started to go down, apparently out of control. I think I must have killed or wounded the pilot when I caught him full plane. I was hit myself directly afterwards by a cannon shell from a ME110 behind me, and I had to bale out from 13,000 feet. I landed unhurt at Boxley Wood near Gillingham."

It seems probable that Beazley's aircraft was shot down by a Bf110 of 5/ZG26 crewed by Obfw Kurt Rochel and Uffz Willi Schöffler. However, the German crew's celebration of their success was short lived as their aircraft (3U+GN) was then attacked by both Hurricanes and Spitfires and, with both engines out of action, the Messerschmitt ditched in the sea off the Nore Lightship; both crew members managed to scramble into their dinghy before their aircraft sank and they were later picked up by a British rescue craft. Meanwhile, Beazley's Hurricane crashed at Eccles Recreation Ground near Rainham. Plt Off Wynn's aircraft (V7352) was also shot down over Rochester at 0740, but by a Bf109E, and he crash-landed near the village of Chartham, with a bullet wound in his neck. Two Bf110s of 6/ZG26 returned to their base having suffered combat damage, each with a wounded gunner, while an aircraft of 5 Staffel crash-landed at Wizernes with both crewmen wounded.

Biggin Hill, Rochford, Eastchurch and North Weald were among the airfields targeted although only minor damage was inflicted. The raiders returned in the afternoon. At 1600, ten Hurricanes, again led by Sqn Ldr Grandy, took off to patrol Southend and Gravesend where they intercepted a large formation of Bf110s from II and III/ZG76, which were escorting Do17s at between 15,000-20,000 feet, the whole formation covering some three to four square miles. They were again joined by Spitfires of 72 Squadron from Croydon. In the ensuing engagement three of the Bf110s were claimed destroyed by 249, including one by Flt Lt Parnall (Red 2), which he chased over Essex:

"After No1 had attacked and broken away I saw two ME110s 1,000 feet above us heading south. I immediately climbed and turned onto the rear ME110 and gave him a steady burst from three quarter below. He immediately turned to the right and went into a vertical dive. At 10,000 feet, something in the machine blew up and the ME110 spun slowly into the ground where it burst into flames by a wood near Billericay — I followed flight of aircraft to 200 feet."

His victim was apparently M8+DM of Stab II/ZG76 which crashed at Frith Farm, Laindon Road in Billericay. The Messerschmitt crashed inverted, at 1640, and burnt out. Oblt Karl Wrede (the Gruppe Technical Officer) and his gunner, Uffz Richard Kukawka, were both killed; Kukawka had only recently recovered from wounds received in action on 15 August. A second Bf110 was claimed by Green 1, Plt Off Meaker, and a third by Sgt Davidson (Green 2), the latter shared with a Spitfire. He reported that it went down near Sutton Valence with its port engine on fire:

"I saw a ME110 below me, flying south on his own. I dived on his tail and as I was about to fire, a Spitfire flew underneath and fired at the e/a, which immediately climbed. As he did so, I fired from 300-200 yards with a two-seconds burst. E/a then dived and Spitfire attacked him again. The procedure was repeated, each of us attacking three times as he climbed. After my last burst, which exhausted my ammunition, I saw e/a going down with his port engine in flames and no further evasive tactics were adopted. I followed him down to about 6,000 feet. In my view he could not have got home, as the engine was well alight."

Meanwhile, Meaker reported:

"Patrolling with the Squadron at about 15,000 feet over Gravesend, engaged a large formation of Do215s [sic] and ME110s. I attacked a ME110 which was circling with another, giving full deflection and firing at plan view of e/a as he turned. I fired two short bursts of about one second each and lost e/a under my nose. When I saw him again, I saw him turn over and go into an inverted dive with his starboard engine and wing on fire. I watched him dive down about 2,000 feet and then looked away as I was being attacked."

He added:

"I feel very cocky again, look for the fight and find it is out of sight. I go home and find that I've only fired 300 rounds."

Another Bf110 was damaged by Plt Off Barclay (Red 3) over the Thames Estuary:

"We ran into some ME110s in defensive circles. They were above us, and we adopted the defensive snake formation. I did an upward full deflection attack from the front — went up into a loop and did an inverted spin out of it! I climbed up again but the 110s went off home hell for leather — one got left behind and I got in a long burst at long-range, one of his engines pouring glycol as he drew away. I couldn't keep up, let alone catch him, so I left him to a Spitfire and rejoined what was left of the snake."

A Messerschmitt of III/ZG76 force-landed near Calais following combat with RAF fighters, and may have been one of those involved in this action, in which the Spitfires of 72 Squadron also made a number of claims. During these afternoon raids several RAF airfields had been targeted including Biggin Hill, Kenley and Hornchurch. RAF Detling was attacked by a small force of Do17s which caused little damage although three aircraft were destroyed on the ground. Bombs which fell on RAF Eastchurch hit a bomb dump and the resultant explosion destroyed many buildings and six parked aircraft.

At 0900 on 3 September, the first anniversary of the outbreak of the war, the Squadron was instructed to patrol a line Chelmsford to Eastchurch but nothing was seen and, after an hour, Sqn Ldr Grandy was ordered to return to North Weald. The Hurricanes were still being refuelled when they were ordered to scramble to engage a large formation of bombers and fighters approaching from the north-east. Not all were ready to take off but the CO led those able to get airborne; others, their tanks only partially replenished, hurried after them and, by the time the raiding force appeared from the north-east, all the Station's serviceable aircraft were in the air, including three Blenheims of 25 Squadron. As the Hurricane pilots struggled to gain height, they witnessed a formation of some 30 Do17s of II/KG2 pattern bomb the aerodrome from about 15,000 feet. The CO commented:

> "We all had the most unsatisfactory experience of seeing North Weald being heavily bombed and being unable to do anything about it."

At least 200 100kg bombs fell on buildings and part of the aerodrome: the Officers' Mess was hit and the floor collapsed; the M/T Section yard was severely damaged and a number of lorries set on fire; a hangar was set afire and two unserviceable Hurricanes parked outside were destroyed; a second hangar was hit and a Blenheim of 25 Squadron was gutted. An airman and a civilian were killed, seven others seriously injured and 30 slightly hurt. Notwithstanding this, although bombs cratered the south and south-west corner of the airfield, the runways remained serviceable.

Meanwhile, the three Blenheims ran into a section of Hurricanes of 46 Squadron, which had been sent to help from the satellite airfield at RAF Stapleford Tawney, about five miles south of North Weald. Tragically, the Hurricane pilots thought the twin-engine bombers were Ju88s raiding North Weald and opened fire; one Blenheim was immediately shot down and crashed near Greensted Green. A second force-landed at Hatfield Heath and the crew survived unhurt (the pilot of this Blenheim, Plt Off Ernest Cassidy, joined 249 the following month). The third Blenheim, although damaged, was able to land back at North Weald.

An afternoon patrol between Eastchurch, Canterbury and Dover — when three Bf109Es were seen but not engaged — was interrupted at 1555 when Sgt Peter Rowell's Hurricane (V6635) was damaged by AA fire when over Dover. Although he was able to reach North Weald, the aircraft was further damaged on landing; Rowell suffered slight concussion. The Squadron received four replacement Hurricanes next day.

After a number of uneventful patrols, the Squadron was again called to action on the afternoon of 5 September. Climbing at 1430 in company with 46 Squadron to intercept a large formation of bombers reported over the Thames Estuary, a Staffel of Bf109Es (possibly 8/JG2) was spotted below. One of 46 Squadron's flight commanders was flying the RAF's first four-cannon Hurricane and he engaged a Messerschmitt which "blew up in the air" following a three-seconds burst.

Flt Lt Barton led his sections to attack the Dorniers (possibly aircraft of II/KG2) over Shellhaven but his own aircraft (V6625 US-K) was hit both by return fire and a Bf109E which had fastened onto his tail. With his engine afire, Barton baled out and landed safely. He was driven back to North Weald in an army car and later taunted by his colleagues for allowing himself to be shot down by a bomber. Barton's assailant was claimed probably destroyed by Sgt Davidson:

> "I gave the e/a a short burst at 200 yards range and he broke away from his attack on Blue 1 [Flt Lt Barton]. I followed him down to approximately 10,000 feet where he pulled out of the dive and began to climb. I immediately gave e/a another few short bursts, whereupon he began to dive for the sea with smoke pouring from his engine. I followed e/a down giving him intermittent bursts down to 2,000 feet without e/a taking any evasive action. At this point my ammunition finished and e/a was still diving towards the sea, heading east."

Plt Off Meaker wrote:

> "Another big day. Over Thameshaven we meet 25 bombers and scores of ME109s. Fired at a Dornier but had to break away when fighters came down *en masse*. Chased bombers for ten minutes but couldn't catch them up. Came home and found Butch had baled out and landed in a garden where a terrified woman looked at him and then ran into the house."

Another Bf109E was claimed probably destroyed by Plt Off Beazley, who reported:

> "Flying as Green 1, I attacked with the Squadron on the bombers' left flank, who were
> proceeding east. I observed no effect from my fire. After breaking away, I saw a ME109 slightly
> above and in front of me, also going east. I climbed up and gave it a short quarter deflection
> shot and then got on its tail and gave it another short burst. A lot of white smoke came from
> it and it began to go down, giving me the impression it was out of action, so I broke away to
> attack another ME109. I consider this ME109 probably had a gun firing aft from the fuselage."

Sgts Davis (Blue 3) and Smithson (Yellow 3) were more successful and jointly claimed severe
damage to three of the bombers; Davis engaged an already damaged Dornier, its port engine
emitting smoke:

> "I fired two bursts and more smoke was observed. The e/a then sank lower in the formation.
> I then broke away and lost sight of the enemy."

Smithson's subsequent report revealed:

> "Flying as Yellow 3 when we sighted a large formation of e/a flying east towards Gravesend.
> Enemy bombers were flying at 20,000 feet with fighters above up to 30,000 feet. Breaking away
> I flew up towards the underside of a Do215 [*sic*]. On coming into range I fired a burst and
> saw tracer bullets going ahead of the bomber's nose. Holding my fire and easing stick back
> slightly, I poured a further four-seconds burst and saw tracer bullets raking e/a from nose to
> tail. Tracer bullets from e/a were passing my starboard mainplane. On breaking away
> I observed large clouds of white smoke pouring from Do215. I lost about 1,000 feet, pulled
> out and carried out the same attack on a second Do215, and on breaking away observed smoke
> trailing from the centre of the fuselage, just behind the cockpit."

On his return to North Weald, Flg Off Wells reported probable damage to a Dornier and a
Bf109E although he observed no positive results. Under the circumstances, although he believed
damage had been inflicted, he did not submit an official claim. However, Group HQ was notified
of his actions.

The Squadron was airborne at 0845 on 6 September, to patrol the Gravesend area in
company with 303 Squadron from Northolt, when a large formation of Ju88s (II/KG76) and
Do17s, complete with an even larger fighter escort, approached east of Maidstone. Sqn Ldr
Grandy led a beam attack on the Ju88s, which were on their way to bomb Kenley, but the
Bf109Es came down before attacks were completed and results were inconclusive, although one
was claimed probably destroyed and two others severely damaged. The probable was later
upgraded to destroyed and was apparently the aircraft attacked initially by Sqn Ldr Grandy
and then by Plt Off Beazley, but the CO was then shot down by Messerschmitts when climbing
to rejoin the fight:

> "After the first attack I found myself over Maidstone on my own after the mêlée, and was
> trying on the R/T to re-form the Squadron. Foolishly, I had not noticed what must have been
> a 109 behind me at this time. There was a loud bang, I was hit in the face (I still have the
> damaged goggles) and there were flames on the cockpit floor. I decided to bale out and,
> I imagine, must have pulled my 'chute too soon thinking I was going to pass out. I think the
> 'chute dragged me out of the cockpit. I never saw my aircraft again and next found myself
> suspended beneath the 'chute with my right leg up around my ear, doing the splits. I managed
> to sort this out before reaching the ground.
>
> I landed in a grass field somewhere near Maidstone and was greeted by a farm labourer
> who looked at me but would not come near. To assure him I was not a German I said to him
> 'For God's sake come and help me out of this f . . . . . g parachute.' He then rolled a cigarette
> which he gave me, and helped as requested. The next event was the arrival by car at the edge
> of the field of a very emotional man who wiped my face with a handkerchief, saying 'This is

blood spilled for England — I shall treasure this handkerchief for ever.' I asked him to forget that and get me to hospital as quickly as he could, which he did. I could not walk on my right leg. On reaching the hospital I sent word both to the Squadron at North Weald, and to my wife."

Meanwhile, other pilots engaged the Bf109Es of which Plt Off Meaker claimed two shot down:

"We nip in before the Hun fighters can get at us and do a quick flank attack. Fighters follow at once. I follow behind the bombers, watching two ME109s coming up behind me. Before they get into range I turn sharp left and whip under them. Unfortunately Crossey, who is following me, gets plugged by one of these guys and has to crash-land. I get into a circle with two 109s and shoot at the second. He starts to dive, so I pull the plug and chase him. Third burst sets him on fire, whole of starboard wing and fuselage.

We are down to 50 feet so I leave him to burn, and climb to 10,000 feet at full bore. Fighting is still going on, and two more 109s come for me. They work in pairs, and it seems fairly easy to get No2. Again I pick him out and we tear down to o feet. We race along the Pilgrim's Way and I fire the rest of my ammunition into him. Both radiators stream glycol, and I can smell him burning. I formate on him when I finish my rounds and he has his oxygen mask off, looking out at me. I leave him to go home and see him crash-land a few miles on. Going home I see a parachute and circle it — a British one. Later it turns out that it was the CO who got shot down by 109s."

A third Bf109E was credited to Sgt Bentley Beard and two others were claimed probably destroyed, possibly by Flt Lt Parnall and Plt Off Beazley. The Messerschmitts were probably from II/JG2; Oblt Hans Hahn and Lt Julius Meimberg each claimed two Hurricanes, while the Gruppe lost one aircraft and pilot in return when Lt Max Himmelheber baled out, and was captured. His aircraft crashed on Plumbtree Farm, Headcorn near Maidstone, possibly the victim of Plt Off Meaker.

Meanwhile, Flg Off Wells and Plt Off Fleming encountered a number of Bf110s of I and III/ZG76, one of which was claimed damaged by Fleming. Wells engaged the same aircraft:

"We had attacked a formation of Ju88s with fighter escort. I did not get a decent shot so did not hit anything and broke down with the rest of the Squadron. Soon afterwards, on my way back to North Weald, I saw an ME110 crossing my path so I went after it at about 5,000 feet. It was heading back to France. I finally caught up with it and got in a good burst which slowed it up and it commenced a dive for the ground with one engine smoking. I gave it another burst after which a crew member on a parachute appeared. It was obviously finished so I watched it hit the ground near a farm; it blew up and burned. I think the crash was near Hailsham. Another Hurricane then appeared, which was Bob Fleming. We got back to North Weald and Bob said he had 'winged' it earlier, which I did not dispute, and back in dispersal I think it was Butch Barton who said 'OK, half each.' "

The accompanying Hurricanes flown by the Polish pilots of 303 Squadron suffered disastrously in this action, losing five aircraft to the Bf109Es and bomber gunners although they claimed two bombers and five fighters shot down in return; one of the bombers was claimed by Sqn Ldr Kellett*, formerly of 249.

Plt Off Barclay, who was not flying on this occasion, wrote:

"The CO was in hospital with some torn muscles in his leg and minor cannon shell wounds. Apparently the Squadron was told to re-form at 15,000 feet over Eastchurch. The CO, on getting the rendezvous, was told to pancake and as they dived down he was shot up by 109s. As is usually the case, he didn't see what got him."

---

* Sqn Ldr Kellett went on to claim five enemy aircraft shot down plus two probables in little over a month while commanding 303 Squadron, and was awarded the DSO and DFC.

At 1735, Flt Lt Barton, now effectively in command of the Squadron, led a dozen Hurricanes to patrol over Shellhaven where the oil tanks were still blazing from the previous day's raid, enveloping the area in smoke haze. 249's Hurricanes were ordered to remain at 20,000 feet and, while at this height, seven Ju87s made a low-level attack on the oil refinery. The dive-bombers were not observed by the high-flying Hurricanes but they did not escape unscathed since Wg Cdr Beamish, who had taken off alone in V6615 GN-B, engaged and claimed two shot down, having pursued them to Rochford *.

At this stage, just when RAF Fighter Command was beginning to feel the effect of the continuous attacks on its airfields, the Germans suddenly changed their strategy and instead targeted London in an attempt to force Fighter Command to commit its remaining fighters in a decisive battle. German Intelligence had assured Reichsmarschall Göring, the Commander-in-Chief of the Luftwaffe, that the RAF was virtually beaten and that its reserve fighters would be destroyed in trying to protect the capital. Thus, satisfied that the battle was almost won, Göring unleased his bombers against London on the afternoon of 7 September.

Until the moment radar began to pick up the plots of the incoming raids, RAF fighter controllers had been mystified by the lack of activity during the morning and early afternoon, expecting the damaging raids against the airfields to continue. By 1615 the vanguard of almost 350 bombers drawn from five bomber groups, escorted by more than 600 fighters, began crossing the coast between Deal and North Foreland, with the capital as their priority target. By 1630, all 21 RAF fighter squadrons within 70 miles of London were in the air or at immediate readiness to take off including a dozen of 249, who were vectored onto the southern bank of bombers over north-east London. Plt Off Barclay wrote in his diary:

"Little did we realize what was in store for us today when we scrambled after lunch. Twelve aircraft took off to patrol Maidstone at 15,000 feet, seven came back."

Flying as Red 2, Barclay recalled:

"We got on patrol and drifted up and down the sky, while the No3s in each section tended to weave less and less. Then suddenly 'Hullo, Ganer leader, Hullo, Ganer leader, bandits on your right — over.' And there sure enough was a tiny slanting black line which we knew were bombers. We turned towards them. I turned the gun button to 'Fire' and looked to see that the reflector sight was working OK. I opened the hood, and immediately I could see 50 per cent better, though it is 50 per cent colder. I saw that the rapidly closing bombers were surrounded by black dots, which I knew to be ME109s. So we were in for it this time! Before we knew where we were, we were doing a beam attack on the Dorniers. All I remember is trying to avoid hitting anyone else as we attacked, and being conscious of ME109s coming down to attack us. I had a long burst at one section of Dorniers and as I broke away noticed at least two lagging behind and streaming glycol or white smoke. These weren't necessarily the ones I had fired at. I never saw another Hurricane anywhere near until I got back to the aerodrome."

As Barclay broke away, two Messerschmitts shot past beneath his aircraft:

"I turned back and fired at the nearest — no result. Had a burst at the farthest and immediately there was a puff of black smoke, a brilliant flame and down he went, slowly turning over on to his back. The whole hood and perspex flew off and the fuselage began to disintegrate. But no time to stop. I turned sharply and found another yellow [nose] 109 on my tail, sitting pretty. I did an aileron turn in a dive to get away and then flattened out and had a good look around. I saw a Hurricane going vertically down pouring smoke (and later the pilot's parachute with another Hurricane circling it to protect him from the Huns)."

---

* Since taking command of North Weald in June, Wg Cdr Beamish had flown operationally whenever possible despite his age (37) and status; by the end of August he had six victories to his credit including three probables, and had been awarded the DSO.

The vanquished Hurricane Barclay had observed may have been that of Sgt Fred Killingback, who baled out wounded over Maidstone, having been shot down by the Bf109Es; his aircraft crashed at Eastling. He reported later that he had shot down a Dornier and probably a Bf109E before he was hit. Plt Off Fleming (R4114) was also shot down over Maidstone, at 1700, his aircraft crashing in open fields near Tong House at Eastling; severely burned, Fleming had baled out on fire and died later of burns and shock. Sgt Smithson (V6574) crashed at Eastchurch with an arm wound after combat with Bf109Es over Maidstone, while Flg Off Wells also fell victim to the Messerschmitts when attacking a He111, which he claimed probably destroyed:

"Followed leader in a beam attack on about 30 He111s. I fired at one and his starboard motor poured out smoke. I broke away and on climbing up again saw this machine flying towards France. I followed and passed him, got in an attack . . . and broke away. I then came around and started a stern attack on port motor. HE111 was then jettisoning his bombs. My aircraft then caught fire so I baled out."

He added:

"I never got any credit for the Heinkel; with one engine stopped and the undercarriage down it was going one way — down."

Wells baled out at 18,000 feet with cannon shell splinters in his head, one hand, both legs and both arms. On his way down he lost his flying boots and landed unconscious at a place known as Dunkirk Bank, just outside Canterbury. Before being taken to Shorncliffe Military Hospital in Canterbury, local soldiers liberated him of his cigarettes and parachute as well as several other personal items. His flying boots were later returned to him in hospital, by a policeman. His Hurricane came down at Goodnestone Court Farm, Faversham.

The Squadron's opponents on this occasion were probably from I/JG2 whose pilots made eight claims at about this time, and included three by Obfw Erich Rudorffer (who survived the war with 224 victories), two by Obfw Günther Seeger and one by the Gruppenkommandeur Maj Helmut Wick, also an ace pilot. The Gruppe lost one aircraft which force-landed at St Radegund's Abbey near Dover where Oblt Ferdy Götz was captured unhurt. Meanwhile, Barclay again encountered the bombers but by now they were about 7,000 feet above him:

"Having lost contact with the Squadron, I climbed up about a mile away on the starboard, watching my tail carefully for the ME109s. Just when I was on the bombers' level and thinking about an attack, the whole formation turned towards me. I did a head-on attack on the leading vic of the bomber formation and, as I broke away downwards, saw a white smoke trail coming from the formation leader's port engine. I claim this HE111 as damaged. I was then forced to land in a field owing to a hit in my engine."

Barclay carried out a wheels-up landing in a field near the village of Potter Street, about four miles from North Weald, at 1705. He was given a ride back to the airfield by some soldiers, who also placed a guard on his Hurricane. Of the six pilots who returned safely to North Weald, Flt Lt Parnall reported sharing a He111 with two Hurricanes over Sheerness:

"I was returning from Eastchurch where one of our aircraft had force-landed due to combat, when at 6,000 feet near Rochester I saw a HE111 heading south at about 2,000 feet, pursued by two Hurricanes. The Heinkel then had his port motor stopped but the other was functioning alright. The Heinkel disappeared into the smoke pall from the oil tanks at Shellhaven, and the two Hurricanes both appeared to lose the Heinkel as I saw them continuing to circle over Rochford looking for it. I immediately turned south and could see the Heinkel from astern, slowly turning east in the smoke — the wind was due west. Heading due east, I gave him a short burst, aiming at the starboard motor. The Heinkel then slowly turned south over Sheerness dockyard. I immediately attacked him again although the AA guns were firing at him. His height was about 1,500 feet then, heading south. I fired another two-seconds burst when the Heinkel turned to the north, rapidly losing height. When he reached the Estuary he steadily turned left and when pointing due south again, crash-landed at Grain, just across the water from Sheerness. The AA fire did not at any time hit the Heinkel. I claim the Heinkel jointly with two Hurricanes."

The Heinkel — A1+DN of II/KG53 — had initially been engaged by two Hurricanes of 253 Squadron following its bombing attack on Thameshaven, before Parnall's attack disabled its port engine. The bomber was actually crash-landed by Oblt Brauer at Old Marsh on the Isle of Grain at 1730, the surviving members of the crew (Obgfr Neumann had been killed) setting fire to the aircraft before going into captivity (with Brauer were Obfw Pizkar, Gfr Urich (wounded) and Uffz Bergmann (wounded). Meanwhile, Plt Off Beazley shared in the destruction of what he believed to be a Do17 but was, in fact, a Bf110:

"I was climbing up with aircraft TM-K [a Hurricane of 504 Squadron] to get enough height to attack bombers again over North Weald. Then I saw the Dornier [*sic*] coming down close towards me. Thinking it was a ME109 I whipped round into it, but saw flames coming from the port engine and underneath. I gave it a burst on the starboard engine and fuselage, and watched it crash near a main road south-east of Onger. I do not know who was responsible for firing the starboard engine."

The aircraft was Bf110 3M+BB of Stab I/ZG2. Three other Hurricane pilots shared in its destruction: the pilot from 504 Squadron, who attacked first and set its starboard engine on fire; Parnall attacked at the same time as did a pilot from 242 Squadron who reported that its port engine caught fire as he engaged, and then, as Oblt Gerhard Granz (the Gruppenadjutant) baled out, a pilot from 73 Squadron gave a burst at which the tail assembly broke away and the Messerschmitt crashed, coming down at Noak Hill, Billericay; Granz and his gunner, Fw Willi Schubel, who also baled out, were taken prisoner.

Meanwhile, Plt Off Neil (Yellow 2) reported shooting down a Bf109E near Ashford, having attacked a vic of three Heinkels first:

"Where were the bombers? Gone! I couldn't see them. But the 109s were there. One was off to my right, coming towards me. Slightly above but flying in the opposite direction. I instinctively turned towards it and, pulling hard, fired. The Hun ignored me, curving away in a slight dive. Emboldened and wildly excited, I shot after him, urging my aircraft on. Faster! Faster! Had he seen me? Surely he must have! Everything straining and shaking, but catching up. I fired again. And again. A few bright strikes. A brief puff of dark smoke. A thin plume of white, then slightly thicker tail of darkening grey. The 109 suddenly looked tired. It leaned slowly to its right and slid downwards gently. I fired again. And again. It sat there, tilting. In a way, pathetic. Then, momentarily, a small puff of debris exploded into the air. It was dying. The aircraft was dying. Like an animal, mortally wounded. Not the pilot or a man, but an aircraft. It fell away. Sadly. The angle steepening, the trail thickening. I let it go. To its death. Watching."

Once rearmed and refuelled, the remaining six Hurricanes were ordered off to patrol Canterbury at 15,000 feet. An estimated 100 Dorniers and Heinkels were seen in three separate waves. Plt Off Neil was delayed taking off but, having done so, climbed after the others:

". . . at about 8,000 feet was surprised to see a parachute above and ahead, drifting down in my direction. I watched it sail by my wing as I laboured upwards. Whose, I wondered? One of ours? It couldn't be. There was no time for them to have reached the raid."

But a Squadron Hurricane it was, Sgt Bentley Beard's N2440 GN-N having been hit by AA fire as he struggled to reach the Dorniers; he baled out over North London and was unhurt. Only Sgt Davidson was able to engage the bombers successfully and claimed a Dornier shot down and a Bf109E damaged:

"I was No2 in Blue Section when, with the rest of the Squadron, we attacked a formation of approximately 40 Do17s. After breaking away I found myself separated from the rest of the Squadron and, climbing up into the sun, I made another attack on three stragglers which were turning over the formation to return east. I fired a good three-seconds burst into the nearest bomber as it was turning and saw the bullets hit the underside of the fuselage and the front part of the perspex nose. The e/a immediately flicked over and dived vertically for the ground, striking the ground in a field approximately one mile SE of Gravesend. On striking the ground the e/a seemed to explode and burst into flame all over the field. After this I again climbed up, with another Hurricane. We had attained approximately 17,000 feet when we were both attacked by approximately six ME109s. A dogfight ensued, during which time I managed to get two three-seconds bursts into a yellow-nosed e/a. White smoke appeared streaming from his engine but I had to break off my attack."

Barclay's final comment on the day's fighting included a tribute to Wg Cdr Beamish:

"The odds today have been unbelievable, and we are all really very shaken! The Wing Commander's coolness is amazing and he does a lot to keep up our morale — very necessary tonight. We all wish the CO was here."

Whilst their colleagues battled for their lives, off-duty pilots Plt Offs Meaker and Loweth had driven to Maidstone to collect Sqn Ldr Grandy from hospital. On the return journey they arrived at the Surrey Docks about five minutes before the bombing got under way. Meaker noted in his diary:

"Coming back we get to the Blackwall Tunnel when the trouble starts raining down all round us — no time to get to a shelter. We stand under an arch and watch the bombers approaching in waves, hear the bombs whistle down and then the explosions. Molotov breadbasket showers incendiaries round us, several in gasworks, which fortunately does not go up. Watch Cockneys put out one incendiary, discover a gloomy type leaning against a lamp-post, who discloses he is waiting for pub to open!

The CO feels a bit hard done by as he's been shot down and wounded yesterday, then gets bombed today. [Loweth] drives like a demon along a street and skids to a halt. We all have stiff whiskies in the Russell. Go back in the dark via Hampstead Heath, fires light up London, and fire engines are coming from all suburbs into docks. Stop at a pub just outside Edmonton and get a riotous reception and lots of beer from excited public bar. I shake hands with everybody and get quite merry."

On his arrival back at North Weald, Sqn Ldr Grandy found that he could not climb into a Hurricane:

". . . my right leg being useless and unable to work the rudder. Very disappointed, I had no alternative but to hand over command of my Squadron to Butch Barton."

Vast areas of London's dockland were devastated as a result of these raids, many of the fires becoming aiming points for subsequent waves of bombers. By 1745 the last of the raiders was on its way home. Almost 1,800 Londoners had been killed or seriously injured during the course of the raids, for which the Luftwaffe paid the price of the loss of at least 40 aircraft; a dozen RAF fighter pilots had been killed defending London during the afternoon raids. That night the bombers returned.

The next three days were relatively quiet for the Squadron, although there was another heavy raid on London on 9 September, which was just as well since A Flight possessed only two serviceable aircraft and pilots, while B Flight could boast just five aircraft. To make good aircraft losses, nine Hurricanes were delivered for the Squadron on 8 September. The Squadron's code letters GN began reappearing on the replacement machines, while the surviving former 56 Squadron aircraft were in the process of being repainted with 249's letters. On this date there occurred only one patrol, carried out in company with 46 Squadron, when a few Bf109Es were seen high above although there was no contact. At this stage, Group decided that squadrons were to operate in pairs or as a wing of three squadrons. For 249 this meant operating with 46 Squadron and, on occasions, with 504 Squadron based at Hendon. Next day the Squadron received an experienced replacement pilot in the guise of Flg Off K.T. Lofts from 615 Squadron, who joined A Flight; a veteran of the fighting in France, Lofts had several victories to his credit. With him came Plt Off W.B. Pattullo of 46 Squadron, who had been loaned to 151 Squadron.

Shortly before 1500 on 11 September, coastal radar detected a build-up of hostile aircraft in the Calais area and, at 1525, 249 was one of six squadrons ordered into the air to meet the bombers — He111s of KG1 and II/KG26 — as they flew up the Thames Estuary towards London. Escorting Bf110s veered off to the Croydon area where they formed defensive circles to await the withdrawal of the raiding force, leaving the Bf109Es to provide close cover, but these were soon forced to return due to lack of fuel.

In company with Hurricanes of 257 Squadron, 249 was ordered to patrol the London Docks and Thames Estuary, where they met 30 Heinkels of KG1 at 19,000 feet shortly after 1600 and, for the first time, the Squadron was able to carry out a head-on attack. The bombers appeared to have only a relatively small fighter escort, flying some 10,000 feet above. Flt Lt Barton, who claimed a bomber damaged in the opening attack, noted:

"Immediately after the Squadron had attacked, at least four Heinkels were seen to break formation obviously in a bad way and pouring out glycol. These were thought to be the same e/a as claimed individually."

Barton's No2, Plt Off Meaker, noted in his diary:

"Head-on into a bunch of HE111s. I do such a violent breakaway that I do an inverted spin. I lose 5-6,000 feet before I can get out of it. Can't find the fight at all after that so I go home fed up."

Red Leader, Flt Lt Parnall, reported:

"Squadron attacked about 30 HE111s and then broke away. I then observed one HE111 that had dropped slightly behind the main bomber formation now heading due south and so climbed up and attacked from the sun, beam to full astern, slightly above. I fired a steady five-seconds burst before breaking away to the sun side again. I noticed no return fire after beginning of burst; e/a then continued on steady course. I then did exactly similar rear to full astern, slightly above, firing a steady burst. Both engines were now only ticking over quite slowly and the e/a went into a steady glide at about 160-170 mph. I felt certain the e/a was about to crash and so flew steady course 500 yards on the rear side of it, ready to fire again if necessary, as I did not wish to waste all my ammunition. At about 5,000 feet or so, other aircraft [flown by Plt Off Pattullo] did astern attacks on the HE111 without any observed effect on its flying ability. At 1,000 feet glycol streamed from one motor and in the same steady glide the HE111 turned east and crashed in a field just north of the Redhill-Tonbridge railway line a few miles west of Tonbridge, when four of the crew climbed out. A parachute streamed from the Heinkel immediately prior to its crashing. At no time did the e/a catch fire."

For his part, Plt Off Pattullo (Green 3), noted:

"Having made a head-on attack in formation with the Squadron, I broke away and attacked one Heinkel which was slightly behind the main formation. The return fire ceased after I had attacked once, and on my second attack one engine gave off white smoke, presumably glycol. During my attacks I noticed another Hurricane attacking this machine, which eventually pancaked in a field by a railway station about five to ten miles SE of London. This machine was definitely destroyed but three [sic] of the crew climbed out after the forced landing. A parachute also broke out when the machine hit the ground. This machine may have been destroyed by either myself or the second Hurricane."

The Heinkel, V4+KL of 3/KG1, had apparently been damaged by AA fire over London and suffered damage to an engine before it was engaged by Parnall and Pattullo. It force-landed at Hildenborough at 1633 and the crew attempted to set fire to the aircraft before being captured. Uffz Steinecke and Uffz Hirsch were unhurt but the other three — Uffz Kramer, Gfr Pfeiffer and Gfr Pümpel — had all suffered wounds.

Blue 2, Plt Off Neil, was credited with shooting down another, while Sgt Davis believed he accounted for a third before his aircraft was hit by return fire. Davis was wounded and his Hurricane caught fire but he was able to bale out and came down at Benenden in Kent at 1620. Wg Cdr Beamish, flying independently, also claimed a Heinkel probably destroyed south-east of the capital. Of the initial encounter, Neil wrote:

> "The line of Heinkels growing magically in my windscreen. My guns ripping and shuddering. Lines of sparks and smoke streaking ahead. Curving. But only briefly. The wing of another Hurricane wobbling crazily by my left ear. Watch out! I was forced to pull away, shrieking expletives. Then, it was all over. I was falling away earthwards, my engine and the wind a high pitched scream."

Having regained composure and altitude, he came upon another group of He111s in a loose and irregular formation, as though they had already been attacked:

> "Deciding to attack from underneath, I was dipping below the tail when the rear gunner shot at me. The tracer came out, a twisting streamer of white which curled lazily towards me . . . I veered away for a second or two before turning back and, pulling up slightly, fired to discourage the man doing the shooting . . . I dropped back a little and fired again . . . A greasy trail began to stream from the starboard engine, not smoke exactly but a darkening stain. I saw that the Heinkel was losing ground and falling away from the formation. Encouraged, I fired again. And again. I followed the Heinkel down as it gradually lost height. A long way, through patches of cloud until, eventually and still under control, it crash-landed in a field alongside a railway line some long way south of London. I circled it several times at about 500 feet and saw one — two — figures emerge from the wreckage. They didn't wave. But then, I could hardly have expected them to."

Despite the onslaught during which ten of the bombers were shot down and at least a dozen damaged, with about 50 aircrew killed or missing and several others wounded aboard returning aircraft, other bomber crews determinedly and bravely struggled on towards London and released their loads. One bomb fell in Lewisham high street and struck a public shelter resulting in about 100 casualties; another struck Deptford Central Hall, where some 50 people were buried in the rubble. Many fires broke out in Woolwich and in the Surrey Docks. Following this latest raid on London, Prime Minister Churchill wrote:

> "These cruel, wanton, indiscriminate bombings of London are, of course, a part of Hitler's invasion plan. He hopes, by killing large numbers of civilians, women and children, that he will terrorise and cow the people of this mighty Imperial city and make them a burden and anxiety for the Government . . . little does he know the spirit of the British nation, or the tough fibre of the Londoners . . . This is the time for everyone to stand together and hold firm, as they are doing."

Replacement pilots and Hurricanes continued to arrive for the Squadron. Sgt W.R. Evans was posted in from 85 Squadron (joining A Flight) together with Sgt C.E. Hampshire from 111 Squadron (who went to B Flight), the latter another veteran of the fighting in France, with three victories to his credit. A third replacement pilot, Sgt G.A. Stroud, arrived from 32 Squadron but lacked operational experience. Three more new Hurricanes were received to bring the Squadron up to operational strength. Sgt Wally Evans recalled:

> "I found myself reporting to Flt Lt Parnall, A Flight commander, and being airborne within

an hour. I just had time to grab a Mae West and the colours of the day before we were scrambled. To my astonishment before we could get airborne, a station wagon came tearing across the airfield and screeched to a halt beside [Wg Cdr] Victor Beamish's aircraft. His erks had it already started and he was off in good time with us."

The Squadron patrolled Dover and although a number of Bf109Es were seen contact could not be made. A stick of bombs was seen to fall outside the entrance to Dover Harbour but no one could see the aircraft from which they were dropped.

The next three days were comparatively quiet generally, due partly to the inclement weather over south-eastern England but mainly because the Luftwaffe was regrouping and replacing its casualties in preparation for the next massed assault. The break was a welcome one for Fighter Command in general and for a depleted 249 Squadron in particular; nonetheless, the Squadron continued to mount patrols although no enemy aircraft were engaged. Plt Off Meaker recorded in his diary:

"Thirteenth and a Friday! More cloud flying expeditions, and everybody very testy about it. Went to B's house about 2200. Drank champagne and some beer. Bombing and AA fire all the time as it was a beautiful night."

Records show that Fighter Command had suffered the loss of at least 70 Hurricanes and almost 50 Spitfires shot down or written off in the preceding week; at least a further 100 Hurricanes and Spitfires had been seriously damaged during this period. A total in excess of 220 frontline fighters were therefore effectively denied to Fighter Command in just one week; worse still, 38 RAF fighter pilots had been killed and a further 34 wounded during this period. The fighters could be replaced fairly rapidly, whereas fighter pilots could not.

Replacement pilots continued to arrive for the Squadron, Sgts C.L. Whitnell and C.A. Rust joining A Flight, Plt Off P.A. Worrall going to B Flight — all three from 85 Squadron — together with Sgt J.P. Mills from 43 Squadron, a pilot with three victories to his credit. A highly successful French campaign pilot, Plt Off A.G. Lewis DFC with eight victories arrived from 85 Squadron on 14 September; he was the fourth South African member of the Squadron*. Arriving at the same time was Sgt G.C.C. Palliser from 43 Squadron; the latter three all joined B Flight. However, Sgt Whitnell was posted back to 85 Squadron within a few days since he was not operationally trained.

249 was not called into action against two attacks aimed at London on 14 September but flew south instead, as Plt Off Meaker noted:

"A trip down to Sussex with another squadron, and saw more of our fighters than I've ever seen before. I got attacked twice, and everybody split up and came home singly or in pairs. Those attacking me must have been HE113s [sic] but everytime I went to attack what I thought were these guys, they were Spitfires! Most foxing!"

Next day (15 September) the Squadron found itself participating in the greatest air battle to date. The day started quietly. At 0925, Flt Lt Barton and Plt Off Pattullo were scrambled to investigate unidentified aircraft. Nothing was sighted and they were recalled within the hour. On their return to North Weald, the Squadron bade farewell to Pattullo who was allowed to return to his former unit, 46 Squadron across the way at Stapleford Tawney, which had suffered losses in recent engagements.

The first major raid of the day crossed the coast near Dungeness at about 1130 and was challenged by 22 RAF fighter squadrons from bases around London, including a dozen Hurricanes of 249 led by Flt Lt Parnall, which patrolled in company with 46 Squadron. Both squadrons were vectored onto a formation of 20 Do17s of I/KG76 south of London, against which a beam attack was carried out. Plt Off Meaker (Blue 2) claimed one Dornier destroyed:

---

* Plt Off Gerald Lewis was born in Kimberley, South Africa, and had learned to fly at his own expense with the Rand Flying Club before travelling to England to join the RAF in 1938.

"Attacked circling formation with Squadron and broke away. On sighting it again, I found bombers heading east but could see no fighter escort. I therefore selected the rearmost Do17 on the left and did a quarter attack, with four-seconds burst. His port engine stopped and I broke away. I saw him leave the formation and start a gentle dive. When he had got away from the formation, I again attacked and concentrated on starboard engine. I was then joined by three Spitfires who also fired at e/a. Large pieces fell off and two crew baled out. E/a crashed about five miles south of Margate."

In his diary Meaker detailed a more lucid and graphic account:

"We go into the bombers but Butch breaks early as he gets hit. I break with him, lose him, then go for the bombers again. Meet them coming home and no Messerschmitts in sight. So I attack one on the edge of the formation. Get him straight away and he leaves the rest of his boys. Follow him, plugging all the time. A quarter attack comes off beautifully, see bullets going in, in a line from the nose back to the tail, at intervals of a foot all the way down. See the rear gunner lying in his seat, probably dead. Dornier is smoking like a chimney, can smell it from behind him. Oil comes back on my aircraft and pieces fly past me. Then three blasted Spitfires horn in and drive me away from my own private and personal Dornier. One guy bales out from the Jerry. He has his arms folded and seems quite resigned. His ship crashes in flames and Spitfires shoot a line all round it . . . They're getting quite a reputation for pinching a bomber when a Hurricane has got it on the run. So I go home first and claim it before they can!"

The bomber, F1+FL of I/KG76, was apparently further damaged by the Spitfires before it eventually crashed in flames at 1240 and exploded in trees at Alcrofts Farm near Sturry, a village just north of Canterbury; Obfw Niebler, Fw Wissmann and Uffz Schatz were killed, while Oblt Karl-Ernst Wilke baled out severely wounded, as did the slightly wounded Uffz Zrenner, both of whom were taken prisoner; Wilke (the navigator) recalled *:

"Unteroffizier Schatz was the first to be killed. His task was to operate the guns on each side of the cabin, to provide defence against attacks from the left or the right. The poor guy was hit during the initial attack. Then I was hit by a bullet from the right, it struck my face just below the nose and blinded me. From that moment I took no further part in the action."

The aircraft then caught fire and only Zrenner (the radio operator) and Wilke managed to bale out. Plt Off Barclay claimed a probable:

"I attacked one of the leading bombers, starting from a frontal quarter attack and developing into a beam attack, opening fire at 300 yards and closing to 50 yards when I had to break over the bombers to avoid hitting them. There being no opposition from enemy fighters, I turned and did a quarter attack on the same Dornier from the opposite side to the first attack. The Dornier broke formation and glided down towards the clouds with glycol pouring from one engine. Both engines were just ticking over. I returned to attack main bomber formation and observed about eight friendly fighters attacking the bomber I originally disabled, about 4,000 feet below."

The "friendly fighters" were undoubtedly from 46 Squadron, whose pilots reported shooting down four Dorniers with a fifth shared. One of their successful pilots on this occasion was Plt Off Pattullo, late of 249. The pilot of one of the shot down Dorniers, having survived a parachute descent, was fatally injured by an angry mob. Of the damaged bombers which managed to reach the French coast, some with dead and wounded on board, two were written off in subsequent crash-landings, one having sustained in excess of 200 bullet strikes.

---

* See *Battle of Britain Day: 15 September 1940* by Dr Alfred Price.

Once refuelled and rearmed, the Hurricanes were ordered off again at 1340 to patrol the same area, this time in company with Hurricanes of 504 Squadron. All 11 Group's squadrons were again airborne, some 300 Spitfires and Hurricanes in the air simultaneously to counter the waves of Do17s of KG2 and KG3 and He111s of KG26 and KG53, a total of 114 bombers steadily approaching London. It was at this moment that Prime Minister Churchill, who was visiting Air Vice-Marshal Park (AOC 11 Group) at his underground Operations Room at Uxbridge, enquired:

"What other reserves have we?"

To which Park replied:

"There are none."

The Squadron almost immediately met 15 Do17s over South London, followed by a formation of He111s. In fact there were three waves of bombers threading their way towards the capital but many were forced to jettison their bombs and turn back. A beam attack on the Dorniers split the formation wide open and a multitude of claims were made, the Squadron being credited with five bombers shot down with another shared, plus eight probables and one more shared, together with three damaged. Of this historic action, the Squadron's diarist wrote:

"One reason for this success was that the German fighters failed to do their stuff, probably due to their attention already being diverted by being attacked from above by Spitfires."

Plt Off Meaker was again successful:

"I attacked with the Squadron, firing a short burst at the starboard leading aircraft of the Do215s [*sic*]. Broke away in face of heavy crossfire and lost 2,000 feet. Then attacked a single Dornier, diving from clouds, their formation having broken up. Fired a five-seconds burst from beam to quarter and e/a burst into flames. Starboard engine and fuselage were blazing and one crew baled out. This aircraft was blazing so fiercely that I claim it destroyed. Breaking away from this, I attacked another Dornier about 250 yards away. Fired two two-seconds bursts, hitting port engine (which later stopped) and fuselage. I was joined by Blue 1 [Flt Lt Barton] in this attack. E/a dived into clouds, where we chased him for some time. He was smoking badly when he eventually went through the clouds."

Meaker was then engaged by two of the escorting Messerschmitts:

"Then I see two ME109s behind me and whip round in a left-hand climbing turn. Horrid moment as I see his cannon winking at me, but he misses. Gradually tighten the turn till I get a shot at No2 from above. See my bullets hit his left wing and he is so shaken he dives into a cloud. Chase these two again and lose them. Then see two fighters coming straight for me. I think they're Spitfires, so don't fire. Dodge under them and find they are the same two yellow-nosed Messerschmitts! Annoying, because they make off, and I can't catch them."

In addition to sharing in the probable destruction of the Dornier with Meaker, Flt Lt Barton claimed a second as probably destroyed:

"I carried out an attack on a Do17 from below and saw a great amount of material fly off front portion of fuselage after a three-seconds burst. Aircraft dived down out of formation. Then attacked Dornier with Blue 2 [Plt Off Meaker] — smoke and oil pouring from engine and aircraft dived into cloud."

Plt Off Beazley claimed another and reported:

"I was Green 1 and carried out a quarter attack with my section and Blue Section on an e/a formation. After a three-seconds burst on the starboard machine of the second one, I noticed one break formation. I carried out a stern chase, firing a second burst, but then saw what I thought to be a roundel on the upper wing. It actually was a yellow and white square. I then gave another burst and the e/a dived into a cloud. Followed it through and saw one member of the crew jump out. I gave the e/a the rest of my ammunition, aiming at the starboard engine. It again went into cloud and another member of the crew jumped out. I noticed brown smoke coming from the starboard engine, and it turned and went vertically down."

Plt Off Crossey, flying in Beazley's section, also claimed one of the Dorniers as probably destroyed:

"Flying as Green 2, I went into a quarter attack with the Squadron. After I had broken I saw a Dornier which had broken formation. I made a head-on attack from above and the starboard engine was put out of commission. I pulled up again and came in from the rear and put a burst into the fuselage and port motor. White smoke appeared to come from this engine and then the bomber went into cloud where I lost him."

Sgt Palliser engaged another Dornier over south-west London:

"I was on patrol with the Squadron over SW London. Became separated from my section and after cruising at 14,000 feet noticed a Do215 [sic] flying in a northerly direction at about 9,000 feet through breaks in the cloud. I dived and made a steep quarter attack and opened fire at approx 350 yards, the burst lasting three seconds. I observed fragments flying from between starboard engine and cabin. This attack was delivered in the wake of a Spitfire which must have hit the port engine of e/a as I could see thick black smoke coming from engine. Four people abandoned e/a by parachute. No return fire noticed."

Following the action, Palliser landed his Hurricane in a farm field at Ingrave near Brentwood, lost and out of fuel. There he was greeted by the farmer's son and taken to the farmhouse. Unable to contact North Weald by telephone, he managed to get through to Hornchurch and explain his plight*. Plt Off Barclay meanwhile engaged three of the Dorniers with some success:

"I attacked main bomber formation with rest of 249 Squadron. I did a beam attack on a Dornier and observed no effect. Dornier then dropped slightly behind main formation and one member of the crew jumped out, his parachute opening immediately. I claim this Dornier as damaged. The enemy bomber formation then broke up and I dived down on a single Dornier. I gave him a five-seconds burst from slightly above and astern, and noticed brilliant flame from its port engine. The Dornier then reached the clouds and I broke off my attack. I claim this Dornier as probably destroyed.

I then attacked another lone Dornier and gave it a seven-seconds burst from its port quarter, closing to about 30 yards when I had to throttle back and swerve to avoid hitting it. I followed Dornier down through the clouds and picked it up again beneath cloud base. Having exhausted all my ammunition I did a feint astern attack and the Dornier went into a steep dive and crashed with a large explosion about three miles west of Vange, north of Shellhaven. This Dornier I claim destroyed."

The Dornier, 5K+DM of 4/KG3, fell at Gladstone Road in Laindon at 1433. Three of the crew, Lt Kurt Dümler, Uffz Maskules and Fw Vogel, were killed in the crash; only Uffz Friebe, who had baled out, survived to be taken prisoner. The bomber had apparently also been attacked

---

* By 1815 an RAF lorry arrived at Ingrave with a 50-gallon drum of fuel, a funnel and a starter trolley. By 1900 refuelling of the Hurricane was completed and Sgt Palliser was able to take off successfully. He beat up the field before setting course for North Weald.

by several other fighters. An eyewitness to the destruction of the Dornier stated that it popped out of cloud followed by two Hurricanes that gave it two or three bursts of fire, one of which may have been flown by Sgt Evans who claimed a Dornier damaged. Aboard one of the KG3 Dorniers was air gunner Fw Heinz Kirsch, who recalled:

"Something struck our machine. 'Hit on the left elevator!' called the radio operator. Like a couple of shadows two Hurricanes swept over us. They came past so quickly we were unable to get them. More hits on our machine. And on top of that there was smoke in the cabin. The Tommies were staking everything they had, never before had we come under such heavy attack. After firing, the fighters pulled left or right to go past us. Some came so close I thought they were going to ram us." *

Having been unsuccessful in the earlier engagement, Plt Off Neil accounted for two of the Dorniers, one of which he shared with a Spitfire pilot:

"Closing, I fired immediately and the whole of the port side of the German aircraft was engulfed by my tracer. The effect was instantaneous: there was a splash of something, like water being struck with the back of a spoon. I fired again, a longish burst . . . two large objects detached themselves from the fuselage and came in my direction, so quickly, in fact, that I had no time to evade. I suddenly recognised spreadeagled arms and legs as two bodies flew past my head, heavy with bulges that were undeveloped parachutes."

Apparently this was 5K+DN of 5/KG3 in which the Staffelkapitän, Hptm Ernst Püttmann, was killed together with Oblt Adolf Langenhain and Fw Franke; only Fw Falke survived to be taken prisoner. Apart from the loss of 5K+DN, 5 Staffel lost three more of its aircraft on this sortie. Out of the five serviceable aircraft which had set out from Deurne airfield near Antwerp on this raid, only 5K+AN returned (5K+HN, JN, GN and DN were lost). A crew member of the surviving aircraft recounted later:

"Above London we were jumped by a bunch of fighters and in a few seconds three aircraft of our Staffel went down smoking, while pieces of other aircraft were dropping all around us. Our own aircraft looked like a piece of lace and, with a boom, our starboard engine caught fire while the other seized up. The aircraft tumbled down towards the rooftops of London but the pilot finally managed to gain control and flew the damaged aircraft, with one engine blazing, back across the Channel to make a wheels-up landing on the French coast near Calais. Apart from a few slight wounds, nobody was hurt."

Meanwhile, Neil had found himself amongst a swarm of Bf109Es and for about 20 seconds fired short bursts as aircraft appeared in his sights:

"Then, as so often happened, they were gone and I was alone. Not alone, exactly, but not immediately threatened. There were perhaps half a dozen aircraft visible . . . including one Dornier. I began to cut the corner and chase after it. It took me perhaps half a minute of hard flying to catch up, by which time I saw that I had another aircraft on my left, a Spitfire."

The Dornier (U5+DS of 8/KG2) disappeared into cloud but then re-emerged, closely followed by both Hurricane and Spitfire; Neil continued:

"The Hun began to dive, not steeply but in a ten degree nose-down attitude. Thereafter, it was easy. Without interference, we took turns in carrying out astern attacks and were gratified to see a translucent stain of dark smoke emerge from one, then both of the engines . . . the Dornier continued to descend, flying eastwards down the Estuary . . . I carried out one careful

* Fw Kirsch's Dornier survived the initial attack but was attacked again on its homeward run and finally crash-landed near Dunkirk (see *Battle of Britain Day: 15 September 1940* by Dr Alfred Price).

attack from astern. The Spitfire approached, fired . . . the Dornier laboured on, barely clearing the masts of a convoy of ships some five miles beyond Shoeburyness, then continued into the open wastes of the North Sea . . . Then all at once, the tail touched, the fuselage lurched forward and the Dornier crashed down in an enormous flurry of white spray . . . Then slowly, gradually, it sank. No one — nothing — remained."

Despite Neil's conclusion, records suggest that two NCOs did survive the ditching of U5+DS and were rescued later by an ASR aircraft of Seenotflugkommando; two other crew members, Fw Dürtmann and Gfr Ertl were however lost. In addition to the Dorniers shot down, claims were made against the Heinkel formation, one of which Flg Off Lofts engaged:

"Whilst on patrol with Yellow Section we were detailed to intercept a raid coming in from the south-east, which consisted of about 20 Dorniers. When the interception was made, I was situated about 2,000 feet below the Dorniers which had an escort of ME109s who started diving on me. I broke away from this attack and when well clear regained height and found a large formation of HE111s on my right, slightly below. I picked out one and did an attack from about 2,000 feet above. I gave one long burst and noticed this e/a break formation and start diving. It was then attacked by several other Hurricanes. It eventually force-landed at West Malling. Damage to my aircraft was due to return fire."

The Heinkel was A1+AN of 5/KG53. It had been attacked repeatedly by a number of Spitfires and Hurricanes before it finally crash-landed. Of its crew, Obgfr Sailler and Gfr Lange had been killed in the air, Uffz Zilling and Fw Lichtenhagen wounded; only the pilot, Fw Behrendt, was unhurt. A pilot of 66 Squadron, one of those who had attacked the unfortunate Heinkel, landed close by and relieved the German pilot of his binoculars. Meanwhile, Flt Lt Parnall claimed a Heinkel probably destroyed over Central London and then damaged a Bf109E south-west of Rochester:

"I was flying over South London by myself as I had lost the rest of the Squadron after first attack on Dorniers, when bomber raid of HE111s was sighted heading due west over Central London. I turned north and did a vertical climbing attack on the last of the formation. I fired a steady burst while climbing vertically. The bullets struck the port motor of the Heinkel and large pieces of metal flew off the port wing. The motor slowed down and was almost stationary when I had to break away vertically downwards to observe what happened to the Heinkel, but he seemed to be rapidly dropping back from the main formation. I claim this aircraft probable.

After breaking away from above encounter, a number of yellow-nosed ME109s came down to 12,000 feet heading north. I was also heading north at the same height but to their west and so I turned right and gave the leader of the 109s a four-seconds burst from the beam to port quarter astern, when a number of pieces fell off the aircraft behind the pilot's seat. I had to break down immediately as there were six 109s diving down on me, following their leader, and so I was unable to observe any further effect."

Another Heinkel was reported shot down by Plt Off Lewis, who claimed a second as probably destroyed:

"Encountered a formation of 18 HE111s in diamond formation at 15,000 feet, with fighters at 20,000 feet, spread over a large area. I found myself with Spitfires, which split up the bulk of the formation. One became separated from the rest. I attacked from slightly below from beam, gave a three-seconds burst, and from here got line astern: set both motors on fire causing undercarriage to drop and the e/a appeared to spiral down in vicinity of Brentwood. As soon as this was down I engaged formation again, which had by now dropped its bombs and was heading towards south coast. I went in after a Spitfire, which broke away, then I closed and set starboard engine on fire. Wheels dropped out and e/a began to spiral down, circled by Spits."

Wg Cdr Beamish also reported sharing in the probable destruction of a Heinkel, which was seen to fall vertically with smoke coming from both engines. Oil from the stricken machine splashed Beamish's windscreen and a piece of wreckage from it dented his wing.

Among the German fighter pilots providing cover for the bombers was Lt Max-Helmuth Ostermann of III/JG54, whose account gives an insight into the problems which faced those on close-escort duty:

> "We clung to the bomber formation in pairs — and it was a damned awkward feeling. From below we looked up at the bright blue bellies of the Tommy planes. Mostly they waited there till our bombers made their turn. Then they would swoop down, pull briefly out, fire their guns, and at once dive on down. All we could do was to shoot off short nuisance bursts while at the same time watching out that there was no one nibbling at our tails. Often we pulled madly on the stick till the ailerons shook, but were then unable to turn round quickly enough and could only watch as the Tommies knocked hell out of one of the bombers . . ."

So ended a day of intense activity. The Squadron had acquitted itself admirably, being credited with six and a half confirmed to add to its growing list, plus nine and a half probables and four damaged, all achieved for the loss of just one aircraft. Fighter Command believed its pilots had initially accounted for 185 of the raiders although this was amended later (post war) to 56 confirmed; a further three returned to France damaged beyond repair and 23 others had sustained lesser damage. A total of 81 German aircrew were killed or reported missing, 63 were taken prisoner and 31 wounded. Though 249 had suffered no casualties, a dozen RAF fighter pilots had been killed, plus one taken prisoner and a further dozen wounded in the day's fighting which had seen 28 Hurricanes and Spitfires destroyed in combat against Luftwaffe claims for 79 RAF fighters shot down. Further signals, praising the Squadron's efforts, were received next day, including one from Sir Archibald Sinclair, Secretary of State for Air:

> "Congratulations on your magnificent fighting yesterday."

Which was followed by another from 11 Group:

> "Well done 249 Squadron, your success yesterday is an outstanding example of the hard fighting which is frustrating the enemy's attack. Keep it up."

While Fighter Command's pilots fought a deadly battle to keep the bombers at bay, they could not imagine what it was like for the civilians in the London boroughs on the receiving end of the horrendous bombing raids. One victim graphically wrote:

> "I had a momentary glimpse of a large ball of blinding white light with two concentric rings of colour, the inner ones lavender and the outer ones violet. The ball seemed to be ten to twenty feet high and was near the lamp-post. The explosion made a noise something like a colossal growl and was accompanied by a veritable tornado of air blast. I felt an excruciating pain in my ears, and all sounds were replaced by a loud singing noise — which was when I lost my hearing. I felt that consciousness was slipping from me, and at that moment I seemed to hear a loud clear voice shouting, 'Don't let yourself go! Face up to it and hold on!' It rallied me, and summoning all my will power and energy I succeeded in forcing myself down into a crouching position with my knees on the ground, my feet against the kerb behind me and my hands covering my face.
>
> Just as I felt that I could not hold out much longer I realised that the blast pressure was decreasing, and a shower of dust, dirt and rubble swept across me. Pieces penetrated my face and something pierced my knuckles, causing me involuntarily to let go my hold on the kerb. Instantly, although the blast was dying down, I felt myself blown slowly across the pavement towards the wall of a building. I tried to hold on, but there was nothing to hold on to. Twice I tried to rise but seemed held down. Eventually I staggered to my feet, and I looked around. The front of the building was lit by reddish-yellow light. A saloon car was on fire to the left

of me, and the flames from it were stretching out towards the building horizontally. Pieces of brick, masonry and glass seemed to appear suddenly on the pavement, making — to me — no sound. Right in front of me were two soldiers, one near a breach in the wall of the building where a fire seemed to be raging. He was propped up against the wall with his arms dangling like a rag doll. I made for the entrance of the building to get help. It was obscured by dust and smoke, and I nearly fell over a large steel plate which was blocking the entrance. Fearing that the car's tank would explode and envelope the injured soldier in flames, I hurried back to him and with him clinging to me we were able to reach the entrance. Soon after that we got help."

Two more replacement Hurricanes arrived at North Weald for the Squadron. Bad weather during the next two days frustrated the German offensive and allowed Fighter Command to lick its wounds and remuster its forces to face whatever the future held in store. There was an increase in Luftwaffe nocturnal activity, London remaining the main target although intruders also roamed virtually unmolested over the southern counties, some also penetrating into East Anglia and the Midlands. At 0230 on the morning of 17 September a solitary bomber dropped two 100kg bombs over North Weald, but these caused negligible damage: one exploded close to the western perimeter track and the other fell in a nearby field.

With bomber losses in particular mounting, the Luftwaffe now employed new tactics by using smaller formations of bombers protected by larger numbers of fighters, particularly Bf109Es flying close support. German fighter pilots were understandably not keen with their new restrictive role. Another role which did not find favour with the fighter pilots was that of the fighter-bomber, introduced by arming specially adapted Bf109Es to carry a single 200kg bomb slung under the fuselage. Initially only II/LG2 was given the task but, later, other units were similarly armed.

The lull did not last long and battle recommenced for 249 just after midday on 18 September. Led by Flt Lt Barton, a dozen Hurricanes carried out a head-on attack against a heavily-escorted formation of 15 He111s over the Thames Estuary near Southend. Two were claimed damaged, one by Barton:

"After carrying out an attack on a HE111 in the rear section from below, oil and puffs of smoke came from port engine. Aircraft lagged behind formation as they returned to France."

A second Heinkel was engaged by Plt Off Neil, who later wrote of his experience:

"Heinkels again! Coming straight for us and at the same height. No climbing up on this occasion. A classic head-on attack. Classic? Head-on attacks didn't suit me at all! Or the Squadron either, from past experience. The familiar stomach-clenching tension and surging wave of excitement. Now . . . fire! Tracer, a mass of it, reaching out. Streaking. Smoking. But only the briefest of bursts before the Huns were upon us. Jesus! We would collide. A moment of terrible suspense as I was hurled violently against my straps. Followed by relief."

Meanwhile, other Hurricanes engaged escorting Bf109Es of I/JG27 near Rochester, one of which Plt Off Lewis claimed shot down:

"Spotted ME109s above us to stern. Attacked a yellow nose heading back, opening fire from slightly below, approaching head-on. Gave short burst of about three-seconds, pulling nose well up beneath e/a. It went down in a flat spiral and following it down saw it crash near a wood. This was confirmed by Plt Off Worrall, Blue 3. Pilot presumed to have baled out as parachute was seen in vicinity."

It seems that his victim was Oblt Rudolf Krafftschick* of 1 Staffel who was, in fact, killed when

---

* Plt Off Lewis may have previously met Oblt Krafftschick in the air over France in May 1940, since the German pilot shot down an 85 Squadron Hurricane in an action in which Lewis was involved. See the author's *Twelve Days in May* published by Grub Street.

his aircraft crashed into Squirrels Wood, Stockbury near Sittingbourne at 1230, although this may also have been attacked by a pilot of 46 Squadron. Two other Messerschmitts were engaged by Wg Cdr Beamish, who was flying alone behind 249. He claimed one probably destroyed and the second as damaged before he was set upon by three others. Beamish returned to North Weald with his aircraft shot full of holes, the hydraulic system shot away and without brakes but was still able to make a safe landing. Of the initial head-on attack against the Heinkel formation, Plt Off Neil recalled:

> "Back at dispersal there were confused reports. Everyone agreed that the Heinkels had been hit — we couldn't have missed them! However, nothing had been seen to go down. Head-on attacks were hopeless. And dangerous, too, by God!"

From this sortie Flt Lt Parnall failed to return; Barclay noted in his diary:

> "Dennis has not turned up from the second trip. He has been missing ever since, but we recall the case of Pat [Wells] who was 'missing, believed killed' for five days and then was found slightly wounded in hospital."

Sadly however, the popular A Flight commander was dead. It transpired that soon after the departure of the Squadron on this operation, he had been obliged to return to North Weald owing to problems with the Hurricane's air pressure system and gun firing mechanism. He had immediately taken off in another Hurricane (V6685) but had been bounced by a Bf109E and shot down near the village of Margaretting at 1325. He may have fallen victim to a Messerschmitt of I/JG3 since Oblt Helmut Meckel of that unit claimed a Hurricane in the area at about this time. The Hurricane crashed and burned out by the A12 near Furness Farm at Furze Hill. An eyewitness reported seeing it enter a spin before it went into a vertical dive with its engine at full boost and pencil thin streams of black smoke issuing from the exhaust ejectors*.

On the fourth sortie of the day the Squadron was vectored onto a formation of withdrawing He111s near Southend Pier, but were unable to reach their height in time to carry out an attack. However, Plt Off Barclay (Red 2) spotted a damaged Heinkel limping home; he wrote:

> "Realising we wouldn't engage the main formation (very infuriating as they seemed to be almost unescorted) I dived down and closed to about 40 yards range. The Heinkel turned left and I saw my bullets rake it from pilot's cabin to tail. A parachute appeared out of the top of the fuselage and flapped around; bits flew off, and a yellow rubber boat bobbed out of the rear top of the fuselage. Then he went down in a vertical dive into the clouds and straight on down, probably into the Estuary near Shoeburyness."

Although believed to have been a Heinkel, Barclay's target was probably a Ju88 — 3Z+HS of 8/KG77 — which had earlier been engaged by a number of Spitfires and Hurricanes before he attacked; when the unfortunate bomber reached sea level the *coup de grâce* was delivered by two Hurricanes of 302 Squadron and it crashed into the Estuary off Sheerness at 1730. Fw Haret baled out and was captured badly wounded but Oblt Hans-Ludwig Weber, Fw Krimpmann and Gfr Neuweg were killed. Sgt Bentley Beard reported shooting down a Bf110 east of Canterbury, although this was possibly a misidentification of another Ju88 or even the same aircraft as attacked by Barclay:

> ". . . a ME110 passed behind, diving in the direction of Canterbury. I followed it and it climbed through the clouds. As I came out of the cloud I opened fire at 500 yards for three seconds with no visible effect. It then climbed eastwards and I closed to 250 yards, about 1,000 feet above

---

* Such was the total destruction of Flt Lt Parnall's aircraft that crash site investigators could not initially establish the identity of the Hurricane or the pilot (who had been decapitated), and whose remains were buried in North Weald's churchyard as an Unknown Airman. Later, when material retrieved from the Hurricane wreck was further examined and its identity was eventually established, Parnall's remains were removed for re-burial at St Gennys in Cornwall, his home town.

the clouds and fired for five seconds. As it went into cloud it burst into flames, going vertically down. I pulled out in cloud and went below but could not see the crash. It may have fallen in the sea as I was very near the coast."

With the death of Flt Lt Parnall, newly promoted Flg Off Beazley was appointed commander of A Flight in his place. Two more experienced replacement pilots arrived at this time, Sgt L.H.B. Pearce from 32 Squadron, and Plt Off W.H. Millington*, a successful Australian with eight victories, who was posted in from 79 Squadron. Both men joined B Flight.

The weather next day (19 September) was very cloudy with strong winds, ideal for reconnaissance machines to race across the Channel to carry out surveys of airfields and keep the defences on constant alert. The Squadron was ordered to send up pairs of Hurricanes throughout the morning, but only Flg Off Beazley and Plt Off Barclay encountered the enemy, south of the Thames-Deal patrol line, after they were scrambled at 0945; Barclay wrote:

"We were suddenly told there was a bandit below us at Angels 10 [10,000 feet]. We dived and there was a Ju88. We broke up and Beazle attacked from astern and got in about a ten-seconds burst. I did a sort of vertical full deflection attack from above, pulled out of the dive and did an astern attack of about seven-seconds burst. The 88 turned slightly to the left and went into cloud with the port engine pouring smoke and bits flying off. I dived after it into cloud and two black bits floated past . . . I never saw the 88 again, though I looked for it below cloud over the Estuary."

Beazley added:

"The e/a took no avoiding action nor did it attempt to go into cloud until both engines appeared to be on fire, and bits flying off it. No return fire was noticed throughout. We appeared to have taken it completely by surprise. Plt Off Barclay and self claim this machine as destroyed as it is reported to have fallen into the sea off Deal."

The aircraft which came down near Deal was 3Z+CH of 1/KG77 in which Gfr Möckel was killed; the other three crew members — Uffz Kunz, Obfw Strahl and Fw Winkelmann — were all reported missing. The Junkers was part of a small formation raiding targets of opportunity. A second aircraft from 1 Staffel (3Z+GH) was chased northwards by Hurricanes of 302 Squadron from RAF Duxford and was shot down at Culford Park near Bury St Edmunds in Suffolk.

There followed another lull in fighting, both sides making the most of the inclement weather to prepare for the forthcoming battle. On 25 September, Plt Offs Meaker and Neil were advised by Wg Cdr Beamish that each had been awarded the DFC, the first decorations for the Squadron. The Squadron's next encounter occurred next day when Flg Off Beazley's section intercepted a Do17 between Gravesend and Folkestone during an afternoon patrol. Beazley reported:

"I was Red 1 leading Red Section above 9/10th cloud, height 14,000 feet. On being vectored to Gravesend, I saw e/a below and about three miles ahead, travelling south. AA fire then opened up for about half a minute and was quite accurate. I dived down to catch e/a. It was travelling very fast. On drawing level, I came out of the sun and delivered a quarter attack developing into a stern attack from the starboard side and gave a five-seconds burst. Red 2 and 3 then began firing from the rear. E/a dived into cloud but came out again and I gave it another five-seconds burst from directly astern. After our combined attacks, white smoke and glycol was seen pouring from the starboard engine. I experienced no return fire. It went into cloud again so I dived through to try and meet it on the other side but did not see it again. My final sight of it was just off Folkestone. Red 2 picked it up under the cloud with one engine steaming but after a short burst it got into cloud again, I claim this with Red Section as badly damaged."

---

* Plt Off Millington was born in England but was taken to Australia by his parents at an early age, and was brought up in Edwardston, South Australia. He returned to England in 1939 to join the RAF.

Burton (Red 2) reported:

> "I followed Red 1, giving a four-seconds burst from starboard quarter, out of the sun. I allowed
> e/a to fly into my fire and saw hits scored."

Palliser (Red 3) added:

> "I dived following leader and made a beam attack, developing into a quarter attack, giving
> two bursts of four seconds. As I attacked I could see white smoke coming from starboard
> engine. There was no return fire. As I broke away e/a dived into cloud."

On their return to North Weald, the pilots were surprised and honoured to be introduced to
Marshal of the Royal Air Force Lord Trenchard KCB DSO, who was paying a visit to the
Station. By now the Squadron's groundcrews, NCOs and Adjutant had arrived from Boscombe
Down, which allowed 56 Squadron personnel to rejoin their unit. The pilots were happy to be
reunited with their own groundcrews.

A land mine dropped on North Weald just before midnight failed to explode. 249 was not
allowed to start an engine, let alone take off, until it had been dealt with. The first scramble on
the morning of 27 September came at 0850 and a dozen Hurricanes were soon in the air, followed
at a distance by Wg Cdr Beamish. They rendezvoused with a similar number of Hurricanes of
46 Squadron in foggy conditions and patrolled Wickford before being ordered to the Maidstone
area where enemy activity was reported. Six Staffeln of Bf110s of V(Z)/LG1 and II/ZG76,
escorted by many Bf109Es, had crossed the coast between Dover and Brighton and were roaming
over Kent and Surrey, their objective to exhaust fuel and ammunition of defending RAF fighters
and thereby allow the Ju88s following them a greater chance to escape interception.

As the Hurricanes approached, 20 Bf110s of V(Z)/LG1 were sighted in a defensive circle
over Redhill and Flt Lt Barton immediately led a diving attack from out of the sun, 46 Squadron
following close behind. A number of Bf109Es were seen high above but, according to the
Squadron diarist, "they showed no inclination to come down and fight." Presumably they had
not seen the Hurricanes. Barton claimed one of the Zerstörer but his own aircraft was damaged
by another over Redhill:

> "Attacked circle of 20 ME110s from up sun, fired four-seconds burst at nearest 110 from above,
> saw port engine stream and pieces fly off. This aircraft was observed by Plt Off Lewis (Blue
> 2) to crash in Redhill sector area. I had to break away as aircraft was damaged."

Barton landed at Gatwick, unhurt, at 0935. Sgt Bentley Beard claimed two more of the Messerschmitts, one of which was credited as a probable:

> "On patrol with the Squadron, I attacked a couple of ME110s. I came in three-quarters on
> one and fired about four seconds. The port engine started falling to pieces and white smoke
> and fluid came away. I saw flames start under the engine. I then lost sight of him. I then
> pursued another ME110 out to sea and fired several short bursts. It then dived into the sea
> about six miles off the coast."

Sgt Palliser engaged three Bf110s with some success:

> "Attacking with Red Section, diving from 19,000 feet split up circle of 20-25 ME110s.
> Separated from section. Attacked single 110 and fired two bursts as he was turning. I saw
> return fire cease as he was doing a steep turn. Smoke and oil issued from starboard engine
> and the machine dived into the sea about four to six miles off the coast south of Redhill. The
> second attack was quarter developing into beam as 110 turned. His port engine ceased and
> started to smoke; no return fire was noticed and machine went into shallow dive in south-
> westerly direction. Did not see him crash. I attacked a third 110 but ammo ran out and I was
> fired at by cannon from rear cockpit. Shell went through rudder."

Apparently Palliser's second victim was later confirmed to have crashed. The first of these two was also engaged by Plt Off Worrall:

> "As No3 of Green Section I attacked with the Squadron, giving one ME110 a head-on three-seconds burst. After breaking away I attacked circle head-on, giving four ME110s one to two-seconds bursts from above; no results were seen. When one ME110 broke out of circle I followed it, preventing it from joining circle. After four-seconds burst port engine smoked and later stopped, e/a diving for ground. I followed, my windscreen oiled up, and with Hurricane and Spitfire followed e/a to coast. After several attacks no return fire was received and starboard engine developed glycol leak."

Their victim was believed to have been M8+XE of Stab/ZG76 flown by Oblt Wilfried von Eichhorn which crashed into the sea off Hastings. The pilot was rescued by the occupants of a fishing boat after two hours in the water, badly burned about the face but his gunner, Uffz Erich Bartmuss, had apparently been wounded and was assumed to have drowned when the aircraft sank. Two more Bf110s, plus a third probable, were claimed by Plt Off Lewis:

> "Sighted circle of ME110s over area near Redhill. Attacked out of the sun and fired two short bursts into e/a following Hurricane down. He billowed smoke and went down steeply. Again attacked circle and put a burst into another ME110 — starboard engine out of action and on fire. Climbed into sun again and again delivered attack on remains of circle. Hit one who dropped out of fight, heading towards coast and, with starboard engine out of action, tried to get home. Forced him down in vicinity of some hills near Crowhurst. He burst into flames on landing in a farmyard."

One of his victims (L1+CK of 14/LG1) was reported to have crashed at Coppice Farm, Dallington near Heathfield at 0950, in which both Fw Friedrich Lindemann and Gfr Artur Hübner were killed, of whom one fell to his death with an unopened parachute. However, this aircraft may have also been engaged by a pilot of 253 Squadron. Yet another Messerschmitt was claimed by Flg Off Lofts:

> "Whilst on patrol with A Flight we encountered a formation of ME110s in a defensive formation. The leader attacked and was followed up by the rest of the flight. I picked on one and gave him a short burst from underneath. He immediately broke away and was then followed by the other Hurricanes who followed and gave him another burst. He finally crashed near Lingfield, Surrey."

This aircraft is believed to have been the same as that attacked by Plt Off Meaker and Sgt Davidson; Meaker reported:

> "Attacked a large defensive circle of ME110s from the sun, diving slightly and going in the opposite direction to the circle. Fired two-seconds burst head-on into one ME110 which immediately broke out of circle. Followed him down in a steep spiral, firing two more short bursts and one long one of six seconds. Port engine was on fire, starboard engine smoking and a piece of what looked like a wing flap came off starboard wing."

Davidson added:

> "We followed him down, firing short bursts periodically, receiving no return fire from the gunner. The e/a crashed in a field near Horne [a village about two miles west of Lingfield]."

L1+LL of 15/LG1 had already been attacked by several fighters and, with both engines damaged, it force-landed near Socketts Manor, Oxted (about five miles north of Lingfield); Oblt Otto Weckeiser and his wounded gunner, Gfr Horst Brügow, were captured; this crew had been credited with four victories. Another Bf110 was claimed by Plt Off Neil:

"I attacked e/a from underneath and from right side. The starboard engine and wing burst into flames and large pieces fell off. The e/a broke formation and fell downward, turning over in the dive. He disappeared into mist at 3,000 feet."

Meanwhile, Flg Off Beazley, leading A Flight, also engaged a Messerschmitt:

"I led Red Section in an attack on circle of ME110s, about 20 in number. One ME110 dived out of the circle. Myself and another Hurricane followed it and gave it bursts from astern. It went down to about 50 feet. Another Hurricane then joined up. I noticed the port engine had stopped."

Beazley's aircraft was then hit by return fire and he was wounded in the left foot. The other Hurricane mentioned in Beazley's report was that of Plt Off Neil:

"I cannot recall which of us in the two Hurricanes fired first, but the result was immediate; the Hun tucked his nose down hard and made for the ground . . . I tumbled down after it . . . when I was more or less in position and preparing to fire, the rear gunner opened up . . . I fired in response and the tracer stopped. I was conscious of the other Hurricane abreast of me and also firing. As I pulled up slightly to take another shot, the rear gunner fired a further burst . . . the Hurricane to my left reared into the air and peeled away to port, leaving me in sole possession . . . No more than 200 yards behind and being twisted about by the invisible hand of the ME110's slipstream, I fired again . . . the 110 began to turn slowly to the right and slacken speed. I fired once more and was rewarded with twinkling strikes."

At this stage Neil had exhausted his ammunition and was obliged to leave the stricken Messerschmitt which was, by then, flying slowly towards the coast streaming a growing trail of smoke from its starboard engine. With his windscreen covered in oil, Neil landed at Detling, there to find that his own aircraft had suffered a routine oil leak and not battle damage as suspected. A few minutes later a second Hurricane landed at Detling, that flown by Sgt Davidson, who had run out of fuel. In his subsequent Combat Report, Neil added:

"E/a [Bf110] is very definitely armoured. When I fired, I had no return fire from e/a, but on ceasing fire and attempting to break away, the rear gunner opened fire. This brings me to think that ME110s have heavy armour and rear gunner shelters behind it when our aircraft open fire but retaliates when fire ceases."

After the pilots had excitedly made their reports, the Intelligence Officer announced that eight of the Messerschmitts had been shot down by the Squadron, with a further five probables. In addition, 46 Squadron claimed four, which prompted the diarist to comment: ". . . it is very much doubted if any of them returned at all." The euphoria was dampened when it was realised that Plt Off Percy Burton was missing. Sgt Palliser reported that he had witnessed the South African pilot's demise:

"I saw his contortions, then I saw him straighten out and fly straight into the German aircraft. I was close enough to see his letters, as other pilots must have been who also confirmed the incident, which in itself caused me to realise that my young life and its future, if any, had jumped into another dimension."

News was received later which confirmed that Burton had been killed. A brief but graphic account of this action suggested that he may have deliberately rammed the Messerschmitt:

"Then above the town of Hailsham was played the last act in the drama. The townspeople came out into the streets and watched the two planes circle and swoop, the Dornier [sic] trying to evade the *coup de grâce*. But the townspeople did not know that the pilot of the Hurricane was mortally wounded, that there was not a single round of ammunition left in his eight machine-guns. He made one last effort. He dived below the Dornier, zoomed up at terrific speed above it, turned and plunged right into it. Both fell like a stone to the ground, only one parachute managing to flutter from the Dornier. When townspeople rushed to the battered wreckage they found [Burton's] body riddled with bullets." *

Meanwhile, the Bf110 with which he had collided — L1+XB of Stab V(Z)/LG1 flown by Hptm Horst Liensberger, the Austrian Gruppenkommandeur, crashed at Simmons Field near Hamins Mill near Hailsham, minus its tail unit which bore four victory markings. Both Liensberger and his gunner, Uffz Albert Köpge, were killed. Their deaths were similarly mourned by their colleagues, one of whom wrote at the time:

"I regarded Horst Liensberger highly as my commander and as a human being and, despite the age difference, I venerated him. I am sure he will come back after the war. Over the radio we heard his last message: 'Both engines are hit . . . am trying to turn . . . it's impossible . . . I will try to land.' Then nothing more."

Once rearmed and refuelled, seven Hurricanes led by Plt Off Lewis, in the absence of both Flight Commanders, were ordered to patrol Maidstone before carrying out a sweep of Hawkinge to Canterbury in company with 46 Squadron. Two formations of Bf109Es were sighted and engaged. Lewis reported:

"As 249 leader, sighted formation of ME109s to north-east of Estuary. Climbed up from 15,000 feet to 20,000 feet but were attacked by second 109 formation from above. In ensuing dogfight was attacked by two 109s, one of which I hit in belly as he passed overhead. He crashed into wood near Canterbury. Put burst into second 109, which attacked soon after the one I shot down, also in belly. I did not observe this one hit the ground but he went down smoking, whereafter smoking fires near the wood in vicinity of Canterbury could have been other aircraft destroyed, as there were no bombers."

His first victim was possibly an aircraft of 8/JG54 flown by Oblt Anton Schön which was severely damaged in combat — the German pilot attempted to force land the Messerschmitt but it hit a fence, somersaulted over the main road and burst into flames at Brenley House, Boughton near Canterbury; Schön was killed. This aircraft was probably also attacked by a pilot of 41 Squadron. Plt Off Barclay reported shooting down another Bf109E, the combat taking place near Ashford:

"I was flying Red 1 when I saw a dogfight going on nearby. Some 109s passed about 400 yards on my port side. I chased a 109 which dived very steeply. I had to use automatic boost to catch up the 109. I lost the 109 in haze owing to its camouflage against the ground, but it suddenly climbed almost vertically out of the haze. I closed to about 150 yards and fired about four bursts, one almost vertically down on the e/a, and two bursts from the beam. The e/a poured glycol. The cockpit roof flew off. The pilot baled out successfully. The e/a crashed (confirmed by Sgt Palliser, Red 3) on a farm SW of Ashford."

This was believed to have been Black 3 of 5/JG52 flown by Fw Herbert Hoffmann who baled out severely wounded. The Messerschmitt crashed at Brick House Farm, High Halden near Tenterden at 1250. Damage was claimed to another Bf109E by Plt Off Worrall, while Wg Cdr Beamish also claimed a Messerschmitt but did not see it crash and was awarded only a probable. He reported that he had seen his fire raking its fuselage at almost point blank range, at which it stalled and went into a spin. Oil on his windscreen prevented further sighting of the German fighter.

With the Hurricanes refuelled and rearmed, the pilots stood by for the next scramble. This

---

* Apparently Plt Off Burton was recommended for the Victoria Cross but it was considered inappropriate to award two VCs to one squadron.

came at 1450 and 11 Hurricanes rendezvoused with those of 46 Squadron in the Hornchurch area. Just on 1530 between 12 and 15 Ju88s accompanied by the usual large formation of Bf110s and Bf109Es were sighted over South London. The Hurricanes quickly manoeuvred to a favourable position and, led by 249, launched an attack. The bombers were flat out which made initial contact difficult. Plt Off Lewis reported:

"As Green leader, attacked formation of Ju88s with Blue Section, and one just dropped out with starboard engine damaged. Closed in and carried out two beam attacks from slightly above and put other engine on fire. Kept after it as it went down steeply towards coast near Selsey Bill. Crashed into sea just near coast. Shot down one ME109 which crossed my sights after engagement with Ju88. Went down in flames, then followed a second ME109 down which I attacked from above and it crashed in wood near Petworth. This is confirmed by Sgt Hampshire of Green Section. Fired short bursts of approx two to three seconds at ME109s and a fairly long burst at the Ju88."

These three victories gave Lewis eight for the day, including two probables, a performance rewarded by a second DFC. The Australian Plt Off Millington opened his account with the Squadron:

"The Squadron attacked formation of 10-plus Ju88s. I climbed 1,000 feet above enemy bombers and made a steep dive quarter attack on the rear e/a. At this time there were only seven or eight left as they were being continuously attacked by Hurricanes. Rear e/a left formation smoking, and I delivered a quarter attack opening fire at 100 yards, closing. Port engine of e/a exploded and e/a dived down steeply to ground in flames. Three fighters, some thousands of feet below, seemed to be following e/a down. E/a crashed SE of Portsmouth.

Bomber formation split up and not one reached the French coast. Plt Off Neil and I attacked the remaining Ju88 at about 4,000 feet which had been attacked by numerous fighters, but was still maintaining height and flying steadily over the coast. I delivered a quarter attack, opening fire from 100 yards closing and the starboard motor of e/a burst into flames. E/a dived steeply over the coast losing height rapidly and Plt Off Neil finished it off with a burst from close range. E/a crashed into sea off Shoreham."

Plt Off Neil had already engaged one Ju88 before joining Millington to finish off the second:

"Wallowing in the slipstream of an 88, I fired a long burst from slightly underneath . . . and had the satisfaction of seeing a succession of vivid strikes on the rudder and starboard wing . . . there was a minor explosion on the right-hand side of the 88 and a shower of debris which produced a thin blade of flame and a developing stream of smoke . . . I watched it slowly drop its nose and drift over onto its side and beyond as though totally uncontrolled.

Curving in pursuit of some Hurricanes ahead of me, I caught up and recognised some of 249, one in particular being flown by our new Australian, Bill Millington . . . we flew together towards a cluster of ack-ack bursts, in the centre of which were some other 88s . . . In turn, we fired at one slightly apart from the rest and the starboard engine was quickly set alight . . . The fire was raging, violent, bubbling red . . . Amazingly the 88 flew on at almost the same speed . . . I followed it down with Millington alongside me and together we shepherded it over the south coast and out to sea where it finally splashed down a mile or so off Shoreham."

Neil added:

"Both [sic] occupants were seen in the water with boat, but all subsequently sank."

Sgt Jack Mills also shared in the destruction of this aircraft:

"I was Blue 3 . . . We attacked and I was able to get in a short burst of about three-seconds at one 88 but it seemed to have no effect; the enemy then turned south and headed for the coast. I made several attacks with two other fighters [believed to have been Sgt Davidson and a pilot from 229 Squadron] on two Ju88s. One of them went down. We carried on with the other one who was left. As we neared the coast he suddenly put his nose down until he got to the water and then flattened out. The two other Hurricanes made astern attacks but it seemed to have no effect so I drew out to the starboard side and made a quarter astern attack of about five seconds. As I broke away the e/a dropped into the sea and sank in about three seconds. No one left the machine."

Flying as Red 3, Sgt Bentley Beard sighted a lone Do17 near Canterbury at 1515:

"I became separated from the Squadron and near Canterbury saw a bomber heading east. I caught it about seven miles out to sea and fired three short bursts; some brown smoke came from the port engine. It began to lose height. I then saw a fighter in my mirror and turned sharply and got behind it. It took little evasive action and my second burst . . . sent it into the sea. I then followed another ME109 near me, turning toward my tail. I had a dogfight with him and after some time fired a burst from the quarter. The machine caught fire and went into the sea. I did not see the bomber again."

Plt Off Barclay (Yellow 3) also claimed one of the bombers shot down, and damaged two others:

"First attack was on a leading vic on the quarter, a five-seconds burst, closing to 100 yards. Two of the four Ju88s left slight trails of smoke and I claim they were damaged. I then did quarter attack on one of the four aircraft; saw the de Wilde ammunition hitting the fuselage. Broke away and did astern attack on same aircraft. It promptly dropped from formation and smoke came from both engines. I stopped firing and immediately the smoke ceased and the e/a rejoined the formation. I opened fire again from astern and again e/a smoked and lagged behind. When I stopped firing the e/a again ceased smoking and rejoined the formation.
    I then closed up to about 100 yards and gave a deliberately aimed burst at each engine. A cloud of black smoke poured out of both engines and oil from e/a came on my windscreen. The e/a then went into a steep dive which it had not pulled out off when I last saw it. I force-landed at West Malling owing to a severed starboard aileron cable. The men at West Malling had seen the combat and confirm that a Ju88 with smoke pouring from each engine crashed in the vicinity. I claim e/a was destroyed."

Since the combat damage to Barclay's aircraft rendered it temporarily unserviceable, he borrowed a Spitfire which had force-landed at West Malling earlier in the day (believed to have been an aircraft of 72 Squadron from Biggin Hill) in which to return to North Weald.
    Another of the bombers fell to the guns of Sgt Davidson, which was apparently shared with Sgt Mills and a pilot of 229 Squadron:

". . . I saw a Ju88 struggling for the rest of the squadron. I carried out a beam attack on this e/a and his starboard engine, which had already been slightly smoking, burst into flame. I carried out another attack and this time e/a's port engine began to smoke and bits of wing and cowling flew off. At this point, pilot of e/a or other member of crew (only one person) baled out and e/a crashed in a field by a road near Chiddingstone, near Penshurst aerodrome."

Their victim was believed to have been 3Z+DC of Stab II/KG77, which had earlier been hit in the starboard engine by AA fire over London. Following the attack by the Hurricanes it crashed in flames at Vexour Farm, Penshurst near Tonbridge at 1530. The crew baled out but only two were recovered, both wounded; Oblt Karl-Heinz Lutze was assumed to have been killed. Another Squadron victim was believed to have been 3Z+DP of 6/KG77 which burst into flames under attack and broke up over Sevenoaks; Oblt Horst Seif, Fw Eichinger and Uffz Gebhardt were killed, with only the wounded Fw Zinsmeister able to bale out. 3Z+GN of 5 Staffel was also believed to have fallen to the Squadron and crashed in the Channel six miles off Beachy Head at 1600. Lt Walter Pflüger, Uffz Grönke and Gfr Reinhardt were reported missing and assumed killed; the body of the fourth crew member, Gfr Max Zott, was washed ashore west of Beachy Head four days later.

The Hurricanes drifted back to North Weald where the returning pilots were saddened to learn of the loss of Plt Off Bryan Meaker (P3834), who was seen to have been shot down east of London by crossfire from a formation of five Ju88s he was attacking; he baled out but hit the tailplane of his Hurricane and fell to earth, his parachute unopened. His body was found at Warren Field near Brightling Park, while the Hurricane crashed at Brake Field, Giffords Farm near Dallington at 1530.

When the score was tallied, the day's claims totalled 21 destroyed, six probables and three damaged. The Squadron's diarist commented:

> "Although two of our most gallant comrades were lost, today was a glorious day in the history of the Squadron."

The survivors of 249 were not to know that they had helped to repulse one of the Luftwaffe's last major daylight raids on London. The German bomber squadrons had suffered heavily during the assault on the capital, losing 56 aircraft with a further ten seriously damaged. But the opposing Spitfires and Hurricanes were not the only threat faced by the short-range Bf109Es, since the return Channel crossing with almost empty fuel tanks presented a major problem, as Lt Ostermann* of III/JG54 recalled:

> "The squadrons had broken up and the separated planes clung to the cloud ceiling trying to save their fuel. Hanging over the water with just a few drops left was a most uncomfortable feeling, and each minute seemed like an hour. Still no land was in sight, and I realised we had crossed the coast far to the west of Dover, where the Channel is very wide. One after another the planes had to go down and ditch, leaving behind a trail of foam, a yellow Mae West, and a green oil stain. At any moment I would have to do the same . . . Then, far ahead I saw something shining. Was it land or just a patch of light? It was the coast indeed."

Since the German High Command could no longer sustain massed formations aimed at the capital and its docks, the Luftwaffe began to rely ever more on fighter-bomber strikes, using Staffels of bomb-carrying Bf109Es and Bf110s. The first major battle in the air had thus been won by Fighter Command's thin blue line, in which 249 had played a prominent part. The planned German invasion was put on hold, although a new offensive was about to commence, for which the main bomber force was given a new role: night terror attacks against the capital and its people.

Although there was a noticeable decline in the number of bombers seen over south-eastern England, the skies nevertheless remained full of danger for the defending fighter pilots. Groups of Bf109Es were seen high above patrols put up by 249 and 46 Squadrons early on the afternoon of 28 September. Ordered up to 25,000 feet over the Thames Estuary, where the pilots found it uncomfortably cold, at least one Bf109E executed a perfect bounce on 249's rear section, shooting down Plt Off Lewis (V6617 GN-R) as he later recalled:

> "We had been patrolling at 26,000 feet, making contrails, and were aware that what we thought were HE113s were slightly above us, also making contrails. On being ordered back to base, we dived, with myself weaving back and forth to cover the Squadron."

Sgt Hampshire, flying as Lewis's No2, added:

> "He and I were tail-end charlies. I'd just had a look into the sun when he shouted 'look out', whereupon I took evasive action and the tracer went over my port wing. Meanwhile they got him and he baled out."

---

* When he was killed in August 1942 in Russia, Lt Ostermann had been credited with 102 victories, of which 93 were claimed in the East.

Lewis continued:

"At about 30,000 feet I was hit by cannon fire, receiving shrapnel splinters in my legs, and the Hurricane caught fire, burning fiercely at the speed at which we were travelling. When I pulled back the cockpit cover the flames roared up round my face and, having just pulled the release of the Sutton harness, I attempted to get out. The suddenness with which I parted company with the plane caused me to be shaken around like an old rag, then the blissful peace and calm of falling free. I remembered what we had been told: don't pull the ripcord immediately on falling free, allow time to separate from the plane, and also to lose initial speed. Brace yourself for the jerk that would follow the opening of the 'chute."

Lewis was admitted to Faversham Cottage Hospital with severe burns; his aircraft crashed at Blacketts Farm, Tonge Corner near Sittingbourne at 1420. Meanwhile, Sgt Bentley Beard gave chase and pursued one of the Messerschmitts to the Dover area where he shot it down into the Channel, about five miles south-east of Dover. The pilot, Hptm Rolf Pingel, Staffelkapitän of 2/JG26 and recent recipient of the Knights Cross, survived the ditching and was rescued by the Luftwaffe's Seenotflugkommando. On his return he reported that he had shot down a Hurricane near Maidstone (his 20th victory), which may have been Lewis' aircraft.*

Next day the Squadron was scrambled at 1600, rendezvoused with 46 Squadron and then patrolled over South London and the Thames Estuary, where heavy cloud was encountered. Sections lost contact with flights, flights with squadrons, and the two squadrons became separated. The Squadron diarist commented "sitting ducks for any ME109s lurking around." After landing back at North Weald, fortunately without loss, 249 invited pilots from 46 Squadron over from Stapleford Tawney after dinner to discuss the mutual problems.

Both squadrons patrolled south of London next day, then flew out over the Thames Estuary, where they tried out their new formations. One squadron was to fly in section vics in line astern while the other remained above in two flights of six, weaving, with the last aircraft of each six also weaving. On sighting enemy aircraft above, the first squadron was to adopt a defensive 'snake' in close line astern and to also commence weaving. After midday, both squadrons again patrolled and many Bf109Es were sighted high above. Meanwhile, a formation of Ju88s sneaked by and reached London but were not seen by any of the pilots, who were concerned with not being bounced by shadowing Messerschmitts. Nonetheless, when the latter did carry out a hit-and-run attack, a Hurricane of 46 Squadron was shot down in flames and its pilot killed.

Two messages of congratulations arrived at North Weald for 249 Squadron in connection with the fighting on 27 September, one from Sir Archibald Sinclair, the Air Minister, stating: "My congratulations on your splendid success in yesterday's operations", and the other from Air Chief Marshal Sir Cyril Newall GCB CBE, Chief of Air Staff: "Congratulations on your continuous additions to a fine record." North Weald also received a visit from Air Vice-Marshal W.S. Sholto Douglas MC DFC, Deputy Chief of Air Staff, who added his own congratulations to the Squadron. Questions were asked as to how soon the more powerful Hurricane Mk II would be available, since it was becoming obvious that the present model was being out-performed by the Bf109E, which the pilots believed had been fitted with a more powerful engine. Assurances of speedy deliveries were given.

Three more pilots were posted in during the closing days of the month: Plt Off J.J. Solak, a Pole, and Sgt J. McPhee, both from 151 Squadron, joined B Flight; Solak had escaped from Poland via France. A Flight received Sgt R.J. McNair from 3 Squadron. In his summary for the month, the Squadron diarist recorded:

"At the end of this month's work all pilots are eager that two very outstanding facts concerning North Weald should be noted in the Squadron's history:

---

* Hptm Pingel was not so fortunate when shot down for the second time, in July 1941; his Messerschmitt crash-landed in Kent and he was taken prisoner. By that time he had been credited with 26 victories.

1. The controlling by R/T here is beyond all praise — all controllers knowing their job extremely well — many of our successes have been due to their excellent co-operation.

2. On a great many of the patrols carried out, the Squadron has been accompanied by the Station Commander [Wg Cdr Beamish] whose enthusiasm and example have been of great encouragement to the Squadron."

The Squadron was notified that it was second in the September list of Fighter Command aerial victories, being credited with 48 destroyed, 29 probables and 21 damaged. The Poles of Sqn Ldr Kellett's 303 Squadron headed the list for September.

Chapter Three

THE BATTLE IS WON — OCTOBER SKIRMISHING

October 1940

"... noticed 109s passing just beneath ... attacked ... one disintegrated — tail struts first, rudder, petrol tank alight and panels falling off. Last seen diving inverted into cloud."

Plt Off Pyers Worrall, 249 Squadron

October started relatively quietly for 249 in particular and Fighter Command in general. On the first day of the month the Squadron carried out patrols over Kent and saw a number of Bf109Es at high altitude, although there were no engagements. Several days of inclement weather followed. However, patrols were maintained by the Squadron. The Luftwaffe, too, was having a rest although the bomb-carrying Bf109Es and Bf110s were now operating in some numbers, posing additional problems for Fighter Command which had to put up many more patrols to counter them. The large number of patrols began to cause maintenance problems, since most of 249's Hurricanes were constantly springing oil leaks due to wear and tear. As a result, an opaque film invariably spread over the offending aircraft's windscreen, considerably reducing pilot visibilty and necessitating an early return to base.

Four new pilots joined the Squadron during this period, two of whom were French: Adjts (Warrant Officers) Georges Perrin and Henri Bouquillard were posted in from 615 Squadron, while Sgts R.H. Smyth and Michal Maciejowski* arrived from 111 Squadron. A native of Huriel, Perrin had served with the Armée de l'Air and had escaped to England on the fall of France, as had 32-year-old Bouquillard, from Nevers. One of the latter's French compatriots wrote:

"He had even fiddled a little with his date of birth to be posted to a fighting unit. He was an excellent pilot, with an almost British imperturbability. I think he was never happier than when he was up in the air, and he just couldn't keep still when a fight was in the offing."

A few days later Sgt Pearce left the Squadron and joined 46 Squadron at Stapleford Tawney, followed by Sgt Hampshire who went to the newly formed 422 Flight at Shoreham. A spate of well deserved decorations were announced for Squadron pilots: a second DFC for Plt Off Lewis (currently in hospital), and the DFC for Flt Lt Barton, Flg Off Lofts (partly for his performance with 615 Squadron prior to joining 249), and Plt Off Millington (mainly for his earlier work with 79 Squadron); in addition, Sgt Bentley Beard received a DFM.

North Weald received a visit from Air Chief Marshal Dowding on 2 October, when he spoke to a number of Squadron pilots. He assured those present that the new Hurricane II would soon be available, which greatly heartened the pilots who were beginning to feel frustrated at not being able to intercept the high flying Bf109Es. Fitted with the Merlin XX engine and armed with four 20mm cannons it was hoped that the new model Hurricane would keep the Messerschmitts occupied.

The bad weather continued unabated although it did not deter a German intruder from locating North Weald at 0500 on the morning of 3 October. Bombs fell near the Officers' Mess but inflicted little damage and no casualties. Flg Off Lofts, who had been given temporary command of A Flight until the return of Flg Off Beazley, attempted to carry out an interception

---

* Sgt Maciejowski was a Pole from a little village near Lemberg. When war broke out he was serving as a Corporal instructor in the Polish Air Force and, following the invasion of Poland, managed to escape to Romania then by sea to France, where he flew Bréguet 693 attack aircraft. Following the fall of France, he and three other Poles stole a French aircraft and flew to England.

but was frustrated by the heavy cloud cover and was unable to sight the bomber. The atrocious weather continued for the next 24 hours, curtailing all flying as far as 249 was concerned but, next day (5 October), there occurred a brief clash over Kent with five Bf109Es which attempted to bounce the patrolling Hurricanes. Both sides escaped unscathed.

Continuing dismal weather prevented the Luftwaffe from mounting any significant attacks, although at least one intruder penetrated the heavy overcast to reach the vicinity of North Weald on 6 October. Plt Offs Neil and Crossey were immediately scrambled and Neil managed to intercept the Dornier north-east of the aerodrome:

> "I instructed Crossey to stay below cloud, then at little more than 1,000 feet, whilst I climbed up through the first layer. Emerging at about 4,500 feet . . . to my utter astonishment, I found a Do17 doing precisely the same less than 400 yards ahead of me . . . I had managed to get to within 200 yards when the Dornier began to slink back into the fringes of the mist. I followed it into the murk, firing at the disappearing silhouette."

Despite searching above and below the clouds, neither Neil nor Crossey were able to relocate the aircraft and returned to base, where it was suggested that Neil may have mistakenly engaged an RAF Hampden bomber since one had been attacked over East Anglia. However, the Squadron was advised later that the damaged Dornier had been caught north of Chelmsford and shot down by two Hurricanes of 17 Squadron from RAF Debden.*

Three patrols were carried out on 7 October, during one of which 20-30 Bf109Es (possibly fighter-bombers of II/LG2) were seen in loose formation north of Ashford, at between 20,000 to 30,000 feet, being engaged by Spitfires. The Hurricanes separated into sections and joined the fight but only Plt Off Millington (Green 1) was able to make a claim:

> "46 Squadron with 249 escorting joined in a dogfight between Spitfires and ME109s at 21,000 feet. Formations broke up and I chased a ME109 which dived steeply down. I left him to a Spitfire and climbed back to about 22,000 feet into the sun and dived down on a ME109 which broke off his attack and turned steeply in front of me, offering a plan view of his underside at point blank range. I gave him a short burst and he turned on his back and dived steeply down, emitting black smoke. I was then tackled by two Spitfires so broke off the engagement. The battle in my opinion broke up due to the Spitfires mistaking Hurricanes for ME109s and attacking them."

The action with the Messerschmitts did not however herald a resurgence of aerial activity, and there followed a further period of mainly uneventful but necessary patrols. On 8 October, 249 was scrambled just after 0800 when two formations of about 50 and 100 aircraft approached the Kentish coast. The Hurricanes patrolled over London as ordered but the Jabo Bf109Es flew high over the south-east of the capital and were not intercepted. Next day there was a scramble just before tea but again no contact was made. Although no enemy aircraft were engaged during the only patrol carried out on 10 October, the Squadron lost one of its newer pilots, as Plt Off Barclay recalled:

> "We climbed up to 24,000 feet with 46 Squadron and were not above the topmost clouds then. We saw some HE113s [sic] above us . . . . at one time the whole Squadron was making white trails. Sgt Bayley, my No2 in Red Section, vanished, and apparently running short of oxygen, he lost consciousness and dived straight into the ground, knocking down two cottages, and unfortunately three people were killed."

---

* Subsequent investigation established that the aircraft attacked by 17 Squadron was indeed a Hampden, L4100 of 106 Squadron on a cross-country flight from RAF Finningley, the crew of which reported being attacked by two 'Spitfires' six miles north-west of RAF Stradishall. The Hampden's co-pilot was killed in the attack although the other three members of the crew were unhurt. That this was the same aircraft as that attacked by Neil seems highly improbable.

Sgt Eddie Bayley's aircraft (V7537) crashed seven miles east-north-east of Gravesend, at Shades House, Cooling at 1547. A new pilot from 32 Squadron married with a baby daughter, Bayley was buried at St Luke's, Bromley*. The Squadron lost the services of another aircraft, albeit temporarily, next day when Plt Off Solak omitted to lower the undercarriage of V6728 GN-Z when landing after a patrol at 1525; the Pole was shaken but otherwise unhurt.

The Squadron carried out a patrol over the Hornchurch-Biggin Hill area at 25,000 feet on the morning of 12 October and encountered a Bf109E formation. One of the French pilots, Adj Perrin (V7313 GN-F) was shot down near Eastchurch, probably by Maj Werner Mölders of Stab/JG51, one of the Luftwaffe's leading pilots; although wounded Perrin was able to bale out, and was admitted to hospital. Only Sgt Bentley Beard (Yellow 3) managed to make a claim:

"I was re-forming with the Squadron after we had been attacked, when I saw a 109 diving on six of our aircraft. One went down taking violent avoiding action. The ME109 then flew in my direction and above. I pulled up the nose and fired for three seconds. I later observed the 109 going out to sea with glycol streaming out behind. He was losing height."

While the Squadron had lost the services of Perrin, it welcomed the return of Sgt Smithson, who had been wounded in the September fighting. The weather deteriorated again over the next couple of days, nevertheless 30 Bf109Es — probably aircraft of I/JG2 — were seen off Folkestone at midday on 14 October, one of which Plt Off Barclay (Yellow 1) engaged:

"Some ME109s dived from 25,000-30,000 feet to attack 249 Squadron at 22,000 feet. Squadron broke up and I climbed in a turn, when I was attacked by four 109s in line astern. I took violent evasive action, diving to 15,000 feet. I turned to look for e/a and one 109 passed across in front of me at 150 yards range. I opened fire with more than full deflection. E/a turned on its back and dived down apparently out of control. I continued firing at e/a with various deflections for 10 seconds; the e/a streamed glycol smoke and continued to dive towards the sea. I was obliged to break off attack when e/a was at about 1,500 feet, upside down, owing to an attack by seven other e/a, so that I did not observe e/a crash in sea."

The next engagement occurred on the afternoon of 16 October during a patrol near Hornchurch. Flg Off Lofts and Adj Bouquillard were ordered to investigate a 'bogey' and came across an aircraft, which they identified as a Do215, near Tenterden; Lofts reported:

"Whilst on patrol I was detailed to intercept enemy raider approaching Maidstone from the south. I was vectored with Red 2 towards the bandit's incoming height to about 12,000 feet and after flying for a few minutes encountered it at 12,000 feet coming head-on towards my section. The bandit evidently saw us and turned steeply to the right and made for the clouds just above us. I detailed Red 2 to go above and myself entered the clouds on the same course as the bandit. I flew for a few seconds and then sighted him straight ahead. I closed to rather a too close a range and opened fire with a burst of about ten seconds. The Do215 dived slightly to the right and I noticed smoke coming from his port engine; he then started to lose height. I then felt a thud against my aircraft and shortly afterwards my engine stopped — no oil pressure. The cockpit filled with flames and smoke but they were not sufficiently overcoming to warrant an emergency descent."

Lofts successfully force-landed the Hurricane at Rolvenden near Tenterden at 1310, and was unhurt. The ever keen and obviously elated Bouquillard added:

"I made a quarter attack astern, closing in from 300 to 100 yards, with a ten-seconds burst.

---

* Although it was assumed that Sgt Bayley lost his life as a result of oxygen failure, when the site of the crash was relocated in 1982 and subsequently excavated, many items came to light including head armour which clearly showed signs of bullet strikes. Presumably his aircraft had been shot down by an unseen Bf109E, probably an aircraft of I/JG2 flown by Fw Reins, who claimed a Hurricane in the area at this time.

The rear gunner fired in my direction for three seconds without hitting me. I had the impression that I silenced his fire. The Do215 dived very steeply with black smoke pouring out of its port engine. At 4,000 feet I made a beam quarter attack from starboard. The Dornier dived gently into cloud and disappeared."

The French pilot was prominent again two days later, when he was obliged to force-land P3463 GN-L at Padfields Farm in Church Road at Thornwood Common at 1630, at the end of a long patrol. He had been orbiting North Weald, waiting his turn to land, when his engine spluttered to a halt. He came down two miles from the aerodrome and although the undercarriage of his Hurricane was damaged, he was unhurt. Sgt Evans experienced a different type of problem on returning from this sortie in V6614 — the wrath of Wg Cdr Beamish:

"Returning one evening from a longer than usual patrol at 30,000 feet or so I landed and ran through a 'filled' bomb crater which I had not spotted on touchdown. The slight jar warned me that I had probably damaged the tail wheel, so I pulled off the runway at the end of my landing run so as to be out of the way of aircraft landing behind me. The Squadron always got down quickly with perhaps two or three aircraft on the same runway at once, and it was essential to get out of the way quickly so that someone else short of fuel did not have to go around again. I then throttled right back to a slow tickover, which was not good for the Merlin engine which would start to burn oil and emit blue smoke if allowed to idle for more than a minute or two. But I wanted to climb down and have a look at the tail to estimate the damage before switching off because it might be possible to taxi if the strut was merely bent, which would save the erks having to lift the aircraft back to dispersal.

    Just as I was examining the damaged wheel on my knees, a very irate voice from beside my ear roared: 'Sergeant, you taxied this bloody aircraft . . . don't you know better than that?' I stood up to confront a red-faced Wing Commander who was quite beside himself with fury. I hesitated and then said that I had not taxied but simply eased off the runway at the end of my landing run to give clearway to the others. 'You did not! I saw, you were taxiing, you bloody fool — look at your engine. Don't you know any better than to throttle back like that?' This time I also lost my temper . . . after all, I was tired, cold and hungry and fed up, to say the least after another hectic day, and I guessed he was too. So I stood up to him and said: 'Sir, if I was not standing here having this stupid conversation with you, the bloody engine would have been switched off long ago.' He turned on his heel without another word, got into his car and drove back to dispersal." *

Despite this heated *tête-à-tête*, Beamish was held in great esteem by all his pilots and was ever keen to take to the air. Flt Lt Barton wrote:

"During those months when we were on readiness at first light and wondering if some of us would make it through the day, Victor's car would come steaming up to dispersal with the Station Commander's pennant flying, and he'd bound out, rubbing his hands, and with a greeting 'A nice day for Huns', when all we wanted was a rest!" *

More new pilots arrived for the Squadron in mid October, Plt Off W.W. McConnell joining from 607 Squadron, followed next day by Plt Off A.R.F. Thompson from 85 Squadron and Flg Off Cassidy from 25 Squadron. The latter had requested a posting to single-engine fighters when his Blenheim unit departed North Weald earlier in the month. Thompson got off to a bad start when he force-landed V6635 at 1805, owing to engine problems when returning from a convoy patrol. The aircraft was Cat 2 damaged. Three days later Thompson was again obliged to carry out an emergency landing due to engine problems, coming down at Fitzwaters Meadows, Hall Lane, Shenfield near Hornchurch at 1509. He was again unhurt.

    Bad weather returned to cause a reduction in flying, although patrols were still sent up. During this quiet period the Squadron acquired a second mascot when Plt Off Millington

---

* See *Wings Aflame* by Doug Stokes.

introduced Wilfred the duck, who soon made friends with Pipsqueak the pup. Apparently Wilfred frequently accompanied off-duty pilots on visits to local pubs in and around North Weald and Epping, when he would consume the odd half pint of best bitter before promptly depositing his calling card *.

The Squadron carried out a patrol north of Biggin Hill during the morning of 25 October, when a formation of 10 to 12 Bf109Es was intercepted. Plt Off Neil and Sgt Davidson fired at three of these but no results were seen. Sgt Maciejowski (V6692) became separated and subsequently lost and landed near Colchester at 1000. He was unhurt and his aircraft undamaged. Flg Off Lofts flew over later in the Squadron's Magister and led Maciejowski back to North Weald.

Shortly before midday a dozen Hurricanes were again airborne and, having rendezvoused with a similar number from 46 Squadron, climbed to 25,000 feet to patrol a line Woolwich-Gravesend-Sevenoaks. A formation of 15 Bf109Es of II/JG26 was sighted but as the Hurricanes approached, the Messerschmitts turned and dived towards the Sussex coast. At the same time the rearguard of both squadrons were attacked from above by individual Bf109Es: three Hurricanes were closely pursued and both Sgt Bentley Beard (P3615 GN-D) and Adjt Bouquillard (V7409) were shot down, probably the victims of Hptm Walter Adolph and Lt Karl Borris. Bentley Beard baled out wounded near Tunbridge Wells and was admitted to Pembury Hospital; his aircraft crashed at Rankins Farm near Linton. The French pilot, also wounded, was able to carry out an emergency landing on Rochester airfield. He was admitted to the RN Hospital at Chatham †.

During the attack on the rear of the Hurricane formation, Plt Off Neil (Yellow 1) saw the Messerschmitt leader overshoot after firing. This he attacked from 50 yards:

"I was able to deliver a two-seconds burst. A large piece broke from the e/a and it jerked very noticeably, finally turning on its back and going down vertically. Owing to further enemy action and cloud, I was not able to confirm [its destruction]."

Meanwhile, other Hurricanes pursued the Messerschmitts and engaged them north of Hastings. Plt Off Millington, who was leading one flight, found himself ideally placed up-sun of an unsuspecting Messerschmitt:

"I carried out an astern attack from slightly below ME109 firing from about 50 yards. E/a unaware of my presence. Large pieces flew off and e/a dived steeply through clouds, large quantities of black smoke pouring from it. Presumably crashed in vicinity or in sea near Hastings."

Plt Off Worrall and four others chased another group of Bf109Es, believed to have been fighter-bombers, to the north-west and was credited with shooting down one:

"As Blue 2 weaving behind, noticed 109s passing just beneath . . . attacked by surprise one of the formation from astern and close: one disintegrated — tail struts first, rudder, petrol tank alight and panels falling off. Last seen diving inverted into cloud."

Worrall noted that his victim's wingman did not attempt a counter-attack. He chased this aircraft southwards but did not see any result of his fire before it disappeared into cloud north of Dover. Over the coastal town he saw six more Messerschmitts circling, apparently waiting

---

* When the Squadron departed for Malta in April 1941, both Pipsqueak and Wilfred naturally had to be left behind. Pipsqueak was apparently looked after by a member of the ground crew who was not travelling with the Squadron, while it is assumed that Wilfred just blended in with the surrounding countryside, his favourite locations being the ditches on the edge of the airfield in which he used to swim.

† Adjt Bouquillard did not return to 249 on recovery from his wounds, but was posted back to his former unit, 615 Squadron at Northolt. Commissioned in February 1941, he was shot down and killed in combat the following month, the first French fighter pilot serving with the RAF to lose his life in action.

to escort bombers returning from an attack on London. He attacked one which immediately dived to avoid him. He reported that none of the other Messerschmitts attempted to engage him, or an unsuspecting Lysander which flew below them.

Hurricanes were scrambled early on the morning of 27 October when a lone Do17 was seen dropping bombs near North Weald. The bomber was chased in and out of clouds before Plt Off Neil caught up with it about ten miles from the Thames Estuary. He fired nearly all his ammunition and saw smoke pouring from both engines before it disappeared into cloud. In another daring attack during mid-morning next day (28 October), a lone Do17 again raided North Weald. It dived through the clouds, unloaded hurriedly and then slipped back into the murk. Just before this attack Hurricanes had taken off and were patrolling above the clouds. Plt Off Millington was Blue 1 and acting as weaver:

> "I was patrolling above cloud with 249 Squadron near Hawkinge. Control reported bandit coming SW about ten miles NE of us. I sighted the Do17 as it broke cloud about three miles to the NE. Started to dive towards it and reported position to leader, Red 1. Two bursts of AA fire close to e/a drew attention of Red 1 to e/a and three more aircraft were despatched. I dived on e/a from above and behind, opening fire at about 200 yards. Bullets could be seen penetrating rear turret and I closed to about 50 yards before breaking away. Lack of fire from rear turret leads me to believe that rear gunner was killed. E/a streamed white smoke and vanished in clouds but smoke had vanished when it again appeared. E/a escaped in clouds.
>
> Yellow 1 [Plt Off Neil] then joined me and, on instructions from Controller, we orbited at 12,000 feet position near Dungeness. We sighted a Ju88 occasionally breaking cloud coming from the north. Waited for it to come into the clear and attacked from above. Yellow 1 came in behind e/a and I carried out a quarter attack from above, allowing full deflection and, with a long burst, fired his starboard engine. As I was out of ammunition I made a dummy attack from above to keep gunner engaged while Yellow 1 continued. Yellow 1 killed rear gunner and there appeared to be a small explosion in rear of fuselage. E/a was heading SE, streaming white smoke. E/a was sighted again by Yellow 3 [Plt Off McConnell] who finished off e/a, crashing in area 10-15 miles SE of Dungeness."

In fact the bomber was attacked not only by McConnell (Yellow 3) but also by Plt Off Thompson (Yellow 2); McConnell, an Irishman, reported:

> "I followed Yellow 1 down when Yellow Section was told to strike. I became separated from the section and a few minutes later when below cloud I picked up Yellow 2 and was orbiting about two miles south of Dungeness when Control said there was one bandit south-west. I proceeded there and at about 4,000 feet saw one Ju88 ahead travelling south-east. I carried out a quarter attack and noticed that the starboard engine was stopped. The e/a went into cloud and I broke away above and the e/a appeared again at 1,000 feet. Carried out and began attack, closing to about 50 yards when smoke streamed from the port engine. The e/a landed on the sea and sank invisible in minutes. There appeared to be two boats on floats but I did not see any of the crew."

Meanwhile, Thompson had also got in an attack before the bomber crashed:

> "I followed Yellow 1 down but after going through cloud became separated. I circled below cloud and eventually joined Yellow 3 at about 4,500 feet. After patrolling for about ten minutes we sighted a Ju88 which we attacked, Yellow 3 leading. The starboard engine was already stopped and the rear gunner killed, as we received no return fire. After two attacks I saw the port engine, which was then smoking, burst into flames. I had used all my ammunition and broke off the attack. Yellow 3 saw the Ju88 sink in the water."

The bomber was probably 9K+MR of III/KG51 from Etampes which failed to return from a sortie to London. The all-NCO crew reported missing, believed killed were Gfrs Erich König, Ernst Kramer, Arnold Hauff and Helmut Zimmermann.

At about 1630 next day (29 October) the Squadron was ordered to patrol the base at 15,000 feet, in company with Hurricanes from 257 Squadron (which had arrived at North Weald earlier in the month), but as the first sections of Hurricanes were getting airborne a dozen bomb-carrying Bf109Es of II/LG2 operating from Calais-Marck airfield suddenly appeared and began dive-bombing the airfield. One large bomb fell in the middle of the aerodrome as Yellow Section was taking off and Flg Off Lofts's aircraft (V7627) was damaged by blast and debris, although he was unhurt and was able to land safely; this was the second such incident to happen to Lofts — he had taken off through a curtain of bombs when RAF Kenley was attacked on 18 August before his posting to 249. The other two members of his section, Plt Offs McConnell and Thompson, managed to get airborne safely but Sgt Palliser's aircraft was hit by flying debris which knocked off part of his propeller. With the engine shaking the Hurricane violently, he circled the airfield and promptly landed. A pilot of 257 Squadron was not so fortunate and his Hurricane crashed. Plt Off Neil was amongst those who witnessed the funeral pyre:

"A Hurricane, pointing west, sat outside our dispersal hut. On its belly and on fire . . . I peered through the smoke and flames. Not our code letters. Must be one of 257's. I turned to Crossey. Where was the pilot? A nod. Inside! As the flames took hold, we watched a blackened and unrecognizable ball that was a human head sink lower and lower into the well of the cockpit until, mercifully, it disappeared. Then the fuel tanks gaped with whoofs of flames, the ammunition began to explode, causing us all to step back a pace, and the fuselage and wings began to bend and crumble in glowing agony. Finally, there was only heat and crackling silence — and ashes."

A second Hurricane of 257 Squadron was also damaged on take-off, but its Czech pilot managed to reach 3,000 feet before he baled out, unhurt. On the ground 19 people were killed and 42 injured, six of the fatalities (and a dozen of the injured) occurring on the airfield, where a hangar was destroyed and a lorry set on fire. 27 bombs were dropped. One bomb exploded between the dining hall and the latrines, shrapnel severely wounding AC1 T.H. Saunders of 249; he was admitted to St Margaret's Hospital in Epping where he died next morning. 257 Squadron lost three men killed outright and two others succumbed to their injuries in hospital. A civilian was also killed.

The Messerschmitts, after their hit-and-run attack, made off due west and Red Section led by Flt Lt Barton gave chase as they skimmed low across the countryside. Barton reported:

"I attacked rear e/a and damaged e/a. I broke as I had to engage new aircraft. Although I attacked six e/a, damaging two (one, glycol streaming from radiator, other a small amount of white smoke from wing root). The third, the petrol tank behind the pilot was hit and set on fire. Pilot baled out OK. Machine crashed on Malden-Goldhanger road."

As noted by Barton, the pilot — Fw Hans Rank of 4/LG2 — baled out but he had been badly wounded in the right thigh; he was taken to a nearby house in Malden and then St Peter's Hospital but died from his injuries and shock the same day. His aircraft, 3X+B, crashed alongside the Goldhanger Road at Malden. Sgt Maciejowski (Red 2) claimed a second of the fighter-bombers:

"I followed Flt Lt Barton, as leader, attacking one of a formation of five at about 4,000 feet. Two of this formation separated and I pursued them. They dived into cloud and I cut through the clouds and found myself 50 yards behind both of them. I gave one of them five- to ten-seconds burst stern attack and it immediately burst into flames and fell to earth, where I saw it burning about 200 yards from the seashore, on land. I could not tell whether it was by the Blackwater River. There were some small boats nearby. I gave the second [Messerschmitt] about five-seconds burst but I then lost it in the clouds."

It seems probable that Maciejowski's victim was Obfw Josef Harmeling, also of 4/LG2, who force-landed 3X+N at Langenhoe Wick where he was captured, slightly wounded. The aircraft, complete with bullet holes, was later put on display for the benefit of the local populace. However, this was clearly not the aircraft Maciejowski had seen burning about 200 yards from the seashore. Sgt Davidson claimed a probable, as did Sgt Stroud, who also claimed one damaged:

> "I got off the ground as the bombs were falling and saw about ten ME109s . . . at about 2,000 feet going in a north-easterly direction. They broke into pairs and I chased one pair which I overhauled . . . and did a beam attack on one of them, above and behind. I saw the bullets enter the cockpit and engine . . . the engine belched smoke and it steadily lost height over the River Blackwater. It probably went down about 12 miles out of the Estuary. I then turned north and came above the clouds to find another ME109 just in front. I gave it a short burst and another in the tail, and saw bits flying off and then lost it in the clouds."

Following hard on the tails of Red Section was Blue Leader, Plt Off Millington:

> "Just after Squadron was ordered to scramble bombs started to fall on aerodrome, so I took off as quickly as possible behind Red Section. ME109s attacked aerodrome and made off due west, diving down to about 500 feet. Red Section chased e/a . . . being a little behind, I opened up to maximum speed and gradually overhauled e/a which had climbed to 3,000 feet. There were four ME109s in front with two HE113s [sic] weaving slightly behind. One ME109 was lagging behind on the right. I formated behind him line astern and opened fire at about 100 yards. E/a immediately dived for haze over the sea and I followed close behind, firing continuous bursts; large pieces flew off e/a and it disappeared, going vertically down into the haze at about 500 feet, emitting large quantities of black smoke. Estimated e/a crashed into sea in vicinity of Buxey Sands."

The aircraft, 3X+S flown by Oblt Hans-Benno von Schenk of 5/LG2, crashed in the sea 12 miles east of the Blackwater Estuary and was believed to have been the victim of Millington or Sgt Stroud, or both; the body of the Staffelkapitän was recovered from the sea off Southend on 3 November.

Having just landed from the last sortie of the day, Wg Cdr Beamish found himself in a difficult situation, as recalled by Plt Off Thompson:

> "The Station siren went again and Victor [Wg Cdr Beamish] saw some navvies [reputedly Irish, as was Beamish], employed on the partially completed runways and bomb crater filling tasks, disappear into a shelter. He drove over in his car, jumped out and ordered them to return to work. They did not respond so he belted the largest of them and laid him out cold — the others went back to work immediately. There were no recriminations!" *

All was quiet early on the morning of 30 October. The first serious radar plots started showing at around 1130. By noon, some 80 German aircraft were flying up the Thames Estuary and these were followed 15 minutes later by two waves of 50 and 60-plus, coming in via Dymchurch. To meet them Fighter Command had ten squadrons of Hurricanes and Spitfires in the air and six of these made contact. 249 was one of them, Plt Off Millington (V7536) finding himself caught up in a series of sporadic actions with Bf109Es of I/JG51 over the Channel. His aircraft was last seen chasing a German fighter out to sea; it is believed that he was the victim of Fw Bielefeldt of 3 Staffel who claimed a Hurricane at about this time. The popular Australian had raised his score to nine and two shared. Other pilots noted that groups of Bf109Es repeatedly flew out to sea and then turned back again as if to entice them to follow. Plt Off Thompson did and when he returned to North Weald he reported that he had shot down one Messerschmitt and damaged a second:

---

* See *Wings Aflame* by Doug Stokes.

"When I was at 26,000 feet I saw eight to 12 ME109s at 28,000 feet going in a westerly direction towards North Weald. They turned. I climbed to 30,000 feet and saw four ME109s in the distance going out to sea . . . over Hastings. They later turned back and one of them attacked me, so I took evasive action. I attacked the left one of the vic from above and behind and gave a long burst of about six seconds; he flicked over on his back and went down. I followed him down . . . he started to pull up again. I gave him a six-seconds burst and his rear tank caught fire and he crashed into the sea. I then felt a cannon shell hit the root of my starboard wing and a few machine-gun bullets pierced the fuselage. I swerved and he overtook me. I gave him the rest of my ammunition and bits fell off his machine but I observed no further effect. I landed at Hastings to refuel and then returned to North Weald."

Sgt Maciejowski force-landed out of fuel at Stoney Field, Blackford Farm near Herstmonceux at 1320 following combat with the Bf109Es over the Channel. On enquiring where he was in broken English, he was at first mistaken for German by the local police; his aircraft was undamaged and once fuel had been acquired and the aircraft refuelled, he flew back to North Weald. On a sweep south of London by 249 and 17 Squadrons during the afternoon, a large formation of aircraft was seen at 30,000 feet but the Hurricanes were unable to reach the height before they turned for France. However, Wg Cdr Beamish, flying above his squadrons, followed and encountered a pair of Bf109Es. He closed on them as they crossed the coast near Dover and fired all his ammunition into one, which dropped from 20,000 feet to 8,000 feet over the Channel streaming glycol, and was credited with its probable destruction.

The month ended with another day of bad weather which curtailed all operational flying.

Chapter Four

ON THE OFFENSIVE
November 1940 — April 1941

"I still had my right hand to pull the ripcord and this I did. Sheets of skin were hanging from my face and legs and the cold really stung the open nerve ends. I could smell roast pork for weeks afterwards!"

Flg Off Pat Wells, 249 Squadron

The first week of November was marred by very bad weather; a combination of weather and a reduction in Luftwaffe activities effectively reduced flying operations, although the Squadron continued to maintain security patrols. On the 5th, Sqn Ldr Grandy accompanied a patrol to the Hornchurch area, his first operational flight since he was shot down two months earlier.

During the late morning of 7 November, Plt Off Barclay scrambled from North Weald when a Do17 was reported to be in the area. Having not sighted the intruder, he made his way back to base where, on arrival at 1205, he saw eleven Hurricanes of his Squadron taking off, and joined up with them as they headed towards the Thames Estuary. Soon after their arrival in this area, a convoy was seen under attack by Ju87s of I/StG3 while Bf109Es from JG26, JG51 and JG53 patrolled overhead. One pilot reported sighting 15 of the dive-bombers in perfect formation of vics of three off Bradwell, apparently heading for France at only 100 feet over the sea. The Hurricanes dived to investigate, meeting Messerschmitts; Barclay recorded in his diary:

"I dived and did a beam attack on one — no result. I saw five 109s at about 2,000 feet streaking for home and, pulling the plug, gave chase. I caught them and had a dogfight with one. Eventually he went into a climb and I saw that his engine had stopped. Whoopee! But then I saw five more 109s between me and the shore, also going home and therefore coming towards me head-on. I gave one of them a burst from below and in front. The whole formation split up and turning I gave the same 109 another burst. He slowed down to about 140 mph and smoking slightly he went on — waggling his wings as he went. I couldn't deliver the *coup de grâce* as I was out of ammo. So two probably destroyed it had to be!"

Meanwhile, Plt Off Neil (Yellow 1) reported that he had also accounted for two Bf109Es, plus a Ju87. In his memoirs, Neil wrote:

"A Ju87! As large as life! The first I had ever seen, close-to . . . I fired, watching the spark-flecked de Wilde curve ahead in smoking fingers to touch first one wing then the fuselage. I found myself pumping the contol column violently in order to keep the German aircraft in my sight . . . A series of brief flickers. Hits! The 87 toppled over in slow motion and passed beneath my port wing . . . Going down — straight down, almost. Into the haze and towards the sea."

The Ju87 was probably the aircraft flown by Lt Eberhard Morgenroth who, although wounded, managed to fly the Stuka back to France and land safely. A second Ju87 was claimed damaged by Plt Off Thompson. Neil was then engaged by three Bf109Es:

"Closing behind one, I gave a short burst. Glycol and smoke came from under fuselage. I further attacked this aircraft from the rear and the white smoke changed to black smoke. Flames came from the cockpit of the e/a which made no evasive manoeuvre but dived towards the sea. I was attacked in turn by the remaining two ME109s, one of which presented itself as a beam target. I fired about three seconds and closed in a quarter attack. The e/a turned over and fell in the sea. The remaining e/a I lost."

Two other Bf109Es were claimed destroyed, one by Sgt Maciejowski, who reported:

"I sighted five 109s attempting to bomb the convoy. They eventually split up into pairs, leaving one straggler in the rear. I attacked the single from behind and above, pouring into him from very close range, approximately a six-seconds burst. The e/a made no attempt to escape and burst into flames. The pilot did not jump. E/a crashed in flames in the sea about eight miles north-west of Margate."

Sgt Palliser may have attacked the same aircraft:

". . . noticed bombs bursting round convoy. When at about 5,000 feet I saw e/a diving below me. I followed him down and waited till he pulled out of the dive. Then I carried out an above stern attack at close range, raking e/a from nose to tail with one long burst. The machine just tattered and spun away out of control and crashed in the mouth of the Estuary, about five miles north-east of Margate. Sgt Smithson, Red 2, who was evidently behind me, witnessed attack and result."

Flt Lt Barton engaged another:

"I attacked a single 109 at 8,000 feet. I fired several short bursts and glycol streamed back from his starboard radiator. E/a flew straight towards cloud and I had to break away as there were several other ME109s above."

A probable was also claimed by Flg Off Wells (Yellow 3), who engaged his opponent about ten miles off Bradwell:

"I met an ME109 from 1,000 feet above, head-on. Turned and dived, and delivered a stern attack on him; gave two-seconds burst and bits fell off. Another two-seconds burst and he emitted black smoke and apparently out of control dived into a cloud layer towards the English coast. At this point I was attacked by another ME109 and had to take evasive action. My aircraft was damaged so I returned to base."

Only one Messerschmitt was reported missing, Yellow 1 of 3/JG26, in which Obfw Wilhelm Müller was lost. Three Hurricanes were claimed by the German pilots, one apiece being credited to Oblt Richard Leppla of I/JG51, Fhr Karl Steffens of II/JG51 and Hptm Bretnütz of II/JG53, all ace pilots. On board a balloon barrage vessel, which was escorting the convoy, an RAF officer noted in his diary:

"1155 hours: This looks bad. About 30 Junkers 87s with an escort of ME109s arrived over the convoy. The procedure is simple. The fighters try to put the balloons down in flames and, like one platoon following another on the parade-ground, the dive-bombers follow. Whether they saw something we didn't, I don't know, but the bombers suddenly veered away, and that was that. But not before our fighters had got a couple of Junkers, and possibly a third."

Notwithstanding this, the Ju87s succeeded in sinking the SS *Astrologer* and damaging two other vessels. Gunners aboard the escorting HMS *Egret* claimed to have shot down one of the dive-bombers and to have damaged a second.

In the evening 249 flew a patrol over the Maidstone area. Wg Cdr Beamish was flying as Red 4 and, without warning, broke formation to investigate something that had caught his eye. His aircraft promptly collided with Plt Off Neil's Hurricane (V7676 GN-J); the latter was obliged to bale out, his aircraft crashing at Woldersdale, while Beamish carried out a crash-landing in V7507 GN-B near Leeds Abbey, five miles south of Detling.

During the course of the next day (8 November), Bf109E Jabo made isolated forays against London, while a force of 40 Ju87s of StG3 and IV/LG1 made their presence felt over the Thames Estuary. There ensued a number of engagements and some heavy combat, but it was not until mid afternoon that the Squadron was called upon, eleven Hurricanes scrambling at 1616, joined by more Hurricanes from 46 Squadron. AA bursts were seen over Sheppey and bombs seen exploding among ships in the Estuary, but by the time the Hurricanes dived down to investigate, the raiders had gone. However, Plt Off Worrall, who was weaving above and behind the Squadron when they dived, had become separated and encountered a number of Bf109Es from I/JG51:

"As weaver above and behind the Squadron at 23,000 feet, I could not see Squadron's objective when they dived, but noticed about 30 ME109s in haze above, at heights from 25,000-30,000 feet, spread out in no formation, heading SE. I climbed after them in company with two Hurricanes (later left behind) following them down coast, catching up with one at 25,000-30,000 feet, three quarters of the way to France on Deal-Gravelines line (other e/a also joining NE of Calais). Gave e/a from behind, at 150 yards closing to 50 yards, all ammunition in two-seconds bursts; three guns jammed (two crossfeeds and one separate case) making aircraft swing on firing. Bullets seemed to hit tail unit, right wing root appeared hard hit, black stuff coming out. Engine stopped and e/a went over on its right side, gliding steeply towards Calais."

Meanwhile, 46 Squadron encountered a "mass of aeroplanes below" and dived on them, assuming them to be Bf109s, the Hurricane leader shooting down the leading 'Messerschmitt' — which turned out to be a Spitfire flown by the CO of 19 Squadron, who was leading the Duxford Wing on this occasion; Pat Wells takes up the story:

"At the time there was no love lost between 11 and 12 Groups, so the CO of 46 Squadron did nothing about it except to ascertain that it was not Wg Cdr Bader leading the Wing on that day and that the leader was uninjured [the Spitfire in fact force-landed at Eastchurch, its pilot unhurt]. 12 Group found out that the deed had been done by one of the North Weald squadrons but was unable to get anything out of 11 Group about it. On the following day [Wg Cdr] Douglas Bader arrived at North Weald and taxied to our dispersal, where we were at Readiness, and started to ask questions in such a nice and friendly way [Bader was Wing Commander Flying, Duxford Wing]. The thing that has stuck most in my memory is that he was sitting on the edge of one of our beds, with his feet off the ground, and I was fascinated to watch him swinging his artificial legs! But nobody would 'talk' so when he left and flew over to 46 Squadron at Stapleford Tawney, we telephoned and warned them. They barricaded all the doors and pulled the curtains, and no notice was taken of his frantic knocking! Bader was fuming, but finally left. The interesting thing about the whole episode is the fate that awaited both 46 and 249 Squadrons later when Wg Cdr Bader's 'pal' Air Vice-Marshal Leigh-Mallory [AOC 12 Group] went to higher places. Both squadrons were shipped off to Malta and 46 had the indignity of having its number changed to 126."

A brief spell of bad weather returned for the next two days, during which the Squadron received four new pilots: Plt Off R.E. Tongue from 504 Squadron, Sgt H.E. Bennett from 43 Squadron, and Sgts A.J. Hughes and Vaclav Foglar (a Czech) both from 245 Squadron. However, their stay was short-lived, all four being posted the following week, Tongue to 46 Squadron and the other three joining 17 Squadron. Within the Squadron, Plt Off Barclay was advised of his promotion to Flying Officer, which was followed by the announcement of a DFC. At the same time Plt Off Neil was awarded a Bar to his DFC.

During the early afternoon of 11 November, the Italians carried out their first major raid against England when the Corpo Aereo Italiano (attached to Luftflotte 2) despatched nine Fiat BR20 bombers of 43° Gruppo BT and 40 Fiat CR42 biplane fighters of 43° Gruppo CT to attack a convoy off Lowestoft, while a smaller formation of five Cant Z1007bis bombers, escorted by 24 Fiat G50 fighters of 20° Gruppo, made a feint towards Great Yarmouth. Two Hurricane squadrons were scrambled to intercept and another, on convoy patrol, was diverted towards the hostile formation. In the ensuing battle no fewer than nine BR20s and four CR42s were claimed destroyed, for two Hurricanes slightly damaged; Wg Cdr Beamish sighted one of the returning CR42s, engaged and claimed it probably destroyed.

At this time, 249 had a number of Hurricanes on convoy patrol duties and one pair was ordered to patrol below cloud, at between 2,000 and 3,000 feet. Here they observed a single-engine aircraft flying low over the sea about 20 miles east of Frinton but, as they dived to investigate, a He59 was sighted. As the Hurricanes approached, the floatplane began taking violent evasive action but was attacked by Flg Offs Barclay and Wells, the former recording:

> "A stern attack turned into a head-on attack. I got its port motor and it had to do turns to the left, against the dead motor. Eventually Pat Wells set the petrol tank in the float on fire and the enemy aircraft landed perfectly, into wind. It gradually burned until, suddenly, the petrol tanks went up and covered it and the sea around with burning petrol."

Wells added:

> "The crew of three were slow getting into their dinghy and the aircraft exploded over them and burnt up."

The He59 was NE+TD of Seenotflugkommando 3 flown by Obfw Herbert Roddey. There were no survivors. At about the same time, a second pair of Hurricanes flown by Flt Lt Barton and Plt Off McConnell noticed an unusual twin-engine aircraft low over the water and broke away to investigate. Climbing above the aircraft, Barton reported:

> "It was a bomber of rather clumsy design with very dark green camouflage (almost black), and the roundels which looked like British ones from a distance were, in reality, white with the black German crosses inside."

Both Barton and McConnell opened fire and the aircraft took violent evasive action, climbing steeply, stalling and diving back towards the sea. Barton then set its port fuel tank afire, following which the German pilot throttled back and the fuel tank exploded. The blazing machine dived into the sea, broke up and sank with no trace of the crew. On return to North Weald, they described the aircraft as probably being a Ju86 but, in fact, it would seem this was a FW58 (OJ+AK) of Stab III/JG51, flown by Uffz Karl Nispel, which had been sent out to search for missing fighter pilots from the morning engagements and did not return.

A dozen Hurricanes were airborne from North Weald at 1025 on 13 November. While patrolling the Maidstone line at 15,000 feet they were vectored onto an enemy aircraft, which was sighted at about 20,000 feet. It was a twin-engine aircraft, probably a Dornier, but as it was being attacked by several Spitfires, they resumed their patrol. Plt Off Worrall was weaving above the Squadron when he saw a formation of five Jabo Bf109Es over Maidstone, which then jettisoned their bombs and turned on him, badly damaging the port wing of his Hurricane (V6635) before he was able to escape. Wg Cdr Beamish, who had climbed up through the clouds to investigate was also attacked, two bullets piercing his cockpit and smashing the instrument panel, others causing damage to the tailplane. Despite the damage, he landed safely at North Weald, obviously shaken as recalled by Plt Off Thompson:

> "This was the only time I ever noticed this and as he walked away briskly towards his car he was heard to mutter 'the little yellow bastards nearly got me that time'." *

Both Hurricanes were claimed destroyed by the II/JG26 pilots, one each by Hptm Johannes Seifert and Obfw Robert Schiffbauer.

---

* See *Wings Aflame* by Doug Stokes.

Next day (14 November) the Squadron was again in action, 11 Hurricanes being ordered off at 1415 to investigate a fighter sweep over the Kent coast by Bf109Es of I/JG51. This was a diversionary action by the Luftwaffe, since a formation of 20 Ju87s of III/StG1 was engaged in bombing Dover, where the harbour, the radar station and coastal batteries were attacked. Near Manston, two Messerschmitts were seen below the level of the Hurricanes; one climbed away but the other — White 8 flown by Fhr Erich Vortbach — dived, followed by a pack of 249 Hurricanes. Flg Off Barclay (Yellow 1) was the first to engage:

> "I won the race to intercept e/a and opened fire at 250 yards. My throttle stuck in fully forward position so overtook e/a very rapidly. I continued to fire at e/a from astern until I had to break away to avoid colliding with e/a. I broke away to the left as e/a did a slight left-hand turn. I opened fire on the left rear quarter, aiming to hit the radiator and glycol system. As I fired, glycol poured from left wing root and black smoke from underneath fuselage. E/a turned towards land, the pilot jettisoning the cockpit hood, and crashed into garden north-east of Manston aerodrome. E/a burst into flames on crashing."

A moment before the crash, Sgt Smyth had swept in behind the Messerschmitt and fired a telling burst which caused it to crash into trees on Sacketts Hill Farm at St Peters near Broadstairs, and burst into flames. Vortbach was killed, having been shot through the head. The unfortunate Smyth was severely reprimanded by Flt Lt Barton for his 'unsportmanship' in continuing to fire at the German pilot, who was obviously about to land. He was posted from the Squadron forthwith, departing for 615 Squadron four days later. Flg Off Barclay was also incensed to discover that a pilot of 46 Squadron had claimed a half-share in this victory, and noted in his diary:

> "It was quite ridiculous of him, as there were six of our Hurricanes dealing with the enemy aircraft. Another 249 Squadron pilot ought to have the half."

The Squadron was advised on 15 November of the award of the Victoria Cross to its former flight commander, Flt Lt Nicolson, still convalescing at the RAF hospital in Torquay from the wounds and burns received on 16 August near Southampton. The investiture took place at Buckingham Palace ten days later. Bad weather again interfered with flying operations and it was not until 21 November that the enemy was again encountered, albeit briefly, when Plt Off Thompson and Sgt Palliser were on convoy protection duty over the Barrow Deep. Just before midday, a Do17 was intercepted and engaged. It jettisoned its bombs over Clacton and escaped, damaged, into thick cloud; Thompson recalled:

> "I got a rocket from [Air Vice-Marshal] Sholto Douglas for not shooting it down! He should have tried himself — in cloud!"

On this date Sgt McPhee, who had joined the Squadron at the end of September, was posted to 17 Squadron at RAF Martlesham Heath. A new arrival was Plt Off J.F. Pain, an Australian who had been shot down and wounded while flying with 32 Squadron at Biggin Hill. However, he did not fly with the Squadron and was posted away three weeks later in preparation for a posting to Malta.

Although the odd high-flying Messerschmitt was seen during patrols when weather permitted, none engaged or were engaged until 28 November, when a dozen Hurricanes took off to carry out a patrol over Kent. At about 1400 several Bf109Es were sighted above, tempting the Hurricane pilots to climb towards them. Flg Off Barclay wrote later:

> "We knew circumstances were ideal for the Huns to pounce on any straggler and sure enough I heard a shout. I looked round and saw a long vertical trail of white smoke and then a little blob far below; a parachute. I tried to think who it might be and came to the conclusion it was Pat Wells."

Flg Off Wells had indeed been shot down and had fallen victim to one of the Luftwaffe's premier fighter pilots, Obstlt Adolf Galland of Stab/JG26, as his 56th victory, whose subsequent report revealed:

"Free hunting. In the area of Detling I saw a squadron of Hurricanes flying with a separate cover. I approached the last Hurricane completely by surprise and shot her in flames from a distance of 120-50 metres. Since I had used relatively much ammunition [64 cannon shells and 132 machine-gun rounds] and since I was not able to have a clear picture of the overall situation, I separated myself immediately."

Flying a few hundred yards behind Galland was Hptm Rolf Pingel, Staffelkapitän of 2 Staffel:

"I saw the attack by [Obstlt) Galland and observed the destruction of a Hurricane by him."

The Germans believed that the pilot of the Hurricane had been killed during the attack, since no parachute was seen. However, badly burned, Flg Off Wells did succeed in extricating himself from the doomed aircraft but not without great pain and difficulty, as he later recalled:

"It was a bright autumn afternoon and there was a lot of enemy activity over Kent, so we were wide awake, me in particular, through previous clashes with 109s. Halfway through the patrol at 23,000 feet I was watching some 109s, some in the sun, but at the time they posed no threat to us and I guessed that the other pilots had seen them anyway so there was no need to alarm anybody. The next thing I knew was an attack from below. I took evasive action and howled on the R/T but nobody heard me nor saw the attack which was a lethal one. I was able to take some evasive action until my controls were shot away. My Hurricane was well alight and I could see tracer bullets going over the left wing and hear bullets rattling against the armour-plate at the back of my seat, so there was no point in baling out into that lot, so I sat and fried. One gets dopey in flames, smoke, fumes and lack of oxygen, so my first attempt to get out was a failure: my right foot got caught under the instrument panel. I climbed back in and tried again, but this time my left foot got caught. A Hurricane diving vertically and on fire is not easy to exit!

As I had earlier seen the sufferings of burned pilots in hospitals, I decided that I did not want to be burned so thought 'to hell with this — I will go down with the aeroplane.' A lot closer to the ground than I would normally have chosen, I was miraculously thrown out of the cockpit. To prove its reluctance to lose me and because of its vertical state, the tail of the aircraft hit me and dislocated my left shoulder. However, I still had my right hand to pull the ripcord and this I did. Sheets of skin were hanging from my face and legs and the cold really stung the open nerve ends. I could smell roast pork for weeks afterwards! I landed in an apple tree which was prickly without its leaves, adding to my discomfort when falling through it." *

Wells was rushed to Leeds Castle Emergency Hospital near Maidstone before being transferred to the special burns unit at East Grinstead for plastic surgery. His Hurricane (V6729 GN-U) crashed at East Peckham. During the mêlée, Sgt Maciejowski reported an engagement with one of the Bf109s in the Maidstone area, claiming it probably destroyed. JG26 did indeed lose one of its pilots in this action, Uffz Heinz Wolf of 2 Staffel, although he apparently ran out of fuel after he had become separated from his colleagues and made a wheels-up landing in Black 2 on farmland at Udimore in Sussex; he was taken prisoner.

Next day (29 November) 249 was ordered off at 1110 to patrol in the Maidstone area.

---

* In 1990, Sqn Ldr Pat Wells DSO and General Adolf Galland began corresponding, which led to a meeting in 1995 at the home of the General, on the occasion of a gathering of members of the German Fighter Pilots Association. In his welcoming speech, he commented: "Pat Wells has just arrived here from Capetown, South Africa, to meet me personally. Isn't it great? Before I continue I have to beg his pardon formally and sincerely for my former rough and hostile actions. Dear Pat, please forgive my rudeness, I will never do it again. I am immensely happy that you've survived." General Galland died in 1996.

Flg Off Barclay and Sgt Davidson were detached to carry out an investigation over Dover. Having sighted nothing unusual, they were ordered to return, but at that point Barclay was shot down:

> "Suddenly four explosions down my right-hand side. I realised that they were cannon shells and as I whipped into a left-hand turn over Davidson, two more explosions, and something hit me hard in the right leg but didn't hurt. I felt waves of hot air and the Hurricane [V6692] went into a spin from which I couldn't recover, so I decided to bale out. All of this was of course in a couple of seconds. Back with the roof, straps undone and lean out and push with feet on dashboard. No result. Back into cockpit, undo oxygen bayonet connection and try again. This time I'm out straightaway and fell forward over the leading edge, missing the propeller by inches."

He landed safely near Tunbridge Wells and was taken to hospital, where the nose of a cannon shell was removed from his ankle. Thus the Squadron had lost two stalwarts on consecutive days. Barclay's victor was Fw Dietrich Koch of II/JG26, who claimed the Hurricane as his third victory*.

There was little flying during the first few days of December as the winter started to take hold, although the Luftwaffe put in an appearance on 5 December. A fighter sweep over southern England was encountered by 249 and 253 Squadrons near Folkestone and a Staffel of I/JG51 bounced 249, Hptm Hermann-Friedrich Joppien shooting down Sgt Stroud's Hurricane (V7677 GN-N) in flames, although the pilot was able to bale out with burns†. Meanwhile, Sgt Maciejowski attacked Joppien's Messerschmitt, which he believed he shot down, although in fact the German pilot managed to get away unscathed:

> "Saw about 15 ME109s about 2,000 feet above us, we being at about 19,000 feet. We formed a circle, going lower and lower while the enemy followed us down. The ME109s dived and attacked as I turned left. I saw a Hurricane shot down. The ME which had shot it down dived steeply, pulled upwards and climbed. In his climb he passed in front of me and I gave him two short bursts as he was climbing almost vertically. He entered a right-hand spin and crashed into the sea almost 500 yards from the seashore."

Since no Bf109Es were lost in this engagement, it would seem that Maciejowski had seen Sgt Stroud's Hurricane crash into the sea and had mistaken that for his opponent. Meanwhile, on returning from this sortie, Sgt Palliser was obliged to force-land his Hurricane (V6565) in a field near Stanford-le-Hope, out of fuel, when it suffered some damage. Flg Off Lofts and Plt Off Crossey both landed at Rochester, Flg Off Cassidy at Redhill and Plt Off Solak at Hornchurch, all similarly short of fuel.

More new pilots arrived at this time, including two Frenchmen from 145 Squadron, Adjts Francois Fayolle and Francois de Labouchère — resplendent in their navy blue uniforms with gold-trimmed epaulettes — and three Poles, Flg Off Henry Skalski and Sgt M. Popek from 46 Squadron, plus Sgt Stanislaw Brzeski. The latter had flown in Poland against the Germans and had claimed two Heinkels shot down before the fall of his country. On reaching England he was sent to an OTU before his posting to 249. Another new arrival was Plt Off A.C.G. Wenman from 32 Squadron, although he moved on a week later, joining 145 Squadron. A similar fate awaited Plt Off R.S. Gaskell who arrived from 264 Squadron. He force-landed at High Ongar after running out of fuel during his first solo on a Hurricane, and was soon on his way to 8 SFTS at RAF Montrose for additional training. Also departing during the month were Plt Offs Worrall and Pain, both of whom were posted to Malta, while Sgts Smithson and McNair left for night flying duties with 96 Squadron, and Sgt Evans was posted to 55 OTU as an instructor.

---

* Fw Koch was shot down and killed four weeks later while in combat with a Coastal Command Blenheim.
† On landing, Sgt Stroud was rushed to Rye Hospital from where he was later transferred to Queen Victoria Hospital at East Grinstead for plastic surgery, where he joined Flg Off Wells.

Early in December news was received that Sqn Ldr Grandy was to be promoted to Wing Commander and posted to Fighter Command HQ *. The Squadron diarist wrote:

"This will be a very sad blow to the Squadron as he formed the Squadron in May and has built it up to an efficient fighting unit through his own personality and initiative."

With the imminent departure of Sqn Ldr Grandy, Flt Lt Barton was promoted to Acting Squadron Leader, and was officially given command of the Squadron which he had effectively led in the air since Grandy's injury. At the same time Plt Off Neil was promoted to Acting Flight Lieutenant to command B Flight. The Squadron welcomed the return of Flg Off Lewis, having recovered from his wounds and burns.

The quiet period was livened by an offensive patrol, sanctioned by Fighter Command, flown by Sqn Ldr Barton (V7538 GN-T) and Plt Off Wynn (V6728) during the afternoon of 29 December. Having set course for France, they made landfall eight miles south of Boulogne, going inland about seven miles before flying due north. They were fired on by flak on the outskirts of Boulogne so entered cloud where the two Hurricanes became separated. Finding himself alone, Wynn returned to North Weald. Meanwhile, Barton followed the Boulogne to Calais road but saw no military transport, so flew to St Inglevert aerodrome where he strafed what he thought were petrol tanks stacked in the west corner of the dispersal area. Although he experienced heavy ground fire his aircraft was not hit and he returned to North Weald safely.

The last few days of 1940 and the first week of the new year remained relatively uneventful for the Squadron, the initial major event of 1941 occurring on 10 January, when the first heavily-escorted day bomber operation (codenamed Circus 1) was undertaken. At noon on that date, six Blenheims of 114 Squadron set out to bomb Fôret-de-Guînes, with Hurricanes of 242 and 249 Squadrons flying forward support sorties; other fighter squadrons provided close escort and top and rear cover. Near Mardyck, the Squadron led by Wg Cdr Beamish encountered a small formation of Bf109Es although there were no engagements at this stage.

Meanwhile, as the Blenheims arrived so 249 withdrew, crossing the coast near Calais, encountering heavy fire from four patrol boats anchored about three miles off Calais. Two Hurricanes were hit: V6728 flown by Flg Off Cassidy returned with a damaged tail, while Plt Off Thompson's V6582 had a piece shot out of a propeller blade. Meanwhile, Beamish dived down and strafed the patrol craft and, as he pulled up, he saw a Bf109E drop onto the tail of Plt Off McConnell's Hurricane (P3579 GN-Y). The Messerschmitt pilot, Oblt Georg Michalek of II/JG3, executed a perfect 'bounce' and McConnell, wounded by splinters, baled out hurriedly; his aircraft crashed into the cliffs near Dover and McConnell was picked up by an ASR craft and taken to St Margaret's Hospital with a broken leg. Beamish later recalled:

". . . half-way over [the Channel] I saw bullet splashes in the sea below me. I looked to the left and saw one of our aircraft being attacked a few hundred feet above the sea. As I closed in I saw that the attacker was one of the yellow-nosed ME109s. I let him have the rest of my ammunition and saw my bullets hitting his machine. But it was not until I returned to my base that I learned I actually got my man. Two of my pilots [Plt Offs Thompson and Crossey] saw him crash in the Channel."

However, Michalek's aircraft was not shot down and the German ace escaped, apparently unscathed. It seems that the two Hurricane pilots had actually seen the demise of McConnell's aircraft and not that of the Messerschmitt. All the Blenheims returned safely although a second Hurricane was reported missing, the aircraft flown by Sgt Maciejowski. However, he turned up

* Sqn Ldr Grandy was posted to RAF Coltishall as Wing Commander Flying, and from there to RAF Duxford to command, where he became involved in the development of the first Typhoon Wing. He later served in the Middle East and in the Burma Campaign, being awarded the DSO. He was subsequently promoted to high rank and given a number of Commander-in-Chief appointments. He became Chief of the Air Staff in April 1967 and, on leaving this appointment in April 1971, was promoted to Marshal of the Royal Air Force.

later having landed at Hornchurch following an exhilarating experience, as his subsequent report revealed:

> "I was on a sweep patrol in the neighbourhood of St Inglevert aerodrome and got temporarily separated from my section, when I saw five Hs126 in line at the south-east corner of what I have since verified through photographs was Guînes-la-Place aerodrome. I came down to between 200-300 feet and machine-gunned the line of aircraft but did not have time to observe the results. I saw two ME109s at about 300 feet flying NNW and climbing. I climbed to 1,000 feet and then attacked the rear ME109, giving him one long and two short bursts from above, 150 yards from behind and above slightly from the right-hand side. He turned steeply and dived vertically towards the ground as if the pilot had been hit.
>
> My throttle had jammed full open and as the other ME109 was climbing steeply, I was unable to follow, so I came down to ground level and made for the coast which I crossed between Cap Gris Nez and Boulogne. As I was approaching this coast, I was fired on by machine-gun posts and Bofors, and from ships as I was almost at sea level. My throttle was still jammed and I came over Hornchurch and switched off the ignition and landed. I later returned to North Weald and landed at 1515."

The Hs126s Maciejowski strafed, without apparent effect, were possibly aircraft of 5(H)/32. There is no evidence to confirm that the Bf109E he attacked was actually damaged. Next day the Squadron received a signal from the AOC 11 Group:

> "The Prime Minister and Commander-in-Chief Fighter Command wish their congratulations to be communicated to all concerned on their very satisfactory ops over Northern France yesterday. I add my own congratulations and look forward to further success in ops of this kind."

An attempt was made on 12 January to fly an offensive patrol over Northern France but lack of cloud cover forced the two Hurricanes to return. Four days later Wg Cdr Beamish, Sqn Ldr Barton, Flg Off Lofts, Flt Lt Neil and newly commissioned Plt Off Bentley Beard travelled to RAF Duxford to receive their respective decorations from His Majesty the King.

Aerial activity increased slightly during the opening days of February, with an uneventful offensive patrol being flown on the second day, while next day an attempted interception of a Ju88 off Dover failed when the reconnaissance aircraft escaped in cloud. A convoy protection patrol flown on the afternoon of 4 February by three Hurricanes of 249 was to prove successful in terms of aerial combat, however. When over Clacton at 10,000 feet, a vector was given on an unidentified aircraft 25 miles out to sea. Shortly after, a Bf110 was sighted over the convoy (codenamed Agent), flying at 2,000 feet just above cloud. As the Hurricanes approached, the fighter-bomber released two bombs which fell wide of the intended target. Sqn Ldr Barton, leading the patrol, dived on it from 10,000 feet and made a head-on attack, then turned onto its tail and delivered a further burst as it entered cloud. Sgt Palliser followed and also fired several bursts. By then, both engines were emitting thick, black smoke and Barton followed it up into clouds, where Palliser waited for it to reappear but as soon as it did, the crew obviously spotted the Hurricane, whereupon it dived back into cloud. Circling below cloud was Plt Off Thompson, who saw a very large splash in the sea. He and Barton flew over the area of impact and observed a circle of foam and oil. The Controller informed Barton that the convoy had seen the bomber crash into the sea. This was Uffz Gustav Drews' Messerschmitt (S9+PK) of 2/EproGr210 in which he died with air gunner, Uffz Steindal.

The Hurricane patrol then flew towards the convoy where AA fire signalled the presence of a second Bf110, which was sighted 2,000 feet above. Sqn Ldr Barton, using boost, climbed and pursued the Messerschmitt — Uffz Josef Roming's S9+EH, also of 2/EproGr210 — and opened fire. The port engine stopped dead as it entered cloud with Barton close on its tail. Firing short bursts, he forced the Messerschmitt down to sea level whereupon it ditched in a cloud of spray near the Kentish Knock Lightship. Although it sank rapidly, the pilot was seen floating in the sea, waving as the Hurricane passed low overhead. However, he was not rescued. A sweep over the Cap Gris Nez to Calais area on the morning of 5 February by Hurricanes of 56 and 249 Squadrons failed to draw the anticipated response, although Fighter Command HQ advised the squadrons that the object of such sweeps was to force the Luftwaffe to maintain standing fighter patrols. Later reports revealed that the objective was being achieved.

With the imminent re-equipment of the Squadron with the new Hurricane MkII, Plt Off Bentley Beard and Sgt Killingback were sent to the RAF aircraft depot at White Waltham for ferrying duties. Next day (7 February), the Squadron was advised that Bentley Beard had crashed while flying a Spitfire and had been removed to Melksham Hospital. Although his injuries were not life threatening he did not return to the Squadron, nor did he remain on operations but transferred to Training Command.

Just after midday on 10 February, Circus 4 got underway, six Blenheims of 139 Squadron detailed to bomb the docks at Dunkirk, with 249 as one of the four escorting squadrons. As the Blenheims bombed, a mixed formation of Bf109Es from IV/JG51 and I/LG2 dived on the formation, bouncing 249 and shooting down Hurricane V7171 flown by newly commissioned Plt Off Davis, who baled out wounded to become a prisoner. He was probably the victim of Hptm Herbert Ihlefeld of I/LG2. The remaining pilots engaged their assailants, Sgts Palliser, Maciejowski and Brzeski each claiming one shot down; Palliser reported:

"Acting as Red 4, I broke away from Squadron over Gravelines with Red 3 and circled to pick out enemy fighters. I saw three ME109s flying at 5,000 feet south of Calais and gave chase but could not catch them. I turned back towards Gravelines and saw a Hurricane being attacked by a ME109. I dived down, giving a quarter attack and about two-seconds burst, which raked e/a. The pilot of the e/a pulled up his nose, trying to make a climbing turn away. At this, I fired about one-second burst into cockpit. E/a dropped its nose and tried to turn once again, so I gave another two-seconds burst which hit engine and side of cockpit. After this, e/a commenced a fairly steep but not very fast dive for the coastline. While following down I made two stern and two quarter attacks, firing in all about six seconds. E/a made no attempt to evade attacks and I judged pilot to be dead.

   Whilst preparing to follow e/a right down, I saw a fighter coming down on my tail, so I turned violently away and commenced turning steeply. Aircraft turned out to be friendly. When I looked for e/a I could no longer see him and judged he had crashed as he was losing height fairly rapidly when I turned. Flg Off Lewis, who was flying as Yellow 2 and who was attacked by same e/a, saw my attacks and substantiates my claim that the pilot was killed and e/a must have been destroyed."

Sgt Brzeski (Blue 2) reported that his victim just cleared the beach at Dunkirk and crashed about 500 yards inland:

"I attacked ME109 at 16,000 feet and while he was taking evasive action, another ME109 dived on me and I was forced to break away. I found myself just out to sea beyond Dunkirk and saw a merchant vessel of about 3,000 tons about one and a half miles west of Dunkirk. I dived onto it from 4,000 feet and machine-gunned it from 500 feet but did not observe any results, nor did I see any sign of life on board. I then climbed to 4,000 feet and saw a ME109 and a Hurricane having a dogfight 1,000 feet below me. This Hurricane was [flown by] Wg Cdr Beamish. I dived with boost and made a stern attack on the e/a from above, giving a long burst of five seconds, breaking off at same level at a distance of 150 yards. He immediately made for the coast, losing height rapidly and emitting fire and smoke. He just cleared the beach and crashed about 500 yards inland."

It would seem that either Brzeski or Palliser (or both) shot down Lt Adolf Steckmeyer of 11/JG51, who was killed when his aircraft crashed at Ardres. Of his combat, Maciejowski (Red 2) reported:

"I was flying at 1,000 feet higher than the leader, who was at 14,000 feet. I saw three ME109s attacking the formation below me. I dived down and did a steep climbing turn and delivered a three-quarter stern attack with deflection. The e/a turned on its back immediately and the pilot baled out although the aircraft had given no sign of injury."

Although Maciejowski reported that he had seen the pilot bale out, his opponent, Uffz Karl Ryback of I/LG2, was lost and his aircraft (White 3) crashed into the sea. In addition to Hptm Ihlefeld's claim, two other Hurricanes were claimed shot down in this brief action, one each by Oblt Hans Keitel and Lt Heinz Wiest of IV/JG51; two Hurricanes (V6582 and V6728) of 249 were indeed damaged but both pilots, Flg Off Lewis and Sgt Davidson, were able to reach North Weald safely. Neil wrote:

> "When I taxied into my hardstanding to stop, I saw Gerald Lewis' Hurricane just ahead of me. He was still in the cockpit as I dropped to the ground and I saw him waving his arms in my direction. When I walked towards him, I could see why. There was massive damage to the left-hand side of his cockpit. No wonder he was upset; it was a miracle he had not been killed or badly wounded."

Neil, naturally upset by the loss of his colleague, Bill Davis, was amongst those who vented his feelings to a sympathetic Wg Cdr Beamish. They demanded to know why the Squadron was still having to fly Mk I Hurricanes on offensive operations when they were at the mercy of the Messerschmitt pilots. Five days later the first batch of 18 brand new Hurricane IIbs arrived at North Weald for the Squadron, some with eight .303s, some with twelve .303s and others with four 20mm cannons. The main advantage of the Mk II over the Mk I was its better performance above 20,000 feet and self-sealing fuel tanks. Neil wrote:

> "Four days later I flew the one I selected — GN-W (Z2638) — and was excitedly impressed. It was tight and bouncy, the engine silk-smooth, and there was the heady, intoxicating aroma of new paint. Super! I could hardly wait to go to war in it."

During the preceding few days the weather had deteriorated, restricting operational flying over the Channel. When it improved, 249 mounted patrols but no enemy aircraft were encountered. New pilots continued to be posted to the Squadron, Sgts C.A. McVean, Ron Rist and R.L. Davies RAAF arriving from 56 OTU on 18 February but, four days later, Flt Lt Lofts departed, tour expired, for 52 OTU. Within 48 hours, three of the five Poles had gone: Plt Off Solak, Sgt Maciejowski and Sgt Brzeski were all posted to the newly-formed 317 Squadron (both Maciejowski and Brzeski went on to become aces). Sgt Popek followed shortly after and joined 303 Squadron at Northolt. Another leaving at this time was Sqn Ldr G.D. Gavin who had arrived a month earlier as a supernumerary prior to taking command of his own squadron. However, old faces reappeared when Flg Off Wells and Sgt Stroud returned from convalescence.

To replace the Poles and tour-expired pilots, there arrived at the beginning of March a batch of operationally inexperienced pilots: Plt Off R.H. Matthews and Plt Off R.H.McK. Munro, a Rhodesian, both from 56 OTU; Plt Off J.V. Marshall from 232 Squadron, Plt Offs M.H. Welmon and C.C.H. Davis from 260 Squadron; and three Sgt Pilots: S.F. Cooper (ex-253 Squadron), E.R. Webster (ex-85 Squadron) and F.G. Sheppard RAAF (ex-605 Squadron). Another new arrival was Capitaine Philippe de Scitivaux, a French former naval pilot who had been serving with 253 Squadron at Kenley*. A change in the command of North Weald took place on 20 March when Grp Capt S.F. Vincent DFC AFC arrived from Northolt vice newly promoted Grp Capt Beamish who was posted to 11 Group as OC Training.

The Squadron carried out another bomber escort mission on the last day of March, six Blenheims bombing two merchant vessels a few miles off Cap Gris Nez. No enemy fighters attempted to interfere and all aircraft returned safely. Although there was little aerial activity

---

* Capitaine de Scitivaux's full name was Charles Jean Marie Philippe de Scitivaux de Greische; he had served in the French Aeronavale and had been shot down and wounded in May 1940 after having first claimed a German aircraft. He eventually reached England via Gibraltar.

during this period, the dangers and hazards of flying were ever-present and the Squadron lost one of its stalwarts on 7 April. When returning to North Weald from a convoy protection patrol at 1930, Plt Off Wynn's Hurricane Z2663 GN-O suddenly fell out of control and crashed into a field at Langford Bridge Farm east of Ongar, killing the pilot. Of the incident, Neil wrote:

"What a tragedy! The smiling, level-headed, experienced Dicky, who had been with the Squadron almost from the start and who had fought bravely for more than six months, being shot down, wounded nastily in the neck, and crashing more than once through engine failure. To die not a victim in battle, but as a casualty in an inexplicable and seemingly needless accident. How grossly unfair that someone as talented and as companionable . . . should have died so casually and to such little effect. A terrible waste."

Having been advised in November that the Squadron had been 'adopted' by the people of the Gold Coast during a local drive for Hurricane and Spitfire funds, and that it was now officially designated 'Gold Coast Fighter Squadron' in recognition of the substantial gift of money from the West African colony, the pilots decided it was time to have a Squadron Crest and submitted a design to the Air Ministry for consideration. This included a central design which depicted an elephant, as portrayed on the official coat-of-arms of the Gold Coast, together with the suggested motto *We Shall Not Fail*, taken from one of the Prime Minister's speeches. However, although the elephant passant was incorporated into the authorised version, the suggested motto was not and the Squadron was granted in its place *Pugnis et Calcibus*, which translated into *With Fists and Heels* although the implied translation was *With Might and Main**.

On 10 April, newly promoted Wg Cdr Ron Kellett, having been appointed Wing Commander Flying at North Weald, accompanied six 249 Squadron Hurricanes on a high-altitude sweep over Le Touquet-Boulogne-Calais area. Flying at 33,000 feet in the unheated aircraft soon began to affect the pilots, as noted by Neil:

"It was unbelievably cold . . . Through the frost-caked metal frame of my hood, some 30 yards away I could see only the top of the helmet of my nearest companion, who was no doubt equally cold."

Such was the cold that Wg Cdr Kellett was posted sick on his return, and was obliged to relinquish his new command. Next day Flg Off Skalski was slightly injured when his Hurricane (Z2450) belly-landed at Marks Tey Hill near Colchester after hitting some high-tension cables. He admitted that he had become lost and was attempting to read his map when the accident occurred. At midday on 13 April, four aircraft of A Flight's Blue Section led by Cne de Scitivaux patrolled over a convoy 40 miles east of Harwich. Fellow Frenchman, Adjt Fayolle, was Blue 4:

"I was weaver . . . when we were informed that there was an e/a in the vicinity. I saw a ME110 at about 10,000 feet going north when we were at 5,000 feet going south. We turned north and climbed. The e/a dived into cloud in a westerly direction. We all followed into the cloud and I turned towards the east. I saw the e/a going east about 1,000 feet below me. He dived full speed into clouds and I could see him weaving in and out. After pursuing him for six or seven minutes, I came below clouds and found myself 250 yards behind e/a. He turned towards the left and I fired three short bursts, with deflection, from astern, closing to 200 yards. I saw the starboard engine emit white smoke and the e/a climbed into cloud. I did not find him again."

A few days later (on 18 April), Flg Off Skalski was again in trouble; he, de Scitivaux and Adjt de Labouchère took off on a formation flying exercise which ended in disaster when all three aircraft collided: Skalski force-landed his Hurricane on the airfield, minus its propeller,

---

* There was also a Gold Coast Bomber Squadron — 218 Squadron, then based at RAF Marham with Wellingtons. In early 1942, newly formed 167 Squadron, a Spitfire squadron, was also named 'Gold Coast Squadron', as was 183 Squadron formed later the same year with Hurricanes and Typhoons.

de Scitivaux nearby but de Labouchère was obliged to bale out of Z2522. None of the pilots was injured. The other two aircraft involved in the collision were repairable.

The comings and goings continued. On 14 April newly promoted Flt Lt Lewis was posted to 57 OTU as an instructor. Then, on 17 April, news was received that the Squadron was shortly to proceed overseas to the Middle East, which accounted for the intensity of movement of pilots to and fro. European pilots — Poles, Czechs, French — were not allowed to serve overseas where they were likely to come up against the Italians, since their countries were not officially at war with Italy, while the Air Ministry decreed that married officers should, whenever possible, remain in the United Kingdom.

Flt Lt F.V. Morello was posted in from 56 Squadron, and was followed by Sgts J.G. Parker, M. Guest and R.W. Lawson from 52 OTU; by the end of the month Sgt D.C.H. Rex had arrived from 1 Squadron. Another new arrival was Flg Off E.J.F. Harrington. Strangely, with the European pilots being posted away, Plt Off Tomas Kozek, a Czech, now joined 249 although he departed again ten days later bound for 242 Squadron at Stapleford Tawney, the unit from which Sgt F.A. Etchells was posted to join 249. In the meantime, both Sgts Palliser and Mills received their commissions. The 'new' 249 was rapidly taking shape although some of the new arrivals soon departed again including Flt Lt Morello, while Plt Off Marshall and Sgt Sheppard left on posting to Malta, and Sgt Webster to 59 OTU for further training. The three Frenchmen also departed, Cne de Scitivaux together with newly commissioned Sous Lieutenants Fayolle and de Labouchère being transferred to 242 Squadron, to which unit Flg Off Skalski was posted.*

249, together with two other Fighter Command Hurricane units, 213 and 229 Squadrons, was ordered to prepare for service in the Middle East. Malta was not mentioned at this stage, although pilots were informed that they would be flying Hurricane Is fitted with long-range fuel tanks off the deck of an aircraft carrier. To prepare them for this daunting episode, two Hurricanes so-equipped arrived at North Weald to enable all concerned to familiarise themselves with the type. Many were dismayed to learn that they were to revert to the Mark I Hurricane after a period flying the superior Mark II. Although there were some last-minute postings-in of personnel, basically the Squadron pilots were the experienced survivors of the men who had established the Squadron as one of the foremost in Fighter Command, including Sqn Ldr Barton, Flt Lt Neil, Flg Offs Beazley, Wells and Cassidy, Plt Offs Crossey, Thompson, Palliser and Mills. Others in the party included recent arrivals Flg Off Harrington, Plt Offs Matthews, Davis and Munro, plus Sgts Etchells, Rex, Lawson, Parker, Rist, McVean, Hulbert and Guest.

Leave was granted, all pilots being ordered to report to London's Euston railway station on 8 May for the journey to Liverpool, from where they were to board the old carrier HMS *Furious*. Of this period, Flt Lt Neil wrote:

> "Our arrival [at Gladstone Dock, Liverpool] was greeted with total indifference. Laden with luggage, we stumbled up the gangway and, as carefully briefed at North Weald, solemnly saluted the quarter-deck, although few of us would have recognised that area of the ship had it been introduced with a fanfare of trumpets. Being a Flight Commander, I rated a cabin on my own — all of six feet square! Within the hour, it was announced that we would be moving out of Liverpool with all haste."

The Squadron's new Hurricane Is were lashed down in the carrier's hangar, while maintenance personnel were kept busy fitting the long-range tanks and testing equipment in readiness for whatever the future held in store. Sqn Ldr Barton noted:

> "HMS *Furious* was escorted through the Atlantic by the ex-target ship HMS *Centurion* (a World War I battleship, her guns made of wood) at one stage of the journey to Gibraltar: no other escorts."

---

* Fayolle was killed in August 1942 during his first operation as CO of a squadron; by then he had three victories to his credit, as had de Labouchère who was killed in action the following month. The third pilot of the trio, de Scitivaux was shot down and taken prisoner in April 1942 as commander of 340 Squadron, the first Free French squadron. He had been awarded the DFC.

Chapter Five

IN MEDITERRANEAN SKIES
May 1941 — February 1942

"Butch Barton slipped away one night aboard a Sunderland in Kalafrana Bay bound for Gibraltar and home. There was no departing binge or palaver, he just went. Quietly. Without fuss. Disappearing as he had always fought, with unassuming distinction . . ."

Flt Lt Ginger Neil, 249 Squadron

HMS *Furious* reached Gibraltar on 18 May. A naval officer aboard the carrier recalled:

"The day before we arrived in Gibraltar we received a signal from Admiral Sir James Somerville of Force 'H', who was in command of the operation, saying that on arrival in harbour we were to berth stern to stern with HMS *Ark Royal* so that some of our Hurricanes could be transferred to her."

During the night of 18-19 May, 249's Hurricanes were duly transferred to *Ark Royal*, as recalled by Sqn Ldr Barton:

"21 Hurricanes of 249 Squadron were transferred to *Ark Royal* at Gib by the simple expedient of lowering a large steel platform between the flight decks of the two carriers and Spanish labourers man-handled the aircraft across without damage."

Meanwhile, ground personnel of all three squadrons were on their way round the Cape of Good Hope, bound via the Suez Canal for Egypt. Sgt Stroud remembered:

"I unfortunately drew the short straw and found myself a member of the advance party to go by ship to the Middle East, en route to Malta. I recall being given seven days embarkation leave from a transit camp in Wirral. Standing on the platform of Lime Street station in Liverpool, during the horrific blitz they had on that city, a pitter pattering sound on the roofing turned out to be shrapnel from the exploding AA shells. Tin hats were very much the order of the day/night. We sailed on either the *Highland Princess* or *Monarch*. Needless to say, we did not arrive in Malta, being posted to a squadron in the Western Desert. Here ended my association with 249 Squadron." *

From Gibraltar the two carriers sailed in company, the Hurricane ferry given the codename Operation Splice. The Hurricanes were ranged on the decks at dawn on 21 May, but on *Furious* the first Fulmar guide failed to start and had to be put below. First off was 213 Squadron, led in sections each headed by a Fulmar. Immediately after take-off of the first flight, the Fulmar crew discovered that their undercarriage would not retract and as this reduced speed and increased fuel consumption, due to the drag created, they led the flight back to the carrier. Another Fulmar was sent off and the flight then set off again with two hours' fuel already gone. Near Pantelleria the formation was fired on, so dived down to sea level where one Hurricane hit the sea and crashed; the pilot was later picked up by the Italians and made a prisoner.

---

* Sgt Stroud was posted to 33 Squadron in the Western Desert, and later joined 274 Squadron before being posted back to the UK in 1943.

The remainder of 213 Squadron reached Malta where, on landing, one aircraft's engine stopped at once as all its fuel had been exhausted, although one guiding Fulmar had been obliged to ditch en route (its crew was rescued by Vichy French and interned). Six Hurricanes from 229 Squadron also reached Malta from *Furious*, but the remaining aircraft of this unit stayed aboard as the carriers had by then been as long in hostile water as was safe to allow*. Meanwhile, 249 had been launched from *Ark Royal*, similarly led by Fulmars. Flt Lt Neil graphically described events:

> "Ahead, the first of the Hurricanes began to take off. Spotted in groups of three, each aircraft moved first to the centre-line, then, under the influence of full throttle and with each rudder giving a brief but defiant wag, one aircraft after another surged forward, tail raised, and took off, rising like a lift in a climbing turn to the left. Then the wandsman again, waving urgently and beckoning in exaggerated gestures. My turn! My mouth dry, I opened up and taxied forward, straightening up on the centre-line. The wands gyrating, urging me to rev up. Up! Up! Then suddenly, with a sweep of the arm — Down! I was off! I set off down the deck at a smart walking pace, my Hurricane feeling ridiculously light. The island drifted by, faces gawping. At this rate I would be airborne in seconds. This really was a stroll! A moment later I was in the air, despite the extra 88 gallons of fuel, the deck dropping away beneath."

The first group, headed by Sqn Ldr Barton (Z4507), had to turn back when the oil tank of the guiding Fulmar split. A relief guide was flown off and the flight reached Malta without further mishap. The second group, with Neil at its head, seemed doomed from the start. No sooner was Neil in the air than the left gun panel in the upper wing surface came loose and stuck up in the air. At the same time wind scooped all his maps out of the cockpit, which was still open. Finding that his aircraft was still controllable, he formed up behind the Fulmar and they set course at low level for Malta. After about an hour the Fulmar suddenly accelerated and climbed away. The Hurricanes lost sight of it and flew around for five minutes, remaining at 400 feet above the water to avoid appearing on the radar screens on nearby Italian-occupied islands.

Finally in despair they turned back, Neil having calculated they should have sufficient fuel to reach Gibraltar but, quite fortuitously, the wakes of ships were seen below and eventually the fleet came into view. On approaching, the ships all scattered under the impression that an enemy torpedo raid was coming in. The Hurricanes flew overhead for 15-20 minutes until their predicament became clear, when *Ark Royal*'s deck was cleared and another Fulmar sent off. The Hurricanes were now nearer to 550 miles from Malta than the 450 intended, and the Fulmar crew announced over the radio that they could not make it, breaking away to land on the carrier again. Neil did not hear this broadcast however, and headed for Malta with his followers, seeing a Ju88 and several other types of aircraft in the distance as they went. After five hours and 35 minutes in the air (probably the longest flight ever made by a Hurricane), they were all desperately short of fuel, but at that moment Malta appeared dead ahead. Neil continued:

> "Malta, when it came, appeared with magical suddenness and in the form of cliffs adjacent to my left ear. They loomed white and brown out of the mist and sea and were almost within touching distance . . . Filfla rock being just ahead, I made a token dart at it before turning north in order to climb up over the cliffs that formed the island's southern boundary."

Neil and his section went straight in to land at Luqa, others landing at Takali and Hal Far, but as Neil approached he saw bombs bursting on the runway: they had arrived in the middle of a raid. Opening up, most managed to complete a circuit, although several ran out of fuel at that point and went down to land at once, while others landed at Takali and Hal Far. Despite everything, all got down safely.

---

* The Hurricanes from 213 and 229 Squadrons which reached Malta soon departed for Mersa Matruh (Egypt), once they had been refuelled and the pilots fed, as they were required for operations in North Africa.

It was now that 249 received the news that it was to stay on the island. The pilots were dismayed, for they had no kit with them, all being aboard ship with the ground party, bound for Egypt. No kit or groundcrew were seen again by the majority of the pilots. Worse was to follow, for they were taken by bus to Takali were they were informed they were to fly the well-worn Hurricane Is of 261 Squadron, which was leaving for the Middle East for a well-deserved rest*. The pilots of the departing squadron were to take most of 249's new aircraft with them. Neil, for one, was not impressed with what he saw, and described the Hurricanes as:

"A poor crowd of battered Mark Is — no squadron markings, some with Vokes filters, some not. A variety of propellers etc."

An eyewitness reported seeing tailwheel tyres stuffed with straw due to lack of spares; the Squadron's inherited Hurricanes were undeniably in a poor state of repair and serviceability. One of the departing pilots, Plt Off John Pain, a former member of 249 who had done very well on the island, agreed with the comment regarding the condition of the Hurricanes left behind:

"By the time we left, aircraft were being repaired with dope-painted linen or cloth from anywhere, and metal repairs were made with the aid of Players 50s tins. And, of course, cannibalisation where practicable."

The day following its arrival, 249 was split into two Flights, one half (B Flight) commanded by Sqn Ldr Barton, the other by Flt Lt Neil. Each flight was to operate for half a day each, allowing 50% of the pilots to be off duty at any one time. A day-on, day-off roster was soon instituted in conjunction with newly formed 185 Squadron, with which it was to share the island's defence.

For the Squadron the first introduction to the real action of Malta came as something of a shock. About ten Hurricanes were gathered round the dispersal tent at Takali on the afternoon of 25 May when, just before 1400, the sirens went; however, the Squadron was not ordered off although the pilots were ready and strapped into their cockpits. Suddenly Bf109Es of 7/JG26 arrived with a crackle of gunfire, shooting-up the airfield. A member of the ground staff at Takali wrote in his journal:

"Machine-gunned by ME109s; eight of them came straight across our 12 machines on the runway, catching two on fire. They burnt out and three others were badly damaged. One of our groundcrew was badly injured and had eight bullets from the thigh downwards . . . A bad show, the Hurricanes should never have been on the deck, they should have been up to meet the 109s."

Flg Off Harrington's aircraft was hit by a cannon shell in the forward fuel tank, another hitting his parachute pack; he was unhurt but his Hurricane burst into flames and was a complete write-off. Sgt Colin McVean leapt from his cockpit in such a hurry that he broke both legs and the unlucky Flg Off Wells suffered a bullet through his right ankle, while three attendant groundcrew were also wounded. Wells recalled:

"This was our first readiness in Malta and whilst sitting in the crew room were astonished to hear the air-raid sirens howling — in the UK we had always been airborne before the sirens sounded. We rushed out to our aircraft and got ready for the scramble which never came. I noticed Flt Lt Neil get out of his aircraft obviously to go to the telephone. I am fundamentally lazy and decided that we would inevitably be scrambled, so it was less effort to remain in my aircraft and wait for it, helmet on and listening to the R/T. The next thing I saw was people running — I still could not hear anything due to my helmet — and on looking round saw the

---

* 261 Squadron had defended Malta since its formation from 418 Flight in August 1940, and had suffered severe losses in the period ending 21 May 1941, when it was effectively disbanded. Although the Squadron was credited with at least 100 victories in Malta's skies, 21 of its pilots had paid the supreme sacrifice. The Squadron was reformed in July 1941 when 127 Squadron at Habbaniya, Iraq, was renumbered.

109s starting their dive on the airfield. I tried to start the engine but the airman on the starter battery trailer had fled, so I could not do a thing except huddle in the cockpit, waiting for the sensation of being hit. The aircraft was burning well and this, plus exploding ammunition, drove me out. Only when I got on the ground and tried to walk did I realise that I had a bullet through the top of my right ankle. The ambulance came and I was filled with delicious brandy, but was instantly sick when I got to Mtarfa Hospital. Here I had the most devoted treatment from an Army surgeon, Major Salisbury, an Australian who was ex-Chief Surgeon on the *Queen Mary*."

The German pilots involved in the attack claimed four Hurricanes destroyed, two by Oblt Joachim Müncheberg, the Staffelkapitän and one of the Luftwaffe's leading fighter pilots, and one each by Fw Hans Johannsen and Obfw Karl Laub; they believed that six had been hit in all from an estimated 15 Hurricanes seen. In fact, two Hurricanes were totally destroyed, two others considered irreparable and a fifth less seriously damaged (believed to have included V6629, V7732 and V7747). This débâcle came as a great blow to the confident pilots of 249, epitomised by its effect on Flg Off Harrington. A few days later an RAF reconnaissance Maryland approached the airfield, looking for all the world like a Ju88. Harrington at once leapt into a slit trench in great haste, only to find it full of barbed wire which inflicted severe lacerations on him. Sympathy was not forthcoming from all quarters, as witnessed by an entry in the Takali airman's journal:

"The trouble with 249 is there is too much class distinction; every time we speak to an officer they tried to make us stand at attention, but we soon cured them of that. The first day they came here, when the warning went and we all rushed to the shelter, one bright bastard said: 'Why do you brave crews run like rabbits when the siren goes?' Sunday's strafing showed them why. Very brave men the 249ers, they run like rabbits themselves now."

The attack on Takali by 7/JG26 was in effect a final fling by the Luftwaffe in Sicily, since German units had been steadily transferring to North Africa to assist with General Rommel's push in Cyrenaica. By the end of the month most German units had gone, leaving the Italians in defence of their own territory. The respite for Malta's defenders was most welcome and allowed the Squadron the opportunity to settle in.

Sqn Ldr Barton recorded 249's first victory over the island on 3 June, when he intercepted a tri-motor SM79 of 56ª Squadriglia BT as it was flying from Sciacca (Sicily) to Libya as part of an air escort for naval vessels. Barton noted:

"SM79 shot down into the sea — on fire off Gozo — no crew known to have escaped."

Ten Franco Miscione and his crew* perished. Having refuelled and rearmed, the CO led a section of Hurricanes to the scene of action and carried out a search for survivors, but to no avail.

Four days later, the Squadron received four pilots on loan from 185 Squadron — Plt Off G.G. Bailey, Plt Off D. Winton, Sgt Sheppard RAAF (who had served briefly with 249 in the UK) and Sgt A. Livingston — mainly because of the latter unit's current shortage of aircraft. Other new postings at this time included Plt Offs B.M. Cavan, R.T. Saunders and D.C.B. Robertson from the departed 261 Squadron.

In the early hours of 8 June, Hurricanes of 249 undertook night patrols as raiders approached the island. Again Sqn Ldr Barton was successful, intercepting a Fiat BR20M (MM22692) of 99° Gruppo BT and shooting it down in flames. He noted:

"I well remember the BR20 I attacked flew for a long time on fire over Valetta and Malta, much to the delight of the local populace."

---

* Serg Dino De Stefani (co-pilot), 1°Av Motorista Amerigo Piragino, 1°Av Armiere Scafati and 1°Av Armiere Mini.

On his return to Takali, Barton set off with his section and carried out a search for survivors of the Italian bomber. Ten Sergio Reggiani and his co-pilot, Mar Guglielmo Mazzolenis, were rescued to become prisoners, but the remainder of the crew* were killed. Mazzolenis told his captors:

> "The Hurricane came in from the direction of the moon. [We] could see him quite well. His attack was very determined and the gunner was unable to return accurate fire, as the Hurricane was weaving across [our] tail. The first burst hit one engine which went up in flames and from that moment the crew prepared to bale out."

A second of the unit's bombers was attacked by Flg Off Beazley and Plt Off Palliser jointly, and was believed to have gone down into the sea 40 miles from the island; the pair were credited with a probable, but in fact the seriously damaged bomber succeeded in limping home having suffered some 50 strikes. Barton added:

> "There seems to be some doubt about the two BR20s being correctly identified; I do not know what else they could have been."

Next day (9 June) four of 249's Hurricanes were sent out after a radar plot, catching four 193ª Squadriglia BT SM79s some 50 miles out to sea, which were being ferried from Sicily to Castel Benito in Libya. Sottoten Marcello Weber's aircraft (MM21852) went down in flames into the water, Sgt Livingston being credited with its destruction, while Flg Off Harrington, Sgt Lawson and Sgt Rex claimed damage to the other three. The latter subsequently had to bale out of Z4087, apparently due to a glycol leak, but was rescued later as was the pilot of the downed Savoia, whom he may, in fact, have shot down. The commander of the rescue launch, Flt Lt Edward Hardie, recorded:

> "We had a very vague idea of where he [Sgt Dennis Rex] was; we knew he was about 50 to 60 miles out . . . visibility was poor and we went on and on — we did not see anything and I was about to give up in despair when I saw something on the horizon that looked like wreckage . . . it was the wreckage of an Italian troopship. It was only the fact that I altered my course like that I came across the fighter pilot swimming like mad and, when I got him on board, I said, Where were you going?' and he said, 'I thought I would give you boys a helping hand in getting nearer Malta.' I told him that he had been heading for Benghazi! He told me before he did ditch he had shot down one of the Italian bombers and he did not know if any of the crew were still alive . . . we looked around and came across one of the wings of the Italian bomber, on which was the very badly burned pilot. When we got him aboard, I had to restrain him because he wanted to shake the hands of the boy who had shot him down. I was nearer to Benghazi than I was to Malta and when I was on the way back I saw something else in the water — a dinghy with two FAA officers in. They had ditched after running out of fuel whilst on a submarine patrol. So I went out for one and came back with four."

Weber's co-pilot, Mar Luciano Fabbri (the co-pilot) was also rescued, but the other four members of the crew were lost†.

Two major engagements were fought over and around the island on 12 June. At 0721, 18 Hurricanes were scrambled — drawn equally from 46 and 249 Squadrons — to intercept an incoming reconnaissance flight, which comprised a single SM79 from 57ª Squadriglia BT and an escort of 15 MC200s of 7° Gruppo CT (led by Cap Saverio Gostini), while 15 more from 17° Gruppo CT provided indirect support. For some reason the British pilots identified the fighters as six Macchis and six Bf109Es, all flying at 16,000 to 17,000 feet. The Hurricanes waded in, Flt Lt Neil identifying his victim as a "Messerschmitt 109 with a light-coloured nose"; he continued:

---

* 1°Av Armiere Lamberto Mariani, 1°Av Montatore Umberto Micheli, AvSc Motorista Antonio Plamiere and AvSc Marconista Nicola Mascellaro.
† 1°Av Motorista Michele Turco, 1°Av Marconista Francesco Minuto and 1°Av Armiere Ugo Binanno.

"I fired. My tracer with its familiar flecks of curving, whipping red, reached out and clutched both fuselage and wings in a brief rippling embrace. After which it was gone. Below my tipping wing. Downwards. Turning. Diving steeply. I followed, violently, keeping it in sight. I was aware of the sea directly beneath. Going like mad now, everything roaring and shaking. Firing! Then a sudden small blob that was a parachute, detaching, a white streak at first, then developing, finally drifting sideways before rushing quickly in my direction and vanishing to my rear. Further below me still, a diminishing silhouette and a sudden slow-motion eruption of water which died quickly into a disc of pale green as the aircraft went in."

Sgt Livingston claimed a probable and pilots of 46 Squadron claimed two MC200s. Neil was adamant that his victim had been a Bf109:

"The aircraft I encountered alongside the Savoia had been a 109. I ought to know as I'd been shooting at the blighters for the last nine months! One or two, including Crossey and Etchells, agreed, but others were doubtful. You couldn't confuse a 109 with a Macchi 200; one had an in-line engine and the other a ruddy great radial. I found myself hoping that the chap in the parachute would be picked up, but by late afternoon there was no news."

However, there were no Bf109s present despite Neil's insistence. It seems there was a fair degree of double claiming, since only the Macchi (MM5354) of 76ª Squadriglia CT flown by Sottoten Umberto Curcio failed to return, while a second flown by Serg Antonio Tirapelle force-landed near Agrigento on return — though possibly not as the result of combat damage. Both were from 7° Gruppo, whose pilots claimed two Hurricanes probably shot down in this action. However, Macchis of 17° Gruppo claimed no fewer than seven Hurricanes shot down and two probables. All 46 Squadron aircraft returned safely, but 249 suffered two losses, Plt Off Rioch Munro being killed when his aircraft (Z4043) crashed into the sea, while Plt Off Saunders (Z4385) baled out, wounded. Fortunately he was located by a pilot of 46 Squadron, who radioed for a rescue launch*. Four Macchis circled overhead during the rescue, but did not attack. A third Hurricane was damaged during this combat, that flown by Plt Off Winton, which force-landed at Safi airstrip.

During the early afternoon an ASR Cant Z506B floatplane — painted white and marked with Red Crosses — was sent out from Syracuse to search for the missing Italian pilot, escorted by two CR42s. These were intercepted by Hurricanes of 46 Squadron, which shot down the Cant, together with one of the biplanes, losing one of its own aircraft. Another Italian rescue aircraft was sent out when the first Cant and the CR42 failed to return. This was another Z506B, bearing the serial number MM45292 and civilian registration I-POLA, which had an escort of nine CR42s from 23° Gruppo and two dozen MC200s from 7° and 17° Gruppos. However, following a general sweep of the area when nothing of the missing aircraft was seen, the fighters left their charge some ten miles south of the Sicilian coast, off Cap Passero, and returned to base. There the Cant was intercepted by seven Hurricanes of 249 led by Sqn Ldr Barton (Z2481) which had been scrambled when the Italian formation had appeared on Malta's radar screens. Sgt Etchells recalled:

"I shot down a Cant Z506 near Sicily, which had red crosses on its wings, and was apparently an air-sea rescue aircraft. Sqn Ldr Barton disapproved but the AOC approved. I did not see the red crosses on its wings at the time and do not know if it would have made any difference had I done so."

One of the occupants was killed and two wounded, although the survivors were rescued later by another Axis ASR craft. Also on this sortie was Sgt Sheppard (in Z2527) who noted simply:

"Mix up with Italian Red Cross seaplane."

---

* Plt Off Saunders did not return to the Squadron but was evacuated to England via Gibraltar on 8 August 1941.

Following these fights little was seen of the Regia Aeronautica for several days — a convenient gap for the defenders, for on 14 June yet another delivery of Hurricanes took place under the codename Operation Tracer. On this occasion *Ark Royal* was joined by the new fleet carrier *Victorious*; on board the latter were 28 Hurricanes of 238 Squadron, desert-bound, while *Ark Royal* carried 20 more such aircraft of 260 Squadron. On this occasion four Hudsons from Gibraltar joined the convoy at fly-off to navigate the Hurricanes to Malta in batches of twelve. Two failed to arrive at Malta, one of which was seen heading for the African coast* and the other crashed into the sea; a third crashed on arrival, killing the pilot. Fulmars, rescue boats and Hurricanes of 249 were sent out from Malta to search for the missing pilots, Flt Lt Neil's section finding an NCO pilot (Sgt Campbell of 238 Squadron) in the sea some 40 miles from Kalafrana. Neil wrote:

"Leaving [Flg Off] Crossey to circle the tiny yellow dot in the water, I returned and made contact with the rescue launch, which was crashing and bouncing its way towards us at maximum speed, and after pointing it in the right direction, flew backwards and forwards endlessly, acting as a guide. After hours, it seemed, we watched it successfully make the pick-up, after which we left, full of warm feelings. It was nice to be able to save a life for a change!"

Nine MC200s from 16° Gruppo CT approached Malta during the early afternoon of 18 June, 249 being scrambled and intercepting 20 miles north of Grand Harbour. Plt Off Palliser and Sgt Sheppard claimed one Macchi shot down between them and a second was claimed as a probable by Plt Off Matthews. The Macchi flown by Mar Sigismondo was badly damaged and belly-landed on return to base, the pilot wounded in one arm. During the fight Sgt Livingston's aircraft (Z4048) was either hit or suffered a malfunction. A particular friend of his amongst the ground personnel, Cpl John Alton, recalled:

"He desperately tried to bring his aircraft back with a glycol leak. When he was over Takali the aircraft caught fire and he abandoned it, alas too late — a couple of hundred feet cost him his life. I was always saddened when we lost a pilot but Jock's death affected me for quite a while."

On 27 June, *Ark Royal* launched 22 new Hurricanes for the island, including a few cannon-armed Mark IIcs; one went missing en route although the pilot was reported later to be a prisoner, while a second crashed on landing. The carrier dashed back to Gibraltar and embarked a further 26 Hurricanes and, in company with *Furious* carrying 16 more, prepared to launch these on the morning of 30 June. Only nine of the latter's complement were able to get airborne however, one Hurricane having crashed on deck on take-off. From these deliveries, 249 received a number of replacement pilots, including Plt Offs P.G. Leggett, J.R.A. Stuart, H.H. Moon, F.C. Hill and G.V. Smith, Sgts A.T. Branch, D. Owen, J.C. Kimberley, A.G. Cairns, H.J. McDowall, D.C. Skeet-Smith, H.W.E. Packham, R.L. Davies RAAF (who had originally joined the Squadron at North Weald in February) and Edwards; welcomed but mainly inexperienced. For example, Sgt Alf Branch, who flew Z3492 from the deck of *Ark Royal* to Takali, was direct from 59 OTU (as were many of the new arrivals) with 56 hours on Hurricanes. Plt Off Harry Moon, from Belfast, was also from 59 OTU and had acquired 52 hours on Hurricanes:

"I had just finished OTU when I (and others) were recalled to do two flights in Hurricanes fitted with long-range tanks. Having completed these, we were told to entrain for Abbotsinch where, on arrival, we were taken to the docks where the carrier *Furious* was anchored. It was the first aircraft carrier I had seen. We were then told that we were going to fly Hurricanes from her deck.

---

* The missing Hurricane turned up at Malta way past its ETA. Apparently the pilot had become separated and lost but eventually sighted land — Tunisia. Having successfully landed and recovered his sense of direction, he was able to take off again just before the arrival of sword-waving Vichy troops, reaching Malta safely and long-overdue, much to the astonishment of his squadron colleagues. However, he overshot on landing and hit a parked Hurricane, damaging both aircraft but not himself.

On arrival at Gibraltar we and our Hurricanes were transferred to the *Ark Royal* and we sailed out into the Mediterranean and were told we were going to Malta. I was due to take off in about the third position but on starting up, my Hurricane [BV163] was enveloped in steam — the coolant cap had been left off. By the time the coolant had been replaced, all the others had taken off and were disappearing into the distance."

Nonetheless, Moon took off and was able to catch up, all Hurricanes arriving safely. With the influx of new pilots, those on loan returned to their units, including Sgt Sheppard. The Squadron received a number of cannon-armed Hurricane IIcs from the latest delivery and Sqn Ldr Barton, who took charge of Z3498, noted:

"Towards the end of June we received some Hurricane IIcs (four cannon), hence cannon firing practice. These aircraft were heavier but had hitting power if you could get the enemy in your sights."

Another Italian raid during the night of 8/9 July was met by a trio of Hurricanes from 249, although only Flg Off Cassidy (a former night-fighter pilot) managed an interception. Ten BR20Ms from 43° Gruppo BT and six SM79s from 10° Stormo BT took part in the raid, one Wellington being destroyed on the ground by bombs at Luqa. Cassidy engaged Ten Vincenzo Petti's SM79 (MM22594) of 56ª Squadriglia south of the island (believing it to be a BR20M) and closed to very short range before opening fire, seeing his victim go down in flames*. Next morning four MC200s and two Cant floatplanes, out from Sicily searching for survivors from the missing bomber, were intercepted by four Hurricanes of 185 Squadron. One Italian fighter was damaged by Plt Off Bailey, who had returned to his own unit following a short spell of service with 249.

The Squadron gained further successes during the late morning of 17 July, when eight Hurricanes led by Sqn Ldr Barton met a formation of about 30 MC200s from 7° and 10° Gruppo CT as they approached the island escorting a reconnaissance SM79. Sqn Ldr Barton shot down one Macchi and Plt Off Leggett a second, while Flg Off Davis claimed a third damaged. Two fighters of 10° Gruppo were lost, Serg Magg Enrico Botti (MM6500) being killed, while Serg Magg Natale Finito (MM5217) was rescued later from the sea by an Axis ASR craft. In return the Italian fighter leader, Ten Col Carlo Romagnoli, claimed a Hurricane shot down, as did Cap Franco Lucchini, commander of 90ª Squadriglia, while Serg Elio Miotto reported shooting down two on his own and Mar Leonardo Ferrulli and Serg Luigi Contarini believed they had probably accounted for two more. Despite all these claims, one Hurricane only was lost when Sgt Maurice Guest (in Z2818) failed to return and was assumed to have been shot down into the sea.

When a flight of six Blenheim bombers arrived at Luqa from the UK, via Gibraltar, on 19 July they brought to the island as passengers two experienced fighter pilots, one of whom, Flt Lt D.W.A. Stones DFC was posted to 249. He had expected to join a new squadron being formed on the island but this had yet to be established. Of his introduction to the Squadron, Don Stones wrote later:

"I rushed out to Takali and met some of 249 Squadron who gave me a bed in a rented house in the village of Mosta. They had just put up a record which must be unique in RAF history. A few days before I arrived, they told me, most of the Squadron had been thrown in jail in Valetta! They were off duty and had gone innocently into a bar from which, unknown to them, some drunken sailors had been evicted a few minutes earlier. Before the 249 pilots could even order a drink, the Maltese Police arrived and promptly arrested them. They were marched to jail and locked in for the night. It took many hours before Air Headquarters could convince

---

* Ten Petti and his crew — Serg Magg Romelio Baldini (co-pilot), 1°Av Motorista Luigi Bellani, 1°Av Marconista Umberto Tedesco, 1°Av Armiere Corrado Cugno and AvSc Armiere Saverio Enna — were all lost.

the civilian authorities that they were not only holding the wrong men, but also half of the island's fighter strength!"

The Squadron's Engineering Officer at this time was Flg Off C.H. Jeffries, who had transferred from 261 Squadron when it left the island, about whom Cpl Alton recalled:

"He had a passion for clean aircraft and to this end pronounced that the rigger with the cleanest aircraft would be rewarded with a flight around the island in a Magister. As may be imagined, with CR42s liable to drop in unannounced, to the airmen it was rather like an invitation to Russian roulette!"

Italian night raiders continued to visit Malta, taking advantage of the good weather, 249 scrambling a section of Hurricanes at every opportunity. Sqn Ldr Barton (Z3462) came close to gaining his third nocturnal victory when the island's searchlights picked out a bomber on the night of 24/25 July, but lost it again as Barton closed in rapidly for the kill:

"Raider illuminated. I fired — out of range as no time to close."

A convoy of six freighters and one troopship reached Malta from Gibraltar on 24 July, having weathered heavy air attack en route by Italian torpedo-bombers from Sardinia and Sicily. Protection for the convoy was provided by *Ark Royal*, her attendant cruisers and a bevy of destroyers. One cargo vessel and a destroyer had been damaged, while *Ark Royal* had lost half of her 24 Fulmars in protecting the convoy although she had successfully launched seven reinforcement Swordfish biplane torpedo-bombers for Malta's depleted Naval strike squadron. Once the convoy had come within protection of Malta's air and naval units, *Ark Royal* and her accompanying force returned to Gibraltar.

On the morning of 25 July, an Italian reconnaissance aircraft was reported approaching Malta, with the obvious intention of photographing the ships of the convoy. With orders to shoot down the intruder at all costs, Sqn Ldr Barton led ten Hurricanes (together with a dozen from 185 Squadron) to challenge the Cant Z1007bis and its close escort of 26 MC200s of 10° Gruppo CT, with 21 more of 54° Stormo CT flying as indirect escort. However, only Flt Lt Stones was able to reach the reconnaissance aircraft in company with five from 185 Squadron, all six pilots engaging the machine. Of the engagement, Stones recalled:

"As I went in to attack, something fell away from our target and nearly hit me. I assumed he was jettisoning a bomb. We set him on fire and down he went into the sea. Only later did we discover that the object which had flown past me was the rear gunner [*sic*] baling out. He survived."

The surviving crew member was, in fact, the observer, Magg Achille Torrerossa (an army officer), who was rescued from the sea and taken to hospital. Ten Alfonso Cinieri and the remainder of his crew perished*. Meanwhile, the other Hurricanes had become engaged with the escort, Sqn Ldr Barton and Plt Off Hill (another Belfast man) each claiming a Macchi shot down into the sea, while Plt Off Matthews reported shooting one down over Valetta. This aircraft, MM8894 of 98ª Squadriglia flown by Sottoten Francesco Liberati, crashed in Kingsway near the Valetta Band Club, the pilot having baled out although his parachute failed to open properly.

The Italians reported that an initial attack by three Hurricanes was driven off, but that approximately 30 more attacked over Malta. Seven of these were claimed shot down, one by Serg Cozzoli, the others by several pilots jointly. On the ground Wg Cdr Carter Jonas, Station Commander at Luqa, who was visiting Valetta, watched Matthews's victim come down:

---

* Apart from Ten Cinieri, those killed were Mar Eschilo Borsini, 1°Av Motorista Santino Alberti, 1°Av Marcon Emanuele Carbone and AvSc Fotografo Clemente Massari.

"Out of the confusion of sound above us, something appeared, tangible and definite. It was a puff of white smoke. A little puff at first, but it grew rapidly and formed itself into a trail of white, like a comet. Then it faded away almost as rapidly as it had come. A moment later there was a new sound. Something terrifying which I could not describe. I had often wondered what a terminal velocity dive in an aircraft would be like. Now my wondering was to be answered. Just below where the white puff had first appeared was an aircraft diving vertically, earthwards. I realized almost immediately that the aircraft would fall into Valetta. Also that it would fall very close to me. Probably fall on the very spot on which I was now standing. I argued to myself that it was too late to attempt to escape into the building, down the stairs to safety. I decided to stay and hope for the best, but now I realised also the meaning of the phrase 'rooted to the spot'. It appeared to be coming straight for my eyes. As it flashed by, diving slightly over the vertical, I recognised it as a Macchi 200. A moment later it hit the ground about 75 yards away. There was a loud report, then silence, followed by the sound of running feet and excited shouts of the Maltese. I straightened up slowly. The pilot had baled out but his parachute had failed to open. He had fallen from the vast Mediterranean sky — in memory of Icarus."

A second Macchi of 98ᵃ Squadriglia was also lost, Ten Silvio De Giorgi (MM6873) baling out into the sea, wounded:

"When we were in sight of the island, I saw a certain number of aeroplanes that, higher and behind us, were diving in our direction. I believed that the planes were our indirect escort, but I was wrong. After the Hurricane assault (because they were Hurricanes), we scrambled all around. I was wounded and moreover I could see many bullet holes in the left wing of my aircraft. I started to feel pain in my leg, so I decided to go home. I wished to have someone to help me, to spot me in case of forced alighting on the sea, so I started to ramble around, looking for an escort.

Suddenly three aeroplanes appeared. The first was a Hurricane. I had the impression that the [other] two were Macchi 200s, and that the Hurricane was trying to attack them. I set aside my intention to return to base and fired a few warning shots towards the Macchis (this was our established signal to warn one another as we had no radio) and prepared to face the Hurricane, by now fully aware of my presence. At the first burst of fire from the Hurricane, I pulled up the nose of my aircraft as if he had hit me, then quickly changed manoeuvre and dived towards the sea, as if I had no control of the aircraft. This manoeuvre confirmed that my plane had no structural damage. Now I could go back to Sicily even without an escort. But suddenly there was a burst of firing and I was surrounded by flames. The Hurricane, of which I had lost sight and which I thought I had escaped from, had instead followed me. There was no alternative but to eject myself. As soon as the parachute opened, an excruciating pain in my chest overcame me. I became completely blind and at that moment I thought my adversary had machine-gunned me. The pain in my chest was terrible and I could hardly breathe."

De Giorgi was subsequently rescued from the sea by a launch from Malta.

It was at this point, with the latest convoy docked safely, that the Italians attempted an audacious raid on Grand Harbour by surface craft. This had in fact been in planning for several months — reconnaissances had been made and only bad weather had prevented the attempt being made a month earlier. Just before midnight on 25 July, the Italian sloop *Diana* hove-to 20 miles north of Malta. She carried aboard two two-man human torpedoes, nine explosive motor boats and their one-man crews and also towed a smaller electric-powered motor boat. Accompanying the vessels were two 60-foot MTBs.

Quite unknown to the Axis — or to many on the Allied side — the British were receiving information through Ultra sources concerning most Italian and German naval movement in the Mediterranean. Thus, when *Diana* was picked up on Malta's radar on arrival at her station, the defences knew at once that something was in the offing. The gun positions covering the harbour area had been put on alert for some time, since noise from the enemy craft moving close to the harbour indicated that the raid was on that night. The searchlights covering the entrance to Grand Harbour were then switched on and the E-boats could clearly be seen. Within a few minutes of the attack being launched, it was all over as the harbour defences, with their 6-pounder twin guns and machine-gun posts, opened fire and succeeded in sinking or damaging virtually all enemy craft in the vicinity of the harbour.

With the coming of dawn on 26 July, Hurricanes of 126 and 185 Squadrons were scrambled to finish off any surviving craft, especially those returning to Sicily. 249 did not participate since it was the unit's day off, although Plt Off Winton, who had flown with 249 briefly in June, was one of those involved in strafing the raiders, only to be engaged and shot down by MC200s sent out to aid the compatriots. After several hours in his dinghy, Winton spotted a stationary motor boat and swam to it, getting aboard to find it occupied by eight dead Italians. A Swordfish floatplane arrived soon afterwards and rescued him. The unsuccessful raid cost the Italians 15 dead and 18 captured — brave men all. It had been a gallant effort, but it had achieved nothing.

The following few weeks were relatively quiet for 249, no interceptions of the regular reconnaissance machines or their escorts being achieved. Towards the end of July a new unit came into being when the Malta Night Fighter Unit was formed at Takali with eight Hurricane IIcs and four IIbs. Pilots for the new 'squadron' were drawn from other Malta-based units, 249 supplying both flight commanders, Flt Lt Stones and newly-promoted Flt Lt Cassidy, together with Flg Off Thompson and Plt Offs Mills and Robertson. Sqn Ldr Barton had a lucky escape on the last day of July when he crashed in Z3492; he noted:

"Engine failure on take-off. I crash-landed from 300 feet — almost impossible at Malta — my lucky day — only suffered second degree burns from acid, glycol and petrol."

The CO was taken to Mtarfa Hospital; Flt Lt Neil wrote later:

"[Flg Off] Crossey and I visited him the day after and found him disfigured, shocked and trembling but profoundly thankful that things had turned out as well as they had. Few people had survived such an experience. Looking tiny and waif-like in his hospital bed, he was childishly relieved at his deliverance. As we left him behind, I was all too conscious of the Squadron's debt to the little man. Small and slight in stature, in no way an heroic figure and unassuming almost to a fault, he was one of the best leaders and fighter pilots it would be my good fortune to meet."

On 2 August the troopship *Leinster* arrived at Grand Harbour, having been escorted from Gibraltar by two light cruisers. Among the new arrivals was AC1 Ken Holroyd, an aircraft fitter, who was posted to 249:

"We operated from the southern side of the strip and being a Fitter 2E I was allocated to the maintenance section of the Squadron. We were responsible for the frequent maintenance procedures which were carried out. There were supposed to be 12 aircraft to a Flight, but I do not recall ever having this total number. There were some Hurricanes that were located in the open between Attard and Mosta. They had been dispersed there and were known as the Command reserve. Unfortunately we suffered one or two night raids by the Italians and three or four of these aircraft were written off at one go, so we lost virtually half of the so-called Command reserve that was at Takali in one night."

Flt Lt Neil, now temporary Squadron Commander, received a telephone call from the Controller on the morning of 17 August, and was informed that an aircraft carrying a 'special passenger' (probably an SOE operative) was due from the direction of Greece. 249 was to provide a section to escort it to Malta. On receiving the order to depart, Neil led Plt Offs Hulbert and Stuart plus Sgt Rex to a designated point north-east of the island, but his own aircraft developed an oil leak. Notwithstanding this, he decided to remain with his section and soon sighted "a twin-engined aircraft of some sort, low down, dark against the sea and flying in the opposite direction". Assuming this to be their charge, Neil turned his section in the direction of Malta and proceeded to escort the aircraft, although he could barely see it. When Malta came in sight, Neil was somewhat surprised that the aircraft did not head for Luqa, but instead approached Kalafrana Bay:

> "At this point, although I had no grounds for suspicion, the faintest shadow of doubt crossed my mind, causing me to look more closely at the aircraft beneath. Whilst I was toying with my doubts, something splashed down into the water and the aircraft upended itself in a steep turn to the right so that it passed directly beneath me."

Their 'charge' was in fact an SM79 torpedo-bomber. On informing Control of the turn of events he was ordered to shoot down the raider, but since he was unable to see clearly, ordered two of his section, who were flying cannon-armed IIcs, to take care of it. Despite using all their ammunition, Hulbert and Rex were unable to shoot it down and, when last seen, it was flying just above the waves, trailing smoke. It was considered unlikely to have reached Sicily and when a subsequent reconnaissance by several more of the unit's Hurricanes found a trail of oil and wreckage, the destruction of the aircraft was confirmed on this evidence. However, it would seem that the badly damaged aircraft — possibly an aircraft of 278ª or 279ª Squadriglia Auto AS from Gerbini — did in fact reach its base, with the crew wounded.

During the month pairs of Hurricanes were despatched on armed reconnaissance flights over Southern Sicily, the pilots briefed to attack targets of opportunity in addition to gathering information. On 29 August Flg Off Beazley and Flg Off Wells (now recovered from his wound, flying BV156) undertook a sortie to Pozzallo, strafing a schooner in the Sicilian Narrows during the return flight. Sqn Ldr Barton returned to the Squadron towards the end of the month and on 30 August made his first flight since his crash, flying Z2794 for just ten minutes. Two days later, early in the morning of 1 September, he led six Hurricanes (in Z2678) to cover two Fulmars of 800X Squadron returning from a bombing and strafing attack on Comiso airfield. No enemy aircraft were sighted.

On the morning of 4 September, 21 Hurricanes from 126 and 185 Squadrons engaged 19 MC200s of 10° Gruppo CT at 22,000 feet off Grand Harbour. The Hurricane pilots claimed seven Macchis shot down and a further two probables for the loss of one of their own, which force-landed. The Italian pilots claimed five Hurricanes shot down jointly, but lost their leader, Ten Col Carlo Romagnoli and one other, and had two other aircraft damaged. In the afternoon of the same day, 20 more MC200s from 54° Stormo CT, operating from Pantelleria and led by Cap Valentino Festa, and ten 10° Gruppo CT aircraft (led by Cap Franco Lucchini) covered a Z506B of 612ª Squadriglia to search for the missing pilots. Eight Hurricanes were scrambled by 249 to intercept, meeting the Italians five miles off Cap Passero at 1546, diving on them and engaging in a fierce dogfight at 1,000 feet. Sqn Ldr Barton later described it as the hardest fight of his career:

> "We attacked, from above, a formation of Macchis escorting what I believe was an air/sea rescue floatplane. We had the advantage but somehow the Italians reacted strongly and an unhappy dogfight ensued — all low down close to the water. I ordered disengage — I doubt if anyone heard — and we ran for home — a most dangerous situation, hence our losses. We should have done better."

Barton himself claimed one probable and one damaged, while Sgts Owen and Parker each claimed one shot down, and Plt Off Matthews one damaged. A third Macchi was reportedly seen to go into the sea, but two Hurricanes (Z3056 and Z3521) were lost when Plt Off George Smith and Sgt Jim Kimberley dived down to attack the Z506B; the seaplane suffered a number of hits before both Hurricanes were shot down by the escorting fighters and the pilots killed.

The Italians, obviously incensed by the loss of Romagnoli, thought they had been attacked by 25 Hurricanes. They claimed no less than 16 shot down — again apparently by all jointly, no individual credits being given — eight damaged and one probable. One 10° Gruppo CT Macchi flown by Serg Luigi Contarini was lost while two more, piloted by Mar Avellino De Mattia and Serg Walter Omiccioli of 54° Stormo CT, were damaged.

On 9 September *Ark Royal* delivered a further 26 Hurricane IIs to a point in the Mediterranean, west of Sicily, for despatch to Malta, but had to return to Gibraltar with a dozen of these still on board as the Blenheims sent to guide them to the island did not arrive. A second delivery of Hurricane IIs was due — via *Furious* — four days later, and *Ark Royal* returned with her complement — a total of 46 flying off, although one crashed into the sea on take-off — these arriving at Malta safely. Of the 59 new arrivals, 35 were destined for Egypt and departed once refuelled.

With the arrival of so many replacements, a number of new pilots were posted to the Squadron to replace those tour-expired, including Flt Lt Morello (who had only recently arrived at Malta) and Flg Off Wells, both of whom departed for Egypt aboard a Sunderland flyingboat. At about the same time, four NCO pilots were similarly posted to Egypt including Sgts Davies, Packham — killed later in a flying accident with 73 Squadron — and Edwards. One of the Squadron's new arrivals was Plt Off D.A. Tedford, one of four American nationals to reach the island from this delivery. Other replacement pilots posted to 249 included Sgt H. Moren.

However, it was not only the RAF fighter squadrons at Malta which were receiving new equipment, but their opponents across the Malta Channel, who were taking delivery of a potent new fighter, the Macchi MC202, which had the same model Daimler Benz 601 engine as the latest model Messerschmitt Bf109F, which was just making its first appearance in North Africa. In the hands of a skilled pilot, the MC202 was more than a match for the Hurricane.

Malta's new AOC, Air Vice-Marshal Hugh Pughe Lloyd agreed to requests for his fighter squadrons to adopt a more offensive role and, as a result, a number of Hurricanes from 185 and 249 Squadrons were fitted with underwing bomb racks capable of holding a total of eight 40lb bombs, to enable them to take the fight to the Italians in Sicily. This adaptation did not please everyone, witness Flt Lt Neil's comment:

"Bombs! What next, mines and torpedos? What were we, fighter aircraft or one-engined Blenheims?"

Thus, at this time, fighter-bombing was becoming *de rigeur* and, on the night of 6/7 October, Flt Lt Neil, in his new Mark IIb, GN-R (the code letters GN had been recently reintroduced to the Squadron Hurricanes), set out to bomb Gela station:

"Fondly hoping that the Italians would reveal their known defensive positions by shooting at me with the red balls, they did nothing of the sort, obliging me to wander about endlessly over Sicily trying to discover exactly where I was. In fact I never did find the railway station but, by sheer good fortune, came across the railway line. I did a gentle dive in that direction and disposed of my load."

That same night Comiso airfield was visited by Sqn Ldr Barton and Plt Off Palliser (in Z4016), who noted:

"First dive-bombing in Hurricane. Target stood out well in moonlight. Bombs fell near dispersals and hangars in south-east corner."

The Hurricanes returned, refuelled and rearmed and set out again for the same target. This time Palliser recorded:

"Set off at 4.30 AM. Much darker. Overshot target and bombed eastern side Vittorio Town, near Comiso."

Hurricanes of the MNFU and two Fulmars of 800X Squadron also operated over Sicily that night, one of the latter being lost when it was forced to ditch in the sea off Syracuse*. Three nights later Palliser (Z4016) was over Comiso again with his flight, noting:

---

* The Fulmar (N4004) has recently (1996) been found by Italian scuba divers, but has yet to be recovered.

"Target stood out very well. Did very steep dive and straddled hangars, dispersals and billets.
Intense flak. Two bombs on Comiso town. No results observed although aerodrome flak, five
miles away, opened up again."

At 0535 on the morning of 14 October, Luqa was strafed by six low-flying MC202s of 9° Gruppo
CT. Five all-black Hurricanes of the MNFU were led off by Flt Lt Cassidy (ex-249), followed
by three each of 185 and 249 Squadrons. Flg Off Thompson, also a former 249 pilot but now
with the MNFU, recalled:

"My 21st birthday! Dawn — scramble! Low flying attack on Luqa by six Macchi 202s. Plt
Off Barnwell and myself jumped. Barnwell shot down one but failed to return himself. The
action took place at dawn and 249 Squadron were also scrambled — Flg Off Leggett fired at
me over Grand Harbour — I seem to remember it cost him at least a couple of beers!"

249 sent Hurricanes out to search for the missing pilot, Plt Off Palliser noting that he found
wreckage but no sign of life. On a second search flight he saw what he thought was a dinghy
but was unable to find the position again. The search for Barnwell (who had in recent weeks
shot down five night raiders over Malta) was eventually called off next day.
    The Squadron found itself in a different role on 17 October, when it escorted six newly-
arrived Blenheims of 18 Squadron to attack Syracuse seaplane base, which was bombed from
12,500 feet. Three MC202s of 9° Gruppo CT scrambled from Comiso to intercept, these being
engaged by the Hurricanes in an inconclusive skirmish. One of the Blenheims was claimed shot
down, but the Italian pilot's own aircraft was hit by return fire and ditched in the sea, from
where the pilot was subsequently rescued by a motor boat; no bombers were actually lost during
this attack.
    Ultra intercepts now warned the British of an imminent increase in air traffic between Sicily
and North Africa, with air transports carrying troops and conveying petrol and supplies. Malta
was requested to despatch long-range patrols in attempts to intercept these aircraft. One such
operation on 19 October was flown by Sqn Ldr Barton and Plt Off Palliser who were briefed to
patrol to the south of Lampedusa Island. Barton recalled:

"Long-range patrol to try and intercept troop-carrying aircraft ferrying to North Africa. As
I remember it we used 44-gallon external tanks (one under each wing) designed for ferrying
only and quite unsuitable for combat."

At 0805 while at 6,000 feet they spotted a lone SM81 bomber-transport 1,000 feet below them,
heading south. Both at once attacked from astern and fired several bursts. The central and
starboard engines at once caught fire and it crashed into the sea where it blew up. Barton added:

"The SM81 soon burned and there was little left by the time it hit the sea — not a pretty sight."

Barton's fine leadership of the Squadron, combined with his continuing run of successes and
admirable fighting spirit following his crash, was rewarded when a Bar to his DFC was
announced at the end of the month. There were those who felt that his leadership warranted
greater recognition.
    After the recent lull in the Italian offensive against Malta, late October heralded an increase
in fighter activity. Obviously the introduction of the new Macchi 202 inspired renewed
confidence amongst the Italian pilots, as 249 found to its cost on the afternoon of 22 October,
when six 9° Gruppo CT MC202s, escorted my eight more, strafed Luqa twice. Although none
of the Hurricanes were hit, three ground personnel suffered injuries during the attack. Nine
Hurricanes of 249 were sent off to intercept, the Macchis diving on them as they were climbing
up over St Paul's Bay. Sgt Owen, who was flying Flt Lt Neil's new Hurricane GN-R, was shot
down in flames, but managed to bale out before his aircraft hit the sea. Sgt Branch (Z4016)
circled above until Owen was picked up safely by a rescue launch. Plt Off Matthews's aircraft
was also hit — in the wing and fuselage — although he was able to land safely. The Macchi

pilots, from 73ª Squadriglia, claimed heavily; two Hurricanes were credited to Ten Pietro Bonfatti and two more to Sottoten Alvaro Querci, and one each to Cap Mario Pluda, Serg Magg Teresio Martinoli and Serg Guerci, while two more were claimed probably destroyed; one Macchi was damaged in the fight.

Strafing and bombing of targets in Sicily, usually by pairs of Hurricanes from all three resident squadrons, continued into November, these generally escaping interception. However, a sortie by Plt Off Palliser (Z4016) and Flt Sgt Etchells on 4 November was caught by six MC202s, after the pair had bombed and strafed Gela station, but they managed to escape in cloud and return to Malta; Palliser noted:

> "Set out to bomb railway at Gela. Bombed railway bridge. No hits observed. Chased out by six Macchi 202s, but got away from them. Chased us for 15 minutes."

A recent arrival at Malta was Wg Cdr M.H. Brown DFC, a Canadian veteran of the fighting in France and over Britain during 1940, who was posted to Takali as Wing Commander Flying. He and Wg Cdr A.C. Rabagliati DFC, whom he was to succeed, planned a fighter-bomber strike against Gela airfield, using all available Hurricanes from 126 and 249 Squadrons. At 0630 on 12 November, four Hurricanes set out to strafe the defences and aircraft on the airfield, prior to the arrival of the Hurribombers; two of the aircraft were flown by Wg Cdrs Brown and Rabagliati, the other two by 249 pilots although one of the latter was obliged to return early, leaving just Plt Off Tedford to cover the Wing Commanders. The trio swept over the airfield, attacking a CR42, a MC200 and a Ju87 on the ground. As Rabagliati strafed the CR42, which caught fire, he saw Brown's Hurricane apparently stall, break away and crash; it had been hit by ground fire and Brown was killed. Rabagliati then saw a Ju87 in the air and shot this down, strafed some troops on horses and then — with Tedford still on his wing — headed for home.

The attack was just an opener and soon 11 bomb-carrying Hurricanes were in the air on their way to raid Gela, each armed with eight 25lb Cooper bombs; the small bombs were dropped individually by means of a bank of switches situated near the pilot's elbow. Six of the Hurribombers were from 249, while a further ten Hurricanes (including four from 249) provided the escort. As the 21 Hurricanes approached Gela they were engaged by three MC202s of 9° Gruppo which had been scrambled from Comiso as a result of the earlier intrusion. All three attacked a Hurricane of 126 Squadron and shot it down into the sea, while a pilot of that unit claimed a Macchi shot down in return, although there were no Italian losses on this occasion. The downed Hurricane pilot was rescued from the sea by an Italian launch and taken prisoner. During the return flight at sea level, with the Hurricanes skimming the wave tops, Plt Off Moon realised that one of his bomb switches was in the upright position. Assuming that he had caught it with his elbow, he flicked it down — thereby releasing a bomb which exploded barely 20 feet beneath his aircraft. Despite the deafening explosion, the Hurricane (Z4016) was not damaged and he, too, landed safely at Takali, wiser for the experience. The raid on Gela was deemed a success and all 249 aircraft returned safely.

Two reinforcement Hurricane squadrons (242 and 605 Squadrons) arrived on 12 November, having flown off *Ark Royal** and *Argus*; three were lost en route, leaving 34 new Mark IIs to reach Malta, where one crashed on landing. The new squadrons' aircraft were to be serviced by groundcrews of 185 and 249 Squadrons — and indeed the pilots were increasingly to fly as integral parts of these units.

The Italians continued to repay Malta in kind, sending over fighter sweeps to attack targets of opportunity but usually strafing the airfields. Hal Far was raided twice on 21 November by MC200s and MC202s, these incursions being disputed by Hurricanes of 185 Squadron. The Regia Aeronautica's assault was stepped up next afternoon (22 November), when ten Ju87s from 101° Gruppo Ba'T set out with an escort of 61 MC200s and MC202s drawn from 54° Stormo CT and 9° Gruppo CT. The close-escort MC200s became unco-ordinated and returned early,

---

* It was following this Hurricane ferry sortie that *Ark Royal* was torpedoed by a German U-boat, finally sinking within sight of Gibraltar.

but the MC202s, which were providing indirect cover, reported engaging 40 British fighters and claimed eight 'Spitfires' shot down.

Twenty-one Hurricanes had in fact been scrambled, 126 Squadron providing top cover to 249. They saw a force of fighters north of Gozo at between 26,000 to 30,000 feet, identified variously as 15 MC202s or 24 Bf109s and Macchis. 126 Squadron engaged in a very violent series of dogfights, its pilots claiming two probables and four damaged for no losses. Lower down, 249 also became involved, the CO claiming a MC202 shot down eight miles north-east of Gozo, the pilot not being seen to bale out. Flg Off Davis claimed a second and then shared another as probably destroyed jointly with Sgt Branch, the latter noting:

> "Sqn Ldr Barton was leading us when we intercepted 12 Macchi 202s at 18,000 feet. Flg Off Davis and myself shared a probable 202. Sgt Skeet-Smith got shot up in the tail and spun down out of control. Machine levelled itself out and he landed OK."

Pilots reported seeing wreckage from one Italian fighter flying through the air and amongst it an object swathed in white, as though the pilot had abandoned his aircraft and become entangled in the folds of his parachute. Only one MC202 (MM7748) was lost in this action, Ten Pietro Bonfatti of 73ª Squadriglia being killed.

Towards the end of November a photo-reconnaissance Mosquito PR1 arrived at Malta, having made a four-and-a-half-hour flight from the UK. Its pilot was a Battle of Britain veteran, who agreed to engage in a mock dogfight with a Hurricane flown by Flt Lt Neil, who discovered to his chagrin that the twin-engine Mosquito could outperform his own aircraft; "it was a good 100 mph faster" was one comment.

With the opening of a major German offensive in North Africa, the Luftwaffe in the Mediterranean was reinforced despite the fact that heavy fighting was continuing in Russia. The onset of winter there would restrict operations in any event, and consequently elements from that front were to be sent south instead, their first duty being the subjugation of Malta. Feld-marshall Albert Kesselring, Commander of Luftflotte 2, was designated Commander-in-Chief Süd (South) at the end of November, while before the end of the month II Fliegerkorps head-quarters moved from the Moscow front to Messina, Sicily. Units drawn from this Luftflotte were also ordered to Sicily, although most of these had first to return to Germany for re-equipment to make good the wastage on the Eastern Front. The force initially allocated the task of attacking Malta comprised three Gruppen of Ju88 bombers, plus two Gruppen of coastal strike Ju88s and a night-fighter Gruppe with Ju88Cs; three Gruppen of the latest Bf109Fs moved to Gela and Comiso. Among the German fighter pilots, fresh from victories on the Eastern Front, were a galaxy of aces including nine pilots with individual scores running into double figures. Faced with such experience and far superior aircraft, the defenders of Malta were soon to be over-whelmed.

The first two weeks of December saw several changes amongst personnel at Malta. At the end of the first week Sqn Ldr Edward Mortimer-Rose DFC arrived from AHQ Middle East, to take over the Squadron from Sqn Ldr Barton, who departed for the UK. During his six months on the island Barton had added five and one shared victories to his total, plus one probable and another shared. Of his departure, Flt Lt Neil wrote:

> "Butch Barton slipped away one night aboard a Sunderland in Kalafrana Bay bound for Gibraltar and home. There was no departing binge or palaver, he just went. Quietly. Without fuss. Disappearing as he had always fought, with unassuming distinction. I suspect he was glad to leave; he had been on the go since September 1939 and was beginning to believe that his luck would shortly run out."

Barton's successor had flown with 234 Squadron during the Battle of Britain and had seven and three shared victories to his credit. Flt Lt Neil was advised that his relief was due from Gibraltar any day, and made his last flight with the Squadron on 7 December, when he bombed Ragusa railway station (flying GN-J); he commented:

"As my target was within spitting distance of the fighter base at Comiso, I half expected to run into a clutch of hostile Macchis or 109s even, but in the event saw nothing, not even a burst of flak."

On 11 December 249 was awaiting the imminent arrival of a small formation of Wellingtons from Gibraltar, one of which was carrying as a passenger the replacement flight commander, Flt Lt Sidney Brandt, but then came a message stating that the Wellingtons were under attack from CR42s of 23° Gruppo Aut CT flying from Pantelleria. Flt Lt Neil, Flg Off Crossey and a few others scrambled to go to their aid, but were too late to intercept the Italian fighters which had shot down two of the bombers and damaged the one in which Brandt was flying, although one of their own number fell to return fire from the Wellingtons; of the incident, Neil* recalled:

"Brandt arrived at Takali in a very sombre frame of mind. His Wellington had been attacked by a group of CR42s and although a passenger, he had manned an extra machine-gun from a makeshift position in the waist of the bomber, firing furiously in its defence. The Wellington had been hit even so, and one or more of the crew wounded."

German reconnaissance aircraft started to make their presence felt over and around Malta during the first half of December, Sgt Branch (BD834) noting that during a dawn patrol on 13 December he intercepted and chased a Ju88 but lost it again in cloud.

On 19 December the Luftwaffe finally made its anticipated appearance. During the morning a reconnaissance Ju88 appeared over a convoy which was just arriving. Hurricanes of 126 Squadron intercepted and claimed damage to the intruder. Somewhat later, at 1045, three Ju88s were seen approaching the ships and on this occasion four Hurricanes of 249 intercepted, as noted by Sgt Branch:

"The new CO [Sqn Ldr Mortimer-Rose] together with Smudge [Sgt Skeet-Smith], Alan [Sgt Cairns] and Risty [Sgt Ron Rist] chased three Ju88s. CO attacked one Ju88 and Alan and Smudge attacked another. Alan was hit by cannon and machine-gun but landed OK. Risty did not fire. One Ju88 was later confirmed and we collected the tail, guns and wings from the kite."

The Ju88 attacked by Mortimer-Rose, R4+HH of I/NJG2, crashed on Gozo; seriously injured Lt Wilhelm Brauns, a six-victory ace, and his gunner, Uffz Erwin Heese, were taken prisoner but Gfr Johannes Mattuschka, the observer, was killed. Examination of the wreck allegedly revealed Italian markings. Uffz Heese told his captors that their task had been to remain over Malta for about an hour and attack any aircraft encountered. The observer's diary revealed that the crew had experienced a combat with two Italian Savoias the previous day, although the outcome of the incident was not recorded.

The real challenge to the Hurricanes came next day (20 December), when four Ju88s returned during the morning to attack shipping in Grand Harbour, but this time with a strong fighter escort of 11 Bf109Fs from the newly-arrived I/JG53, together with a number of MC202s (presumably from 9° Gruppo CT). A dozen Hurricanes of 249 were scrambled at 1036 to challenge the incoming formation, which was assessed to be 40-strong. Plt Off Palliser (flying a cannon-armed IIc) attacked one Ju88 head-on, opening fire when only a few yards away. He saw his shells hit its starboard engine and reported that the wing then detached and fell away. The stricken bomber went straight down but was lost from sight when it entered cloud. Before he could follow he was attacked by a number of Messerschmitts, one of which he believed he probably damaged; in the meantime, the bomber was seen to crash into the sea by coastwatchers. All three of the remaining bombers were claimed damaged before the escorting Macchis and Messerschmitts intervened.

---

* Shortly after this flight, tour-expired Flt Lt Neil, together with Flg Off Harrington, a long-time sufferer of 'Malta Dog', and Flt Lt Cassidy of the MNFU, departed Malta aboard the SS *Sydney Star* bound for Egypt.

The Hurricane flown by Sgt Howard Moren was believed to have collided with the Ju88, although it seems probable that he fell victim to a Messerschmitt; he was killed. Meanwhile, Flg Off Crossey fired at a Macchi, hitting its starboard wing; he reported that it gave a 'quick flick' and went straight down. Another Macchi was attacked by Sgt McDowall, who reported that it spun down apparently out of control, disappearing into cloud. The Squadron suffered a second fatality when Plt Off Brian Cavan's Hurricane was shot down from a height of 20,000 feet. The Hurricane fell like a stone and Cavan was killed and was one of three claimed by the pilots of I/JG53, one each being credited to Oblt Friedrich-Karl Müller (his 31st victory), Hptm Herbert Kaminski (his 6th) and Lt Werner Schow (his 4th).

During the late morning of 21 December a further raid approached, comprising four Ju88s and 20 escorting fighters — both Bf109Fs and MC202s. Ten Hurricanes of 185 Squadron and eight of 249 were scrambled, led by Wg Cdr Rabagliati in 249's Z4005. The Hurricanes were unable to reach the bombers and became embroiled with the escort, Flg Off Davis claiming a Macchi probable while both Flt Lt Beazley and Flt Sgt Etchells claimed damage to Bf109Fs; 185 Squadron pilots reported shooting down a Macchi and probably a second, but lost one of their own, who was killed. 249's Flg Off Leggett was also shot down by a Bf109F, baling out over Grand Harbour and suffering minor abrasions, while Flt Sgt Owen's aircraft suffered damage to its engine, the pilot gliding in to Takali for a dead-stick landing from some ten miles out. One Hurricane was claimed as his 51st victory by the Kommodore of JG53, Maj Günther von Maltzahn, and a second by Oblt Gerhard Michalski of 4 Staffel (his 23rd).

The Germans were back again during the afternoon of 22 December, Hurricanes of 126 and 249 Squadrons being scrambled when reports were received of Bf109Fs strafing fishing boats off Grand Harbour. A Messerschmitt was spotted by Plt Off Robert Matthews, who dived to the attack. A pilot of 126 Squadron witnessed the action:

> "Matthews got the Messerschmitt as it climbed from the sea for new altitude, but another German was hard on his own tail chasing him towards the shore. Matthews was hit and crashed into the sea wall at Valetta, where his aircraft [BV156] exploded and started to burn."

Matthews's body was recovered later from the sea and interred in Capuccini Naval Cemetery. Sgt Branch (BD703) reported meeting four Messerschmitts, but spun whilst engaging. Two Hurricanes were claimed by pilots of 2/JG53, Oblt Klaus Quaet-Faslem reporting shooting down one at 1536, his 10th victory, while Lt Heinrich von Schwerdtner claimed another at 1550 (his 6th).

Christmas Eve brought four alerts but only one interception. Wg Cdr Rabagliati led off 17 Hurricanes of 126 and 249 Squadrons after four Ju88s which dive-bombed Grand Harbour; this was the 25th raid in seven days, an indication of the level of activity that the arrival of the Luftwaffe had brought. Sqn Ldr Mortimer-Rose had decided that 249's aircraft should take off and climb in pairs, so as to give the impression (to the Germans) that large numbers of Hurricanes were climbing up to engage rather than the few available. Plt Off Moon recalled:

> "I was one of the last to take off and, as I climbed, I could see the CO's aircraft virtually standing on its tail as he fired at a bomber. A pencil-thin line of smoke or vapour appeared from one of its engines, but this had ceased before I lost sight of it."

The CO was joined in the attack on the Ju88 by Plt Off Palliser and the bomber, 3Z+EP of 5/KG77, was sent crashing into the sea in flames some 20 miles east of Zonqor Point, Lt Siegfried Tack and his crew (Obgfr Walter Kersken, Obgfr Hermann Kunz and Fw Nikolaus Wand) all perishing. A second Ju88 was claimed shot down by the combined attacks of Flg Off Crossey and Flt Sgt Etchells, who were also joined by Palliser. Their victim had apparently been damaged by AA fire and when last seen, five miles north of Malta, was losing height with smoke pouring from both engines. It seems probable this was M7+HK of KGr806 flown by Uffz Werner Lessner, which also failed to return from the raid. A third bomber was pursued to Sicily by Plt Off Moon:

"I saw a Ju88 leave the formation. I was 2,000 feet below and chased it towards Sicily but before I could catch up, it entered a thundercloud. I followed, held steady and luckily met it on the other side. I fired at long range, but nothing observed. Fired again and the 88 started weaving. I caught up and fired again, saw strikes and it fell away. My No2, Sgt Lawson, then appeared and I told him to follow it down to observe the crash but when I got back I found that he had followed me instead."

This was clearly an aircraft of 4/KG77 flown by Fw Otto Bude which crash-landed on return to Catania, one member of the crew (Obgfr Paul Müller, the observer) having been fatally wounded during the combat. Meanwhile, some of the Hurricanes were engaged by escorting Bf109Fs of 5/JG53, Sqn Ldr Mortimer-Rose's aircraft being shot up (possibly by Oblt Kurt Brändle, who claimed a Hurricane at 1308 for his 29th victory), necessitating a crash-landing at Luqa, where it was found that the CO had a bullet lodged in his heel. Palliser's aircraft was hit in the glycol tank during the action, but he was able to return to Takali safely. 126 Squadron lost a pilot in the engagement.

With Sqn Ldr Mortimer-Rose wounded, command of the Squadron passed to Flt Lt Beazley, who was duly promoted, A Flight being taken over by newly promoted Flt Lt Davis. Christmas Day proved peaceful, but on 26 December the raiders were back over Malta. Four alerts were sounded and during one Luqa was heavily attacked and a number of aircraft were destroyed or damaged on the airfield. An official communique issued at 1700 that evening simply stated:

"During the course of the day five alerts have been sounded. During the first and second alerts enemy aircraft crossed the coast, but dropped no bombs. In the third alert a number of enemy bombers escorted by fighters crossed the coast and were engaged by our fighters. One enemy bomber was definitely destroyed and two others were damaged. One enemy fighter was destroyed and another damaged."

Sgt Branch (Z2698) was among the 249 pilots scrambled to meet the raid:

"We joined up with 126 Squadron and climbed to 25,000 feet. CO left formation as his engine was cutting. Four attacked one Ju88 and destroyed it. Risty [Sgt Rist] had his first squirt in action. Flg Off [sic] Davis and Plt Off Tedford had a poop at a 109 and believed to have damaged it. Flt Sgt Owen had his time cut out getting out of the way of 109s. Flt Lt Carpenter of 126 Squadron claimed a Ju88 with 249. One Hurribox shot up, but no damage or casualties apart from this. Not a bad day."

Squadron Hurricanes were scrambled again on 28 December when Ju88s and their escort were reported approaching the island. Branch (Z3757) wrote:

"Saw Ju88 but jumped by Messerschmitt 109s as unable to get height. Squirted at by 109. Dave Owen had a nasty experience. Shot up by 109s, he baled out and landed in a very rough sea five miles out. Kalafrana rescue launch kept on and finally found him, after two of the crew had been knocked out and the boat battered to blazes. Lucky man Dave. This makes the second time in three months and he still has 27 pieces of shrapnel in his shoulder."

Old faces were rapidly disappearing, Owen having been with the Squadron since May. Worse was to come, however.

29 December was to see the heaviest day of fighting over Malta since the return of the Luftwaffe to Sicily, and a costly one for the defenders. There were five scrambles during the day, three of which developed into major combats. The first of these occurred soon after 0945, when 36 raiders approached, 16 Hurricanes being sent up (although none from 249). Two Hurricanes collided in mid-air soon after take-off, one pilot losing his life and the other baling out into the sea, from where he was rescued. The remaining Hurricanes engaged Ju88s and

Bf109Fs, one of the latter being claimed probably destroyed and a second damaged; in return three Hurricanes were damaged.

Eighteen Hurricanes were again sent up soon after 1430 to intercept two dozen raiders, one Messerschmitt being claimed shot down and three damaged by 185 Squadron for the loss of one Hurricane and its pilot. An hour and a half later 249 scrambled four Hurricanes, led by Flt Lt Brandt, to investigate a report that five fighters were attacking the Gozo ferryboat, the schooner *Marie Georgette*. On arrival over the Gozo Channel they saw that the ferryboat was in fact on fire and the Bf109Fs were still in the vicinity. These engaged and Lt Joachim Louis of Stab/JG53 promptly shot down one of the Hurricanes (his 1st victory), but failed to notice Plt Off Stuart closing on his tail; Louis was wounded and struggled to reach Sicily but eventually ditched his damaged aircraft just off the coast, from where he was recovered by an Axis rescue craft. Meanwhile, Oblt Michalski succeeded in shooting down a second Hurricane. Both Brandt and Sgt Roy Lawson were lost in this engagement, their aircraft (BD834 and BE344) falling into the sea. At the first opportunity an RN Swordfish was despatched from Hal Far to search for the missing pilots, but returned after a fruitless three hours.

The damaged ferryboat, which had a normal crew of ten, was carrying a dozen passengers. When attacked, Marcel Theuma, the skipper, had rushed to the bridge, taken the helm himself and succeeded in heading the vessel towards St George's trenches. The Messerschmitts returned to the attack and Theuma was struck by a bullet; one of the crew was killed as was a passenger. The vessel was beached and the survivors jumped into the sea and all bar one were saved when rescuers — soldiers in the vicinity — formed a human chain to get them ashore. The severely wounded master was taken to St Patrick's Military Hospital where he died the following day. The schooner did not sink and was later recovered, repaired and put back into service.*

The last combat of the year for 249 occurred during the morning of 30 December. Just before midday ten Hurricanes from 126 and 249 Squadrons were sent off, led by Takali's new Wing Leader, Wg Cdr W.A.J. Satchell. The official communique relating to the action noted that the bombers attacked Luqa, Takali and the Dockyard on this occasion. The Hurricanes engaged five Ju88s of KGr806 near Luqa and Satchell pursued one out to sea and was credited with its destruction; a second was claimed shot down by 249:

> "Another Junkers which was set on fire by a Sergeant Pilot [Sgt Rex] was also seen to crash into the sea. Black smoke was pouring from the port engine of another, which was trying to make for home after it had been attacked by a Sergeant Pilot [Sgt McDowall]."

Sgt Branch added his own comment:

> "A good ending to the old year!"

At 0840 on 3 January, 14 Hurricanes — seven each from 126 and 249 Squadrons — scrambled from Takali, followed ten minutes later by eight more from 185 Squadron. Climbing to 20,000 feet, the leader spotted two or three Ju88s (again aircraft of KGr806) at 15,000 feet over Luqa, with an escort provided by a dozen Bf109Fs of II/JG53. The unaccustomed height advantage was not to be wasted and the Hurricane pilots made the best of this rare opportunity. Two pilots of 126 Squadron jointly shot down one of the bombers, a second being attacked by 249's Plt Off Hulbert and a pilot of 126 Squadron; with its port engine on fire and the other pouring black smoke, the bomber was last seen in a dive. An airman at Luqa noted in his journal:

> "Four Ju88s and several 109s came over . . . The first Ju88 just blew up in mid-air directly our Hurribird fired it. The second one circled our 'drome twice and during that time three Jerries baled out while all the time smoke was pouring from his tail. Eventually he piled in."

---

* The *Marie Georgette* is still soldiering on at the time of writing (1997); it has been extensively remodelled however and has been renamed *The Buccaneer*. As a pleasure craft it is actively employed conveying tourists from St Paul's Bay to nearby Comino island.

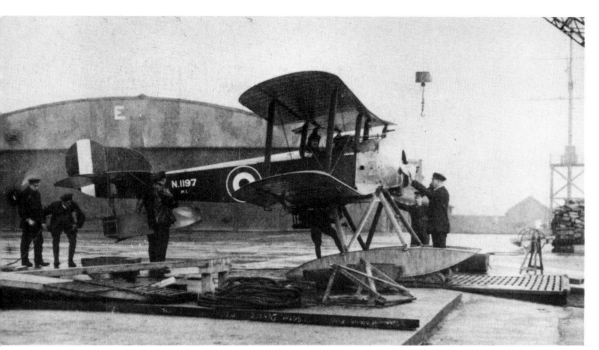

Top: Sopwith Baby N1197, Dundee 1918.
(GS Leslie via AS Thomas)

Middle: Short S184, **Dundee 1918.**
(GS Leslie via AS Thomas)

Above: Flg Off Young (IO), Sqn Ldr Grandy,
Off Lohmeyer DFC. *(Wg Cdr TF Neil)*

ght: Plt Off Ozzie Crossey with
Cs Bill Bones (left) and Len Hiscocks
side Ops Hut. *(WG Bones)*

Top: Salvaged from 249's first victory. *(Wg Cdr TF Neil)*

Above: Flg Off John Young, A Flight. *(Author's collection)*

Above right: P3154 GN-H following its force-landing on 20 July 1940.

(AS Thomas)

Right: B Flight groundcrew.

(WG Bones)

Top left: Flt Lt James Nicolson, awarded the Victoria Cross. *(Author's collection)*

Top centre: Sitting on the fence, Boscombe Down. All smoking pipes except Bryan Meaker smoking a tent mallet! (left to right): George Barclay, Percy Burton, Wells, Bryan Meaker. *(Sqn Ldr PHV Wells)*

Top right: Visit by the Duke of Kent to Boscombe Down, August 1940 (left to right): George Barclay, Bryan Meaker, Dennis Parnall, Pat Wells, Duke of Kent, Sqn Ldr Grandy. *(Sqn Ldr PHV Wells)*

Bottom left: Plt Off George Barclay.

(Sqn Ldr ARF Thompson)

Bottom right: Flt Lt Barton on returning to North Weald after being shot down simultaneously by return fire from a Do17 and a Bf109 on his tail during the afternoon of 5 September 1940. *(Wg Cdr TF Neil)*

Top left: Sgts George Stroud, Charles Palliser, Dusty Mills and Harry Davidson. *(Wg Cdr TF Neil)*

Top right: Irish-born Plt Off Bryan Meaker, killed in action 27 September 1940. *(Wg Cdr TF Neil)*

Middle left: GN-C and GN-A taking off from North Weald, September 1940. *(G Perrin via AS Thomas)*

Middle right: Tail unit of Hptm Horst Leinsberger's

Bf110 with which Plt Off Percy Burton collided on 27 September 1940; there were no survivors from either aircraft. *(Author's collect)*

Above: Plt Off Percy Burton, Flt Lt Butch Barton, F Off Lew Lewis, Plt Off Ozzie Crossey, Plt Off Ginge Neil, Flg Off John Beazley, Sqn Ldr Grandy, Plt Off George Barclay, Flg Off Keith Lofts, North Weald early September 1940. *(Wg Cdr TF l*

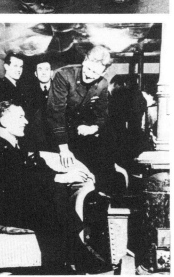

Top left: Flg Off Pat Wells and Plt Off Ginger Neil with Wilfred.

(Wg Cdr TF Neil)

Top right: Flg Off Bill Millington (with Wilfred) and Plt Off Neil
(with Pipsqueak). *(Wg Cdr TF Neil)*

Above left: Plt Off Dicky Wynn and Flg Off Ernest Cassidy with
Squadron mascots. *(Wg Cdr TF Neil)*

Above centre and right: Hptm Rolf Pingel of I/JG26 was shot down by Sgt
Bentley Beard on 28 September 1940 just after he had shot down Flg Off
Lew Lewis, pictured above (left) with Plt Off Crossey; both pilots survived.

(Author's collection)

Left: Newly commissioned Plt Off Bentley Beard and newly promoted
Flt Lt Ginger Neil, with Sgt Popek and Flg Off Skalski in the background.

(Wg Cdr TF Neil)

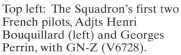

Top left: The Squadron's first two French pilots, Adjts Henri Bouquillard (left) and Georges Perrin, with GN-Z (V6728).

(G Perrin via AS Thomas)

Top right: Sgt Micky Maciejowski shot down one of the Bf109s which attacked North Weald.

(Author's collection)

Middle left and right: Flt Lt Keith Lofts was fortunate to survive the attack on North Weald by Bf109s of II/LG2 on 29 October 1940 when his aircraft was damaged by a bomb as it was taking off.

(both Wg Cdr TF Neil)

Right: Obfw Josef Harmeling's Bf109 of 4/LG2 which force-landed at Langenhoe Wick following an attack by Sgt Maciejowski on 29 October; seen here on display to raise funds for the war effort.

(Michael Payne)

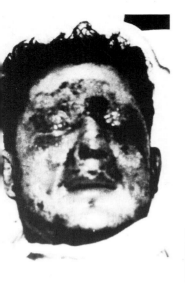

Top left and centre: Pat Wells was shot down and badly burned on 11 December 1940 by Obstlt Adolf Galland of Stab/JG26; following treatment at the special burns unit at East Grinstead he made a remarkable recovery, as testified by the second picture taken just three months later.
(Sqn Ldr PHV Wells)

Top right: Plt Off Bill McConnell, the Squadron's first casualty of 1941.
(Wg Cdr TF Neil)

Middle left: Winter 1940 (left to right): Sgt Mills, Sgt Sheppard RAAF, Sgt Palliser, Sgt Davidson, Flt Lt Lewis, Sqn Ldr Barton, Flg Off Lohmeyer (Adjt), Plt Off Crossey, Flg Off Wells, Plt Off Wynn, Plt Off Thompson, Flg Off Cassidy, Flg Off Woolmer (IO), Flt Lt Neil, Flg Off Robertson (EO).
(Wg Cdr TF Neil)

Above: Plt Off Tommy Thompson.
(Wg Cdr TF Neil)

Left: North Weald, 1941 (left to right): Unknown Sgt Plt, Flg Off Beazley, Flt Lt Neil, Sqn Ldr Barton, Flg Off Davis, Sgt Parker, Sgt Mills, Flg Off Wells, Sgt Guest; (front): Plt Off Munro with Pipsqueak. *(WG Bones)*

Top left: Welcome to Malta! The wreck of one of the Squadron's Hurricanes at Takali following a strafing attack by Bf109s of 7/JG26 on 21 May 1941. *(NWMA)*

Top right: Sgt Fred Etchells.
(FA Etchells)

Middle left: 249 at Takali following arrival of reinforcements (front, left to right): Flg Off Beazley, Sqn Ldr Barton, Flg Off Harrington, Plt Off Leggett; (rear, left to right): Plt Off Tedford, Plt Off Palliser, Sgt Rist, Plt Off Matthews, Sgt Skeet-Smith (behind), Sgt Branch, Sgt Parker, Plt Off Hill, Sgt Owen, Flg Off Davis. *(Wg Cdr RA Barton)*

Middle right: Flt Lt Don Stones.
(Sqn Ldr H H Moon)

Above: Sgt Maurice Guest, killed in action 17 July 1941.
(R Rist via AS Thomas)

Right: Sgts Alf Branch and Jim Kimberley (the latter was killed in action 4 September 1941).
(AT Branch)

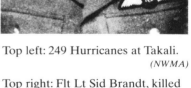

Top left: 249 Hurricanes at Takali.
(NWMA)

Top right: Flt Lt Sid Brandt, killed in action 29 December 1941.
(F Margarson)

Middle left: Slight mishap! U of 249 Squadron. *(AT Branch)*

Middle right: Plt Off Jimmy Stuart, killed in a flying accident on 9 February 1942.
(Sqn Ldr HH Moon)

Far left: Plt Off Jack Hulbert, killed in action 4 February 1942.
(Sqn Ldr HH Moon)

Left: Sgts Dave Owen, Ron Rist and Hugh McDowall (the latter was killed in action on 4 February 1942). *(R Rist via AS Thomas)*

Top left: Plt Off Harry Moon from Belfast.　*(Sqn Ldr HH Moon)*

Top right: Sgt Roy Lawson, killed in action on 29 December 1941.
(NWMA)

Middle left: Flg Off Davis, Sqn Ldr Mortimer-Rose, Flt Lt Beazley, December 1941.
(PG Leggett via Chaz Bowyer)

Middle right: Flg Off Graham Leggett and Plt Off Bob Matthews (the latter was killed in action on 22 December 1941).
(PG Leggett via Chaz Bowyer)

Right: Sqn Ldr Stan Turner.
(NWMA)

Far right: Plt Off Don Tedford, the Squadron's first American pilot, killed in action on 24 February 1942.
(NWMA)

Top left: AB264 GN-H, one of the first Spitfires to arrive.

(NWMA)

Top right: Flt Lt Buck McNair RCAF. *(Author's collection)*

Middle left: Flt Lt Norman Macqueen, killed in action on 4 May 1942. *(NWMA)*

Middle right: Sqn Ldr Stan Grant. *(NWMA)*

Left: Sgt Dave Ferraby.

(DL Ferraby)

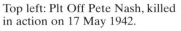

Top left: Plt Off Pete Nash, killed in action on 17 May 1942.
(Wg Cdr PB Lucas via NWMA)

Top right: Flg Off Raoul Daddo-Langlois, a Channel Islander.
(Daddo-Langlois collection)

Above: Flg Off Buck Buchanan from Rhodesia.
(Wg Cdr PB Lucas via NWMA)

Above right: Plt Off Jeff West RNZAF. *(NWMA)*

Right: Plt Off Ray Hesselyn RNZAF.
(NWMA)

p left: Plt Off Paul Brennan RAAF.   *(NWMA)*

p right: Plt Off Doug Leggo, another Rhodesian,
led in action on 20 March 1942.

(NWMA)

Above left: Plt Off Jimmy James, wounded on 26 April
1942.   *(Wg Cdr PB Lucas via NWMA)*

Above right: Plt Off Owen Berkeley-Hill, an Anglo-
Indian, killed in action on 12 July 1942.

(Mrs Rosamund Hills)

Top left: Plt Off Jack Rae RNZAF.
(NWMA)

Top right: Plt Off Johnny Plagis
from Rhodesia, with Flt Lt Ron West.
(NJ Ogilvie)

Above: Sqn Ldr Laddie Lucas.
(Wg Cdr PB Lucas via NWMA)

Above right: Plt Off Ossie Linton
RCAF and Flg Off Les Watts.
(Daddo-Langlois collection)

Right: Flt Lt Johnny Plagis.
(NJ Ogilvie)

Top left: Plt Off George Beurling, the Squadron's Canadian top-scoring ace. *(NWMA)*

Top right: Plt Off Ernie Budd. *(NWMA)*

Middle left: Flt Sgt Bob Middlemiss RCAF. *(NWMA)*

Above: Sgts Micky Butler (killed in action on 25 August 1942) and Gerry De Nancrede, both Canadians. *(NWMA)*

Left: Flt Sgt Murray Irving Gass, killed in action on 4 October 1942. *(NWMA)*

Top left: Flt Lt Frank Jones RCAF.
(Daddo-Langlois collecti

Top right: Plt Off Al Yates RAAF.
(Daddo-Langlois collecti

Left: Plt Off Allen Stead RNZAF.
(NWM

Above right: Flt Lt John McElroy RCAF.
(Daddo-Langlois collecti

Other pilots were unable to engage, Branch (Z3757) noting:

"Reached bombers' height — chased them out to sea but jumped by 109s."

It was the same story next day when Hurricanes from 249 were scrambled, Branch annotating his logbook thus:

"Ju88s escorted by Messerschmitt 109s at 21,000 feet. Got height but 109s sitting above us again — chased by two 109s."

By now the airfields were short of petrol and oil bowsers for refuelling the aircraft, most having been destroyed in recent air raids. AC1 Ken Holroyd, who had just returned to the Squadron at Takali having been hospitalised after breaking a leg, recalled:

"I then got seconded to the Station's workshop. We had to make a bowser. We had an old bus chassis on which we mounted a 250-gallon oil tank and fitted a couple of hand recipro-cating pumps. The idea was to trundle this round the airfield, but we found that operation of the hand pump was not successful, and it was not speedy enough to do a turn around on aircraft. We had to return back to the four-gallon drums. The only wheels on the Station were owned by Wg Cdr Satchell, who had a little James two-stroke motorcycle. We did have small carts — donkey carts with either a donkey or a mule owned by local farmers — and these were our only means of transport. We shipped ammunition, petrol and things like that, but they were not useful for transporting personnel."

During mid-month 249 bade farewell to another stalwart when Plt Off Palliser was posted to 605 Squadron at Hal Far as Acting Flt Lt to take command of a flight. The announcement of a well-deserved DFC followed soon afterwards. He renewed his association with the Squadron shortly after however, when he was best man at the wedding of Flt Lt Crossey and Miss Lilliana de Giorgio, daughter of Malta's Regional Protection Officer. The marriage took place at St Paul's Church, Rabat:

"While the bridegroom's Hurricane squadron roared into action to break up enemy bomber formations, which were dropping bombs all around [the church], the bride calmly walked down the aisle to the altar, ignoring the thunder of bomb explosions and anti-aircraft fire which all but swamped the church organ's Wedding March."

The newspaper report continued:

"On the second day of the honeymoon, Flt Lt Crossey was recalled to duty . . ."

The Hurricanes continued to go up after the swift Ju88s without undue success. The speed differential was marginal, while the armour of the bombers was so effective that only cannon-armed Mark IIcs had any real chance of success. It was a frustrating but common experience for the pilots of the IIbs to struggle within range of a fleeing bomber, only to fall back as the recoil of twelve .303 Brownings slowed their aircraft down without inflicting commensurate damage to the target. Flt Sgt Etchells commented later:

"On several occasions, as I recall to my disgust, I saw an odd Ju88 unescorted and just asking to be shot down, but with all power on and nose down by 15°, it was able to increase distance between us."

Etchells, who had been on the island since the previous May, also summed up the defensive attitude of mind required to survive in the dangerous Malta skies at this time:

"In retrospect, I realise that Malta had to take a very low priority for good and modern fighters, and fear that a lot of our time was taken up by attempting to survive in well-used Hurricane Mk Is and later Mk IIs — again very second-hand. We were quite aggressive as a fighter squadron, but soon learned that it was more necessary to keep a good lookout behind and above, than looking for victims, as the 109s in particular had many thousands of feet advantage over us, plus an enormous speed advantage."

In order to help lift flagging morale, a mini pre-emptive early morning strike was launched on 19 January against Comiso airfield, home of bombers of KG77 and the fighters of JG53. It was carried out by four Hurricanes led by Wg Cdr Rabagliati, which took off at 0730, each aircraft carrying eight 20lb fragmentation bombs. The other three aircraft were flown by Sqn Ldr Beazley, Flt Sgt Etchells and a pilot of 126 Squadron. A surprise attack was carried out, when buildings and aircraft were strafed. A fire was started and 65 drums of aviation fuel were burned, while two Ju88s were claimed probably destroyed. Beazley's aircraft (BV174) was hit by ground fire and he subsequently force-landed at Luqa on return.

Shortly after midday, a 70-plus raid was plotted on the radar screens as the Luftwaffe launched a heavy raid against a convoy which was approaching Malta; other bombers headed for the airfields. Hurricanes from 126, 242 and 249 Squadrons were patrolling over the ships as the Ju88s — aircraft of KüFlGr606 — arrived and Flt Sgt Etchells joined two of 126 Squadron in an attack on one, but could only claim damage before it escaped. Three other pilots from 126 enjoyed greater success and shot one of the bombers into the sea. Meantime, Flg Off Leggett and Sgt Branch were attacked from astern by three Bf109Fs of II/JG53 over Luqa. Branch (Z3757) noted:

> "Jumped by three 109s at 2,500 feet and had starboard aileron control shot away. Got two bursts at 109. Claimed damaged — landed at Luqa OK."

His Hurricane was nonetheless claimed shot down by Oblt Brändle of 5 Staffel. Due to the prompt intervention of the Hurricanes, no co-ordinated attack could be made on the convoy by the raiders, and none of the ships was hit, but both Takali and Hal Far airfields were bombed and strafed. At Hal Far a Swordfish was destroyed, while at Takali four airmen were killed, including 249's Cpl John Small, when their rock shelter received two direct hits; a Hurricane and two Blenheims were badly damaged. A mile to the north-east of Takali lies the ancient town of Mosta (famed for its awe-inspiring church which possesses the third largest unsupported dome in the world), its very location placing it in the front line. During the raid a number of bombs missed the airfield and exploded in and around the town, killing 13 civilians, while four more of the seriously injured died later.

The first raid on 22 January approached the island just after 1100, 17 Hurricanes being scrambled, seven of these from 249 with Sqn Ldr Beazley at their head. Three Ju88s from I/KG54 and five escorting fighters — identified by the RAF pilots as MC202s, but in all probability Bf109Fs — were sighted at 10,000 feet, ten miles east of Kalafrana. In the ensuing skirmish one bomber was shot down by 126 Squadron, a second damaged and one of the escort probably destroyed. Meanwhile, the third bomber was attacked by Flt Lt Davis and Plt Off Tedford, together with a pilot from 126 Squadron, but it escaped serious damage. Next day (23 January) Flt Sgt Etchells was one of a dozen 249 pilots scrambled to intercept a raid by five Ju88s. He engaged one of the bombers and fired a five-seconds burst, claiming some damage. Another of those engaged, Plt Off Moon, recalled:

> "There was a steady stream of Ju88s and 109s in thick cloud. Saw twin-engined aircraft and attacked but thought then it might be a Blenheim and broke away. Later heard that a dinghy was seen and feared that I had shot down the Blenheim after all, but it turned out to be the crew of an Albacore shot down by 109s. The aircraft I attacked was in fact a Maryland flown by Flt Lt Warburton [the legendary reconnaissance pilot of 69 Squadron]. I later apologised but Warburton seemed unconcerned."

In the afternoon of 24 January a major interception was attempted at 1325 as raiders approached the island, heading for the airfields at Luqa and Hal Far once more. A total of 23 Hurricanes (five from 249) took off, intercepting three Ju88s (from III/KG77) and eight Bf109Fs at 17,000 feet. Moon engaged one of the bombers, gaining hits, but his own aircraft was then shot up by a Messerschmitt:

> "The cockpit filled with smoke and I opened the hood, ready to bale out, but the smoke cleared so I glided back to Luqa with a dead engine and landed with the wheels down. One propeller blade had a cannon hole through it the size of a man's fist, and a bullet hole through the canopy beside my head."

His Hurricane (BP612 GN-H) had probably been damaged by Oblt Michalski of 4/JG53, who claimed one shot down at this time. Meanwhile, the blip on the radar screens indicating the bomber Moon and a pilot of 185 Squadron had jointly attacked ultimately faded and they were credited with its destruction. This was undoubtedly an aircraft of 8/KG77 which crashed at Castelvetrano on return, in which Lt Ernst Fischer and his crew were killed.

The defending fighters were hit hard next day, when a maximum effort was called for to provide cover for two empty supply ships which were departing Malta with an escort of destroyers. To ensure minimum interference as the eastward-bound convoy left Grand Harbour, seven Hurricanes from Hal Far were to provide low level protection, while eight others from 126 and 249 Squadrons were to act as top cover, but three of the latter were forced to return early, including Moon who managed to glide back to Takali in BD789 GN-G with a dead engine when the supercharger sheared. As the ships passed Delimara Point, four Ju88s and a dozen Messerschmitts were seen approaching. The Hal Far Hurricanes had just engaged the bombers when the Messerschmitts struck. Bouncing the top cover, Maj von Maltzahn's Staff flight of five Bf109Fs rapidly shot down three of the Hurricanes (all 126 Squadron machines), killing one pilot and obliging the other two to bale out. In addition, Flt Lt Crossey's aircraft was badly shot up. The Messerschmitts then dived on the lower level Hurricanes, shooting down one from which the pilot baled out, and seriously damaged four others, three of which crash-landed; one pilot was slightly injured. An airman at Kalafrana was among those who witnessed the unequal battle:

> "A real dogfight between Hurricanes and Messerschmitts right overhead. Saw four fighters come down and three pilots bale out. Can't say which side they belonged to. One machine was flying itself round and round, upside down, and at last landed upside down and burned."

Of the attack on the top cover Hurricanes which included the 249 section, Maj von Maltzahn recalled:

> "I drew towards them from behind with my five aircraft. Then coming at them from the rear from out of the sun in wide curves, I set up the first attack against the five Hurricanes. This worked well. We came in unnoticed, with me attacking the Hurricane laying on the extreme left. She was hit, went down immediately, and broke up in flames into the sea. Whereupon I collected together my flight and set up a second attack. The Hurricanes increased speed over the land and tried to climb above us. I allowed a little time in order to let my planes end their attack. Just then I saw two of the somewhat higher situated Hurricanes had curved around, apparently in order to position themselves behind us. But they didn't do this, though — on the contrary they flew towards land. As a result, I was able to push forward with the second attack without any harassment. Again I fixed my sights on the plane laying on the extreme left, thus allowing my comrades also to get going once more. Again the Hurricane received a direct hit. The pilot baled out. I saw him immediately afterwards, falling away from me over my cabin roof."

The five pilots of Stab/JG53 claimed eight Hurricanes shot down, two by von Maltzahn, whose final comment was:

"We must put it down to good luck that we came out of this combat completely unharmed and returned to base without a single casualty."

The Hurricane pilots engaged in this action, on the other hand, were lucky under the circumstances to have suffered only the one fatality, while the ease with which the Messerschmitts disposed of their opponents must have been almost the last straw for the defenders in their outclassed Hurricanes. Morale was undoubtedly shaken.

The first engagement of the new month for 249 occurred on 4 February, when several raids were made on the island, culminating in a heavy bombing attack on Takali. At 1225 four Hurricanes from 249 (plus two from 126 Squadron), scrambled after two Ju88s south of Kalafrana. One of these was attacked by Flt Lt Davis, who gained hits on both engines before Sqn Ldr Beazley and Plt Off Tedford joined in, the bomber finally escaping in cloud. This was possibly an aircraft of 2/KGr806 which crash-landed at Scalea; one member of the crew, Obgfr Heinrich Pfitzner, was injured.

At 1450 another scramble was ordered, 11 Hurricanes from 126, 242 and 249 Squadrons taking off, but failing to make contact with the bombers, which commenced to bomb Takali. Serious damage was caused to the airfield buildings and there were a number of casualties, including the Squadron's LAC Alex Robinson, who was mortally wounded. Meanwhile, in the air the 249 section led by Flt Lt Crossey was joined by a pilot of 126 who had become separated from his own section, but the Hurricanes were bounced by Bf109Fs from Stab/JG53, which promptly shot down three of the five Hurricanes; Plt Off Moon narrowly missed a similar fate:

"Crossey shot up into the clouds but the first I knew of an attack was when I looked either side and saw both Hurricanes falling in flames. Two Messerschmitts sped past without hitting me and I became involved in a series of dogfights for about 15 minutes, squirting at several 109s. Once they had departed Control ordered me to orbit the oil slicks where the Hurricanes had gone in. I said there was no point, there were no survivors but was ordered to remain as a rescue launch was on its way. After about 15 minutes I called Control who told me to return since the rescue launch had been shot up by 109s."

Both Plt Off Jack Hulbert (Z4003 GN-S), a 19-year-old from Woodgreen in Hampshire, and 21-year-old Sgt Hugh McDowall (Z4016) from Manchester were killed; they probably fell to Lt Karl-Heinz Preu (his 6th victory) who claimed a Hurricane at 1650, and Maj von Maltzahn who claimed another three minutes later, for his 56th victory. The 126 Squadron pilot was also killed. Four Hurricanes, two Swordfish and HSL129 were sent out to search for the missing pilots, the launch heading for a point four miles south-south-east of Benghaisa Point but two Bf109Fs of 6/JG53 swooped on the rescue craft. Although badly damaged it managed to return to Kalafrana under its own steam but with two dead and two wounded on board. No sign of the three missing pilots was found.

The Squadron lost another pilot on 9 February when Plt Off Jimmy Stuart was killed during an air test; his Hurricane, Z3526, dived into the ground on take-off from Takali and burst into flames. One of the groundcrew at Takali, LAC Bill Metcalf, noted in his diary:

"Three raids in two hours — in the last the photographic and sick bay were hit. Three bodies so far recovered and a number of casualties. Detailed for Plt Off Stuart's funeral tomorrow, he was flying GN-F — the kite crashed and he was burned to death."

At 1715 on 15 February, Sqn Ldr Beazley took off at the head of seven Hurricanes — a mixed force drawn from 249 and 605 Squadrons and 1435 Flight — to provide protection for a returning Maryland. However, they failed to rendezvous with the reconnaissance aircraft, which had developed engine problems, and turned northwards, but were then bounced by a Staffel of Messerschmitts from III/JG53, as Sgt Branch noted:

"Seven of us went out to intercept the Maryland being attacked by 109s. Visibility was very

poor and the cloud was very low. We were jumped by 109s 15 miles south-east of Kalafrana
— a tough scrap — 109s were cutting us from the island."

One of the 605 Squadron machines was shot down with the loss of its pilot, but everyone else landed safely.

Torrential rain during the middle of the month flooded both Takali and Hal Far airfields, necessitating 249 moving its Hurricanes to Luqa as a result. The Squadron received a new Commanding Officer at this time, tour-expired Sqn Ldr Beazley being advised of his imminent departure to the Middle East. His successor was Sqn Ldr P.S. Turner DFC, who had just arrived on the island aboard a Sunderland flyingboat*. Turner was a tough, no-nonsense Canadian — nicknamed 'Bull' — of whom one pilot wrote:

"Turner is not precisely a man of refinement and hardly ever uses polite language when he utters an opinion on something. It is not easy to discuss things with him or to contradict him. After he has drunk a few glasses he would scare off a regiment of Polish infantry."

At 1135 on 22 February, six Hurricanes of 249 (joined by two from 126 Squadron) were scrambled on the approach of three Ju88s of I/LG1 and their escort of six Bf109Fs from II/JG3, which were encountered at 16,000 feet over Filfla. Plt Off Moon attacked the right-hand bomber of the trio but saw no results before his own aircraft (Z4002 GN-M) was attacked by a Messerschmitt:

"Squirted Ju88 but got shot up by a 109. Landed OK even though tyre on tailwheel shot to pieces. Some bullets had glanced off the armour plate and passed under the seat, others had glanced off the footrest."

Moon's No2, Sgt Branch, pursued the same bomber, closing from 300 to 75 yards, but the tail of his Hurricane (BE583) was damaged by a Messerschmitt, and he broke away. He noted:

"Got four bursts into one 88 — saw strikes. Got shot up by 109, landed OK."

A third Hurricane was damaged when Sgt Cairns attacked another — or the same — Ju88, while Sqn Ldr Turner and Flt Sgt Etchells each reported strikes on the Messerschmitts with which they became entangled. One Messerschmitt returned to Sicily with fairly substantial damage, while Uffz Leopold Münster claimed a Hurricane shot down for his 10th victory — possibly believing Branch's aircraft had fallen out of control as it broke away from the attack on the Ju88. Messerschmitts from III/JG53 also appear to have been present, Lt Fritz Dinger claiming a Hurricane at 1205 as his 13th victory.

All three airfields came under heavy attack on 23 February, two Wellingtons and a Blenheim being destroyed at Luqa, while the pilots' dispersal at Takali was hit by a bomb-carrying Bf109F of 10/JG53, where a pilot of 242 Squadron was killed and two others injured, as were three airmen and a civilian. LAC Metcalf recorded in his diary:

"We were leaning against the wall when the Messerschmitt dropped a bomb, but he had given a burst of cannon fire which told us what to expect. We all dived for the hole and just made it."

The Squadron lost another Hurricane during the day when BP612 GN-H crash-landed at Luqa following engine trouble while being air tested by Flg Off Leggett. This was BP612's first flight since it had been damaged in combat on 24 January when being flown by Plt Off Moon. The pilot survived the impact.

At 1510 on 24 February, radar screens picked up the blips of approaching aircraft and eight

---

* Other fighter pilots aboard the Sunderland included Flt Lt P.B. Lucas, Flg Off R. Daddo-Langlois, a Channel Islander, Flg Off R.W. McNair RCAF, Flg Off G.A.F. Buchanan, a Rhodesian, and Plt Off J.G. West DFM RNZAF, all of whom would be posted to 249 when the Spitfires arrived in early March.

Hurricanes from 249 were scrambled, these separating into pre-arranged pairs. Sqn Ldr Turner and his No2, Plt Off Tedford, were vectored to the reported height of four 'hostiles', but were unable to see them. The Controller informed Turner that they were dead ahead, but had apparently confused the two plots on the radar. The four 'hostiles' — Bf109Fs from Stab/JG53 — were in fact behind, and the Hurricanes were consequently bounced. Tedford's BG771 was shot down into the sea by Lt Franz Schiess (his 16th victory), while Turner's aircraft (Z3580) took hits in the cockpit and engine, which caught fire. Unable to open the damaged cockpit hood to bale out, the slightly wounded Turner dived his aircraft steeply, whereby the flames were extinguished, enabling him to make a belly-landing at Luqa. What the irascible Canadian later told the unfortunate Controller has not been recorded. An American pilot of 126 Squadron, Plt Off Howard Coffin, a close friend of Tedford, noted in his diary:

> "Two 109s intercepted Sqn Ldr Turner DFC. Crash-landed wheels up at Luqa aerodrome. Bullet clipped his goggles from helmet. Plt Off Tedford, one of the four Americans on this bloody island, shot down and was last seen to have crashed in the sea. Words cannot express how I feel at this moment. I've lost a buddy and the air force has lost a wizard pilot."

Apparently Tedford had called Control to say he was wounded and was baling out. When Coffin heard the news, he went off to search for him:

> "Nobody ever blamed me for leaving my post of duty that day. At Takali I managed to get a plane into the air that was no good for fighting, but was serviceable for patrol, and went looking for Tedford. I searched the sea until dark. I found no sign of life down below."

249 was effectively disbanded on 26 February, its aircraft together with the majority of its pilots being transferred to 126 Squadron, pending their postings to the Middle East. Sqn Ldr Beazley was the first to go, leaving on 2 March; Flt Lt Crossey, also tour-expired, followed three days later and Flt Lt Davis soon afterwards*.

The defence of Malta was now about to take a new turn, for the carrier HMS *Eagle* was on its way from Gibraltar with 16 Spitfire Vbs for the island. In preparation for this historical and much-anticipated event there had been considerable movement of pilots between the resident squadrons, following the recent spate of new arrivals. 249 was to be promptly resurrected and re-equipped, and in consequence those recently-arrived pilots with Spitfire experience were to be concentrated in 249 Squadron. The arrival of the Spitfires was in the nick of time, for the island's defences had almost ceased to exist — current availability was just 21 serviceable Hurricanes.

---

* Three of the Squadron's tour-expired pilots — Flg Off Leggett, Flg Off Hill and Plt Off Moon — were sent to Aden where they helped form the Aden Battle Flight, comprised mostly of Malta veterans. Another to join the Flight was Wt Off Stroud, one of the Squadron's Battle of Britain pilots.

Chapter Six

SPITFIRES ARRIVE IN THE NICK OF TIME
March — April 1942

"I recall registering strikes in the wing roots and the tail unit of the 88 . . . and the next thing I remember was falling head first towards the harbour sans aircraft . . ."

Flt Lt Nip Heppell, 249 Squadron

Thus, early on the morning of 7 March, 15 Spitfires (the 16th having developed mechanical trouble) lifted off the deck of *Eagle*, then at a position 700 miles west of Malta, and set course for the four-hour flight to the beseiged island. The Spitfires were in two flights, one of eight and the other of seven, led by Sqn Ldr S.B. Grant DFC and Flt Lt N.C. Macqueen. One of the new pilots, Flt Sgt D.W. Ferraby recalled:

"'Don't know how we were chosen for take-off order, but I know I was the eighth. There was only room on deck for eight Spitfires at a time, to leave sufficient take-off run, so we went off in two lots."

On approaching Malta, the Spitfire pilots found Hurricanes in the air, patrolling to cover their arrival and landing at Takali, but of the Luftwaffe there was no sign.

The Spitfires were immediately stripped of their long-range fuel tanks and full servicing began in preparation for their introduction to operations; the aircraft and their pilots were absorbed into 249, still under the command of Sqn Ldr Turner, who now found himself not only with Sqn Ldr Grant as his supernumerary, but with no less than five relatively-experienced Flight Lieutenants. Flt Lt Lucas was given command of A Flight and Flt Lt McNair took over B Flight. The inflated Squadron now comprised 29 pilots with Spitfire experience, as listed below (those marked with an asterisk had flown from the carrier):

Sqn Ldr P.S. Turner DFC	
*Sqn Ldr S.B. Grant DFC	
Flt Lt P.B. Lucas	(from 185 Squadron)
Flt Lt R.W. McNair RCAF	(from Air HQ)
*Flt Lt P.W.E. Heppell DFC	
*Flt Lt N.C. Macqueen	
Flt Lt W.C. Connell RCAF	(from 126 Squadron)
*Flg Off N.W. Lee	
Flg Off W.R. Daddo-Langlois	(from 185 Squadron)
Flg Off G.A.F. Buchanan (Rhodesian)	(from Air HQ)
Flg Off J.C.M. Booth	(from 126 Squadron)
Plt Off J.G. West DFM RNZAF	(from Air HQ)
Plt Off H.M. Fox	(from 1435 Flight)
Plt Off R.H. Sergeant	(from 185 Squadron)
Plt Off R.W. James	(from 126 Squadron)
Plt Off D.W. Kelly	(from 126 Squadron)
*Plt Off P.A. Nash	(flew AB336 to Malta)
*Plt Off K.N.L. Murray RAAF	
*Plt Off J.J. Guerin RAAF	
*Plt Off J.A. Plagis (Rhodesian)	(flew AB343 to Malta)

*Plt Off D.C. Leggo (Rhodesian)
*Flt Sgt D.W. Ferraby   (flew AB331 to Malta)
*Flt Sgt I.M. Cormack
*Sgt J.L. Tayleur
*Sgt V.P. Brennan RAAF
*Sgt R.B. Hesselyn RNZAF
*Sgt R.J. Sim RNZAF
Sgt J. Berchamps   (from 185 Squadron)
Sgt H.T. Freeman RAAF   (from 1435 Flight)

Of the newcomers, newly promoted Sqn Ldr Grant had served with 65 Squadron in the UK and had been credited with three victories; Flt Lt Heppell also had three, gained while flying with 616 Squadron, the same unit with which newly commissioned Plt Off West had similarly gained three victories, while Plt Off Nash had two from his service with 609 Squadron. The majority of the others had little operational experience.

On the morning of 10 March came the moment for the Spitfires' debut over Malta. This occurred at 1020 when seven aircraft (wearing GN code markings, which had been applied using white paint!) took off from Takali in company with eight 126 Squadron Hurricanes, together with four more from 185 Squadron from Hal Far. A pilot of the latter unit noted in his diary:

> "The Spitfires have arrived and are now doing top cover for us, which is a great help. It rather shakes you up to see one on your tail 'cause they look so much like a 109."

The objective of the scramble was to intercept an incoming raid of nine Ju88s, of which three crossed the coast to bomb Luqa, where a Wellington was destroyed. The Spitfires climbed to 19,000 feet, three led by Sqn Ldr Turner and four by Flt Lt Heppell. On reaching altitude, Heppell's section saw the Ju88s and their escorts below them, and at once bounced the unsuspecting Messerschmitts. Heppell fired a long burst at one which was seen to crash into the sea; this was Fw Heinz Rahlmeier's Black 11 of 8/JG53, in which the pilot was killed†. Other Messerschmitts were attacked by Plt Offs Nash and Plagis, both of whom claimed probables, the latter having attacked one on Nash's tail. Meanwhile, Flg Off Daddo-Langlois claimed one damaged, having knocked pieces off its tail, and Flt Lt Lucas (AB337) chased another without success. None of the bombers was shot down, but one Hurricane was lost and another damaged. Uffz Hans Schade of 8/JG53 claimed a Spitfire during this action, but was probably responsible for shooting down the Hurricane.

Attempts to intercept two more raids during the mid-part of the day failed, but at 1632 an estimated 40 'hostiles' were plotted approaching to attack Luqa and Hal Far, Ju88s of I/KG54, II and III/KG77 and LG1 taking part. Eleven Hurricanes and four Spitfires were scrambled. Both Flt Lt Macqueen and Flg Off Buchanan claimed damage to bombers, but the aircraft (AB343 GN-D) flown by Plt Off Ken Murray was attacked by Bf109Fs and shot down, apparently by Hptm Karl-Heinz Krahl, Gruppenkommandeur of II/JG3 (his 24th victory) — the first of the Spitfires to be lost. Murray baled out at high altitude, but his parachute failed to open properly. He sustained severe injuries on hitting the ground and the 20-year-old Australian from Toorak, Victoria, died in hospital that evening; initially his colleagues believed that he had been shot whilst descending. His Spitfire crashed at Ta'Zuta near Rabat. Flt Lt Lucas witnessed the brief action:

> "We spotted, far away to port, a single Spitfire obviously looking for a mate. As we turned to go to his aid, a lone 109, diving very fast out of the sun, pulled up unseen, under the Spit. From dead astern, the pilot delivered a short, determined burst. Relieved, we saw a parachute open. As we watched the silk canopy floating down in the distance, with the pilot swinging on its end, another single 109, diving down out of broken cloud, made a run at the 'chute,

---

† It would seem that Heppell's victory was the Squadron's 100th 'confirmed' although the occasion was apparently not celebrated.

squirting at it as he went and collapsing it with his slipstream as he passed by. The canopy streamed, leaving the pilot without a chance."

Since it was first believed that Murray had come down in the sea, three Spitfires went out to cover him while a launch was despatched to pick him up. During the subsequent search, Buchanan was attacked by Messerschmitts and suffered superficial wounds to his right leg when AB262 GN-B was hit, necessitating an emergency landing at Takali. During the raid only one Ju88 had actually been hit, a 4/KG77 machine returning with two wounded on board; however, this was probably a victim of the Hurricanes. Additionally, a Ju88 from 2/KG54 crash-landed at Gerbini on return, but reportedly due to undercarriage malfunction.

There was only one raid during 11 March, when at 1135 two Ju88s of 5/KG77 escorted by six Bf109Fs approached the coast. The Ju88s turned back without bombing, one of which crashed on landing at Comiso and was completely destroyed. Sixteen Hurricanes and four Spitfires scrambled, the latter in pairs led by Sqn Ldr Grant and Flt Lt Connell, and a number of dogfights ensued. Grant attacked two Messerschmitts at 10,000 feet over Grand Harbour and one was seen going down inverted towards the sea; he was credited with its probable destruction. Connell and Sgt Hesselyn also engaged the escorting fighters, with the former claiming damage to one. Another Messerschmitt attacked his Spitfire, which suffered a bullet strike two feet behind the cockpit. Meanwhile, Hesselyn's reflector sight and R/T failed, which effectively put him out of the fight, while Flt Sgt Ferraby also engaged a fighter but observed no result. Later a few Spitfires were scrambled and ordered to climb to 25,000 feet since Bf109s were reported to be in the area. Plt Off Sergeant recalled that none were sighted but two Hurricanes mistaken for Messerschmitts narrowly escaped being attacked.

Takali was raided twice on 12 March and neither raid was intercepted. During the second attack at 1635 by three Ju88s, one Spitfire was slightly damaged on the ground, as was a Hurricane and a Blenheim. The airfield was raided again next day (13 March), when a Hurricane and a petrol bowser were burnt out. The Squadron also suffered a fatality when LAC Gordon White was killed.

14 March heralded not only further action for the Spitfires of 249, but a change in command as Sqn Ldr Turner handed the reins to Sqn Ldr Grant, when the Canadian was promoted to take command of the Takali Wing. Four Spitfires were sent off at 1030 on the approach of three Ju88s of II/KG77 escorted by about 20 Bf109Fs. A trio of Messerschmitts was seen orbiting Gozo, apparently part of a search party looking for two pilots missing from a morning sortie. Flt Lt Macqueen dived on one, attacking from 275 to 50 yards and fired all his ammunition, reporting strikes along its fuselage. The Messerschmitt pilot took no evasive action, continuing a slow climbing turn as the Spitfire broke away in front of it. Macqueen believed that it dived into the sea and this would seem to have been an aircraft of 7/JG53, from which Uffz Adolf Jennerich baled out. The skipper of ASR launch HSL107 was refused permission to go out when the Messerschmitt was seen to fall in flames a mile outside Kalafrana Bay, owing to the threat posed by the large numbers of other Bf109Fs at low level.

The downed pilot, Jennerich, was however rescued from the sea by an Axis ASR craft in the afternoon, cover to this operation being provided by more Messerschmitts; two of these were seen orbiting Gozo at about 1535 by Flt Lt Lucas and Flg Off Daddo-Langlois, the former reporting strikes on the fuselage and tail of the one he attacked before others drove him away. Meanwhile, Daddo-Langlois' aircraft (AB332 GN-N) had developed an oil leak which prevented him from engaging in combat. Fw Josef Kröschel of 8/JG53 claimed a Spitfire at 1610 for his first victory, possibly believing that he had shot down either Lucas or Daddo-Langlois as they dived away. Between 1550 and 1750 an estimated 16 Bf109Fs were reported patrolling to the west and south-west of the island. Taking off again, Lucas and Daddo-Langlois initially escorted a Maryland departing on a reconnaissance sortie before encountering two Messerschmitts. Lucas fired all his ammunition and saw hits on the fuselage of one, reporting a trail of black smoke as it dived away; again he could claim only a damaged.

On 15 March three Ju88s with fighter escort raided Luqa and Valetta shortly before lunchtime; eight persons were killed, including two soldiers. Four Spitfires led by Flt Lts Connell and Heppell, together with seven Hurricanes, were up and intercepted the raid in low cloud. Heppell claimed a Bf109F damaged after seeing his cannon shells strike the underside of its fuselage, and from which his No2 saw pieces fall off into the sea; he then attacked a second Bf109F and a Ju88, but without result. One of the bombers was attacked by Plt Off West and Sgt Tayleur, who jointly claimed some damage before being driven away by the escort. The escorting Messerschmitts of III/JG53 claimed two Spitfires shot down during this engagement, one apiece by Oblt Helmut Belser (his 19th) of 8 Staffel and Obfw Werner Stumpf (his 31st) of 9 Staffel, although none of the defending fighters was lost on this occasion. At 1320 three Ju88s and seven Messerschmitts raided Zabbar, and were met by four Spitfires. Connell claimed one bomber probably destroyed, and it seems likely that this was an aircraft of 3/KGr806 (M7+ML) which failed to return from an operational sortie over Malta, Uffz Rudolf Max and his crew being reported missing.

Between 0730 and 0945 on 17 March, 23 Ju88s struck at Luqa, where four Wellingtons were destroyed and five other aircraft damaged, including a Spitfire. A petrol bowser was burnt out, two civilians killed and three injured. Bombs also fell on Sliema, Tigne and Cospicua, where 23 more civilians and two policemen were killed and 40 civilians seriously injured. Four Spitfires and 11 Hurricanes were scrambled, the 249 quartet climbing to 20,000 feet, where six Ju88s and a number of Bf109Fs (of II/JG53) were seen 10,000 feet below. Sgts Brennan and Tayleur were approached by two of the Messerschmitts, but the latter's aircraft went into an uncontrollable dive as the seat had come off its hinges and jammed the control column; the aircraft fell to 8,000 feet before Tayleur was able to get it back into place and pull out. It seems probable that Oblt Michalski of 4/JG53 had also fired at Tayleur's aircraft, since he claimed a Spitfire shot down at about this time. Brennan meanwhile attacked a Messerschmitt from dead astern, closing from 150 to 100 yards and seeing strikes on the fuselage behind the cockpit and on the port wing root. It turned on its back and went down, initially being credited as damaged only. However, the claim was apparently upgraded later, Brennan's appropriate logbook entry stating:

"Shot down one, confirmed as destroyed. My first."

At 0955 seven more Ju88s and four Bf109Fs crossed the coast, a further four Spitfires led by Flt Lt Heppell attempting to intercept. Unable to gain position, Heppell instructed the others to dive for home, which they did, but Flt Sgt Ian Cormack (in AB330 GN-C) failed to pull out and was killed when his aircraft crashed straight into the sea off Filfla. Of the incident, Flt Sgt Ferraby recalled:

"Why they didn't just turn towards the 109s, I don't know. Cormack blacked out and spun in. He was a black-haired, slightly built chap from Elgin in Scotland, and another good buddy."

During the afternoon and early evening an estimated 56 raiders approached Malta at intervals, including 25 bombers which attacked all three airfields. A dozen Hurricanes, with two Spitfires as top cover, were scrambled. While the Hurricanes engaged the bombers, Sqn Ldr Grant and Plt Off Plagis each claimed damage to Messerschmitts they encountered.

18 March proved to be another day of heavy combat, which began around 0900 when two Bf109Fs crossed the coast at low level, covered by more higher up. This marauding pair strafed the Gozo ferry boat *Royal Lady*, which had just docked at Marfa with 209 passengers aboard although only one civilian and two soldiers were wounded. The Messerschmitts were away again before Malta's fighters could be scrambled. Lunchtime was interrupted by four Spitfires scrambling to intercept five Messerschmitts patrolling off the coast, while another four took off to escort a returning reconnaissance Maryland, but instead engaged two of the German fighters at sea level south of Delimara. Flt Lt McNair attacked one at which Wg Cdr Turner also fired, reporting strikes, while McNair then attacked and damaged the other.

The bombers were back during the early evening, two dozen Ju88s of I/KG54, KüFlGr606 and KGr806 — in five waves with large fighter escort — bombing the airfields, when in excess of 14 tons of bombs were dropped. At Hal Far an Albacore was destroyed and several others hit by debris, and at Luqa three damaged Wellingtons were now destroyed. Four Spitfires and

11 Hurricanes were scrambled, but at 12,500 feet the 249 quartet was jumped by four Bf109Fs of III/JG53 and Plt Off Harry Fox's AB334 GN-J was hit; the 20-year-old Liverpudlian baled out into the sea, but was lost. Plt Off Sergeant noted:

> "Ju88s with escort. Four of us mixed up with several 109s east of Gozo. I also met two 109s near Filfla and squirted, one 109F damaged. Harry Fox went straight in. Two bullet holes in my machine."

Flt Lt Macqueen attacked a Messerschmitt which he believed had just shot down Fox, opened fire from 100 yards, whereupon it smoked, shed pieces and dived into the sea close to where Fox's Spitfire had splashed, about three miles off Wied iz-Zurrieq. The other two 249 pilots, Flg Off Lee and Sgt Berchamps, claimed damage to a Ju88 and a Bf109F respectively. Immediately following this action, ASR launch HSL107 was sent out to search for the missing pilots (two Hurricanes of 185 Squadron had also been shot down into the sea), escorted by two Spitfires. More Messerschmitts were encountered, one of which was claimed probably destroyed by Plt Off Sergeant who reported:

> "Mac and I out over launch and picked up Plt Off Lester [of 185 Squadron]. Seven 109s over, which took no notice. Jumped by two. Got on tail of one about to attack Mac and dogfought. Last seen heading out to sea with slight white smoke. One bullet in my machine."

The launch also located the German pilot shot down by Macqueen — Lt Kurt Lauinger of Stab III/JG53, who had been wounded and had also suffered a broken leg. He subsequently told his interrogators that he had shot down a Spitfire in this action:

> "[We] were flying over Malta at 12,000 feet in two pairs stepped up in an echelon when [we] sighted three Spitfires below and dived to attack. [I] fired a burst at one of the Spitfires and then did a climbing turn in order to keep at the same height as section leader. By this time one of the other Spitfires had turned inside [me] and attacked, shooting away [my] rudder. [I] baled out, landed in the sea and was picked up after dark by a rescue launch."

On 19 March there was just a single raid by an estimated 15 Ju88s and a dozen Bf109Fs on Takali, which destroyed a Beaufighter and damaged four other aircraft including another Spitfire. 249 was rapidly running short of aircraft; of the 15 Spitfires delivered, three had been shot down and a further two damaged on the ground, all within the space of ten days. Another was lost next day (20 March), when four Spitfires and a dozen Hurricanes were sent off at 0805 to intercept an incoming raid. Flt Lt McNair encountered a Messerschmitt at which he fired, reporting that pieces fell off as it went down in a spiral dive; a splash was seen in the sea south of Delimara and this was undoubtedly Uffz Josef Fankhauser's White 4 of 7/JG53. Meanwhile, Plt Off Doug Leggo was lagging behind when another Messerschmitt came out of the sun and shot him down from 50 yards range. The Rhodesian was killed and his Spitfire, AB337, crashed in a field near Qrendi. Claims for Spitfires in this engagement were submitted by Lt Hermann Neuhoff (his 38th) and Lt Ernst Kläger (his 11th), both of 7 Staffel.

A heavy raid on Takali at dusk, when in excess of 60 Ju88s pounded the airfield and rendered it temporarily unserviceable, prompted Sgt Branch (temporarily attached to 126 Squadron) to write in his journal:

> "I was on watch and I must say Jerry is getting to be a nuisance. The drome was dive-bombed by Ju88s and He111s [sic], making the fourth day in succession. Approximately 30 bombs dropped in one go during one raid. The Mess had a near shave; at the same time an amusing thing happened. The two bombs dropped close to the Mess were approximately 1,000lbs each. These bombs were very close to an old well and the blast sucked all the mud and water out of it — and poured it down on the building, shaking the occupants who thought the lot was coming down on top of them!"

The dusk raid was followed next morning (21 March) by an even heavier attack by over 100 Ju88s. Neither of these fighter-escorted raids was opposed by the handful of Hurricanes and Spitfires remaining, although relatively little long-term damage resulted from the first example of carpet-bombing the island had experienced. Soon after the bombers had departed, eight Bf110s of III/ZG26 appeared overhead to bomb and strafe Hal Far, under an umbrella of Bf109Fs. Amongst the four aircraft damaged on the ground was one of 249's Spitfires; the Squadron was now down to just two serviceable aircraft.

Ground personnel at Takali immediately got to work clearing the rubble and in-filling bomb craters, ready to receive more Spitfires winging their way in from the west, nine aircraft having been launched from *Eagle*; it had been the intention to fly off 16 Spitfires, but the Blenheim escort for the second flight failed to arrive. One of the new arrivals, Sgt Jack Yarra RAAF, who had been aboard *Eagle* when the first Spitfires had flown to Malta but whose aircraft had gone unserviceable and was therefore left behind, wrote in his diary:

> "We landed at Takali and put the aircraft away. I then went up to the Mess to get a drink and find out how the rest of the boys were. I learned that Mac [Cormack], Fox, Leggo and Murray were all dead and that, out of the 15 Spitfires they had brought in, only two were left."

At 1435, the third major raid to be centred on Takali within 24 hours began when the first of 70 Ju88s (with a large fighter escort) bombed the airfield, while wayward bombs also fell on Rabat, Mosta, Gzira, Boschetto, Tigne, Attard and Birkirkara. At Rabat, a large bomb fell just outside the front door of the Point de Vue Hotel, which had been requisitioned to billet RAF officers stationed at nearby Takali, where a number of officers had gathered to watch the raid; six were killed outright and another died in hospital. Among the dead were two of the Squadron's pilots, Flg Off John Booth and Plt Off Jimmy Guerin. Flt Lt McNair had just entered the building with Flt Lt Connell and Flg Off Ron West (126 Squadron) when the bomb exploded:

> "When I came to I didn't know where I was. I didn't feel I was dead, but I didn't feel whole. My eyes were open, but my jaw and chest didn't seem to be there. There was no pain . . . As I became more conscious, I found I was upstairs. Then I realized I had been blown upstairs either through a door or through an opening at the turn of the staircase. I'd been blown up 20 or 30 feet. I went down the main staircase which was barely hanging in place. I saw the bodies lying at the foot of it. They were in a heap. Heavy dust covered the bodies. One was headless . . . I heard a moan, so I put my hand gently on the bodies to feel which of them was alive. One of them I noticed had a hole, more than a foot wide, right through the abdomen. Another's head was split wide open into two halves, from back to front, by a piece of shrapnel . . . How the man managed still to be alive, I don't know. I thought of shooting him with my revolver. I heard Bud Connell's voice behind me. Ronnie West appeared. We decided to get drunk. When we got over to the Mess, the orderly refused us anything to drink and wouldn't open the bar. We broke our way in and each took a bottle of White Horse. We drank gulps of it straight."

On the airfield itself two Spitfires, four Hurricanes and three other aircraft had been destroyed, while five Spitfires and 15 Hurricanes were among the 21 damaged in this latest attack. However, many of the damaged Hurricanes had been written-off as a result of earlier raids and were thus non-operational. Takali appeared to be so severely bombed that returning Luftwaffe bomber crews reported that the base looked as if it had been subjected to volcanic eruption! Air Vice-Marshal Lloyd, the AOC, had to agree that it resembled a WWI battlefield and it was feared that it would remain unserviceable for at least a week. However, troops worked throughout the night and all next day and, by the evening of 22 March, all serviceable Hurricanes and Spitfires were able to be flown to Luqa.

The new Spitfires and their pilots were intended to re-form 126 Squadron in a similar manner to that which had occurred with 249. Because of the losses of Spitfires to date, however — four lost in the air and two destroyed on the ground — 249 and 126 Squadrons were going to have to share the remaining aircraft. This left the two units with a preponderance of pilots to aircraft, while the remaining Hurricane unit, 185 Squadron, was very low on pilots. Consequently after about a week, a trawl was made of Spitfire pilots to establish who had Hurricane experience. Hence, newly-arrived Sgt Yarra, having been posted to 249, was one of those soon to be transferred to fly Hurricanes, together with Flt Sgt Ferraby, Sgt Berchamps and Sgt Sim.

The arrival of the new Spitfires and new faces brought with it a debate on tactics. Initially it had been the policy to send 249 up as cover to the Hurricanes, their task to hold off the Messerschmitts while the latter sought to deal with the Ju88s. But experience had shown that the Hurricane IIbs were too slow and too lightly-armed to have great effect against the swift, heavily armed bombers. Few cannon-armed IIcs now remained, and of those that did, most had had two of their four cannons removed to increase their speed although thereby reducing their fire-power by half. 249's initial experience had been to lose as many of their own aircraft to the Bf109Fs as they were able to claim — hardly a profitable ratio given the dire circumstances prevailing. It was agreed, therefore, that in future both Spitfires and Hurricanes would concentrate their efforts against the bombers and avoid the escorting fighters wherever possible.

The two-day period 22-23 March witnessed much action out to sea, east of Malta, as a convoy from Alexandria fought its way to the island. The cruiser HMS *Penelope* and a single destroyer from Malta (Force 'K') set out to escort the four merchant vessels, once its naval escort had turned back, aircraft from Malta providing cover. Initially long-range Beaufighters attempted to keep the Axis bombers at bay, but once within appropriate range, Spitfires and Hurricanes took over protection of the valiant ships, one of which had already been lost. Even as Force 'K' set out from Malta, all available FAA torpedo-bombers on the island had been ordered to prepare to attack Italian warships assembling to engage the convoy.

At 1755 on 22 March therefore, five Albacore biplanes took off, escorted for the initial part of their flight by three Spitfires that had been made serviceable, flown by Flt Lt Macqueen, Plt Off James and a pilot of 126 Squadron. No sooner were they on their way when two Bf109Fs attempted to intercept out of the setting sun, one diving on the 126 Squadron pilot's tail. Macqueen turned towards this, but then saw the other Messerschmitt firing at an Albacore and attacked this instead, sending it down in a shallow dive. James reported that he saw the aircraft turn on its back at 50 feet above the sea, and Macqueen then observed a splash; on the basis of this circumstantial evidence he was credited with its destruction. By now low on fuel the Spitfires turned back, leaving the biplanes to their fate, but after a further two hours these were recalled and the operation cancelled.

There were several skirmishes over and around Malta on 23 March as the surviving merchant vessels reached the island, but not until the afternoon was 249 in action. Shortly after 1300, small formations of Ju88s attempted to reach the ships, being met by sections of patrolling Hurricanes and Spitfires. One pair of Spitfires, flown by Flt Lt Macqueen and Plt Off Sergeant, joined two Hurricanes in engaging a trio of Ju88s, claiming damage to all three bombers before they escaped in cloud. Sergeant noted:

"Exceedingly low cloud. Mac and I attacked an 88 and set both engines on fire, will most probably be confirmed."

One of the bombers attacked — B3+LL of 3/KG54 flown by Lt Hermann Janzik — was shot down, returning crews reporting that it fell victim to four Spitfires . Two other Spitfires patrolled four miles east of Grand Harbour, where a further pair of Ju88s was intercepted, one of which was claimed damaged by Plt Off Plagis.

The Luftwaffe launched a determined raid against the berthed ships in Grand Harbour on the morning of 24 March, some 40 Ju88s and a strong fighter escort arriving over the island at 1140. Six Hurricanes and three Spitfires, two flown by 249 pilots, were scrambled, but only Flg Off Buchanan was able to make a claim when he damaged a Messerschmitt. An accompanying Spitfire, flown by a 126 Squadron pilot, was shot down by Messerschmitts and crash-landed at Luqa. At least three Hurricanes were damaged in combat during the day, leaving just nine serviceable fighters — Spitfires and Hurricanes — at the end of the day.

Rather surprisingly there was little hostile activity over Malta until the afternoon of 25 March, but then at least 30 Ju88s, 25 Ju87s (of III/StG3) and 13 Bf109Fs were reported over the island between 1540 and 1725. To meet these raids eight Hurricanes and six Spitfires (of which four were flown by 249 pilots) got into the air, and a number of claims were made, primarily against the Ju87s, with Sqn Ldr Grant and Plt Off Plagis reporting shooting down one apiece. The Rhodesian claimed strikes on a second before his aircraft (BP850) was attacked and damaged by Fw Max Fischer of Stab II/JG3. Fischer's joy was short-lived however, for the CO was soon on the tail of the Messerschmitt and shot it down into the sea off Gozo. The German pilot managed to bale out and was rescued later by a Do24 from Sicily. Meanwhile, Flg Off Lee gained strikes on another Ju87, while Plt Off Nash initially claimed one as a probable, only to have this upgraded later to a confirmed victory; he noted in his logbook:

> "30+ Ju87s. Terrific! Ju87 probable. A marvellous party! We caught them over Grand Harbour. Hurricanes also got some."

Although four Ju87s were claimed shot down, with two more probables, records suggest that only one was lost, Lt Klaus Heemann's T6+CC falling into the sea about five miles east of Marsaxlokk; a second aircraft returned to Sicily with a wounded gunner.

The initial bomber raid on the morning of 26 March was intercepted by seven Hurricanes, inflicting negligible damage. At 1355 four Spitfires — the only fighters then available — scrambled to engage the second formation, which comprised an estimated 15 Ju87s of III/StG3 and three Ju88s of I/KG54, with escorting Bf109Fs. Sgt Brennan attacked the trio of Ju88s as they dived in formation, seeing cannon strikes on one, which turned away. Flt Lt Connell, who was leading the formation, claimed to have shot the tail off another, but this was probably the same aircraft as that attacked by Brennan, which Flt Lt McNair then attacked, reporting that it went down disintegrating into the sea half a mile off Xlendi Bay, Gozo. Connell then joined McNair in attacking the Ju87s, the latter claiming one of these probably destroyed, this subsequently being upgraded to a confirmed victory. The pilot of the shot down Ju88, Lt Johannes Rottmann, told his captors:

> "We were attacked by two Spitfires off Gozo. The first attacked from above and was driven off by fire from the top rear gunner; the second attacked from slightly below, the bottom rear gun jamming. The starboard engine was set on fire and there was a probability that this would reach the petrol tanks, so I decided to land on the sea."

Amazingly all members of the crew survived and scrambled into their dinghy before the aircraft sank; they were rescued later by local police and one crew member was taken to Victoria Hospital, suffering nothing more serious than a strained knee.

The next major series of assaults came in between 1630 and 1857, when 24 Ju88s and 18 Ju87s, with fighter escort, were reported over Grand Harbour and Kalafrana, while three Messerschmitt-escorted ASR Do24s searched near Gozo for the crew of the missing bomber. Four Spitfires and six Hurricanes were scrambled to meet these latest raiders. As the Spitfires approached a formation of Ju88s, Plt Off R.E. McHan (AB346 GN-K) — an American recently posted in from the MNFU — found himself targeted by the AA guns, his aircraft being peppered by shrapnel; he managed to reach Takali and land safely. The other three engaged the bombers, four of which were claimed damaged — one each by Flt Lt Connell and Flg Off Buchanan, the other two being credited to Flt Lt McNair — before the escorting fighters forced them away. A Ju88 (M7+AA) of 3/KGr806 crash-landed at Comiso on return, having been damaged by fighter attack, during which the rear gunner (Obfw Gustav Reimers) was killed.

Following a relatively quiet 36 hours, a quartet of Spitfires flown by 249 pilots engaged a reconnaissance Ju88 just after midday on 28 March. Although all four — Sqn Ldr Grant, Flg Off Lee, Plt Off Plagis and Plt Off Nash — attacked the aircraft some 20 miles north of Grand Harbour, they were unable to shoot it down despite using all their ammunition. Nash noted:

> "All attacked him from less than 50 yards but he wouldn't go down. He jettisoned bombs in the sea."

The Junkers streamed smoke from both damaged engines, Lee continuing to follow for some 25 miles northwards, hoping to see it crash. He then realised that his own aircraft had been hit in the engine by the rear gunner, and prudently turned back. The four were credited with the probable destruction of the reconnaissance machine, but it would seem to have regained its base.

A further batch of Spitfires arrived from *Eagle* on 29 March, the balance of the earlier delivery, although seven additional Spitfires were obviously not going to save Malta from the onslaught. The arrival of the latest delivery did not go unnoticed by the Germans and soon after midday nine Ju88s approached the island, crossing the coast singly or in pairs to attack and depart under cover of heavy cloud, but failed to inflict any damage on the airfields. There were no raids on Malta next day, although a reconnaissance Ju88 was intercepted by Flt Lt Macqueen and Flg Off Daddo-Langlois just after 1400. Having chased it to within a few miles of the Sicilian coast, both pilots attacked, Daddo-Langlois using all his ammunition, but they did not see it crash. However, a Ju88 of 5/LG1 ditched in the sea east of Catania with engine damage, Uffz Heinz Pfeiffer and his crew of two being killed, and may have been their victim, although Luftwaffe records put the loss down to an accident.

During the course of the 20 days since their operational debut over Malta, 249's Spitfires were credited with 14 enemy aircraft shot down, plus one shared, six probables and 20 damaged which, when compared with the handful of probables and damaged claimed by the Squadron's Hurricane pilots since the beginning of the year, emphasised the combat superiority of the Spitfire V over the Hurricane II. As March drew to a close, British intelligence revealed that Hitler had issued orders for Malta to be seized during April, to safeguard the sea lanes for supplies to Rommel's Afrika Korps preparing for the North African offensive. Malta was thus forewarned of imminent invasion.

1 April was 249's day to man the Spitfires and, at 1315, six were scrambled to intercept four Bf109Fs apparently on a reconnaissance flight. One broke away as the Spitfires turned towards them, Plt Off Plagis giving chase, his logbook entry merely stating:

"Chased and shot down ME109 south-east of Grand Harbour."

It would seem that his victim was one of III/JG53's leading pilots, Fw Hans Schade of 8 Staffel, a 13-victory ace; his aircraft crashed into the sea and he was posted missing. Thirty-five minutes later, just as the flight landed, four were immediately scrambled again. This time they encountered 15 escorted Ju88s of I and II/KG77, diving through the AA barrage to get at them. Some way behind followed six Hurricanes of 185 Squadron. Plagis noted:

"Shot down Ju88 bomber quarter mile north-west of Grand Harbour. Also shared a probably destroyed Ju88 with Hurricane."

In fact, two Hurricane pilots of 185 Squadron reported sharing a Ju88, so presumably all three attacked the same bomber. Meanwhile, Plt Off Nash attacked another of the bombers, which he claimed to have hit in the fuel tanks and reported that it flicked onto its back in flames and spiralled into the sea. On the ground at Takali, other pilots of 249 were watching including Sgt Hesselyn:

"We saw Pete's [victim] burst into flames and head straight for the sea, sending up a column of water as it crashed."

Sqn Ldr Grant claimed damage to another bomber, but Flg Off Lee's aircraft was shot up by a Messerschmitt and he force-landed at Takali with a shell splinter in his ankle. His probable victor was Maj von Maltzahn of JG53, who claimed a Spitfire at 1445 as his 60th victory.

At 1630 a Do24 flyingboat was seen five miles north-east of Grand Harbour, under an umbrella of Bf109Fs, apparently searching for missing aircrew; four Spitfires and a Hurricane were sent off to investigate. Plt Off Plagis — on his third sortie of the day — claimed one of the Messerschmitts shot down into the sea six miles north of Grand Harbour; Sgt Hesselyn also claimed a fighter shot down, the CO and Flg Off Buchanan each claiming one damaged. Hesselyn wrote:

> "Stan [Grant] led us down until we were directly behind the enemy and about 5,000 feet above. Then he told us to go in and take our pick. I chose the one on the extreme right, and as I dived on him I could see the rest of the boys going in, line abreast. I quickly caught my 109, but I was coming in too fast and overshot him. However, I got a good bead on the one ahead. It was a lovely break. This 109 was turning at the time and I had him dead in my sights. Opening fire from about 50 yards, I gave him a four-seconds burst. He flipped on his back immediately and went straight in. I was as excited as hell. I told everybody, including Woody [Grp Capt A.B. Woodhall, Senior Controller], that I had shot down my first, screaming over the R/T."

Hesselyn began circling the Messerschmitt down in the sea, but was attacked by two more, streams of tracer just missing his port wing. On landing he discovered that in his excitement he had pressed the wrong firing button, using only his four .303 Brownings to shoot down the German fighter, rather than his cannons. It would seem that he or Plagis — or more likely both of them — had shot down Uffz Gerhard Kitzenmaier's Black 5 of 5/JG53. In return Oblt Belser of 8/JG53 claimed a Spitfire at 1701 for his 20th victory.

No sooner were the Spitfires down than another raid began approaching, some 70-plus aircraft including 54 Ju87s, making for the Dockyard and Hal Far. Two Hurricanes had been sent up at 1700 to cover the returning Spitfires, and these were joined by five more at 1800, and then by five Spitfires half an hour later. The Ju87s were encountered over Grand Harbour, six of which were claimed shot down (two by the AA defences), five more as probables and three damaged. Of these, Plt Off Nash, Plt Off Plagis and Sgt Hesselyn claimed one apiece, Sqn Ldr Grant a probable and a damaged and Flg Off Buchanan a probable. Plagis reported setting his opponent's engine on fire, whereupon it spun down in flames, while Nash saw his target blow up and fall into the sea. Of the action, Hesselyn wrote:

> "We each got onto a bomber's tail. Pete [Nash] was slightly ahead of me and I could see him firing before I opened up. His shells were striking and suddenly his 87 blew up. I had no time to see any more. I was within 100 yards of my 87 and, pressing the right gun button this time, I gave him everything I had. In a couple of seconds he burst into flames and dived into the drink."

Hesselyn was jumped by a Bf109F as he approached to land with wheels and flaps down, but was able to retract these and turn steeply, the attacker missing his opportunity; the Messerschmitt climbed away after overshooting, allowing the New Zealander to land safely.

It seems likely that the AA gunners claimed the same aircraft as those attacked by the fighters. Two Ju87s were actually lost, T6+FN of 8/StG3 crashing on the seashore at Delimara Point with the loss of the gunner, Gfr Wilhelm Neubauer. The pilot, Uffz Winfried Gunther, managed to bale out and was blown out to sea; he was soon picked up by ASR tender ST338. A second Ju87 from this unit came down in the sea five miles north-east of Valetta, the pilot, Oblt Kuhn, being rescued later by an Axis ASR craft, although his gunner (Gfr Helmut Suchlich) was lost. A third aircraft, from 7 Staffel, was hit during this operation and its pilot, Obfw Kurt Auer, was wounded. While RAF and Military personnel were inspecting the wreck of T6+FN at Delimara Point, a bomb aboard the aircraft exploded and killed a number of those present.

Spitfires of 249 were required to scramble after one raid only on 3 April, Sgt Yarra engaging a Ju88 without tangible success; this was Yarra's last flight with the Squadron, for next day he was posted to 185 to employ his previous experience on Hurricanes advantageously. During an afternoon raid by Ju88s bombs fell on Takali, where Spitfire AB418 was destroyed and three others damaged, including AB420 which was damaged beyond repair.

On 4 April Ju87s and Ju88s targeted the damaged cruiser *Penelope* at dock in Grand Harbour, but she suffered only minor damage. An evening raid by 60 Ju88s was intercepted by four Spitfires and six Hurricanes, Flt Lt Macqueen leading a stern quarter attack on one of the bombers, seeing its starboard engine catch fire. He then shot at the port engine and the bomber turned on its back and dived vertically. Another bomber was claimed damaged by Plt Off Sergeant, who reported an apparent dead rear gunner following his attack, with the aircraft last seen rolling onto its back; however, this may have been the aircraft under attack by his leader, a Ju88 of 5/KG77 belly-landing at Comiso on return, having been badly damaged by fighters. A third bomber was claimed damaged by Flg Off Daddo-Langlois, whose own aircraft sustained one bullet strike from the rear gunner.

There was only one major — unopposed — raid on Easter Monday, 6 April. At least 20 Ju87s and up to 55 Ju88s attacked Grand Harbour, the Dockyard and the airfields. Luqa came under heavy attack and five Hurricanes and two Spitfires (AB338 and AB454) were damaged beyond repair. The other Spitfire unit, 126 Squadron, recorded that nearly all its former Hurricane pilots had now departed, including those transferred from 249 earlier, although Flg Off Ron West (who had previously flown Spitfires) now joined 249. Of this period of heavy air attack, LAC Metcalf at Takali confided to his diary:

> "This Easter has been one that I'll remember (should I be one of the lucky ones to get away with it!). From dawn to dusk wave after wave of 88s, 87s and other gash kites to make weight have bombed and better bombed. During one lull I bobbed my head above the slit trench and suddenly spotted a fresh wave of 88s coming in over St Paul's. I counted 27, but when the leader put his nose down and started a power-dive straight for my slit trench — what a sensation — I could neither speak nor move! Luckily he came a few feet too low and the bombs went over the top of the trench."

Raids on 7 April found the fighters grounded again. The first raid concentrated on Grand Harbour and the airfields. At Kalafrana an ASR Swordfish floatplane and a Walrus amphibian were damaged, while Spitfire AB262 GN-B, under repair at Takali, was seriously damaged. Metcalf's diary continued:

> "And still they come, in all their might. God in Heaven alone knows what's going to happen next or where this is all going to end. Its a pity we haven't some fighter protection, but what we do have, have done wonderful work and each pilot deserves a VC at least. To send the last few up alone would be murder in the first degree. The ack-ack boys too are great and I hold my hand out to each of them."

A severe form of dysentery was rife on Malta at this time and was known locally as 'Malta Dog'. One of 249's chief sufferers was Plt Off Jeff West, who went down with a bout every ten days or so, but was ever keen to fly as soon as he was feeling better. According to Flt Lt Lucas, the well-rehearsed dialogue went something like:

> Sqn Ldr Grant: "And how are you today, Jeff?"
>
> Plt Off West: "Better sir, thank you. I could do a trip of 40 minutes, no more."
>
> Sqn Ldr Grant: "But Jeff, can you fart yet without danger? That's always the test."
>
> Plt Off West: "Not yet sir, but I don't want to."
>
> Sqn Ldr Grant: "Right then, you're still stood down."

Apparently West was feeling somewhat better by 8 April, since he was one of a trio of pilots ordered off at 1330 on the approach of another raid. Joined by seven Hurricanes, the three Spitfires engaged six Ju88s at 14,000 feet over Kalafrana. West attacked one bomber head-on and saw strikes on the cockpit. He then turned on the tail of a Messerschmitt and closed, firing all his ammunition and causing black smoke to appear; this may have been a 6/JG53 aircraft flown by Lt Hans Möller which crashed into the sea off Valetta; Möller was picked up later by an ASR craft from Sicily, when he reported that he believed he had been hit by AA fire.

Meanwhile, Flt Lt Heppell attacked another bomber, seeing strikes on wings and fuselage, then fired at a second, hitting the cockpit, fuselage and starboard engine, which gave off smoke. He fired another six-seconds burst from astern and then broke away due to the attentions of another. A splash was observed in the sea, convincing Heppell that his victim had gone in. A Hurricane also claimed a Ju88 in similar circumstances and it would seem that both had attacked an aircraft of KüFlGr606 which ditched after having been hit by fighters, the crew later also being picked up by an Axis ASR aircraft. The third member of the trio, Plt Off Kelly, claimed damage to yet another bomber.

A bigger raid developed at 1500, no fewer than 57 Ju88s and 26 Ju87s being reported, together with many fighters. Grand Harbour and Luqa were apparently the main targets. Flt Lt Heppell again led off three Spitfires, which were joined by nine Hurricanes. Flying AB346 GN-K, Heppell attacked a Ju88 over the harbour at 8,000 feet; he wrote later of his experience:

> "I recall registering strikes in the wing roots and the tail unit of the 88 . . . and the next thing I remember was falling head first towards the harbour sans aircraft. When my parachute opened it seemed that I was on some sky-hook, and not apparently losing height, with bombs falling past, ack-ack exploding and a continuous rattle of machine guns all around. I crashed into a bomb hole, still conscious but unable to move. I was given a shot of morphia by a MO and taken to Mtarfa Hospital. Shortly afterwards I was on the operating table about to have the gashes in my head and legs sewn up."

Although initially it was believed that Heppell's aircraft had hit an aerial mine, it was established later that it had received a direct hit from an AA shell and that he had been blown out of the aircraft, the remains of which fell into a cemetery near Sliema. Meanwhile, the bomber attacked by Heppell — probably an aircraft of 6/KG77 which crash-landed at Comiso on return — was probably the same as that engaged by Flg Off Ron West and a pilot of 185 Squadron.

With the approach of dusk, three of the Squadron's Spitfires were again scrambled, this time after an ASR Do24 of 6 Seenotdienststaffel, which was operating offshore under a screen of Messerschmitts, obviously searching for survivors of missing aircraft. The flyingboat was seen taxiing on the water with six Bf109Fs overhead and six Ju88s in the general area, Flg Off Ron West at once diving to attack the Dornier. Strikes were seen all along the fuselage and the rescue craft caught fire, the crew escaping unhurt and were themselves later rescued. Plt Off Kelly meanwhile had attacked one of the Ju88s from quarter astern, claiming strikes on the port engine and cabin, before following West down to attack the flying boat. As West pulled up from his attack, he was bounced by some of the escorting fighters, but succeeded in getting a deflection shot along the fuselage of one as it overshot. A patrolling Hurricane pilot apparently reported that he had seen both the Messerschmitt fired at by West and the bomber attacked by Kelly, hit the water; consequently both were credited as having been shot down.

The famous Mosta Church was damaged by bombs at 1640 on 9 April during a raid by Ju88s, one bomb penetrating the nine-feet thick dome before bouncing twice off the interior wall, but it failed to explode. It then skidded along the floor of the nave and came to a standstill. There were some three hundred of the congregation present, although most had scattered to the side chapels and corridors for shelter as the bombs began falling, and none was hurt, even by flying debris. LAC Jim Somerville of 249 was in the vicinity of the church and recalled seeing a lady emerging from the building, bringing the news that there was an unexploded bomb on the floor of the rotunda. He and two or three soldiers entered the church and proceeded to roll the bomb outside, from where it was taken away on an army pick-up truck. Seconds later Somerville was wounded in the leg by shrapnel from another bomb which exploded nearby.

The first raid on 10 April came at 1245 and met no defenders. The bombers returned in greater strength at 1745, an estimated 65 Ju88s and 20 Ju87s attacking Grand Harbour, Hal Far and Takali. Four Spitfires flown by 249 pilots scrambled to join a dozen Hurricanes, meeting ten Ju88s of III/KG77, one of which Flt Lt Macqueen claimed shot down; two of the crew appeared to bale out, but in fact, the gun position had been blown off the cabin of 3Z+HS, this and the body of the gunner, Uffz Paul Boger, falling on Takali airfield. The 8 Staffel machine was also claimed by AA gunners. Of the incident, LAC Metcalf wrote:

"The rear gunner of an 88 was shot out of his kite complete with turret and landed roughly 50 yards from our trench. He wasn't greatly disfigured although his neck was broken."

Meanwhile, Flg Off Buchanan dived out of the sun on a Messerschmitt over St Paul's Bay as it was pulling up after firing at a Hurricane. He fired from long range and, to his surprise, the aircraft burst into flames and the pilot baled out; he was credited with its destruction, although a pilot of 185 Squadron claimed a Bf109F in similar circumstances and was also credited with a victory. Only one Messerschmitt was lost, the pilot none other than III/JG53's leading Experte, Lt Hermann Neuhoff* in Yellow 1 — who now became a prisoner; only the previous evening he had been promoted to lead 6 Staffel. Neuhoff subsequently asked to meet his victor, and was introduced to Buchanan. However, the returning pilots of JG53 believed that Neuhoff had been shot down accidentally by a pilot of 1 Staffel, who had apparently admitted firing at a Messerschmitt in error during the heat of the battle. However, Neuhoff told his captors:

"[I] sighted a Hurricane below and dived to attack, leaving [my] No2 to protect [my] rear. This, however, [he] failed to do and when diving on to the Hurricane [I] was attacked by a Spitfire from behind."

Other claims were submitted by Flg Off Lee for a Ju88 probably destroyed and one damaged, and by Plt Off Nash for a Ju87 probable; he recorded:

"My Ju87 gave off lots of black smoke when I attacked from just under his tail. Then bounced by six 109s. Got strikes on wings and rear of cockpit from one. Not sorry to get down again today!"

His attack on the Ju87 would seem to have been successful, for one Ju87 of 8/StG3 crashed into the sea north of Valetta after being attacked by a fighter, both Uffz Gerhard Bode and Gfr Josef Seidl, the gunner, being wounded although both were later rescued.

During the next few days the defending fighters were not able to achieve much against raiders who targeted the airfields. At Takali on 11 April two Spitfires and a Hurricane were damaged on the ground, the other two airfields suffering similar losses to dispersed aircraft. Next day a Spitfire and a Hurricane were destroyed at Takali. The first raid on Malta on the morning of 14 April was by six Ju88s which targeted Takali. Immediately thereafter, three Spitfires of 249 took off to provide protection for a departing reconnaissance Maryland of 69 Squadron, but were promptly engaged by Bf109Fs. Plt Off Kelly claimed one damaged before being shot down himself — probably by Maj von Maltzahn of JG53. Kelly baled out of AB342 from about 800 feet, three miles west of Hal Far, but his parachute failed to open properly and he hit the water very hard, suffering severe bruising. He also became entangled in the shroud lines, and lost his dinghy whilst freeing himself. Two more Spitfires were at once scrambled to search for him, the two Wests locating him and circling overhead, some two miles offshore. Kelly was seen to be swimming strongly and even found the strength to raise two fingers to his colleagues as they passed low overhead. HSL128 was despatched to the rescue, covered by a pair of Hurricanes. Coxswain Flt Sgt L.G. Head wrote:

"Two Hurricane pilots warded off Messerschmitt 109s who were attacking the launch whilst

---

* The loss of Lt Neuhoff was a blow to JG53; he was one of the most successful Luftwaffe fighter pilots to be shot down over Malta during the whole siege. He had claimed 40 victories, 21 of them over Russia, although only five over Malta. Interrogation obviously uncovered details of claims since it was soon realised that Neuhoff had probably shot down Plt Off Leggo on 20 March.

proceeding to base at Kalafrana after rescuing a Spitfire pilot, Plt Off Kelly. One can only speculate on Kelly's thoughts — to be attacked and brought down in his plane and then to be attacked in the rescue boat after being pulled out of the sea. He must have wondered whether the Gods were being unkind to him particularly bearing in mind the fact that Plt Off Kelly's parachute failed to open when he baled out of his crashing Spitfire." *

Another two Spitfires were off at 1300 to cover the returning Maryland, finding it being pursued by two Bf109Fs. Flt Lt Macqueen and Plt Off Sergeant attacked at once; the latter wrote:

"Cover for Maryland. Attacked by two Messerschmitts with three below. A good squirt at one and a quick squirt at another. A 109 went in so Mac and I split the bag — half 109F destroyed, half 109F damaged."

An aircraft of 8/JG53 crashed into the sea as a result of this combat, the pilot subsequently being rescued by the Axis ASR service.

And so it went on, day after day. The numbers of serviceable Spitfires and Hurricanes dwindled to a mere handful. When seven Hurricane reinforcements arrived from North Africa on 19 April, it had been four days since Malta's fighters had been able to operate, and the situation was truly desperate. While the delivery of the two initial batches of Spitfires to the island had brought some relief, it was obvious that the small numbers involved would not allow sustained operations to be maintained for long — as indeed had been the case. But help was on its way and, on the morning of 20 April, the first of 46 Spitfires touched down on Malta having flown from the American carrier USS *Wasp*. The flight had proved uneventful for the majority of the pilots although one failed to arrive, its American pilot having landed in Algeria. The new arrivals comprised two complete Fighter Command squadrons (601 and 603) rather than a collection of pilots drawn from many units and, while the initial intention was that half the new aircraft would go to reinforce the existing Spitfire units on the island (126 and 249 Squadrons), events over the next 48 hours soon put an end to these plans.

Such a large number of aircraft flying from the west had not gone unnoticed by the Axis on this occasion, their presence having been plotted on radar and picked up by radio intercepts. A major effort was at once prepared by the Luftwaffe and, during the remainder of the day, no fewer than 272 bomber sorties were flown against Malta's airfields. The first of the new Spitfires had arrived at around 1000, but it was 1230 before the initial German raid was plotted coming in, comprising 32 Ju88s and 20 Ju87s. These hit all three airfields but without causing undue damage: at Takali one newly-arrived Spitfire was badly damaged, three others and a Hurricane were slightly damaged. With the approach of the raid, six Spitfires flown by 249 pilots were scrambled and were joined by three Hurricanes, soon becoming entangled with the escort. Flt Lt Lucas, leading the flight, wrote:

"Around 1300 hours, six of we old hands really got stuck into what turned into one of the heaviest raids to date. There were pickings all round, although Junior Tayleur had the cockpit canopy of his aircraft shattered by cannon fire from a ME109 which had attacked him from head-on. Despite being badly cut about the face and bleeding freely, Junior had carried doggedly on, probably destroying an 87 before landing his Spit, with wheels and flaps down, at Takali and immediately being carted off to hospital at Mtarfa.

Raoul [Daddo-Langlois] had a similarly unnerving experience — he saw one coming straight at him, head-on, with guns blazing. Returning the fire, he held his bead on the German. Each refused to give way and, with a closing speed of some 500 or 600 mph, neither broke in time. They collided, the tip of Raoul's starboard wing catching the root of the 109's wing, severing it completely and sending the aircraft spiralling earthwards. Only the outer section of the Spitfire's wing had been severed. Bringing the aircraft in with excess speed, Raoul had let it run down the strip until he saw he was going to overshoot. Then, as the undercarriage was whipped smartly up, the run was brought to a halt with the pilot leaping

---

* Plt Off Kelly did not return to 249 on recovery but was posted instead to 1435 Flight at Luqa.

from the cockpit just as four 109s were beginning an aggressive run across the airfield, all guns firing."

The Messerschmitt which collided with Daddo-Langlois's aircraft (GN-C) had apparently been hit first by Flt Lt McNair; the I/JG53 pilot was seen to bale out south of Delimara and was later picked up by an Axis ASR craft. Daddo-Langlois noted:

"Squirted at Ju87, Ju88 and 109s. Collided with 109 head-on. Pranged on landing. 109 confirmed."

Meanwhile, McNair engaged a Ju88 and saw strikes on this also, claiming it damaged. A Ju87 was attacked by Flg Off Ron West, which turned over and was seen to go down five miles south of Delimara; he also claimed damage to a second Ju87 before gaining strikes on a Ju88, another of which Plt Off Sergeant damaged:

"Dived on two 109s which I lost due to oiled windscreen. On my own, so attacked Ju88 over Grand Harbour but cannons jammed. Ju88 damaged."

Hurricanes attempted to provide cover for the Spitfires as they came in to land in the face of strafing Messerschmitts, as recalled by LAC Somerville:

"Airmen were encouraged to fire at low-flying enemy aircraft. It had become a habit for enemy aircraft to follow our Spits into Takali when they [the Spitfires] had run out of fuel and/or ammo, with the object of shooting up an easy target. Drill was to collect from the armoury a rifle and belts of .303 machine-gun ammunition — ammo supplies unlimited. Imagine the effect when the 109s saw tracer bullets converging on them from all round Takali — tracers, armour-piercing, incendiaries, the lot! It was not haphazard banging away with guns — the task was taken seriously as the airmen had been advised they were first line of defence should there be an invasion! As a matter of fact two enemy aircraft destroyed were credited to small-arms fire at Takali."

One of the damaged Spitfires attempting to evade the strafers was that flown by Flg Off Daddo-Langlois; Sgt Hesselyn was watching from the ground:

"I noticed one Spit with its wingtip sheared off. He was flying low down with a bunch of 109s above, and was whistling around the circuit, waiting a favourable moment to come in and land. His damaged wing was plainly visible from the ground. About 18 inches of it was missing, and instead of the usual elliptical section of a Spit wing, it looked rather like the square-cut wing of a 109E. Eventually the Spit came in, but was hit. It went running past dispersal when the pilot whipped up his undercart, and skidded the aircraft along on its belly . . . It came to rest in a cloud of dust. Brennan ran towards it, but the 109s swooped down and started to beat up the aerodrome. Brennan dodged behind some sandbags, and Buck [Buchanan] and I ran towards a slit trench. Before we could reach it, the 109s were overhead and we had to fling ourselves on the ground. As we did so I saw Raoul Daddo-Langlois leap from the cockpit of the Spitfire and make a bee-line for dispersal. Machine-gun bullets ploughed into the ground all round us, and a cannon shell burst within a few yards of Buck, but luckily we were not hurt."

As evening approached radar warned that another big raid was brewing. At 1700 two Spitfires of 249 took off to provide airfield defence, flying out to sea to enable them to offer cover when the main interception force returned to land. As Flg Off Buchanan and Sgt Hesselyn climbed to 10,000 feet, they skirmished with a number of Bf109Fs which were approaching ahead of the main force, and were obliged to engage these. Hesselyn got onto the tail of one and attacked, chasing it across the island and giving it a four-seconds burst as it passed over the coast at St Paul's Bay, following which the Messerschmitt nosed down and apparently went vertically into the sea. Hesselyn was then jumped by others but evaded these and fired at some Ju88s, seeing strikes on one. Buchanan, meanwhile, also chased a Bf109F and claimed to have shot this down into the sea in the same area — witnessed by Hesselyn — but the two were then attacked by others. An aircraft of I/JG53 did, in fact, crash into the sea off Valetta, from which the pilot was later rescued by an Axis ASR craft.

The evening raid came in at 1715 and was, indeed, a major affair, including an estimated 64 Ju88s, 25 Ju87s and more than 30 Bf109Fs, accompanied by an ASR Do24. At 1720 six Spitfires from Takali flown by 249 pilots and six from Luqa manned by 126 Squadron were scrambled, meeting Messerschmitts south-west of Gozo at between 15,000 and 17,000 feet covering Ju88s which had just bombed Takali, where two Spitfires were destroyed on the ground and three others damaged. Flt Lt Macqueen reported shooting down one bomber which he believed crashed into the sea, while Plt Off Sergeant claimed a second north of Grand Harbour:

> "Hell of a dogfight with 109s over Gozo, one squirt. Attacked an 88 over Grand Harbour and set port engine on fire. Last seen diving down flaming and smoking. Ju88 destroyed."

One of the escorting fighters was claimed by Sgt Brennan and was seen to fall into the sea seven miles west of Gozo by Flg Off Ron West; Brennan then attacked a Ju88 over Mtarfa, which was also observed — by Flt Lt Connell from the ground — to crash into the sea with both engines afire. Return fire from this aircraft hit Brennan's Spitfire but he was able to land safely. A second Messerschmitt was claimed probably destroyed by Flt Lt McNair, who believed he had shot away most of its tail, while Flt Lt Lucas gained strikes on a third. It seems that the bombers were from KüFlGr606 and KGr806. One aircraft from the former unit was crash-landed at Catania in a badly damaged condition by Fw Winfried Böhlen, two of the crew having been wounded, while an aircraft from the latter Gruppe also crash-landed at Catania. Meanwhile, the 126 Squadron flight had suffered at the hands of the Messerschmitts, losing two aircraft with both pilots being killed.

Air Vice-Marshal Lloyd, the AOC, had been delayed getting to Takali to welcome the new arrivals due to a bomb splinter puncturing a tyre on his car, but when he did arrive he found many of the new pilots almost speechless at the exhibition of concentrated bombing. Lloyd feared that Takali would be unserviceable for three or four days, so severe appeared the damage. But soldiers and airmen again worked through the night and by first light next morning the runways had been cleared, filled and rolled, allowing Spitfires which had landed at Luqa or Hal Far to return. Nine other Spitfires remained trapped in their pens by debris, however, and could not be moved for the time being. To help fill the gaps in 249's ranks, four of the new arrivals — Plt Offs L.W. Watts, O.M. Linton RCAF, C.B. McLean RCAF and F.E. Almos RCAF, an American — were posted in from 603 Squadron, while Plt Off H.A. Milburn moved across from 185 Squadron.

Despite all efforts, only 27 Spitfires could be made serviceable by dawn on 21 April to oppose the anticipated onslaught on the airfields, the first raid approaching at 0730 when an estimated 37 Ju88s and 34 Bf109Fs began a series of attacks on Grand Harbour, the Docks, Luqa and Takali. Ten Spitfires, including four flown by 249 pilots, and five Hurricanes were scrambled shortly after 0830. Six Ju88s which had just bombed Luqa were encountered, and one of these was engaged jointly by Sqn Ldr Grant and Plt Off Plagis; the bomber was last seen diving steeply towards the sea with both engines pouring black smoke and they were credited with its destruction. Plagis also claimed damage to a Messerschmitt, as did Sgt Hesselyn, while Flg Off Buchanan gained strikes on another Ju88.

At 1210 a second raid approached: 20 Ju88s, 15 Ju87s and 36 Bf109Fs being reported making for Takali, Hal Far and the Grand Harbour. As a result of the attack on Takali, two more Spitfires were destroyed and one damaged. Plt Off Nash ran across to see if he could help extinguish a burning Spitfire in its pen, but was caught by the blast of an exploding bomb and rendered unconscious for 15 minutes although otherwise unhurt. 249 had scrambled six Spitfires and these enjoyed some success when they got amongst the Stukas. Sgt Hesselyn claimed one in flames as it was attacking Takali and then took a snap shot at a Messerschmitt, which was hit by his cannon fire and also considered destroyed. He was then chased down to 2,000 feet by another, which Plt Off Plagis drove off his tail and claimed probably destroyed. Flg Off Buchanan claimed a second Ju87 shot down. One of the new pilots, Plt Off Watts, reported strikes on the Messerschmitt he attacked.

The third and final raid began at 1559, with an estimated 60 Ju88s, 20 Ju87s and 40 Bf109Fs approaching to attack the airfields and Grand Harbour yet again. Nine Spitfires of 249 scrambled at 1645, and two of these dived on a formation of Messerschmitts but were then attacked by other fighters, possibly MC202s of 10° Gruppo CT; a pilot from this unit claimed a Spitfire shot down although none was lost. At 1720 the Spitfires encountered a number of Ju88s and their escorts as they were diving in line astern from 12,000 feet, heading for Filfla after attacking Takali. Flt Lt Macqueen claimed one Bf109F shot down and a bomber damaged, but was then set upon by two more Messerschmitts as he came in to land. The first missed its opportunity and the second did not attack, driven away by Bofors fire. Sgt Brennan claimed to have set fire to a Ju88 over Filfla and was credited with its probable destruction, but was then attacked by a Bf109F; a cannon shell hit his cockpit as he went after a second bomber, and he was attacked repeatedly as he went down to land but was not hit again. Another Junkers was claimed shot down into the sea by Flg Off Buchanan, but his aircraft was shot-up in the circuit as he was endeavouring to land; despite the damage he got down safely. Plt Off Sergeant's Spitfire was also hit when six Messerschmitts attacked:

"Chased 109 but was jumped by six others and badly shot up with cannon in empennage — landed OK but very frightened. More 109s than ever."

Among 249's opponents in this clash were Oblt Brändle of 5/JG53 who claimed his second Spitfire of the day at 1739 to raise his score to 35, while Fw Rudolf Schmidt of 7 Staffel claimed another as his sixth, and Lt Rudolf Müller of 8 Staffel, a third. On the ground the evening attack had taken a heavy toll. Some 150 bombs had struck Takali, and while not rendering the airfield completely unserviceable, had destroyed two Spitfires and damaged four others. Flt Lt Connell and Flg Off Lee were among seven pilots who departed under cover of darkness in a Wellington bomber heading for Egypt; they had been instructed to collect replacement Hurricanes and to ferry them to Malta.

When the first raid approached the island at 0930 on the morning of 22 April, no more than 17 Spitfires could be made ready for operations. The raiders again headed for the airfields and, as a result of the attack on Takali, one Spitfire was destroyed; in addition, two soldiers were killed and six wounded. First off at 0915 to meet the raiders were four Spitfires with Flt Lt McNair leading three inexperienced new arrivals. They gave chase to a lone Ju88 — almost certainly Uffz Wilhelm Schreiber's 3Z+FM of 6/KG77 — at which all fired. McNair observed many strikes during his attack and was probably responsible for its destruction. There were no survivors.

At 1010 seven Spitfires were scrambled, again led by McNair, the pilots intercepting 20 Ju88s approaching St Paul's Bay. Flg Off Ron West claimed two bombers damaged and Sgt Brennan another, although he was then attacked by Messerschmitts and his own aircraft hit in the lower cockpit area, his flying boots being ripped to shreds by cannon splinters. 126 Squadron took over the Spitfires after midday but were unable to prevent an evening raid on Takali which saw the destruction of three more Spitfires on the ground. Two more were wrecked during morning and evening raids next day (23 April), making a total of 13 Spitfires written off in this manner in the preceding four days, and a further dozen or so damaged, while nine more had been shot down. The situation was again becoming very serious for the defenders.

The last raid of the day on 24 April saw a handful of Hurricanes and Spitfires intercept 15 Ju87s over Grand Harbour, Plt Off Nash leading two inexperienced pilots on their first sorties from Malta. However, immediately after getting airborne, Nash's aircraft suffered engine failure and crash-landed on the clifftops near Rabat; although understandably shaken, he was not injured. It seemed as though nothing could stop the Luftwaffe from pounding the airfields and destroying the few remaining serviceable fighters. Up to 85 Ju88s and 15 Ju87s were reported attacking Luqa on the morning of 25 April; there was a repeat raid by similar numbers of bombers soon after midday, resulting in more than two dozen fatalities among the gunners and others defending the airfield. A few defending Hurricanes and Spitfires managed to get airborne, four of 249 meeting Ju87s and Ju88s, one of the latter being engaged by Sgt Brennan over Naxxar but he was in turn attacked by six Bf109Fs. He pulled up into these and all but one overshot:

> "I pulled up 30 or 40 feet underneath him. It was point-blank range, and every detail of his machine stood out vividly. I could see his markings, his twin radiators, his retracted wheels, even the rivet heads on his fuselage. I gave him a second and a half with all four cannons. The result gave me a terrible fright. His starboard wing snapped off near the fuselage. It folded back, and banged against the fuselage. For a moment I thought it was going to tear away from his machine and come hurtling into my aircraft."

The Messerschmitt pilot, Uffz Heinrich Becker of 8/JG53, managed to bale out into the sea from where he was later rescued by an Axis ASR craft*. Brennan then attacked a Ju88 from dead astern at 200 yards range and saw this catch fire, reporting that it crashed into the sea (confirmed by groundcrews at Takali, who were watching the aerial battle). However, Brennan's Spitfire had taken a number of strikes from the rear gunner of the bomber and it went out of control. After a few anxious moments however, he managed to regain control and headed back to Takali, but there Bf109Fs were in the circuit and he heard the Controller call for Spitfires to cover Hurricanes as they attempted to land at Hal Far.

In response to the call for help, both Brennan and Flt Lt McNair arrived over Hal Far to keep the Messerschmitts at bay, but as two Hurricanes attempted to land simultaneously, one took the other for a Bf109F and pulled away, while the other mistook the Spitfires for Messerschmitts and also hesitated. An irate McNair called over the R/T that he would shoot down the over-cautious pilots himself if they did not land quickly! When McNair finally landed at Takali, he reported that he had damaged two Messerschmitts, a Ju88 and a Ju87. However, Brennan recorded that McNair got two confirmed during this sortie and it seems likely that the claims for the two bombers were upgraded.

The next big raid came on the afternoon of 26 April, with 55 Ju88s and 15 Ju87s attacking Valetta and Kalafrana from 1430 onwards. Six Spitfires and four Hurricanes were scrambled, three of the former flown by 249 pilots although the leader, Plt Off Nash, was forced to return when his electrical systems failed. The remaining two, Sgt Hesselyn and Plt Off James, engaged Bf109Fs over St Paul's Bay, one of which Hesselyn claimed damaged before his own aircraft was hit by another. He was then warned of Ju87s diving on Takali and engaged one at 8,000 feet, firing a four-seconds burst. The aircraft was seen to catch fire and the crew baled out; two parachutes were seen over Naxxar as the Stuka crashed into the sea. Meanwhile James, after attempting to attack Ju88s over Grand Harbour, was also attacked by Bf109Fs and his Spitfire (BR199) was badly damaged; cannon splinters wounded him in the neck and left leg but he succeeded in belly-landing the aircraft at Takali. Despite his wounds he was able to scramble clear of the wreck as Messerschmitts swooped down to strafe.

Although there were three raids on each of 27 and 28 April, the Squadron was not involved, and over the next two weeks raids proved to be much smaller affairs. The respite would give groundcrews time to carry out repairs to the remaining Spitfires, and Army personnel to repair the airfields. By the end of the month no more than seven Spitfires and a handful of Hurricanes remained serviceable. It was estimated that Takali had been on the receiving end of 841 tons of bombs during April, compared to 482 tons in March and 120 tons in February; the other two airfields had received similar tonnages. 339 civilians and 208 servicemen had been killed during the April assault on Malta; in addition, some 550 civilians and many servicemen were injured.

Defending fighters were credited with 53 victories during the month of April, plus a dozen probables and 118 damaged, of which 249's pilots claimed 38 destroyed (including the Do24 on the water), nine probably destroyed and 26 damaged. Actual German losses were substantially fewer than this, however. The Squadron saw the departure of the injured Flt Lt Heppell and the sick Plt Off Jeff West at the end of the month, while Sqn Ldr Grant, Flt Lt Lucas, newly promoted Flt Lt Ron West, Flt Lt McNair and Flg Off Daddo-Langlois were flown to Gibraltar

---

* Records suggest this was the Squadron's 150th 'confirmed' victory.

aboard a Hudson to assist with the next Spitfire delivery, as Lucas recalled:

"After the disaster of the first lot of Spitfires from USS *Wasp*, arrangements had apparently been made at high level to allow the US Navy's huge carrier to make a second run down the Med with a further batch of 48 Spitfires on board."

The AOC had decided that it was essential for the next reinforcements to be led in by experienced Malta pilots.

Chapter Seven

BATTLE FOR SURVIVAL

May — June 1942

"After firing one burst I received a shot into my cooling system. I intended to fly as far away from Malta as possible, bale out and wait for the rescue Do24, but my cockpit rapidly became red hot. I baled out and was picked up by a launch."

Lt Dr. Heiner Jörg, II/JG53 ace shot down by 249 Squadron

On Malta, May opened with a number of small fighter sweeps. The first of these was intercepted at around mid-morning by two Spitfires flown by Flt Lt Macqueen and Plt Off Watts, who were advised of the presence of Messerschmitts nearby while on an air test near Filfla. Four Bf109Fs of 6/JG53, all carrying long-range tanks, were spotted. Giving chase at once, Macqueen and Watts jointly shot down one Messerschmitt which carried out a successful ditching in the sea off Cap Scaramia; the pilot was later safely picked up by an Axis rescue craft. Watts also reported strikes on a second Messerschmitt.

The afternoon of 2 May saw a raid by a dozen Ju88s on Luqa and Safi, with escort provided by Bf109Fs and Macchis. Of the four 249 Spitfires that managed to scramble, only Flg Off Buchanan succeeded in gaining strikes on a Messerschmitt before others drove him and his section away. Next morning (3 May) the Ju88s were back, seven bombers raiding Hal Far at midday. Five of 249 were scrambled while two others covered the aerodrome. Plt Off Nash, who was flying with Plt Off Milburn (known to his colleagues as D'Arcy), noted:

"D'Arcy and I were 'drome defence section. Came in at 12,000 feet just under 9/10th cloud and jumped four 109s over Hal Far. D'Arcy lost me during subsequent manoeuvres. Chased two and shot the No2 down at sea level. Was then jumped by two more so came home five miles west of Kalafrana. Only had port cannon working."

Milburn claimed a second Messerschmitt as damaged. Plt Off Watts also claimed one damaged. Eight Spitfires, including four of 249, were scrambled during the afternoon of 4 May to counter a raid by five Z1007s escorted by five MC202s and ten Bf109Fs. Sgt Brennan wrote:

"Caught as we head up sun, a little south of Gozo. The 109s were everywhere. Linny [Plt Off Linton] and I were at once separated from Mac and Almos [Plt Off Almos]. The last I saw of Linny was when he was in a vertical dive, skidding and twisting like blazes, with four 109s hotly pursuing him. It seemed to me as if I had been throwing my aircraft about for an hour . . . when a Hun blundered. He made a belly attack on me, missed and overshot. He was a sitting target. I gave him four seconds. He went into a spin, pouring glycol . . . Almos called up that Mac was in trouble and wanted to land."

Meanwhile however, Plt Off Linton had escaped his pursuers and landed safely, but the other two were in trouble. Having arrived too late to catch the bombers, Flt Lt Macqueen had apparently suffered an R/T failure and, consequently, was unable to hear warnings of approaching danger. Watchers on the ground saw a Bf109F bounce him, but miss and overshoot. The German No2, Uffz Walter Manz of III/JG53, then pulled up underneath and gained strikes on Macqueen's aircraft (BR226); his demise was witnessed by many including the CO of 603 Squadron, who wrote:

"Several of us saw it happen from the Mess verandah. We saw the 109's tracer going right into Norman's machine. His Spitfire lurched and gave out a thin smoke trail. For some time it seemed to be under control and circled downwards as if he hoped to land. Then suddenly the nose went forward, and the machine dived like a stone into the ground, bursting into flames as it hit. I felt a lump come into my throat."

Witnesses were of the impression that the inexperienced Almos, an American, had been too close to properly protect his leader's tail from this attack. He soon himself transferred to 126 Squadron in which an all-American flight was being formed.

At 1225, Flg Off Buchanan and Sgt Hesselyn were scrambled to provide cover for a returning photo-reconnaissance Spitfire being pursued by Italian fighters. No sooner were they airborne than they were warned of two low-flying Bf109Fs over Hal Far. Unable initially to find these, they saw a pair, probably the same, being fired upon by AA over Grand Harbour. Catching up with one, Hesselyn opened fire for two seconds before his cannons jammed. The Messerschmitt dived steeply for Takali and at first appeared about to crash, but at the last moment pulled up and flew off northwards. Hesselyn was credited with damaging the fighter, but as it sped away it passed over a bus full of Maltese, which was trundling down the Rabat to Takali road. Thinking they were about to be strafed, the passengers piled out of the bus, seeking cover. One man dived through a window, cracked his skull on the road and died shortly afterwards from the resultant fracture.

After several days which had been much quieter than those of late April, 8 May heralded the start of another intensive Luftwaffe offensive against the island. Only a dozen Hurricanes and Spitfires remained seviceable, and as these were being preserved to support an imminent Spitfire delivery, no fighters rose to intercept. The raiders hit Takali where Flt Lt Connell and Flg Off Buchanan found themselves caught in the open, the Canadian being wounded by shrapnel or debris.

Help was not far away, however. The USS *Wasp*, with 50 Spitfires embarked, had departed Gibraltar on the night of 7/8 May, and was joined by *Eagle* carrying a further 17 Spitfires for Malta. Sqn Ldr Grant and Flt Lt Ron West were on board *Eagle* and were to lead the first two flights to Malta; the other three 249 pilots sent to Gibraltar for similar duty were held back to assist with a second operation, planned for 18 May. That decision did not go down well with Flt Lt McNair, as recalled by Flt Lt Lucas:

"Buck McNair nearly did his nut: he was a restless, aggressive Canadian who wanted to be in the thick of the fighting all the time. He could be rude — even to a Wing Commander! And he was certainly rude to Mac [Wg Cdr J.S. McLean, in charge of the Spitfire delivery] in Gib. 'Goddam, Sir, are you really asking Laddie, Daddo and me to sit on our arses here in Gib for another ten days while they'll be the hell of a party going on over the island? Sir, Goddam, I'm brassed right off . . .' He got no change out of Mac who was surprisingly calm with him. Daddo-Langlois and I (and Mac) had nearly ten days of Buck's bitching and binding before we went aboard *Eagle* to lead in the next 17 Spitfires to Malta."

Malta was ready for the Spitfires this time. Pilots at Takali were advised that every new Spitfire was to be back in the air within 15 minutes of its arrival. Five men were to be allocated to each aircraft pen, plus an experienced pilot to take over the aircraft. Long-range tanks would be removed first, and each pen would contain all that was necessary to rearm and refuel the fighters, the fuel being kept in four-gallon cans protected by sandbags. Every incoming Spitfire would have a large number/letter combination painted on its fuselage, and each pen allocated a specific aircraft so identified, which had to be led in regardless of the situation at the time. Whatever the rank of the new arrival, the Malta pilot in the pen was in command, and was to take over the aircraft at once and get it back into the air with all speed. If the aircraft happened to be damaged, it was to be taxied to repair pens at the rear. The pilot, if not wounded, was to return to the airfield to take over a more junior pilot's aircraft.

Sqn Ldr Grant was airborne from *Eagle* by 0643 on the morning of 9 May and set course for Malta, his flight to land at Takali; meanwhile the pilots of Flt Lt West's flight, who were to follow, were briefed to fly to Luqa. The American carrier began launching her flights at about the same time, but one Spitfire failed to gain sufficient flying speed and crashed into the sea and a second returned with a faulty long-range fuel tank. Against orders and to the amazement of the crew, the pilot made a successful landing aboard the carrier, eventually coming to a halt six feet from the bows. As the flights of Spitfires approached the island, fighters from Malta provided cover as Messerschmitts attempted to engage the new arrivals on their landing approaches. In the mêlée, two Messerschmitts were claimed shot down for the loss of a defending Spitfire.

All of the first batch of Spitfires landed safely and within a few minutes several had been refuelled and fully armed. At 1055, 11 of the new Spitfires took off, flown by 249 pilots and led by Sqn Ldr Grant. The formation almost immediately encountered Messerschmitts, as Plt Off Nash recorded:

> "I was leading D'Arcy [Milburn], Almos and Linton. Sent to Hal Far to deal with 109 trouble. We bounced them at 3,000 feet from 15,000 feet. Mine went into the sea off Hal Far. Formed up again and attacked by three 109s. One stuck around above us. Got up to him and gave a short burst. Spun down, lots of black smoke, five miles east of Malta."

Nash was credited with one confirmed and one probable, but Plt Off Milburn was shot down and killed as he attempted to land; jumped by four Bf109Fs at 1,000 feet, his Spitfire (BP845) crashed in a field near Safi. He was possibly the victim of 5/JG53 since Fw Rollwage and Fw Kneuer each claimed a Spitfire shortly after 1100. Meanwhile, Flg Off Buchanan engaged a Bf109F at 10,000 feet, five or six miles south-east of Kalafrana, claiming a probable when it dived away streaming glycol but then lost sight of it near the sea.

At 1115, Spitfires were again scrambled as Flt Lt West's flight from *Eagle* approached Luqa, having attempted to formate on a patrol of Bf109Fs over Grand Harbour by mistake. A Messerschmitt promptly attacked West's aircraft and shot a large piece out of its fuselage, although he was able to force-land safely. The leader of a flight from the *Wasp*, having landed safely at Hal Far, took off again to provide cover for others, only to strike a dispersal pen as he became airborne and crashed. When the Messerschmitts finally departed and the dust had settled, it was realised that two Spitfires from the last flight had failed to reach Malta*.

Throughout the remainder of the day the Axis air forces returned repeatedly in an effort to catch the new arrivals on the ground. At 1315, some 15 Ju88s and 18 escorting Bf109Fs approached, making for Hal Far and Takali. A strong formation of 24 Spitfires took off, eight of which were flown by 249 pilots but they were unable to reach the bombers before becoming engaged with the escort off Dingli. Plt Off Nash claimed one damaged:

> "We were scrambled too late to catch the bombers. Saw two 109s below so bounced them. Only one cannon worked."

A reconnaissance Ju88 with two Bf109Fs as escort appeared at 1530 and caused four 249 Spitfires to be scrambled, but they were unable to engage and were ordered to patrol off Sicily instead. Towards the end of their allotted time, as they headed back to base, the quartet met Ju87s over Grand Harbour, part of a force which had been attacking Luqa and the harbour. Plt Off Nash claimed a probable:

> "Chased recce Ju88 but unable to find him even over Sicilian coast. Stuck around at 27,000 feet for big raid. Bounced 87s over Grand Harbour. Only one cannon [operative] again. He [a Ju87] went on his back belching black smoke."

Shortly after the Spitfires had landed and were being refuelled, six Ju88s swooped on Takali. Pilots leapt from cockpits and headed for slit trenches; one large bomb exploded 20 feet from one trench crammed with pilots and groundcrew, but no one was hurt although two Spitfires

---

* The fate of the two pilots remained a mystery until a study of records revealed that they had in fact collided while attacking an Italian floatplane en route to Malta.

were riddled by shrapnel. Sgt Brennan twice tried to take off between raids but was prevented on the first occasion by a flat tyre, just reaching a trench before the bombs fell. On the second occasion he was fully strapped in as the Ju88s appeared. He ripped off his straps although in panic forgot the dinghy cord, which jerked him back and for a few seconds had him suspended on the wing root of his Spitfire. Again he was fortunate and reached cover just before the first bombs exploded. Raids continued throughout the late afternoon, most being successfully repelled by the defenders, the last coming in at 1840 when seven Ju88s and a dozen Bf109Fs attacked Takali. Three of 249 were airborne but were not able to make contact.

The day had been almost the success planned for. A total of 61 Spitfires had arrived safely although three others had been lost during the operation. In the frantic fighting over Malta during the day, four more had been shot down and six damaged to some extent on the ground. Nonetheless, counting those already on the island, nightfall saw the defenders with at least 50 undamaged Spitfires to hand, with another dozen or so repairable, together with a handful of Hurricanes; the defences had never been in better shape. As a back-up to the successful delivery of Spitfires, the fast minelayer-cruiser HMS *Welshman* had made an unescorted run from Gibraltar carrying quantities of AA amunition, smoke-making cannisters, aircraft engines, powdered milk, canned meat and dehydrated foodstuffs, as well as 100 RAF technicians to aid in servicing the additional fighters. The Squadron received a handful of new pilots from this latest consignment including Plt Offs E.L. Hetherington, A.S. Yates RAAF, and O.W.H. Berkeley-Hill; Flt Sgts J.W. Williams RCAF, B. Butler RCAF, H.J. Fox RCAF, an American, and L.A. Verrall RNZAF; Sgts C.G.S. De Nancrede RCAF, J.C. Gilbert, and J.C. Gray.

On 10 May the defenders were ready for the Axis raiders as never before. Two early morning reconnaissance sorties caused Spitfires to be scrambled, during which Plt Off Plagis claimed damage to a Messerschmitt. However, it was 1020 before a major raid approached, some 20 Ju87s and ten Ju88s making for Valetta to attack the *Welshman* under a heavy fighter escort. A smoke screen helped prevent the vessel from being hit, while 37 Spitfires and 13 Hurricanes rose to challenge the raiders — an unprecedented reception. 249 contributed five of the Spitfires led by Flt Lt Lee and, as they climbed steeply, they were attacked by Bf109Fs over Filfla. While Lee and Flg Off Buchanan engaged the Messerschmitts, the other three went after the dive-bombers, Plt Off Nash claiming two shot down:

> "Terrific party over Grand Harbour. All the Ju87s missed the target (two cruisers). Everyone got something. The Stukas stuck! Starboard wing came off one, the other disappeared into smoke screen at 200 feet!"

Sgt Brennan claimed another:

> "87 attacked — he literally flew apart . . . his radiator fell off, the air scoop broke away, the pilot's hood whirled off in one piece, and bits of the fuselage scattered in every direction — into the sea off Grand Harbour. Confirmed; another damaged; another 109 and 87 attacked — no results."

Plt Off Plagis claimed a further Stuka shot down north-east of Grand Harbour, but had initially experienced difficulty in finding a suitable target:

> "Flew seven miles out to sea to find Ju87 which didn't have a Spit on its tail."

Having evaded the Bf109Fs, both Lee and Buchanan engaged the Stukas and claimed one probable and one damaged, respectively. Frustratingly for him, Sgt Hesselyn (the sixth member of the flight) had suffered a flat tyre as he attempted to take off, and was obliged to watch the action from the ground:

> "The Hun was getting a hiding. I counted 12 opened parachutes drifting towards the sea. They were floating down lazily, presenting a curious contrast to the diving, twisting and turning aircraft. I watched two 109s crash, one by St Paul's Bay, the second at Naxxar. The latter burst into flames as it hit the ground."

His exuberance was somewhat stifled when it was later realised that the parachutes seen did not actually carry unfortunate German aircrew but parachute mines, released by the Ju88s.

After a minor alert at midday, the Luftwaffe returned at 1400, seven Ju88s covered by at least 30 Bf109Fs again raiding Grand Harbour, but again all bombs missed their target, the *Welshman*. 20 Spitfires, of which eight were from 249, were scrambled, accompanied by six Hurricanes. Only 249 reported decisive engagements, Sqn Ldr Grant claiming one bomber shot down in flames, while a probable was credited to Flg Off Buchanan. Sgt Hesselyn dived on the Ju88s and had just selected a target when a cannon shell burst in the cockpit of his Spitfire. Splinters tore his helmet, while another shell struck the port wing root. At that moment a Messerschmitt overshot him — probably his assailant — and he fired at this from 20 yards:

> "My shells struck first on his starboard wing and, as he flew across my line of fire, travelled right across his cockpit and then crashed into his port wing. Pieces flew off him in all directions. He seemed to be cut in half. His machine literally collapsed and went down in varying sizes."

Despite this graphic description, there were no witnesses and Hesselyn was credited only with a probable. However, it seems likely that his victim was Yellow 3 of II/JG53, from which Lt Dr. Heiner Jörg baled out into the sea; a launch set out from Malta to pick him up and he was rescued unhurt. The 35-year-old German pilot recalled:

> "Seeing three Spitfires below, I dived to deliver a frontal attack while my No2 manoeuvred into an up-sun position. After firing one burst I received a shot into my cooling system. I intended to fly as far away from Malta as possible, bale out and wait for the rescue Do24, but my cockpit rapidly became red hot. I baled out and was picked up by a launch."

He told his interrogators that he had shot down four aircraft during the brief Polish Campaign in 1939, but was then invalided for a year and only returned to flying operations in the autumn of 1941. He was posted to Sicily in December of that year and had since claimed two Hurricanes shot down over Malta.

As evening approached, another raid began to build up on the radar screens, and at 1740 ten Spitfires were sent up in readiness. As the raiders approached — five Z1007s with an escort of MC202s and Re2001s, followed by Ju87s and Ju88s with a large escort of Bf109Fs — more Spitfires were scrambled, including eight of 249 led by Flt Lt West. While other units engaged the bombers, the 249 flight was vectored on to the Messerschmitt escort, one of which was claimed shot down by Plt Off Watts; Plt Off Hetherington claimed a probable and Flt Lt West a damaged. The Squadron suffered no losses.

First Axis aircraft to appear over Malta on the morning of 11 May was a reconnaissance Ju88 with fighter escort. Four Spitfires of 249 scrambled at 0725, but Sgt Brennan at once force-landed with a faulty engine while the remaining three pursued the intruder back towards Sicily. On approaching the coast, eight Re2001s of 2° Gruppo CT — incorrectly identified by the Spitfire pilots as MC202s — were encountered and these attacked Plt Off Plagis, who had become separated; he later related:

> "I thought my last minute had come and decided to sell my life dearly. I flew straight at the nearest machine with the intention of ramming it. I did not fire a shot, but the Macchi pilot, suddenly realising his number might be up too, took violent evasive action, stalled and crashed into the sea."

One of the Italian pilots claimed hits on Plagis' Spitfire but, although his aircraft was not damaged, the Rhodesian was fortunate to get back safely due to lack of fuel, and landed with just three gallons in his tank.

Up to 15 Ju88s and about 40 Bf109Fs approached just before 1030 and 23 Spitfires were scrambled, including eight from 249 which were vectored onto a section of three bombers south-east of Kalafrana Bay. As Plt Off Plagis and Flt Sgt Williams dived on one of the bombers, eight Messerschmitts came down on them. Sgt Brennan called a warning and immediately engaged the attackers, becoming involved in an intense struggle during which he gained strikes on one but was almost shot down himself. He yelled over the R/T for help, Plt Offs Nash and McLean arriving to chase away his assailants, but at this point Brennan heard that more Bf109Fs were off Grand Harbour, and gave chase:

> "Chased two 109s and caught them about 20 miles north of Gozo. I gave the rear one a short burst, but saw no result. He began to turn. I turned inside him, and gave him another very short burst. He could not have been more than ten feet from the water, and suddenly his right wing hit the sea. He cartwheeled on his wingtips and tail once or twice, then blew up."

Meanwhile, Nash had claimed one of the Messerschmitts with which Brennan had previously been engaged:

> "Got one of them two miles off Grand Harbour — went straight in from 5,000 feet. Only fired 20 rounds cannon all from one gun from 50 yards."

McLean claimed another Bf109F damaged, while Williams believed he had probably destroyed a Ju88. At least one Messerschmitt fell in this action, no less a pilot than Maj von Maltzahn of JG53 being obliged to bale out into the sea off Valetta. Immediately his loss was known an intensive search was carried out, and he was successfully located towards evening in his dinghy, being safely picked up by a Do24.

While a handful of 249 was thus engaged, other bombers struck at Takali where a number of off-duty pilots were watching the blitz from the roof of Xara Palace, one of whom recalled:

> "As the attack went in and the bombs were falling, the Bofors batteries blazing away and the Spitfires mixing it up above with the 109s and 88s, Bob Sergeant came running up the stairs on to the terrace. He had barely called out 'what's happening?' when he was hit by a stray bullet which fell from the sky. It clipped his lower lip and jaw before lodging dangerously in his chest. It was a chance in a million, but an object lesson in the sense of tin-hat wearing."

Plt Off Sergeant was evacuated that evening to Gibraltar aboard a Hudson transport, and from there was flown to England by Sunderland a few days later.

12 May proved to be a day of more sustained fighter combat. After an initial abortive attempt by three patrolling Spitfires at intercepting an early morning reconnaissance aircraft, 30 Spitfires (including eight from 249) and two Hurricanes were scrambled at 1055 to engage six Ju88s and a dozen Bf109Fs of III/JG53 raiding Hal Far. Immediately after take-off, Sgt Hesselyn discovered that he had no oxygen supply and signalled Sgt Brennan accordingly. Consequently, Brennan stayed on his wing and the pair remained at low altitude. Here they witnessed a Spitfire of 603 Squadron crash into the sea, and immediately gave chase to its attacker, pursuing it out towards Sicily; Hesselyn reported:

> "I saw my shells striking the water behind the fleeing 109. I realised I was firing too low. I pulled up the nose of my aircraft and gave him another quick squirt. This time my shells must have hit him, although I did not see them do so. His speed slackened perceptibly . . . I throttled back to avoid overshooting him. His speed continued to slacken as we skimmed the sea at about 50 feet. I fired another burst, checked for skid, and gave him another and longer burst. This time I hit him squarely. He flicked over on his back, hung poised for a second, and dropped straight into the drink. I circled around him to see if the pilot would get out. He didn't."

Meanwhile, as Hesselyn was so engaged, Brennan was under attack by three others, all of which overshot without hitting him but the first then turned for a head-on attack. A cannon shell hit the portside of the Spitfire's armour-glass windscreen, which splintered, some of the splinters hitting Brennan in the left arm; his aircraft (BP953) flicked over and as a result went into a spin. The Messerschmitt departed, the pilot presumably believing that the Spitfire had been shot down, but Brennan was able to recover control and land at Takali. As Hesselyn returned to Malta he engaged another Bf109F and "blew half its tail off" but it dived away, covered by two others. The bombers had not escaped unscathed, one being claimed probably destroyed by Flt Lt West, who shared in damaging a second with Plt Off Linton.

Stukas returned to Malta on 13 May, 16 aircraft of III/StG3 escorted by 26 Bf109Fs raiding Hal Far at lunchtime. Eight Spitfires of 249 were among the dozen or so scrambled, but as Flt Lt West's section took off, Messerschmitts swept over and attempted to strafe them, albeit without result. Sgt Hesselyn, having escaped this attack, saw another Bf109F pass close by as he was climbing. Turning after it, he fired but failed to gain any strikes before he saw two more at the same height and got on the tail of the No2. Opening fire at 100 yards for two seconds, he reported that it dived straight into the sea, pouring smoke. R/T chatter then reported action over Kalafrana Bay, and on arrival there he spotted another Messerschmitt on a Spitfire's tail:

> "I went in at once, attacking from the starboard quarter. I could see my shells striking its fuselage. He turned on his back. I turned on mine, firing all the time. He started to go down in a gentle dive, and I kept firing to make sure of him. He crashed into the bay and, as he hit the water, Ronnie West's voice came to me over the R/T: 'Spit that just shot down that 109, thanks a hell of a lot!' "

The first main raid on 14 May was plotted approaching at 0900, when 28 Spitfires including eight from 249 were ordered off to intercept three Ju88s of 1/KGr806 and a number of Bf109F Jabo, all covered by a large fighter escort. The bombers raided Takali and Luqa, while the fighter-bombers also attacked Takali. Flt Lt West's section of four saw the Ju88s some 30 miles out and about 1,000 feet below their level. West attacked the centre bomber of three, claiming to have shot it down before firing at the port aircraft, which was also attacked by Plt Off Linton; they reported seeing it make off with an engine on fire. West then became involved with the Messerschmitt escort and claimed strikes on one before it evaded and escaped. Sgt Hesselyn attacked the bomber on the right of the section, seeing strikes along the fuselage and cockpit area, whereupon it blew up. It seems that he and West actually fired at the same aircraft, for apparently only one Ju88 — M7+FH flown by the Staffelkapitän, Hptm Emil Braun — failed to return. Flt Sgt Williams, meanwhile, pursued a Bf109F for some distance but was obliged to break away after registering some strikes. On returning to Takali he belly-landed, having exhausted his fuel.

Shortly after 1700, a further trio of KGr806 bombers approached, again under cover of a large fighter escort. Seven Spitfires of 249 were first off, well in advance of the raiders' arrival, and these at once attacked a number of Jabo Bf109Fs which had just bombed and strafed Hal Far. Flg Off Buchanan claimed one probably shot down, while Flt Sgt Harry Fox, an American from New York, called over the R/T that he had also shot one down; moments later, however, his Spitfire (BP878) crashed into the sea, victim of another Messerschmitt, probably that flown by Obfw Stumpf of 9/JG53*.

The Italians were back on the morning of 15 May, three S84s of 4° Gruppo BT, escorted by 30 MC202s of 4° Stormo CT, heading for St Paul's Bay at 0915, the crews briefed to bomb Fort Campbell barracks. A dozen Spitfires were scrambled including six from 249 and engaged the formation shortly after it had bombed, but only Flt Lt Lee was able to reach the bombers, claiming one damaged. Other Spitfires engaged the escort and newly commissioned Plt Off Verrall was able to get a telling burst into the Macchi flown by Cap Alberto Argenton, commander of the 91ᵃ Squadriglia, who was killed. Two hours later, a flight of 249 was scrambled to engage a fighter sweep by an estimated 40-50 Bf109Fs. All returned safely with Sgt Gray reporting engagements with two Messerschmitts, both of which he claimed damaged.

Early on the afternoon of 16 May a single Ju88, covered by an estimated 26 Bf109Fs (including five Jabo) and 15 Re2001s of 2° Gruppo CT, attacked Kalafrana. Six 249 Spitfires were scrambled at 1440, followed by five more from another squadron. Flg Off Buchanan

---

* By strange coincidence, Flt Sgt Harold J. Fox was the second 'Harry Fox' lost to the Squadron in a matter of weeks, Plt Off Harold M. Fox having been killed in action on 18 March.

claimed an Italian fighter shot down, which he believed was a Macchi, while Sgt De Nancrede reported gaining strikes on a Messerschmitt. Plt Off Plagis and Plt Off Nash engaged another with greater success. Nash recorded:

> "Damn good party with 109s off Kalafrana Bay. They attacked in pairs but Plagis and I fixed one from 300 yards. This is the 100th e/a destroyed on Malta by 249 Squadron."

It would seem they had shot down White 6 of JaboStaffel 10/JG53, although the pilot of this machine, Uffz Dr. Felix Sauer, thought his aircraft had either been hit by AA fire or that the subsequent explosion in his engine had been caused by a technical problem; he recalled:

> "Four Spitfires suddenly appeared. I moved to counter-attack but there was an explosion in the engine, which goes dead. I dived and escaped but there was nothing left to do, so I descend from 3,000 metres to 700 metres and take to my parachute. My comrades fly round me and make me understand that they have seen me, and that they will try to get some help. While baling out I hurt my chin and for a while was stunned. The cold water soon restored my senses. I detached myself from the parachute and inflated my small rubber boat." *

Two Spitfires of 249 were scrambled after a lone reconnaissance Ju88D from 1(F)/122 at 0700 on 17 May. They were expertly vectored onto the intruder, and Oblt Günther Steppmacher's F6+LH was intercepted over Valetta by Flg Off Buchanan and shot down into the sea; there were no survivors. A pair of Spitfires were again scrambled at 1155, joining six more from 603 Squadron, on the approach of a fighter-bomber raid. Plt Off Nash and Plt Off Verrall each reported shooting down a Messerschmitt, while Verrall claimed another damaged. Only one was lost, however, Lt Wolfgang Herrmann of 5/JG53 failing to return in Black 8. A second pilot of this unit baled out over Cap Scaramia, but allegedly as a consequence of technical problems. Another Messerschmitt then shot down Plt Off Peter Nash, who crashed to his death in BP951 near Dingli; the loss of the popular 20-year-old ace, with 11 victories to his credit, was a hard blow. He fell to either Uffz Erich Paczia or Lt Hans Märkstetter, both of 6/JG53, who each claimed Spitfires at more or less the same time; probably both fired on his aircraft.

An Italian ASR Z506B was out during the evening, protected by 19 Re2001s of 2° Gruppo, the formation being engaged by Spitfires of 601 Squadron. A series of dogfights ensued and 249 scrambled seven aircraft to assist. Having pursued the Italians out to sea, Plt Off Plagis fired at one of the Reggianes, which he identified as a MC202:

> "Chased a Macchi which strafed Hal Far. Caught up with him, fired every round at him 200 yards — and he got away — never forgive myself. Only damaged him."

Misidentifying the fleeing fighters as Messerschmitts, Sgt Brennan reported:

> "Exchanged shots with some 109s, but without result either side. Shot at by Spit."

Early on the morning of 18 May, 16 MC202s and eight Re2001s of 2° Gruppo CT set off towards Malta as cover for a number of Italian MTBs operating off the island. Four 249 aircraft were ordered to investigate, but at the last moment Sqn Ldr Grant's Spitfire became unserviceable. He rushed over to Sgt Brennan's aircraft and ordered him to lead the remaining trio then taxiing for take-off; they were soon followed by Flt Lt West, who scrambled to bring the flight up to strength, but when he caught up with the others he allowed Brennan to continue leading. About ten miles east of Zonqor, four fighters — believed to have been Macchis — were spotted 2,000 feet below and Brennan led an attack on these. He fired a short burst at one, seeing strikes on the port wing, but this pulled away and flew right across the nose of Sgt Gilbert's aircraft. The

---

* Uffz Dr. Felix Sauer would spend eight long days in his dinghy before he was rescued by an Italian craft from Sicily (see *Malta: The Spitfire Year, 1942* by the author with Christopher Shores and Nicola Malizia, published by Grub Street).

latter also fired and the Italian fighter fell away, pouring coolant. Brennan, meanwhile, was attacking another:

"He promptly went into a vertical dive. I followed him, caught him as he was pulling out of his dive at 2,000 feet and, getting dead behind him, gave him a long burst. He hung there for a second, rolled on his back, and hit the sea. As he crashed I saw another aircraft spin into the sea half a mile away. As I thought it might be one of our boys, I called up the others, and Ronnie [West] told me he had just shot down one of the Eyeties . . . The one Johnny [Gilbert] had hit force-landed at Zonqor Point, and it was then we learned that the Eyeties had not been Macchis, but Reggiane 2001s."

The force-landed Reggiane had been flown by Ten Remo Cazzolli, the leader of the 152ᵃ Squadriglia flight, who recalled:

"There were many Spitfires and few Re2001s, so when I ordered my pilots to break formation and engage, I found myself surrounded by Spitfires! As I opened fire, I saw before me in planform, like a cross, a Spitfire. I took aim and fired, seeing a long, black trail — possibly a sign that I had hit him . . . suddenly there was a terrible noise like thunder and my engine stopped; it was the fire of 20mm cannon, which overwhelmed my senses. I realised at once the situation, and my face was covered with blood; by instinct I sought to open the cockpit canopy, but it was stuck, a shell having struck behind the seat armour and crushed the canopy forward against the windscreen. I thought it was the end. I was in an aircraft with no power, a radiator shot away, a shattered aileron fluttering, with the earth of Malta coming up inexorably to meet me! I tried to recover control. I do not know what condition the tail of the aircraft was in, but the aircraft seemed to have a life of its own; it would not kill me! I saw a rock flush in the sea, there was an indescribable crash, and I passed out." *

Later the same morning, Sgt Gilbert was again successful in an action in defence of one of Malta's high-speed rescue launches which had just plucked from the sea two pilots, one British, one German, but was now being harrassed by other Bf109Fs. The Squadron despatched five aircraft at 1145 and these engaged a number of Messerschmitts, one of which Gilbert claimed shot down while Sgt Gray claimed a probable.

Far to the west of Malta there was further aerial action, as a naval force sailed eastwards to undertake the delivery of 17 more Spitfires to the island via *Eagle*. The first flight began taking off at first light, led by Flt Lt McNair. Flt Lt Lucas, who was to lead the second section, wrote:

"Buck's formation was off first in the early morning, all his aircraft disappearing ominously, one after the other, beneath the bows of the carrier as they left the flight deck before appearing as the undercarriage of each Spitfire came up and its airscrew bit into the air. We, who were to follow, would have preferred not to have witnessed this disturbing scene!"

Despite Lucas' misgivings, all the Spitfires got away safely and all arrived at Malta, three and a half hours later, where they landed at Takali.

The arrival of the latest Spitfire reinforcement coincided with a major withdrawal of Luftwaffe forces from Sicily for service in Libya and on the Russian front. One Bf109F Gruppe and two of Ju88s had already departed at the end of April, and were now followed by others, leaving only the Messerschmitts of II/JG53 and the Ju88s of KüFlGr606 and KGr806, plus the Regia Aeronautica units, which were soon reinforced from mainland Italy. The reduction of Axis strength on Sicily caused a sudden and most notable falling-off in activity over Malta.

---

* Ten Cazzolli was recovered from the wreck of his aircraft which had made a reasonable crash-landing near Fort St Leonard, and was taken to Mtarfa Hospital where he was wrapped in a plaster cast from head to toe, having suffered many fractures and contusions. He was later sent to the UK and was repatriated to Italy in 1943 in exchange for an RAF prisoner, and eventually made a good recovery (see *Malta: The Spitfire Year, 1942*).

During 19 May small numbers of Bf109Fs swept over the island, followed by three Z1007s escorted by a dozen Macchis, but 249 was not involved in any engagements. That night a raid on Takali destroyed one of the Squadron's unserviceable Spitfires, BR106, but caused very little damage otherwise. Next day, the Squadron was advised of the awards of DFCs to Sqn Ldr Grant, Flg Off Buchanan and Plt Off Nash (deceased), while Sgt Hesselyn received a Bar to his DFM, plus a commission.

The Squadron saw limited action again on the morning of 22 May when 20 Bf109Fs crossed the coast, four bombing Hal Far. Eight Spitfires scrambled and four from 249 intercepted two of the Messerschmitts off Kalafrana, Flt Lt McNair claiming one shot down. There followed another quiet period before the Squadron engaged in further combat during the afternoon of 25 May, eight Spitfires meeting three S84s of 4° Gruppo Aut BT escorted by 16 Re2001s with a dozen Bf109Fs as indirect cover. In the ensuing series of dogfights south-east of Takali, Flt Lt West claimed a Reggiane shot down and Sgt Brennan reported strikes on another, while Flt Lt McNair and Sgt De Nancrede each damaged Bf109Fs; McNair reported:

"As Green 3, when going to attack bombers, I saw an aircraft on my tail. I turned and found it to be a ME109. I gave fight and managed to get in two bursts on quarter astern attack: both seemed to be effective. The fight carried on until I lost him in cloud. Claim ME109 damaged."

Flt Lt Lee managed to penetrate the fighter screen and fired at one of the bombers, claiming it badly damaged; the same aircraft was also attacked by a pilot of 126 Squadron. All three of the bombers were in fact hit, two returning to Sicily with wounded on board. Flt Lt West's latest claim raised his personal tally to six and he was recommended for a DFC. He was somewhat of a character, as described by a 185 Squadron pilot, a relative newcomer to the island, on the occasion of the latter's visit to 249's Mess at Takali:

"When I went into the Mess there was a swarthy individual sitting in the hallway, naked except for his shorts and a towel wrapped around his head like a turban. He was sitting cross-legged and in front of him was a basket with a hunk of rope dangling over the side to represent a snake. This person was swaying back and forth and playing a clarinet, and rather well, too. I stopped and asked the pilot with me what the score was. He introduced me to the snake charmer, who was none other than Ronnie West, and who assured me, with a very straight face, that it was just a matter of time until all pilots went just as crazy as he was. After what we had gone through in the past weeks, this was easy to believe!"

The last week of May continued to prove relatively quiet for the defenders in general and for 249 in particular. Four of the Squadron's Spitfires were scrambled on the afternoon of 26 May, in company with others, but failed to engage a small Italian fighter sweep, two of which were shot down by another squadron. Next day, only four small formations of Bf109Fs were reported over the island; no interceptions were achieved by those Spitfires that were scrambled. Although the Squadron continued to put up patrols when required, no trade came its way until the beginning of the new month. May had seen the Squadron's tally rise by 31 confirmed, together with 11 probables and at least 24 damaged.

During the early morning of 2 June a raid was reported forming up over Sicily, and just after 0910 a total of 20 Spitfires — seven drawn from 249 — took off and climbed out to sea, encountering the incoming force some 15 miles east of Kalafrana. The raiders were three S84s escorted by almost two dozen Re2001s with 32 MC202s as indirect escort; their target was Safi. Although there were engagements, none of the 249 contingent made claims. Next day (3 June) saw the arrival of more reinforcements, 31 Spitfires being flown off the deck of *Eagle*. One flight was led by Plt Off Plagis who had been flown to Gibraltar with two other Malta veterans for the purpose. All went well with the launch of the Spitfires but on this occasion — for the first and only time — a dozen Bf109Fs of II/JG53 from Pantelleria made a successful interception of a Spitfire ferry and shot down four of the reinforcements, two near Pantelleria and two near Gozo. Aircraft from 249 and 601 Squadrons were scrambled to cover the new arrivals and to search for missing pilots. Flg Off Daddo-Langlois spotted one in the sea off Gozo, orbiting for an hour overhead, but sadly no help was forthcoming and the pilot drowned. It remains a matter of conjecture whether British Intelligence suspected the possibility of interception on this occasion, especially with having sent three particularly experienced Malta pilots to lead the new arrivals in. According to one of the survivors, Plagis had not performed very well during the ferry flight and two of those lost were his charges:

> "Near Pantelleria we saw some Messerschmitts sitting out there watching us for five minutes. I could see them getting in position, saw them closing. I recall 'T' [Flt Sgt Tom Beaumont] shouting the 109s were attacking. I saw them coming. Plagis suddenly rolled over and dived for the sea. He left the rest of us up there like sitting ducks. Those 109s flew in behind us and shot 'T' out of the sky. I had one or two on my tail and they followed me right down to the sea. I remember zig-zagging madly across the water, and in the finish I was on my own. I didn't know where I was, but I knew I had to steer a certain course which might bring me to Malta. It did." *

On his return to the island, Plagis learned that he had been promoted to Acting Flight Lieutenant and was posted to lead a Flight in 185 Squadron, as had Flt Lt West. The Squadron received a further three replacement pilots from the new delivery, all RCAF: Plt Off F.E. Jones, Wt Off C.B. Ramsay, and Flt Sgt R.G. Middlemiss.

At 0445 on the morning of 6 June four 249 aircraft were scrambled on the approach of two 'hostiles'. While climbing to gain altitude, a section of Spitfires from 185 Squadron spotted a Ju88 at sea level which they attacked. As the 249 section approached, Flt Lt Lucas, who was leading, reported that he believed he had seen the bomber fall into the sea. Two more Ju88s were then seen and attacked by the 249 quartet, Lucas and Plt Off Jones shooting down one and Plt Off Linton and Flt Sgt Butler jointly claiming the second. Of the action, Lucas wrote:

> "We got our attacks spot on. With all the advantage of height, each pair made a nicely judged, beam-to-quarter attack from opposite sides, pressed right home to near point-blank range . . . The shooting was good, so one attack from each side was enough to do it. As, first, Jonesie and then Micky [Butler] pulled away, I saw the port Ju88 start terraplaning over the water before rearing up and sinking in a cloud of spray."

The second quickly followed suit; Lucas continued:

> "We circled the spot for a full five minutes, climbing up to give fixes for the ground station (and, no doubt, the enemy) to pinpoint the area. There was no sign of survivors, only two patches of spreading oil and debris. I was sorry, for each crew and, in particular, each rear gunner had fought the attack in the best tradition of the Luftwaffe. But such is war."

The rear gunner of the aircraft attacked by Lucas had gained a hit on the engine of his Spitfire (BR109 C-30) before his own demise, necessitating an emergency landing at Hal Far. Records show that two Ju88s of KüFlGr606 were lost, 7T+HK flown by Uffz Heinz-Wolf Bartels and 7T+BL commanded by Lt Werner Dielas.

A second scramble was called an hour later, four more 249 aircraft and 11 from 603 Squadron going off to intercept five 50° Gruppo Z1007bis bombers (two from 210ª Squadriglia and three from 211ª Squadriglia) which attacked Safi, escorted by 24 MC202s of 155° Gruppo and a dozen Re2001s of 2° Gruppo. Wt Off Ramsay and Sgt Gilbert each claimed a Reggiane shot down; one, or both, had attacked Ten Leonardo Venturini of 358ª Squadriglia who radioed that he was about to ditch off Malta, but was lost. Sgt Gray claimed damage to a fighter he identified as a Bf109F, while Gilbert and Plt Off Watts reported damaging one of the bombers. This was the same aircraft attacked by two pilots of 603 Squadron; the bomber sustained damage

---

* Apparently two of the missing pilots, but not those from Plagis' flight, had encountered a FW58 communications aircraft which they shot down into the sea before the Messerschmitts engaged.

to its fuel tanks and engines but managed to return to Sicily. One of the Macchi pilots involved in this action was Ten Giovanni Ambrosio of 378ª Squadriglia, who had initially experienced engine problems but was then able to rejoin his flight:

"In the instant I retook my position, all the Macchis scattered in the sky. The aircraft were darting through the air. Were there enemy fighters? I had a moment of hesitation and once more found myself alone. Overhead I saw five to six fighters diving. I thought they were our Re2001s so I pulled up to join that flight. I realised when one was near me that it was a Spitfire, with coloured cockade and number on fuselage — I was his target. It tried to get on my tail but I took the advantage and fired a burst at one who seemed to be the leader. My tracers bent behind the tail of the enemy. I fired once more. This time I saw rounds enter the fuselage and 'crackle' over the engine of the Spitfire; black smoke emitted around the fuselage. After a swift reversal and in a dive, I unscrewed my neck to see if I was under the fire of other Spitfires."

By diving to sea level, Ambrosio evaded further attention and reached Gela safely. He had survived his first combat.

The day was still young, however, and at 0920 an estimated 20 Axis aircraft were reported searching to the east of Malta; in fact, 11 Re2001s led by Ten Col Aldo Quarantotti were out searching for the missing Venturini. They spotted some possible wreckage and oil where his aircraft was believed to have ditched but of the pilot there was no sign. While so engaged and flying low, they were attacked by four 249 Spitfires which had been scrambled, Flg Off Daddo-Langlois and Plt Off Jones each claiming a Reggiane shot down, while Plt Off Linton and Flt Sgt Butler each claimed one damaged. Four more 249 Spitfires, which had scrambled at 1020, then arrived and Wt Off Gray claimed damage to a Re2001 while Flt Lt Lucas reported strikes on a Bf109F. Daddo-Langlois recorded:

"Section met four Re2001s east of Zonqor. Jones destroyed one. I got one destroyed. Linton and I were jumped by four 109s. Running fight to Kalafrana from 15 miles out. These yellow-nose boys know their stuff."

One Reggiane flown by Ten Arnaldo De Merich had gone down at once and crashed into the sea, while a second — flown by Cap Salvatore Teia — had been seriously damaged and belly-landed on return to Caltagirone.

During the afternoon of 8 June, a dozen Spitfires of 249 were scrambled to intercept a dozen Bf109Fs, of which four were encountered, resulting in Butler's aircraft (BR312) sustaining damage; the Canadian crash-landed in a field near Takali and was slightly injured. He was possibly a victim of Oblt Michalski of 4/JG53.

Far to the west a further Spitfire reinforcement operation was underway — the third in less than a month — as 32 Spitfires were ferried towards the island aboard *Eagle*. Early on the morning of 9 June the Spitfires were launched. The flight was made safely and landings began at Takali from 1000 onwards. One aircraft, flown by future 249 notable Plt Off John McElroy RCAF, had damaged its tail on take-off and subsequently crashed on landing. The angry Wing Commander, not fully aware of the facts, immediately grounded the luckless Canadian and threatened to have him posted to the Middle East.

Among the new arrivals posted to 249 was another Canadian (a member of the RAF), Sgt George Beurling, already with two victories to his credit. He had achieved some notoriety and had not endeared himself to his superiors; with an obvious disregard for discipline, his posting to Malta was seen by some as a last chance for the young extrovert. Of the flight to Malta he later recalled:

"The weather was cloudy but we were told to expect excellent visibilty at Malta. The Wing Commander had said 'Keep your eyes peeled for Jerries as you near home. The last time we came down this way the blighters lay in wait between Tunis and Pantelleria and shot down three or four of them. Knocked every one of them into the sea and every pilot killed — just because he didn't keep his eyes peeled.' By 0605 the first eight were on the way, leaving the flight deck about two minutes apart. As each plane became airborne it climbed and made left-hand circuits of the carrier until joined by its mates. At 20,000 feet they formed up over the ship, then legged it for Malta, climbing hard. I went away with the third flight at 0630. Malta came into view at 0950 from 20,000 feet. My gang made Takali, all right side up, at 1030. Right then the war began in earnest for Sergeant Beurling!"

Others posted to the Squadron from the latest batch of new arrivals included Flg Off John Smith; Plt Offs J.H.R. Paradis RCAF, a French-Canadian; Harry Kelly, an American in the RAF; C.H. Lattimer RNZAF, and B.W. Spradley RCAF, another American; Flt Sgts L.G.C. de l'Ara, a former test pilot, and M.E. Tomkins; Sgts A.E. Budd, C.L. Baxter RAAF, and C.E. Mutch RCAF. Also posted to the Squadron was Wt Off J.D. Rae RNZAF, who had recently been discharged from hospital following an argument with a Messerschmitt while flying with 603 Squadron. Beurling continued:

"I was assigned to 249 Squadron, proud of its record as the fightinest outfit in the RAF, with 180 German and Italian aircraft in its bag when I joined. The Squadron Leader was Grant, a swell Englishman and a swell pilot. The Flight commanders were Laddie Lucas and Buck McNair, both top-drawer guys."

Ten 249 Spitfires were sent off at 1100 on 10 June when ten Bf109Fs and MC202s were reported attacking a patrolling minesweeper. During the ensuing skirmish, Wt Off Gray reported shooting down a Macchi, but on returning to Takali he undershot as he came in to land and crashed, although he suffered only minor injuries. A little while later an escorted Do24 approached the island and a dozen Spitfires were ordered off to investigate. Wt Off Ramsay claimed a Bf109F probable out of a dozen met, while Flt Lt Lucas and Plt Off Linton reported damaging the flying boat. During this engagement Obfw Rudolf Ehrenberger of 6/JG53 claimed a Spitfire shot down.

At 1810, eight more Spitfires took off led by the CO to cover the arrival of a formation of nine Beaufort torpedo-bombers flying in from Gibraltar, which had radioed that they were under attack by a single fighter. Before the Spitfires could reach them, however, they were diverted onto an incoming raid and met five Z1007s escorted by 27 MC202s and 19 Re2001s, with indirect support provided by Bf109Fs of II/JG53. A dozen more Spitfires were scrambled to assist those of 249. Sqn Ldr Grant claimed a Reggiane shot down (bringing his victory tally to at least five) and was undoubtedly the machine flown by Serg Giovanni Dringoli of 150ª Squadriglia; the pilot was believed to have been mortally wounded and his aircraft was seen to crash into the sea. Flt Sgt Williams claimed a second as damaged — probably Ten Agostino Celantano's aircraft which was badly damaged but managed to reach base — while Flt Lt McNair claimed a Bf109F for his eighth victory, seven of which had been claimed with 249; his victim may have been Uffz Heinrich Sedlmaier of 5/JG53 who was reported by the Luftwaffe to have been shot down north of Valetta, allegedly by AA. Wounded, he baled out and was subsequently rescued by an Axis craft.

An early morning raid on Luqa developed on 12 June, two Ju88s and 15 Bf109Fs carrying out the attack; little damage was done to the airfield. Fighters only comprised the next intrusion, eight Bf109Fs crossing the coast during mid-morning. 249 scrambled a dozen Spitfires and a number of dogfights developed. Sgt Beurling opened his Malta account when he claimed to have blown the tail off a Messerschmitt he attacked, but it was not seen to crash and he was credited only with a damaged. Wt Off Rae was also credited with a damaged, while Flg Off Daddo-Langlois recorded:

"Found myself alone with three [Bf109Fs], 15 miles out. Got shot up."

His aircraft (BR107 C-22) was hit in the tail, wings and fuselage, although he was able to fly it back to base.

Reduced Luftwaffe presence in Sicily and the regular deliveries of Spitfires by aircraft carrier had enabled the defence of Malta to be strengthened greatly by early June. Taking advantage of the improved situation provided by the increase in Malta's fighter defence, an important convoy had left the UK with the intention of resupplying the beseiged garrison. It passed through the Strait of Gibraltar in the early hours of 12 June, where it picked up a strong naval escort which included *Eagle* and *Argus*; on this occasion the carriers were not ferrying Spitfires but had embarked Sea Hurricanes and Fulmars for the defence of the convoy. As the convoy steadily progressed towards Malta, its fighter escort was involved in many aerial encounters with Axis reconnaissance aircraft, Sicily-based bombers and Italian warships though not without cost. As the two surviving freighters, of the five which had set out, came within range of Malta Spitfires, sections were despatched to provide added protection.

Activity over the convoy increased in the late morning of 15 June, when a strike force from Malta at last arrived to engage the Italian cruisers. Only two serviceable Beaufort torpedo-bombers with very inexperienced crews were available, together with four vulnerable torpedo-armed Royal Navy Albacore biplanes. The small formation had departed Malta at 0930 with the benefit of an escort of 16 Spitfires provided by the Squadron, but the latter had insufficient range and endurance to escort them the whole way. Despite an attack by two Macchis, the small strike force survived the action and all returned safely to Malta.

At 1800, four Squadron Spitfires were scrambled, followed by others from 185 Squadron. Three Messerschmitt-escorted Z1007bis were intercepted over the convoy — still 30 miles out — south-west of Gozo. Flt Sgt Williams claimed a Messerschmitt damaged and Flg Off Smith a bomber damaged. One of the quartet, BR364, crash-landed on return but the pilot was unhurt and the aircraft only slightly damaged. The final interception of the day occurred in the late evening when four Spitfires took off at 2105 — Plt Offs Linton, Jones and Watts led by Flt Lt Lucas — to intercept about a dozen KGr806 Ju88s heading for the ships, apparently relying on the dusk to protect them. Control ordered the Spitfires to orbit the convoy at 17,000 feet until the bombers came within range, but with dusk rapidly approaching Lucas realised the raiders would not be seen against the dark sea and took his section down to lower levels. The bombers were consequently sighted against the light western sky, as he later recalled:

> "The Ju88s were flying straight and level in quite tight boxes of four aircraft each. They hadn't seen us coming out of the darkening eastern sky. I gave the instructions . . . Lint and Watty would take the starboard box, and Jonesie and I the one to port. Then both pairs would have a go at the centre formation if we could. Our assault came off to a T. The rear gunners never saw us as we attacked upwards from underneath, against the dark waters below . . . It was difficult to see the results, but Watty and I reckoned that we had shared an 88 between us, Jonesie got another — a flamer — while Lint and I felt we had severely damaged an additional 88 apiece."

There seems little doubt that two of the bombers, M7+HL and M7+FK, flown by Uffz Heinz Kaufmann and Oblt Kurt Kehrer (the Staffelkapitän) respectively, were shot down in this action.

Malta had lost five Spitfires defending the convoy although none of these losses had occurred within 249. The ensuing few days were anti-climatic and the Squadron was not called into action again until the afternoon of 23 June, when a dozen Spitfires were scrambled at 1750 to intercept an incoming Italian raid of some size. This comprised three S84s from the 4° Gruppo BT, escorted by 27 MC202s of 155° Gruppo CT, with indirect support provided by 18 Re2001s of 2° Gruppo CT. The bombers were misidentified as Z1007s and Plt Off Lattimer fired at the one in the centre, reporting strikes. Meanwhile, Sgt Baxter engaged two of the Reggianes, reporting that one appeared to 'shake' after he had fired at it. AA shrapnel damaged the Spitfire flown by newly commissioned Plt Off Brennan as he approached the bombers but he landed safely. Despite these attacks, the bombers were able to release their bombs over the Takali area and three persons were killed in nearby Mosta, where a further six were injured.

Flt Lt Lucas was promoted to command the Squadron on 24 June, vice Sqn Ldr Grant, who was promoted to Wing Commander Flying at Takali. Daddo-Langlois was promoted to take over Lucas's Flight. Of this period, Lucas wrote:

"One June dawn, soon after I had taken over command of 249 Squadron from Stan Grant, I was sitting in my Spitfire at Takali at advance readiness. It was barely light, but already our radars were picking up the enemy moving south from Sicily. I heard a heavy thump on the fuselage of my aircraft. Looking down I was astonished to see the Governor and C-in-C [newly arrived Lord Gort VC], by himself, red tabs and all. Whipping my flying helmet off, I made as if to get down from the cockpit only to be met with a brusque, 'Stay there, Squadron Leader, stay there, please.'

Gort nipped up on the port wing of the Spitfire and held out his hand. 'Good morning, Squadron Leader, my name's Gort. I'm the Governor. I just called in to see the Squadron. I know how well 249 has been doing and I wanted to say so to you personally. Keep it up and good luck with the Squadron.' With that, he jumped down off the wing and started to talk to my groundcrew clustered around the blast pen. He knew their worth and, I gathered afterwards, saw to it that they understood it. Gort knew there was only one place from which to lead — from the front . . ."

Nothing much happened over Malta on 25 June until the late evening, when nine Bf109Fs on a fighter sweep approached the coast; at 2010 the Squadron was ordered to scramble a dozen Spitfires and these intercepted the Messerschmitts over Gozo. Plt Off Berkeley-Hill attacked a section of five, and grey smoke was seen to pour from the fuselage of one which turned over and dived away; it was seen by Sgt De Nancrede to stream coolant and Berkeley-Hill was credited with its probable destruction. Plt Off Lattimer attacked another from 100 yards astern, which poured black smoke and apparently went down out of control, then fired on a second from quarter astern and slightly below: he reported that "it blew up in the air". This was undoubtedly an aircraft from 4/JG53 which crashed in the sea near Gozo, from which the pilot was later rescued by an ASR craft from Sicily. Flt Sgt Maurice Tomkins was not so fortunate; he endeavoured to nurse his damaged Spitfire (BR382) back to Takali, as recalled by Sgt Beurling:

"Tommy Tomkins's Spit was pretty badly shot up and he was hit in the engine and radiator. He pulled out of the mix-up and tried to make Takali, instead of going over on his back and baling. At that he nearly made it. He came in over the island streaming glycol and trying his damnedest to stretch his glide. He cut it too fine and suddenly flicked into a spin at 150 feet, bursting into flames as he hit the ground."

Another to witness the crash was a pilot of 603 Squadron:

"This afternoon I was sitting in my kite ready to take-off when I heard a Spit in a power dive. Looked up and saw it coming down with glycol pouring out. The pilot made for the 'drome, did a circuit and started to fly across the 'drome at low speed. About half-way across, his motor cut dead. His wings started to wobble as he lost speed, heading straight for my kite. When almost directly overhead he tried to turn; he stalled at about 60 feet and spun. The aircraft immediately burst into flames. The fire tender was about to approach but the ammo started to go off so they stopped. The kite had nearly burnt itself out before they went near it. I went over to have a look and saw the pilot caught in amongst the wreckage . . . I could smell his clothes burning. It was Flt Sgt Tomkins, who sleeps next to me."

Four Squadron Spitfires scrambled during the morning of 27 June, led by Flt Lt Daddo-Langlois, and encountered a seaplane identified as a Do24 (which was in fact a Red Cross Z506B) with an escort of a dozen MC202s provided by 51° Stormo. They were searching for a Macchi pilot shot down the previous day. The Spitfire pilots reported bouncing eight 'Re2001s' 15 miles south-east of Sicily, Wt Off Rae claiming one shot down and a second probable, Flt Sgt Middlemiss one and a damaged, and Plt Off Verrall yet another. Apparently the wreckage of three of the Italian fighters was seen in the water within 200 yards of each other. In return, a Spitfire was claimed by one of the Italian pilots.

Two Spitfires, and two Beaufighter night fighters, took off at 0455 on 29 June to intercept raiders approaching the coast. Although they themselves were unsuccessful, the Spitfire pilots witnessed a Ju88 fall into the sea in flames, one of the two victims of the Beaufighters. The month ended with a brief skirmish with Bf109Fs when Plt Off Berkeley-Hill and Plt Off Lattimer had their aircraft damaged in combat, both having been bounced from the sun. Both force-landed at Takali, shaken but otherwise unhurt.

During the month of June, 249 had increased its tally by 15 confirmed, three probables and 18 damaged. Aircraft allocated to the Squadron, which up to now mainly carried the codes applied while aboard the delivery aircraft carriers, had the code letter 'T' painted on the fuselage for identification purposes. With the influx of new faces, a number of stalwarts left the Squadron including tour-expired Flt Lt McNair, together with two of the Squadron's more successful pilots, the inseparable Plt Offs Hesselyn and Brennan. Within the Squadron Wt Off Rae received his commission as did Flt Sgt Williams.

The relatively quiet spell which followed the arrival of the June convoy did not last long. The Regia Aeronautica was now planning a resumption of activities to be launched as the second major Italian assault against Malta, and due to commence on the first day of the new month. To support their allies, the Germans had also taken steps to reinforce Fliegerkorps II in Sicily, two bomber Gruppen arriving from France, together with a fighter Gruppe, I/JG77, from the Eastern Front. Commanded by Hptm Heinz Bär, credited with 113 victories, the three Staffels of I/JG77 boasted a sprinkling of aces including Oblt Fritz Geisshardt (82 victories), Oblt Siegfried Freytag (49) and Lt Günther Hannak (41).

Chapter Eight

BLOODY JULY

July 1942

". . . three streaming balls of smoke and flames falling slowly from the sky to the south of the island told the story. All three Cants [*sic*] had been destroyed."

Sqn Ldr Laddie Lucas, Commanding Officer of 249 Squadron

July opened fairly quietly with a reconnaissance Ju88, heavily escorted by Macchis and Messerschmitts, sweeping over the island during mid-afternoon. Spitfires rose to intercept although 249 was not called upon. Next day (2 July), however, the Squadron was heavily engaged, a dozen Spitfires led by Sqn Ldr Lucas being scrambled at 0920, in company with eight from 603 Squadron, on the approach of five Z1007bis of 33° Gruppo BT escorted by 24 MC202s of 51° Stormo and 15 Re2001s of 2° Gruppo CT. The Spitfire pilots misidentified the Italian fighters for Messerschmitts, one of which Flt Sgt T. Parks RCAF (recently transferred from 126 Squadron) claimed shot down; this was probably Sottoten Giuseppe Riccardi's Macchi of 351ª Squadriglia which crashed into the sea about 18 miles south-east of Valetta. A second was claimed probably destroyed by the CO while Plt Off McElroy damaged another.

Several of the Spitfires evaded the close escort and attacked the bombers, but could only claim damage before being forced away. Sgt De Nancrede joined three Spitfires of 603 Squadron in an attack on one Cant, gaining strikes, as did Wt Off Ramsay who attacked another. Both Canadians then engaged the escort each claiming strikes on their opponents before being chased away. The next raid — by three Ju88s of III/KG77 closely escorted by four Bf109Fs — was picked up on the radars at 1415; Luqa was the target for the attack where two civilians and two soldiers were killed, two others being wounded. Fifteen Spitfires were scrambled of which seven were flown by 249 pilots. The Squadron's Texan pilot, Plt Off Harry Kelly (BR184 T-C) failed to return, shot down by Messerschmitts of the escort, one of which Flt Sgt Middlemiss claimed. Of Kelly's loss, Beurling commented later:

"He'd been feeling like hell for days — a touch of the Dog, I guess — but wouldn't go sick. Getting into the action he had lagged out of formation for a moment and some watchful Hun had spotted him and dived. Over the R/T I heard somebody yell Harry's identification call. But the call came too late and one short burst got him."

Meanwhile, Plt Offs Linton and Spradley were joined by a pilot of 185 Squadron (Sgt Sim, a former member of the Squadron) in attacking a vic of bombers, two of which they claimed damaged. Flt Lt Daddo-Langlois pursued another for 40 miles before being able to shoot it down into the sea; members of Fw Herbert Leiwelt's crew of 3Z+JT were seen to bale out.*

The final attack of the day occurred between 1945 and 2020 when three S84s, with a close escort of ten MC202s of 151ª Squadriglia, approached. Seven 249 Spitfires had already been scrambled and these were joined by four more from 185 Squadron. Two of the fighters, again misidentified as Messerschmitts, were claimed damaged by Sqn Ldr Lucas and Flt Sgt Parks, though the aircraft (BR377 T-K) flown by Sgt De Nancrede was hit during a head-on attack and crash-landed at Takali. He was probably the victim of Cap Doglio Niclot, who claimed a Spitfire shot down during this action.

---

* Flt Lt Daddo-Langlois' victory was recorded as the Squadron's 100th while flying Spitfires, and its 199th to date; the 200th was registered on 4 July in an action when the Squadron claimed three S84s shot down.

Ten 249 Spitfires were up to meet the early morning raid on 4 July when three Z1007s and 14 fighters were reported approaching the coast just before 0900. The attacking force actually comprised three S84bis of 4° Gruppo BT, escorted by 22 MC202s of 51° Stormo, while a further 17 Macchis accompanied them as indirect escort. Before take-off, Sqn Ldr Lucas had briefed his pilots to go for the bombers, each section being instructed to tackle a given target:

> "Red Section — my section — would take the bomber on the port side; Blue Section, led by
> Raoul Daddo-Langlois, the one to starboard. Yellow Section, with Jack Rae in the lead, would
> split into two pairs to cover Red and Blue Sections from the fighters as they went in, and then
> if they were still disengaged, go for the leading bomber. The Squadron went straight through
> the fighter screen, unseen and unmolested, and closed fast with the bombers . . . In a few
> seconds all of us were diving straight for the ground with the fighter cover spreadeagled all
> over the sky above us. As we pulled out at deck level . . . three streaming balls of smoke and
> flames falling slowly from the sky to the south of the island told the story. All three Cants [sic]
> had been destroyed."

One was credited to Sqn Ldr Lucas, another to Plt Off Rae, the third falling jointly to Flt Lt Daddo-Langlois and Flt Sgt Middlemiss; MM24008 of 14ª Squadriglia flown by Serg Magg Romolo Cristiani, fell in flames near Takali, crashing into a field. The bodies of three crew members were found in the wreckage. A second bomber, MM23998 of 15ª Squadriglia flown by Ten Raffaele Notari, crashed into the sea some miles from Marsascala, but the third (also of 15ª Squadriglia), although badly damaged by fighter attack and AA fire, limped back to Sicily, its gunners claiming to have shot down a Spitfire. Three more Spitfires were claimed by the Macchis, one apiece being credited to Ten Col Aldo Remondino, Cap Ricardo Roveda and Mar Ennio Tarantola. Although the Spitfires flown by Daddo-Langlois and Middlemiss were shot-up, both made safe landings at Takali. There were two survivors from the shot down bombers including a gunner, AvSc Marc Arduino Perneschi from Cristiani's aircraft, who was rescued from the sea by HSL128; the coxswain, Flt Sgt Head, recorded:

> "This man, when found floating in his Mae West, appeared to be holding in his hand a white
> handkerchief. When rescued it was found that the 'white material' was the remains of his
> shattered hand, which had been washed clean of blood by the sea water. He had a resigned
> and pitiful look on his face which simply mirrored the horrors of war."

Perneschi told his captors:

> "[My aircraft] was one of three S84s which came over on a bombing/photo-recce raid. After
> releasing our bombs we ran into an AA barrage and the aircraft was hit several times and
> damaged. I was severely wounded by one of the bursts and jumped before the fighter attack
> which set the aircraft on fire."

The following day, Sqn Ldr Lucas, Flt Lt Daddo-Langlois and two others visited the survivors in the Military Hospital at St Patrick's Barracks, as Lucas recalled:

> "As I walked over to the bed occupied by one of the two survivors [Perneschi], a good-looking
> Italian in his middle to late twenties looked up at me with sad, plaintive dark eyes which seemed
> to be appealing for sympathy. As he gazed at me, he slowly and painfully lifted a heavily
> bandaged arm. The hand and a part of it had been blown off by a cannon shell during the attack.
> Sickened, I bent down and held the Italian's other hand in mine, shaking my head in sympathetic
> belief as I did so. I then turned away and at once withdrew to wait at the door of the ward while
> my other Squadron colleagues finished their conversations with the Italian through an inter-
> preter. The same evening, I told my two flight commanders that the Squadron's practice of
> visiting badly wounded prisoners — German or Italian — in hospital must cease forthwith.
> Those with commonplace and non-evocotive wounds were a different matter. I explained that
> a repetition of my emotive experience that afternoon could only harm morale."

Shortly before 2000 (on 4 July) the Italians were back, when five Z1007bis serenely sailed over Malta at 20,000 feet, their substantial escort provided by 20 Macchis of 20° Gruppo and ten Re2001s of 2° Gruppo. Eight 249 Spitfires were already up to meet this armada, Sqn Ldr Lucas again at their head, and were soon joined by a dozen more from 126 Squadron. The 249 formation engaged the escort, Plt Off McElroy claiming a Reggiane as probably destroyed, while Flt Sgt de l'Ara damaged another. Messerschmitts were also about, one of which attacked Lucas' aircraft (BR324 T-R), as he noted:

> "Shot up by a 109 and bounced by Reggianes while attacking five Cants!"

He was, however, able to land safely at Takali. His assailant was possibly Oblt Michalski of II/JG53 who claimed two Spitfires over Malta on this date, one in an earlier action against 603 Squadron.

Spitfires of 603 Squadron engaged the early morning raid on 6 July but could not prevent Ju88s bombing Takali, where a Spitfire was damaged in its blast pen. No sooner had 603 landed than 11 of 249 were off to meet the next raid, which comprised three Z1007bis of 9° Stormo BT with 14 Re2001s of 2° Gruppo CT as close support, and 24 MC202s of 20° Gruppo CT as indirect support. Yet more Macchis of 151ª Squadriglia flew a sweep in advance to clear the way for the bombers.

Flt Lt Lee led the Spitfires in a head-on attack on the Cants, causing them to jettison their bombs into the sea; four pilots — Lee, Flg Off Smith, Plt Off McLean and Sgt Beurling — claimed strikes as they swept past, although none of the bombers were seriously damaged. 20° Gruppo then engaged the Spitfires, Ten Francesco Montagnani claiming one but Serg Francesco Pecchiari of 352ª Squadriglia was shot down, almost certainly by Beurling. The Canadian reported shooting down in flames a Macchi attacking Smith's aircraft, before he engaged another, which also tried to get on Smith's tail; this was chased down vertically from 20,000 feet to 5,000 feet where it suddenly blew up. Flt Lee claimed another — or possibly the same — shot down in flames; it would seem that one of these claims actually related to an Re2001 rather than a Macchi since Sottoten Romano Pagliani of 152ª Squadriglia was shot down. He was seen to bale out although his No2 reported that his parachute failed to open. The stricken Reggiane crashed near Zejtun, five other 2° Gruppo aircraft returning with varying degrees of damage including that flown by Ten Col Quarantotti.

Meanwhile, the Macchi pilots of 151ª Squadriglia reported meeting five Spitfires apparently trying to cut off the escape route of the retreating bombers. Cap Doglio Niclot claimed one shot down, which his No2 reported crashed north of Valetta — this would have been Pagliani's Reggiane he had seen crashing rather than a Spitfire; a second Spitfire was claimed by Ten Michele Gallo, but 249 suffered no losses although the aircraft (BR246 T-J) flown by Plt Off Yates was shot-up, as was that flown by Sgt Beurling (BR323 T-S), whose two victories were confirmed by Flt Lt Lee. In the early afternoon, Beurling was called to fly escort for HSL128 searching for survivors and he reported that the two pilots he had shot down earlier were both recovered, but:

> "One died that night in hospital, badly burned. The other had been hit in the leg by a cannon
> shell and in the shoulders and arms with machine-gun bullets. The doc had to amputate the
> leg. The pilot survived."

However, available records suggest that only one of the Italian pilots was picked up from the sea, about three miles out from Kalafrana, by HSL128; possibly another craft picked up the other or the pilot actually came down on land, as seems more likely in Pagliani's case.

The final raid of the day occurred at 2030 when three Ju88s of II/KG77 swept in at low level to bomb Takali, escorted by Bf109Fs of II/JG53 and I/JG77, the latter unit making its first sorties over the island. Twenty Spitfires were scrambled including eight of 249. On this occasion 603 Squadron made a successful interception, shooting down three Ju88s and claiming two of the fighters. A third Messerschmitt was claimed by Sgt Beurling, who wrote:

". . . two ME's dropped on me, but I did a quick wing-over and got onto one's tail. He saw me coming and tried to climb away. I figured he must be about 800 yards away from me when I got him in the sights and let go at him. It was a full deflection shot, and I had to make plenty of allowance for cannon-drop. I gave him a three-seconds burst, smack on his starboard flank, and got him in the glycol tank. He started to stream the stuff, leaving a long white trail of smoke . . . I followed my man down to sea level, where he burst into flames and went into the drink."

Beurling's victim was probably Fw Anton Engels of 1/JG77 whose White 4 was reported to have crashed into the sea, although according to Lt Armin Köhler of 3/JG77 it was believed to have been shot down by AA fire.

Eleven 249 Spitfires were joined by six of 185 Squadron at 0730 on 7 July to intercept a dozen Ju88s heading for Luqa, escorted by two dozen Bf109Fs of II/JG53 and 30 MC202s. A swirling dogfight developed, the Messerschmitts and Macchis reacting strongly. Flt Lt Daddo-Langlois, flying BR565 T-U, noted:

"Three of us went for the bombers but 109s prevented us getting them. Shot up again. Bob [Middlemiss] baled out OK."

Plt Off Rae added:

" . . . jumped Blue Section from all angles. Flt Sgt Middlemiss shot down — OK, Flt Sgt Parks hit by flak — OK."

While Sqn Ldr Lucas noted:

"Shaky do with 88s and 109s. Paul [Brennan] and Lint [Linton] got 109s, Mac [McElroy] a Macchi."

It was Plt Off Brennan's last operational flight of his tour:

"Scramble. I intercepted six Ju88s with heavy fighter escort. Head-on attack on Ju88. No result observed. Attacked and shot ME109 down into sea. Damaged another."

Brennan's victim, his 10th, was seen to go down into the sea in a vicious spiral; a second was claimed by Linton, while McElroy claimed a Macchi and Flt Sgt Parks damaged a Ju88 but his aircraft (BR165 T-Y) was hit by AA fire directed at the bombers, which blew off its tail and he baled out, coming down on land near Zebbug with nothing worse than a bruised eye. Middlemiss was shot down by the Messerschmitts and sustained slight injuries when he baled out of BR251 T-E into the sea; he was seen to scramble into his dinghy. Spitfires were soon out searching for him, covering the sea south and east of the island; he was located by Plt Off Brennan and Flt Sgt de l'Ara to the east, and was soon on his way back to the island in the care of HSL128. 185 Squadron also lost a Spitfire in this action.

The next raid proved just as costly for the defenders, when Spitfires from 249 and 126 Squadrons clashed with 18 Messerschmitts. Plt Off Rae reported that the pilot baled out of the Messerschmitt he attacked head-on, but two Spitfires were also shot down including BP990 flown by Sgt De Nancrede, both pilots being picked up by the crew of the hard-working HSL128. De Nancrede had been attacking a Ju88 from below and had seen strikes on its belly and wing roots when the German gunner replied with an accurate burst, hitting his engine. Two other Spitfires were hit and were both obliged to crash-land on return, including BR347 T-Z flown by Flg Off Hetherington, who escaped unscathed, his aircraft also having been hit by return fire from the Ju88 he was attacking, which he claimed badly damaged.

The morning of 8 July began with a raid at 0730 by seven Ju88s on Luqa, the bombers escorted by Bf109Fs of I/JG77 and 21 MC202s of 20° Gruppo. This formation was intercepted by 24 Spitfires, eight of which were from 249 although these were sent off after the attack had commenced. By the time the Squadron joined the action, two Spitfires had already been shot down and two others had crash-landed. As they attempted to engage the bombers, the 249 flight became entangled with the escort. A Bf109F passed closely above Plt Off Hesselyn's aircraft: he pulled up, fired and saw the Messerschmitt turn on its back and go straight into the sea. Sgt Beurling got his sights on another and fired a two-seconds burst; black smoke poured out and he too reported that it went into the sea, three miles off Gozo, confirmed by two Hal Far pilots. Meanwhile, Plt Off Williams damaged another while Sgt Baxter belly-landed BR295 T-H at Takali, although on this occasion not due to combat damage but to lack of fuel.

The Luftwaffe was back just after midday, a total of 23 Spitfires intercepting seven Ju88s of II/KG77 and a dozen escorting II/JG53 Messerschmitts; the bombers again attacked Luqa. 249 was in the forefront and broke through the fighter screen to reach the bombers, Plt Off Hesselyn gaining strikes on one, causing an engine to catch fire, which he claimed shot down for his 12th and last victory whilst flying over Malta; he went on to damage a second. Plt Off Williams reported damaging another, which turned for home. He kept after it, attacking until it crashed in flames off Filfla. One of these was undoubtedly 3Z+GR flown by Oblt Erich Behr, the Staffelkapitän of 7 Staffel, who was reported lost with his crew. A fourth bomber was damaged by Plt Off Berkeley-Hill, while another was fired at by Sgt Beurling who reported seeing flames appear from its starboard engine, before he was himself attacked by five Messerschmitts. He claimed strikes on one which dived for Filfla with its engine apparently on fire, and was credited with its probable destruction.

Flg Off John Smith and Sgt Johnny Gilbert were also attacking the bombers when a number of Bf109Fs dived on them. Smith's Spitfire (BR233 T-Q) caught fire and was then hit by two more Messerschmitts before he could bale out, and blew up. The same fighters then attacked Gilbert's aircraft (BR227 T-T), which turned on its back and went into the sea off Wied iz-Zurrieq. Both pilots were killed. Sgt Beurling wrote later:

> "Smitty took fire on the first burst. Two more Messerschmitts bored in and pasted him again, blowing his Spit to bits and giving Smitty no chance to bale out, if he was still alive. The same gang got Gil in the same second of sudden death. He simply went over on his back and fell headlong into the sea."

Plt Off McLean claimed one of the Messerschmitts damaged, but others badly damaged the aircraft flown by Flt Sgt Butler although he was able to land safely. It seems likely that they had been engaged by Messerschmitts flown by Oblt Michalski, Fw Paczia and Uffz Egbert Willenbrink, each of whom claimed a Spitfire shot down. Sgt Beurling was successful in driving off other fighters when they attempted to attack Plt Off Williams, as the latter pursued another Ju88, which he claimed damaged.

Seven Ju88s raided Luqa and Safi at 1300 on 9 July, while escorting Macchis from 20° Gruppo and Bf109Fs of I/JG77 clashed with Spitfires, although Plt Offs McElroy and Rae broke through the fighter screen and jointly claimed a bomber shot down; a second was damaged by Plt Off Paradis before his own aircraft (BR128 3-W) was attacked and damaged by a Messerschmitt. Following his attack on the Ju88, Rae then engaged a Macchi which he claimed probably destroyed. Takali was the target for six Ju88s during an evening raid which approached the coast shortly before 2000, escorted by Bf109Fs from both II/JG53 and I/JG77. Eight 249 Spitfires were among the 35 scrambled at intervals but, on this occasion were held back from the main action. There occurred a brief skirmish with Messerschmitts and one was claimed damaged by Plt Off Jones.

Nineteen MC202s of 20° Gruppo and six of 155° Gruppo CT, together with Bf109Fs from II/JG53, provided cover for 14 Ju88s raiding Takali on 10 July. Spitfires first engaged when the raiders were still some 20 miles off Malta, then the fighters clashed south of Rabat, including seven of 249. Plt Off Lattimer reported damaging a Messerschmitt and shooting down a Macchi, probably Mar Ennio Tarantola's aircraft which was badly damaged in the fuselage and fuel tank; the Italian pilot was however able to reach base safely. Meanwhile, Sgt Beurling engaged a Messerschmitt which he hit "in the belly"; apparently the burst killed the pilot as the aircraft reportedly dived straight into the sea. This was possibly Lt Hans-Jürgen Frodien of Stab/JG53 who was shot down near Rabat, his demise witnessed by a pilot of 126 Squadron:

"Stood on porch watching raid and we saw a long spiral at about 2,000 feet — a 109 had been shot up. Pilot baled out. The aircraft came streaking down and crashed straight into rock about 300 yards from us. We could see the markings clearly. Got tail wheel as souvenir."

At 1115, six 249 Spitfires joined a dozen others to meet the next raid, comprising six Ju88s with an escort of Messerschmitts from I/JG77 and a small number of MC202s from 20° Gruppo. The 249 flight led by Flg Off Hetherington dived onto a formation of Macchis, one of which Sgt Beurling engaged:

"The Eyetie went into a steep dive, pulled out and twisted away, rolled and pulled into a climb. Finally he went into a loop at the end of this climb and I nabbed him just at its top. A two-seconds burst blew his cockpit apart. The pilot baled out in a hell of a hurry. I circled over him as his parachute opened. He seemed to be healthy, so I gave 'May Day' on the R/T, specifying that the gent was Italian, not one of our boys."

It would seem likely that Beurling's victim was Serg Magg Francesco Visenti of 378ª Squadriglia, who had just shared in shooting down a Spitfire of 126 Squadron. He baled out wounded in an arm and leg and was rescued from the sea three hours later by a Z506B floatplane from Sicily. This latest victory raised Beurling's Malta tally to five in just four days. Plt Off Williams was credited with a Messerschmitt and Flt Sgt Butler gained strikes on another; a Bf109F crash-landed at Comiso on return and may have been involved in this action.

There was a short, sharp raid on Takali by 13 Ju88s between 0925 and 0955 on 11 July, when a petrol bowser was destroyed and a steam roller damaged. Only a few of the dozen 249 pilots vectored to intercept them were able to make claims, the large fighter escort — 23 MC202s and two dozen Bf109Fs — successfully warding off attacks. Sqn Ldr Lucas gained strikes on one bomber while Plt Off Yates and Wt Off Ramsay shared in the claimed destruction of a Messerschmitt. Flt Lt Daddo-Langlois also claimed one, an aircraft of Stab/JG53 which crashed near St Julians: he recorded:

"Bounced fighters escorting 12 Ju88s. Got a 109. Pilot baled out on land."

The uninjured 22-year-old Lt Heinz Riedel was taken prisoner by soldiers from the nearby Ta'Giorni AA battery. He later told his captors:

"I was in a section of two and was about to engage Spitfires flying below when I was hit [he believed his aircraft had been hit by AA fire]. I told my section leader I was returning to base but then received another hit. My aircraft went out of control and I baled out."

249 was not involved in the afternoon raid but was called into action at 1810 on the approach of ten Ju88s, 16 Macchis and two dozen Bf109Fs, the bombers heading for Takali. There ensued a series of engagements with the escorting fighters, Plt Off Jones claiming one Messerschmitt shot down and another as damaged. Two more were damaged by Plt Off Paradis and Flt Sgt Parks, but a fourth Canadian, Wt Off Charles Ramsay was shot down in BR111 T-M and lost. Beurling commented:

"Nobody saw what happened. When we all came home Chuck just wasn't there . . . old Mother Mediterranean had claimed another good Canuck."

The badly-damaged Spitfire (BR347) flown by Flt Sgt de l'Ara was escorted back to Takali by others, where it crash-landed, slightly injuring the pilot. Two more 249 Spitfires were despatched to search for the missing Ramsay, but nothing was sighted. Macchi pilots claimed two Spitfires shot down including one by Cap Doglio Niclot, while the Messerschmitt pilots claimed three: Oblt Geisshardt of 3/JG77 was credited with his 83rd victory while Uffz Simon Pohlein, also of

3 Staffel, claimed his first, over Gozo; the other was credited to Lt Karl-Heinz Preu of Stab/JG53.

A dozen Ju88s attacked Takali on the morning of 12 July, but patrolling Spitfires failed to find them and had just landed to refuel as the bombers swept overhead, resulting in damage to six of the Spitfires. One of those on the ground at Takali was LAC Metcalf, who wrote in his diary:

> "Flt Sgt Matthews and myself were in a slit trench outside the dispersal hut when it got hit with a 500lb HE. The joint collapsed like a pack of cards. In our trench Chiefy and I did two complete loops and a half-roll before we hit the deck. What a to-do it was. We both thought we'd had it for certain. I was thankful for the corrugated iron sheet over the top of the trench. It saved us both a cracked skull."

Meanwhile, 249 attempted to engage as the raiders raced out to sea again, but were frustrated by the strong fighter escort comprising 18 Macchis, 16 Reggianes and a dozen Messerschmitts, which prevented them from reaching the bombers. One section spotted Ten Francesco Vichi's 358ª Squadriglia Re2001 about 25 miles north of Gozo, Sgt Beurling firing a one-second burst at this, following which the pilot baled out. Apparently this aircraft was also attacked by Flg Off Hetherington, as witnessed by Plt Off Berkeley-Hill who called over the radio "I saw it, Hether old boy!", but Berkeley-Hill's aircraft (BR324 T-R) was then attacked by two fighters, reported to be Messerschmitts, and was shot down; the 20-year-old Anglo-Indian was killed.

Despite bad weather, Ten Col Aldo Quarantotti, commander of 2° Gruppo, at once led three others to search for the missing Tenente Vichi, but as they flew low over the sea one Reggiane was forced to return early with engine trouble. Fifteen minutes later, Mar Antonio Patriarca returned to Gela on his own. Neither Quarantotti nor Ten Carlo Seganti came back, and it was believed by the Italians that they might have collided; in fact, both had been shot down by Sgt Beurling. The Canadian and his section leader, Flg Off Hetherington, on returning from the earlier sortie, had volunteered to search for their missing colleague, Berkeley-Hill, when the two low-flying Italian fighters were seen in low cloud. Although misidentifying these as Macchis, they correctly assumed that they were also searching for their own missing pilot. Hetherington climbed to give cover while Beurling pursued one which was lagging:

> "The boys must have been intent on the search for their missing sidekick, for I swear neither had seen me yet. I simply sneaked up behind the tail-ender [probably Seganti] and gave him a one-second squirt. He burst into flames and went down. Without further ado I whipped around on the other lad . . . I came right underneath his tail. I was going faster than he was; about 50 yards behind. I was tending to overshoot . . . I closed up to 30 yards and I was on his port side coming in at about 15° angle. I could see all the details in his face because he turned and looked at me just as I had a bead on him."

Beurling fired a short burst which apparently decapitated the pilot, adding:

> "He dived in beside his mate. From the firing of the first shot until both Macchis [sic] went down no more than six or seven seconds had elapsed. Things happen fast in this racket." *

An even larger force of bombers — two Staffeln from II/KG77 comprising 18 Ju88s — were briefed to carry out the early morning raid on Luqa on 13 July, arriving over the airfield at about 0800. Two dozen Spitfires from 126, 185 and 603 Squadrons rose to the challenge, claiming at least two bombers before the escorting Bf109Fs, MC202s and Re2001s intervened. Eight 249 Spitfires were scrambled late — too late to catch the bombers and instead engaged Macchis of 20° Gruppo, although Plt Off Rae identified his victims as Reggianes, one of which he claimed shot down before gaining strikes on two others, while Plt Off McElroy identified both his opponents as Messerschmitts, claiming one destroyed and one damaged. Pilots of 126 Squadron

---

* Neither Ten Col Quarantotti nor Ten Seganti survived; both were posthumously awarded the Medaglia d'Oro, Italy's highest award for bravery.

also claimed a Macchi shot down and a probable in this action, although only two were lost in which Sottoten Rosario Longo and Sottoten Pietro Menaldi, both of 151ª Squadriglia, were killed. 126 Squadron lost a Spitfire from which the pilot was rescued, slightly wounded, and three other Spitfires were damaged, including BR565 T-U flown by Sqn Ldr Lucas:

"It always used to be said that if you could actually recognize a 109 in the mirror, it was too late. Now, I could identify not one but four of them in line astern, coming in from five o'clock and a little above in a fast curving arc. As I whipped my aircraft over into a tight diving turn towards the attack, a salvo of 20mm cannon shells hammered into the starboard wing of the Spitfire with strikes from 7.9mm machine-gun incendiaries along the side of the engine.

As the smoke and heat increased in the cockpit, tiny flames started to lick the engine cowlings along the top of the nose in front of me. I was still at 18,000 to 20,000 feet over the sea, five or six miles south-east of the island, losing height in tight diving turns. I tugged at the black rubber toggle at the top of the cockpit to release the canopy. The bobble came away in my hand. The hood was stuck fast. I was now at 15,000 feet, still over the sea, two or three miles out from Kalafrana Bay; the heat and smoke were intensifying. Then, astonishingly, as I went on diving, the smoke in the cockpit began to thin and the heat perceptibly to lessen. The flickering flames at the side of the nose seemed to have gone out."

The CO headed for the nearest airfield, Hal Far, where he successfully landed downwind without flaps and amid a shower of red Very lights, in the path of two Swordfish which were just taking off:

"The aeroplane came to a stop 20 yards from what had once been a hangar or a store. I must then have blacked out, with the noonday sun blazing down on the cockpit and the effect of the delayed shock, for the next thing I was conscious of was an airframe fitter on either side of me, with tools, trying to lever the canopy backwards along its runners . . ."

A flight of seven 249 Spitfires was airborne during the late afternoon but failed to sight raiders which bombed Takali at about 1730; nonetheless, Plt Off Jones was bounced by an unobserved fighter and had his elevator controls shot away, but got down safely.

The second Italian offensive against Malta, though not officially over, was now almost at a standstill. Italian bombers had practically ceased operating and the steam was certainly going out of their fighter force. The first raid on the morning of 14 July was by seven Ju88s of KüFlGr606 which bombed Luqa shortly after 1000. A large force of Spitfires from all four squadrons — 30 aircraft — were waiting to ward off the raiders, two of which were promptly shot down before the fighters clashed. Plt Off Williams damaged one of the Messerschmitts, but two of the seven 249 Spitfires were hit in return, Flg Off Hetherington being obliged to force-land BR379 T-V at Hal Far, while Sgt Beurling (BR130) was wounded in the heel by shrapnel from an explosive bullet:

". . . I spotted a batch of Macchis, travelling in a tight V about 500 feet below me and a mile away. I went in to break them up. As I did, three Messerschmitts and two Reggianes came out of the sun at me from opposite angles, putting the scissors on me. I had to break one way or the other in a hurry, so I decided to let the Reggianes shoot at me, as they have less fire-power than MEs. The bastards riddled the old Spit! They put better than 20 bullets through the fuselage and wings.

An explosive bullet nicked my right heel. I did a half-roll and went away in a hurry as another bunch of Reggianes ganged me. From that moment the Spit was in no shape to fight, but I messed around and kept our friends as busy as I could, keeping clear of any close-in action. I limped home to be kidded to death by the rest of the guys for getting myself shot up."

As the assault on Malta cooled, stock could be taken. Since the beginning of the month — in just two weeks of concentrated fighting — the defenders had lost some 36 Spitfires destroyed or badly damaged in action. This represented about 40% of all available fighters with half as many again having suffered damage of a lesser degree. Although losses of pilots had been at a much lower level, the rate of attrition of Spitfires was indeed severe. Of this total, 249 had suffered eight aircraft totally destroyed with five pilots killed; a further five Spitfires had force-landed and at least ten others had sustained varying degrees of combat damage, with two pilots injured or wounded, albeit not seriously.

Help was on the way however, for *Eagle* had again sailed from Gibraltar with a deck cargo of 32 Spitfire Vcs, 31 of which reached Malta safely on the morning of 15 July; one crashed on take-off. One flight was led to the island by Flg Off Watts, who had been flown to Gibraltar aboard a Hudson, with others, for the task. With the arrival of so many replacement pilots, all the Spitfire units received an influx of new faces to replace those tour-expired, several of whom were posted to the Squadron including Plt Offs K.C.M. Giddings, J.L. Lowry RCAF (an American), V.K. Moody RCAF, R.P. Round RNZAF, Flt Sgt G.A. Hogarth RCAF, Sgts H.G. Brydon RCAF, V.H. Wynn RCAF (another American), W.S. Shewell RCAF, D.F. Ritchie RCAF, and M. Irving Gass.

Another new arrival was Air Vice-Marshal Sir Keith Park MC DFC, former commander of RAF Fighter Command's 11 Group, who was now to take over as AOC Malta from Air Vice-Marshal Lloyd. The new AOC soon issued his 'Fighter Interception Plan' which called for interceptions to be made north of the island, well out to sea, before the bombers could reach their targets. This strategy was now possible with the numbers of Spitfires being made available by the carrier deliveries. The plan necessitated three squadrons working together; one to intercept the high cover, the second to engage the bombers' close escort, while the third would make a head-on attack on the bombers about 10 miles from Malta's coast. If a fourth squadron was available, it would be responsible for the interception of any bombers which broke through the fighter screen.

To meet the afternoon raid on 18 July, eight of 249 scrambled at 1405, followed by eight more from 126 Squadron 15 minutes later. The former chased a single Ju88, obviously a reconnaissance aircraft, and 15 escorting Bf109Fs at sea level, but Plt Off Chuck McLean was bounced by others and his aircraft (BR323 T-S) was hit and caught fire. It took the Canadian a full minute to escape from the inferno, by which time he was badly burned about his arms, thighs, groin, chest and face, and was barely able to pull the ripcord of his parachute. On splashing into the sea about four miles off Gozo, he was too weak to inflate his dinghy and floated instead in his Mae West — fortunately for only 15 minutes — until HSL107 came speeding to his aid. The launch had been alerted by Sgt Brydon, who had witnessed McLean's plight and had circled him on his way down. A second Squadron aircraft was also hit in this encounter and Plt Off Lattimer was slightly wounded, but he managed to crash-land BR107 at Takali without further injury. The Luftwaffe fighter pilots, from both II/JG53 and I/JG77, were credited with three victories, one of which was claimed north of Valetta by Lt Heinz-Edgar Berres of 1/JG77, a second by Oblt Freytag, the Staffelkapitän's 60th victory, while the third was credited to Lt Franz Schiess of Stab/JG53.

The Squadron was in action again on the afternoon of 20 July, eight Spitfires being scrambled to assist those of 185 Squadron engaged with Ju88s and Messerschmitts off the coast. Although they intercepted the bombers there were no tangible results, except that Sgt Wynn found himself under attack by a Bf109F of I/JG77 which damaged his aircraft (BP867 T-E) and slightly wounded him in one leg.

Next day (21 July) saw the successful arrival at Malta of a further 28 Spitfires which had been ferried from Gibraltar by *Eagle*; one of the flights was led by 249's Plt Off Jones who had been flown to Gibraltar with three other Malta veterans for the task. These new arrivals more than restored the strength of the defences and allowed some changes to be made. At Luqa, 1435 Flight was re-formed, this time as a day fighter unit equipped with some of the surplus Spitfires. Among the pilots posted to this unit were 249's Plt Off Lattimer (now recovered from his wounds) and Sgt Baxter. Among new pilots posted to 249 were Flg Off D.G. Newman, a Malta veteran formerly with 603 Squadron, plus newcomer Sgt R.W. Lamont RCAF. There was now a complete change of command for 249, Sqn Ldr Lucas and his Flight commanders, Flt Lts Daddo-Langlois and Lee, preparing to leave for the UK. The news had been broken to them in the bar, as Lucas, who had been awarded the DFC earlier in the month, noted:

"Leaving 249 which, for months, had been my life, and where I found friendship, kindness and loyalty, was just like going away to school. I longed suddenly to be picked up from the bar, parcelled up and, without anyone else noticing, deposited by some magic spirit in London, without having to say any goodbyes. I didn't know how I was going to face them. I was close to tears when I put my head on the pillow of my bed that night. Exhaustion leaves you with no resistance once you let go."

Newly promoted Sqn Ldr R.A. Mitchell was posted in from 603 Squadron to take over command, Flg Offs Hetherington and Watts being promoted within the Squadron to take over the Flights. The new CO had run up an impressive tally since his arrival at Malta in May, being credited with four confirmed plus two shared, two probables and eight damaged; he had also survived being shot down into the sea.

Fourteen Spitfires from 126 and 249 Squadrons intercepted the late morning raid on 22 July, when still some 20 miles off Zonqor Point, but two promptly fell to I/JG77's escorting Messerschmitts including Plt Off Jean Paradis, the Squadron's French-Canadian. Paradis had just spotted three Ju88s which formed the nucleus of the raid, and yelled excitedly over the R/T, when his aircraft (BR128) was bounced and shot down. A pilot of 126 Squadron saw the Spitfire splash into the sea and orbited the point of entry, only to be shot down by another Messerschmitt; both pilots were lost. Paradis had been a particular friend of Sgt Beurling, who reflected:

"Jean and I had always been good friends. Only a couple of days before his last scramble we had gone swimming together at Sliema — we were just a couple of kids who lived within 100 miles of each other back home."

Eight Spitfires led by Sqn Ldr Mitchell were the first to be engaged during the mid-morning raid on 23 July when three Ju88s and a dozen fighters — estimated as seven Bf109Fs and five Re2001s — were met at 15,000 feet, heading for Luqa. Diving from out of the sun, through the top cover, the CO reported shooting down one bomber which apparently dived straight into the sea; two more were damaged by Sgt Beurling and Flt Lt Hetherington, both of which were left with smoke streaming from their starboard engines. Beurling then engaged a Reggiane which dived on him, and reported blowing off its port wing with a deflection shot, the wreck crashing into the sea. The Squadron was again involved in the afternoon raid when five Ju88s bombed Luqa. Flt Lt Watts led his flight after the bombers but the Messerschmitt escort kept them busy, one of which Watts and Plt Off McElroy jointly claimed probably destroyed; McElroy claimed a second damaged and another was damaged by Plt Off Round.

Following three quieter days, six of 249 were ordered off at 0855 on the morning of 27 July, joining with 16 other Spitfires to engage a formation of nine Ju88s heading for Takali, but arrived too late to prevent an attack on the airfield. Two Spitfires were badly damaged on the ground; later, when a delayed action bomb exploded, a further two together with a pair of Hurricanes were also damaged. As Spitfires of 126 Squadron pursued the bombers out to sea, escorting Macchis moved in to provide assistance but were spotted by the 249 flight; the indefatigable Sgt Beurling later recalled:

"I spotted four Macchis running in line astern and took Number Four. They saw me coming and pulled into a climbing turn to the right. As they did I came up on my man's starboard quarter and let him have a burst. It was a straight deflection shot which went into his engine and radiator. He flicked into a spin, but managed to pull out and crash-landed on Gozo, able to walk away from the mess."

The Italian pilot, Serg Magg Falerio Gelli of 378ª Squadriglia, who had claimed three Malta Spitfires during his tour, later told his captors:

"I saw one Spitfire firing at me but felt no hits. I took violent evasive action and when disengaged noticed that the engine temperature was mounting rapidly. I turned north in an effort to reach my base but soon realised I could not do this as my oil tank was hit, as well as my radiator. I turned back and force-landed on Gozo, getting away with a few bruises." *

Having disposed of the Macchi, Beurling immediately latched onto another, which was seen to waggle its wings as he closed in and opened fire:

"The poor devil simply blew to pieces in the air."

So died Cap Furio Doglio Niclot, commander of 151ª Squadriglia and one of Italy's leading fighter pilots, having claimed six victories plus three more shared. The 34-year-old former test pilot was killed instantly†. Andrenalin must have been pumping into Beurling's veins as he moved towards the next Macchi, only to be distracted by a couple of Messerschmitts he spotted below. He immediately half-rolled and pulled up under them, getting in a full burst into the fuel tank of one. He reported that it, too, went down and he still had sufficient ammunition remaining to knock pieces off the wings and tail of the other one before it evaded and disappeared from view. Other pilots of the flight were also engaged with the Messerschmitts: Sgt Brydon believed his attack killed the pilot of the one he engaged as it was reported to have dived straight into the sea from 20,000 feet, and Plt Off Williams claimed another.

Lunch was interrupted at Takali by the approach of five Ju88s, but defending fighters prevented them from reaching their objectives. All four squadrons had aircraft up, a total of 25 Spitfires including six from 249, in an attempt to comply with the new AOC's latest instructions. On this occasion, the 249 flight was tasked to engage the escorting Bf109Fs, a number of which were spotted circling around the descending parachutes of crew members of three shot down Ju88s. Plt Off Williams and Sgt Brydon dived on these but the former's aircraft (BP976 T-C) was attacked by another and shot up quite badly. As Williams headed back to Luqa he spotted a lone Messerschmitt below him which he attacked in a dive: a quick burst and he reported that the German fighter burst into flames and went into the sea. Sgt Beurling joined the fight and saw two Messerschmitts:

"I started chasing one of them around in tight turns and we split-arsed uphill and downdale until he went into a dive to get away. I went along, picked him up in the sights and put a one-second squirt into his glycol tank. He rolled over and went into the sea from 1,000 feet. During the mix-up I had been on the second ME's tail for a split second, just long enough to give him a quick one. He streamed black, oily smoke from his engine."

Either Williams or Beurling had attacked Uffz Heinrich Freckmann's Yellow 11 which fell into the sea off Cap Scaramia as a result of combat; the 6/JG53 pilot was posted missing. The final raid of the day occurred just before 2000, three Ju88s being escorted towards Luqa by Bf109Fs and MC202s of 51° Stormo. Again 249 was involved in the interception, seven Spitfires joining eight others from 603 Squadron, but only Plt Off Rae was able to make any definite claims; he reported the probable destruction of a Messerschmitt before he went on to damage a Macchi, which he misidentified as a Reggiane.

At 1130 on 28 July, five Ju88s with an escort of 16 Bf109Fs and four MC202s were intercepted well north of the island by 23 Spitfires of 185 and 249 Squadrons, only two of the raiders eventually crossing the coast to attack Hal Far. 249's pilots reported intercepting three bombers, eight Bf109Fs and two Re2001s, obviously misidentifying the Italian fighters; there were no conclusive results of the ensuing action in which Sqn Ldr Mitchell claimed one bomber probably destroyed:

"I sighted three Ju88s 5-6,000 feet below us and dived sharply on them. I attacked first, full beam, closing to astern and observed strikes on both mainplanes and fuselage. As I broke

---

* Sgt Beurling later visited Serg Magg Gelli in hospital.
† Cap Furio Doglio Niclot was awarded the Medaglia d'Oro posthumously.

away I observed both engines pouring black smoke and the aircraft diving steeply. This was observed by Plt Off McElroy, No3 of my section."

Plt Off Rae and Sgt Irving Gass shared the probable destruction of a second of the bombers, as Rae reported:

"I carried straight in on the bombers opening fire on the rear one from about 300 yards on the beam, closing to almost astern; strikes were observed on the fuselage. I broke down and underneath this e/a. The fire from the rear gunner ceased before breaking away. I then came up underneath the leading bomber, opening fire for about three seconds from almost dead astern. E/a commenced smoking from starboard engine and wing root. Sgt [Irving] Gass also attacked this e/a observing it smoking before attacking."

Plt Off Yates damaged one more. Others tangled with the escorting fighters, Flt Sgt Parks being credited with a Messerschmitt probably destroyed, while Sgt Wynn and Plt Off McElroy damaged two more; the latter also claimed damage to an Italian fighter.

The following morning (29 July), seven 249 Spitfires were scrambled at 0915 to intercept a sweep by an estimated 16 Bf109Fs and four MC202s, which came in after an earlier raid had turned back before reaching the island. After an initial skirmish, one fighter dived out of the sun on Sgt Beurling's Spitfire (BR301 UF-S), shooting off the cockpit canopy. Beurling immediately turned onto the tail of what he believed to be the aircraft which had just attacked him, and from 450 yards fired a one-second burst which hit the engine of the Messerschmitt. At once it went down in flames into the sea 500 yards off Sliema Point, as Beurling's subsequent Combat Report revealed:

"As Tiger Blue 1, I attacked 15 ME109s over Grand Harbour. Dogfighting ensued for 15-20 minutes. Made an attack on one e/a from port quarter below; gave a three-seconds burst cannon and machine-gun fire; large pieces of e/a came off, then e/a's gas tank exploded and the aircraft burned. E/a struck the sea one mile north of Grand Harbour."

His victim on this occasion was almost certainly Uffz Karl-Heinz Witschke flying Yellow 2 of 3/JG77, who had claimed his own third victory a day earlier. The action was witnessed by a pilot of 126 Squadron:

"Watched a Spit attack a 109 while on the beach bathing. It went down in flames and crashed about half a mile out to sea. Pilot baled out but apparently his 'chute burned because he splashed in shortly after from several thousand feet."

It seems unlikely, however, that Witschke had been the pilot who attacked Beurling's aircraft, for two claims were submitted by the Luftwaffe, one by Oblt Geisshardt of 3/JG77 (his 86th victory), and the other by Obfw Rollwage of II/JG53. One of these apparently related to Beurling and the other to another member of the 249 flight, Sgt Budd, who returned to Takali with a damaged aircraft (BR131 T-O) and crashed on landing, although he was unhurt. He reported shooting the fin and rudder off a second fighter, which he believed was another Messerschmitt, and this also fell into the sea. It seems likely that he had misidentified his victim, for Serg Domenico Manini baled out of his 378ª Squadriglia Macchi about three miles south of Marsascala, from where he was picked up by a British minesweeper and taken to Malta.

Although the Squadron was involved in two scrambles on 30 July, contact was not made with the enemy on either occasion. Shortly before 1600, at least six Axis fighters crossed the coast at great height, but again no contact was made by the four 249 Spitfires which were up at the time. The Spitfires were actually escorting a captured Cant seaplane* from Zonqor to Kalafrana, where it would be repaired, serviced and given new colours. It was intended that from now on it would serve Malta as a rescue craft.

The Squadron was not called upon during the last day of July, a month which had opened with two weeks of intensive operations before a slackening in aerial activity. Indeed, this was now the end of the Regia Aeronautica's offensive: all further operations by Italian fighters were suspended due to low serviceability caused by excessive vibration problems being experienced with the Macchi 202s when they dived after, or away from, Spitfires. One aircraft had already been lost in this manner when its pilot baled out over the Sicilian coast.

During July, Malta's Spitfire pilots had flown 1,780 sorties and had claimed 137 aircraft shot down, of which 249 was credited with 43, almost equalling its previous highest monthly total (September 1940). The price had been high, however: 38 Malta Spitfires had been lost from which almost half the pilots had been saved. The Squadron had suffered ten of these aircraft losses in which six of its pilots had been killed and another severely burned. On a brighter note, the Squadron's outstanding Canadian pilot, Sgt Beurling, received two DFMs and a commission; he was now the island's leading fighter pilot with 17 victories, 15 of which had been scored during July.

---

* The Cant Z506B had been highjacked by the crew of a Beaufort torpedo-bomber which had been shot down off southern Greece two days earlier. The crew had been rescued by the Italians and flown to Preveska, a Greek mainland harbour. The following morning they were put aboard another for the flight to Italy and imprisonment but managed to overpower the guard and crew, then ordered the pilot at gunpoint to fly to Malta where, on arrival, the Cant was attacked by a flight of Spitfires and forced to alight on the sea where it remained until HSL107 came to its rescue: see *Malta: The Spitfire Year, 1942* for the full story.

Chapter Nine

THE FINAL BLITZ — THE BATTLE IS WON
August — October 1942

"... I think that it was the pilot's unlucky day for his 'chute never opened and I remember
him flashing past my eyes to disappear in a cloud of dust 50 yards distant."

An eyewitness report of a 249 Squadron victory during the October blitz

The first day of August was notable by its lack of aerial activity over Malta; it was not until three
hours before midnight that the air raid alarms sounded in earnest, which heralded a small scale
raid by half a dozen Italian bombers. Although there was limited action over the island during
the ensuing week, 249 was not actively involved until 8 August when seven Spitfires scrambled at
0830 to intercept a small formation of Bf109Fs of I/JG77; two of the Spitfires were obliged to return
early but the remaining five engaged the intruders. Newly commissioned Plt Off Beurling fired at
one as it headed northwards, but was jumped by two more. He claimed that he hit one in the
glycol tank and engine with a two and a half-seconds burst, and that it went straight into the sea.
This was apparently confirmed by his section leader. Beurling's aircraft (EN973 T-T) was then
hit and the engine almost seized; having decided against baling out, he carried out a successful
belly-landing in a ploughed, stoned-walled field, as he later recalled:

"As I came close in over the wall I put the left wing down to take up the bump and bellied
down into the ground. The wing absorbed the wallop and stopped me cold. The far wall was
too near for comfort. I climbed out, unhurt except for a superficial cut in one arm."

Plt Off Jones (BP867 T-E), who was leading Blue Section, also claimed a Bf109F shot down:

"Six enemy aircraft passed overhead . . . we turned towards e/a and saw two more coming
down on our tails. I told Blue Section to spiral down to draw e/a down. I saw e/a attacking
Blue 2, Sgt Budd, and warned him. He broke in front of me followed by the e/a which appeared
in front of my nose at less than 15 yards, presenting his belly to me at point-blank range.
I fired a burst of one second and then was forced to break as I was being fired at myself. E/a
disappeared and was seen by my No3 [Beurling] to be going down smoking and in obvious
distress. I fired a short burst at close range at another ME109 but saw no results."

Sgt Budd claimed damage to one more but his own aircraft (BR131 T-O) was also hit and
damaged, and he sustained shoulder wounds. Despite his injuries, he succeeded in landing safely.
A number of Spitfires of 126 Squadron were scrambled at 1020 to aid those of 249, but lost one
and its pilot in the action. The Luftwaffe reported later that 20 Bf109Fs of II/JG77 and II/JG53
had encountered 30 RAF fighters and claimed three shot down, Oblt Freytag and Fw Otto Pohl
of the former unit being credited with one apiece (probably the 249 aircraft), while the third
was claimed by Obfw Rollwage of II/JG53 as his 30th victim.

On the evening of 9 August, Flt Lt Hetherington and Plt Off Beurling were despatched to
search the southern coastline of Sicily for signs of a reported MTB flotilla. Although nothing
untoward was sighted on this occasion, packs of such Italian and German craft were indeed
active and would cause havoc when let loose amongst an approaching convoy.

The ending of the second Italian offensive against Malta coincided with preparations to
run a further convoy through the Western Mediterranean. The arrival of only two damaged
freighters in June had done little to alleviate the ultimate problem facing the defenders —

starvation, both in terms of food and fuel. Hence, a large convoy comprising 13 heavily laden freighters and the American tanker *Ohio* had departed the Clyde in late July, heading for Gibraltar where a strong naval force, including four aircraft carriers (one of which carried 38 Spitfires for Malta), was being assembled to escort the convoy towards its destination. The convoy and its escort finally sailed from Gibraltar at dawn on 10 August, the Spitfires being flown off during the early afternoon of the following day; all but one reached Malta safely. Several of the new arrivals were posted to the Squadron including Flt Lt E.N. Woods DFC, who took command of the Squadron on 18 August vice tour-expired Sqn Ldr Mitchell; others were Plt Offs R. Seed, J.G.W. Farmer, A.F. Roscoe RCAF (an American), Flt Sgts J.G. Sanderson RAAF, E.T. Hiskens RAAF, B.C. Peters, and Sgts E.F. Crosswell and P. Carter RCAF.

Meanwhile, German and Italian reconnaissance aircraft had located the convoy and a ferocious series of bomber and torpedo-bomber assaults were launched. The defending Sea Hurricanes, Fulmars and Martlets, together with the escort's guns, gallantly repelled raid after raid but could not prevent the loss of nine of the 13 merchantmen. In two days' fighting, the Fleet Air Arm pilots claimed 39 Axis aircraft shot down and several more probables for the loss of seven Sea Hurricanes, four Fulmars and two Martlets; eight pilots, one observer and two TAGs were killed.

By the morning of 13 August, the leading vessels of the convoy at last found themselves within range of Malta's fighters, and during the course of the day flights of Spitfires were despatched at intervals to provide some protection. A flight from 249 led by Flt Lt Watts saw action at about 1430 south of Pantelleria, when two S79s of 30° Gruppo were sighted. Before they escaped, Watts managed to get in a burst of fire at what he identified as a Fiat BR20, slightly damaging the 55ª Squadriglia bomber. A further section of Spitfires had followed at 1400 to patrol over the convoy, but the aircraft (BR246 T-J) flown by Flt Sgt Parks was hit by AA fire from the convoy's escorts; he baled out into the sea, slightly wounded, and was picked up by a destroyer from which he was eventually disembarked at Gibraltar. The Squadron was not immediately notified of his rescue and Parks had been posted missing for some time before details of his whereabouts were received at Malta*. A later patrol encountered a lone reconnaissance Ju88 of 2(F)/122 at about 14,000 feet, some 15 miles east of Linosa, which Plt Off Jones attacked at once; his head-on pass peppered the nose and wings, while Sgt Wynn gained strikes on the fuselage. Plt Off Beurling then waded in and shot out the starboard engine; the Junkers, F6+KK, went down in flames. Uffz Hans-Joachim Schmiedgen and his observer were lost, though two others baled out and were both rescued from the sea including wounded Fw Johann Brenner, who was picked up by a Fiat RS14 floatplane.

Another Italian floatplane was operating to the west of Malta at about 1515 on the afternoon of 14 August, although this was the captured Z506B now wearing RAF colours. With Wg Cdr Satchell at the controls and with an escort of four Spitfires provided by 126 Squadron, it was searching for a missing Beaufighter crew, shot down while supporting the convoy. Three of the escorting Spitfires were distracted by three Italian fighters, leaving the remaining two to protect the Cant but one of these had to return to Malta with engine problems. Shortly after 1530, a section of 249 Spitfires, flying cover for the tanker, spotted the floatplane and Flg Off Newman led Flt Sgts de l'Ara and Hogarth plus Sgt Lamont into the attack. Fortunately for the Wing Commander and his crew, the Spitfires suffered iced-up windscreens which prevented an accurate attack being carried out and the floatplane was not hit.

During this traumatic period of time, Malta did not remain entirely raid-free. At 1825, Spitfires of 249 were scrambled, the pilots meeting a trio of Bf109Fs over Hal Far, probably on a reconnaissance. Flt Sgt Hiskens claimed damage to one but another, flown by Oblt Michalski of 4/JG53, surprised Flt Sgt Hogarth and shot down his aircraft (EP207), from which he baled out safely into the sea, being rescued by HSL128.

---

* A colleague wrote of Flt Sgt Thurne (Tommy) Parks RCAF: "Tommy was a tough hard-nosed kid. He took exception at the food served to the Sergeant Pilots on board the ship taking him and others to the UK from Canada, and led a rebellion against the ship's company. As a result this was classed as a mutiny and he ended up at the OTU as a Corporal pilot. He actually joined an RAF squadron as a Corporal but the RAF CO had this rectified in short order."

With all surviving vessels of the convoy safely gathered in by the evening of 15 August, stock could be taken. Although the convoy had almost been annihilated and 300 merchant seamen had lost their lives, the four freighters which reached Malta had on board some 32,000 tons of provisions, while the severely damaged tanker limped into harbour, supported by two destroyers and towed by tugs. Malta now had food, ammunition, fuel and more Spitfires — she could fight on. On 17 August a further batch of reinforcement Spitfires arrived, having flown from the carrier *Furious*, which made her second run from Gibraltar; 29 of the 32 launched reached Malta safely, although one crashed on landing; one flight was led by Flg Off McElroy who had been sent back to Gibraltar specifically for the task. The influx of reinforcing pilots allowed further releases of tour-expired pilots, and among those leaving the island were Flt Lt Watts and Plt Off Linton; newly promoted Flt Lt Jones took over Watts' flight. Also leaving the Squadron at this time was Flg Off Newman, who joined 229 Squadron only to be killed in action a few days later. Of the latest batch of reinforcing pilots to arrive, only Sgt A.B. Stead RNZAF joined 249. This was Stead's second attempt to reach Malta. He had been aboard *Furious* earlier in the month (11 August) but on becoming airborne on that occasion had discovered that his long-range tank was not feeding through. Initially, the pilots had been told that should they experience problems immediately following take-off, they were to bale out ahead of the nearest destroyer which would pick them up if not too busy! This was greeted with so much adverse comment that it was agreed that should problems arise, a landing could be attempted on the nearest carrier. Stead favoured the latter option, and having carried out a low pass over HMS *Indomitable* (which was escorting *Furious*), successfully landed at the second attempt.

20 August was to herald a new era for Malta's fighter pilots: the first official offensive fighter sweep over southern Sicily; its objective was to draw the enemy into the air. Grp Capt W.M. Churchill DSO DFC, who had recently arrived at Malta, led the 18 Spitfires from 229 and 249 Squadrons, but the operation proved to be something of an anti-climax, as Plt Off Beurling recorded:

"We formed up south of the island and whisked across the water in three layers . . . we swept into Sicily over Cap Scaramia and took a look at each of the main enemy airfields at Comiso, Biscari and Gela. Not a Jerry stirred. Not a drop of flak was poured up at us. We rolled along, coming out over Cap Scaramia and beetled home. Nothing much to it, bar the pleasure of sticking your nose into the enemy's country for a change."

A second offensive sweep was carried out the following afternoon by a total of 23 Spitfires from four squadrons, including a quartet from 249. Axis fighters again refused to be drawn up to challenge. But they were there, as recent aerial reconnaissance of Sicilian airfields had revealed about 175 fighters and in excess of 100 Ju88s plus at least 50 Italian bombers. Since there was no bomber force at Malta to attack these concentrations of aircraft, three redundant Hurricanes were each fitted with two 250lb bombs and were made ready to operate as fighter-bombers, flown by FAA volunteer pilots. The first such raid was carried out against Gela and Biscari airfields on the afternoon of 23 August, the Hurricanes escorted by eight 249 Spitfires and four from 229 Squadron; one Hurricane was obliged to return early but the other two released their bombs over their respective targets. The covering Spitfire pilots spotted two Bf109Fs but no contact was made.

24 August proved to be a quiet day for the defenders, although Beauforts and Beaufighters from Malta attacked an Axis convoy off the southern tip of Corfu during the afternoon. One Beaufort was shot down and a second badly damaged, the latter struggling back to Malta with an ailing engine. When it was detected on Malta's radars, two 249 Spitfires were scrambled to investigate; Plt Offs Beurling and Farmer encountered the crippled aircraft 40 miles east of the island and escorted it back to Luqa, where it successfully belly-landed.

Even though 25 August was relatively uneventful for Malta's Spitfires, 249 lost two aircraft and both pilots. At 1130, the Squadron scrambled ten aircraft when at least 30 Bf109Fs were reported approaching Grand Harbour. Three of these were spotted at 21,000 feet and two promptly turned into the sun and dived on the Spitfires, one getting on the tail of the aircraft (BP976 T-C) flown by Plt Off Reg Round, shooting it down into the sea; the New Zealander was killed, a pilot of 126 Squadron witnessing his demise:

"He was hit high up and slowly glided in swooping circles, throttled back or engine quit, into
the sea off St Julian's Bay, where our Mess was, and where we were swimming. I guess he
was killed high up, poor chap."

Ten Squadron Spitfires took off at 1745, together with nine more from 229 Squadron, for a sweep
over southern Sicily, when they were to also escort three RNAS Hurricanes to raid Biscari.
Shortly after take-off, the Hurricanes were recalled owing to adverse weather conditions,
although the Spitfires continued the sweep. As the force headed northwards, Flt Sgt Basil Butler
(known to his friends as Micky) called out that his aircraft had suffered a malfunction of its
hydromatic propeller, and that he was going to bale out. However, before he could do so, the
Spitfire (EN695) dived vertically into the sea.

Greater things were afoot, however, for a major strike against Sicilian airfields had been
planned following the lack of reaction during recent fighter incursions. Just before 1000, ten
Spitfires of 185 Squadron headed for Comiso, followed five minutes later by eight from 229
Squadron bound for Biscari. Finally, Sqn Ldr Woods took off at the head of a further eight from
249 five minutes after the departure of 229 Squadron; their target was Gela where, on arrival
at low level, Red and Blue Sections attacked the west and east dispersal pens respectively. They
turned away across the barracks north-west of the aerodrome, re-crossing the coast at 300 feet
over Gela town.

During the strafing attack, one Ju88 was claimed destroyed on the ground by Plt Off Seed,
and an MC202 by Sqn Ldr Woods; it was believed that three airmen seen working on the Macchi
had been killed (in fact, one airman of 155° Gruppo CT was killed and two of 102° Gruppo
wounded). Plt Off Williams was credited with the probable destruction of a Ju87, apparently
an aircraft of 102° Gruppo which was destroyed by fire but not before three of the unit's ground
personnel had managed to remove the 1000kg bomb with which it was armed. Sgt Brydon was
credited with probably destroying a Ju88 and Sgt Shewell a Bf109F, while another Messerschmitt was claimed damaged by Flt Lt Hetherington. The CO reported:

"We approached the aerodrome from the south-east corner and attacked four Macchi 202s
parked on the perimeter. I saw strikes all along the fuselage and cockpit, then an explosion.
I turned left at 0 feet and attacked a group of soldiers or airmen, killing or wounding them.
There were no more suitable targets, so I set course for base. After crossing the Sicilian coast
on our return, a very large column of black smoke was seen coming from the aerodrome."

Of his part in the operation, Plt Off Seed (Red 3) recalled:

"I saw a Ju88 parked outside a hangar on the north-west corner of the field. I opened fire at
about 400 yards and gave a four-seconds burst. I saw many strikes and the aircraft caught
fire. Several mechanics who were working on the port engine on a ladder fell to the ground.
I turned to port and followed Red Leader out to sea over Gela Town. About three miles out
to sea I attacked a two-masted, motor-driven cutter of about 80 feet. I saw cannon and
machine-gun strikes from the water line to the bridge. Tiger Blue 4, who was a distance behind,
reported smoke coming from it."

While attacking Comiso, 185 Squadron lost an aircraft which force-landed with its pilot taken
prisoner, while Grp Capt Churchill, flying with 229 Squadron against Biscari, was shot down
and killed. Apart from these losses, the operation was considered a great success.

Next day (28 August), during a scramble by seven Spitfires of 249 and nine more of 229
Squadron, the aircraft flown by Plt Off Roscoe was involved in a collision with one from the
other squadron shortly after take-off, but both pilots were able to land safely; the American
Roscoe was posted to 229 Squadron as a flight commander shortly after this incident.

September opened quietly for the defenders and there were no operations of any note on
the first day, but action returned next day (2 September) when four of 249 took off at 1305 for
an offensive reconnaissance over Sicily, passing inland west of Licata some 25 minutes later.
Macchis from the 51° Stormo were scrambled from Gela to intercept, and near Cap Scalambria

one of the these, flown by Sottoten Emanuele De Seta, was seen at 16,000 feet. The Spitfires were at the same height, so they split up and Flt Lt Hetherington made a stern attack from 50 yards while Wg Cdr A.H. Donaldson DFC AFC (Wing Commander Flying, Takali) fired several bursts from 200 yards, and Plt Off Farmer then made a beam to stern attack, closing to within about ten yards. All three gained hits on De Seta's aircraft and the tail came off as the Macchi went down streaming coolant. The Italian pilot was able to bale out and was picked up safely from the sea.

There was little activity over Malta during the next few days, but on the morning of 5 September an incoming plot caused six 249 Spitfires to be scrambled at 0855, followed ten minutes later by five of 185 Squadron; one of the former was obliged to return early when the cockpit hood blew off. Four Bf109Fs were spotted over the Grand Harbour at 25,000 feet, then six more at 32,000 feet; the latter were attacked by 249, Plt Offs Williams and Giddings each claiming a damaged.

Just as 249 was starting to get a taste for the offensive forays over Sicily, orders arrived from London effectively curtailing such freelance operations in an effort to conserve Malta's dwindling stock of aviation fuel. In spite of these instructions, later that morning Wg Cdr Donaldson led 19 Spitfires of 229 and 249 Squadrons on a sweep over southern Sicily but only two fighters were seen and these promptly fled. Apparently Donaldson received a mild rebuke from the AOC on their return for his complete disregard of the Air Ministry warning.

The second week of the month was unusually quiet and relatively uneventful for Malta's defences, only the occasional offensive reconnaissance sorties by small groups of high-flying Bf109Fs causing alarm. The Luftwaffe at last returned to the skies over Malta early on 15 September, when nine 249 Spitfires were scrambled at 0825 to patrol over Zonqor at 21,000 feet. Three-quarters of an hour later, two Bf109Fs suddenly dived out of the sun and shot down Flt Sgt Bernard (Pedro) Peters' aircraft BP867 T-E, which crashed into the sea with the loss of the 22-year-old pilot from West Wickham in Kent, who was reputed to have flown as a volunteer in the Spanish Civil War (hence the nickname). Plt Off Beurling later recalled:

> "A bunch of Macchis [sic] tried to gang us. One of them caught him with a wild-eyed deflection shot, clear out of nowhere, and Pete never knew what hit him. He simply fell off the end of the line-abreast formation and dived into the sea from 20,000 feet. Another of the well-liked guys gone home!"

It would seem, however, that Peters was the victim of a Messerschmitt flown by Oblt Günther Hess of 6/JG53, who claimed a Spitfire at 0853. Later that same morning, two Spitfires of 229 Squadron were lost in combat with I/JG77's new and more powerful Bf109G-2s, two Spitfires of 249 being despatched to search for the missing pilots. At 1215 an empty dinghy was sighted about 25 miles north of St Paul's Bay and, as they flew at low level to investigate, a body was seen face down in the water nearby, dressed in white, but was not considered to be one of the missing pilots.

During the early evening of 16 September, nine of 249's aircraft were again on patrol when eight Bf109s were encountered at 1745. A series of dogfights ensued, Flt Lt Hetherington and Plt Off Beurling being engaged for nearly an hour before the Messerschmitts broke away; Beurling's aircraft (EP706 T-L) received damage to its starboard wing and tail, while Hetherington claimed one of his opponents damaged. Next day, at 1115, a total of 22 Spitfires were scrambled including a flight from 249 to investigate groups of MC202s and Bf109s approaching the island. About 10 miles north of Comino, at 25,000 feet, 229 Squadron engaged the Macchis with some success. However, the Messerschmitts of I/JG77 caught 249 off guard, Oblt Freytag gaining a number of strikes on Plt Off Farmer's Spitfire (EP663), forcing him into a power dive with his controls shot to pieces. Following a desperate struggle, Farmer managed to bale out at about 450 mph but pulled the ripcord too soon; the jerk of the parachute opening dislocated his shoulders, broke one arm and gave him a slight rupture. He came down in the sea and, fortunately for him, was soon rescued by HSL107.

Ten 249 Spitfires scrambled at 1120 on 25 September, joining two others of 1435 Squadron to intercept a plot reported as 15 to 20 miles north-east of Grand Harbour. A dozen

Messerschmitts were encountered orbiting 30 miles north-east of Zonqor Point, and attacked from up sun although only Plt Off Beurling enjoyed any success:

> "As Tiger White 2, attacked two ME109s of a formation of 12, from starboard quarter above. Fired one-and-a-half seconds burst from 300 yards. Enemy aircraft disintegrated. Attacked No2 aircraft from astern. Two-seconds burst, 350 yards. E/a emitted black smoke from engine with pieces coming off cowling, then glycol followed afterwards. Attacked third e/a five minutes later, six miles east of previous position, from port quarter, slightly above, 250-300 yards. Fired two-seconds burst. E/a enveloped in flames, dived vertically, striking the sea. Enemy pilot was seen going down by parachute, and was fired upon by ME109, causing the parachute to stream."

Two of his victims appear to have been the new Bf109Gs of I/JG77, Obfw Georg Ludwig of the Stab (Staff Flight) and an unidentified pilot (flying White 8) both getting back to Sicily with damaged aircraft, but the identity of the pilot seen to bale out is not known. The third aircraft attacked by Beurling had been firing at the Spitfire flown by Plt Off Budd who was unhurt, although Plt Off Moody's aircraft, EP136 T-P, was hit, and he crash-landed at Takali. Two claims for Spitfires were submitted by the Luftwaffe, one by Lt Berres of I/JG77, and one for which there was no witness. For some unexplained reason, the German pilots thought their opponents to have been American aircraft, while 249 noted that the German fighter sweeps were getting bigger and tougher.

The Luftwaffe had been building up its forces in Sicily during the preceding few weeks, in readiness for a new offensive against Malta. These included a further three Kampfgruppen of Ju88s, plus the return of I/JG53's Bf109Fs from the Eastern Front, followed by I/SchG2 equipped with Bf109F fighter-bombers, and I/JG27 with Bf109Gs.

October started off relatively quietly for Malta's defenders, but all on the island were aware that something was again brewing on Sicily. The second day of the new month was marked by a minor historical event — the first operational use of bomb-carrying Spitfires — when six of 229 Squadron set out to raid Biscari aerodrome. Whilst these and their escort were operating over Sicily, nine of 249 patrolled off the southern coast to cover the withdrawal. At 1005 two MC202s were sighted going south at 19,000 feet, then two sections each of four Bf109s were spotted. Sqn Ldr Woods and Flt Sgt de l'Ara attacked one of the Macchis, the latter claiming strikes before it evaded and dived away.

The Luftwaffe put in an appearance during the morning of 4 October, at least 20 Bf109Gs of I/JG77 approaching the coast which only a few crossed. Sixteen Spitfires, drawn equally from 185 and 249 Squadrons, were airborne, Red Section encountering four of the intruders at 26,000 feet over Grand Harbour. Before these could be engaged, however, about a dozen more dived out of the sun, attacking in pairs. Sgt Irving Gass (EP700 T-Q) who was straggling, was shot down into the sea off Filfla; he did not survive. A second Spitfire, BR379 T-V, was damaged; seriously wounded in the head, Flt Sgt George Hogarth struggled back to the island, only to crash-land in a field near Qrendi as he was approaching to land. The Spitfire skidded into the only building around, where a number of airmen were sunning themselves; no one was hurt apart from the 21-year-old Canadian pilot from Winnipeg, who was further injured and rushed to hospital, where he died. HSL128 was sent out to search for Sgt Murray Irving Gass but found only a Mae West and wreckage. One of the Spitfires was shot down by Lt Hans-Joachim Gläss of 3/JG77 for his sixth victory.

Two dozen Axis fighters approached Malta from the north shortly before 0800 on 10 October, some of which crossed the coast. Eight 249 Spitfires were airborne, one of which was flown by Sqn Ldr M.M. Stephens DSO DFC and Bar, a highly successful pilot with some 15 victories to his credit, two of which had been claimed in 1941 whilst flying Hurricanes with the Turkish Air Force. He had recently arrived on posting from the Middle East and was attached to 249 as a supernumerary to gain experience of local conditions. Four 229 Squadron Spitfires were also patrolling off the coast and these were attacked by the Messerschmitts which shot down one of the Spitfires before being driven away by three of 249; Stephens opened his Malta account by claiming one damaged. Sometime later, Plt Off Beurling was carrying out an air test when Ops reported that two Bf109s had sneaked in at low-level and were apparently searching for ground defences on the south-side of the island. Beurling flew out to sea in a wide arc, sweeping back in close to Filfla, where the two Messerschmitts were seen at about 1,000 feet, flying in line abreast:

> "I dropped in on them. I went down and down, clean under the starboard fellow, and rolled up under him, giving him a quick burst into the engine. He pancaked right smack down on his belly on the island and flipped over onto his back. The other fellow tried to circle away but I stayed with him. He turned out to sea, then whipped back across Filfla again. As he did, I moved onto his starboard quarter and let him have it. The burst caught the gas tank and the 'ship' blew up, complete with pilot."

These latest victories brought Beurling's Malta tally to 21 confirmed, with another shared, and his overall total to 23 and one shared. A DFC would soon follow to add to the DFM and Bar already awarded.

At 1040 up to 50 aircraft including two Ju88s were reported approaching, some of which crossed over Gozo, where they were intercepted by Spitfires; the bombers jettisoned their bombs, some of these falling on the little Gozitan town of Sannat where 16 persons were killed and 60 injured. A total of 23 Spitfires were up but only the 249 flight, joined by Wg Cdr P.P. Hanks DFC (Wing Commander, Flying, Luqa), made contact, initially meeting a dozen Bf109Fs at 20,000 feet, 15 miles north of Gozo. Attacking head-on, one Messerschmitt was claimed shot down by newly commissioned Plt Off Sanderson for his first victory, his own aircraft sustaining slight damage. He noted:

> "Gozo bombed. Intrepid! All-in dogfight with 12 ME109s. One Messerschmitt 109F destroyed."

Another was claimed shot down by Flg Off McElroy, who also claimed a second damaged:

> "Attacked head-on; e/a dived to right so turned on their tails. Caught another 109 climbing with two others in line astern. I attacked head-on from above quarter, fired a half-second burst, and observed cannon shells hit leading edge of e/a's wing. A large piece of wing blew off. I fired at other 109s, closing from 100 yards to 20 yards, but observed no strikes. I broke right on to another 109, 250 yards line astern, and fired a three-seconds cannon and machine-gun burst, observing hits on engine and wing roots, with heavy black smoke and pieces coming off; the e/a half-rolled, so I followed it down and gained on him in the dive; the aircraft tried to pull out at 5,000 feet, so I closed to 200 yards and finished my cannon, observing strikes and glycol. I continued to attack with machine-guns down to 50 feet from the sea, 15 to 20 miles south of the Sicilian coast; e/a still diving towards sea, streaming glycol and black smoke."

Sqn Ldr Stephens claimed another Bf109F as probably destroyed, having observed strikes on its starboard wing following "a two-seconds burst with everything I had", while Sgt Stead also claimed a probable. Two others were claimed damaged by Wg Cdr Hanks and Sqn Ldr Woods. The increased activity in Malta's skies during the preceding few days was but a foretaste of what was to follow.

The new blitz opened at 0720 on the morning of 11 October, when seven Ju88s of I/KG54 escorted by MC202s and Bf109Fs approached the island, a few bombers crossing the coast to release bombs on Hal Far and Benghaisa Point. Nineteen Spitfires were scrambled, although none were from 249. Nor was the Squadron involved in repelling the next raid at 1000, or at all during the two afternoon raids, since it was being held in reserve. Meanwhile, the other squadrons claimed a total of seven Ju88s, five Bf109Fs, three MC202s and two Re2001s shot down during the day for the loss of one Spitfire and its pilot, three Spitfires crash-landed and at least seven damaged. Of the new blitz, LAC Metcalf at Takali wrote:

> "Our boys knocked hells bells out of Jerry and even then we got three bashings at Takali, two

at Luqa and one at Hal Far. For the first two raids I stayed on the runway but for the third (some killed) my nerves weren't up to much so I ran for the big hole! Most of the chaps were pretty shaky at supper and couldn't eat anything. I wonder what we'll be like if we have, say, a month of this?"

At the conclusion of the day's hard fighting Lord Gort, the Governor, sent a message of congratulation to Air HQ, which read: "Well done. The Spitfires have produced a fine opening score." Pilots of 249 were peeved to have not been involved.

The first raid on the morning of 12 October arrived soon after 0620. Eight Spitfires of 185 Squadron and four more from 229 Squadron intercepted the first wave of Ju88s, some of which bombed Takali and Luqa, while ten of 249 engaged as the bombers departed. Sqn Ldr Woods claimed a Ju88 probably destroyed before attacking an escorting Bf109 which he claimed damaged, while Sgt Stead attacked and damaged a second; the latter then reported shooting down another Messerschmitt which Sqn Ldr Stephens had already attacked. Stephens meanwhile engaged another of the escort, also claiming this shot down. Finding himself alone following the action, he attempted to join up with a second Spitfire but was bounced by a lone Bf109. The engine of his Spitfire (AB377 T-E) seized after being hit:

"After my engine cut I had plenty of time to transmit for a fix before baling out. I spent a long time in the water floundering around, as the air bottle in my dinghy was flat, but eventually managed to climb aboard and finish inflating it with bellows. I had a grandstand view of quite a number of combats during which I saw four aircraft shot down. I was quite confident throughout that I should be picked up by our Air/Sea Rescue service, which was quite magnificent. Eventually I was rescued by a seaplane tender [ST280], since all the ASR boats were already out. There was quite a swell and I was as sick as a dog after I had been picked up."

Four of the bombers were claimed by pilots of 126 Squadron, who also lost their CO in the action. The raiders were back at 0910, seven Ju88s and a dozen MC202s crossing the coast. Bombs fell on Luqa, where some aircraft were damaged, and at Takali. The formation was intercepted on the way in by eight Spitfires of 229 Squadron, while nine from 249 engaged the indirect escort comprising Bf109Fs from II/JG53, stepped from 21,000 to 30,000 feet. Flg Off McElroy reported:

"I got my sights on one and let him have it fair and square, and then engaged another. But the Jerries had had enough and they broke off and headed for home."

He was credited with shooting down one Messerschmitt, but his own aircraft (AR488 T-S) also sustained damage. A probable was claimed by Flt Sgt Hiskens, while both Plt Off Sanderson and Sgt Stead reported damaging two others. Hiskens also engaged a Ju88 which he and Flt Sgt de l'Ara jointly claimed probably destroyed.

Eight Ju88s approached the island at midday, covered by ten MC202s of 51° Stormo and 20 Bf109Fs. They were intercepted south of Sicily by 15 Spitfires including eight of 249, all led by Wg Cdr Donaldson, who reported:

"I was leading 229 Squadron with 249 Squadron as high escort . . . I sighted eight Ju88s escorted by 30-plus fighters, five miles south of Gela, coming south . . . made a head-on attack on leading Ju88. No hits were observed. I broke upwards and did a stall turn and turned into a Ju88 which I singled out. I made an astern attack from 200 to 80 yards. Port engine smoked and burst into flames. Aircraft dived vertically and crashed into the sea in flames."

Sqn Ldr Woods led a diving attack on the bombers, two of which were claimed shot down by Flg Off McElroy and Flt Sgt Hiskens; a third was claimed probably destroyed by Flt Sgt de l'Ara, who damaged a second, while both the CO and Plt Off Lowry reported hits on the aircraft they attacked. By this time the escorting Macchis and Messerschmitts had joined the action, as

Donaldson's report revealed:

> "I then saw a ME109F and got on his tail. I fired a two-seconds burst and he burst into flames
> and crashed vertically into the sea. No parachute. This was witnessed by Plt Off Sanderson
> [of 249]. I was then attacked by an unseen aircraft and hit in rear fuselage by one bullet."

The CO also reported shooting down a Messerschmitt, while Plt Off Sanderson claimed a
probable and Plt Off Yates a damaged. Pilots of 229 Squadron reported shooting down one
bomber and probably a second, plus two Bf109s, the action inspiring Donaldson to write:

> "It was the most spectacular sight I have ever seen. The whole sky was filled with enemy
> aircraft in severe trouble! I saw three flaming Ju88s and another three flaming ME109s, and
> counted no less than ten parachutes descending slowly, three of them from the Junkers I had
> shot down."

The survivors turned back. It seems that several of the combats with 'Messerschmitts' were, in
fact, with MC202s, two of which were damaged in this engagement, one pilot suffering a leg
wound.

The Squadron was not called into action against the two afternoon raids. Conclusion of
operations at dusk indicated a considerable victory for the defenders, who had claimed 27
confirmed victories plus 13 probables and many damaged, for the loss of seven Spitfires and
three pilots. Records suggest that 12 Ju88s and four Bf109s were shot down during the day's
fighting. 249's share totalled six confirmed and five probables for the loss of Sqn Ldr Stephens'
aircraft.

At 0635 on the morning of 13 October, eight Spitfires of 185 Squadron and eight of 249
were scrambled as seven Ju88s of II/LG1, under an umbrella of 30 Bf109Fs, approached the
island. While the 185 Squadron formation tangled with the escort, Flt Lt Hetherington led 249
to engage the bombers, then three miles north of St Paul's Bay. Plt Off Beurling reported:

> "As Tiger Red 3, I attacked eight [sic] Ju88s, taking a straggler from slightly above to the
> right with a two-seconds burst of cannon and machine-guns. Pieces came off the starboard
> wing. I broke away to port and down and saw one ME109 closing in from port above. I broke
> left and then turned onto him [and from] 50 yards astern fired one-and-a-half-seconds burst
> of cannon and machine-guns. Enemy aircraft burst into flames. A second ME109 came down
> from starboard quarter above. As enemy aircraft pulled out ahead at 250-300 yards, I gave
> him a four-seconds burst with machine-guns; observed no strikes but pilot baled out. At this
> time I saw first e/a strike the sea."

Plt Off Seed claimed another Messerschmitt as damaged and also one of the bombers as
probably destroyed, and others were damaged by Hetherington, Plt Off Giddings and Sgt
Shewell. Despite the attention of the Spitfires, some of the bombers reached Luqa and released
the loads; two civilians were killed. As they sped northwards, Beurling was able to get on the
tail of one, catching it about eight miles north of Zonqor:

> "I attacked a Ju88 from starboard quarter above, 300 yards, with cannon and machine-guns,
> two-seconds burst, and observed strikes on roots of starboard wing, and black, oily smoke
> poured out. I gave it the remainder of my ammunition into the fuselage. Enemy aircraft did
> a diving turn to the right, striking the sea."

This was probably Fw Anton Wilfer's L1+KP which was reported shot down over Valetta and
crashed into the sea just off the coast. Meanwhile, Plt Off Yates crash-landed his damaged
Spitfire at Takali, EN954 skidding into the building housing the Squadron Armoury, but he
escaped unhurt.

The Squadron was not involved in repelling the next raid, which came in during mid-
morning, although seven Spitfires were scrambled following the raid when further activity was

detected but this turned out to be an Axis ASR operation and it was not engaged. The bombers were back shortly after lunch when six Ju88s and a massive fighter escort approached, but again 249 was not called to action. The respite did not last long, however, and eight Spitfires were scrambled during mid-afternoon when a further seven Ju88s were detected, covered by no fewer than 30 MC202s and 42 Bf109s. The bombers were intercepted 20 miles north of Gozo, but only Sqn Ldr Stephens was able to make a positive claim:

> "We saw Ju88s and escorting fighters among AA bursts, flying south near Filfla. I dived after them through AA and they turned east. I attacked one Ju88, hitting the starboard engine which began to smoke nicely, but then disengaged as the Macchis were after me. This Ju88 was seen from Qrendi Strip by the Squadron Adjutant to be diving from about 1,000 feet with his starboard engine in flames. I then attacked two more Ju88s and was closing in on them when I was warned to break, which I immediately did and a 109 flashed by."

Sgt Stead reported inflicting damage on a second bomber but was chased away by the escort, four of which were claimed shot down by Sqn Ldr Woods' flight, two by the CO himself (both Bf109s), one by Flt Sgt Hiskens (a Macchi) and the other by Flg Off McElroy, who identified his victim as an Re2001. Stephens also engaged a Macchi:

> "I then attacked an MC202 observing strikes on starboard side of the engine. Plt Off Nash of 229 Squadron watched these attacks and saw the aircraft crash and the pilot bale out after I was forced to break away."

The same aircraft was also attacked by Flt Sgt de l'Ara, who was credited with a share in its destruction. By this time Spitfires from both 229 and 1435 Squadrons had joined the battle, and pilots from these units claimed two bombers and a Macchi shot down. During the fight 153° Gruppo lost two MC202s, Cap Enzo Radini and Ten Felice Mezzetti both being reported missing. Radini had baled out badly burned and was later picked up six miles south-east of Delimara by HSL128. With the close of hostilities for the daylight hours, Sqn Ldr Stephens was posted to command 229 Squadron when its CO was taken ill.

Although attacks against Malta were to continue unabated for several more days, already the mini blitz was effectively over, for the Axis Command had now accepted that it was failing in its intended aim. Feldmarschall Kesselring later revealed:

> "The assault in the middle of October had not been the success we hoped for; I broke it off on the third day because, especially in view of the expected landings [the Anglo-American landings in Vichy-controlled North-West Africa], our losses were too high. The surprise had not come off, and neither had our bomber attacks against their air bases. Instead, the battle had to be fought against enemy fighters in the air and their bomb-proof shelters on the ground."

During the preceding three days the Luftwaffe had lost 16 Ju88s and two He111s, the latter during night raids, with a further nine Ju88s written off in crashes or crash-landings on returning to Sicily; 68 aircrew had been lost, a crippling rate of attrition to the fairly small forces involved.

At least eight Ju88s with a high escort of some 40 fighters stepped up to 28,000 feet approached soon after 0700 on the morning of 14 October, the majority crossing the coast. Twenty-nine Spitfires including eight of 249 were airborne to meet the raid, the first engagements occurring at 0720. Led by Sqn Ldr Woods, 249 intercepted the bombers over Grand Harbour, carrying out a stern attack as they headed for Takali, but only the CO and Flt Sgt de l'Ara were able to make claims, for a probable and two damaged respectively. Plt Off Sanderson noted:

> "Large party of ME109s kept us very busy. Hottest fight yet. [AR488 T-S] hit in wing."

Bombs fell on Takali, doing little damage but temporarily rendering the airfield unserviceable; there were two civilian casualties. The bombers returned shortly after 1000, but 249 was not called into action on this occasion. The pilots rested until 1310 when seven were scrambled to accompany 14 others as more Ju88s approached, Flt Lt Hetherington leading an attack just south of Zonqor; he claimed one probably destroyed while two more were damaged by Plt Off Giddings and Sgt Brydon before Messerschmitts from I and II/JG53 intervened. In the ensuing series of dogfights, Giddings claimed one shot down, Sgt Wynn a probable and Plt Off Williams two damaged. It was Beurling who once again stole the show however, though this time at cost:

"As the action opened I spotted five fighters pulling up high, as if to get ready to dive on Giddy [Plt Off Giddings] and Hether [Flt Lt Hetherington]. I called into the mike and we soared up to 24,000 feet, just as the five ME's got there. The 'Schmitts' promptly peeled off and dived . . . and away we went, right among the bombers . . . We each picked a Ju. I took the one on the starboard rear position of the V and gave him a two-seconds burst from starboard. He burst into flames and we went headlong toward the sea. As I nabbed the bomber, Hether came whipping just under me, diving away from eight ME's on his tail. I went down in a hurry with them, right past my flamer, and lashed into the leading Hun, just as he was going to let Hether have it. As I passed the burning bomber the rear gunner took a shot at me, peppering the port side of my fuselage and the port wing. I picked up about 30 bullet holes, I guess. Explosive bullets were snapping through the cockpit and one nicked the left middle finger of my throttle hand. Another stabbed my left forearm. I'd picked up two ME's on my own tail and still had Hether to worry about . . . I took a long shot from about 450 yards from above and to port. I got the bastard in the engine and he dove for the sea, streaming smoke and shedding pieces . . . One of the ME's on my tail riddled my port wing like a sieve and put a couple of bullets through the perspex hood, right over my head, while the other blasted my starboard wing full of holes.

A call for help came over the R/T . . . My own position was right above Kalafrana, so I rolled over and had a look down, to see a swell mêlée going on below. I went down vertically, hitting almost 600 mph in my riddled crate and at 14,000 feet pulled up under a Messerschmitt, just as he was all set to pot 'Willie the Kid' [Plt Off Williams]. I gave the Hun a two-seconds burst and blew his whole left wing off at the root. He flicked over, and that was that. Just as I shot Willie's pal down, another ME nailed me from behind. He got me right in the belly of the Spit [BR173 T-D]. A chunk of cannon shell smashed into my right heel. Another went between my left arm and body, nicking me in the elbow and ribs. Shrapnel spattered into my left leg. The controls were blasted to bits . . . I threw the hood away and tried to get out, but the spin was forcing me back into the seat. The engine was streaming flame by this time, but somehow I managed to wriggle my way out of the cockpit and out onto the port wing, from which I could bale into the inside of the spin . . . At about 1,000 feet I managed to slip off."

Plt Off Seed had seen Beurling's predicament and followed him down; now, as Seed circled the wounded pilot who was struggling to get into his dinghy, he called Control and requested that a rescue launch be sent out immediately. Within 20 minutes HSL128 had arrived, and Flt Sgt Head — the coxswain — was subsequently able to record another side of Beurling's rebellious and obstinate character:

"Immediately on gaining the deck of the launch he was very, very concerned with the fact that he could not find his bible. This small volume was quickly located and handed to him whereupon he became more composed, and explained that it had been given to him by his mother and under no circumstances would he fly without it. In the launch on the way back to base he told the crew that he would be flying again that afternoon but it was obvious to the crew that this would not be so. Beurling has a nasty dull blue closed wound in the heel which indicated a possible bullet lodged deep in the flesh."

A piece of cannon shell had indeed penetrated Beurling's right heel, and this effectively ended his participation in Malta's defence. Although not the easiest of men to live and fly alongside, the Canadian's outward fearlessness and undeniable success had proved an inspiration to many of the other pilots, and he was hero-worshipped by many of the ground personnel. His three final claims had raised his person total to 29 and one shared, all but two whilst flying with 249 from the island. One Messerschmitt of I/JG 53 was damaged in this action, the wounded Obfw Josef Ederer crash-landing his 2 Staffel machine at San Petro, where another I Gruppe aircraft was damaged when it was rammed by a landing Macchi. Three II Gruppe aircraft were reported to have been damaged in landing accidents at Comiso, possibly having suffered combat damage.

Six Ju88s swept in to bomb Luqa during the morning raid on 15 October. Although 28 Spitfires were airborne, they failed to intercept the raiders prior to their arrival over the island. 249's eight Spitfires, which had been ordered to patrol north of Zonqor Point, were attacked by Bf109s before the bombers were sighted. These were fended off however, Sgt Wynn claiming one shot down. The bombers were then seen near Kalafrana and pursued, Plt Off Moody claiming one, Plt Off Williams reporting a probable, and Plt Off Giddings a damaged.

Soon after 1000 eight Ju88s and eight bomb-carrying Bf109Fs — probably from the newly-formed I/Schlachtgeschwader 2 — were escorted towards the island by 25 MC202s, with more Messerschmitts as high cover. The presence of intercepting Spitfires caused the bombers to turn back before reaching Malta, whilst the fighter-bombers were engaged out to sea by 15 Spitfires including eight from 249. Several were seen to jettison their bombs as they crossed the coast, one of two falling on Mellieha where a civilian was killed and two injured. Before the Spitfires could engage however, they were bounced by other Messerschmitts. Sgt Brydon had his leg broken by a cannon shell which penetrated the cockpit of BR254 T-E; in great pain, he managed to bale out into the sea. The aircraft (EP135 T-Z) flown by Plt Off Moody was also hit, although he managed to return to Takali where he crash-landed. Both pilots may have been victims of 3/JG77's Staffelkapitän, Oblt Geisshardt, who claimed two Spitfires shot down, or of Oblt Freytag, Staffelkapitän of 1/JG77, who also made similar claims. In return, Sgt Wynn was able to claim strikes on one of the Messerschmitts and it seems likely that his victim was one of the fighter-bombers, for such an aircraft crash-landed at Comiso on return. Subsequently HSL128 was again sent out, the crew finding Brydon clinging to his partially inflated dinghy an hour after he had been shot down.

The Squadron scrambled seven more Spitfires to meet a further fighter-bomber raid just after midday, meeting the raiders five miles off St Paul's Bay at 20,000 feet. Four were seen to jettison their bombs immediately and turn away, but the remaining three were harried as they attempted to attack Takali, their bombs falling wide of the target; no claims were submitted however. Six Ju88s were back mid-afternoon, escorted by 30 Bf109s of I/JG53 and 31 Macchis of 51° Stormo and 153° Gruppo. Sqn Ldr Woods led the Squadron in a head-on interception off Kalafrana as the formation approached from the north-east of Zonqor, when once again bombs were seen to be jettisoned into the sea. The CO reported:

> "I sighted ten [sic] Ju88s with about 30 fighter escort at about 19,000 feet, flying south. We turned towards them and I led my section down in a quarter head-on attack. I opened fire at about 400 yards, firing cannon and machine-guns. I saw strikes on the leader and his No2, who was echeloned to port of him. I turned to starboard and came underneath another Ju88 and opened fire at about 100 yards and saw strikes on the belly. I received no return fire but was forced to break off and down as an ME109 was attacking me from the stern. I found myself in the middle of about 20 ME109s, one of which broke to port and up, right in front of me. I opened fire at about 100 yards, gave it a two-seconds burst and saw no strikes but the engine started to smoke and then burst into flames. At this point I stalled and spun down. I came out of my spin behind and below the bombers and climbed up after them, four of which jettisoned their bombs into the sea. Two Ju88s were smoking badly from both engines and four Spitfires were attacking the remainder from all angles and, as I climbed up, I saw strikes on practically all the bombers. The bombers started to dive down and I dived down on one who was straggling, and opened fire at about 200 yards; both cannons jammed but I exhaused my machine-guns, closing to point-blank range and silencing the rear gunner."

Although he had seen strikes on four of the Ju88s he had attacked, Woods was credited with one damaged only, in addition to the destruction of a Bf109. Sgt Stead claimed a Messerschmitt probably destroyed, having earlier attacked a Ju88 in conjunction with Plt Off Yates which was also credited as probably destroyed. Another probable was claimed by Plt Off Sanderson, while Flg Off McElroy reported shooting another into the sea — probably 3Z+CL of 3/KG77 flown by Uffz Herbert Gross which failed to return from this raid; this aircraft may also have been attacked by a pilot of 185 Squadron. McElroy claimed a second bomber as damaged, as did Flt Sgt Carter.

The escorting Messerschmitts attempted to come to the rescue of their charges, Uffz Marian Mazurek of 1/JG53 shooting down the Spitfire (EP340 T-M) flown by Flt Sgt Ed Hiskens for his 30th victory, the action confirmed by his wingman, Uffz Heinz Loch; the German ace reported:

> "Before the Ju88s were able to drop bombs, they were attacked by six to eight Spitfires. I followed them immediately and fired my machine-guns from a far distance. I managed to place myself in a good shooting position behind a Spitfire. As I came closer I started to fire with all my weapons out of a left turning. After that the plane tumbled down without control and hit the sea 15 kilometres from Valetta and sank."

The 21-year-old Australian was killed. Flg Off McElroy's aircraft was also badly shot-up and he was slightly wounded in one leg by shrapnel. With the aircraft diving out of control and the cockpit full of smoke, he decided it was time to jump but then discovered that the hood was jammed shut. Struggling to regain control, he managed to level out and reach Takali, where he crash-landed BR373 T-N without further injury.

Next day (16 October) during the morning raid, 249 patrolled up sun, 20 miles north-east of Zonqor, in order to intercept any high cover but saw nothing. The Squadron achieved better success during a follow-up raid later that same morning, Sqn Ldr Woods leading six Spitfires against a small formation of Ju88s and their escorts near Hal Far. One of the bombers was claimed shot down by Flt Sgt de l'Ara and two others were damaged by the CO and Flg Off McElroy. The escorting Messerschmitts of I/JG53 then attacked, inflicting damage to Woods' aircraft (AR466 T-R) and shooting down EP338 T-A flown by Flt Sgt Pete Carter, who was killed. His victor may have been Fw Heinz Golinski of 3 Staffel, who was seen by other JG53 pilots to shoot down one Spitfire before being shot down by another. Golinski, victor of 46 combats in Russia, was killed and may have fallen to Plt Off Lowry, the American claiming one of the attackers; alternatively he may have been shot down by a pilot of 1435 Squadron who claimed a Messerschmitt at about the same time.

The bombers were back three hours later. Seven Ju88s of KG77 accompanied by 42 Macchis and 40 Bf109s including at least six fighter-bombers, crossed the coast in six waves. The Spitfires were late in making contact on this occasion and consequently Luqa was bombed and Takali was attacked by the Jabo where the airfield was rendered temporarily unserviceable, and two civilians injured. Flt Lt Hetherington led eight Spitfires in a head-on attack just after the bombers had crossed the coast on their way home, claiming one damaged as did Plt Off Budd; Plt Off Williams was more successful and reported the one attacked was shot down, while Sgt Wynn claimed a probable. For the second day running McElroy was obliged to crash-land at Takali, having been bounced by a Bf109 before he could reach the bombers. In return, Plt Off Sanderson claimed a Messerschmitt shot down.

The defenders had noticed a change in the tactics employed by the Axis during the day's fighting. Many formations were now attacking on a wide front and approaching from several directions simultaneously. While several raids had thereby got through, they had failed to inflict much damage on the airfields. As daylight faded, Air Vice-Marshal Park despatched a message to the Spitfire squadrons:

> "Grand work fighter boys. Your magnificent fighting in the last five days is being watched not only in Malta but by the RAF on other fronts as well, as well as by our Russian allies. Although heavily outnumbered last May, the Malta Spitfires came out on top and I am confident that you will win the second Battle of Malta. Some of the enemy bomber squadrons have already shown they cannot take it. Keep it up and in a few days the other German bombers will throw

in the sponge. Replacement pilots and Spitfires are on the way but there is still some stiff fighting to finish the job. Good luck to you and good shooting."

The AOC did not forget the hard-working maintenance personnel either and sent congratulations to them also, but added:

"Your part in the present Battle of Malta greatly appreciated but serviceability of Spitfires continues to fall. You can and must get it up again. Where you have worked hard you must work harder and faster. Give the fighter boys Spitfires and they will drive the Hun out of the sky."

Five 249 Spitfires were airborne early on the morning of 17 October when seven Ju88s approached the island, but their task was to search for the high-flying Messerschmitt escort. Two were sighted at 25,000 feet orbiting ten miles east of Zonqor but these avoided combat. The midday raid was ten minutes late, but when it did appear it comprised eight Ju88s of II/LG1, nine Jabo Messerschmitts from I/JG27 and a heavy escort provided by 41 Bf109s and 31 Macchis. Again the Spitfires were late in getting off and by the time they had intercepted, the attacking force had reached the Comino-St Paul's Bay area. Despite vigorous attempts to intercept all the diverse groups of raiders, the fighter-bombers could not be prevented from attacking Takali. Little damage was inflicted however, although bombs also fell on Mosta where three civilians were killed and six injured. The bombers released their bombs in the Birkirkara area, where several houses were demolished or damaged.

Two Ju88s were shot down by the Spitfire pilots, one by a pilot of 126 Squadron and the other by Plt Off Giddings, while Plt Off Seed claimed a probable. There were no survivors from Lt Ottokar Fritscher's L1+CP of 5 Staffel, which went into the sea about 12 miles south-east of Sicily. Italian pilots had watched as the pilot struggled in vain to keep the aircraft flying on one engine whilst the other belched flames. The other Ju88, L1+YC, crashed into the sea off Valetta. On board was the Gruppenkommandeur, Maj Gerhard Kollewe, who baled out with the rest of the crew but was lost, as was the observer. Two survivors were picked up by HSL128 and, on being pulled aboard, the W/Op, Obfw Martin Assum, claimed that a Spitfire had swooped on the defenceless airmen in the sea and machine-gunned Kollewe (a recipient of the Knights' Cross and Oakleaves) and the observer, Fw Bernhard Mahler, both of whom had been killed. A third bomber returned with a wounded gunner on board.

With the bombers under attack, the escorting Messerschmitt and Macchi pilots did their utmost to frustrate the Spitfires, shooting down a 229 Squadron aircraft and damaging three other Spitfires. In return the Spitfires claimed three Bf109s shot down, one each by Flt Lt Hetherington and Plt Off Giddings, while Plt Off Budd claimed a probable. During an afternoon scramble, seven 249 Spitfires were bounced by a number of Bf109s but, on this occasion, managed to avoid any damage. The Messerschmitts were gone before any of the pilots could react.

Despite Kesselring's suspension of the bombing assault against Malta, the island was not yet spared further attack. Just as the end of the daylight bombing raids over England in September 1940 had brought several weeks of fighter sweeps and pinprick fighter-bomber attacks — designed to draw up the British fighters for destruction in the air — this now became the pattern for Malta.

The first such raid on the morning of 18 October came in at 0640 when an estimated 50 fighters approached the island. These were met by Spitfires although 249 was not involved. Thirty-five Messerschmitts, including a number of Jabo, returned mid-morning and bombs were dropped on Takali but without causing much damage or any casualties. The attack was over before interception could be made. At 1355 an estimated 20 Bf109s were reported and although these were engaged, 249 was again not involved, nor was it able to intercept any of the small groups of Messerschmitts, up to 75 aircraft in total, which crossed the coast between 1545 and 1700.

The Squadron fared better next day (19 October) when, at dusk, 40 unescorted Ju88s from II/LG1 and III/KG77 approached the island in two formations. It was still light enough, however, for a standing patrol of three 249 Spitfires to spot the KG77 aircraft 25 miles out to sea as they approached from the west. The Spitfires were joined by two 89 Squadron Beau-fighters, whereupon a number of bombers were seen to jettison their loads and turn back. Flt Sgt de l'Ara led his section to intercept the other formation, which was encountered 15 miles east of Malta and again bombs were seen to be jettisoned, as de l'Ara recorded:

"Whenever I manoeuvred my section nearly within range of a bomber in these groups, they would jettison their bombs and dive into cloud. I was vectored onto one bomber which I recognised as a Ju88, about 400 yards ahead, and crossing my starboard bows. I brought my section round behind it. The top gunner fired at me at about 200 yards but I had closed to about 150 yards and fired a three or four-seconds burst at the port motor. The engine gave a flash, caught fire and streamed a considerable amount of black smoke. The gunner stopped firing and I noticed a glow inside the cockpit, then I broke right to avoid ramming. Immediately I broke, my No2 [Sgt Stead] opened fire from astern. The e/a turned slightly to the right, then flicked over and spun into cloud."

Only three bombers had in fact crossed the coast and it was one of these, 3Z+GS flown by Uffz Gerhard Demuth, which fell to de l'Ara and Stead. It seems probable that Plt Off Sanderson also participated in this action; he noted:

"Many Ju88s around. Fired at one in the dark. We got two between us. Ju88 destroyed. Night landing."

Bombs fell near Luqa and Hal Far but caused no material damage. Amongst those watching from the ground was a pilot of 89 Squadron, who related:

"The Ju88s are still in formation and are just starting to open up and dive on the 'drome now. One has been hit, a Spit got him and one engine is on fire. Two of the crew have baled out. Christ, here come the bombs also. The Ju88 that was hit has just hit the ground and blown up about a mile from here. Three of the crew are coming down in parachutes."

Another eyewitness wrote:

". . . about a hundred feet from the deck she [the crippled Ju88] levelled out, crashing 500 yards away. I think that it was the pilot's unlucky day for his 'chute never opened and I remember him flashing past my eyes to disappear in a cloud of dust 50 yards distant."

A second Ju88, an aircraft of II/LG1, was pursued north-eastwards by one of the Beaufighters which shot it down into the sea. The crew was later rescued by HSL128. For his leadership during this interception, Flt Sgt de l'Ara was awarded an immediate DFM. A number of other awards were forthcoming at this time, including a third DFC for Sqn Ldr Stephens, now leading 229 Squadron, a second DFC for Sqn Ldr Woods, DFCs for Flt Lt Hetherington and newly promoted Flt Lt McElroy and, rather surprisingly, a DSO for Plt Off Beurling. The latter award evinced some sharp comment, not everyone considering that the award of a medal normally associated with outstanding leadership was appropriate in this case.

Heavy rain during the next two days caused a dramatic reduction in operations, 249 not being called upon until the morning of 22 October when, between 0955 and 1030, at least ten Bf109s, two dozen Macchis and three Re2001 fighter-bombers raided Takali. Eight 249 Spitfires were airborne and encountered 14 fighters at 24,000 feet north of Grand Harbour. Flt Lt McElroy and Plt Off Lowry jointly claimed a Bf109 shot down while Plt Off Sanderson identified his victim as a MC202. A Messerschmitt was claimed probably destroyed by Sqn Ldr Woods, who claimed a second damaged, as did Sgt Stead, who also reported strikes on a Macchi.

The Squadron was in action again during the afternoon of 24 October when at least 40 Bf109s and MC202s approached, these being intercepted by seven Spitfires about 25 miles north of the island at 1610. Attacking head-on, Plt Off Giddings claimed one Macchi shot down and a second probably so, while Plt Off Williams reported shooting down a Messerschmitt, possibly an aircraft of 6/JG53 from which the pilot was rescued by an Axis ASR craft; Giddings reported:

> "I attacked one gaggle of Macchis in line astern, when the last three rolled onto their backs and dived down. I fired at No3 aircraft of the remainder with cannon and machine-guns for about three seconds. Glycol poured from it and there was a violent explosion around the cockpit and the fuselage broke up. I then fired a long burst at the No4 of the formation and saw a thick stream of glycol pour from it. At that moment I was forced to break away and aileron-turned down to 2,000 feet. In my dive I saw an e/a streaming black smoke crash into the sea. This was probably the 109F claimed by Tiger Blue 1 [Plt Off Williams]."

On 25 October the first two of 15 long-range Spitfires arrived safely at Malta following a five-and-a-quarter-hour flight direct from Gibraltar. Each aircraft was fitted with a 170-gallon jettisonable slipper tank beneath the belly, together with an extra 29-gallon tank in the rear fuselage, plus a larger than normal oil tank. Meanwhile, *Furious* was on its way from Gibraltar with the final carrier-borne reinforcements for the island.

The Squadron's final combats of the month occurred on 27 October, eight Spitfires led by Sqn Ldr Woods engaging a Jabo raid on Takali just after 0700. During the brief skirmish two of the Messerschmitts were claimed damaged, one by the CO and the other by Plt Off Moody. There followed a similar engagement during the afternoon when three Spitfires encountered another fighter-bomber raid, during which Flt Lt McElroy claimed one damaged. However, on this occasion, an escorting fighter attacked the Spitfire (BR529 T-D) flown by Sgt G.D. Cameron RCAF, a new pilot, who was slightly wounded in the head. Despite his injury, he was able to land his damaged aircraft at Takali.

Two days later, on 29 October, the latest (and final) carrier-borne Spitfire delivery was made, 29 aircraft reaching the island safely from *Furious*. Their arrival did not pass unnoticed and between 1000 and 1120 more than 40 Bf109s were reported to be airborne in an effort to intercept the delivery aircraft, about half of these crossing the coast. AA guns opened fire and 27 Spitfires were scrambled, but no engagements were reported and all the delivery aircraft landed safely. However, two of the Spitfires ordered to provide cover crashed on take-off, including AR488 T-S flown by Plt Off Giddings. His aircraft collided with a truck which had just delivered building materials to Takali; Giddings broke his wrist and several small bones in his arm but Emanuel Grech, one of the Maltese labourers unloading the lorry, was killed instantly and another, Michael Zerafa, was seriously injured.

The Squadron received a number of new pilots during the month, including Plt Off F.E. Fowler, who was made a Flight Commander on the 26th vice Flt Lt Hetherington; others included Flg Off J.J. Lynch, yet another American; Plt Offs G. Newberry, W.J. Locke RCAF, W.J. Cleverly and J.A.N. Dawkins, plus Flt Sgts D.L. Rawson, Sgts A. Notley, W.B. Weir, N. Bage, J.E. Roberts, W.J.B. Stark, J.H. Waterhouse RAAF, M.J. Costello RNZAF, J.C. Hughes RCAF, E.D. Kelly RCAF and W.D. Wendt RCAF, the latter also an American.

With no action for Malta's defenders for 48 hours, the end of the 29th month of the siege allowed stock to be taken. Although losses of Spitfires during October's battles had been high, pilot casualties had not. The month's claims by Malta's Spitfires were assessed at 126 confirmed, 62 probables and 162 damaged, of which 249 was credited with 40:19:37 for the loss of seven Spitfires shot down and five crash-landed, with the deaths of four pilots killed plus four wounded. However, for two of the Squadron's more successful pilots — survivors of numerous air battles in Malta's skies and now tour-expired and on their way back to England via Gibraltar — fate was yet to deal a deadly blow.

During the evening of 31 October, a Liberator transport aircraft (AL516 of 511 Squadron) departed Luqa bound for the UK with two dozen tour-expired or wounded pilots, together with ten civilians, two of whom were young children. On arriving over Gibraltar in the midst of a violent storm, the Liberator overshot the runway and flopped into the sea about 100 yards offshore. The aircraft broke its back and sank like a stone. Of the ten civilians on board, eight were drowned or died of injuries, including the children, and the survivors were both injured. Five pilots were drowned, including Plt Off John Williams of 249; additionally, Flt Lt Eric Hetherington died of his injuries. He was seen to be conscious and apparently not in difficulties when rescuers arrived, and even suggested they help others first, but seconds later he died, presumably from internal injuries and/or shock.

The wounded Plt Off Beurling, despited his foot encased in plaster, managed to extricate himself from the wreckage and was rescued from the sea. Amongst the survivors was a former 249 pilot, the American Flt Lt Roscoe, who had been wounded during the October battles; he remembered:

> "Beurling was in the water near me and offered to help me, with my arm being in a sling, but I told him I was OK and he swam off toward shore. I was a good swimmer but didn't trust my bad arm. The aircraft had settled to the bottom of the shallow bay, resting on the extended undercarriage, with the wing just awash. I climbed onto the wing and tried to help others up. Some of those in the water were all right, others dying or already dead. The army put rafts out from shore and soon we were all taken off, drenched and cold, many suffering from shock."

In addition to Beurling, who went on to achieve even greater fame and notoriorty, the survivors included Plt Off Yates and Plt Off Farmer, both late of 249.

Chapter Ten

THE TURNING TIDE

November 1942 – October 1943

"I was too low to bale out, so had to ditch — a bit dicey in a Spitfire. By good luck I managed to get the tail down first, to help break the impact . . ."

Sgt Ken Browne, 249 Squadron

The first day of November was marked by a single scramble by one of the other squadrons, 249 not being called upon until 1340 the next day (2 November). Four patrolling Spitfires were ordered to investigate two dozen fighters which overflew the island although no sightings were made. Just over two hours later another fighter sweep approached the coast but only six crossed, two of these bouncing a flight of five 249 Spitfires, Sgt Weir's aircraft (EP448 T-F) sustaining some damage and the pilot suffering multiple flesh wounds; he crash-landed at Takali on return. A scramble by Blue Section on 9 November resulted in the interception of a PRU Baltimore.

Although patrols were maintained every day, little trade came the Squadron's way although the losses continued. At 1025 on 15 November, three Beaufighters of 46 Squadron were ordered to fly to Malta on detachment from the Western Desert, but all three failed to arrive. During the afternoon four Spitfires from 249 carried out a search for the missing aircraft, but from this operation Sgt John Roberts, a 21-year-old Welshman from Rhosllanerchrugog, failed to return. It was assumed that his aircraft (EP199 T-K) had crashed into the sea although the cause of its loss was undetermined.

The Squadron moved from Takali to a new strip at Qrendi on 18 November and was among those units which began taking the war to the enemy, Spitbombers carrying out a series of raids directed initially against the airfields at Gela and Comiso. Sqn Ldr Woods led the first raid by three Spitbombers at 1450 on 22 November, covered by seven more of the Squadron; four bombs were seen to explode on the runway and two others among aircraft dispersal pens. Three Spitbombers again led by the CO returned to bomb Gela two days later although two returned early when the target was found to be obscured by thick cloud. During the afternoon of 25 November, the CO led six Spitbombers back to Gela and all bombs were seen to explode within the aerodrome perimeters. Wg Cdr Grant (former CO and now Wing Commander Flying Takali) led the escort although no enemy aircraft were sighted. Earlier in the day four Spitfires had taken off for a weather patrol and intercepted two Bf109s, one of which Flt Lt Seed claimed to have damaged. This may have been an aircraft of 9/JG53 flown by Lt Gerd Bottcher, who was on his way to Tunisia from Sicily. On arrival at Bizerta his aircraft crashed and he was killed.

At 0730 on 29 November, five Spitbombers and four escort set out to raid Comiso where light and inaccurate flak was encountered. Just before midday six Spitbombers with two escorting fighters set out to attack Gela. Over the target the American Sgt Willy Wendt's aircraft (BR293 T-M) was hit by flak although it was last seen going down under control and other pilots believed a crash-landing was a possibility; he was in fact captured*.

During the morning of 1 December, six 249 Spitbombers led by Flt Lt Seed (BR373 T-N) took off to carry out an attack on Biscari airfield, closely escorted by four more led by Plt Off Sanderson (EP833 T-F). Bombs were seen to burst near buildings and aircraft pens. Gela airfield

---

* Sgt Wendt remained a prisoner until the Italian Armistice in September 1943, when he escaped captivity and made his way through German lines to meet the advancing Allied armies. He remained in the RCAF rather than transfer to the USAF, was commissioned but was then killed in action flying Mustangs with 19 Squadron.

was again targeted during the afternoon, Sqn Ldr Woods (EP343 T-V) leading six Spitbombers while four others acted as close escort, and a further eight from 229 Squadron flew top cover. Bf109s of I/JG53 engaged the top cover, shooting down one, but the fighter-bombers took the defences by surprise. Several aircraft were damaged on the ground during the attack; three personnel were killed and five wounded.

There followed a period of relative inactivity although patrols and sweeps were maintained, but this dramatically changed on 11 December, when eight 249 Spitfires led by Wg Cdr Grant, which were escorting six Beaufighters of 272 Squadron on an offensive patrol of the Pantelleria-Lampion-Kirkenna area, encountered a formation of 32 Ju52s of KGzbV.1 near Lampion. The lumbering troop transports were flying at sea level with an escort of three Bf110s of III/ZG26 and two Ju88s 1,500 feet above them; a lone four-engined aircraft was also seen. The Beaufighters went for the transports, claiming five shot down and three damaged for the loss of one of their own, while the Spitfires tackled the escort. There was an element of double-claiming since four Bf110s were reported shot down by the Spitfires, Sqn Ldr Woods and Flg Off Lynch claiming one apiece, Woods also sharing a Ju88 with Flt Sgts Hughes and Costello.

Another Bf110 was shared by Grant and Plt Off Locke, while a similar claim was made by Flt Lt Seed and Plt Off Cleverly. The Spitfires then attacked the transports, Grant and Seed each claiming one, Lynch a probable, Seed and Costello each one damaged. At least two Ju52/3ms of 2 Staffel (1Z+6K and 1Z+DK) were lost. In addition, the Bf110 flown by Fw Hermann Breitenbach crashed into the sea with the loss of pilot and gunner (Gfr Günther Reinecke), while Obfw Willy Reaker and his gunner (Obfw Helmut Schön) were killed when their aircraft crashed on Pantelleria; the third Bf110 was also believed to have crashed on the island, although the crew apparently survived.

Next day (12 December), Wg Cdr Grant's Spitfire crashed when landing at Qrendi on returning from a patrol; although he was unhurt, his aircraft ER622 T-P suffered some slight damage. Action came again on 13 December, when four Spitfires flew a reconnaissance at 1550, meeting ten Bf109s and three Ju88s over Pantelleria at 1,000 feet. One of the bombers was pursued by Flg Off Lynch and newly commissioned Plt Off Stead, who claimed to have inflicted damage before it escaped. A late morning convoy patrol led by Wg Cdr Grant ended when Sgt Bage (EP557 T-R) was obliged to bale out owing to engine trouble; he was soon rescued from the sea, none the worse for the dunking.

On 14 December five Spitfires escorted the Beaufighter Squadron's commanding officer on a reconnaissance over the Lampedusa area. At 1040 a Ju88 of II/KG30 was seen to the south-west, proceeding northwards, and was engaged by all six fighters, although the Beaufighter's cannons jammed and it was eventually shot down by the combined fire of Flg Off Lynch, Plt Off Stead and Sgt Stark; the survivors were observed getting into a dinghy. At 1305 four Spitfires set out to again escort 272 Squadron's CO on another mission to the same area, meeting another Ju88 of II/KG30 west of Lampedusa. The Beaufighter was joined by Sqn Ldr Woods and Flt Lt Seed in making stern attacks on the bomber until it caught fire and spun into the sea. One of the bombers was 4D+DM of 4 Staffel, flown by Oblt Karl Raunacher, the other was 4D+EN flown by Lt Walter Klause of 5 Staffel; there were no survivors from either machine.

On returning from an offensive patrol at 1125 on 15 December, Sgt Waterhouse's aircraft, EP343 T-V, sustained minor damage when it swung off the runway on landing; the pilot was unhurt. Eleven Spitfires, led by Sqn Ldr Woods (AR559 T-W), and five Beaufighters set out on offensive reconnaissance at 1100 next day (16 December). A flight of three twin-engined aircraft were seen and as the Spitfires closed, they were fired upon, Flt Lt Seed's aircraft (EP708 T-U) sustaining damage. Seed returned the fire but broke away on recognising the bombers as Bostons (*sic*) — they were in fact Marauders of 14 Squadron — which then identified themselves by firing the colours of the day. By then, however, it was too late for the aircraft fired at by Seed, Sgt L.A. Einsaar's FK367 CX-J, which crashed into the sea 15 miles off Benghazi, with the loss of four of the crew: Sgts Exell, Ploskin, Watts and Cockington. The Australian pilot was rescued by an ASR launch after two hours in the sea, as was Sgt Dixon (who suffered a broken ankle) and Sgt Willcocks, the latter suffering from burns. A further similar tragedy occurred three days later when a Halifax of 138 Squadron, en route from Egypt, was shot down into the sea by AA fire as it approached Malta; all on board were killed.

Six 249 Spitfires set off on 17 December as escort to four of the Beaufighters, one Spitfire returning early with technical problems. At 1020 two Ju88s of Erg/LG1 from Catania — L1+RV of 11 Staffel flown by Obfw Gerhard Meyer and L1+DW of 12 Staffel (Lt Dieter Hahn) — were seen east of Cap Passero, their destination Castel Benito (Libya). All fighters attacked. Flg Off Lynch and Flt Sgt Costello shared one with a Beaufighter piloted by a Belgian. Lynch then joined Plt Off Locke to assist the Beaufighter leader to shoot down the other. All members of the two crews were killed*.

During the afternoon Sqn Ldr Woods led four Spitbombers to Lampedusa where the landing ground was bombed. Light inaccurate flak was experienced over the target. Two days later (19 December), four 249 Spitfires escorted two Beaufighters on an offensive reconnaissance at 0840; soon after 1100 a Do24 of 6 Seenotstaffel and two Ju88s of 8/KG76 were seen near Delimara at between 500 and 1,000 feet, and at once the CO shot down the flyingboat:

"Offensive recce — east of Malta. Dornier 24 destroyed. Hit in elevators by return fire. OK."

Meanwhile, Plt Off Locke and Flt Sgt Hughes engaged one Ju88 and shot this down with assistance from the Beaufighter leader; the other Ju88 was shot down by the Beaufighters. The two bombers were F1+LB flown by Obfw Otto Schuler and F1+OB flown by Obfw Otto Bombel; there were no survivors. Flt Sgt Costello (EP835 T-Z) crashed on landing at Qrendi on return although he was unhurt.

On Christmas Eve (24 December) eight Spitfires carried out a patrol between Lampedusa and Pantelleria. Although the ORB states "no sighting", Plt Off Sanderson noted in his logbook:

"Searched Lampedusa area. Shared ME110 with Jimmy. Good party. Huns gave us a little sneak raid for Xmas! Nice types."

Next day the CO led Locke, Costello and Hughes on an offensive patrol over southern Sicily, sighting two locomotives about 20 miles inland. Both were strafed: many strikes were seen followed by much steam and both were claimed probably destroyed. The Squadron's fighter-bombers returned to Lampedusa on 26 December, where two bombs were seen to burst among aircraft and buildings. Four Spitfires again escorted four Beaufighters on 29 December, carrying out a sweep of the Gulf of Hammamet area; at 1529 a Ju88 of II/KG54 was seen near Pantelleria and was shot down by the Beaufighter leader before the Spitfires could engage. Locke crash-landed EP728 T-S on return from a convoy patrol but was unhurt.

New arrivals during the month included Flg Off E.F. Clarkson, Plt Off I.F Kennedy RCAF, Wt Off W.J. Bentley, Flt Sgts D.E. Cruse and Petchay, and Sgts K. Browne, D.E. Nicholson and G.A. Hardy RNZAF. On their way back to the UK, tour-expired were newly commissioned Plt Offs Wynn† and Moody, while newly promoted Flt Lt Lynch took command of B Flight from Flt Lt Fowler, who had become sick.

Eleven 249 Spitfires, four of which carried bombs, attacked Lampedusa landing ground on 4 January 1943, Sqn Ldr Woods leading the dive-bombers while the escort included two flown by Wg Cdr A.V.R. Johnstone DFC (BR177 T-E), Qrendi's new Wing Leader and former Battle of Britain pilot, and Wg Cdr F.H. Tyson (BR119 T-B), who frequently flew night sorties over Sicily in a Hurricane, dropping urgently needed supplies to agents. Next day four Spitbombers raided Comiso, Wg Cdr Grant leading the escort. On returning to Qrendi, Flt Sgt Bage crash-landed EP140 T-M although the aircraft was not badly damaged.

---

* Apart from Obfw Meyer, the crew members of L1+RV were Uffz Walter Pierskalla, Uffz Horst Sellke and Obgfr Karl Amann; the crew of L1+DW comprised Lt Hahn, Uffz Gerhard Abendroth, Uffz Engelbert Binger and Uffz Ferdinand Sacht.
† Soon after his return to the UK, Plt Off Vasseure Wynn transferred to the US 8th Air Force and joined the 4th Fighter Group; he claimed two further victories, plus a third shared, before he was shot down and became a PoW in April 1944. On release he remained in the USAF and served in the Korean War when he claimed a MiG-15 damaged whilst flying an F-84E jet fighter-bomber.

At 1405 on 6 January six Spitfires left Malta for a sweep over southern Sicily, where three Bf109s and five MC202s attacked from astern. Flg Off Jack Dawkins' Spitfire (AB465 T-R) was seen to go down under control pouring white smoke, and although it was believed by his colleagues that he would survive, Dawkins was in fact killed. The body of the 20-year-old from Southend-on-Sea was recovered from the crash site by Italian soldiers and interred in the cemetery at Syracuse. Of Dawkins' loss, Plt Off Kennedy wrote:

"There were some Messerschmitt pilots at Comiso who were masters of the hit and run tactic. They would attack from high above, usually directly out of the sun, at high speed, one very quick pass only, then disappear, impossible to catch. If the victim was lucky, he could bale out; if not, there wasn't a word. So it was with Jack Dawkins. The yellow-nosed ME109 flashed between us, and black crosses on pale blue wings disappeared far below. Perhaps one second had elapsed. Not a word from Jack, his aircraft leaving a long trail of smoke."

Sqn Ldr Woods led five Spitbombers to attack a sulphur factory at Licata on 7 January. A number of large explosions were seen and one Spitfire (BR463) suffered flak damage, causing it to hit a bowser on landing at Qrendi. Although an undercarriage leg collapsed the pilot was unhurt. The Squadron saw the arrival during the day of Flt Lt M.G. MacLeod RCAF, a 25-year-old Nova Scotian who transferred from 229 Squadron at Takali. He was to take command from Woods who was posted to Air HQ. At about the same time Plt Off Cleverly was promoted to command A Flight vice tour-expired Flt Lt Seed. There were other changes during the month: on 11 January, Flg Off Clarkson left the Squadron on posting to the Middle East, while Flt Sgt Petchay was transferred to Air HQ, followed on 19 January by the departure of tour-expired Plt Offs Stead and Sanderson, together with Sgt Crosswell. New arrivals included Plt Offs B.J. Oliver RNZAF and A.F. Osborne, plus Sgt R. Keating.

The remainder of the month saw a continuation of the fighter-bomber attacks on targets in Sicily: Sciacca on the 12th; a chemical factory near Pachino on the 16th; a power station near Porto Empedocle two days later; a barracks at Licata on the 21st; Porto Empedocle power station again on the 24th; and a military warehouse at Scicli on the 28th. No aircraft was lost during these sorties.

The Spitbomber sorties continued into February, the railway and warehouses at Pozzallo being targeted on the 3rd with the new CO leading the attack but as the month progressed, fighter-bomber attacks were carried out by pairs or sections rather than larger formations of bomb-carrying Spitfires. Early on 7 February two Spitfires took off on a low-level sweep over the Gela-Licata area. Flt Lt Lynch and Plt Off Kennedy first attacked a train about six miles west of Gela, then turned south and when at zero feet a Ju52/3m was seen north of Riesi at 1,500 feet. They climbed up to a position behind and below the transport, and Lynch opened fire, setting the port engine on fire. Kennedy followed and raked the fuselage, and the Ju52 slowly turned to the left and dived towards the ground with flames spreading along the fuselage. It crashed on a hillside 15 miles north-east of Licata just after 0845, blazing from stem to stern. Kennedy recalled:

"As Flight Commander, he [Lynch] had the privilege of attacking first, and he set one engine on fire before I had a crack at it. I knew that he was generous to share it with me."

Next day (8 February) two Spitfires again flew a sweep over Gela and Licata, beginning at 1715. During this operation, Flg Off George Newberry's aircraft (BR373 T-N) was hit by machine-gunfire at Gela; dropping his bombs, he force-landed between a road and the railway ten miles west of the target, but was able to tell Flt Lt Cleverly over the R/T that he was unhurt, before he was taken prisoner. On landing, Cleverly found that his own aircraft (BR177 T-E) had also been hit by ground fire.

Six aircraft from the Squadron joined four Spitbombers of 229 Squadron in an attack on targets located at Pachino and Marzameni, the 249 flight led by Sqn Ldr MacLeod with the escort led by Wg Cdr Johnstone. One aircraft returned with minor flak damage. A message of congratulations was received from Air Vice-Marshal Park:

"The AOC Commanding congratulates the Qrendi Spitfire Wing on their successful bomb and cannon attack on a chemical factory in Sicily on 13th February. Next to destroying enemy aircraft these bombing attacks are of the greatest importance in preparing the way for the Med offensive."

On returning from an unsuccessful search for MTBs reported off the south coast of Sicily on 16 February, Flt Sgt Hughes' aircraft (EP708 T-U) developed problems and he diverted to Luqa, where an emergency landing was achieved. There was not much aerial activity during the ensuing week, but the end of the month saw a resumption of fighter-bomber raids on targets in Sicily: a factory on the coast at Pozzallo was bombed on the 25th, Wg Cdr Tyson leading the escort. All returned safely but next day a Spitfire and its pilot were lost. At 1630 on 26 February, four Spitfires set out to cover fighter-bombers from 126 and 1435 Squadrons to attack targets in Sicily. At 22,000 feet, when about 40 miles north of Malta, they were suddenly attacked by two Bf109s and newly commissioned Plt Off Tony Notley, a 22-year-old from Watcombe in Devon was shot down in AR559 T-W and killed, the victim of the new Staffelkapitän of 8/JG53, Oblt Franz Schiess*, who recorded:

"I took off with my Kazmarek (wingman) and soon we were in a battle with four Spitfires. There were only two of us but we took them by surprise and they didn't spot us until one of them was already going down on fire and were satisfied with that and a fine introduction to my Staffel as well as a birthday gift. No38 for me, again over Malta."

On the last day of February six Spitbombers, with two others as escort, bombed the power station at Cassibile. On the return flight a submarine with its hatch fully open was seen about five miles east of Ayela, and was promptly strafed. Strikes were seen all over the conning tower and hull, followed by a flash and clouds of smoke from the tower itself.

By the end of the month replacement pilots Plt Offs N.C. Holmes and D.A.S. Colvin, Sgts B.W. Sheehan RNZAF, J.A. Denman, J. Meadows and T. Hennessy had joined the Squadron ex-UK, and Sgt Weir (who had been wounded on 2 November) reported to Qrendi to resume flying duties. The Squadron was also notified of the award of the DFC to Flt Lt Seed.

Four Spitfires from 1435 Squadron took off from Malta at 0815 on 3 March to sweep over southern Sicily. About six miles south of Comiso they were attacked from behind and above by six Bf109s of 5/JG27, three of the Spitfires being shot down; the surviving pilot saw one of his colleagues bale out into the sea; one of the other pilots also baled out, landing on the beach, but the third crashed into the water with his aircraft. From Malta an ASR launch — HSL107 — put out from St Paul's Bay to search for the missing pilots, and at 1005 four 249 Spitfires took off to cover this. Five minutes later the pilots saw a Ju88 of Stab I/KG54 (B3+BB) at 800 feet, going north some 12 miles from Pozzallo. The launch commander recorded in his log:

"At 1010 a Ju88 was sighted at about 500 feet and circling boat quarter mile radius clockwise direction. Aircraft were heard on R/T to mention this machine. One minute later Spitfires shot this machine down in flames."

The 249 patrol was led by Plt Off Oliver, who attacked the Ju88 from astern but, as Plt Off Kennedy, who was leading the second pair, later recalled:

"The leader of our section of four aircraft went in to attack but the fire coming at him was so strong, he broke away. His No2 [Sgt Stark] went in next and was shot down but managed to bale out. I was No3. The 88 was at 700 feet so I elected to go under him at sea level, and attack from underneath at high speed, setting his starboard engine on fire. I broke straight up, but he got me in the tail even though I was going at 400 mph and I came home with half a dozen holes in the Spit [EP343 T-V]. Because the 88 was on fire, the No4 [Flt Sgt Cruse] did not attack. The [pilots] from 229 Squadron who were relieving us saw the scrap and when

* Oblt Schiess raised his score to 67 before he was killed in action over Italy on 2 September 1943.

we got back to Malta the Intelligence Officer decreed that the No3 aircraft had in fact shot down the 88 'because 229 Squadron had reported that whoever had attacked third was the one who had destroyed it.' "

Despite this, Kennedy was apparently awarded only a third share of the destroyed Ju88, from which one crew member was seen to bale out, but too late, hitting the water with a partially-opened parachute: Oblt Anton Vögl, Uffz Klaus Unterecker, Uffz Georg Sareiter and Uffz Hermann Wessels were all reported missing, presumed killed. Having already successfully rescued one of the missing Spitfire pilots, HSL107 was directed to search for Stark. The launch's log reveals:

"1055 — Message passed through escorting aircraft for launch to proceed to position 0152. 23 miles, Grand Harbour. Course was immediately set for this position and ETA at position was given as 1120.

1120 — Two Spitfires were sighted two miles south-west of launch. Contact was established by R/T and information passed that they were orbiting round a second airman in the water, in Mae West, no dinghy.

Reached this position and picked up second pilot (Sgt Stark) at 1145. This airman very cold and slightly shocked, having been in the water for approximately one hour. He rapidly revived following applications of hot blankets, hot water bottles and a dose of brandy. Sgt Stark stated that a parachute cord fouled his dinghy as he opened the control valve of the bottle and while attempting to clear the cord he forgot to turn off the control valve, with the result that the dinghy received too much air in one place and split."

The pilots of the circling Spitfires, having observed Stark's plight, had dropped their own dinghies but they fell too far away for Stark to retrieve one. The launch arrived in the nick of time. Four more Spitfires were sent to provide cover and to escort it back to Malta, but one of these (EP140 T-M) crashed on landing when it hit an obstruction, tipped onto its nose, injuring its pilot, Sgt Jack Meadows.

Sqn Ldr MacLeod and his No2 carried out a search off the southern coast of Sicily during the afternoon of 9 March, investigating an earlier sighting of two canvas canoes seen 24 miles north of Malta. Nothing was sighted however, owing partly to poor visibility. Two days later (on 11 March) the CO accompanied Wg Cdr A.D.J. Lovell DFC from Air HQ on a sweep over Sicily at 0920, and in the Comiso area a goods train was sighted and attacked, but Sqn Ldr MacLeod's aircraft (EP519 T-C) was hit by AA fire and crashed into the sea. He was the Squadron's first (and only) Commanding Officer to be killed in action. Flt Lt John Lynch, a 25-year-old American from Alhambra, California, was promoted to take his place, while Flt Lt K.B.L. Debenham, a Battle of Britain pilot, arrived from 185 Squadron as the new flight commander.

From Malta at 1445 on 20 March, two Spitfires of 185 Squadron flew a sweep over southern Sicily, during which one was hit by flak and the pilot was compelled to bale out into the sea; his companion radioed his position and a Walrus amphibian set off from Malta to pick him up. In the meantime however, the surviving Spitfire circling the downed pilot in the sea was also shot down when intercepted by two Bf109s from II/JG27. At 1540 four 249 Spitfires took off to escort the Walrus searching for the missing pilots; they saw it alight on the water and pick up the original downed pilot, as recalled by Sgt Ken Browne, who was flying BP869 T-Z:

"We circled the Walrus at about 1,000 feet or so. I did not realise that my R/T was not working until one colleague flew close by me, apparently trying to warn me of enemy aircraft above. Before I could take action, ie pull into a tighter turn, I was hit (I think) by a single cannon shell in the port wing, right where the oil cooler was situated."

His victor was undoubtedly Hptm Wolfgang Tonne of I/JG53*, flying one of the new, more powerful Bf109Gs with which the Gruppe was being equipped; Browne continued:

"I headed for Malta but only got about five or six miles when the engine seized up and the prop stopped dead. I was too low to bale out, so had to ditch — a bit dicey in a Spitfire. By good luck I managed to get the tail down first, to help break the impact, and only got a bad knock on the forehead from hitting the reflector sight due to the sudden deceleration and the effect of Newton's law of motion. I managed to get out complete with parachute and K type dinghy pack before the plane sank — about 30 seconds or so. I then detached the dinghy and blew it up with the CO_2 bottle provided. The parachute sank. Then, after some difficulty, I managed to get in. Unfortunately, the emergency rations were missing from the dinghy, so I had nothing to eat or drink. It was a bit cold at night, but during the day the sun was warm, and I had a nice view of the top of Mount Etna in the distance, and wished I could have a handful of the snow-covered peak!"

Flg Off Bill Locke, a 20-year-old Canadian from Newfoundland (in BR345 T-W), also failed to return and was apparently the victim of Hptm Paul Sommer† of II/JG27 who, together with his wingman, had arrived on the scene. In the skirmish Flg Off Colvin (EP712 T-C) and Flt Sgt Hughes (EP201 T-D) believed they jointly damaged one of the attackers. Of the action, Sgt Don Nicholson recalled:

"The shooting down of Ken Browne was once again the result of being jumped by 109s. They really were very efficient at this type of attack — a dive out of the sun, a quick burst of fire and away. Partly our own fault of course as we were perhaps too intent on watching the Walrus pick up the pilot from his dinghy."

Meanwhile, Browne was left bobbing up and down off the coast of Sicily in his dinghy, devoid of water and food, praying that he would soon be rescued:

"On 25 March, a Dornier 24 flyingboat flew overhead. It landed, the crew no doubt thinking I was their man [a pilot of II/JG 27 was also missing]. When they came alongside, they said 'Ach, Englander' and I thought they might leave me, but they took me aboard and treated me very well — put me in a rescue suit (sort of track suit) and gave me soda water laced with brandy. I was taken to a Luftwaffe sick quarters in Syracuse, where I was fed well, and young German airmen came along to practice their English on me. I learned that I had been shot down by a Messerschmitt 109G, the latest of that mark and certainly one up on the older Spit VBs we had in Malta. After a week they transferred me to a Luftwaffe-run hospital at Catania as I was suffering from the effects of exposure and dehydration. While there I got quite pally with a NCO ME109 pilot."

On 24 March, when landing at Takali, BP961 T-G hit a truck which had been abandoned by its terrified Maltese driver when he saw the Spitfire about to land. Fortunately, Sgt Keating was not hurt. Next day (25 March), three Spitfires took off at 0825 to escort an ASR search for the crew of a Wellington bomber which had crashed into the sea. Thirty minutes later a Ju88 — believed to have been an aircraft of KG77 — was seen 15 miles south-west of Porto Empedocle at 200 feet and was shot down by Flg Off Kennedy and Flt Sgt Kelly. Kennedy's aircraft suffered a few holes from the rear gunner's machine-gun before the bomber crashed into the sea. It would seem that this was the Squadron's 300th victory.

Three replacement pilots posted to the Squadron during March were Sgts J.H. Hingston, A.R. Lifford and W.L. Yahonitsky RCAF. With a reduction in enemy activity and a surplus of fighter pilots at Malta, some of those who had been on the island for a few months were allowed leave, as recalled by Sgt Don Nicholson:

* Hptm Tonne ended the war with 122 victories.
† Hptm Sommer, a Danish volunteer, was reportedly tried and shot in Denmark after the war.

"Early in April it was arranged for some of the aircrew from the fighter squadrons in Malta to have a few days leave in Tripoli as the campaign in North Africa was drawing to a close. I was amongst the first to go, together with four other Sergeant Pilots. Whilst we were flying from Malta to Tripoli in a DC-3 Dakota, as passengers, we were attacked by a Beaufighter who had mistaken the DC-3 for a German plane. Luckily we sustained only slight damage from a couple of hits before the pilot of the Beaufighter realised his mistake — no one was injured in the attack and it was quietly hushed up. We later received an apology from the Beaufighter pilot (a Squadron Leader) and no more was said."

For the Squadron, April's activity opened on the second day of the month when two bomb-carrying Spitfires led by Flt Lt Debenham departed Malta at 1635 to attack the power station at Cassabile in Sicily. Both claimed direct hits but on the return flight two Bf109s attacked and damaged BR177 T-E flown by newly commissioned Plt Off Costello who, despite inoperative brakes and flaps, carried out a successful landing at Luqa.

At 0615 on 7 April, two 249 Spitfires took off to sweep south of Sciacca in southern Sicily; when 40 miles south-east of this point at 0700, flying at sea level, a Ju88 was seen one mile ahead, flying eastwards. Sqn Ldr Lynch made a starboard rear quarter attack, firing a one-second burst and seeing pieces fly off, at which the bomber burst into flames and dived into the sea; this was probably an aircraft (F1+6R) of III/KG76, in which Oblt Hans Merden and his crew were reported missing. Eight Spitfires, four of which were carrying bombs, together with a similar formation from 229 Squadron, set out at 1500 to attack Comiso airfield. Although all 249 aircraft returned safely, 229's CO was compelled to bale out into the sea during the return flight; despite an intensive search, he was not found.

Two days later, on 9 April, ten Spitfires carried out a sweep of southern Sicily, crossing the coast at Cap Scalambria then flying over Comiso, Ragusa and Noto and back. One Spitfire had turned back earlier before that (BR131 T-O) flown by Sgt Wally Yahonitsky suffered engine failure when eight miles off Scalambria; Yahonitsky baled out but the rescue craft were unable to find him. The body of the Canadian pilot was later recovered from the sea and buried in Malta's Capuccini Naval Cemetery.

Sgt Lifford returned from a sweep on 12 April when his R/T failed but when he attempted to land at Qrendi in a strong crosswind, an oleo leg collapsed resulting in some damage to EP132 T-J. Next day at 1430, four Spitbombers led by the new Wing Leader, Battle of Britain ace Wg Cdr J. Ellis DFC (flying 249's AB535 T-Z), accompanied by four others from 229 Squadron, set out to bomb Pantelleria, arriving over the island an hour later. The formation had been spotted on the island's Freya radar and six of the new MC205s from 17° Gruppo scrambled to intercept. An aircraft of 229 Squadron was engaged by the Macchis and claimed shot down, although the damaged Spitfire was able to return to Malta. Meanwhile, dive-bombing attacks were carried out from 16,000 to 10,000 feet, and bombs were seen to explode among four Ju52s and other aircraft parked in the south-west corner of the airfield. Four covering 249 Spitfires were unable to engage the Italian fighters although a pilot of 229 Squadron reported damaging one.

Four Spitfires set off at 0645 on 16 April to escort two destroyers to the island; these were found at 0730, 15 miles from Sciacca, one burning, the other stationary in the water. At the same time a Ju88 of III/KG76 (F1+BS), flown by Hptm Heinrich Oldendorf, Staffelkapitän of 8 Staffel, was seen flying towards Sicily, and all Spitfires attacked. Flg Off Kennedy and his two companions — Plt Offs Oliver and Costello — reported gaining hits and the bomber ditched in the sea off Sciacca with its starboard engine on fire, but not before return fire had damaged Kennedy's aircraft, who reflected later about his engagements with Ju88s during the previous few weeks:

"I had attacked three Ju88s, a German bomber with excellent rear gunners and on each occasion all of them had put holes in my Spit before they went down into the sea."

Two long-range Spitfires of 249 departed Malta at 0610 on 22 April to carry out a low-level sweep off the Sicilian coast. At 0700 when five miles off Riposto, a transport aircraft identified as a Ju52 was seen, and this was attacked by Kennedy from the rear quarter; it crashed in the sea in flames. This was probably an SM82 of SAS, on its way to Pantelleria, which was reported missing in the area. Half an hour later three more tri-motor transports were sighted near Alicudi in the Lipari Islands, flying west at zero feet. Within seconds all three were reported down in the sea in flames, two being claimed by Sqn Ldr Lynch and the other by Kennedy. These were in fact Ju52s, but since only two of the transports were actually shot down, it would seem that one was attacked jointly by Lynch and Kennedy.

These victories took the CO's score since joining the Squadron to four and four shared. Further success was to come his way three days later, when, at 0740 on 25 April, he and Flt Sgt Cruse encountered a Caproni Ca313 torpedo-reconnaissance bomber flying at 700 feet over six small vessels, ten miles west of Cap Milazzo. Lynch climbed from zero feet to make a quarter head-on attack, seeing strikes on the fuselage; he then attacked twice from astern and pieces flew off. A fire broke out along the starboard side of the fuselage and in the port engine, and the aircraft dived into the sea in flames.

The Squadron reverted to its dive-bombing role on 26 April, six Spitbombers accompanied by six of 229 Squadron and led by Wg Cdr Ellis again striking at Lampedusa. Six bombs were seen to explode near seven dispersed aircraft, believed to have been SM81s, on the west side of the airfield. Another burst within 50 yards of a large aircraft believed to have been a Fiat G12 parked on the south side. No aircraft were seen to take off during the attack although one aircraft was seen up sun as the Spitbombers headed back towards Malta, but it did not engage.

Sqn Ldr Lynch and Plt Off Osborne were airborne at 0535 on 28 April for a sweep of the Sicilian coastline, sighting a Ju52/3m at sea level five miles north of Cap Cafafu. Lynch attacked from the rear quarter with a four-second burst, seeing strikes on the fuselage and centre section; the aircraft trailed a stream of petrol from the starboard engine and made for the coast, but suddenly dived into the sea. Osborne then saw another Ju52 one mile further out to sea, and made a full beam to quarter astern attack, gaining strikes on the fuselage. Lynch attacked the same aircraft head-on and saw his fire hitting the windscreen and fuselage before Osborne fired a second burst from the port quarter. The transport dived into the sea. On his return, Lynch reported:

> "As soon as my Junkers crashed, I went off to see how my No2 was doing. I found him attacking his Ju52 and we finished it off together."

These two victories were assessed to be the 1000th and 1001st aircraft shot down by Malta-based units since the start of the war. Soon after they landed, the CO received a congratulatory message from the AOC:

> "Congratulations to your Squadron on destroying the thousandth Bosche shot down by the Royal Air Force, Malta. The Squadron has kept up its magnificent record."

Partly as a result of this achievement, Lynch was awarded an immediate DFC, having raised his personal score to six destroyed plus a further seven shared destroyed, of which five and a half had been shot down during April.

The Squadron lost another pilot on the last day of the month when four Spitfires carried out a low level strafing sweep of the Sicilian coastline. Flt Sgt Don Cruse failed to return, his aircraft (EP188 T-Y) last seen at 1235 near Marzamemi, where it eventually crash-landed; Cruse was taken prisoner. It was assumed that he had fallen victim to ground fire since no enemy fighters were observed. However, Bf109s of II/JG27 were in the vicinity and Fw Josef Brändl claimed a Spitfire shot down west of Pantelleria, which may have been Cruse's aircraft. Flg Off Kennedy's aircraft (EP343 T-V) was hit by ground fire in the engine bay although he was able to get back to Qrendi safely.

The first week of May was relatively quiet for the Squadron, four Spitbombers raiding Lampedusa in company with 229 Squadron on the 3rd, although results were not observed owing to heavy AA fire over the target area. Early on 10 May, two Spitfires flown by Sqn Ldr Lynch and Flg Off Holmes took off on an offensive sweep. At 0710 two Cant Z506B floatplanes of 186[a]

Squadriglia RM (flown by Cap Antonio Blengini and Sottoten Amedee Fiorillo), which had just taken off, were seen at 500 feet, five miles east of Riposto. Lynch promptly shot down one into the sea, Holmes similarly disposing of the other one. A Ju52 was then sighted by Holmes, but his guns jammed, so Lynch shot it down. Another floatplane was sighted, identified as another Cant Z506B, but was in fact a Fiat RS14 of 170ª Squadriglia RM; Lynch attacked and sent this spinning down in flames with the loss of Serg Magg Residori and his crew. Three Messerschmitt 210s of III/ZG1 then appeared and Lynch attacked one with machine-guns only (his cannon ammunition being exhausted); he saw strikes but he and Holmes were forced to return to Malta. III/ZG1 reported one of its aircraft damaged north-east of Catania, in which Oblt Ferdinand Glanz was wounded.

Fighter-bomber raids continued to be carried out by the Squadron against various targets in Sicily: the power station at Porto Empedocle on the 8th; the sulphur refinery and railway installations at Licata next day; a hutted military camp five miles east of Pozzallo on the 16th; Lampedusa airfield on the 23rd. In between, two bomber escorts were flown: Sqn Ldr Lynch led a dozen Spitfires as escort to Liberators raiding Augusta on the 13th when five enemy fighters were seen, although these did not intercept; and again on the 25th when nine Liberators were escorted back to Malta following a raid on a target in Sicily.

However, for Malta's fighters generally this period was very much quieter, although on 21 May the Luftwaffe launched a surprise dawn raid on the island by FW190 fighter-bombers of III/SKG10 from Sicily, escorted by more FW190s and Bf109s — 36 aircraft in all. Hal Far was targeted, where three Albacores and a Spitfire were destroyed. AA defences shot down one fighter-bomber which crashed on the edge of the airfield, killing its pilot. Both 229 and 249 Squadrons managed to scramble aircraft, the former unit claiming three of the raiders shot down. Four patrolling Spitfires of 249 made contact with four to six FW190s at 9,000 feet heading northwards, one of which Sgt Keating attacked and claimed damaged; it was last seen in a steep dive. Flg Off John Beatson RAAF, a six feet five inches tall Australian from Toora, Victoria, known as Shortie, noted:

"Four FW190s off Gozo. Intercepted badly and they got away easily."

Beatson was one of five replacement pilots posted to the Squadron during May, the others being Flg Offs K. MacBain RCAF and O.L.V. Gervais RCAF, plus Sgts R.E. Pride and D.E. Chambers. Leaving the Squadron, tour-expired, were Flt Lt Cleverly who passed command of A Flight to newly promoted Flt Lt Colvin, and Plt Offs Costello, Oliver and Hardy, together with Flt Sgt Kelly. By the end of the month a second DFC was announced for the CO, the citation for which concluded:

"Squadron Leader Lynch is a highly successful squadron commander whose personal example to his pilots is outstanding. The excellent work carried out by his squadron is due in a great degree to his determination to seek out and destroy the enemy at every opportunity."

Plans for the invasion of Sicily were by now well advanced and, since heavily-fortified Pantelleria, and Lampedusa, lay on the direct invasion route to southern Sicily, it was desirable that the threat they posed be removed. Therefore, British forces landed on Pantelleria on the morning of 11 June where they met little resistance and, at midday, the demoralised garrison, comprising 11,100 Italians and 78 Germans, surrendered. The garrison on Lampedusa surrendered the following day. With the islands thus subdued, all efforts could then be concentrated against Sicily and, to assist in this, Malta's capacity for handling aircraft was being greatly increased, with airfields being enlarged.

Since early May the heavy bombers of the Strategic Air Force had been launching a regular series of attacks on airfields in Sicily, Sardinia and southern Italy, and against ports and submarine bases in the area. Following the fall of Pantelleria and Lampedusa, the medium bombers were also directed on to the assault on Sicily, formations of Bostons, Baltimores, B-25s and B-26s, escorted by Malta-based Spitfires and P-40s becoming an ever-more familiar sight as they winged their way to and from the targets.

One such escort mission was undertaken on 13 June by a dozen 249 Spitfires led by Sqn Ldr Lynch, plus a similar number from 229 Squadron, which departed Malta at 1105; their task to cover Liberators briefed to bomb Gerbini. When leaving the target area after the bombing, three Bf109Gs of II/JG53 attacked the Spitfires from astern, shooting down the Wing Leader (Wg Cdr Ellis, who survived as a prisoner) and a pilot of 229 Squadron. It is believed that Ellis was shot down by Hptm Gerhard Michalski for his 57th victory. In addition, Flt Sgt Hughes' aircraft (EF539 T-F) suffered damage and crashed on landing at Luqa. 249's Sgt Bernie Sheehan (ER811 T-J) also failed to return and was similarly taken prisoner. Later, on his release, he reported that he had been engaged by several MC202s, one of which he claimed to have shot down and damaged a second, before falling victim to a third. Of those who returned to Malta, only newly commissioned Plt Off Nicholson was able to make a claim:

> "The 109s were spotted coming down on us from the rear and we broke right to turn towards them. I had just straightened up when I saw in front of me a 109 coming towards me from my left. I just pushed the firing button and the 109 flew through my line of fire. I saw a couple of strikes near the cockpit and then it was gone — all very sudden and over in a few seconds. I did not see it go down but John Beatson confirmed seeing it diving vertically and also seeing an aircraft hit the ground. This may have been my victim or could have been that of Sgt Sheehan. Anyway, the Intelligence Officer said 'probably destroyed' — who was I to argue!!"

Of the missing pilots, Flg Off Beatson noted:

> "Sgt Bernie Sheehan and Wg Cdr Ellis failed to return. Later Y Service report a Wing Commander and a Sergeant Pilot entertained at a German Air Force Mess in Sicily." *

On 20 June the people of Malta were in for a pleasant surprise, for His Majesty the King had chosen to visit them, to see for himself the results of the heavy bombing to which it had been subjected. The visit lasted only one day however, during which time the King and his staff were driven through the various towns and villages that had been most heavily bombed. His Majesty also toured the docks and Luqa airfield, as well as the Palace in Valetta, where he appeared on the balcony to wave to the thousands of well-wishers who had gathered on the Palace Square in the hope of catching a glimpse of him.

The Squadron had been relatively inactive for the first half of the month, but participated in attacks against Comiso on 26 June when a Ju52 was seen taking off although it escaped. Comiso was visited again two days later and on this occasion a MC202 attacked one of the Spitbombers which evaded and turned the tables although no results were seen. Comiso was again the target on 29 June, when a dozen Spitbombers, six each from 249 (led by Flt Lt Debenham in EF646 T-F) and 229 Squadrons, with similar number of escort drawn equally from the two units set out for Sicily. Top cover was provided by eight of the new Spitfire IXs of 185 Squadron. A total of two dozen 250lb bombs were dropped before up to 20 enemy fighters were reported attempting to intercept as the formation fled for Malta; claims were submitted for one Macchi destroyed, one Bf109 probable and three damaged, although the only claim for 249 was by Flg Off Beatson, who claimed damage to a Bf109.

During the month the Squadron had received a number of new pilots: Flg Offs L.W. Humphrey RCAF and A.R. Speare; Flt Sgt V.H. Twomey and Sgts K.L. Dale, RCAF, C.J. Shenberger RCAF, J.A. Felton RCAF, W. Docherty, J.D. Sheeran, R.W. Kimmings and J.S. Simmons. Those who departed during the month, tour-expired, were Flt Sgts Hughes and Bage. The new arrivals coincided with the delivery of the first four Spitfire IXs, EN306 T-A, EN350 T-D, EN456 T-P and ES107 T-L operating in Squadron markings for the first time on 1 July.

Thirty-eight Spitfires, including a dozen from 249, rose from Malta's airfields late on the morning of 4 July, their pilots tasked to escort heavy bombers to Sicily but the bombers failed

---

* Wg Cdr Ellis and Sgt Sheehan, both uninjured, were taken to JG53's Mess where they were entertained by Oblt Friedrich-Karl Müller, Gruppenkommandeur of I Gruppe, who spoke good English. Next day the two prisoners were flown to Germany.

to rendezvous. A similar misunderstanding occurred the following morning, although in the afternoon USAF B-26s were escorted to Biscari where they unloaded their bombs. Many enemy fighters engaged over the target area but these were tackled by 185 and 229 Squadrons and 249 did not become embroiled. The operation was repeated on 6 July, when 249 Squadron — again joined by Spitfires from 229 Squadron — provided escort for B-26s bombing Biscari. Although 249 was not attacked by the defending fighters, the other unit was. Flying with 229 was a future CO of 249, Flt Lt Jack te Kloot RAAF, who recalled:

"Jumped by FW190s, being on the outside of a turn after the Mitchells dropped their bombs and turned for home. Lost CO and a Flight Sergeant. I was shot up. Three cannon shells through starboard wing. My first introduction to the enemy in the air."

Next day (7 July), eight 249 Spitfires, together with others from 229 and 185 Squadrons, escorted USAF B-17s to bomb Gerbini. A number of MC202s attempted to interfere but only the Wing Leader was able to make a conclusive claim, a second being damaged by a pilot of 229 Squadron. Further escorts were provided to B-17s raiding Gerbini on the 8th, and for B-26s bombing Biscari on the 9th. No enemy aircraft were sighted on either occasion.

By this time the impending assault on Sicily had brought to Malta additional British and American troops and armour. Anchored off the coast were several warships of all kinds as the harbours were already overflowing with landing craft, aircraft carriers and similar-sized ships. Troops were kept on troopships and were also billeted all over the island, many under canvas. The airfields which a year earlier had been subjected to daily bombings, were now packed with aircraft. So much so, that an additional strip had to be laid out on the neighbouring island of Gozo by American engineers, who within three weeks of the landing of their earth-moving equipment at Marsalforn Bay, had cleared an agricultural site at Xewkija and had it operational. Malta had never seen such military activity.

All was set for the invasion, codenamed Operation Husky, for 10 July, when the weather unexpectedly deteriorated. But as the number of craft and troops involved was so great, the order to go ahead was given, since most of the invasion fleet from east and west had sailed from their rendezvous near Malta. Some 3,000 ships and major landing craft, carrying 115,000 British and Commonwealth soldiers and 66,000 American troops, 14,000 vehicles, 600 tanks and 1,800 guns headed towards Sicily. The airborne troops left from six landing strips in Tunisia on board USAF C-47s, RAF Dakotas and Albemarles, together with Halifaxes and Stirlings which were towing Waco and Horsa gliders carrying men and anti-tank guns. The strong wind was not the only obstacle of the day. Through some tactical error, Allied naval vessels opened fire on the troop-carrying transports when close to the Sicilian beaches. Several were shot down whilst others were damaged and had to return to North Africa. In order to avoid being hit, some pilots altered course and dropped their troops away from their appointed sites, some as far away as the Italian mainland. Notwithstanding this and the freak storm, the Allies established a number of beachheads and advanced inland. Aerial protection was afforded from the Maltese islands and the newly-occupied Allied airfield on Pantelleria; the bombing of Sicily, intensified a week before the invasion, was sustained after the actual landing, by British and American bombers operating from Tripolitania, Tunisia and Malta. Spitfires from Malta were continually airborne over the beaches.

During the first three days of the invasion, 249 flew a number of offensive patrols in the Gela-Scalabria area, as noted by Flg Off Beatson:

"Cover for invasion forces landing in Sicily. American Army on west; 8th Army on east. Amazing number of ships. Several fires but otherwise quiet. Operation appears very successful. Went well north of front line. Nothing up."

On 13 July, he wrote:

"Escort to Mitchells — Caltagirone. Operation stopped when on the way in. Target in process of being taken by land forces."

However, the Squadron did gain a success on another operation during this day, when twelve Spitfires — six IXs and six Vs — escorted P-40 Kittybombers to raid Lentini, departing Qrendi at 1800. Three FW190s were sighted south of Catania at 12,000 feet and one of these was claimed shot down into Catania Harbour by Sqn Ldr Lynch. More aircraft were sighted by another 249 patrol, but they proved to be friendly, as Flg Off Beatson noted with a certain amount of disappointment:

> "Sweep along front, Caltagirone-Lentini area. Saw, hoped, prayed that they would be FW190s. They were Lightnings."

Despite this early success, the Squadron was not called upon to take part in offensive operations during the invasion, being held back for the defence of Malta.

Within 38 days of fierce fighting, Sicily was occupied. As soon as Sicilian airfields fell into Allied hands, Malta-based fighters crossed over to set up base there. During the height of the Sicilian Campaign, on 25 July, the news of Mussolini's downfall was broadcast. King Vittorio Emanuele III assumed the role of Head of State and appointed Maresciallo Pietro Badoglio his Prime Minister. The morning of 17 August saw Sicily entirely in Allied hands. Over 1,000 enemy aircraft were reported to have been taken on airfields. Guns, tanks, rifles and machine-guns lay scattered all over the island. The enemy had lost 167,000 men, of whom 37,000 were German. The Allies lost 31,158 killed, wounded and missing. The capture of Sicily was an undertaking of the first magnitude.

The Allied Chiefs had earlier agreed that action against Italy should be decided in the light of the fighting in Sicily. The Americans had plans for the capture of Sardinia but were made to understand that, in the event of severe and prolonged enemy resistance in Sicily, it might not be possible. But, should Italian resistance prove to be not as strong as anticipated, then invasion of the Italian mainland could be contemplated. At that time there were 74,000 British prisoners in Italy, together with about 30,000 Yugoslavs and Greeks. The Allied commanders were fearful that some of these prisoners would be deported to Germany. Detailed plans had already been made between the British and American governments about the probable surrender of Italy. Early in August, the Badoglio Government cautiously approached the British Ambassador in Lisbon and explained that, although the King and Government wanted peace, they had to make a pretence of continuing the fight in order to avoid a German *coup d'etat* in Italy. The British made it clear that there was no room for negotiation. Unconditional surrender was required. Meanwhile, the war continued.

The Squadron underwent a further change of personnel, starting at the top. Shortly after being awarded his second DFC, Sqn Ldr John Lynch resigned his commission in the RAF and transferred to the USAAF in the Mediterranean, being granted the rank of Lt Colonel. With this unexpected departure, Sqn Ldr Woods was recalled from Air HQ to take over command once again. The Squadron also lost its other high-scoring pilot when Flg Off Kennedy, recently awarded the DFC, was posted. Others leaving the Squadron at this time, tour-expired, were Plt Off Nicholson, Flt Sgts Weir, Stark, Meadows, Keating, and Sgt Waterhouse. More replacement pilots arrived during this period: Flt Lt P.F.T. Wakeford (posted sick soon after arrival and did not return to the Squadron*), Flg Off L.J. Foubert RCAF, Plt Off J.O. Gray RCAF, Flt Sgt F.F.E.J. Potvin RCAF, A.H. Lamb RNZAF, and Sgts A.R. Fulton, C.F. Jacobsen RNZAF, L.K. Till, N.F. Houghton RCAF.

This was a period of training, the new pilots familiarising themselves with their new mounts — more Spitfire IXs had by now arrived — and the theatre of operations. Sgt Docherty suffered concussion when he crashed in ER819 T-M after its engine had cut but he was soon discharged and back with the Squadron.

At 0825 on 22 August four Spitfire IXs were scrambled when an intruder was reported in the area. Climbing to 30,000 feet, a reconnaissance Ju88 of I(F)/123 was sighted 20 miles north-

---

* Although Flt Lt Wakeford, who had been wounded earlier in the war when flying Blenheim bombers, did not rejoin the Squadron at Malta he was, however, re-posted to 249 in early 1946 when it was equipped with Baltimores at RAF Eastleigh, Kenya (see Chapter Thirteen).

east of Grand Harbour at 0840 and was attacked from astern and below by Flt Lt Debenham. The port engine of 4U+DH caught fire and, before it crashed into the sea, the three crew members baled out. The Spitfires orbited the survivors until relieved by a section from 229 Squadron, which covered the rescue launch coming out from Malta. The seriously wounded pilot, Uffz Heinz Krösing, a Knights Cross holder, subsequently told his captors:

"On becoming aware of presence of four fighters, a hurried oblique photograph of the Grand Harbour and coastline was taken, and the aircraft headed due west and then north in a wide sweep. The W/Op signalled base that [we] were being attacked by fighters. One of the Spitfires closed in and his first burst broke [my] arm and wounded [me] in the legs. The lower gun position and the boost lever were also destroyed. The attack from underneath was sudden and unexpected; the W/Op was momentarily unsighted and no evasive action could be taken."

The W/Op, Uffz Günther Lehmann, was less seriously wounded, while the observer, Lt Günther Wissel, a double Knights Cross recipient, escaped with only a dunking. Flg Off Beatson noted:

"Deb bagged a Ju88. Air gunner later entertained in Mess. Pilot shot in arm and base of spine. Belly gunner also shot up in same burst."

Five days later (27 August) the Squadron accounted for another reconnaissance Ju88 (probably also from I(F)/123), which was to be its 317th and last victory while flying from Malta. Four Spitfire IXs were scrambled at 1710 and 45 minutes later contacted the aircraft flying at 36,000 feet, 20 miles east of Kalafrana. Flg Sgt Lifford was the first to sight the Junkers some 2,000 feet below, then Flg Off MacBain yelled "Tally-ho!" and dived to attack. The German machine dived away with MacBain following closely and after three short bursts, both engines caught fire. Two crew members were seen to bale out as it spiralled down to crash into the sea. Although both Lifford and Plt Off Gray also attacked and reported hits, the destruction of the Ju88 was credited to MacBain. The fourth member of the section, Sgt Houghton, had become separated and took no part in the action.

The skipper of rescue launch HSL128 recorded:

"Call out 0605 (on 28 August) — Search for two men seen in a dinghy in position 35N 14E. ASR Beaufort taking off shortly. 0634 Beaufort passed overhead on same course."

Three and a half hours later HSL128 had reached the position indicated and commenced a square search. Aerial assistance was requested and by midday three Wellingtons and a Swordfish were seen in the area. Eventually a sighting was made, as noted in the launch's log:

"1445 — Sighted object on starboard bow and turned towards it. Seen to be a man sitting on an a/c wheel in middle of large oil patch.

1448 — Picked up German pilot (Gerhard Horch) with broken ankle. Informed by him his W/T operator about one kilometre away. Gave him first aid and commenced search for second man.

1542 — Picked up second German floating in life jacket, one mile NW. Dead when brought aboard (drowned). Removed personal effects from body and buried it at sea."

Next day the AOC sent a message of congratulations for the successful interception. The Squadron was now ordered to revert to its original code markings of GN and all aircraft were rapidly repainted, including the four additional Mark IXs just received: EN256 GN-B, EN392 GN-V, EN456 GN-P and MA500 GN-Z.

3 September saw the invasion of the Italian mainland. At dawn the British and Canadian divisions of the Eighth Army crossed the Straits of Messina — without opposition. Reggio was speedily taken. The Allied armies pushed northwards, where they were to fight over difficult

mountainous terrain in a campaign which was to become the battleground of some of the fiercest fighting in the war. On the night of 8 September as the Allied armada approached the Salerno beaches, they heard the announcement of the Italian surrender. They were however, warned not to expect a walkover since German forces would offer strong resistance. While the Salerno battle was raging, the Royal Navy steamed boldly into Taranto harbour and deposited 6,000 British airborne troops. Again there was no opposition. The terms of the Armistice with Italy provided for co-belligerency and the surrender at Malta of the Italian Fleet. This sailed from La Spezia and Taranto under the vigilance of the Royal Navy. En route the flagship *Roma* was sunk by a German radio-controlled bomb, with the loss of many men, the first ships arriving on 10 September.

September had proved to be a quiet month for the Squadron, highlighted on the 9th when Flg Off Humphrey crashed at the end of the runway on take-off. He was unhurt although his aircraft EN456 GN-P suffered some damage. On 27 September the Squadron moved from Qrendi to Hal Far and was advised of imminent movement to a new base in southern Italy. There was a further change of personnel, five Canadian pilots — Flg Off Foubert, Plt Off Gray, and Sgts Felton, Houghton and Shenberger — departing, their replacements in the guise of Flg Offs J.W. Brooks DFM RCAF and R.G.F. Chase, Plt Off A.J. Sykes RNZAF, Wt Off P.V. Waddell RAAF and Flt Sgt J.G. Belec, arriving a few days later. Brooks had won his DFM while flying with 607 Squadron in the UK.

The Squadron's Malta sojurn came to an end on 27 October 1943 when 16 Spitfires — including six Mark IXs — departed Hal Far on 27 October for Grottaglie airfield in southern Italy. The first flight of eight arrived at 1240:

Flt K.B.L.Debenham	JK465 GN-X
Flg Off K. MacBain	EN256 GN-B (IX)
Flg Off J. Beatson	EP728 GN-K
Flt Sgt A.R. Fulton	JL346 GN-F
Flt Sgt V.H. Twomey	BP978 GN-O
Flt Sgt C.F. Jacobsen	ER774 GN-T
Flt Sgt J.D. Sheeran	EN350 GN-D (IX)
Flt Sgt D.E. Chambers	ER591 GN-M

A further seven arrived at 1310, the remaining aircraft having been delayed by engine problems at Hal Far:

Flt Lt D.A.S. Colvin	EN392 GN-V (IX)
Flg Off N.C. Holmes	MA500 GN-Z (IX)
Flg Off L.W. Humphrey	LZ811 GN-P (IX)
Flt Sgt R.E. Pride	EN306 GN-A (IX)
Flt Sgt J.S. Simmons	BR118 GN-W
Flt Sgt F.F. Potvin	BR380 GN-N
Flt Sgt A.R. Lifford	ER878 GN-H

Newly commissioned Plt Off A.H. Lamb followed as soon as his aircraft (ER549 GN-U) was ready, arriving at Grottaglie at 1545. Ground personnel and spare pilots travelled by sea and disembarked at Taranto, from where they proceeded by road to the airfield.

Thus, 249 ended its illustrious association with Malta after almost two-and-a-half years, a period which had seen a resolute defence of the island by its pilots, of whom 44 had made the supreme sacrifice; in addition, four ground personnel members of the Squadron were killed in bombing raids on Takali. During this period 249 had increased its score of enemy aircraft to 317 confirmed, with a further 441 probably destroyed or damaged, of which 245 confirmed (plus 357 probables/damaged) had been claimed in defence of Malta.

A new era was about to begin.

Chapter Eleven

THE BALKANS: SPITBOMBER OPERATIONS
November 1943 – August 1944

"I flew in front of them, waggled my wings, fired a burst across their nose and almost yelled at the pilot through his window, but he wouldn't go in to the shore. I got so furious I thought quite seriously of shooting the Cant down into the water."

Flt Lt Shortie Beatson RAAF, 249 Squadron

In September, following the Italian surrender, the Germans occupied the islands of Corfu, Cephalonia and Zante to strengthen their hold on Yugoslavia, and the following month with the invasion of Italy well in hand, units of both Coastal and Tactical Air Forces began to operate on occasions over this area and in support of Marshal Tito's Partisan forces in Yugoslavia. The mountainous and forested terrain of the Adriatic regions of the three Balkan countries was highly favourable to guerilla warfare. Historically too, it had affected the development and way of life of the inhabitants of those regions, especially of the peasantry. There were few major roads and railway communications were limited and restricted. Distances were commonly calculated by time and not by mileage. Movement was mostly by foot or mule or animal-drawn transport.

Following the successful establishment of the Allied armies in southern Italy, 249's operations were almost entirely to be in support of Partisan forces in Greece, Albania and Yugoslavia. With its arrival at Grottaglie, the Squadron came under the control of the Coastal Air Force and, with 126, 185 and 1435 Squadrons, formed 286 Wing as part of 242 Group. Although operations over the Adriatic — and along the coastline of Yugosalvia, Albania and Greece — opened in a fairly small way, the Squadron's stay in Italy was to be extremely active, with sections flying every day during daylight hours on bombing and strafing operations, whenever weather permitted. When the weather was unfavourable, but with the possibility that there could be areas where there was enough broken cloud cover to make operations feasible, sections were then sent on weather reconnaissance. Regular operations in the Balkan theatre in which the Squadron participated were instituted in the autumn of 1943. A characteristic peculiar to the Balkan war was that air crew who were forced down during operations were frequently and easily able to make contact with local Partisans and so to be quickly returned to their squadrons.

On 2 November the Squadron took part in its first action in the new theatre of operations, a Wing sweep led by Grp Capt E. Rhys-Jones in a 249 aircraft (BR118 GN-W), when a RDF station north of Durazzo in Albania, was attacked. Flg Off Beatson (JL346 GN-F) noted:

"RDF station Durazzo. 22 Spits. Target pranged and on fire. Durazzo bombed by Navy following night."

Ten days later Sqn Ldr Woods (JK465 GN-X) led the Squadron on an escort to USAF B-26s tasked to bomb Berat. Woods noted:

"Wizard bombing — shot up two schooners on return and did air-sea rescue on crew of Mitchell in the drink. Successful — four bomber boys picked up."

The Squadron was instructed to fit bomb racks to its Spitfire Vs, thus enabling each aircraft to carry two 250lb bombs, and then moved to the coastal airfield at Brindisi, from where they would be able to range the Valona and Durazzo areas of Albania. Brindisi had earlier seen the arrival of an ancient French aircraft of WWI vintage, which had initially been flown to Tortorella airfield (further up the coast) by an escaping member of the Croat Partisan Forces. Another unusual aircraft to arrive at Tortorella was a Caproni Ca311bis which had narrowly avoided being shot down by two SAAF Spitfires as it crossed the Adriatic from the direction of Sarajevo. On board were seven Yugoslav officers who had kidnapped the Croat pilot and aircraft.

Under the terms of the Armistice, the Regia Aeronautica was required to transfer its aircraft to Allied bases in Sicily and Tunisia. Despite the lack of fuel, great distance and the presence of German troops on many Italian airfields, some 200 aircraft succeeded in reaching Allied airfields, where the aircrews were given the opportunity to continue the fight, but now on the side of the Allies against the Germans. Many did, and so the Italian Co-Belligerent Air Force came into existence. However, many of those based in the north of Italy felt differently and refused to surrender. They chose to carry on under the control of the Luftwaffe. A number of Co-Belligerent units were based at Brindisi, including squadriglie equipped with MC202s and MC205s, plus two squadriglie operating Z501 and Z506 seaplanes, the latter being co-opted for ASR duties.

The Italians had already shown a keenness to fight their former allies, Macchis and Re2002s having bombed and strafed the German airfield near Lake Scutari in Albania in mid-October, and by the end of that month had carried out several dive-bombing missions, losing three aircraft but claiming a Ju52 and a Bf109 shot down. Italian SM82 converted bombers also carried out supply-dropping sorties, escorted by USAF P-38s from Foggia.

The first 249 Spitbomber operation from Brindisi took place on 16 November, when six aircraft were in action along the Shkambin river valley, south of Tirana. Sqn Ldr Woods (JK465 GN-X) noted in his logbook:

"Bombing bridge SE of Durazzo. Six direct hits. Plenty of flak."

Next morning, a section of Spitfires took part in a protective escort of an ASR Walrus of 284 Squadron off the coast of Albania, searching for the crew of a USAF B-25 which had ditched in Kneta Bay. Flt Sgt Sheeran (EF638 GN-K) suddenly reported enemy aircraft above and gave the 'Tally-ho' but was then shot down by a Bf109 of 12/JG27 flown by Lt Hans Hetzler, operating from Kalimaki in northern Greece. Sheeran's companion, Flt Sgt Dale (EN256 GN-B) was engaged by another Bf109 which attacked from astern, although he managed to evade. Subsequently Dale saw a Messerschmitt 'on the deck', dived and opened fire on it at a range of 150 yards, hitting its starboard wing; he saw black smoke coming from its fuselage before he was forced away when he saw another Messerschmitt coming to attack him. He turned in towards this aircraft, which veered away. He then saw the aircraft he had attacked losing altitude and going down in slow diving turns, still pouring black smoke, but he did not see it hit the ground. This was in fact Lt Hetzler's aircraft, the pilot having been wounded but he was able to return to Kalimaki. Thereafter, Dale circled Kneta Bay for 15 minutes, calling Sheeran. Receiving no reply, he returned to base.

Meanwhile, the ASR Walrus had spotted the wreckage of the B-25 but as it alighted on the sea it struck a submerged obstacle 200 yards offshore and had settled on the seabed. Thus the crew, together with a survivor of the American bomber, awaited rescue. Another Walrus was despatched in the afternoon, escorted by four more 249 Spitfires, and successfully completed the rescue; however, nothing more was heard of Flt Sgt Dennis Sheeran, a 21-year-old from Elland, Yorkshire, whom it was assumed had crashed into the sea.

Next day, 18 November, the Squadron lost the services of one of its Spitfire IXs when EN306 GN-A suffered engine failure when in the circuit two miles south of Brindisi and crash-landed, Flt Sgt Kimmings suffering slight injuries. The Squadron lost another pilot on 19 November when Flt Sgt Ken Dale was killed, two days after his victory over the Bf109. He was flying No 2 in a section of four Spitfires, when Sqn Ldr Woods (JK465 GN-X) led a strafing attack on three lorries and a staff car parked on a road in the area of Fier, south of Tirana. Woods warned the section to be careful of tall poplar trees lining the two sides of the road, but Dale's aircraft (BP978 GN-O) struck one of them. Its starboard mainplane was torn off and the aircraft flicked over, on fire. It crashed, slid along the ground and exploded. The remaining two pilots broke off the attack and returned to base with the CO, who noted:

> "Two petrol storage tanks exploded, one lorry on fire."

Operations against road transport intensified towards the end of the month, the CO's logbook annotated accordingly:

> "21 November: eight lorries on fire — six more destroyed — bombing poor. 23 November: 15 lorries destroyed — plenty of flak — five aircraft hit."

That the flak was becoming a nuisance was verified by Flg Off Beatson, whose logbook revealed:

> "23 November: Several lorries set on fire. Accurate light flak. Hit in tailpane (GN-O); 25 November: Field day. Covered road from Elbasan to Durazzo. Hit in wing (GN-T); second sortie: Kullzh to Bushnesh (GN-N). Squadron total for three days approx 70 vehicles. 26 November: Bombed and shot-up supposed RDF. Flak holed behind my cockpit (GN-T)."

November was proving to be a bad month for 249, the Squadron losing its third pilot in ten days on 26 November. Six Spitfire fighter-bombers and one fighter had bombed and strafed a gun position near Fier and, as the flight was crossing the coast on its way back to Brindisi, Plt Off Sykes reported that his aircraft's engine temperature was rising. Soon afterwards he baled out of JL346 GN-F and came down in the sea about five miles from the coast of Albania. He succeeded in getting into his dinghy, which was then orbited by three of his colleagues until they were relieved by a section of two more Spitfires. When the Spitfire-escorted Walrus arrived, the crew spotted Sykes in his dinghy north of Sasens Island, but the amphibian was unable to alight, so dropped a marker float nearby. Flg Off MacBain, leading the escort, also dropped his Mae West near the dinghy.

Throughout the next day aircraft and ASR launches continued to search for the dinghy, but without success. The weather deteriorated, with poor visibility. The search was resumed for a third day, again without success while the following day the weather precluded flying. Plt Off Allen Sykes, a 24-year-old New Zealander from Auckland, was subsequently listed as missing, presumed killed. The actual cause of his death remains unknown. The Squadron lost its popular CO for a second time when Sqn Ldr Woods was promoted on 30 November to lead 286 Wing, Flt Lt Colvin taking his place with newly promoted Flt Lt Beatson given command of B Flight.

249 gained another success on 1 December, during a mission when four Spitfires led by Flg Off Brooks (JK366 GN-H) were providing escort for a squadron of USAF P-39s* from Sicily on a strafing mission in the Alessio-Shegas area of Albania, as Brooks later reported:

> "Red Section was escorting P-39s over Albania. Spitfires were at approximately 2,000 feet and P-39s were about 1,500 feet, in front. We were approximately five miles north of Shegas when I saw a Ju52 below, flying south at 500-1,000 feet. I dived down and delivered a shallow deflection attack from starboard quarter. I saw hits along the side and before I finished firing, it was on fire around the cockpit area. I saw, before I attacked, that the Ju52 was trying to make a crash-landing but it caught fire at approximately 100 feet and crashed. I also saw one P-39 attacking from astern as I attacked. The Ju52 [an aircraft of II/TG4] tipped up on its nose and burned up. I saw nobody get out."

The US 15th Air Force credited 1/Lt Robert H. Wagner of the 92nd Fighter Squadron with shooting down the Ju52, totally ignoring 249's participation, although Brooks sportingly conceded that the American had shared in its destruction. Some of the P-39s strafed the blazing wreck, in which Obfw Walter Brädler and two of his crew were killed, together with four passengers; however, three other passengers survived, although all suffered injuries and burns.

---

* It has been suggested that the P-39s were Italian Co-Belligerent aircraft, but 4° Stormo did not receive the type until the following year.

Next day (2 December) seven 249 Spitfires set off on a sweep at 1405. They flew to Corfu but there the weather was bad so they did not strafe and instead flew north and crossed into Valona Bay. Heavy AA fire was experienced but no aircraft was damaged. Between Saseno and the headland, Sqn Ldr Colvin (JK817 GN-Z) sighted a Messerschmitt at 500 feet, flying north-eastwards:

> "I immediately gave chase and when approximately five miles south of Fier I identified the aircraft as a ME109F or G with a belly tank [it was in fact a Bf109G of 1/NAG12, a reconnaissance unit]. I was then about 250 yards, line astern to him. He must have seen me because he started a slow turn to the left. I gave him a two-seconds burst with cannons and machine-guns, and observed strikes along the whole length of the fuselage. With smoke pouring from him he stopped turning, jettisoned his hood and baled out. His 'chute opened successfully. The aircraft dived into the ground and burst into flames."

The CO's No2, Flg Off MacBain (JK625 GN-K), also opened fire at the Messerschmitt. The pilot, Oblt Hans Marquardt, although seen to bale out, was reported missing.

On 4 December at 0900, Flt Lt Beatson (JK465 GN-X) and Flt Sgt Jacobsen (ES306 GN-T) were scrambled from Brindisi on receipt of information reporting aerial activity in the vicinity of Berat. They crossed the coast at low level over Valona Lagoon and flew to Berat, orbiting at 500 feet east of the airfield, waiting for the opportunity to strike. Beatson reported:

> "I saw a Ju52 [also an aircraft of II/TG4] take off from the 'drome and, as it was climbing north and at about 400 feet, we attacked from over the top of the hills. I approached from starboard and slightly above and opened fire at 150 yards from an angle of 30°, giving a two-seconds burst of cannon which set the port motor on fire and the aircraft proceeded to glide gently towards the hills. My No2, Sgt Jacobsen, attacked, setting the central motor on fire. The machine went completely out of control and crashed in flames. No one got out of it."

Two hours later Wg Cdr Woods (MA701/ENW) and Flg Off Brooks (ER783 GN-L) crossed the Albanian coast at Bar and flew southwards at 50 feet to Podgorica airfield. On his return, Woods reported:

> "I was on the northern side of the aerodrome at zero feet when I saw a Ju87 [probably an aircraft from 13/StG151] coming towards me at 500 feet. Just at this moment all the ground defences opened fire and I was hit almost immediately by a Bofors in the airscrew, causing the whole aircraft to vibrate intensely. I climbed to underneath the Ju87 who dived for ground level and took evasive violent action, while the rear gunner opened fire completely out of range. I chased the enemy aircraft for about five miles, and opened fire at about 250 yards with about half-ring deflection. I gave a fair second burst. A large lump came off the starboard wing. I also saw strikes on the cockpit; return fire ceased and the aircraft dived into the ground and blew up. Green 2, who witnessed this, reported the return fire was fairly accurate. Camera was carried and the film exposed. While circling Podgorica aerodrome I saw six Ju88s dispersed on the eastern perimeter, two which looked like Do217s on the north, and two single-engine fighters on the west side. Intense and accurate flak came from the northern perimeter, also heavy from the surrounding hills."

Woods (flying 249's JK465 GN-X, since his personal aircraft was under repair) was in action again on 16 December, when he led four Spitbombers with six Spitfire fighters as escort to attack a factory-type building (believed to be a distillery) near Uleing, not far from the north-west coast of the Gulf of Drin. After what appeared to be a successful bombing of the target, the fighter-bombers strafed the buildings. They next successfully strafed motor transport along the road from Kullzh south to Shegas. Flt Sgt Docherty's aircraft (ES306 GN-T) was hit and he had to force-land about a mile west of Rozge, near the coast. He came down in a field and was seen to run towards the coast. As other aircraft flew back to base, the pilots encountered light

AA fire from the direction of Vorre and heavy fire from Durazzo, one aircraft being damaged, with its tailwheel shot away. Flt Lt Beatson (EN256 GN-B) noted:

"All bombs hit the distillery. Five trucks destroyed, six damaged. Docherty hit by flak, force-landed near coast. OK, hiding in shrub. Flak punctured my starboard wheel and shot away tailwheel."

Having changed aircraft (now in ER673 GN-F), and accompanied by Flt Sgt Belec, Beatson took off again almost immediately to search for the missing pilot. They encountered a Co-Belligerent ASR Cant Z506 (probably from 141ª Squadriglia, out from Brindisi), the pilot of which patrolled about ten miles off the coast, but did not fly in closer. With the arrival of two other Spitfires, these from 126 Squadron, Beatson and Belec flew to the Rozge area, where Docherty was sighted at the river mouth near Rozge, waving a red scarf. Beatson and Belec returned to the Cant and tried to force the Italian pilot to go closer to shore, as the former recalled:

"I flew in front of them, waggled my wings, fired a burst across their nose and almost yelled at the pilot through his window, but he wouldn't go in to the shore. I got so furious I thought quite seriously of shooting the Cant down into the water."

The 249 pair once more made for the coast and soon sighted Docherty on the ground, hiding in some shrubbery. Just then, when off the headland west of Bize, two Bf109s of 10/JG27, operating from Kalimaki in northern Greece, appeared; Beatson continued:

"Saw two 109s and attacked one. I turned into them and was promptly shot down by a third. I was lucky enough to be able to bale out, my parachute opening no higher than 300 feet. I came down in the water only a few hundred yards from the shore. Water very cold."

He had been shot down by Lt Holger Lummerding, the German pilot's first victory. Meanwhile, Belec chased the Bf109 but it climbed and drew away. Belec then orbited his Flight Commander, who started swimming inland aiming to meet up with Docherty, but then a Spitfire-escorted ASR Walrus (W3012 flown by Sgt Lunn) arrived and alighted nearby; Beatson continued:

"As it taxied up to me one of the crew, Flt Sgt Pickles (the air gunner), grabbed me and started to haul me up the side. I nearly swallowed the whole Adriatic while hanging on to the strut as the pilot taxied to get out of range of the small-arms fire. Just then a German machine-gun post opened up from the shore. A bullet passed smartly between me and my rescuer, hitting him in the fleshy part of his upper arm. It was the arm that was holding me, and he never let go! Self grazed on shin."

Seeing the Walrus under fire, Belec strafed the position and was joined in this task by the three 249 Spitfires, plus one other from another squadron, that had escorted the Walrus. Having completed the strafe they then flew north to search for Docherty. The Walrus meantime returned to its base, escorted by Belec and the two 126 Squadron Spitfires.

The search aircraft looked for Docherty in the Rozge area but saw no sign of him. During this time, another section from 249 engaged in the search for the missing pilot, but, despite a thorough reconnaissance, were similarly unsuccessful. As they searched they encountered heavy ground fire from the south of Rozge, plus light AA fire from the area of Rozge itself; two of the Spitfires were hit, but both pilots were able to fly back to base.

When news of the engagement with the Messerschmitts reached Grottaglie, Wg Cdr Woods immediately scrambled, accompanied by 126 Squadron's new CO Sqn Ldr Ken Debenham (former 249 flight commander). Neither aircraft returned and it was believed that they had collided over the sea. Flt Lt Beatson believed their intention had been:

". . . to slip across the sea to Yugoslavia, and under cover of the hills, lay off behind the

German fighter base waiting for the enemy aircraft to land . . . . it was an old trick we used
to play."

ASR aircraft and launches, protected by sections of Spitfires, searched for the missing pilots but
to no avail. Woods had been flying his 301st operational sortie and had been credited with nine
victories plus three others shared. His position as Wing Leader of 286 Wing went to Wg Cdr
J.C. Freeborn DFC, a Battle of Britain ace.

Next day the search for the three missing pilots was resumed. A flight of seven 249 Spitfires
led by Flt Lt Beatson were airborne early to escort an ASR Walrus, which flew at sea level with
the Spitfires in two sections, each flying about five miles distant from the Walrus. Once in the
Rozge area, three of the Spitfires dropped to sea level with the amphibian, while the other four
flew at 1,000 feet to give top cover. At about the same time six Spitfire IXs of 1435 Squadron
arrived in the area, keeping to a height of 10,000 feet. The three Spitfires flying at sea level began
another thorough search for Docherty, and he was seen by Flt Sgt Pride, again at the river mouth
where Beatson had seen him on the previous day. The pilot of the Walrus was contacted following
which the ASR machine alighted on the sea and taxied towards shore. Docherty, a non-swimmer,
started to wade towards his would-be rescuers, but was still 200-300 feet from it when the aircraft
grounded on a sand bank and could be taxied no further. Beatson continued:

> "Doc didn't seem to have his Mae West and he had never learned to swim. There was nothing
> to be done. It was all the Walrus could do to free itself — and take off. Poor Doc had to be
> left on the shore . . . it was a hard ending." *

At 0950, four Bf109s of IV/JG27 suddenly appeared and two dived from up sun to attack the
Walrus, but they were engaged by two 1435 Squadron pilots, who shot both down. One Messerschmitt fell into the sea and the other crashed on land, killing both Lt Lummerding (victor over
Beatson the day earlier) and his wingman, Fhr Friedrich Thiel. The remaining two Messerschmitts were then also engaged and shot down by 1435 Squadron, with the loss of Lt Rolf
Heissler, Staffelkapitän of 11/JG27, and his wingman, Uffz Rolf Andre. With the danger passed,
the Walrus now took off and was escorted back to Italy, but the 249 flight had to leave the escort
to 1435 Squadron when about 15 miles from the Italian coast owing to fuel shortage; six landed
at Brindisi and the other at Bari.

249 returned to Grottaglie in December. For several weeks — from the latter part of
December and well into January of the new year (1944) — operations were largely restricted to
convoy protection patrols. There were several days when bad weather curtailed all flying.
Towards the end of January the Squadron again became active with bombing and strafing, the
targets and target areas being chiefly in Albania and north-west Greece. Such operations
continued until toward the end of May, when thereafter they were extended increasingly to
Yugoslavia in support of Marshal Tito's Partisans.

The Squadron received the first two of a steady stream of South African pilots on 4 January
with the arrival of Lts M. McCardle and I. Robertson. During the month the Squadron also
carried out several attacks against enemy shipping in Valona and Corfu harbours, plus dive-
bombing strikes on the radar station at Durazzo and the aerodrome at Berat while, on
24 January, Flt Lt Beatson guided an ASR launch to two dinghies which contained ten American
airmen, the crew of a ditched USAF B-17. The other squadrons of 286 Wing were equally active,
bombing and strafing, but only 1435 Squadron met any German aircraft during the month,
claiming four Bf109s shot down in three combats. A further unit arrived at Grottaglie for
operations during the month, 6 Squadron equipped with rocket-firing Hurricane IVs. Plt Off
Twomey and Flt Sgt Fulton were sent on 19 February to search for the crew of a crash-landed
B-17. The aircraft was located on the beach at Fiumenica Point, near the village of Cariati, but
there was no sign of the crew so they returned to base.

Wg Cdr Freeborn led five of 249 on a fighter-bomber sweep over Corfu Harbour on
3 March. A large two-masted schooner was observed near the harbour boom and was attacked

---

* Flt Sgt Walter Docherty was taken prisoner.

by bombs and cannon; at least two bombs were seen to explode close by. Andrew Stamatopoulos, a young Corfiot schoolboy, maintained a journal during this period:

"At 1120 hours six Spits appeared flying from north to south over the sea at the height of 200 metres, distance about one and a half kilometres from the town. They then turned to the north towards my house while gaining height. I was watching them from the highest point of the house, while they were fired on by flak, so I took partial cover lest some flak splinters would hit me. The Spits turned then to port, just in front of my house and flying from south to north they dropped each two bombs near the northerly mouth of the moat of the Old Fortress. The bombs rather glided than dropped on the way down and caused little noise while exploding. The tactics were for the aircraft to effect a shallow dive during the attack and to follow each other in a line — also to strafe the target while dropping the bombs. I was told that the bombs exploded in the sea close to the north side of the Old Fortress, causing no damage to the enemy, or any casualties of any sort."

On 30 March, six 249 Spitbombers and six of 126 Squadron unsuccessfully bombed the airfield at Tirana, in the face of intense light and heavy AA fire. Later the 249 flight strafed a hutted camp near Vorre, towards the Adriatic coast. As they were returning to base at 1030, light AA fire was encountered in the area of Durazzo. The Spitfire (JK532) flown by Lt McCardle was hit in its overload fuel tank. The South African pulled his aircraft up to 1,200 feet and then baled out, after which he was seen in the water in his Mae West, about 500 yards offshore near Durazzo. Other aircraft of the section orbited above him until relieved by two aircraft of 87 Squadron. Small-arms fire was reported to be directed at McCardle and the circling aircraft. Shortly afterwards, a Cant ASR aircraft (probably from 141ª Squadriglia) was sent to where McCardle had ditched, the seaplane escorted by ten Spitfires including four from 249, but he could not be located; all that was visible was a patch of fluorescence. Intense light AA fire was experienced and Wt Off Waddell reported over the radio that his aircraft had been hit; the Spitfire (AR596 GN-D) was seen to crash into a wooded hillside near the seashore. No parachute was seen. Neither was Johannesburg-born McCardle seen again and he was presumed to have also perished. A double blow for the Squadron.

A few changes in flying personnel occurred during March and April. Flt Lt Holmes, B Flight commander, had become tour-expired on 27 March and was replaced as A Flight commander by newly promoted Flt Lt MacBain, while on 1 April Flg Off Brooks was posted to 185 Squadron, from which unit Flg Off D. Sinclair RCAF, who had recently shot down a Ju88 over Malta, joined the Squadron. Other new arrivals included Lt R. Whittingham SAAF and Wt Off A.G. Bowman.

Corfu Harbour was again the target for the Squadron's Spitfires on 3 April, a number of bombing and strafing sorties being undertaken, Flt Lt Beatson alone flying three sorties in GN-S:

"Harbour and shipping in rather worn condition. Flak fair. Partisans later reported extensive damage."

Andrew Stamatopoulos wrote in his journal:

"At 0625 hours there came from the south-east six Spits at the height of 5,500 feet, exactly as on the previous day. They dropped their bombs at the foot of the New Fortress, where there are some German ack-ack guns, while strafing the target. They departed towards the west. Two houses nearby had been severely hit. Once again the Spits failed to hit their targets. No Germans hurt; only two Greeks wounded.

At 1015 hours, while I was at school, there was an air raid alarm and the flak began to rattle. My school mates ran to the basement for protection. I stayed in my class room as I believed that since the Spits were small aircraft and friendly and their bombs small, there was no danger. A minute later they were heard diving. Two distant explosions were heard and soon after, a close explosion caused breakage of window panes in the classroom. I then rushed to the classroom for protection. After three to five minutes the aircraft were heard no more, so I got out of doors and saw that bombs had opened four craters at the next block of houses, not far from a car repair workshop commandeered by the Germans. Then I saw a column of black smoke billowing up from the direction of the harbour which burned for an hour. Some said that 40 drums containing heavy oil had been hit and set alight. This was the end of school lessons, as the raids began to be dangerous. It was rumoured that the second front will be opened in Greece . . .

Again at 1450 hours, ten Spits came from the south-west at the height of 5,000–5,500 feet. They dove as usual but they dropped their bombs from the slightly higher altitude of 1,500 feet. This time the bombs fell in the heart of the town, damaging several houses as well as the roof of the Royal Palace used by the Germans. A small vessel was damaged near the moat separating the Old Fortress from the town; the ammunition carried by it caught fire and burnt for one to one-and-a-half hours. I was told that three Greek civilians had been killed on that day and 15 more wounded, while it was rumoured that several Germans had been wounded."

On 6 April, eight 249 Spitfires were sent on an armed reconnaissance of roads leading towards Tirana, the capital of Albania. The pilots reported seeing several AA guns along one road and then, on the road from Vorre to Tirana, they sighted a dozen vehicles. Four of these were strafed and left smoking. Soon afterwards they were met with light flak and Flt Sgt Belec called out that he had been hit. His aircraft (EF607) was seen to crash into a field from about 500 feet and catch fire. He was reported to have been killed in the crash.

The last week of April proved a very busy one for the Squadron in general and for Flt Lt Beatson in particular. On the 25th, the Squadron escorted Hurricane fighter-bombers to Corfu; Beatson commented:

"Hurris clueless! We bombed their target and strafed the alternative."

Two days later, Beatson flew two sorties bombing and strafing M/T east of Elbasan:

"Amazing do! Approximate 200 trucks seen — 108 clobbered."

During his third sortie on the 27th, Beatson (GN-S) led an offensive patrol to bomb and strafe in the Scutari area. He jettisoned his bombs when a Fi156 was seen near Scutari, which he promptly shot down before strafing a truck with his remaining ammunition.

Changes in personnel continued: on 18 April Wt Off Potvin and Plt Off Twomey transferred to 73 Squadron at Foggia, the latter being promoted to flight commander. Their departure was followed by that of Flt Sgt Chambers and Wt Off Lifford. New arrivals included Flt Lt P. Quine from 242 Group who had earlier flown with 152 Squadron at Malta, Lt R. Briggs SAAF, Plt Off G.C. Nichols, Wt Offs M.V. Lalonde RCAF and A.L. Fox RAAF, plus Flt Sgt C.N.V. Davey.

At 1500 on 7 May, Flt Sgt Simmons (ES311) and Wt Off Lalonde (JK817 GN-Z) were despatched from Grottaglie to search for survivors of an American bomber. About 20 miles north of Bari they located two dinghies containing nine or ten airmen, above which were circling three USAF B-24s and a B-26. A launch arrived to pick up the survivors. Flt Lt Beatson (JK817 GN-Z) led 11 of 249 two days later to escort Italian Co-Belligerent Air Force SM82 transports from 88ª Squadriglia to Potom, where supplies were to be dropped. On arrival over the area, the transports circled for about 20 minutes, but no supplies were observed to be dropped!

At first light on 20 May, four Spitfires flown by Flg Off Hingston (Red 1 in ER874), Wt Off Bowman (Red 2, JL220), Flg Off Sinclair (Red 3, ES284) and Lt Whittingham (Red 4, JK678) were airborne on a reconnaissance for E-boats north of Port Palermo. Sighting nothing in this area the pilots turned to the north-east of Corfu Island. Soon after 0600, an E-boat was sighted there, moving at about ten knots, and was attacked, the aircraft dividing into two sections, one section approaching the craft from the port side, the other on its starboard; Hingston attacking to port, had his aircraft hit and was forced to bale out at 2,000 feet, alighting in the sea. The following machine, flown by Bowman, was also hit in the propeller, but was not forced down. Sinclair, having completed his attack, then circled above Hingston, who was quickly into his dinghy, and dropped his Mae West. The three Spitfires continued to circle the downed pilot for some 30 minutes, Bowman climbing to 5,000 feet to give a fix for his position. About an hour after baling out, an ASR Catalina, escorted by two more of the Squadron's Spitfires, picked up Hingston, who thus was back at base in time to return for a late breakfast.

Meanwhile, the damaged E-boat was observed to have stopped, but then resumed movement, making for the mainland at about two knots. When last seen it was smoking heavily. The young Corfoit, Andrew Stamatopoulos, wrote in his journal:

"An aircraft was heard patrolling at great height over the northern part of the island from 0800 to 0830 hours. At 1535 hours I saw from the country two Spits which passed at 2,500 feet over the village of Kalafationes to the west of where I stood, flying from south to north, but they soon turned to their right, to the east, and were lost from sight. I was told that they encountered a German E-boat and three caiques coming to Corfu Town from the Albanian port of Santi Quaranta (Porto Edda). The E-boat had been set afire and sank between Kouloura and the island of Vido."

At dawn on 25 May, German forces carried out a surprise parachute and glider attack on Tito's headquarters at Drvar, the operation supported by bombers and fighters. All available Allied air support was given by Strategic, Tactical and Coastal Air Forces. Six 249 Spitfires departed Vis at midday and crossed the coast at Rogoznica to fly to Ripac. Sqn Ldr Colvin led the flight, which included the four pilots who had been involved in the strike against the E-boat a few days earlier, and Flt Lt Quine. Once over Ripac they patrolled from east to west until Flg Off Hingston (Red 4 in JK450) sighted two Hs126 Army tactical reconnaissance machines of the Nahaufklärungs Staffel Kroatien. The whole flight gave chase but only Hingston was able to get in a burst at one aircraft, which crashed into trees on a hillside; nobody was seen to get out. Meanwhile, the second machine had turned back and was being chased by Colvin (EF720), who gave it several long bursts. His shells could be seen exploding amongst trees all around the low-flying aircraft although none appeared to be hitting it! All six Spitfires pursued it for about ten minutes, making many attacks and scoring hits until finally Red 2, Lt Whittingham (JK678), got in a telling burst and the Henschel crashed. Again no survivors were seen.

At that point Flg Off Sinclair (Red 3, JK101 GN-U) sighted three more Hs126s and fired at the rear aircraft. When last seen the machine was on its back in a nose down attitude at about 100 feet from the ground. It was not seen to crash but all agreed that it could not have recovered. The remaining two Henschels were now chased by the whole flight, Wt Off Bowman (Red 4, JL220) firing at one, followed by Colvin, Whittingham and Quine (ES299). One airman was seen to bale out before a wing broke away from the crippled machine. The remaining Henschel evaded further detection and escaped. These aircraft were used by the Germans to harrass Partisan forces, the slow-flying and highly manoeuvrable machines being ideal to flit in and out of valleys and ravines. To lose four such aircraft in one sortie must have been a severe blow to Luftwaffen Kommando Südost.

By the end of May it seemed that the enemy transport had been practically driven off the roads by day, as a result of the attacks of the past six months. To allow the Squadron's Spitfires to cover new territory, they were fitted with 90-gallon overload fuel tanks, enabling excellent hunting ground to be found in Serbia and beyond Lake Ohrid. The beginning of June saw a considerable change in the Squadron's flying personnel. The many hours flown in April and May had meant the completion of several operational tours, which resulted in both Flight Commanders, Flt Lts Beatson and MacBain, being posted away; both received DFCs for their performaces with the Squadron, Beatson being given command of 242 Group's Communications Flight. Flt Lt Quine also left the Squadron on posting to 32 Squadron. Sqn Ldr Colvin had also completed his operational tour and was awarded a DFC, handing over the reins on 1 June to Sqn Ldr Jack te Kloot RAAF, an Australian from Queensland who had served with both 229 and 185 Squadrons at Malta and had more recently commanded the latter's B Flight then operating from Palermo, Sicily. Of his arrival he recalled:

"My old friend Shortie Beatson gave me a great welcome when I arrived. He had completed his tour, having stayed on 249 Squadron throughout that period. Shortie stayed on hand for a few days to show me around and introduce me to all the Squadron members — as well as an operational trip where Shortie thought we could get some good shooting, but in fact we saw nothing to shoot."

The new CO participated in an offensive sweep on the day of his arrival, flying Wg Cdr Freeman's Spitfire JFC to Vis, from where his section patrolled the Kenin area. Several M/T were seen of which he claimed damage to two. Three days later, two Spitfires of 249 and two from 87 Squadron flew on a road-strafing operation over north-west Greece, after crossing the coast near Sarange in southern Albania. In their search for targets, the two sections separated. The pilots of 87 Squadron damaged six stationary M/T near Vatadles, and soon afterwards damaged another. They then rejoined the 249 section and the four pilots flew towards Yannina, where Flg Off Chase was lost. Flt Sgt Davey (Blue 2, ES284) reported that he had seen Chase's aircraft (EF567) making a steep turn round a hill south of Serviana, a small town south of Yannina. In fact his aircraft had been hit by AA fire. The CO recalled:

"Charlie Chase baled out; on landing in Albania he was quickly rescued by Partisans who dressed him as a woman and sheltered him until he could be transported out to Italy."

The Balkan Air Force came into existence on 7 June under Air Vice-Marshal W. Elliot DFC, with headquarters at Bari in southern Italy. The new air force was formed from a nucleus known as Special Operations Air Force, which had encompassed 334 Wing at Brindisi, and was initially allocated eight squadrons (including 249) and one flight, a strength which was very rapidly increased. The prime task of the Balkan Air Force was to support Tito and his Partisans against enemy forces in Yugoslavia, while continuing to attack the enemy in Albania and Greece, both of which countries had their own Partisan guerillas.

Air support to Tito's forces at Drvar had made all the difference, and within a week the Germans were on the defensive again. A small ground detachment, known as 2 Balkan Air Terminal Service, was sent to join Tito and to find landing strips into which supplies could be flown and casualties evacuated from. One such strip was discovered at Kupresko Polje. Immediately a Red Air Force Dakota flew in and air lifted Tito, together with the British and Russian missions, to attend a conference at Bari. At the same time Tito's staff and 118 wounded were brought out by USAF C-47s of 60th Troop Carrier Group. The purpose of the conference was to arrange much closer air support for the Partisans and, to this end, a Red Air Force detachment of a dozen Dakotas and a dozen Yak 9 fighters arrived at Bari to operate over Yugoslavia, under Balkan Air Force command.

Sqn Ldr te Kloot chalked up 21 hours of operational flying in his first seven days of command, strafing M/T on 6 June (GN-F) including a staff car and its occupants, and leading a fighter-bomber sweep two days later (JK817 GN-Z); he reported:

"Bombed M/T on road and missed. Strafed hutted camp and four other stationary M/T near Melissopetra. Lt Briggs destroyed one Hs126 [presumably another aircraft of NAStf Kroatien] on the ground. Light flak from hillside."

On 10 June the Squadron lost another pilot when Wt Off Fox was brought down during a bombing and strafing operation by four Spitfires. The target was an M/T park, debris from an exploding hut damaging his aircraft's glycol system. Climbing to 8,000 feet west of the target, he baled out of JK266. On landing he was immediately helped by Albanian Partisans, but was unable to get back to the Squadron until 2 August. The CO's aircraft, JK817 GN-Z, received three hits from rifle fire during this sortie, during which he claimed four M/T destroyed, but he was able to return safely.

Entries in the CO's logbook provide an indication of the Squadron's continuing intensive operations against road transport during this period:

"13 June: strafed three M/T south of Korca. Missed one, destroyed one, damaged one. Staff

Top left: October 1942 (from left to right): Plt Off John Williams RCAF, Sqn Ldr Padre Lamb, Flt Lt Eric Hetherington, Flt Lt John McElroy RCAF, Flt Lt Eddie Glazebrook RCAF; all four pilots had just received the DFC. (NWMA)

Top right: Sgt Keating's BP961 T-G which hit a truck that had been abandoned by its terrified Maltese driver when he had seen the Spitfire about to land, Qrendi 24 March 1943. (DE Nicholson)

Above: Unauthorised but hard-earned addition to the Squadron badge. (NWMA)

Above right: Trio of 249 Spitfires Takali. (Peter Arnold via NWMA)

Right: Sgt Bill Weir's mishap in T-H. (DE Nicholson)

Top left: Flt Lt Robin Seed.
(NWMA)

Top right: Flt Lt Jock Colvin in T-T; a future CO.
(DE Nicholson)

Above: Flg Off Hap Kennedy RCAF posing with T-B.
(DE Nicholson)

Above right: Sgt Don Nicholson shared the same aircraft.
(DE Nicholson)

Right: Sgt Jack Hughes RCAF with Jock.
(DE Nicholson)

Top: EP188 T-Y was shot down on 30 April 1943 and force-landed in Sicily; Flt Sgt Don Cruse was taken prisoner. *(AS Thomas)*

Above left: Sqn Ldr John Lynch was credited with Malta's 1000th. *(NWMA)*

Above: Sgt Bernie Sheehan RNZAF was shot down and captured on 30 June 1943. *(DE Nicholson)*

Far left: Flt Lt Ken Debenham wore gloves to protect hands burned in the Battle of Britain. *(DE Nicholson)*

Left: Sgt Joe Hingston was later commissioned and served with the Squadron in the Balkans. *(DE Nicholson)*

Top: One of the Squadron's first
Spitfire IXs, MA700 T-Z.
(NWMA)

Above: Sqn Ldr Timber Woods.
(NWMA)

Above right: Wg Cdr Woods
ruefully inspects propeller blade
following combat on 4 December
1943 when he shot down a Ju87.
(Author's collection)

Right: GN-U displaying symbols
representing 33 bombing sorties.
(DW Southwell via AS Thomas)

left: Flt Lt Shortie Beatson (centre) with Sqn Ldr
vin on right.

(Sqn Ldr J te Kloot)

right: Flt Lt Red Sinclair posing with 185 Sqn
fire at Malta prior to his posting to 249 at Grottaglie.
(Sqn Ldr J te Kloot)

dle left: Nose log of Sqn Ldr Colvin's aircraft
568 showing 26 bombing sorties plus a single air
ory symbol. *(Sqn Ldr DAS Colvin via AS Thomas)*

Middle right: Captured Fiat CR42 at Grottaglie wearing
249's code letters.

(Sqn Ldr DAS Colvin via AS Thomas)

Above left: Flt Lt Clive Jacobsen RNZAF was lost on
23 June 1944; he was killed while a PoW.   *(Paul Sortehaug)*

Above right: Behind German lines in Northern Greece
a detachment of 249 operated from a secret airfield at
Deskori, known by the codename Piccadilly Peggy.
GN-E (HB946) being camouflaged.   *(Sqn Ldr J te Kloot)*

Top left: Posing at Piccadilly Peggy on 21 September 1944, from left to right, Flt Lt Alf Dryden (killed next day), Sqn Ldr Jack te Kloot, Flt Sgt Eddie Davison, Capt Rick Whittingham.
(Sqn Ldr J te Kloot)

Top right: Capt Rick Whittingham SAAF. *(Sqn Ldr J te Kloot)*

Above: Sqn Ldr Jack te Kloot in the cockpit of a Mustang.
(Sqn Ldr J te Kloot)

Right: Flt Lt Tom Ashworth with his groundcrew and GN-B (KH682); note elephant insignia. *(JW Gardner)*

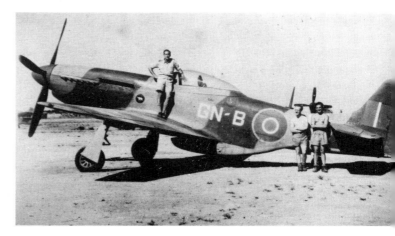

Top left: Spy Boulton, Intelligence
Officer. *(Sqn Ldr J te Kloot)*

Top right: Lt John Malherbe SAAF.
(Sqn Ldr J te Kloot)

Middle left: Flt Lt Nobby Noble
(Canadian), Lt John Malherbe
(South African) and Flt Sgt Dobbie
Finlay. *(Sqn Ldr J te Kloot)*

Above: Flg Off Ginger Gardner
(in cap) and Flg Off John Dickerson
(centre) with groundcrew;
Dickerson shared 249's 328th
and last air victory.

(J Dickerson)

Left: Sqn Ldr te Kloot (in bush
hat) with 249's Armament Section;
Wt Off Thorne on his left.

(Sqn Ldr J te Kloot)

Top left: Flt Lt Nobby Noble, who shared 249's final air victory, with Sqn Ldr Jack te Kloot.
(Sqn Ldr CE Edmondson)

Top right: Flg Off Mac McCaig on his return to 249 after being shot down. *(Sqn Ldr DPF McCaig)*

Middle: Still from Flt Lt Muir's camera-gun during an attack on a train near Zagreb on 3 February 1945. *(Sqn Ldr J te Kloot)*

Right: Flt Lt Jock Muir was killed in action on 1 March 1945.
(Sqn Ldr J te Kloot)

p left: Group of pilots early 1945 (rear): Sgt DA
ardiner (3rd from left); Sqn Ldr Charles Edmondson
th from left); Wt Off Dick Wheeler (5th from left);
t Lt Tom Ashworth (extreme right); Plt Off Eric
eddes (2nd from right, front).

(Sqn Ldr CE Edmondson)

p right: Wt Off Dick Wheeler RAAF – "none ever
me better" wrote his CO.   *(Sqn Ldr CE Edmondson)*

Middle: The wreck of GN-F (KH543) following Flg Off
Gardner's take-off accident.   *(JW Gardner)*

Above left: Flt Lt Geoff Nichols, champion
M/T strafer.   *(Sqn Ldr CE Edmondson)*

Above right: Plt Off Eric Geddes, a Scot.

(E Geddes)

Top: 249 received Spitfire IXs (for the second time) in April 1945; GN-X (MH956) and GN-Y (MJ730) at Prkos airfield, Yugoslavia. *(JW Gardner)*

Middle left:Sgt Ted Ramsbotham was 249's last wartime casualty, killed in action on 29 April 1945.
(Sq Ldr CE Edmondson)

Middle right: Group of 249 officers and NCOs at Brindisi just prior to disbandment: (astride nose) Sgt DA Gardiner; (rear): Flt Lt "Doc" (2nd from left);

Flg Off Spy Boulton (3rd from left); Flg Off Ginger Gardner (8th from right); Flt Lt Tom Ashworth (6th from right); Flt Sgt Bill Monkman (3rd from right); Plt Off Maurice Smith (extreme right); (squatting): Flt Sgt Shandy Beer (4th from left); Plt O Tilley (6th from left); Plt Off Sharpe (4th from right); Flg Off Morrison (EO, extreme right). *(JW Gardn*

Above: Baltimore V GN-B (FW714) in storage at Kisumu, Kenya. *(AS Thom*

Top: Aircrew pose with first Mosquito FB26 delivered to the Squadron. Wg Cdr HJD Matson (the CO) is ated centre, with Sqn Ldr DC Davies on his right and n Ldr EJF Harrington on his left. *(JW Chilton)*

iddle left: Mosquito FB26 GN-Q (KA370) at astleigh. *(AS Thomas)*

iddle right: The Squadron's first Tempest pilots (left right): Flt Sgt Jock Sutherland, Wt Off Paddy

Hanrahan, Flt Lt Peter Steib, Sqn Ldr JI Kilmartin, Flt Lt Mike Fisher, Flg Off John Capel, Wt Off Mike Buxton. *(Wg Cdr PF Steib)*

Above left: Tempest GN-J (NX245) undergoing servicing at Habbaniya. *(Wg Cdr PF Steib)*

Above right: Tempest GN-E which Sqn Ldr Steib force-landed near Habbaniya in November 1947.

(Wg Cdr PF Steib)

Right: En route to Palestine, May 1948 (left to right): Paddy Hanrahan, Sqn Ldr Peter Steib, Flg Off Geoff Bradshaw, Wt Off Mike Buxton. *(Wg Cdr PF Steib)*

Below left: Vampire FB5 VX473/B wears original yellow/blue 'check' marking. *(AS Thomas)*

Below right: Forlorn Vampire FB9 (WL606/C) force-landed at Amman by Flg Off Leighton Fletcher on 9 August 1954. *(LA Fletcher)*

Bottom: Pilots of 249 at Nicosia, Cyprus April/May 1954 (standing, left to right): Colin Smith, Geoff Leach, Kiwi Kjestrup, Keith Duro, unknown APC staff member, Andy Keeley, John Tetley, Pete Broughton, Peter Cock; (seated left to right): John Vardy, Capt Norman Waddell (GLO), Sandy Sanderson (A Flt commander), Wing Co Flying, Nicosia, Sqn Ldr Gibbons (CO), OC 26 APC, Johnny Coleman (B Flt commander), Jimmy Budd, Leighton Fletcher; (seated on the ground): Les Walters, Tony Gronert. *(LA Fletcher)*

Top left: Cpl Bob Byrne with a Venom FB4.

(Bob Byrne)

Top right: SAC Roy Jones also posing with an FB4.

(R Jones)

Middle left: Venom FB4 with elephant insignia painted nosewheel door. *(Sqn Ldr TS Syme)*

Middle right: Suez! Pilots at Akrotiri dispersal (left to right): George Garner, Denis Moyes, Alec Webster, Andy Anderson, Keith Bridge, Pete Purnell, Peter Warden, Doug Dallison, Tam Syme, Tony Gronert, Ron Etheridge. *(Grp Capt DG Slade)*

Above: B Flight pilots with groundcrew (pilots, left to right): George Garner, Dave Elford, Andy Anderson, Tam Syme, Mick Waterhouse, Peter Purnell, George MacIntosh. *(Sqn Ldr TS Syme)*

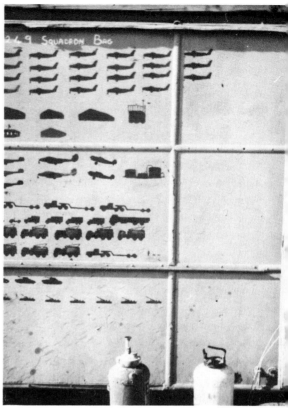

Top left: Sqn Ldr Jock Maitland (centre) with Flt Lts
Pete Warden (left) and Mick Goodwin.   *(Bob Byrne)*

Top right: Squadron scoreboard denoting claims for
Suez operation.   *(Bob Byrne)*

Above: Christmas 1960, Officers' Mess, Akrotiri
(left to right): Dicky Byfield (with guitar), unknown,
Mrs Henharen, Don Henharen, Muriel Gill, Dave
Wyman, Terry Gill, Doug Barfoot (CO), Rhoda
Kissane, Jerry Turner, Roger Kissane, Pam Barfoot,
Maurice Bendall, Mike Knight.   *(JN Turner)*

Above right: Flt Lt Jerry Turner, Flg Off Bryan
Montgomery, Flg Off Dicky Byfield.
          (JN Turner)

Right: Canberra B2 WH650 (note elephant insignia
on wingtip tank).   *(AS Thomas)*

Top: Canberra B16 (WJ783) at Akrotiri, 1965.

(AS Thomas)

Above: Canberra B16 (WJ777) at Akrotiri; in addition to the elephant insignia, WJ777 also bears RAF Akrotiri's flamingo crest.

(AS Thomas)

Far left: Presentation of the Squadron Standard by Air Chief Marshal Sir John Grandy to Standard Bearer Flg Off JV Evans, On 7 October 1965 at Akrotiri.

(Akrotiri Sun via ACM Sir John Sutton)

Left: Sir John Grandy with Sqn Ldr John Sutton (CO).

(ACM Sir John Sutton)

Top left: Sqn Ldr Alan Hastings, 249's last CO.
(Grp Capt TA Hastings)

Top right: Flg Off Barry Dove, navigator.
(Wg Cdr Barry Dove)

Middle right: Disbandment Ceremony, RAF Akrotiri February 1969. 249's Colour Party in foreground: Flg Off John Beard (Standard bearer), Flt Sgt AW Swan (Standard warrant officer), Sgts J Agnew and J Holden (Standard escorts), J/T V Silvester (Standard orderly).
(Group Capt TA Hastings)

Above left: Sqn Ldr Hastings leading 249's flypast.
(Grp Capt TA Hastin)

Above: Laying up of Colours, St Clement Danes 6 Ju 1969. Sqn Ldr Hastings handing over Standard to Chaplain-in-Chief, the Venerable LJA Ashton. Behin is Sqn Ldr Alan Ginn, CO of 73 Squadron.
(Grp Capt TA Hastin)

car south of Permet damaged and another M/T damaged south of Tepelene. Lively flak around Permet (GN-R). 15 June: One trailer damaged west of Kodadash. Two trucks damaged east of Kodadash. Personnel strafed at Stugra. One flamer, one damaged M/T east of Stugra. One truck damaged main street Ohrid. Lively 20mm and MG at Ohrid. One truck damaged south of Berat (flying JCF, Wg Cdr Freeborn's aircraft). 15 June, second sortie: All bombs in target area, M/T park Ohrid; destroyed two M/T previously claimed damaged and damaged one more. Strafed road north of Valona (GN-S). 16 June: Caught six M/T entering Korca from east. Four flamers, two damaged total (self one flamer, one damaged). Hangars strafed Korca aerodrome (GN-V). 17 June: Dropped 90-gallon overload tanks west of Monastir. Swept roads to Florina and then to Korca. Total 12 M/T destroyed, 13 damaged; one loco destroyed, one damaged (self four flamers, four damaged, one loco destroyed). Light flak (GN-F). 20 June: Swept road and rail to Monastir. Seven flamers and five M/T damaged. Two locos destroyed, one steam roller destroyed, artillery and ammunition dump strafed (self three and half flamers, four M/T damaged, one and a half locos destroyed (GN-F)."

During the middle of the month, the Squadron was joined by the four 'Ps' — Sgt Pilots H.G. Pallett, R. Penny, R.S. Perry and D.A. Preece; plus Sgts P.A. Ouston and A.W. Manning. On 22 June, Perry flew his third operation, as Red 2 to Flt Lt Sinclair (who had taken over command of B Flight), with Lt Whittingham as Red 3 and Penny (Red 4). The operation was to strafe transport along the road to Elbasan and Lake Ohrid. The pilots flew inland about 20 miles when Perry's aircraft (JL368) was hit by light AA fire near Peqin and he himself seriously injured in one leg. He turned back to base, followed by Sinclair, who had been unable to contact him by radio. Perry* landed safely at Brindisi, Sinclair flying on to Grottaglie. Meanwhile, Whittingham and Penny continued on the operation to Struga, north of Lake Orhid, about 20 miles further north returning to the Adriatic coastline due west of the Lake. During this flight they destroyed or damaged seven motor vehicles. Sqn Ldr te Kloot (JK723 GN-V) led another section:

"Swept road and rail to Monastir and Florina. Total four M/T destroyed, 18 M/T damaged. One loco destroyed, one damaged. Two rail wagons smokers. Radar station strafed, large HQ strafed."

Next day, 23 June, four of the Squadron's Spitfires, each equipped with a 90-gallon overload fuel tank and led by Flt Lt Jacobsen (who had been promoted to take command of A Flight) flew to Struga on a road-strafing operation. Seeing nothing on the roads, they flew north, then east and reconnoitred the railway lines in the area linking Greece, through the Vardar River valley, with Yugoslavia. South of the Orse they sighted a stationary train with no locomotive, of about 20 open and closed wagons. Each aircraft made two attacks on the wagons. One of these blew up, giving off a sheet of red flame followed by grey-black smoke. Six other wagons were damaged. During the second attack Jacobsen, flying as Red 1, reported that his aircraft (ES299) had been hit. He flew westward and had just passed Bir, when he had to bale out, which he did from about 5,000 feet. The pilots of the other three aircraft followed him down. They saw that he had disposed of his parachute on landing and was seen running towards a wood, waving and apparently uninjured. With that, the three remaining Spitfires returned to Grottaglie where Sgt Manning's aircraft was found to have been hit in the fuselage by a .303 bullet. As none of the pilots had seen any AA fire, it was presumed that Jacobsen's aircraft had also been damaged by small-arms fire†.

---

* Sgt Ron Perry was detained in hospital for some months and was eventually returned to England about the end of October, his injury not having recovered. However, he regained its partial use after the war.
† Nothing more was heard of Flt Lt Clive Jacobsen RNZAF until after the war had ended. A commission of enquiry, appointed to seek news of airmen missing in the Balkans, was informed that he had been captured by Bulgarian soldiers when he attempted to cross the Belick Mountains in an effort to reach the Partisans. Circumstantial evidence led to the acceptance of the grave of an unknown airman found near Kicevo, as being that of Jacobsen. He was Mentioned in Despatches posthumously.

Sqn Ldr te Kloot led three further highly successful bombing and strafing sorties at the end of the month:

"28 June: To Pec-Prizren. 19 M/T destroyed, 18 M/T damaged; 12 mules destroyed in army camp, 20-plus bods liquidated (GN-U). 29 June: Belecevac to Mitrovica. One diesel loco and two steam locos destroyed. Pec-Prizren, seven M/T destroyed, 27 M/T damaged, one bowser damaged, one steam roller damaged, one hutted camp strafed (GN-V). 29 June, second sortie: Four locos destroyed, four damaged, two oil wagons destroyed, one M/T destroyed, 16 M/T damaged (GN-V)."

Led by Flg Off Humphrey, four Spitfires set out at 1545 on 30 June to strafe in the Skoplje-Veles-Izyer area, during which the aircraft (JK725) flown by Lt Briggs suffered a hit in the fuselage from AA fire. However, the damage was not serious and north-west of Ibrammoye he sighted a Ju52, an aircraft of II/TG4 which he immediately attacked from astern. The transport's gunners returned his fire before the aircraft burst into flames and crashed north-west of Veles; there were no signs of survivors.

A further batch of new pilots had arrived by the end of June, including two South Africans: 2/Lts W. Shields and H.K. Rachmann, plus three NCOs: Sgts A.W. Gordon, R.C. Larcombe and T.D. Finlay. They were followed a few days later by Flt Sgts R.E. Thomas, J.A. Sawyers and R.W. Taylor, although the first two were almost immediately re-posted to 1435 Squadron. With the influx of new blood, several tour-expired pilots now departed including Flg Off Hingston, Flg Off Lamb and Wt Off Fulton. Sadly, Sgt Taylor was killed within days of his arrival when his Spitfire (JK929) crashed during dive-bombing practice.

On 4 July Sgt Penny was lost in the area of Pholarina in northern Greece, east of Lake Prespansko, when flying as Red 4 to Sgt Oustan, who had to return early because of difficulty with his overload tank. Over the target area, the remaining three aircraft were subjected to small-arms fire, both Flg Off Humphrey's aircraft and that of Plt Off Nichols sustaining damage. Penny was heard by Nichols to acknowledge his message that his aircraft (LZ873) had been hit, but nothing further was seen or heard of him; it was assumed that he too had been hit by ground fire and subsequently crashed. On his return to base, Humphrey was found to have had a remarkable escape. A bullet had passed into his cockpit and gone through the elbow of one of his sleeves, had then struck against the armoured back of the seat, from which it ricocheted to pass through the elbow of the sleeve of his other arm and then out through the other side of the cockpit.

The CO (JK723 GN-V) led another highly successful sortie on 11 July:

"Strafed mule train at Dragas (panic). Two M/T damaged at Blace, hutted camp strafed at Stinlje (damaged). One hut of petrol and six petrol dumps set on fire at Urosevac, also tented camp and stores dump causing chemical fire. Railway buildings strafed and one M/T damaged south of Urosevac. Three locos destroyed, one damaged near Kacanila. 19 petrol wagons strafed, no visible results. Two locos pulling six coaches (troopers) attacked with MG — troops panicked."

249 was finally incorporated into the Balkan Air Force on 15 July, as one of its fighter-bomber formations, transferring from Grottaglie on this date to Canne airfield (which had a pierced steel planking runway) near the small town of Campomarino, a few miles south of Termoli. The Squadron flew its first operations from Canne on 16 July. The target areas that day were inland from the southern Yugoslavian coast. The second operation of the day was flown by three Spitfires led by Flt Lt Sinclair to strafe targets along the roads linking Sucevici, Bihac, Olviac and Gospic. The pilots saw nothing to attack and encountered no ground fire. As they were on their return flight, Sinclair reported that his aircraft (LZ822) had developed a glycol leak. He was compelled to bale out, close inshore. His No 2 circled him for ten minutes, and saw him paddle ashore and land. An ASR launch was despatched immediately, with two of the Squadron's Spitfires giving air cover. As the launch approached Sinclair's dinghy it was attacked by heavy machine-gun fire from the neighbouring shore. The escorting pilots dived and silenced the guns. They also reported that the dinghy was empty.

With the enemy guns silent, Flt Lt Watts, the skipper of the launch, then went ashore in the launch's dinghy. Here he was confronted by a solitary German soldier who informed him that Sinclair had been taken prisoner. Watts returned to the launch, but then went ashore again to retrieve Sinclair's seat pack and dinghy. Having done this he proceeded to make another trip with the intention of reconnoitring a fort on the area, to check the German soldier's statement if he could, but when the crew reported to him that the covering aircraft were running short of fuel and would have to fly back to Vis, Watts withdrew. As his launch got under way it came under heavy fire from 155mm shore guns although it was not hit.

In the middle of the month the Germans launched a heavy assault on the Partisans' II Corps headquarters in Montenegro, air support for the operation given by about two dozen Ju87s and some Fi156s and Hs126s, plus fighter cover. Heavy fighting ensued, the Partisans counter-attacking, closely supported by Balkan Air Force units, driving back the Germans, who suffered heavy losses.

A Combined Services operation was carried out on 29 July against the German garrison at Spilje, near Himara, in southern Albania. Eight 249 Spitfires were flown to Leverano, on the heel of Italy, as were others from 32 and 253 Squadrons. The fighters were required to provide cover for the operation, to engage in tactical reconnaissances and to aid by bombing and strafing. The operation was reported to have had much success. Of particular interest to 249 was that pilots on the second support operation were able to make contact with Wt Off Fox (the Squadron's Australian pilot who had baled out over Albania the previous month), who was acting as a liaison officer with the ground controller. Following the operation, the Squadron resumed flying from Canne in aid of the Yugoslav Partisans (with the use of the forward field at Vis), while detachments at Leverano and Brindisi gave continued support to Albanian Partisans, as well as operating over adjacent north-west Greece.

More new pilots arrived during this period including Flg Off P.F. Noble RCAF and Wt Off K. Russum from 1435 Squadron, to which unit Wt Off Lalonde was posted; other new arrivals were 2/Lt A.J. Malherbe SAAF, Flt Sgts E.J. Clarke and E. Ray RAAF and Sgt D.A. Gardiner. They were followed by Flt Lts A.H. Dryden RNZAF, who took command of B Flight, and O.B. Andrews, Flg Offs T.H.E. Ashworth and J. Dickerson.

On 3 August two 249 Spitfires, each carrying two 250lb bombs, were sent on a bombing and strafing operation in the coastal area from Valona to Sarande. After an apparently successful bombing of a bridge near Sarande they flew northward towards Valona, strafing road transport. Just north of Valona, Flg Off Noble reported that he thought his aircraft (JK718 GN-Z) had been hit by ground fire. He baled out into the sea about 10 miles west of Himare. Not long afterwards he was picked up by Greek destroyer L91, which Flt Sgt Ray (Noble's No2) had directed to him. On landing at Leverano, Ray found that his aircraft (JL328) had also been damaged by AA fire. Noble returned to the Squadron nine days later.

Sqn Ldr te Kloot (GN-F) was in the thick of the action again on 5 August, leading an offensive sweep east of Korca:

"East of Korca one volkswagen damaged (tree, shot down, falling on target). One Tiger tank a flamer, two M/T destroyed, one damaged, one loco destroyed south of Florina. Two locos destroyed pulling trains loaded with M/T (M/T cargo strafed). One fast loco destroyed north of Monastir. One guard hut destroyed near bridge, one M/T damaged north of Ohrid. Self shot up in prop and tail."

Five days later (10 August) four Spitfires from Leverano crossed the Albanian coast south of Vis and flew northward to a road in Yugoslavia, south of Pec. The section was led by Lt Briggs and flying No2 was newly arrived Flt Lt Andrews, on his first operation with the Squadron. North of Decani, the pilots attacked a convoy of three motor vehicles and damaged all three, but Andrews misjudged his attack and his aircraft (MA332) flew into the ground. Beyond Pec the three remaining pilots continued to search for targets and east of Mitrovica they attacked and damaged one vehicle and another north-east of Durakovac. Following this they saw yet another motor vehicle south of Lausa, then turning back towards Pec they sighted a convoy of almost 20 vehicles west of Ruddnik and moving south-west. As he led the Spitfires in an attack on the convoy at 0730, Lt Briggs' aircraft (JK660) was hit in its overload fuel tank. It caught fire, crashed near Ruddnik and burnt fiercely. The other two pilots, Wt Off Russum and Sgt Preece, flew back to base*.

249 lost another Spitfire next day (11 August), when a section of three (Flt Sgt Davey, Sgt Preece and Sgt Gordon) from Leverano crossed the Albanian coast near Himare and flew to Yannina and Trikkala in Greece. South-west of Dhemation, the pilots sighted a convoy of about 50 M/T moving towards Yannina, but an overhanging cliff prevented an attack from being made. West of Mt Lakasion they saw another convoy, this of 15 to 20 vehicles carrying troops, which was attacked. They were greeted by intense light AA fire, Sgt Gordon's aircraft (JK214) taking a hit in its radiator, compelling the pilot to bale out south-east of Mt Lakasion. The other two returned to base. On his return to the Squadron a few days later, Gordon said that he had immediately been helped by ELAS (Communist) Partisans and had sat with them on a neighbouring mountainside, watching the Germans extinguishing fires in the convoy.

On 18 August two Spitfires were airborne in the late afternoon from Vis. Flg Off Nichols and 2/Lt Rachmann, were to make a reconnaissance of Korcula Island and of Hura Island and to continue along the Peljesa Peninsula to Ston and thence on to Dobrovnik. They were also to drop leaflets. Searching along the south coast of Korcula they saw nothing. Turning northwards they dropped leaflets at Cara, about the middle of the island, then continued along the north coast of the Peljesac Peninsula, dropping leaflets at Duva and Trpanj. Accurate 40mm AA fire greeted them at Trpanj, a shell hitting Rachmann's aircraft (JK723 GN-V) in the fuselage, severing the rudder controls. On reaching Vis he attempted to carry out a landing but was unable to control the aircraft, so went round again to make a second attempt. This failed too, so he called Canne to enquire whether he could reach the airfield by nightfall. Having been assured that he could, the two Spitfires however arrived over the field in darkness, Nichols landing at 2040.

To assist Rachmann with his landing, Grp Capt A.H. Boyd DFC (OC 281 Wing) ordered all available mechanical transport to positions where, with their headlights full on, they could give directing light onto the runway. Rachmann orbited the airfield several times, meanwhile jettisoning his overload fuel tank, but could not get his machine to touch down under control. Grp Capt Boyd ordered him to make one more attempt, and if this failed, he should bale out into the Adriatic offshore. This time Rachmann crashed his Spitfire onto the steel planking runway. The aircraft skidded along with a loud metallic rasping noise and then swerved violently to the right and stopped on the adjoining ground. He survived unhurt.

Rather more than 60 miles due north of Cetinje in Montenegro lies the town of Polje, in wooded, mountainous country, well suited to guerilla warfare. Yugoslav Partisans had established themselves in force in the terrain there until the Germans made a major effort to destroy them and had succeeded in encircling them. The Partisans had to struggle to make a way through the enemy ring, but they were handicapped by having a large number of their forces severely wounded. They dared not leave any wounded to be captured, if they could avoid doing so, for the war in the Balkans was savagely cruel. On 22 August, therefore, operations were undertaken by the Balkan Air Force to bring out as many of the wounded Partisans as possible, flying them to safety in Italy. Spitfires of 249, together with those of 253 Squadron and Mustangs of 213 Squadron (the latter from 254 Wing at Biferno) — totalling 18 fighters on two operations and 19 on the third — flew as escort to Dakotas, which were able to land on an airstrip at Polje already prepared by Partisans for the receiving of supplies and the movement of liaison officers and agents. Six Dakotas of 267 Squadron and 24 C-47s of 60th Troop Carrier Group from Bari took part in each of the three rescue operations. These aircraft had a considerable carrying capacity and so were able to bring away a very large number of casualties.

During the afternoon, two 249 pilots flew to the Polje airstrip to drop a message asking the Partisans there whether more Dakotas would be able to land to evacuate more wounded. An affirmative reply was signalled from the ground and two canopies laid out as guiding markers. The pilots then climbed to make height for relaying the message to Brindisi by R/T. The last section of 249 Spitfires landed back at Brindisi at 1925, well on towards dusk. A contemporary

---

* Lt Ron Briggs' body was recovered later and taken to Belgrade for burial.

newspaper reported:

> "Wave after wave of Dakota aircraft flew across hundreds of miles of German-held territory in daylight to land on an airstrip in Yugoslavia within sound of gunfire and evacuate more than 900 Partisans. The biggest evacuation flight of this kind ever made was carried out in response to an appeal from the Partisans. The Dakotas, not one of which was lost, were escorted by fighters. The officer commanding the medical side of the operation said: 'As we loaded wounded, we could hear shelling over the hill. A great sea of wounded men was lying around the strip, most of them in a pathetic state of malnutrition.' "

Throughout the day the Dakotas evacuated altogether 940 men, the RAF squadron carrying 219 of these. That night the Russian Dakotas went in and brought out a further 138 wounded men.

With this problem off their minds, the Partisans once more counter-attacked, but no sooner was this well under way, than a powerful German attack was thrown in, and defeat seemed inevitable. At this point however dramatic events further north changed the position utterly and unexpectedly. In the face of the mighty Red Army offensive of summer 1944, Romania and Bulgaria sought armistices, and by the beginning of September both had joined the Allies, Russian troops pushing forward to the Romanian-Yugoslav border. Threatened from behind so suddenly and decisively, the Germans had no recourse but to cease their offensive and pull back rapidly, to try and hold the Russians.

Among the replacement pilots arriving for the Squadron at this time were Flg Offs J.R. Muir and D.P.F. McCaig, Plt Offs J.W. Gardner and E. Geddes, Sgts P.W. Amis, J.R. Davis, E. Davison and P.C. Jones. Flg Off Dennis McCaig hailed from Suva in the Fiji Islands, about whom the Squadron's Intelligence Officer, Flg Off W.H.A. Boulton (known to his Squadron colleagues as Spy), noted:

> "Flying Officer McCaig, while in camp, would wear a pith helmet across the front of which was inscribed in large capital letters: 'First Fiji Contingent'."

On 5 September four Spitfires, each carrying two 250lb bombs, flew on an armed reconnaissance from Brindisi. Crossing the southern Albanian coast near Pigeras, they continued on into north-west Greece to Dholana, where they were met by heavy AA fire. From Dholana, they flew on to Metsovon and here encountered light ground fire from the roadside south of the town. Soon afterwards, Sgt Preece reported that his aircraft (MA900) was affected by high temperature and set course for base; Flg Off Nichols accompanied him as escort. Both pilots jettisoned their bombs in the sea. When about 40 miles due east of Brindisi, Preece baled out from about 10,000 feet into the Adriatic. Nichols covered his aircraft until he saw Preece bale out, then continued to circle the location for about 45 minutes, meanwhile giving repeated fixes of his position. Running very short of fuel, Nichols accordingly flew on for base when he was informed that aircraft were being sent by 1435 Squadron. He sighted the relief aircraft immediately on leaving his colleague, who was soon afterwards picked up from his dinghy by an ASR Cant Z506B of 141ª Squadriglia from Brindisi.

From late July until well into October, the duties of the Squadron related to the withdrawal of the enemy's forces northwards from Albania and Greece. In the middle of all this activity, the Squadron started to receive new equipment in the form of the Mustang III.

Chapter Twelve

THE BALKANS: MUSTANGS ARRIVE

September 1944 — August 1945

"I saw them in the blink of an eye, the first a perfect blue silhouette, a Focke Wulf 190 — I couldn't believe it, PR jobs; the second, just behind, showed tailplane and cockpit canopy. Squeezing the trigger exploded my .5s in a spray, all four guns roaring . . ."

Flg Off Mac McCaig, 249 Squadron

Early in September 1944, 249 began converting from Spitfire Vs to the Mustang III (the North American P-51C), moving to Biferno airfield, right by the shore line near Campomarino. Biferno airfield was laid out on a sandy marsh and hence was of pierced steel planking throughout — the north-south runway, the taxiing approaches and the dispersal areas. The Mustang III was a faster, more strongly-built aircraft than the Spitfire, but not so manoeuvrable. It could carry two 500lb bombs against the Spitfire's bomb load of two 250-pounders, and was armed with four .5-inch machine-guns. One of the Squadron's newer pilots, Flg Off McCaig, wrote:

"They took our Spits out and we got the latest Mustangs, capable of hitting anything in the Balkans, with longer-range fuel tanks, more speed, greater operational flexibility. We'd loved the Spits but they belonged to an earlier part of the war. That game was over. We changed our tactics to aggressive recces, going out at first light, sweeping far and wide, seeking any late night movement in the early dawn. Marauding sections of four planes went south each day to raid out across Albania, hunting over the Greek plains, foraging for the enemy where he'd been unmolested overlong."

Notable features of the conversion were that it took place without an accident and well within the time allowed for the change. In fact, the time taken to convert the whole Squadron was 18 days, of which four days flying were lost owing to adverse weather conditions. From experience gained in training A Flight pilots, it was decided in the case of B Flight to concentrate on giving each pilot a greater number of landings and less general flying. This was done arming the Mustangs with 100lb practice bombs each time they landed, thereby increasing bombing practice also. It was found that a pilot could take off, drop his bombs, and land again, in 15 to 20 minutes. However, the transition from Spitfire to Mustang did not progress without a hitch or two, as Plt Off Gardner had good reason to remember following a practice dive-bombing flight in Mustang HB941 GN-E:

"I dived the machine from some 10,000 feet. When I attempted to pull out of the dive I found I could not — the controls were rigid. Feet on instrument panel and all the strength I could muster. I managed it when almost in the sea. No forward visibility through oil from propeller; wing root bolts sheared; radiator flap torn off, which hit the tailplane. Near speed of sound?"

The Squadron's first operations with the Mustang took place from Brindisi on 13 September. At first light, 0600, Sqn Ldr te Kloot (HB928 GN-A) and 2/Lt Shields (HB926) were airborne on an operation along the Vardar River valley. They crossed the Albanian coast near Mifol and flew eastward towards the Salonika region, where they turned north, following the course of the Vardar, to Krilovak and Veles, strafing suitable targets. They claimed damage to four locomotives, an armoured car and a railway wagon. In mountainous territory they flew into low cloud and rain which obliterated all vision. The CO, flying by instruments, broke clear of the cloud, but Shields continued to fly blind, while he waited for what he thought would be a fatal crash. Suddenly he found himself in clear sky, with a blanket of cloud above him and between the steep sides of the valley; both returned to Brindisi safely.

The CO decided a second operation should be flown during the afternoon, thus Shields found himself airborne again at 1515. On this flight they crossed the Albanian coast north of Sarande, near the frontier with Greece, bypassing Yannina and Kharditsa, covering the road towards Larissa. The village of Taousani, west of Larissa, was burning and near the town they attacked a convoy of about 20 vehicles going north. One M/T was left burning and a second was damaged before they turned south to Almiros and then west to Thomokos. On the road from Thomokos to Lamia they came across "a convoy of several hundred M/T" moving northward. They made two attacks, but Shields' aircraft (HB926) suffered damage to its glycol system. He climbed to 12,000 feet and flew south-west before baling out about 10 miles south-east of Agrinon. On touching down he was soon helped by Greek Partisans, who took him to a town north of Missolonghi. That night the town was bombed by RAF Wellingtons from southern Italy. With the help of the Partisans and a British undercover officer, Shields eventually reached Taranto on 21 October, but then went down with a serious attack of malaria. He eventually returned to the Squadron in January 1945.

Sqn Ldr te Kloot (HB952 GN-F) led 15 Mustangs including two sections from 213 Squadron on an offensive sweep to Prilep on the morning of 17 September. En route, he was warned of an unidentified aircraft in the vicinity and despatched Green Section of 213 Squadron to investigate and soon a Bulgarian Air Force Do217 was encountered, which was promptly shot down. The remaining Mustangs bombed and strafed positions between Prilep and Monastir, the CO strafing two staff cars which he claimed damaged.

Early in the morning of 21 September, Flg Off Ashworth (HB937) and Sgt Manning (KH422) were airborne from Brindisi, their take-off time being 0500. They crossed the coast south of Valona Bay and flew to Larissa, about 35 miles east of Trikkala. When about 10 miles north of Larissa they dived to 500 feet and then swept across the airfield at 300 feet. Manning, who was leading, strafed a Ju52 and set it on fire; Ashworth, following closely on his tail, strafed a second transport aircraft, which blew up. Unable to break away in time, he flew through the explosion, which tossed him to starboard, his Mustang suffering damage by debris. On looking back, he saw Manning's aircraft flying through a curtain of 20mm and 40mm flak; the Mustang took hits in the rudder, fuselage and radiator and had its hood shot away, but continued to fly until some distance from Larissa when Manning was compelled to bale out. He landed on a hilltop near Kritsini and was helped by Greek ELAS Partisans soon after he landed. Within a few days he was returned to Italy in a Dakota from a landing strip not far from where he baled out. He did not return to the Squadron as he had injured his back when baling out, and was posted to the United Kingdom. He was advised later of the award of the DFM.

At 1400, four Mustangs flown by the CO (KH465), Flt Lt Dryden (KH468), newly promoted Capt Whittingham (KH425) and Flt Sgt Davison (HB952 GN-F) departed Brindisi for a secret landing strip codenamed 'Piccadilly Peggy', which had been prepared in woody mountainous territory about 10 miles from Trikkala, northern Greece. So secret was the strip that an attempt the previous evening by the four Mustangs to find it had failed! A servicing party, their kit and necessary equipment and supplies had already been flown to the airstrip by Dakota. On landing, the Mustangs were immediately concealed with tree branches.

The course of the war was now forcing the Germans to withdraw completely from Greece and subsequently from Albania and Yugoslavia. From Greece their main line of withdrawal was along the Vardar River valley. Thus it was planned that the Mustangs would be airborne at first light the next morning to engage in strafing operations along roads and railways, hoping to catch the enemy by surprise. They were off at 0455, Sqn Ldr te Kloot and Flt Sgt Davison flying to Dhomerli, Flt Lt Dryden and Capt Whittingham setting out for the Gulf of Salonika. At Dhomerli the first pair damaged a locomotive pulling 20 open wagons. The standing order to pilots when attacking trains was always to go for the locomotive unless they sighted ammunition or oil wagons, these then to be their primary targets. After the strafing at Dhomerli, the CO and Davison followed the road to Lamia, thence on by the Gulf of Maliair and along the north-west coast of Evvoia to Cape Sounion, then westward to Methana and northward to

Megara. On the landing strip here they strafed and destroyed two Ju52s, both being set ablaze. They then flew north-west and near Thivai saw three companies of marching men, about 30 in each, one of which they strafed, causing several casualties. Continuing their flight, they next attacked a convoy of ten M/T, destroying two and setting a third on fire. Further on they damaged a second locomotive and following this damaged a solitary motor vehicle. Later two more locomotives were destroyed and some oil-laden wagons, which were pulled by one of them, were left burning. Finally, at Kati Kalvia, they damaged yet another locomotive. Both pilots landed at Brindisi at 0815. The CO noted:

> "Two Ju52s destroyed on Megara LG near Athens. Two locos destroyed, three locos damaged. Several oil wagons fired. Three M/T destroyed, one M/T damaged. One bullshit parade liquidated."

This operation was the first in what proved to be a series of unusually successful attacks on the enemy's transport as he withdrew his forces northward, but there were attendant losses: neither Dryden nor Whittingham returned. However, just before midnight, the South African arrived at Brindisi aboard a Dakota. He reported that they had strafed the marshalling yard at Lamia and had destroyed a locomotive and damaged another; west of Lamia they destroyed another and shortly thereafter two more. Yet another pair were destroyed, but the second blew up and apparently debris brought down Alf Dryden's aircraft; the New Zealander from New Plymouth was killed. Whittingham circled the area, searching for his missing companion, then followed the railway line northwards, destroying two more locomotives. However, his aircraft suffered damage from debris as he overflew his second victim. Losing coolant, he set course for the secret airstrip but was obliged to bale out when about 20 miles short. The Squadron's IO, Flg Off Boulton wrote:

> "On landing he [Whittingham] soon found himself helped by local Greeks. They mounted him on a donkey, which they equipped with a wooden saddle. It was a long and painful ride along precipitous mountain paths. He arrived at 'Piccadilly Peggy' in the early afternoon, and immediately lay down on the ground and slept for three hours. In the evening he was brought out by Dakota."

On the morning of 23 September, Sqn Ldr te Kloot (KH465) and 2/Lt Malherbe (HB946) took off from the 'Piccadilly Peggy' airstrip (having flown there the previous afternoon) and headed for Brindisi, where they landed at 0725. Having refuelled they set out for Larissa, on to Volos, thence to the peninsula leading to Athens, where they attacked two trains, each pulling 15 wagons laden with oil drums. They destroyed both locomotives and fired all the wagons, thick black smoke rising from them to 1,000 feet and more. On the road and railway to Athens they strafed several targets, but attempted to save their ammunition for what they might find at Athens/Tatoi airfield. As they swept in at low level they saw 20 to 30 Ju52s dispersed in the north-west corner of the field and four photo-reconnaissance Bf109s in blast-proof pens. In a quick attack they destroyed five of the transports. More aircraft were sighted on Athens/Eleusis airfield, but these were left alone. Returning along the peninsula they attacked yet more road and rail transport. They overflew the area of their earlier attack on the two oil trains, arriving in time to see an explosion with huge flames rising high in the sky.

Following two or three days of severe thunderstorms and heavy cloud which reduced flying, operations were resumed on 27 September with four Mustangs carrying out offensive reconnaissances west and north-west of Salonika. Flt Sgt Davey (HB924 GN-D) and Flg Off McCaig (KH425), forming White Section, successfully attacked railway and road transport before Davey sighted the airfield at Prokhama; McCaig recalled:

> "My No1 called, his voice full of his message, words tumbling out in excited haste: 'Airfield — four o'clock — two aircraft on it.' Aircraft down there, for our taking — too good to be true! He [Davey] went in first, stirring the hornet's nest — they'd know we were here — airfields were the highest risk targets. Squeezing down the tension, I checked guns to FIRE,

gunsight on. This was going to be hairy, the place would be alive with the best flak arrangement they had: the Luftwaffe did not expose its few remaining planes.

Out of the corner of a sharply alert eye I saw smoke, his guns were blazing. I saw them in the blink of an eye, the first a perfect blue silhouette, a Focke Wulf 190 — I couldn't believe it, PR jobs; the second, just behind, showed tailplane and cockpit canopy. Squeezing the trigger exploded my .5s in a spray, all four guns roaring. The nearest one was smouldering, the second took my bursts, leaping and jumping all over its engine cowling and cockpit. A whole world of armament was coming up at us, lines of arcing tracer; vicious, bright in the shrouded light, each projectile cutting directly for me; pretty colours, full of menace; bigger black puffs from heavier guns."

There were at least three FW190s on the airfield, one of which Davey believed he destroyed, while McCaig reported that the two he attacked were severely damaged. Meanwhile, the other pair — Plt Off Geddes (HB933 GN-X) and Flt Sgt Ray (KH476) flew south from Nea Pella towards Larissa, having successfully attacked three locomotives and in the station near Ambelakia they destroyed another and damaged a fifth. These attacks were countered by intense and accurate light AA fire, which damaged both Mustangs as Eric Geddes recalled:

"Eddie [Ray], who was leading, went in attacking a group of locomotives sitting in a railway station, making four or five runs against very heavy opposition and although we destroyed a good number of locos between us, his attacks eventually stopped when he was hit in the glycol, which streamed out as he climbed up. By this time I had been hit with a 20mm shell through the aileron which had jammed it so that I couldn't turn the aircraft in both directions. I lost sight of Eddie. My troubles weren't over as I'd still to make my way back to Brindisi across the Adriatic in a series of wide turns and, to make matters worse, the R/T had gone on the blink. I heard afterwards that Eddie's body had been found. Evidently he'd baled out but his 'chute hadn't opened."

Next day (28 September), Sqn Ldr te Kloot (HB952 GN-F) and Flt Lt Noble (HB912) visited Salonika, where the CO had a lucky escape:

"Strafed main aerodrome at Salonika — one Ju52 destroyed, one Iti destroyed, one He111 destroyed, one Go242 glider damaged. Flt Lt Noble three enemy aircraft damaged. Four locos destroyed, two damaged. Received 40mm cannon shell in wing. Aircraft write off on return to base."

Partly because of bad weather, sorties flown during September amounted to about 130 (compared with in excess of 400 sorties flown in May and June) yet the results were relatively better than the Squadron had previously achieved from strafing. Of particular interest were the number of aircraft attacked on the ground, 15 being destroyed and eight damaged. 47 locomotives were also destroyed and 23 damaged, while 38 railway wagons, nearly all oil-laden, were destroyed together with 112 M/T destroyed or damaged. This score was almost entirely achieved in northern Greece. As has been seen, these results were not achieved without loss, five Mustangs falling to ground fire, the Squadron's highest monthly loss for the year. In October, operations were again affected by bad weather. The changed military situation had its effect, too, escorts to supply missions being a principal feature of the work.

At dawn on 8 October two Mustangs were airborne from Brindisi for a strafing sweep along the railways from Edessa to Verria, thence to Llanovergi and Eleotherokhorion, on the west coast of the Gulf of Thermai. The pilots, 2/Lt Rachmann (KH538) and Flg Off McCaig (HB933 GN-X), then followed the railway northward to Polykastron. They saw no movement anywhere on the railways, but encountered inaccurate light ground fire north of Eleotherokhorion, where a viaduct was being repaired. Moving south near Evropos and about five miles north of Nea Pella was one motor vehicle, which they attacked but saw no results. Near Gephyra, east of Nea Pella, they were again met by light ground fire and McCaig's aircraft was apparently hit as later, when north of Polykastron, he noticed he was losing glycol:

"A stream of white vapour was coming back over the clear perspex of my cockpit canopy. As I watched, the streamer widened and I called to Rachmann that I was climbing for altitude and the mountains. As the Mustang climbed, the sinister white plume thickened just before the engine spluttered twice, then stopped. My sleek P-51C shuddered its death throes, dying at the point of stall. My time was now. To live I must get out. Tugging frantically, I pulled at the canopy release, smashing upwards to make the hood go. Bashing, thrashing, the canopy whipped away; a bewildering maelstrom of blasting air took over. Moving the stick across, violently, I rolled the dying Mustang on to its back; letting go, falling into a vast, terrifying emptiness of space. A thin white streak against the stark emptiness below picked out my Mustang. Delivered only six weeks ago, now it curved ever downwards for the mountains, a terminal dive to end in smashed metal, ravishing a hole in the earth."

McCaig came down near Megala Leivadia, about 15 miles west of Polykastron and was knocked unconscious on landing. When he came to he saw a number of men approaching. They asked if he was English and when he replied in the affirmative they became very friendly. Then a policeman arrived and took charge of his revolver before he was taken into the village of Skra, where he was given a drink while being examined for injuries by a local doctor. After the medical examination he was taken out to look at the wreckage of his Mustang, which was buried about 15 feet in the ground. The following day it was discovered that certain parts of the wreck had been stolen. Although not of military importance, McCaig was again taken to the site and made to identify the stolen material. The guilty persons were marched off to the local gaol.

Having spent the rest of the day and night in the village, McCaig was taken to Mount Paikon, where he was handed over to British agents. That same evening he has taken to a landing field at Ardea, where a Dakota from Italy was expected, but no aircraft arrived. With assistance from Greek Partisans he evaded capture from a pursuing German patrol and, some two weeks later, after helping to construct a rough grass landing strip for the Dakota to fly in at night, he was flown back to Bari, where he later rejoined the Squadron.

On 14 October Sqn Ldr te Kloot led an offensive sweep to the Lamia-Larissa area of northern Greece:

"To Lamia marshalling yards — three locos destroyed, two locos damaged, two M/T destroyed, three M/T damaged, two troop concentrations strafed, one flak wagon destroyed. My No2, Sgt Amis, shot-up my starboard wing."

Two days later, at 1055 on 16 October, three Mustangs were airborne from Biferno, the section led by Capt Whittingham. The trio crossed the mainland from the Pasman Channel west of Lake Vransko and flew northward towards Sisak to patrol the territory east of the town. En route, about 20 miles east of Bihac, they saw a USAF Liberator, apparently in good condition, on the ground but not on a landing ground. While following the railway running south-east from Sisak they sighted, at Zivaja, a train of one locomotive and a dozen mixed wagons, two of which were flak wagons. The gunners opened fire, but the Mustangs did not attack the train, instead they flew to Jasenovac, where they attacked a locomotive pulling two wagons. No flak was seen during the course of this incident, but immediately after the attack Whittingham's aircraft (KH532) appeared to have a glycol leak.

The section set course for Biferno. At about 1340 Whittingham baled out about five miles north-east of the Tremiti Isles, which lie approximately 25 miles east by north of Termoli. His aircraft fell into the sea with its engine on fire. 2/Lt Malherbe and Sgt Pallett circled Whittingham who was afloat in his dinghy and gave fixes by radio of his position. At about 1430 an ASR Catalina arrived to pick him up. By the time they landed at Biferno, Malherbe and Pallett had flown their aircraft almost to the limit of their endurance. Whittingham was back with the Squadron the same afternoon, seemingly quite unperturbed by his experience, but having had to bale out three weeks earlier, he was now stood down by order of Grp Capt D.S. MacDonald DFC, OC 283 Wing.

Three Mustangs were airborne from Brindisi at 0930 on 19 October, flown by Wt Off Davey (KH428), Plt Off R. Andrew (a new pilot, in KH530) and Flt Sgt Clarke (KH422), their task to bomb the railway at Amyntaion in northern Greece, and then to strafe roads to the southern end of Lake Ohrid. At Amyntaion they saw 30-plus wagons in the railway sidings, which they bombed. The weather looking unfavourable westward, instead of flying towards Lake Ohrid, Davey decided to lead his section to the north-west, following the road to Bitolj in Yugoslavia. Here they destroyed a staff car on the road then, north of Bitolj, sighted and attacked a stationary locomotive with a wagon attached. The locomotive was destroyed and the flak wagon damaged. Next they flew north-west following the road to Kicevo, where they attacked a convoy of over 30 M/T moving northwards. One of the vehicles was left in flames and two others damaged. The convoy responded with 20mm flak and small-arms fire. The trio turned east towards Prilep. Sighting another convoy, of about 15 vehicles, they attacked again in the face of moderate flak and damaged two. They then turned west for base. Over Albania was a thick cloud layer and Clarke lost sight of his companions about 15 miles north-east of Tirana. He made several attempts to call the two pilots, after which he crossed the coast at Lalze Bay and reached Brindisi with the aid of homing directions. Three days later the Squadron received news that Andrew was safe and unhurt. He had baled out when his fuel became exhausted, but of Davey nothing more was heard. Of his loss, Flg Off Boulton wrote:

> "With his fair colouring and close-curled hair went a lively disposition. He used to say that, when the war was over, he was going to spend holidays among the Dalmation Islands. He had been seized with their beauty, their sandy beaches and the bright water surrounding them."

On 24 October a section of four Mustangs, led by 2/Lt Rachmann, were airborne for a road sweep in the coastal region of Albania north of Durazzo. The pilots crossed the coast at the north end of Lalze Bay and flew to Bushnesh and southward to Vorre and Durazzo, but saw nothing. Then over the R/T they heard a pilot's call that there was a convoy between Skegas and Alessio. Flying back they found and attacked the convoy; four M/T were set ablaze and two more damaged, but Rachmann's aircraft (HB941) was seen to hit the ground. Subsequent reconnoitring revealed that the Mustang was in some bushes, with smoke coming from it, but that it did not appear to be broken up. However, 20-year-old Rachmann from Durban died in the crash. During the attack light flak had been fired from the convoy, but there were no reports of aircraft having been hit and the three remaining Mustangs were found to be intact when back at Brindisi. Plt Off Gardner recalled:

> "I was his No3. Rachmann failed to pull out of a dive. I wonder if this aircraft had done any more diving attacks since 18 September. If not, was there an inherent fault with HB941?"

Six days later, eight Mustangs were flown from Biferno for an offensive sweep over southern Yugoslavia — from Bitolj to Prilep, Veles and Skoplje — covering part of a principal route for the retreating German forces making their way northward, following their withdrawal from Greece. The Mustang leader was Grp Capt MacDonald, while 213 and 249 Squadrons provided four and three aircraft respectively. There was extensive cloud over Yugoslavia and the pilots flew above this to the Skoplje area. As they came down through the cloud, the Squadron pilots became separated from their leader, as recalled by Plt Off Geddes (KH561 GN-B):

> "Over the target area the weather was extremely bad, even worse than that on the outward journey which was 9/10th cloud. Over the mountains it was 10/10th cloud. Eventually Grp Capt MacDonald put the formation into line astern, presumably to help keep in contact. No7 and No8 in the formation were barely scraping over the mountain tops! Then somewhere around where the target area was likely to be, the leader spotted a hole in the cloud and dived through it into the valley below with the cloud immediately closing behind him. The speed of the dive effectively split up the formation which was still in line astern and the order was given to carry on, on an individual basis, with the offensive sweep; which is what happened. I was lucky enough to come out of the low cloud in a valley and followed a railway line to the target area but apart from frightening some stationary railway wagons to no great effect, no other targets were seen."

Others flew northwards from Skoplje, following both road and railway. North of Lipljan a stationary convoy of about 20 M/T and carts was sighted. Intense light flak was encountered from the area and the 213 Squadron section leader was shot down. Geddes continued:

> "Then, from somewhere, I heard a call on the R/T for everyone still in the area to make his own way back to base, and I was able to find my way back through the cloud and set course for Biferno where I landed some three hours after take-off. On landing I found that two aircraft of 213 Squadron had arrived back early. Grp Capt MacDonald had just landed safely but had apparently burst a tyre. A pilot of 213 Squadron had got into difficulties and become disorientated in the 10/10th cloud over the Adriatic on the way home. He believed he was flying upside down, with the aircraft out of control and tried to bale out, only to find his parachute had become entangled in the cockpit, at which point the aircraft appeared to right itself and he was pulled back into the cockpit and eventually, with difficulty, found his way back to base."

Sgt Ouston (KH532) found his compass made unserviceable by the intensity of the storm but was able to fly around it and steered for Italy by the sun. He landed at Giulia, 200 miles south of Biferno. While in the storm area, Ouston thought he saw Sgt Pallett (KH437) and called to him to fly south. There was no reply. One of the 213 Squadron pilots reported that he had heard another pilot saying that he would have to bale out. It was thought that this must have been Harry Pallett, of whom nothing more was seen or heard. When last sighted, he was about ten miles south of the island of Lagosta. ASR searches for him during the next two days proved fruitless. The weather meanwhile continued stormy and the sea rough.

On the last day of the month, two Mustangs set out at dawn for an armed reconnaissance, Flt Lt Noble (KH427 GN-V) and Flg Off Dickerson (KH575) crossing the coast near Divjake. They flew over the lakes to Floriana and swept along the Bitol-Prilep and Durazzo-Scutari roads, but no M/T was sighted. However, north of Bitol they encountered a low-flying Fi156 Storch, which both attacked, as recalled by John Dickerson:

> "I have no recollection of any R/T exchanges, though there must have been some. Flt Lt Noble, who was at least 1,000 yards ahead of me, fired on the Storch, which was flying very low, though I didn't see the fire as we didn't use tracer ammunition — the effects of ricochets when attacking ground targets was rather alarming. I followed in from a different angle and remember feeling surprised at how like the official Aircraft Recognition cards the Storch looked.
>
> The pilot didn't seem to realize he was being attacked, as he was turning gently to port. I was closing very rapidly on him and managed to get in a brief optimistic burst of fire at a narrow deflection angle, without obvious results, before overshooting and pulling round sharply to avoid the wooded valley side. As I came round I looked back and saw the Storch had struck the hillside. There was no fire or explosion, and the wings were folded back over a bent fuselage."

This was the Squadron's 328th — and last — air victory of the war.

October had proved less rewarding and more punishing; for a total of about 20 locomotives destroyed and 55 M/T destroyed or damaged, the Squadron had lost six aircraft and three pilots. However, the Squadron's achievements were recognised by the award of DFCs to Flt Lts MacBain and Sinclair (who was a PoW), Capt Whittingham and Wt Off Simmons. With good results, the enthusiasm of the groundcrews was also well sustained and, as in the Malta days, they worked uncomplainingly for long hours to keep the aircraft flying.

Throughout November and December, Balkan Air Force units concentrated on transport targets in an effort to prevent as many Germans as possible from extricating themselves from the morass. In November the Germans were bombed and strafed northward from Albania and the Skoplje area to Visegrad, east of Sarajevo. Bad weather continually hampered flying and results did not compare with previous months. Nevertheless, large concentrations of M/T were found when weather permitted, and were effectively attacked. For example, on 15 November Flt Lt Noble (KH561 GN-B) led eight 249 Mustangs, operating with sections of Mustangs from

213 Squadron, and bombed a large M/T convoy near Tirana. While bombs were believed to have exploded in the target area, there were no claims made for the damage or destruction of any of the transport, as none was observed. Four days later, on 19 November, a report was received from a British agent in the area of the target that the combined attacks of Partisan forces there and of Balkan Air Force had almost completely destroyed the convoy. Approximately 1,000 of the enemy were reported killed and a prisoner of war later affirmed that there were about 100 dead from the air strikes, and that the convoy had not moved after the bombing and was abandoned.

Good results were achieved on 23 November, when 25 M/T were destroyed or damaged. This destruction was to a convoy moving northwards from Prizren to Visegrad and then west to Sarajevo. Many of the survivors had to make their way on foot along the snow-covered mountain roads and arrived in Sarajevo in a very bad plight. Next day (24 November) eight of the Squadron's Mustangs were airborne at 1110, tasked to reconnoitre from Podgorica to Spuz but ever increasing cloud was experienced until there was complete cover extending up to 15,000 feet and the operation was aborted. As the formation returned, Sgt Amis' aircraft (HB928 GN-A) was seen to be giving off black smoke and the pilot reported glycol and oil on his windscreen was obscuring vision. Immediately after this he baled out into the sea about 50 miles east by north from Biferno. He was seen to get into his dinghy and three of his fellow pilots remained over him until he was picked up by an ASR Catalina.

The Squadron was now regularly taking bombs on its missions, by contrast with its first use of the Mustang, when operations were chiefly restricted to strafing. The Mustang proved much steadier in the dive than the Spitfire. It had once been remarked that when the Squadron was bombing targets such as bridges, the enemy ran on to them for safety. The point of the quip was lost with the Mustang. Four replacement pilots arrived towards the end of November: Flt Sgt M. Smith and Sgts F.J. Weed, E.A. Beer and W.J. Monkman RCAF.

Throughout the late autumn and on into the winter, the Squadron's activities had been hampered by adverse weather. At the end of November reports were received of a large-scale movement of the enemy in the Podgorica area, north of Lake Scutari. This convoy was under heavy attack throughout nearly the whole of the month. 249 played its full part in the onslaught and was very successful. The results were all the more creditable in that the pilots continually sought out the head of the convoy so as to block the narrow roads to all traffic.

On the first day of December, 2/Lt Malherbe (HB912 GN-A) and Sgt Monkman (HB884 GN-D) were briefed to fly an armed weather reconnaissance to the area of Podgorica. On becoming airborne from Biferno they followed the coast of Italy to south of Vieste Point and, with the cloud improving to thin stratus at 7,000 feet and with breaks in it, they set course for the target area. Over the target area the cloud base was about 9,000 feet, but was now unbroken. South of Bioce and a few miles north-west of Podgorica, Malherbe sighted between 300 and 400 M/T dispersed on both sides of the road, but was unable to indicate the target to Monkman because the latter's R/T had gone unserviceable. The pilots, therefore, set course for base and jettisoned their bombs in the sea. On seeing a storm in their direct route, they flew northward until they received a homing signal from Vis Island. As he turned for Vis, Malherbe lost sight of his companion so continued alone and landed safely. Shortly afterwards a call was heard from Monkman saying that he was going to bale out over land near Split, well north of Vis. He came down in friendly territory and was soon returned to Italy.

Next day eight Mustangs led by the CO in KH427 GN-V were sent to attack a road bridge near Bioce. This bridge had been the target earlier in the day for an operation by six of the Squadron's Mustangs. With four bombs falling about 20 yards from the bridge and the other dozen inside a radius of about 200 yards, the bridge was claimed as damaged. Immediately after the attack new pilot Sgt Weed, who was flying KH472 GN-E, was found to be missing from the section*. There had been a light barrage of 20mm flak around the target which had ceased completely after the first action of four aircraft had bombed. This operation was to be the last for Sqn Ldr te Kloot, who had completed a highly successful tour, which had brought remarkable results. He was later awarded a DSO for this work. His successor was Sqn Ldr Charles

---

* Sgt Weed was later reported to be a prisoner of war.

Edmondson RAAF, another Australian, who had served previously with a number of squadrons, including 451 Squadron RAAF in the Western Desert and 450 Squadron RAAF in Italy.

On 18 December, Flt Lt Noble (KH594 GN-Y) led eight pilots on an armed reconnaissance along the road at Bioce, including Sgt Monkman, recently returned following his bale out. Near Matesevo were numerous M/T, all stationary and concentrated. The pilots observed several fires among the vehicles before they attacked. With all their bombs falling as direct hits or very near misses, they succeeded in intensifying the fires. After their attack the pilots saw three other fires burning somewhat further on in the same area. Three days later, on the morning of 21 December, two Mustangs set out on a weather reconnaissance, but Sgt Gardiner's aircraft (HB896 GN-Z) developed engine trouble and the section returned early. On landing at Biferno, Gardiner overshot and crashed; the aircraft was written off although the pilot was unhurt.

Christmas came and went; the war continued. On 27 December four Mustangs flew on an armed reconnaissance about due north of Lake Scutari in the area of Kisilici and Mojkovac, on towards Plevlja and Prijepolje. Flying as leader was Flg Off Muir (KH561 GN-B), with Flt Sgt Smith (FB330), Flg Off Geddes (FB308 GN-E) and Sgt Sharpe (a new pilot, in FB306 GN-C). As they flew north the pilots encountered some inaccurate light flak from near Mojkovac. Some miles north of Plievlja they bombed a stationary convoy of rather more than 20 M/T, six of their eight bombs missing the target. The remaining two hung up on the aircraft and were jettisoned live in a dive. At this stage Geddes reported his compass unserviceable and his fuel consumption high. He was ordered to return to base, with Sharpe to accompany him as escort. Muir and Smith proceeded to strafe the convoy, destroying one vehicle and damaging two more. They attacked from 8,000-5,000 feet in the face of accurate, intense light flak and Smith's Mustang was hit in the glycol system. The attack was broken off and he was escorted by Muir towards Niksic; they had flown but a little more than 20 miles when Smith's engine cut and he had to bale out. He was last seen at about 1,500 feet, with his parachute not yet open. The area where he descended was mountainous and covered in snow. Muir, although now alone, returned to the target area, making observations and attacking where practicable. Along the roads near Kisilici he observed a small number of dispersed stationary M/T camouflaged and elsewhere two separate convoys of about 50 vehicles, also camouflaged. He was fired upon by inaccurate 20mm flak as he observed the second of these large convoys. Having destroyed one vehicle, which he saw moving alone, he followed this with an attack on four stationary vehicles, destroying two and damaging the other two; he reported that three of the four vehicles appeared to be large removal vans.

Meanwhile, Smith's parachute had opened in time and he had landed safely. He set to walk down the mountain slope and, as he did so, noticed animal tracks in the snow and wondered whether they were bear or wolf footprints. He presently arrived at a cottage, which he entered, where a bearded, elderly man was seated inside, smoking a pipe. Convinced as he was that he was in Partisan-held territory, Smith spoke to the man:

"Ja sam Britanski." (I am British)

And added that he wanted help. The man sat silent so that Smith turned to leave the cottage. At this, the man spoke in perfect English:

"Damn it, man, what do you want?"

Smith explained his predicament and that he wished to have help from the Partisans. The man — probably a British undercover agent — arranged to have a message sent to the nearest Partisan unit and, while they waited for transport, he entertained his unexpected guest with walnuts and wine. Smith's unusual experience ended when Partisans arrived and guided him to safety; he was back with the Squadron within a few days.

Meanwhile, on 29 December, Flg Off Gardner was one of two pilots briefed to fly on an armed weather reconnaissance but he crashed on take-off in KH543 GN-F:

"I swung on take-off and hit sand bank at side of strip. Propeller went first, then undercarriage plus two 500lb bombs, followed by the engine. Both wingtips ripped off and fuselage broken behind petrol tank. Wing and fuselage tanks were full. No fire, no explosion, no injuries. Someone looking after me. On getting out of the wreckage unhurt, shouted to approaching pilots and groundcrew 'Bombs not gone off.' "

Flg Off Geddes also remembered the incident:

"I immediately ran towards the crashed plane and was surprised to find all the airmen in the vicinity running towards and past me. Anyway, I continued running to the plane and helped John out of his harness and, finding he was more shocked than injured, helped him back to dispersal. He kept mumbling something and it was several minutes before I could make out what he was saying. It was 'Bombs! Bombs!'. The bloody aircraft had crashed with two 500lb bombs — thankfully undamaged. That was why the exodus was in the opposite direction."

During December an estimated 155 M/T, nearly all part of the vast convoy in the Podgorica area, were judged to have been destroyed or damaged solely by strafing and bombing. When the Partisans with a British force moved into the Podgorica pocket — as it came to be called — about 1,000 M/T were counted on the road leading north to Matesevo and Prijepolje. These had been abandoned, as destroyed or damaged or without fuel.

By the end of the year Russian forces were well into Hungary and had surrounded Budapest, but the new year found the weather so bad that few sorties could be made by the Balkan Air Force. On 13 days in January bad weather stopped all flying. With the European war entering its final stages the enemy continued his steady retreat northwards through Yugoslavia, harassed in the western regions of the country by the 4th Yugoslav (Partisan) Army and by the activities of the Balkan Air Force, whose aircraft had thus increasingly to fly further from their bases. New ground was broken, the Squadron operating to the Austrian border and beyond for the first time. Sorties were now the longest in its history, 600 miles and more being frequently flown. Targets ranged from Sarajevo to Zagreb, Maribor and Dravograd. Attention to railway communications were the prime targets, very few M/T being attacked.

Flg Off Geddes (HB907 GN-G) participated in an attack on the harbour at Pola on 18 January, when three E-boats were attacked and two claimed destroyed. One of these was claimed by Geddes who also damaged a second. Bombs were seen to explode on a warehouse and the harbour. There was intense heavy flak but all aircraft returned safely. Newly promoted Flt Lt Muir (KH619 GN-H) led four Mustangs on an armed reconnaissance on 25 January to Novska, Brod, Doboj and Sarajevo where, east of Brod, two aircraft were seen. The Mustangs jettisoned their bombs and gave chase, but on closing found the aircraft to be Marauders and broke away. A locomotive pulling wagons was sighted near Brod, this being strafed and twenty wagons left in damaged condition. Accurate 20mm flak was experienced, Flg Off Ashworth's aircraft (KH561 GN-B) suffering a hit which also wounded the pilot in the thigh. However, he was able to return to base safely. The month's most successful operation occurred next day (on 26 January), when nine Mustangs destroyed or damaged eight locomotives and numerous railway wagons, besides strafing a troop train and inflicting many casualties as its occupants fled from the coaches. Other targets this month were shipping at Pola and Lussino Island, and the coastal guns at Lussinpiccolo which were proving a nuisance to the Royal Navy craft operating among the northern Dalmatian Islands.

The improved weather in February made it possible for the Squadron to fly nearly double the number of sorties flown in January. The month opened well, 27 locomotives being destroyed or damaged in the first week. On 2 February, six Mustangs, operating in two sections of three, flew on an armed reconnaissance to the area of Dravograd, Celje, Maribor and Zagreb, thus approaching close to the Austrian border with Yugoslavia, their targets being the railway system and railroad rolling stock. The pilots' first objective was to bomb the railway bridge at Laska, south of Celje, on the line from Austria to northern Italy. In this they claimed some success, with several near misses if not direct hits, which cut the track north of the bridge. Thereafter rolling stock was strafed along the railway system north-west from Zagreb to Celje and north to Maribor. Considerable flak was experienced and Flt Sgt Monkman's Mustang (KH467) was hit in the fuselage. Flg Off McCaig (HB912 GN-A) called over the radio to the No3 pilot, Lt R.V. Jacobs (FB308 GN-E), that he would escort Monkman back to base. Jacobs, a South African from the Orange Free State who had recently joined the Squadron, replied "Good show", but that was the last that was ever heard of him. It was assumed that he, too, fell victim to the intense and accurate light flak.

On 7 February two sections, each of six Mustangs, were flown successively, one in the morning (led by Flg Off Nichols) and the second in the afternoon (led by Flt Lt Muir), on armed reconnaissance along the railway from Laska, to Celje, Maribor and Dravograd. A message from a field source in the area subsequently reported that Allied fighters that day had destroyed five locomotives between Celje and Maribor. It was agreed that three of these should be credited to the Squadron and two to 213 Squadron. In addition, Squadron pilots claimed one locomotive destroyed, four disabled and three damaged between Laska and Dravograd.

Three days later Flg Off Gardner took off on an air test in Mustang KH427 GN-V:

"When landing, the starboard brake seized and the tyre burst soon after touch down. Managed to hold the aircraft straight and came to an abrupt halt on the strip. Wing Commander Flying (Wg Cdr W.A. Laurie) appeared and was heard to say 'Not you again!' I thought I had done fairly well! Local Italian farmers were summoned and lifted both wings and deposited me and kite off the runway, as more aircraft were waiting to land."

Sqn Ldr Edmondson (FB306 GN-C) led a strike against Berge airfield on 15 February, where the six Mustangs (the others flown by recent returnee Lt Shields SAAF, plus Flt Sgts Gordon, Gardiner, Jones and Clarke) strafed three Ju52s, claiming these damaged. Earlier during the sortie, a bridge at Celje had been bombed and a locomotive pulling twenty wagons north of Pragersko, strafed; half the wagons were claimed damaged, as was the engine, before a road convoy was attacked and 20 M/T left damaged.

On the morning of 26 February, at 0625 hours, Flg Off McCaig, with Flt Lt J.D. Younie DFC (recently posted in from 241 Squadron) as No2, were airborne for a weather reconnaissance along the Dalmatian coast, from Lussino northward to Fiume. There they were to check the harbour for the ship *Kuk-Kuk*, a 4,200-ton minelayer, which pilots of the SAAF Beaufighter squadron attached to 283 Wing had attacked and claimed to have sunk two days earlier. Over the Fiume area was a thin layer of stratus cloud, its base at 5,000 feet, the visibility above it being unlimited and below it about 10 miles. McCaig (HB912 GN-A) flew low over the harbour looking for signs of the vessel, but instead sighted four camouflaged E-boats clustered round the jetty; he wrote later:

"I squeezed viciously on the trigger — a long, deadly burst — the .5s stabbing and leaping out into the jetty, the water around it, into the boats. 'Flak-flak-flak six o'clock. Coming up thick. Coming from the E-boats, the harbour, like bloody confetti.' Red 2's voice cut my wandering thoughts, the sky around me full of menace. Vicious yellow and black balls passed me on all sides, below and above, floating beyond, terminating in puffs of smoke. A flak hit my rear end, but how bad it was I had no way of knowing. I kept her going on, up still, clawing for height, weaving, my life depending on it, waiting for any indicated reaction, heart skipping a thousand beats, a knot of fear tightening my gut."

McCaig gave the order to break away and to fly south, out to sea. Younie (KH561 GN-B) confirmed that McCaig's Mustang was trailing white smoke. McCaig, who had been shot down four months earlier, continued:

"My whole being shuddered, there it was, all over again. The worst thing he could say. My radiator punctured. I was for it, but how fast this time? How long would it take to overheat? The four, big life-giving propeller blades slowed, grinding to a shuddering full stop. One minute all the powerful thrust needed, the next a deadly aerodynamic baffle impeding what remained of vital flying speed. At 15,000 feet she juddered on a stall. I pushed the nose down, picking up a few knots. I was in space with the sudden stillness about me, the euphoric feeling of weightlessness, no movement downwards, no sensations, only gently swishing shroud lines, overhead the umbrella 'chute. I didn't want to go through this again, the wide deep sea awaiting me below. A down-plunging silver shape curved round me, the mortally wounded Mustang spiralling with grace to an underserved fate, slowly twisting through an arc as if to evade its end."

Younie, having observed McCaig scramble into his dinghy about 500 yards off Pernata Point (Cherso Island), called 'Mayday' and reported his position. He then flew low over the dinghy and saw McCaig fire a red Very cartridge and wave his arms, after which he paddled towards shore. Control advised Younie that two Spitfires were being sent out and would be at the scene in about half an hour. At 0815 Younie made radio contact with the Spitfire pilots and arranged to meet them at 4,500 feet at the position where he had seen the dinghy. He then led them in line astern to fly north along the coast to where he indicated the beached dingy and McCaig's fluorescence marking along the shore's edge. The Spitfire pilots saw McCaig fire his second red Very cartridge and wave to them from a small sandy cove, near where he had baled out. Younie, having been advised that an ASR Catalina was on its way, set course for base. But McCaig was not rescued. Flg Off Spy Boulton wrote:

"The bid to rescue Fiji [Flg Off McCaig] was an odd failure, inexplicable at the time. The Catalina duly arrived and Fiji was seen to come to the shore line. With him were some civilians, evidently island inhabitants. He was not being molested and it was easy enough for him to paddle out to the Catalina. The Spitfires were still overhead and there was no sign of any enemy anywhere. Yet, instead of setting out for the rescue aircraft, after what seemed some talk with the islanders, he waved to the Catalina'a crew, turned and walked inland, still accompanied by the islanders. It was not until after the end of the war in Europe that the Squadron received the explanation of this strange incident."

The 'islanders' were in fact Italian soldiers manning a German air observer post and, keen to extricate themselves from their untenuous position and the war, invited McCaig to take the surrender of the entire Italian outpost:

"I couldn't believe it. These guys wanting me to take them back in the Air Sea Rescue plane, my prisoners of war!"

However, when the Catalina arrived and circled offshore, it flashed a morse code message instructing McCaig to "come out 200 yards" but the Italians would not allow him to paddle out to the flyingboat, on the grounds that if they did, they would suffer reprisals from the Germans. After some time, the circling Catalina flashed a further message advising that it would return at dawn. McCaig's captors were happy with that and, in the belief that they too would be flown to Italy aboard the flyingboat, produced some bottles of wine with which to celebrate their impending freedom:

"Drink wasn't something I needed but friendly persuasion swept aside my resistance and the glass in my hand became bottomless, each filling tasting better. They showed me another brew, insisting I try it. This was stronger stuff, raw spirit. Slowly I drifted into a pleasant coma, not caring about anything. Some dreamy time in the night I came half awake, conscious of voices sounding around me, getting louder. The group moved towards me, torches flashing, the beam slammed into my sensitive eyes. It was nothing to do with my Italian friends playing around but the full might of a German Unteroffizier backed by armed soldiers in field grey . . ."

McCaig spent the remainder of the war as a prisoner, the Squadron's 10th — and last — pilot to be so incarcerated.

Later that same day, six Mustangs ranging far and wide disabled or damaged six locomotives, destroyed two passenger coaches, damaged five railway wagons, destroyed or damaged five M/T and damaged three torpedo boats. In his report on the Squadron's activities for the month of February, Sqn Ldr Edmondson wrote:

"During the month the Squadron continued its attacks against enemy communications in Yugoslavia, chief attendance being given to railway bridges and rolling stock. Tactics employed for strafing consisted of formations of four aircraft flying at or below hilltop height, one pair each side of the line, taking advantage of their camouflage against the mountain background, and attacking alternately at high speed. Only one pilot was lost on strafing missions but considerable damage was effected against the enemy."

With the war in its final stages in Europe, the enemy's forces in the Balkans were nearing their vacation of that theatre of activities. On 1 March three Mustangs led by Flt Lt Muir were airborne on an armed reconnaissance north of Zagreb, German troops having been reported moving northward in that area. Along the road leading north-east from Zagreb to Varazdin they bombed ten M/T moving northwards. All ten vehicles were claimed destroyed. In subsequent attacks, as the trio continued northward, they strafed various M/T and six laden, heavy-duty vehicles. Their claims from these attacks were another six M/T destroyed and one damaged and four of the heavy-duty vehicles damaged. The pilots encountered small-arms fire from the roadside during the attack on the first convoy. A few miles south of Varazdin a locomotive, with steam up, was sighted pulling five wagons and moving southwest. Muir was seen going into attack, when his machine (HB851) flew straight into the ground from a height of about 40 feet. It exploded and then burst into flames and was completely destroyed. No flak had been seen and he had not reported that he had been hit. His fellow pilots thought that he must have been struck by small-arms fire.

In the face of the Russians' tremendous gains, the Germans now launched a strong offensive in an effort to save the Hungarian oilfields and the industrial area of eastern Austria, but by mid March this attempt had failed, part of the German forces in Vienna being cut off from those in Italy and Yugosalvia. Early in March the Germans brought in the 7th SS Division to clear the main route to Brod, and heavy fighting again flared. The Yugoslav General Dropin was now about to open an offensive in Croatia with his newly-formed 4th Yugoslav Army, in an effort to clear the Gospic-Bihac area and the coast and the northern Dalmatian Islands.

On 16 March six Mustangs, led by Flt Lt Younie (KH640 GN-T), bombed gun positions on the island of Rab. Eight bombs struck the target area, the other four falling as near misses. Only light flak was experienced but, during the return flight, Lt Peter Hill SAAF, a new pilot flying his first operational sortie, reported that the engine of his aircraft (HB859) was running rough, possibly as a result of flak damage. Flt Sgt Clarke (KH619 GN-H) was ordered to escort him to Ancona, on the coast of Italy. Hill then reported that his oil pressure had gone off the clock and, at 1520, about 20 minutes after he had first reported his engine difficulty, he baled out over the Adriatic. He was then at 6,000 feet and his parachute was seen to open at 4,000 feet. His escort, Clarke, who had immediately called 'Mayday', orbited where Hill had gone down in the sea and saw him, in his Mae West, moving in the water but did not see his dinghy. Clarke then flew to a small motor vessel about a mile away and then back again to Hill, to indicate where he was but, on going back over the fluorescence, where Hill had been, could not see him or his parachute. The fluorescence and oil patches were in relatively the same positions as before. Clarke was then joined by two Spitfires, which had been sent in response to his 'Mayday' call. Together the three pilots searched the area, but with no result. The motor vessel, to which Clarke had previously flown, also arrived on the scene, a dinghy being lowered from it, which was seen to approach the oil streak where the Mustang had entered the water, but nothing more resulted from the search either there or in the general area thereabouts. As Clarke returned to base he sighted an ASR Catalina, an ASR high speed launch and more vessels arriving to join in the search for the missing pilot, but nothing more was ever seen or heard of Hill.

Another notable operation took place next day (17 March), when Flg Off Gardner (HB952 GN-F) led Flg Off Dickerson (KH427 GN-V), Flt Sgt Clarke (HB869 GN-W) and another new pilot Flt Sgt O.G.L. Tilley (KH594 GN-Y) along the railway east of Zagreb, where they damaged six locomotives and destroyed or damaged five laden oil tankers and six ammunition wagons. All returned safely. Three days later (20 March) six Mustangs were airborne at 1450 for an armed reconnaissance along the railway communications south-west from Zagreb to Brod, and south from Brod to Doboj. After a bombing attack at 1550 by four of the pilots on the railway sidings at Sijekovac, about three miles south of Brod, Flt Sgt Monkman (KH619 GN-H) and Sgt Beer (KH594 GN-Y), who had both taken part in the bombing, separated from the remainder of the section and operated south towards Doboj. The other four pilots, two of whom had not yet used their bombs, now worked along the railway from Brod toward Zagreb, led by Gardner (KH640 GN-T). At 1600 Monkman and Beer sighted a stationary locomotive with steam up and about 30 wagons near Darvenja, south of Brod. Monkman led the attack:

"When we sighted the train, I went down to strafe the locomotive with Sgt Shandy Beer following, but as I made my approach, I saw that some of the wagons were loaded with oil drums. I therefore decided to attack these instead. I remember firing a sighter burst at a flat-car carrying oil drums as I was not yet within normal firing range, aiming slightly above the target. The thought running through my mind was that there may be a hell of a bang here as the train was unusually long (30 plus carriages) and had the character of a supply or ammunition train. My air gunnery proved to be on the mark. There followed an immediate and tremendous explosion, with a mass of flame rising to a thousand feet or more. My instinctive reaction was to get away from the target so I pulled hard on the stick, initiating a loop and while going up vertically I could feel and hear debris hitting the aircraft. I have a vivid picture in my mind of an axel with two railway wheels going by. I rolled the aircraft 'off the top' and checked for damage. All the instruments were reading normally, particularly the glycol temperature and oil pressure gauges which are usually the first to spell trouble."

On seeing the explosion, Beer broke away sharply and noticed Monkman climbing steeply to avoid the flame and debris.

"Shandy then called me and asked if I was on fire. I looked up and behind me and saw smoke issuing from the rear fuselage. As there was still fuel in the fuselage tank immediately behind me I made the decision to go, albeit reluctantly as the aircraft was operating so normally. As a result of my manoeuvre to avoid the explosion I was already heading in a westerly direction and I only had a short turn to make to get on my tract for home. Events now moved quickly. Smoke started to fill the cockpit so I jettisoned the hood, took off my helmet and mask, stuffing this equipment down by the seat, undid the seat harness and wound the elevator trim nose heavy. I pulled the nose up slightly and rolled. The exit was clean and moments later the 'chute deployed successfully. I was worried on my descent as the ground appeared to be entirely covered with coniferous forest, not considered to be the best sort of vegetation on which to make a parachute landing. There was practically no wind so I made no attempt to guide the 'chute. At the last moment however I saw I was going to land on a fairly wide trail and freeing myself from the parachute harness a group of peasant women came running down the trail towards me. I was so astonished I just sat stupified and, to my amazement, they ran past me as though I wasn't there and pounced upon my 'chute and started to cut it up into pieces. I stood up and saw what was obviously a guerilla soldier walking towards me. When we met he was very friendly and although I couldn't understand his Serbian he repeated the word 'Chetnik' several times and I tumbled to the fact that he wasn't a Partisan."

On returning to base, Sgt Beer reported on events and said that he had seen Monkman's parachute open, but had not spotted him on the ground. Within a few days following the loss of the Canadian, however, radio messages were received advising that he was safe and uninjured. Flg Off Boulton wrote:

"The messages were passed to the Squadron, but there was no indication of their source. It was thought that they were transmsitted from somewhere in the area of his baling out."

Meanwhile, Monkman had been taken to the local Chetnik HQ where he met some USAF survivors of a raid on the Ploesti oil refinery. The Chetniks were on friendly terms with the local German garrison, this evidently arising from their mutual antagonism to the Partisans, yet they would not hand over their British and American prisoners to the Germans. A bizarre incident at this time concerned a football match played between two teams of Chetnik soldiers, to which the local German Commandant was an invited guest, as were the American and British prisoners. Monkman recalled:

> "Giving the Chetnik guard the slip, I made my way unobserved to the group behind the Commandant. I stood for a little while and then whistled 'Tipperary' right through. The conversation stopped and there was complete silence. Feeling encouraged by this, I stepped out in front of the group so that my Flight Sergeant's stripes and crown and pilot's brevet could be clearly seen by him. The Commandant threw up his arm in the Nazi salute and said 'Heil Hitler!' I gave him the best salute I could."

Later, following a skirmish between the Chetniks and Partisans, Monkman found himself a 'prisoner' of the latter but eventually reached Belgrade and safety.

In the meantime, on 21 March, Flt Lt Ashworth (FB328 GN-X) and new arrival Wt Off R.N. Wheeler RAAF (HB952 GN-F) departed Biferno at 1605 and flew to Prkos airfield near Zara, where they landed 45 minutes later. Next day they took off from Prkos at 0520 to carry out an offensive sweep of Maribor, Dravograd, Zeltweg and Bruck, rather less than 100 miles due south-west of Vienna. This operation was the furthest into enemy territory of any made by the Squadron. They strafed numerous targets, chiefly along the railway linking the towns and claimed two locomotives destroyed, two disabled and five more damaged, together with ten railway wagons damaged. At Zeltweg they attacked the airfield where, in the south-west corner, was a Ju88, partly under tarpaulins, with men working on it. The bomber swung round sharply when hit and a small fire was started under the fuselage and it was claimed probably destroyed. They next strafed and damaged the control tower, which was located on the south side of the airfield. In the south-west corner were two hangars, one with an aircraft, believed a Bf109, standing outside its closed doors. The Messerschmitt swung back against the hangar as it was hit and was claimed damaged. Both that hangar and the other were strafed as was a barracks hut just outside the airfield. On nearing Twimberg they strafed a factory building and south of Bruck they strafed and damaged a motor vehicle pulling a trailer, travelling north-east towards that town.

Two days later, on 23 March, four Mustangs led by Flt Lt Younie (HB869 GN-W) flew on an armed reconnaissance from Ljubljana to Celje, Maribor and Dravograd, to attack railway targets. Going north-west, about five miles from Radece, a small town south of Celje, was a train, with the locomotive pulling about 20 wagons. Younie's bombs hit the locomotive and destroyed it. Some seconds later a series of explosions ran the length of the train, giving off brilliant vari-coloured flashes, mostly red, others green, blue, orange and white, with little or no smoke. Blast waves were clearly seen in the mist thereabouts as the explosions took place. The train was evidently laden with ammunition and was claimed completely destroyed.

Nearer to Radece, a second train going northwards was seen and attacked by two more of the Squadron's new arrivals, Wt Off A.J. Rogers RNZAF (FB327 GN-S) and Sgt E. Ramsbotham (HB907 GN-G). A dense cloud of steam with blackish debris rose to between 200 and 300 feet, but the results of the bombing were not clearly visible because of mist. The locomotive was claimed probably destroyed. About 40 miles west of Maribor a locomotive with 20 wagons, going north, had just entered the station at Lavamund. This blew up on being strafed and was claimed destroyed. Three wagons, in one of which a fire started, were claimed damaged.

Next day an offensive sweep was made against the airfield of Gornji Stupnik, near Zagreb, where a large force of enemy aircraft was reported to have been seen the previous day. The sweep was made by eight Mustangs, four each from 213 and 249 Squadrons, the latter each carrying two napalm bombs — known to the pilots as fire bombs — the Squadron having recently introduced this type of weapon in the European theatre of war. The bomb was in fact a 110 US gallon overload fuel tank filled with petrol and napalm, and was a terrifying weapon of considerable destructive power. Flg Off Geddes led the 249 section in HB869 GN-W:

> "We were to drop the bombs as we crossed the main railway line. I had some concern about

what would happen when we dropped these at such a low altitude, although I had actually used them on a number of previous occasions. The Wingco Flying had greeted me at the briefing with 'I hope you've got your tin pants on'. Apart from the apprehensions about the bombs, I thought we had a good plan of attack.

Indeed, everything went fine for 249's section except that there were not the number of enemy aircraft targets we had been led to believe would be there. When the bombs were released — there was a train passing at the time — the trim of the aircraft altered badly, the nose tried to rise and the trimmer had to be used quickly but we were aware of this. At this point I saw out of the corner of my eye one of the 213 Squadron planes on fire and rising rapidly to about 200 feet. Then we were onto the perimeter where right in my line of fire was a FW190 with covers on it (probably left behind u/s) which burst into flames, and to the right a Ju88 with personnel working on it. I had to use heavy right rudder to get onto the target but got a long burst into it and saw people fall over. By this time the flak was really coming up but as we were flying at zero feet it seemed to be going over our heads. I continued to fire at where the flak was coming from, particularly at the outskirts of a small wood where orange-coloured 20mm was being fired. In fact, by this time at least one of my guns had overheated and was firing on its own.

Having passed the danger area we quickly gained altitude into the sun and a feeling of exhilaration gripped me and, as I had seen another aircraft on the other side of the airfield out of my line of fire, I was thinking about having another run across to get it. Fortunately, I was brought down to earth when my No2 John Malherbe reported over the R/T that he had been hit by flak and his plane was vibrating. No3 Dobbie Finlay also reported he had an oil leak. So more sensible notions came into play. I asked No3 and No4 to return to base, and I would take No2 to Zara [where a base had recently been established], but a brief call to John seemed to confirm that his plane was still airworthy and we returned to base — only to find that there was much more damage to his aircraft than the holes in the wings he had noticed."

On landing back at Biferno, Malherbe was surprised to find a hole in each of two opposing propeller blades equally disposed, a hole in the spinner and two holes in the engine cowling of his aircraft, KH594 GN-Y. However, he reported that he had strafed a sky-blue FW190 — apparently a photo-reconnaissance variant — and an unidentified single-engined aircraft with Italian-type camouflage. The two aircraft were parked outside the perimeter near the north-west corner. He saw the FW190 catch fire as he strafed and claimed it destroyed. The unidentified aircraft was also hit, but did not flame and was claimed only as damaged. Despite the oil leak obscuring his vision, Flt Sgt Finlay (FB327 GN-S) had nonetheless carried out a strafing attack but made no claims. The fourth member of the section, Wt Off Wheeler, strafed the east corner of the airfield, hitting buildings and a barracks block. He saw three aircraft on the south perimeter to the right of his line of fire but was not able to attack these. Geddes continued:

"213 Squadron, although they lost one of their own, also accounted for a 190. The Group Captain and several others from HQ came down to the airfield to find out how we got on and were naturally disappointed that the larger number of enemy aircraft they expected to be at Gornji Stupnik had gone (if they had ever been there). But they seemed quite pleased with the results."

The Squadron was asked to provide two pilots to ferry Tiger Moths from Brindisi to Zara, as part of the programme instituted by the RAF to train selected members of Tito's forces. The training school was to be set up at Zara, to where Tiger Moths and Harvards were to be flown. Flt Sgt Jones was nominated to fly NM149, departing Brindisi on 4 April, reaching Zara next day via Bari, Nuova and Iesi; he was followed next day by Wt Off Smith in MN881. Smith and Jones were both flown back to Brindisi; the latter commented on his return:

"My idea of what flying should be. Evidently some political importance behind this flight."

Sqn Ldr Edmondson (HB869 GN-W) was briefed to lead a section of four to attack an observation post on Pag Island in the Dalmatians on 4 April, each aircraft carrying two napalm bombs. The attack was made in bad weather in a dive from 500 feet down to 100 feet, as he recalled:

> "We were plagued by fog en route to Pag and my radio was not performing well, finally packing up as we neared the target. I signalled to John Younie to take over and positioned myself at the tail, which proved ideal for observation. As the bombs ahead exploded I was reminded of lava pouring from an active volcano. It was impossible not to feel compassion for the small but stubborn force which, well dug in, had for some time resisted the efforts of the Yugoslav forces to dislodge them. The official report from the field confirmed that the operation had been successful."

Next day, a section of Mustangs carried out an armed reconnaissance of the Jasenovac-Brod-Doboj area. South of Dervenja a locomotive and several trucks were damaged and, shortly afterwards, Flg Off Geddes (GN-U) spotted what he initially thought was going to be an addition to the Squadron's tally:

> "Biplane sighted. Red [Air Force] markings. Aircraft probably a U2 Russian Army Co-op. Not shot down."

A few days later (on 11 April), Geddes (KH640 GN-T) again encountered an aircraft in the air when flying an armed reconnaissance in the Macjlag area:

> "Sighted aircraft flying near Doboj. Chased aircraft — had Red Star painted on fuselage. Believed Russian MiG-3. Not shot down."

Mustangs were out again on 6 April, attacking a large convoy retreating from Sarajevo to Doboj and Brod. Some 60 M/T were claimed destroyed or damaged. A further 36 vehicles were claimed destroyed on 10 April. Next day, three Mustangs led by Flg Off Gardner (FB327 GN-S) departed at 1605 on an armed reconnaissance from Vraca northwards to Brod. About 10 miles north of Vraca they bombed 20 parked M/T, claiming three direct hits and two near misses and estimated that they destroyed ten and damaged five of the vehicles. Some 20mm and 40mm flak was experienced. They then made towards Doboj, strafing other vehicles, four of which Gardner claimed as 'flamers' and five more damaged. Sgt Ramsbotham (KH520 GN-B) claimed two more as 'flamers', two as damaged, and two heavy duty vehicles damaged, while Flt Sgt Jones (HB869 GN-W) claimed damage to four M/T and an armoured car. Near Zepec the pilots were met with small-arms fire and Gardner's aircraft was hit in the coolant system:

> "After we had completed our strafing attacks and had set course for base, my No2 [Sgt Ramsbotham] reported that white smoke was coming from the underside of my aircraft, and that he had lost his rudder control. I advised him to land at base fairly fast and on his wheels, then to control his landing direction with his brakes. Assuming I had a glycol leak, I altered course in the hope of making landfall on the strip at the island of Vis. Just after leaving the Yugoslavian coast, my engine became rough and flames appeared from the exhaust stubs. I was then over the island of Brac at 8,000 feet and knew that I should have to bale out. I informed the section of my intention and unplugged oxygen and R/T connections, trimmed hard forward, released the hood and pushed the stick hard forward — and left the aircraft abruptly. As I floated down I could see my plane burning on the ground and hear the ammunition exploding."

Gardner's No3, Jones, witnessed his leader's plight:

> "It was the first and only time I experienced being at the same height as someone abandoning an aircraft — most spectacular. When he left the Mustang he came out like a cork leaving a bottle of champagne, turning somersaults in the air before his 'chute opened. His plane went

into a vertical dive, going at a terrific rate of knots. I thought the wings would have left the fuselage. When it was almost out of sight it then did a vertical climb, falling just short of its original height. I was concerned for his safety: to be clobbered by four and a half tons of Mustang at 8,000 feet is not a funny thing."

Having witnessed Gardner land safely, the remaining two pilots returned to Biferno where Ramsbotham's aircraft was found to have been hit in the starboard tailplane, the port elevator and the rear fuselage. Meanwhile, Gardner landed in a clearing near a building. Gathering his parachute, he was approached by the owner of the building and, on enquiring on the where-abouts of any Germans, was told they had left the island:

"I was invited into the building and given some food. Later another man appeared and indicated that I should go with him. Outside was a donkey with a wooden saddle. Eventually we came to a hamlet, Nerezisce, where I was greeted by most of the population. Eventually two RAF chaps arrived and we motored down to Milna, where a HSL was waiting to take me to Vis. We arrived there after an uneventful sea trip. Americans there gave me a bed for the night. [Next day] they took me down to where a full Dakota bound for Italy was about to take off. An Army officer of superior rank to myself was asked to get off so that I could get on board. He was not pleased. On take-off a tyre burst and I began to think my luck was running out. However with a new tyre fitted we took off across the Adriatic and I was dropped off at Biferno just about 24 hours after I had left there."

An earlier strike against the same convoy resulted in claims for 38 M/T destroyed or damaged, taking the day's total to 74 vehicles disabled. Napalm bombs were again used.

On 14 April the Squadron broke camp at Biferno, ready to move by road to Bari en route for the airfield of Prkos, near Zadar in Yugoslavia. Due to a critical shortage of Mustang IIIs elsewhere, 249 handed most of its remaining aircraft to 213 Squadron, re-equipping once more with Spitfires, 16 Mark IXs being flown in the same day by ferry pilots, who were to take them to Prkos. The Squadron was posted back to 281 Wing, already based at Prkos. Next day the Squadron travelled to Bari, where it was divided into two parties. On 16 April one party embarked on a landing craft at Barletta and sailed in the evening to Zadar, from where it travelled on to Prkos airfield. The other party embarked with the Squadron's M/T and all its equipment on another landing craft at Bari. This party arrived at Zadar two days later and then moved on to Prkos. From 19 to 21 April the Squadron was occupied with establishing itself at the airfield. During the next three days the pilots were engaged in converting to the Spitfire IXs. At 1050 on 24 April Lt Malherbe crashed his Spitfire (JG123 GN-A) immediately after taking off. Flg Off Boulton noted:

"His aircraft was shattered and it was said that he had been killed, a report that may have caused more concern as no pilot had been lost in this way from the time the Squadron moved to Italy. A little later the Intelligence Office received a telephone call from Wing HQ requesting that Lt Malherbe's parachute kit be collected from there. Flt Lt Tom Ashworth was with me at the time and we immediately set off in the Squadron jeep. We collected the parachute and saw that it had a large reddish stain. Immediately afterward the Wing Medical officer appeared and we asked him where Malherbe had been taken. To our surprise and relief he replied: 'He'll be all right. He'll be back with the Squadron in three week's time!' He had been saved by the Spitfire's cockpit having remained intact with him still seated in it when it crashed. The red stain on his parachute had been caused by its having been dumped on red earth, characteristic of the land of the region!" *

With the Spitfire IXs operational — and the war in its last two weeks — the field of operations

---

* Lt Malherbe suffered nothing worse than burns to his right shoulder and upper arm, and bloodshot eyes; however, since the war in Europe was over he did not return to the Squadron, but was flown back to Italy and immediately released to return to South Africa.

was over the northern Adriatic, the Istrian Peninsula and territories north of Fiume. Duties included escorting motor torpedo boats, Dakotas, and armed reconnaissance patrols. On 29 April, Flg Off Gardner led four of the new Spitfires on an armed reconnaissance from Lippa (ten miles north-west of Fiume) to Trieste and Senosencekia. Gardner (MK478) and his No2, Sgt Ramsbotham (MH980), bombed two motor vehicles west of Lippa, but with low cloud approaching Gardner ordered the other two to jettison their bombs safe. About ten miles south-east of Trieste, Gardner and Ramsbotham strafed one of three vehicles seen and when Ramsbotham fired, the truck blew up and then burnt fiercely, as if it had been carrying ammunition. The pilots continued to reconnoitre the area but, when they were near Senosencekia, Ramsbotham reported that his engine was running rough and that he would have to bale out. Evidently he had a glycol leak which it was thought must have been caused by debris from the explosion of the strafed M/T. Ramsbotham's aircraft was then at 4,000 feet and with rain cloud ahead, he and Gardner turned to avoid this cloud. His own turn completed, Gardner could not see Ramsbotham's aircraft and saw nothing of his parachute. He then circled the area for ten minutes searching, but with no result. Following the loss of Ramsbotham, the other pilots turned for base. When they were less that five miles east of Trieste, Gardner's aircraft was hit by small-arms fire. On landing at Prkos he was found to have had a bullet-damaged radiator and overload fuel tank. As for Sgt Teddy Ramsbotham nothing more was heard of him. With this incident the Squadron suffered its last wartime loss of a pilot and aircraft.

During the final week of April, the 4th Yugoslav Army, closely supported by the Balkan Air Force, broke through north of Istria and reached the River Isonzo. Here it met the advancing spearheads of the British 8th Army from Italy, at Montfalcone. This was the end for the Germans, and resistance began to fade away rapidly. By 6 May the German withdrawal from Slavonica was almost over and that evening all enemy troops north-west of Fiume surrendered. However, for 249 the war was not quite over, as remembered by Sqn Ldr Edmondson:

> "After being stood down following the surrender of the Germans in Europe, we were stood to again and continued operating whilst the Germans in our area continued to resist the Russians, preferring to wait for the Kiwis' arrival before surrendering. Presumably they had never seen the All Blacks in action!"

Still at Prkos when hostilities in Europe came to an end, the Squadron was ordered to return to Biferno on 16 May, when Marshal Tito gave orders for all British forces to be withdrawn forthwith; the former Anglo-Yugoslav alliance had turned so violently that RAF fighter squadrons were required to provide cover to the ground forces as they withdrew by road to Zara. Sqn Ldr Edmondson was posted to the Middle East for repatriation to Australia, and Flt Lt Tom Ashworth assumed temporary command; he wrote in his official report:

> "May was of course a month of anticipation, celebration and movement and changes. Bonfires and bursts of small-arms fire on the hillside on the eve of the 1st caused much speculation until someone found out or remembered it was Labour Day. After the announcement of the surrender of the German armies in Italy, our aircraft were forbidden to attack ground targets and had the job of trying to build up a picture of events of the chaos that existed. For VE night some splendid liquers were got from a well-established firm in Zara. This enabled everyone to get as drunk as they wished without any bad effects on health."

He added:

> "There was a natural reaction [to the end of the war] and as many of the airmen found the lack of urban amenities trying, it was hard to get the Squadron down to a routine training, the intention being to work to as near a peacetime programme as possible."

On its return to Biferno, the Squadron converted again, this time receiving two Mustang IIIs (FB328 and KH640) initially, used to convert pilots who had no experience on type, before 13 brand new Mustang IVs, together with three more Mk IIIs (KH424 GN-V, KH512 GN-U and

HB921 GN-C), were delivered between 5-14 June. Several more South African pilots were posted to the Squadron about this time, including Lt F.C. Mortimer from 94 Squadron, Lts M.H. Pitcher and M.C. Stevens from 9 SAAF Squadron, and Lt E.W. John. At this stage, the Squadron was advised of the award of a DFC to Flg Off Geoff Nichols, who had achieved a total of 56 M/T destroyed in recent operations. Flt Sgt Bill Monkman was awarded a DFM, the first such decoration since the Squadron's arrival in Italy. Further decorations for the Squadron were gazetted in August, Sqn Ldr Edmondson receiving a DSO, while Flt Lt Tom Ashworth received a DFC and Flt Sgt Dobbie Finlay a DFM. Later, in October, a DFC was announced for the deceased Flt Lt Jock Muir, then later still, in February 1946, the Squadron's final decoration of the war was announced when Flg Sgt Hugh Manning received a DFM.

The Squadron had completed a career which stands to the credit of all who were privileged to serve in it, and which had ranged from Britain to Malta and Sicily, and from Italy to Greece, Albania, Yugoslavia and Austria. The cost had been high, however. The Squadron suffered the grievous loss of 73 pilots killed between July 1940 and April 1945, all but a handful killed in action; a further ten spent time as prisoners of war.

On 30 June, the Squadron moved to Brindisi and spent its short peacetime stay in Italy in practice flying. It reached such a high standard that it was selected to take part in an air display over Athens, but was unable to do this due to its disbandment on 18 August 1945. News of imminent disbandment was received at the beginning of August and was followed by a widespread feeling of disappointment. But there was no time for reflection. All personnel were advised of their postings and many had departed before it was announced that the number 249 was not to disappear, as noted by Flt Lt Ashworth:

"It was to be transferred to 500 Squadron, a light bomber squadron in the Desert Air Force and all our documents are to be immediately sent to them. Nothing more remained to do except wish 500 Squadron the best of luck with their new number and hope that success and good fortune would attend their progress."

Chapter Thirteen

AN UNEASY PEACE

August 1945 — January 1950

"The Tempest seemed OK . . . so I flew it back to Habbaniya, without a parachute and with my cap pulled fully down over my ears, sitting on the three-tonner's removable seat."

Sqn Ldr Peter Steib, Commanding Officer 249 Squadron

Having flown successively Ansons, Blenheims and Hudsons with Coastal Command's 16 Group until late 1942, 500 Squadron had been transferred to the NWAAF, later re-equipping with Venturas and then Baltimores before joining the Desert Air Force in December 1943 as a light bomber squadron initially based at La Senia in Italy. It remained in a night interdiction role until the end of the war, which found the Squadron based at Villaorba near Udine. With the arrival of peace, the Squadron was involved in communications flights until Transport Command took over its duties, and it was then advised of an imminent move to RAF Eastleigh in Kenya, East Africa, where it was to undertake its new peacetime role, that of photographic survey using the standard F24 camera. At the same time the Squadron received a new Commanding Officer, Wg Cdr H.J.D. Matson AFC.

The ground parties began leaving Villaorba on 24 August 1945, one party of mainly maintenance personnel heading for Lecce from where they were to be airlifted to their new base, while the M/T party travelled to Trieste, where loading of vehicles began on the 27th. The first eight Baltimores, led by Wg Cdr Matson, flew to Malta via Bari on 13 September, followed next day by the remaining six. By the 18th all had reached Egypt, landing at Cairo West aerodrome, from where next day four set out for Kenya. On arrival at Eastleigh, the home of the RAF's Anti-Malarial Flight also equipped with Baltimores, Wg Cdr Matson found that the advance party had already established a base, as recalled by the Squadron Gunnery Leader, Wt Off Joe Chilton:

"I was ordered, whilst detached from 500 Squadron in Cairo, to receive an advance party from the Squadron and take them by air to Eastleigh. I did this, eventually overcoming 'base-wallah' resistance and establishing our hangar and workshops for the Squadron, which flew in from Italy. When we (the advance party) arrived at Eastleigh, it was pleaded that there was not enough vacant accommodation. The corporals and airmen were OK but senior NCOs including myself were directed to a former Polish displaced persons' hutted compound near the guardroom, and there the Wt Off/NCO aircrew stayed as long as I recall. This all led to some feeling. We tarted it up and installed a bar and mess in due course."

On arrival at Eastleigh, the CO was advised that he was also to take over the duties of Station Commander vice Wg Cdr P.D.R. Hutchings, and that 500 Squadron was to be renumbered as 249. On 1 October, seven more Baltimores set out from Cairo West for Eastleigh. The first three aircraft arrived via Malakal and Juba on the 4th, followed by two more next day. The remaining two, both of which had developed problems en route, arrived later in the month.

With his new role as Station Commander occupying his time, Wg Cdr Matson effectively passed day-to-day command of the Squadron to the senior Flight Commander, Sqn Ldr D.C. Davies DSO DFC, on 23 October; B Flight was commanded by Sqn Ldr Harrington, who had originally flown with the Squadron in 1941 at Malta. During the month four NCOs and 16 airmen arrived at Kisumu aerodrome by BOAC, from where they travelled by train to Eastleigh. A further contingent arrived aboard an RAF Dakota under the command of the Squadron

Engineer Officer, Flt Lt Y.L. Rabin. The Baltimores were to be responsible for all photographic tasks in East Africa, including Kenya, Tanganyika, Uganda and Somaliland. Wt Off Chilton continued:

"The Anti-Malarial Flight did the dangerous job of chasing locusts as well. They were established separately, the aircraft permanently fitted with extra tanking and spraying kit from the bomb-bay. I had several friends who flew with it and constantly hoped that wind changes would not alter the locust 'flight plan'; at least one crash occurred through air intakes becoming filled with locusts. Early sprayings with experimental chemicals killed a lot of fish in the lakes!"

However, before any serious survey work could be undertaken from Eastleigh by 249, the authorities decided that the main runway would have to be widened and therefore all flying was suspended for a few days, then only limited flying would be possible for the ensuing two months until the work was completed. To enable crews to familiarise themselves with the vastness of their new command, three aircraft were detached to operate from Nairobi civil airfield for a few days at a time. Of this period, Sqn Ldr Davies commented:

"Although adverse weather prohibited photography for almost half the month [of November], hours flown in aerial survey show an advance on October times; long-range flights covered obliques of airfields in Tanganyika."

One aircraft was held on standby at Eastleigh for 'jungle rescue' duties to deal with any forced landings. On 26 November the first such occasion arose and Wt Off Burrell and his crew were scrambled when news arrived of a 1414 Meteorlogical Flight Spitfire down near the Thika river. However, the Spitfire pilot had made a successful emergency landing and telephoned his base to confirm that he was unhurt. The Baltimore was thus recalled. By late November the Squadron was well into its stride, as revealed in a local newspaper report:

"Many areas in Kenya and the adjacent territories have already been surveyed for Government Departments, and for Military Survey. There are still many areas to be photographed and this work is going on whenever weather permits; obviously heavy overcast prevents an accurate survey of any sizeable stretch of country being made. The headwaters, catchment areas and the courses of the Thika and Athi rivers have been surveyed. The enlarged photographs show accurately the contours, nature of the ground, degree of erosion and the extent of denudation of vegetation, and saves many months which would be required for ground survey. Surveys by air have also been made for the medical authorities with the object of aiding anti-malarial work. The photographs show the concentration of bush and vegetation, water courses and swampy ground, and potential [mosquito] breeding areas.

The RAF photographic unit also went as far afield as Nganda to survey a blockage in the waterway from Kimolo to Lake Salisbury, the breaking up of which have endangered communications for many miles around. One of the most important jobs of all will shortly be undertaken in the form of an aerial survey for the Forest Department. It will show the extent of the forest reserves, the concentration of timber, where cutting out of tree growth has been too heavy, where young trees are dying off. Air survey is by no means a cheap method of doing the job but is far more rapid than normal methods. The chief problem in East Africa is the prevalence of low cloud which renders many days useless for photography. It is essential to get as much work done as possible on clear days, entailing long hours in the air."

Excellent weather during the first two weeks of December enabled the Squadron to improve on its total of photographic hours. Mosaics of Lake Maivasha and Ol Donyo Sapuk were completed, while many hours were spent on pin-points for the Anti-Malarial Flight. Towards the middle of the month these areas were given priority. But it was not all work and no play, as Wt Off Chilton recalled:

"Wg Cdr Matson was certainly busy but needed, like all of us, his days off. He instituted what he called 'goodwill flights.' His brother was British Consul-General in Tanganyika, at Dar-es-Salaam. He asked me if I could DI [Daily Inspection] a Baltimore — after three and a half years on the type I could build one — and if so, we would take off on Friday afternoon and go to Dar [return on Monday morning]. I was to stay at the New Africa Hotel in Dar. This we did more than once. I heard that a 'goodwill flight' even got to Johannesburg."

However, since Baltimores were Lease/Lend aircraft, the Squadron was advised that it was to be re-equipped with Mosquito FB26s and, on 16 December, the first two Mosquitos arrived although it transpired that these aircraft were in fact intended for 114 Squadron based at Aden, to where they were later despatched, but not before Sqn Ldr Davies had taken the opportunity to fly one. Operations came to a virtual standstill at the end of the month as the majority of the Baltimores were due their inspections, which normally took ten to fourteen days. Two of these, FW609 and FW866, had already been withdrawn from Squadron service and sent to Kisumu for storage. Another, FW880 GN-T, suffered some damage on 21 January when it collided with another Baltimore, FW554 of the Anti-Malarial Flight, while taxying at Eastleigh. Early in the new year Wt Off Chilton* carried out a mounting and levelling test on a K17 camera set experimentally fitted to Wt Off Snow's aircraft, but this did not seem to offer any advantage over the standard F24 in use. At the end of February, Sqn Ldr Davies wrote:

"The first three months saw the main of the Squadron's photographic commitments fulfilled, but bad weather towards the end of the month stopped some tasks being rendered complete."

March opened with the arrival at Eastleigh of Sqn Ldr J.M.O. Dyer DFC AFC, who was to take temporary command of the Squadron vice Sqn Ldr Davies. The latter was due for release from the Service and returned forthwith to the UK. Another new arrival who was to take command of one flight was Sqn Ldr Wakeford OBE, who — like his predecessor Sqn Ldr Harrington — joined the Squadron for the second time. He had originally been posted to 249 at Malta in late 1943, but had been taken ill on arrival, hospitalised and on being discharged was posted to another squadron.

On 16 March Flt Lt Mason† was scrambled in the 'jungle rescue' Baltimore when news arrived of a force-landed Dakota at Shinyanga. However, on arrival, the crew and passengers of the downed aircraft were seen to be in good hands and no supplies were dropped. A number of Mosquito FB26s plus a Mark III trainer had by now arrived and conversion training was under way, one of which Flt Lt J.T. Black crashed on take-off on 22 March during his first solo. He was unhurt and later the same day completed his solo in another aircraft. By the end of the month only one Baltimore was serviceable. Mosquito conversions proceeded at full speed and within a few weeks most pilots were fully converted, although not without incident. On 4 April Wt Off M.G.R. Del-Rosso experienced engine failure while practicing a solo landing and crash-landed on the runway. The aircraft caught fire but the pilot escaped with minor injuries. Next day Flg Off Sheldrick's aircraft suffered a burst tyre on take-off although he was able to make a safe landing.

A further change in command occurred on 14 April with the arrival of Wg Cdr J.H. Player DSO DFC, a New Zealand-born, wartime night-fighter pilot. He took over from Wg Cdr Matson whose responsibilities as Station Commander precluded him from giving the Squadron his full attention. Sqn Ldr Dyer now became Acting Squadron Commander. A few days later, he found himself in the role of Acting Station Commander following the departure of Wg Cdr Matson and the imminent arrival of the new Station Commander, Wg Cdr Craven. However, the latter's

---

* Wt Off Chilton left the Squadron in January 1946 and returned to the UK. The following year he was advised that a commission recommended in 1945 had been awarded and back-dated to April 1945: "I had to repay my Warrant Officer gratuity (difficult) and then received an officer gratuity, a triumph of admin genius!"

† Shortly after the end of the war, Flt Lt Mason's aircraft had been forced down by Russian fighters near Graz when flying a communications sortie; he, his crew and aircraft were released after three days of internment.

arrival at Eastleigh was temporarily delayed when the Ventura conveying him from the Middle East force-landed near Tororo in Uganda. Two Mosquitos flown by Sqn Ldr Wakeford and Flg Off MacFadyen were scrambled from Eastleigh and carried out a search during which the Ventura was located. However, MacFadyen's aircraft suffered a bird strike which damaged its nose and necessitated a landing at Kisumu for repairs. He was followed in by Wakeford's Mosquito which had developed an engine problem. Both aircraft were made serviceable by the morning and returned to Eastleigh, followed shortly afterwards by Wg Cdr Craven who was none the worse for his experience.

With Mosquito conversion complete, the Squadron anticipated resuming its duties but this was not to be. All aircraft were grounded on 27 May following the discovery of faulty bolts fitted to the main undercarriage. Replacement parts were flown to the Squadron and by the middle of June flying re-commenced. Sqn Ldr Wakeford left during the month to take command of the East Africa Communications Squadron and was later replaced as Flight Commander by Sqn Ldr Whitaker. The Squadron was now re-classified as a long-range fighter-bomber unit and instructions were received for an immediate transfer to RAF Habbaniya in Iraq, where there was political unrest. The first three aircraft departed on 27 June, accompanied by a Dakota and led by Wg Cdr Player; three more Mosquitos and a second Dakota followed. The following month exercises in conjunction with the RAF Armoured Car companies based at Habbaniya began. Mosquitos took part in a search for an overdue French Ju52 believed down in the desert wastes but which was found later to have landed safely at Beirut.

The heat of Iraq had a disastrous effect on the wooden Mosquito and skin shrinkage soon became a problem. So serious was it that all Squadron aircraft were grounded on 28 August. Wg Cdr Player and all aircrew were posted away, while groundcrew were temporarily employed by other units at Habbaniya awaiting a decision on the Squadron's future.

The months following the end of the Second World War had found the MEAF's ground-attack squadrons equipped with obsolete Spitfires, lease-lend Mustangs due for return, or unsuitable Mosquitos. The Air Ministry therefore decided to continue production of the Tempest — one of the fastest piston-engined fighters ever produced, which had helped see off the Luftwaffe in Northern Europe during the closing months of the war — with which it would re-equip certain MEAF units. To assist with the conversion of pilots due for posting to the new Middle East Tempest squadrons, 54 Squadron based at RAF Odiham, which operated the Tempest briefly in 1946 before re-equipping with the Vampire jet, was selected as a conversion unit. As and when Tempests and pilots became available for the MEAF, small flights of aircraft were ferried to the MU at Fayid in Egypt, ready for allocation to the new squadrons, one of which was to be 249 languishing at Habbaniya. Without aircraft, pilots or even officers, the seemingly forgotten unit was held together by its admirable SNCOs, Flt Sgts Cooper and Anderson.

Sqn Ldr J.I. Kilmartin DFC, a wartime fighter ace, had been nominated to command the revamped Squadron, with Flt Lt P.F. Steib DFC (a former wartime Typhoon and Mustang pilot) as his senior Flight Commander. On reaching Fayid they found five pilots awaiting their arrival, but only five Tempest F6s, therefore Flt Lt Steib and Flt Lt M.P. Fisher DFC went on ahead as passengers aboard a Lancaster staging through to Habbaniya, Sqn Ldr Kilmartin leading Flg Off J.S. Capel, Wt Offs M. Buxton and V. Hanrahan, plus Flt Sgt J.W. Sutherland in the Tempests, arriving two days before Christmas 1946. During the flight from Egypt, Hanrahan's aircraft, NX126, developed an oil leak and was fortunate to reach Habbaniya where, on inspection, it was found necessary for a new engine to be installed.

The Air Ministry decided that 249 was to be re-formed on a cadre basis, with eight Tempests and one Harvard T2 (FS741), ten pilots and 50 ground personnel, and that it was to have a fighter-bomber role with rocket projectiles as the main armament. Three more Tempests arrived during January to bring the Squadron up to strength but it was not until April that R/p training got under way. The Squadron's GN code letters were painted on the new aircraft: red letters outlined in white, while on the fin base was painted a white arrowhead with a gold disc and black elephant within, the detail extracted from the Squadron crest.

Exercises were flown in conjunction with the Army but these were considered to have been of little benefit to the Squadron. Oil leaks continued to plague the Tempests and one aircraft was damaged in an emergency landing when its reduction gear sheered. The middle months of 1947 passed relatively uneventfully with continuous training. Towards the end of the year however, in November, Flt Lt Steib experienced a freak accident and was obliged to carry out a wheels-up forced-landing in the desert:

> "I had taken GN-E up for a gun test — no targets, just firing into the desert, but when at about 1,000 feet a ricochet pierced the radiator. My No2, Mike Buxton, advised me of a glycol leak. I headed back towards Habbaniya, having decided to carry out an emergency landing when the engine temperature reached 135. This I did, with only minor damage to the tips of the blades. The aircraft was later towed back on its own wheels the 20 miles to Habbaniya."

Sqn Ldr Kilmartin left the Squadron at the end of November "after a series of farewell parties", command passing to newly promoted Sqn Ldr Steib.

Three new pilots arrived in January 1948, Plt Off M. Searle from 213 Squadron and Flg Offs G. Bradshaw and D.A. Harragan from 208 Squadron. Daily routine was livened on 18 March when two aircraft were scrambled to intercept a Lincoln from Shallufa, a sortie which was considered to have been successful. The exercise was successfully repeated four days later when two pairs of Tempests were scrambled after three Lincolns. During one sortie Flg Off Capel radioed to say that his engine was giving cause for concern and he eventually landed in the desert, some 20 miles from base, from where he was picked up by an Army unit. Meanwhile, Sqn Ldr Steib and an inspection team drove to the scene in a three-ton lorry, as the CO recalled:

> "Following inspection, when the engine was run at full throttle, the Tempest seemed OK. John had already departed, taking his parachute and helmet . . . so I flew it back to Habbaniya, without a parachute and with my cap pulled fully down over my ears, sitting on the three-tonner's removable seat."

249 received a visit on 7 April from Grp Capt John Grandy DSO, the Squadron's 1940 Commanding Officer, who gave a lecture on the training scheme followed by a talk on the Squadron's early history. Before his departure from Habbaniya, Grp Capt Grandy took up a Tempest on a local flight. Six days later, on 13 April, a signal was received at 1000 to the effect that four Tempests were to be sent to Palestine for a possible rocket attack on a target near Jerusalem, the scene of angry clashes between Jews and Arabs. By 1300, an Anson with five groundcrew on board departed for Ramat David airfield. An hour later a Ventura departed, loaded with rocket heads and motors, oil and spares, and, by 1430, three Tempests fitted with long-range tanks and armed with four rockets apiece, departed Habbaniya and arrived at Ramat David at 1650. They were followed by two more Tempests early next morning. However, the strike was cancelled and one aircraft returned to Habbaniya on the 21st, leaving four Tempests on duty at Ramat David, from where sector recces were flown. During an air test on the 23rd, Flg Off Geoff Bradshaw's aircraft was fired upon by an unseen enemy on the ground and one bullet passed through the port aileron.

The detachment returned to Habbaniya on the 27th, the groundcrew flying in a Dakota, but two days later the Squadron was ordered to send four Tempests back to Ramat David. All were ready by 0800 including the Dakota with ground personnel, although low cloud prevented take-off until 1130. Daily reconnaissances were flown, climaxing on 14 May with the withdrawal of the last British ground forces from Palestine, which became the new state of Israel as from midnight. The RAF maintained a presence at Ramat David until the 17th when all four Tempests departed at 0740 for Habbaniya; however, Sqn Ldr Steib's aircraft developed a glycol leak and he was obliged to land again, followed by the other three. The three serviceable aircraft took off at 0845 flown by Flg Off Bradshaw, P2 Hanrahan and P2 Buxton; the CO's aircraft was left behind to have its engine changed and he returned to Habbaniya aboard a Dakota. The Dakota later flew back to Ramat David with new engine, together with P2 Grimes, who eventually flew the repaired aircraft back to Habbaniya. Despite the occasional problems with glycol leaks, Sqn Ldr Steib and his pilots were satisfied and happy with their mounts.

The remainder of the year for the Squadron was relatively uneventful. Training continued with a new batch of pilots joining during the second half of the year, including Flg Off D.G.L. Heywood, Plt Off D.M. Scrimgeour, P2 C. Peters, P2 Brown, P4 G.A. Hunt, P4 J.J. Smith and P4 J. Hatton, while Sqn Ldr Steib and Flg Off Bradshaw departed, both tour-expired. Flt Lt Fisher assumed temporary command until the new CO arrived.

P2 Colin Peters* had been with the Squadron less than two months when he was killed in a flying accident on 24 August, the Squadron's first flying fatality since the end of the war. His Tempest, NX209, stalled and crashed 14 miles south-east of Habbaniya while on an air-to-ground firing practice flight. His death was followed by that of P1 Alex Rollo* who was taken ill with severe bronchitis on 3 September and admitted to hospital, where he died eight days later. In October, Flg Off Harragan, P2 Brown and P4 Hunt returned to the UK to ferry back to Habbaniya three new Tempests for the Squadron, the shortage of aircraft being increased when newly promoted Flg Off Scrimgeour force-landed NX142 GN-G with a glycol leak caused by a ricochet during air-to-ground training on 16 November. The pilot was not hurt and his aircraft was towed back to Habbaniya for repairs. A second Tempest made a safe landing when a serious oil leak developed.

The Squadron was also suffering from a shortage of pilots, since the three sent to the UK for ferrying duties had yet to return; neither had the new CO arrived and, in his absence, Flt Lt Fisher assumed the role of Acting Squadron Commander. Despite these problems, the Squadron put on a demonstration of air-to-ground firing for the Iraqi Air Force, watched by HRH the Regent, following which an Iraqi Fury and its pilot joined 249 the following day for air-to-ground firing on the Markab Range. Shortly after this, the Squadron participated in Operation Labourer, an exercise in co-operation with RAF Levies when Tempests attacked targets specified by the Army.

The new year of 1949 started on a sombre note. Following the arrival on 5 January of Sqn Ldr J.R. Baldwin DSO DFC, a notable wartime fighter pilot, to take temporary command of the Squadron pending the arrival from the UK of the designated commander, Flt Lt Fisher, who had been unwell, was admitted to hospital, where he died of pneumonia the following day†. On 26 January, two Tempests were scrambled to assist in the search for a missing Iraq Communications Flight Proctor carrying, as a passenger, the commander of the RAF Iraq Levies. The aircraft was located, upside down in the Euphrates, at Hit; there were no survivors. The new Squadron Commander, South African-born Sqn Ldr C. Scott-Vos DFC, another notable wartime fighter pilot, finally arrived on 9 February.

The three replacement Tempests had also reached Habbaniya but the oil leak problems continued, the engine of P3 Hunt's aircraft seizing on landing following dive-bombing practice. Three further incidents marred March's flying programme, P3 Smith putting up a black when he forgot to lower his undercarriage when landing, causing severe damage to his aircraft. This was followed by a second wheels-up landing although, on this occasion, due to engine failure. P3 Hatton was obliged to come down in the desert 30 miles south-west of the aerodrome and although "he made a very good job", NX141 was considered beyond repair. A week later, on 21 March, all three aircraft involved in a live firing exercise against a ground target — a written-off Proctor, which went up in flames — returned to Habbaniya with their aircraft unserviceable. One had suffered an oil leak, the second had a damaged windscreen, while the third had lost a wing panel.

Earlier in the month Sqn Ldr Scott-Vos had received instruction to move the Squadron to the RAF Station at Deversoir in the Suez Canal Zone, where it was to join 324 Wing. Thus, on 29 March, five Tempests and the Squadron's Harvard, together with four Dakotas carrying ground personnel, spares and equipment, departed from Habbaniya for its new location. Three unserviceable Tempests were left behind. However, the Squadron was still plagued by problems and en route the Harvard, flown by Flg Off Harragan, lost power and with an escort provided

---

* P2 Colin Peters and P1 Alex Rollo had both flown Tempests during the closing stages of World War II and had both been shot down and taken prisoner.

† Wg Cdr Steib is of the opinion that the deaths of both Flt Lt Fisher and P1 Rollo were probably due to what is now known as Legionnaires' Disease.

by three Tempests, force-landed safely at H3 airstrip. Harragan and his passenger, Flg Off Heywood, were driven to Amman from where they were flown by Dakota to Deversoir two days later.

Once installed at Deversoir, the Squadron received a new Flight Commander, Flt Lt M.J. Gray DFC, whose duty was to form a second flight, while the Squadron was to receive nine new Tempests supplied by 107 MU at Kasfareet, plus one redundant Tempest formerly the property of 39 Squadron at Khartoum. One of the replacement aircraft was sent to 109 MU at Fayid because after inspection "it was found to be three inches longer than it should have been!" The Squadron carried out exercises with the other two resident Tempest units, 6 and 213 Squadrons and, on 19 May, whilst landing from a cine-gun exercise, Heywood braked too hard to avoid a native working on the runway lighting. The Tempest, NX150 GN-H, cartwheeled onto its back but Heywood's only injury was to his left hand.

The Squadron received a number of replacement pilots during this period including jet-trained P2 R.E. Maxwell, who flew his first Tempest solo shortly after his arrival at Deversoir. At the end of June, all twelve Squadron aircraft flew to Nicosia, Cyprus, for APC led by Sqn Ldr Scott-Vos; groundcrews and equipment followed in six Dakotas. The Tempests proudly wore the new Squadron emblem — a black painted elephant on a yellow background — which adorned the radiator inspection panels (later transferred to the tail fairing). Additionally, all aircraft had red and white spinners, red undercarriage spats and D doors, and red code letters outlined in white. The six-week long stay at Cyprus was well received and all pilots benefitted from the air-to-ground practice facilities, although on one occasion the CO was obliged to make an emergency landing on the airfield following loss of coolant, and RAF Nicosia's Wing Commander Flying, Wg Cdr R. Deacon Elliott DFC, using the Squadron's NX268, force-landed on the beach at Morphou Bay. The detachment returned to Deversoir on 8 August.

Soon after the arrival of three new pilots in September (P3 Burrage and P3 Chiswick, both jet-trained, and P3 Leslie), the Squadron participated in a 324 Wing exercise. On returning to Deversoir with a suspected oil leak, P3 R. Watson's aircraft also suffered an undercarriage malfunction and swung violently on landing. The undercarriage collapsed, severely damaging NX233 GN-H although the pilot was unhurt. At the beginning of October, two more new pilots arrived: Flg Off F.G. Rayner-Sharpe, a former instructor, and Flg Off W.P. Dale, ex-Fleet Air Arm. Their arrival signalled the departure of two of the recently arrived NCO pilots and P3s Chiswick and Adlington were posted to understrength squadrons. A further new arrival was Flt Lt R.L. Cameron from 208 Squadron to take command of B Flight. The second half of the month witnessed three serious incidents; on the 18th, P3 Hunt experienced hydraulic malfunction when landing and, without flaps or brakes, NX126 GN-A ran off the end of the runway where the undercarriage collapsed. Next day, when on the ground, a practice rocket was inadvertently fired from a Tempest, causing fatal injuries to a member of the groundcrew. Ten days later, there occurred a further serious accident when P2 Maxwell, leading a section, tried to cross under another section, instead of over, in a crossover turn. His aircraft (NX182 GN-Q) collided with the No2 of the other section, damaging Flg Off Dale's propeller and wings although he was able to land NX281 safely. Meanwhile Maxwell, despite having lost his rudder and part of an elevator, carried out a successful wheels-up landing at Kabrit.

The year ended on a fairly uneventful note although the Tempests continued to be plagued by problems, mainly hydraulic failures, and pilots eagerly awaited their first jet, the Vampire FB5, with which 324 Wing was being equipped. 213 Squadron had already received its initial batch and on 5 January Flt Lt Gray flew one of these. Five days later Sqn Ldr Scott-Vos flew the Station Commander's Vampire in which he made a safe landing despite barostat failure. As more Vampires arrived at Deversoir, so 249 began its conversion. A new era had begun.

Chapter Fourteen

INTO THE JET AGE

January 1950 – August 1956

"I soon spotted the tug and glider combination. As I gazed upon its squat, black, clipped outline my imagination transformed it into a Heinkel silhouetted against the off-white haze of the horizon, and it was 1940 and my Vampire was a Hurricane about to attack the intruder sneaking up the Thames to drop its load of death and destruction upon the capital."

Plt Off Leighton Fletcher, 249 Squadron

By the end of January 1950, the Squadron had received its first four Vampire FB5s and conversion was well under way, albeit with the odd minor mishap as witnessed when P2 Smith scraped the tail and booms on take-off during his solo flight. On 10 February, Air Marshal Sir John Baker KCB MC DFC, the new AOC-in-C MEAF, paid 324 Wing a visit and a flypast was staged by all three squadrons. 249 Squadron put up three Vampires and six Tempests but soon after take-off Tempest NX252 flown by P2 Ron Watson started giving trouble and white smoke was seen to pour out. He tried to reach the airfield but the aircraft stalled, crashed and caught fire. Airmen quickly on the scene attempted to extricate the pilot but were unable to do so.

A number of new pilots joined the Squadron about this time including Flg Off J.P. Talbot, P2 R.E. Hillard, P2 Jankowski, a Pole, and P4 C. Firmin, plus Flg Off R.A. McPhie*, a Canadian who had ferried a Vampire from the UK. By March the Tempests were beginning to disappear, three being ferried back to the UK on the 6th by P2s Hunt, Smith and Rose. The Squadron's last two, also the last two at Deversoir, departed on the 10th, one destined for Kasfareet, the other (piloted by Jankowski) flew over HQ MEAF, Deversoir, HQ 205 Group and the remainder of the Canal Zone airfields in a farewell salute, with an escort of three Vampires on either side. By the 16th the Squadron could boast a complement of 16 Vampire FB5s; two more were on their way from the UK but Flg Off Dale damaged his aircraft when landing at Istres in France.

In April six members of the Royal Egyptian Air Force arrived at Deversoir on a seven-day attachment to 249, and a programme of lectures was drawn up for their benefit. The Squadron also received three more new pilots during the month, Flt Lt T.P. Calvey, Plt Off D.J.S. Foard and P3 D.J. Evans. Training continued and on 2 May the Squadron flew no fewer than 30 sorties comprising air-to-ground firing and air-to-air camera-gun practice; a night-flying programme was planned. A few days later a series of dive-bombing sorties were undertaken which left all pilots involved "favourably impressed". A few weeks later the Squadron completed a rocket-firing sortie, the first Canal Zone Vampire squadron to achieve this.

The first serious incident concerning the Vampire in Squadron use occurred on 27 May when Flg Off Heywood accompanied the Station Commander, Grp Capt V.S. Bowling CBE, on a flight to Cyprus. During the course of the return flight, just before crossing the Egyptian coast and when flying at 30,000 feet, the cockpit canopy of Heywood's aircraft exploded. The pilot was shaken but not hurt and was able to land safely at Deversoir "though feeling considerably cooler that he had done in the past few weeks", wrote the Squadron diarist.

Towards the end of June the Squadron departed for its annual APC at Nicosia, where it joined 6 and 213 Squadrons, beating both in air-to-ground firing practice. During one such sortie Sqn Ldr Scott-Vos's aircraft was hit in the wing by a ricochet. Closer inspection showed it to

---

* Flg Off McPhie was another former wartime Tempest pilot who had been shot down and taken prisoner just before the end of hostilities.

be an incendiary bullet which had pierced the fuel tank and failed to explode — "the Boss's lucky day" was the general comment. However, a month later on 3 August the Squadron lost one of its newer pilots, P3 Chris Firmin, whose Vampire (VV553) failed to pull out of a bombing dive and crashed into the sea off Morphou Bay. It was the Squadron's first fatality since P2 Watson had been killed in a Tempest crash in February. The Squadron returned to Deversoir the following week.

New pilots continued to join, replacing those tour-expired, including P3 M.D. Howlett, P3 MacMillan and P4 Drake; shortly after, Plt Off W.L. Bull arrived from the UK, fresh from RAF College Cranwell, and was followed by Sqn Ldr R.L. Boulding on 24 October as the new CO vice Sqn Ldr Scott-Vos, who departed for Southern Rhodesia. Sqn Ldr Boulding was a former Battle of Britain pilot who had been shot down in 1941, being imprisoned by the Germans until his release in 1945. He had just completed a course at the Central Fighter Establishment.

Plt Off Bull excelled in dive-bombing and on his first such sortie turned in a remarkably good average of 20 yards; and to prove it was not a fluke he recorded an average of 16 yards on his second sortie. Sadly, ten days later, on 8 December, his Vampire (VV622/P) hit the ground when pulling out of a firing pass on the Abu Sultan ranges, killing the promising pilot instantly. Another accident occurred six days later when Sgts* Evans and Hatton were taking off from Deversoir on a strike during Exercise Noel. When both aircraft were well along the runway, the pilots were instructed to abandon take-off due to a suspected technical fault with Hatton's aircraft. He was able to stop in time but Evans, in order to do so, had to retract his undercarriage, causing considerable damage to his aircraft.

The Squadron was somewhat depleted when Christmas 1950 arrived, four of its pilots being absent on ferrying duties to the Far East Air Force, delivering Vampires to units of that Command. At about this time the Squadron was requested to prepare to send an aerobatic team to appear at a flying display at RAF Negombo in Ceylon planned for the beginning of February, Flt Lt Calvey, Flg Off Rayner-Sharpe and Sgt A. Brandon being selected for formation aerobatics while Flt Lt McPhie was to undertake the solo performance.

The Squadron received a new pilot on 11 January, Plt Off Elliott having arrived from the UK, another Cranwell graduate. On the same date Flt Lt Talbot rejoined the Squadron following the ferry flight to Singapore. Two more pilots departed on ferry flights next day, Flg Off Foard and Sgt Evans flying to RAF Ramat David initially for pre-flight planning and briefing. Meanwhile, Flt Lt Talbot accompanied Grp Capt Bowling when two Vampires were scrambled from Deversoir to search for two missing pilots, one RAF and one Egyptian, whose aircraft — a Vampire of 213 Squadron and an REAF Fury — had collided during an exercise. The RAF pilot was spotted in the desert 25 miles north-east of the base; both he and the REAF pilot were rescued.

The Ceylon detachment comprising five Vampires and two Meteor T7s (WA596, WA627) under the command of Grp Capt Bowling departed on 27 January for RAF Negombo. In support were three Valettas of 216 Squadron. These carried three crews, plus one standby crew and their own servicing party of one NCO and five airmen, in addition to 24 airmen. Sqn Ldr Boulding led the Vampire and Meteor formation. The route decided upon was Deversoir to Mafraq and Habbaniya on the first day, then Habbaniya to Bahrein and Sharjah next day, followed by Sharjah to Mauripur, Mauripur to Poona, and finally Poona to Tambaram and Negombo on the last day of the month.

Due to runway repairs at Deversoir it was necessary for the Vampires to proceed to Fayid to fill their long-range tanks, this process taking considerably longer than expected. Shortly after take-off, fuel was seen to be leaking from the Vampire flown by Sgt Howlett and he returned to base in order to change into one of the reserve aircraft. After refuelling at Mafraq the aircraft headed for Habbaniya, from where Grp Capt Bowling decided to pilot one of the Vampires rather than travel in the back seat of a Meteor. The Vampires delayed their departure in order to await the arrival of Sgt Howlett. Bahrein was reached without any trouble and after refuelling set course for Sharjah. All aircraft completed this leg satisfactorily, although it became apparent

---

* The RAF had recently reverted to its former system of ranks for NCO aircrew, abandoning the unpopular Pilot/Navigator 1, 2, 3 and 4 grades for Sgt, Flt Sgt and Warrant Officer.

that the Meteors would have to refuel at Jiwani on the return flight. The distance from Sharjah to Mauripur is 648 nautical miles and with head winds of between 80-100 knots the safety margin was almost non-existent.

Everyone was favourably impressed with the friendliness and co-operation shown by the Indian Air Force at Poona. An early start was made next morning and Tambaram, 16 miles from Madras, was reached successfully. After refuelling of the aircraft and refreshments for the pilots, the aircraft departed for Negombo where all landed safely following a flypast over Colombo. The detachment was greeted by the AOC, several of his staff and representatives of the local press.

The rehearsal carried out in the afternoon of 1 February went according to plan and the display took place two days later, attended by an estimated 100,000 people. It proved to be a great success, as was the Independence Day flypast over Colombo two days later, followed by dinner at the Governor-General's residence for the officers and a dance for the airmen at the Garden Club in Colombo. All were granted a few days leave before the detachment made its way back to Poona where a flying display was put on for the benefit of the Indian Air Force. About 3,000 attended and it was considered by the Squadron as the 'best yet'. The detachment set course for Deversoir next day and arrived on 21 February minus Flt Lt Calvey's Vampire, which had been left at Jiwani with a broken turbine blade, Calvey travelling in the back of Sgt Hillard's Meteor. On 28 February, Flt Lt Cameron and Sgt Burrage departed from Deversoir in a Meteor T7 to collect the repaired aircraft. The Squadron claimed a number of 'firsts' as a result of the detachment's flight to Ceylon and back: (a) the first to have flown Meteors along this route; (b) the first jet fighter squadron to have been to Ceylon; (c) the first Vampire squadron to have flown westward along this route.

The Squadron bade farewell to four tour-expired pilots, Flt Lts Scrimgeour and Talbot together with Sgts Hatton and Leslie leaving for the UK. There was now a shortage of pilots and replacements from the UK were keenly awaited. March saw the annual Army training exercise (Exercise Sandgrouse) when a total of 143 sorties were flown during a six-day period. At the end of the month Flt Lt McPhie flew to Mafraq to complete arrangements for use of the firing ranges by a detachment of Vampires. Each of the nine aircraft carried eight rockets when the detachment set out on 16 April. All aircraft participated in gun-firing sorties next day, followed by a sector reconnaissance of the area to be used for an exercise with the Arab Legion (Exercise Jet). The first two-day phase of the exercise saw 27 ground-attack sorties flown, ending with a strike by four aircraft firing live rockets at the objective to be 'captured' by ground troops; next day a further eight sorties were flown. A bad dust storm prevented a flying display for HM King Abdullah and the detachment arrived back at Deversoir on 26 April. Four days later two new pilots arrived on posting from the UK, Plt Off Sankey and Sgt P. Spinks, effectively replacing Flt Lt Cameron and Sgt MacMillan who had recently departed, tour-expired.

May saw the aerobatics team now led by Flt Lt McPhie, while Sgt Drake joined as No4 pilot when the team was increased to four. The highlight of the month was an attempted (but unsuccessful) interception on the 26th by a Squadron Vampire of the de Havilland Comet jet airliner, in the Middle East on a proving flight. A second attempt during the afternoon was slightly more successful. The Squadron was now increasingly carrying out rocket-firing sorties and by mid-June the Vampires were often armed with the full complement of eight rockets. On the evening of 20 June eight aircraft carried out a dummy dive-bombing attack on an objective in the Gulf of Suez. This intense training was appreciated when the Squadron was informed that it was to proceed to RAF Shaibah in Iran, owing to the local oil crisis at Abadan.

A dispute in mid-June 1951 between Britain and Persia, when the Anglo-Iranian Oil Company's refinery at Abadan was seized and promptly nationalised, gave cause for grave concern for the safety of British nationals. As a result, 27 Hastings aircraft of RAF Transport Command were flown to Fayid in Egypt, ready to airlift troops to safeguard and help carry out a mass evacuation of the threatened civilians, should the need arise. To provide air cover for the transports, 6 and 249 Squadrons were ordered to Shaibah where they were to be joined by Brigand-equipped 8 Squadron from Aden. Thus, all 16 of the Squadron's Vampires departed for Shaibah on 13 July, refuelling at Mafraq and Habbaniya en route. Once installed at Shaibah, two sector recces were made by the Flight Commanders before all pilots carried out reconnaissance sorties on 17 July. The area covered included Kuwait, the head of the Persian Gulf, the estuary of the Shatt-el-Arab and along the western bank of the river past Abadan to Basrah, plus the marsh area and islands to the north. An RAF presence in the area was maintained for the next three months. The monotony was broken in early August by boat trips on the Shatt-el-Arab using landing craft provided by HMS *Messina*, followed by a trip aboard the destroyer HMS *Chieftain*. For most of the pilots it was their first time aboard a warship.

On 9 August the Squadron 'defended' the aerodrome against a 'strike' by Brigands of 8 Squadron escorted by Vampires of 6 Squadron. Squadron pilots claimed that all the attacking aircraft were intercepted well before reaching the target. The following week saw further exercises carried out in conjunction with 6 Squadron, as a rehearsal should the squadrons be called to intervene in the Abadan oil crisis. Training included rocket firing against a target towed by HMS *Chevron* in the Persian Gulf. During a test flight by Flt Lt Calvey, the canopy hood of the Vampire shattered and although pieces of perspex and metal frame caused considerable damage to the tailplane, he managed to land safely.

Sqn Ldr Boulding flew to Deversoir on 25 August, intending to return with a replacement Vampire. On arrival at Habbaniya, however, his aircraft became unserviceable so he continued his flight to Egypt aboard a Valetta transport. At Deversoir he was allotted a "very second-hand" replacement Vampire, which reached Habbaniya without incident but en route to Shaibah the engine started to lose power although a safe landing was made at Shaibah after dark.

Flt Lt Gray departed at the end of the month, tour-expired. Earlier in the month the Squadron had received a new pilot, Sgt Hill. September opened with a visit by the AOC-in-Chief who informed the Squadron it would be returning to Deversoir at the end of month: "The news does not appear to have caused any regret", was the Squadron diarist's comment.

After so many months of accident-free flying, the Squadron lost a pilot on 7 September. Sgt Stefan Zagroba, who had recently joined from 213 Squadron, was executing an unauthorised slow roll in Vampire VX989/R at low altitude over the dispersal area and when he attained the inverted position he lost height rapidly and hit the ground. The aircraft exploded and caught fire on contact*.

A shortage of spares and fuel at Shaibah reduced the Squadron's flying programme during September, the problems not being eased until the end of the month. The highlight during October was a simulated attack on ships of the Royal Navy in the Persian Gulf, 21 such sorties being flown on 10 October alone. The attacks were well synchronised and highly successful. The exercise was arranged at the request of the Senior Naval Officer, Persian Gulf, and it was considered that the Squadron gave the Navy a very realistic impression of attack by jet fighters. The Squadron's return to Deversoir was delayed owing to an outbreak of typhoid in the region, but eventually flew back on 24 October — straight into another local crisis.

In October the Egyptian Prime Minister announced that his country was abrogating the Anglo-Egyptian Treaty of 1936. Four days later Britain, France, the USA and Turkey offered Egypt a partnership in their new Middle East Defence Organisation, but as Egypt was still trying to get foreign troops out of the country this ill-timed proposal was rejected. The country had no wish to see the British presence in the Suez Canal Zone replaced by four non-Arab armies. The fact that one of these armies would be Turkish did nothing to help. Egyptians, like most other Arabs, still considered the four centuries of Ottoman Turkish occupation that had so recently ended as a long period of cultural oppression. Almost at once trouble flared up in the Canal Zone, where several British soldiers and a number of Egyptian policemen were killed as the cycle of terror intensified.

While the Squadron was at Shaibah, the mother of the late Plt Off Bull — killed in a flying accident in December — arrived at Deversoir to visit the Squadron and the site of her son's grave. Sqn Ldr Boulding and Flg Off Elliott, who had been a personal friend of the deceased pilot, flew to Deversoir to meet and escort her during her stay. She presented to the Squadron a trophy, thereafter known as the Bull Trophy, in memory of her son, to be competed for between the Flights in all sports for which teams could be raised.

---

* Early in 1949, during his jet conversion course in the UK, Polish-born Sgt Zagroba had successfully landed a Vampire after its engine had exploded in flight, for which he had been commended.

With the return of the Squadron to Deversoir, training continued including joint exercises with the other squadrons based there. Bomb racks were fitted to the Vampires and dive-bombing practice commenced. Air-to-air firing was also included in the day's programme on 20 November, a Beaufighter towing the target; however, as the diarist commented:

> "Not one pilot managed to hit the target but as it was the first and only shoot for about 12 months for most pilots, this is not surprising."

Mid-December saw two mishaps for Squadron pilots, both of whom made safe landings when engine problems were encountered. On the 20th, Sgt Burrage made a successful landing on the airfield after his barostat had failed, and then, next day, Sgt Spinks made a creditable landing after his engine had failed when at 30,000 feet over Kabrit. He had been escorted back to Deversoir by Flt Lt Calvey.

The first day of 1952 was marred by an unusual but fortunately minor accident to Flt Lt McPhie. A bomb fell on his index finger when he was assisting in 'bombing up'. He was admitted to Fayid Hospital for treatment. Rocket-firing practice continued, using the Abu Sultan range. When taking off from Deversoir on 10 January, Flt Lt Dale suffered engine failure in WA102/O. He raised the undercarriage to avoid hitting a hedge and belly-landed as his subsequent report of the incident revealed:

> "I opened the throttle for take-off and got full power from the engine. At 70-75 knots I noticed that the power was fading. I checked the throttle setting and revs . . . I decided to abandon take-off and, as I considered that at that speed I could not pull up by using brakes without overshooting the runway, I adopted the emergency procedure of retracting the undercarriage whilst on the ground. The aircraft sank on its belly and decelerated."

The wave of Egyptian anti-British violence reached its peak in the new year, starting on 25 January 1952 with a British Army attack against the barracks at Ismailia which housed Egyptian military police, whom the British believed were turning a blind eye to the many acts of terrorism being carried out. The one-sided battle, during which tanks went into action, lasted several hours before the garrison surrendered shortly before midday; almost 900 policemen threw down their arms, following the deaths of 41 of their comrades with a further 73 wounded. Three British soldiers were killed and 13 wounded in the action. When news of this latest humiliation reached Egyptian hard-liners in the various militant organisations, leaders of these groups planned an immediate response. Early next morning violence erupted in Cairo: hordes of young men burned and looted European businesses, restaurants and cafes, resulting in the deaths of 17 civilians, mainly European, and 50 Egyptian police officers. It was not until 1700 hours that the Egyptian military put in an appearance, then 150 soldiers attempted to restore some form of order amongst the tens of thousands on the streets. But the troops refused to open fire on their countrymen, although looting was rife and fires continued to break out. Late that evening came the announcement over the radio of a curfew and martial law.

At local level retaliation by British troops was severe, including burning at least one Egyptian village, thought to be harbouring some of the ring leaders of the riots, while Britain's response was to send more troops and aircraft to the Canal Zone, a squadron of Lincoln bombers and two Vampire squadrons arriving at Deversoir in January 1952, 6 Squadron from Habbaniya and 73 Squadron from Malta. Contingency plans were even drawn up for an attack on the REAF to cover a British ground advance against Cairo. Meanwhile REAF aircraft flew fully armed with other armed aircraft held on standby. The AOC 205 Group, Air Vice-Marshal V.E. Groom CB CBE DFC, was reported as saying:

> "With regard to the Royal Egyptian Air Force, [we will] take no deliberate action against them, and relations between the RAF and REAF had always been most cordial. [My] men have been instructed to take no action which might be construed as hostile towards the Egyptians, unless they attempt to stop the British from carrying out normal work and duties."

With the increase in tension, 249 was ordered to disperse its aircraft at dawn on 28 January because of the possibility of a surprise attack by the REAF. However, weapons and flying training continued unabated although the Squadron remained on alert. As part of the emergency training, the Squadron carried out a simulated strike against Kabrit airfield on 7 February to give the attackers and defenders a realistic experience in case the local situation worsened. Much was learned from the attacks and associated briefings and debriefings. Next day an exercise was undertaken jointly with the Guards Brigade. Later in the month saw the start of Exercise Hightime with 249 playing the role of defenders against waves of Lincoln bombers and Brigand fighter-bombers escorted by Meteor FR9s. The result of the first day's action was that 249 claimed one Meteor and one Lincoln 'destroyed', two Meteors 'probably destroyed' and one Meteor 'damaged'. Next day (27 February) claims were submitted for one Lincoln 'destroyed', one Meteor 'probable', two Meteors and one Brigand 'damaged'. On the third and final day four Lincolns were claimed 'destroyed', three Meteors and one Lincoln 'probably destroyed' and one of each 'damaged'.

On 17 March, when 27 training sorties were flown, Flg Off Elliott's aircraft (VZ123/N) was lost to the Squadron when it suffered brake failure on landing; Elliott retracted the under-carriage to prevent an even more serious accident. The highlight of the month was a demon-stration of ground attack given to the Army and included the strafing of a three-ton lorry which was left in flames. Meantime, Flt Lt Dale left the Squadron, tour-expired, to be replaced by Flt Lt P.R. Sanderson, while Plt Off J.R. Coleman was posted in from the UK.

April saw Exercise Happy Hunter against ground targets, and Exercise Lookout when the Squadron defended Deversoir against an attack by Meteor F9s and Mosquitos; the Squadron claimed one Meteor 'destroyed' and four 'damaged', plus one Mosquito 'damaged'. During the second half of the month the Squadron left for Cyprus for R/p and gunnery practice; a dozen Vampires, two Meteor T7s and four Valettas had arrived at Nicosia by the afternoon of 16 April and the programme began five days later, using the range at Morphou Bay. All pilots also participated in an Escape and Evasion exercise while at Cyprus before the Squadron returned to Deversoir on 9 May. Sqn Ldr Boulding in his subsequent report concluded:

"The long awaited detachment has already proved most beneficial both in terms of experience and morale. It is considered that the new type of course, of which this is the first, is too short. Furthermore, whilst the situation in the Canal Zone remains tense, Cyprus is the only place where it is possible to really relax and future squadrons, if they arrive and depart on schedule, will have very little time to relax."

On 12 May the first four of the Squadron's new Vampire FB9s arrived at Deversoir and by the 23rd all 15 had arrived. It was decided that the new aircraft should have Squadron markings consisting of blue and yellow diagonal bars painted on either side of the roundels on the booms, and that A Flight aircraft would have the nose-wheel door painted red, and B Flight blue. Air Vice-Marshal David Atcherley CB CBE DSO DFC, the new AOC 205 Group (whose connection with the Squadron dated back to its formation in 1940) paid a visit at the end of the month.

During June it was decided that the three squadrons of 324 Wing should practice a formation consisting of the letters 'DEV' (for Deversoir). Each squadron was allocated a letter and that assigned to 249 was 'V'. The pilots soon realised that a difficulty was the fact that the 'V' had to be flown in the opposite direction to that in which the apex was pointing. However, with practice a fairly satisfactory result was achieved. When not involved with such disciplined flying, the Squadron was able to participate in an exercise against Lincoln bombers from Shaluffa which carried out simulated attacks at relatively low level (not exceeding 5,000 feet) when a fair number of successful interceptions were achieved. During one formation practice, Flg Off Richardson's canopy burst while flying at 30,000 feet and a fragment struck the leading edge of the tailplane, causing a large dent. After a rapid descent Richardson was able to return to base and landed without further incident.

The first day of July saw all Canal Zone squadrons, and visiting naval squadrons of Sea Furies and Fireflies from HMS *Glory*, participate in a large-scale exercise. Flying as part of the Deversoir Wing, 249 contributed a total of 44 sorties in defence of its base and was credited with 'shooting down' a dozen Sea Furies, six Meteor FR9s and PR10s and two Lincolns, for an assessed 'loss' of two Vampires with a further four 'damaged'. However, it was deemed likely that under actual battle conditions the Wing would have suffered considerable damage from the hit and run tactics employed by attacking Mosquitos and Sea Furies. Flt Lt Calvey noted:

"The Squadron enjoyed manoeuvres with HMS *Glory*'s aircraft which proved that the Sea Fury, unless handled to the limits of its performance, was no match for a Vampire 9 in the hands of a determined pilot."

The main event during the first week of August was the provision of eight Vampires towards a Wing escort for 18 Valettas simulating a bomber stream. This was followed on the 15th by a visit by the Secretary of State for Air, Lord de L'Isle and Dudley VC, when the Squadron aerobatic team put on a display which finished with a simulated attack on the airfield defended by the RAF Regiment's 40mm Bofors firing break-up shot.

The Squadron received a new pilot in the guise of Sgt Stutt from 208 Squadron, who immediately carried out a successful first solo flight in a Vampire but departed within a few days on posting to 213 Squadron. However, Plt Offs R.J. Renshaw and J.R.W. Vardy joined the Squadron on arrival from the UK. For Sqn Ldr Boulding the month had not been a particularly good one:

"This month has been a struggle. Lack of spares resulting in low serviceability, preparations for B Flight's forthcoming detachment and cancelled air-to-air programmes, have all made life difficult. However, Vampire flying hours task was exceeded and the Meteor hours flown were high in relation to their serviceability."

On 5 September Flt Lt Calvey led six Vampires of B Flight to Khartoum via Wadi Halfa, where an aerobatic display was to be staged for British troops stationed in the Sudan, before the aircraft flew to Nairobi to participate in the forthcoming Battle of Britain display at RAF Eastleigh. Following the aerobatic display, two Vampires carried out a simulated ground attack of the airfield. Calvey was later personally congratulated by the Governor-General and GOC, Kenya Colony. With the B Flight detachment preparing for the return journey, Vampire WA108 went unserviceable and departure was delayed until the appropriate spare parts were flown to Eastleigh by a Valetta.

Meanwhile, back at Deversoir the Vampires of A Flight also participated in Battle of Britain celebrations and joined Vampires of 32 and 213 Squadrons, together with Meteors of 13 and 208 Squadrons, in a formation flypast. Deversoir was visited by representatives of the Egyptian Air Force towards the end of the month, 249 staging a close formation flypast followed by a dive-bombing demonstration, which suitably impressed the visitors. Four days later, on the 26th, while on a Wing formation practice flight, Flg Off Coleman observed a crashed C-46 Commando transport, an aircraft of the EAF's 7 Squadron based at Helwan.

October was a relatively quiet month for the Squadron, training flights continuing without incident. Another new pilot joined the Squadron on arrival from the UK, Plt Off N.J. Budd, while Flt Lt Calvey and Flg Off Foard departed, both tour-expired. November opened with Exercise Triangle when the Squadron flew 33 sorties attacking, in the main, army formations south-west of Suez. This was followed, mid-month, by an attack on HMS *Vigo* in the Gulf of Suez; two of the aircraft were flown by visiting pilots of 14 Squadron RNZAF, a Nicosia-based Vampire unit. A further strike was carried out by four aircraft a few days later on a RN destroyer in the Gulf.

At the beginning of December the Squadron received a new Flight Commander to take command of B Flight, when Flt Lt F.D. O'Brien arrived on posting from 185 Squadron at Habbaniya. The Squadron was also joined by Wg Cdr J.F. McPhie AFC from HQ 205 Group, who was attached for flying duties for two weeks. The Squadron diarist smugly noted:

"Wg Cdr McPhie scored 25% in today's air-to-air firing programme on a flag. Squadron average was 86%."

There occurred only one minor incident during the month when WR130 suffered a hydraulics failure. Despite this, the pilot carried out a successful flapless landing when the aircraft sustained only minor damage. Christmas 1952 came and went. Squadron life continued and the start of the new year (1953) saw the departure of three NCO pilots, Sgts Brandon, Drake and Howlett, causing Sqn Ldr Boulding to note:

> "We are now down to 14 pilots with no replacements in sight. Manning strength in groundcrew trades is becoming an acute problem."

The Squadron also lost the services of Flg Off Coleman who had volunteered for a tour of duty in Korea, where the struggle between United Nations forces and those of the Communists was at its height.

On 5 February, 249 provided eight aircraft for a Wing interception and dogfight with Meteors of 208 Squadron. During the mêlée, one Meteor pilot lost control of his aircraft and was obliged to eject, landing safely. 249 duly recorded the 'victory' and, during the afternoon, sent three Vampires to search for the wreckage, which was successfully pinpointed. Five days later, the Squadron's 15 Vampires and two Meteor T7s flew to Nicosia for APC, where a Meteor pilot from 13 Squadron was attached to 249 for the duration of the course. The pilots enjoyed firing at four gliders towed by Beaufighters at 20,000 feet, two of which they shot down. The detachment returned to Deversoir on 3 March.

The high point during the month of March was Exercise Session, but there were very few interceptions during the four-day exercise although, on the final day, a number of Varsity twin-engine transports were successfully intercepted. Two new pilots joined the Squadron during the month, Plt Offs J.C. Butler and G. Leach arriving from the UK. The Squadron was more successful the following month, four Vampires led by Flt Lt O'Brien intercepting a Canberra at 42,000 feet as it flew towards Khartoum. Later, at the end of April, the Deversoir Wing intercepted Meteor NF11s of 219 Squadron from Kabrit, escorted by Meteor FR9s of 208 Squadron from Abu Sueir — and claimed all the FR9s 'destroyed'. The Squadron received a new Commanding officer on 20 April, Sqn Ldr J.R. Gibbons AFC taking over from Sqn Ldr Boulding who was tour-expired.

May saw a visit by representatives of the Canadian National Defence College, the Squadron staging an aerobatics display in their honour, which included a simulated dive-bombing demonstration and solo aerobatics by the new CO in a Meteor. A few days later, eight Vampires provided an escort for the USAF Constellation carrying American Secretary of State Foster Dulles, who was on a Middle East goodwill tour. The Squadron's next duty was to smile for the camera when representatives of the *Daily Express* visited. Another tour-expired pilot departed at the end of the month, Flt Lt Elliott returning to the UK.

June opened with further visits to the Squadron by the media, NBC filming a formation practice for American TV; two days later it was the turn of the *New York Times* to film and photograph the Squadron and its aircraft. These visits were in connection with the Wing's Coronation Flypast which was undertaken on 5 June. Initially a formation representing 'ERII' was flown, followed by an arrowhead. The Wing landed, its aircraft fitted with smoke bombs and rockets, and took off again to carry out a ground attack. The *Daily Express* air correspondent was of the opinion that the formation flypast was the best he had ever seen. 249 returned to Deversoir minus one aircraft however, Sgt Baker's Vampire having suffered a hydraulics failure. Notwithstanding this, he was able to carry out a successful landing at Kabrit where the aircraft was speedily repaired.

Later in the month the Squadron was called upon to investigate aircraft not keeping to the designated air safety lanes and, on the 21st, among those intercepted was an EAF Sea Fury whose pilot did not apparently see the Vampires although he did eventually return to the correct course. Next day, pairs of Vampires intercepted a Trans Jordan DC-3 and a French civilian Lanquedoc airliner which had also strayed. Three days later another Egyptian Sea Fury was intercepted, its pilot under no illusions that he had veered off course since he was given a close escort until clear of the Canal Zone, as was an Egyptian DC-3 encountered over the Sinai. At the end of the month Sqn Ldr Gibbons led 11 aircraft on a weekend detachment to Habbaniya, seven aircraft returning via Mafraq on the 29th. Of the remaining four, two had been unable to start and had been left behind at Habbaniya while the other two had developed hydraulic problems after landing at Mafraq. However, all four were soon serviceable and were back at Deversoir within a few days, where two new pilots had arrived on posting to the Squadron, Plt Off R.S. Kjestrup, a New Zealander, and Plt Off Cook.

An exercise in co-operation with HMS *Bermuda* at the beginning of July was followed by another with HMS *Gambia*, before the month ended with Exercise Lookout II when the Squadron intercepted high-level 'bombers' from Kabrit, in the guise of Meteor FR9s, and Vampires from Deversoir. August passed by relatively quietly except for a minor mishap when Meteor T7 WA596 swung on landing and its undercarriage collapsed, followed a few days later by the force-landing of WR132 at Kasfareet in the hands of Sgt Spinks, following engine failure. September saw the Squadron's 'Touring Team' comprising Flt Lt O'Brien, Flg Off Butler, Plt Off A.F.W. Keeley (a new pilot) and Sgt Hill, set out for Malta via El Adem and Idris, although Hill was forced to return with an unserviceable drop tank. At RAF Idris the pilots were able to examine the new Supermarine Swift which had arrived in Libya to have a crack at the World Air Speed Record then held by a Hunter.

Other new pilots joining 249 at this time included Plt Offs R.P. Broughton, Colin Smith, K.T. Duro and J.F.H. Tetley, while the Squadron welcomed the return of Flg Off Coleman on completion of his tour in Korea, where he had flown Meteor F8s on operations with 77 Squadron RAAF. Two of the new pilots experienced minor accidents at the beginning of November, Plt Off Keeley bursting a tyre on landing following partial hydraulic failure, a problem which also affected Plt Off Duro's landing shortly afterwards. Training continued unabated and included further exercises with the Navy as well as interception sorties. The weather was so bad over the Christmas period, effectively curtailing all flying, that some of the pilots made use of the break to re-decorate the aircrew room.

Early in January 1954, the Squadron had a visit from a CFE team who gave lectures on the comparative merits of the Russian MiG-15, the American F-86 and the Venom, with which the Squadron hoped to be re-equipped. Later in the month the Squadron participated in a Wing flypast for the AOC, followed by another at the beginning of February on the occasion of the visit of the Chief of Air Staff. A continuation of Exercise Lookout II at the end of the month, when the Squadron claimed several intercepted aircraft 'destroyed' or 'damaged', was followed by Exercise Chatterbox II when 18 strike sorties were flown against ground targets.

Three more pilots joined the Squadron at the beginning of March, Plt Offs A. Gronert, W. Barker and L.A. Fletcher fresh from the UK, followed shortly after by Plt Off P.G. Cock, a Cranwell graduate who had been awarded the coveted Sword of Honour; Leighton Fletcher recalled his introduction to the Squadron:

"I landed at Fayid airfield as a passenger on an RAF Hastings transport. I was one of a dozen replacement pilots fresh from OCU destined for one of the ground-attack squadrons in the MEAF. There were two other officers in the tent, Tony Gronert, who had arrived with me last night and who was now sitting up scratching his head vigorously and gazing at his mug of tea with an expression close to disgust, and a stranger who was asleep when we arrived and was still in a comatose state as his tea cooled beside him. The chap in the third bed began to stir and Tony wished him a good morning. He was an air traffic controller and had arrived a couple of days before us.

After breakfast in the Mess, all the pilots in our group were told to report to the medical officer. No one knew why, which caused considerable speculation among us. On our arrival at Sick Quarters we were informed to our combined relief, that we were simply required to have our thighs measured: 'What the hell for?' Tony asked the bespectacled medical sergeant in the white coat: 'For the Venoms, sir.' He seemed surprised that we didn't already know: 'All the Vampires are going to be replaced by Venoms, and they have ejector seats, and anybody with a thigh length over 25 inches will leave his kneecaps behind if he has to eject.'

Later that day we were all summoned to an office where we were told our postings. Bill Barker, Tony and I were lucky enough to be joining the same squadron. We were delighted, and after getting our gear together, prepared for departure next day. So here I was, joining a famous fighter squadron, 249, as one of its 20 pilots. After an entertaining evening in our new Mess, Bill, Tony and I found ourselves outside our new Squadron Commander's office, about to introduce ourselves. We were clad in our best uniforms. Sqn Ldr Gibbons AFC was a fairly big sandy-haired chap in his early 40s. We introduced ourselves and he went on to tell us that he commanded the best squadron in the RAF, what he expected of us as pilots, and what he expected of us as officers."

The Squadron took part in a further naval co-operation exercise on 25 March, nine sorties being flown during which 20mm attacks were carried out on a drogue towed behind HMS *Delight*. The Squadron diarist wrote:

"The Squadron was disappointed when the Navy could not produce any more targets after the first drogue was shot off the towline."

Before flying to Nicosia for APC on 20 April, the Squadron aerobatic team comprising Flg Offs Renshaw, Vardy, Budd and Leach gave a display at the opening of the new terminal building at Khartoum Airport, followed by solo aerobatics performed by Sqn Ldr Gibbons. Two congratulatory messages were later received, one from the AOC Aden and the other from the Governor-General of the Sudan. During its stay at Nicosia, the Squadron also performed extremely well. For Plt Off Fletcher the highpoint was the 'shooting down' of a towed glider target:

"I was briefed to actually lead a section of four aircraft in an air-to-air firing sortie against a 25-foot metal glider towed behind one of the Meteor tugs. These gliders were almost indestructible and we fired only ball (non-explosive) ammunition using just two out of four cannons. The target was airborne ahead of us and I led my section in a battle formation climb up to 20,000 feet over the sea, where I soon spotted the tug and glider combination. As I gazed upon its squat, black, clipped outline my imagination transformed it into a Heinkel silhouetted against the off-white haze of the horizon, and it was 1940 and my Vampire was a Hurricane about to attack the intruder sneaking up the Thames to drop its load of death and destruction upon the capital."

Despite misjudging the angle of attack, by pulling so tightly that he almost blacked out, he was able to fire a short burst at the glider:

"There was something like a spark at the port wing-root and, as I zoomed up and away from it, I rolled again to the left and looked back over my shoulder in time to watch its port wing fold upwards and almost gracefully detach itself from the fuselage. Immediately the glider rolled violently to the left, twisting the tow cable until it snapped and then fell in a crazy spiral, with its amputated port wing fluttering down like a dead leaf half a mile away. I didn't want to fire another shot as I wanted to find out when I landed how many rounds it had taken me to deliver the death blow — it turned out to be seven. The next day when the cine film of my attack was developed, I was told in no mean terms that I should never have fired after such an awful attack. But deep inside I knew, that whatever my mentors might say, however right they may be, the fact remained: I shot the bloody wing clean off . . . that Heinkel wouldn't have reached London."

Before returning to Deversoir on 28 May, the Squadron was joined by two new pilots, Plt Offs W.G. Hancock and L.C. Walters. Following the APC, the C-in-C MEAF, Air Marshal Sir Claude Pelly KCB CBE MC, sent a message of congratulations to the Squadron:

"The results obtained in air exercises are highly commendable and are indicative of a very successful and profitable year's work. No less commendable is the notably low incident of armament failures. Great credit reflects upon the servicing personnel concerned."

A message from the AOC, Air Vice-Marshal J.G. Hawtrey CBE, added:

"I would be grateful if you would congratulate your PAI [Pilot Attack Instructor], Flg Off Budd, on his excellent individual scores and his work as Squadron PAI which is obviously mirrored in the excellent results obtained. I should also like to congratulate Flt Sgt MacPhail of whom you say in your report 'much of the credit for the armament servicing goes to him.' "

There was no mention of the stir caused by one of Flg Off Budd's more graphic performances while carrying out aerobatics over Cyprus, as recalled by Plt Off Fletcher:

"One of our most experienced pilots, Jim Budd, a brilliant pilot and excellent shot, got himself into a spot of bother one morning by demonstrating his ability to write in the sky. He climbed his aircraft over Cyprus until he found a height at which his engine produced a strong vapour trail."

Budd then proceeded to draw an 'object' in the sky which was considered by some observers as being obscene or offensive; Fletcher continued:

". . . when completed [the artistic creation] remained stationary over the island stretching from the pan handle to Morphou Bay, and undoubtedly witnessed by the whole population. It stood out in brilliant white outline against the deep blue of the Mediterranean sky, so perfect in its geometry and obvious in design, and so still and persistent that even after he had landed Jim was able to admire his work from the ground — until he was called for by the Wing Commander, as three Meteors from the Target Towing Flight were scrambled to scribble it into obscurity with their own condensation trails."

News was now received of an imminent move to Amman in Jordan and, on 1 June, Sqn Ldr Gibbons flew to the newly upgraded station to inspect accommodation and facilities, where he was soon joined by the Advance Party aboard two Valetta transports. On 8 June, 16 Vampires set out for their new home, thereby replacing those of 6 Squadron which moved to Habbaniya. Two more Valettas conveyed ground personnel, while others travelled by convoy. The Squadron also learned that Sqn Ldr E.C. Gough was to replace tour-expired Sqn Ldr Gibbons as Commanding Officer, taking over the reins on 17 June.

On arrival at Amman, the Squadron took over the billets recently vacated by airmen of 21 LAA Squadron of the RAF Regiment, who had been detached to Aden for temporary duty. Within days of 249's arrival, the gunners returned. They were not happy at having lost their billets, as recalled by gunnery NCO Cpl Terry Gladwell:

"A tented site had been erected for 21 Squadron by the Advance Party, who had arrived several days before us. They had found no room at the inn, for our former billets on the Station had been commandeered by 249 Squadron, who were now firmly fixed at Amman. As well as collaring our billets, they had acquired a fair slice of our former heritage, including the hangar, taken over completely. Even Station Flight was no longer resident in the ancestral home. As for Bofors guns, why, the hangar was for aircraft, not for a load of Regiment junk! What a homecoming! Kicked out of house and now living like gypsies! Washing facilities were provided on site. For baths, we were allowed back on the Station at certain times. Meals, too, were strictly timed for Squadron personnel. Behind this smokescreen was probably a desire to keep our people from those of 249 Squadron, due to the considerable resentment we felt at being ousted from our former homes. Harsh words had been said and one or two minor fracas had resulted."

The Squadron's Vampires were still suffering occasional canopy pressure problems, Flg Off Broughton being the latest to experience this when flying WR104/W on 1 July. However, he was able to land safely. Another new pilot posted to Amman was Plt Off D.J. Rowe, the Squadron diarist recording the pilot strength as 21, of whom three were non-operational. A more serious incident occurred on 9 August when Flg Off Fletcher belly-landed WL606/C at Amman following engine failure at 16,000 feet, which necessitated a 20-mile glide to reach the airfield which was successfully accomplished. The accident enquiry revealed that the aircraft had been only partly refuelled; the airman responsible was court martialled, found guilty and sentenced to 28 days detention.

The August jinx continued next day (10 August) when a Vampire suffered damage as a result of a rocket which failed to leave the rails and burned the underside of the wing. Then, on Friday the 13th, Flt Lt Coleman was forced to bale out of R-for-Roger when the aircraft caught fire during a high-level sortie. The fire went out but then the engine seized. Coleman attempted to glide back to the airfield but when still some distance short, decided to bale out, as recalled by Flg Off Fletcher:

> "We all knew how to bale out of a Vampire but had little confidence in the procedure. If any could do it though, JC could. He lowered his seat fully, pulled down his goggles and reaching his right hand forward, ducked his head and pulled the canopy jettison handle. The canopy lifted up and over his tailplane and toppled away behind us to the ground below. He looked at me, his face now totally covered with helmet, oxygen mask and goggles and gave me a V sign. We watched him trim his aircraft nose down with his left hand, then he raised the nose slightly and rolled the machine to the left until it was almost inverted. At this point he fell out and lost control. Unfortunately he didn't fall all the way out, his legs appeared to be trapped, and he finished up spread-eagled on his back, arms outstretched, over the rear fuselage with his legs still inside the cockpit.
>
> The inverted Vampire nosed up slightly, paused then headed earthwards rolling as it did so with Johnny still spread-eagled half in and half out of the cockpit. The Vampire continued its rolling plunge earthward and I watched fascinated as the increased speed caused it to curve out of the dive, now upright, and zoom upwards in a kind of lazy loop. Then, near the top, Johnny somehow separated from his machine and described an arc towards the earth."

Coleman landed safely with nothing worse than a sprained right ankle, and was soon picked up and on his way back to Amman. His aircraft narrowly missed impacting onto the oil pipeline that runs parallel with the road from Iraq to the Mediterranean. The run of bad luck continued and culminated in the death of Flg Off Les Walters when his aircraft, WR192, crashed into the ground while attempting to recover from a dive on a target on the Mafraq range; Fletcher wrote:

> "Les was a very close friend. Apparently he fired very late in the attack and, as he broke away from the target, either flicked out of a high speed stall, or in banking to avoid flying debris, had touched the ground with his wingtip. It was all over in a second. He was buried with full Military Honours in the small cemetery on the airfield. The women wept behind dark glasses, and one by one his fellow pilots paused at the foot of his grave to give a farewell salute to this lad from Leicester who loved bananas, horror comics, flying and a girl in England whom none of us had ever met. We had one more farewell party at our flat, when the whole Squadron come down to consume two cupboards full of booze. Les Walters' 21st birthday was celebrated even though he never quite made it."

The promised Venom re-equipment materialised on 16 October when the Squadron received its first two FB1s (WR472 and WR495), followed by two more (WR296 and WR307) two days later, together with two new Flight Commanders, Flt Lt D.M. Dallison, a New Zealander, and Flt Lt J. Birnie, to replace tour-expired Flt Lts Coleman and Sanderson. Another new pilot to arrive at this time was Plt Off R.C. Etheridge. In the meantime, the Vampires soldiered on, Flg Off Keeley experiencing an engine failure while flying WR103 but was able to land safely, while Flg Off Fletcher was lucky to escape a landing misjudgement in early October when he touched down too close behind his leader, Flg Off Hancock:

> "My aircraft was about 50 yards astern and a little to Curly's left when the full fury of his jet efflux hit me, flicking me over like a piece of paper, and to my horror I crossed the threshold

with my wings vertical. My swift frantic attempts at recovery were futile and with a bone jarring crump my left wingtip 'graunched' into the runway. By all the natural laws the aircraft should have cart-wheeled which, in a Vampire, would almost certainly have been fatal, but she just bounced into the air while my right foot was hard down on the top rudder pedal."

In the days that followed, the number of Venoms increased to five and the Vampire number decreased accordingly. Then, out of the blue, came an order to ground all Venoms, as Fletcher recalled:

"The reason, we managed to establish, was that they were apparently blowing up in mid-flight. The grounding was swiftly followed by an instruction to remove all tip tanks and continue flying. This left the Squadron in a hybrid state operating both Vampires and tipless Venoms for the next five months while the experts investigated the problems. The Boss got us together and warned us should a Venom catch fire in the air, it would almost certainly explode with very little warning. Apparently within seconds of the fire-warning light illuminating.

In the event of the fire-warning light coming on, the drill was to execute a rapid turn through 360 degrees to see if there was any smoke. If there wasn't any, and the instruments looked OK, then suspect an electrical fault. The CO said, 'If the warning light comes on, you have my permission to eject at once. But, for Christ's sake be sure the light is actually on before you get out. We don't want to leave perfectly serviceable Venoms up there on their own — we've only got five'."

However, the number of Venoms was soon reduced by one when WR307 went out of control while performing aerobatics on 19 October, Flg Off Cock successfully carrying out the Squadron's first ejection. The stricken aircraft crashed across the border in Syria, but the pilot floated down into Jordanian territory north of Mafraq. Fletcher remembered:

"Peter, after successful separation from his seat, made a safe parachute landing, without injury. A rescue vehicle from Mafraq met him walking towards them leading a party of wandering Arabs who had insisted on carrying his battered ejector seat — and demanded financial reward for their efforts."

Cpl Gladwell of 21 LAA Squadron added:

"249 didn't have an easy time converting to the Venom after the docile Vampire, and lost a couple in the process. One of the pilots, Flg Off Cock, was a real hotshot. The Syrians wouldn't even let the RAF have the bits of the wreckage [of his aircraft] back."

Flg Off Duro experienced a flame-out, due to fuel starvation, in another Venom when flying at 5,000 feet on 28 October, but was able to land at Mafraq without damaging the aircraft. Two days later, Duro's aircraft suffered a cracked canopy. Next day Flt Lt Birnie's aircraft landed with a similar problem. Then Flg Off Fletcher found himself in trouble again when, on 5 November, his Vampire (WR126/A) suffered an engine failure when flying at 40,000 feet near the Iraqi border, some 80 miles from Amman. He started to glide back towards base, escorted some of the way down by Sqn Ldr Gough and Flg Off Leach. Realising that he would not be able to reach Amman, and having entered dense cloud, he decided to bale out when at 10,000 feet. However, at the last moment, he broke clear of the cloud base to find himself within sight of Dawson's Field, a huge dried-up salt lake. He decided upon a wheels-up landing:

"A thousand feet now and still coming down quite steeply. It certainly looked good and I felt now that I couldn't miss the field if I tried. I tightened my straps. Five hundred feet and still heading for that point. I began to reduce my rate of descent and the airspeed slipped below 140 knots. Two hundred feet and plenty of room all around me as I close with the ground. Speed 120 knots and I held that until I levelled her off at around twenty feet and let the speed come down a little further as she continued to sink gently. More by luck than judgement, its belly gently made contact with the ground and I was down scraping along like a sled at about 90 mph. No brakes and no means of controlling the beast at all. Then, with the speed fallen to around 40, the nose slewed to the left and the plane careered sideways, coming to halt with its nose pointing about 60 degrees to the left of its final path."

Before long the Station Anson arrived and made a landing close by, picked up Fletcher and whisked him back to Amman. After lunch, he accompanied the CO and both Flight Commanders back to Dawson's Field aboard an Arab Legion Rapide, where they discovered that the Squadron Technical Officer, Sqn Ldr Robertson, and his team had jacked up the Vampire and were running the engine. Having been pronounced flyable, Sqn Ldr Gough gamely flew WR126 back to Amman, wheels down, but there the aircraft was eventually scrapped.

King Hussein paid Amman a visit on 10 November, when an aerobatic display was arranged. Cpl Gladwell of 21 LAA Squadron wrote:

"For dash, verve and sheer accomplishment this almost-impromptu performance can seldom have been surpassed. For a few days previous, we had watched training for this demonstration, aghast at the expertise of these quite ordinary run-of-the-mill squadron pilots. On the day itself, it belied adequate description.

Impressed as we had been, some days later there was a repeat presentation, almost over the top of 21 Squadron's gun-park. A BBC film crew had arrived to record one of our Bofors in make-believe action against a single Vampire flown, I believe, by Flg Off Cock. The gun-crew freely admitted that they had been dead meat from the moment the Vampire took off, in a split-arse climb, followed immediately by a vertical dive straight down the barrel of the gun. A violent pull-out at near ground level was succeeded by a 180 degree turn, to come back at the Bofors at nought feet and 500 mph. The whole gamut of ground-attack profiles was perpetuated against the hapless target then, which itself was incapable of being traversed quickly enough to lay sights on the fleeting aircraft. It was as well this was a dummy run for the benefit of the cameras and the aircraft was unarmed, instead of carrying high-explosive rockets and 20mm cannon shells."

December passed relatively uneventfully, but on 10 January 1955 the Squadron lost the services of another of its Vampires when WR122/H was caught in the slipstream of another on take-off, dropped a wing and slid along the runway at Fayid. Although Flg Off Leach was unhurt, the aircraft was badly damaged. Another Vampire was rendered temporarily unserviceable on the 21st when WR155 suffered a bird strike near Amman. The Squadron bade farewell to Flg Offs Renshaw and Vardy, both tour-expired.

Exercises with, and demonstrations for, Arab Legion forces were carried out during this period, Sqn Ldr Saunders, seconded to the Arab Legion, flying one of the Squadron's Vampires during January and later accompanying Flt Lt Birnie to Nicosia in the Squadron's Meteor T7. During a visit to Amman in February, King Hussein flew the Squadron's Vampire T11, also accompanied by Flt Lt Birnie. Two new pilots arrived during the month, Plt Offs R.C.K. Alcock and D.L. Shelcott.

The Squadron participated in Exercise Down Under on 9 and 10 March, intercepting Canberras, Meteors and Vampires from the Canal Zone and Nicosia. Although only 23 sorties were flown on the first day, a number of 'kills' were recorded. The main complaint from the pilots was that they were kept at two minutes' readiness for up to two-and-a-half hours in some cases. Many more 'kills' were claimed on the second day of the exercise during the course of a further 48 sorties. The Squadron suffered another fatality on 23 March when new pilot Plt Off David Shelcott crashed three miles north-east of Amman in Venom WR472/E, as recalled by Flg Off Fletcher:

"Several pilots watched Shelcott take off and noticed that during a climbing turn to port, something, possibly a tip tank, fell off the aircraft. One of those watching called the tower on the phone and informed the controller, who in turn asked Shelcott if he'd lost a tip tank. He replied 'So I have.' Apparently Sqn Ldr Gough was in the tower at the time and took over from the controller, telling Shelcott to climb away and carry out the Mach runs as briefed; the remaining tip tank would be empty on his return and present no problem when landing. Shelcott didn't reply, instead he positioned himself down wind and lowered his wheels. The CO continued to instruct him to climb away and continue his detail, but again received no reply. In fact, David never spoke over the R/T again and didn't respond to Gough's instructions. When eventually he turned into finals, Sqn Ldr Gough ordered him to drop the tank but he didn't do this and continued his approach to land. As he slowed down he would have found it difficult to hold up the 'heavy' wing and should have kept his speed up. He was seen to make a normal approach and simply rolled over, impacted with the ground and exploded. There was much conjecture about the reason David apparently lost contact with the tower, but we shall never know the truth."

Flt Lt Birnie led four aircraft to Aden for a short visit during the middle of April, all arriving safely. However, the Squadron lost another Venom on the 21st when Flg Off Kjestrup ejected from WR343 after an elevator jammed, coming down 11 miles east of Amman. Flg Off Fletcher again takes up the story:

"The Boss ordered Kiwi [Kjestrup] to eject and Kiwi replied, in best theatrical tradition, that he would do no such thing while there was a risk of his abandoned machine crashing onto the garrison town of Zerqa immediately ahead of him. So Kiwi stayed with his machine, and with his apparently limited control, managed to manoeuvre it clear of the town before ejecting at about 300 feet. He parachuted down into Zerqa while his Venom crashed into nearby hills. Kiwi badly sprained both ankles, and was cast in a new role — the wounded aviator enjoying the sympathy and close attention of all the ladies as he hobbled his way around the Mess on crutches. At least, for a while, we were spared the Maori war dance he and Dallison felt obliged to entertain us with after a few pints and the drop of a hat."

On 26 April, the Squadron despatched aircraft to search for a missing Anson which had failed to show up anywhere in the region after leaving Amman the previous day. 21 sorties were flown before news was received that the Anson had landed in Saudi Arabia. Another Venom — the third in as many months — was lost on 13 May when Plt Off Alcock abandoned WR358/G when he was unable to recover from a spin during aerobatics at 40,000 feet, as noted by Fletcher:

"His attempts at recovery failed, and after spinning for about 15,000 feet he became a little disorientated and decided to eject. This was a big mistake, since it found Chris sitting in his ejector seat at about 24,000 feet which was much too high for his superiors, who felt that he should have persevered with his spin recovery efforts for a lot longer. Chris fell like a brick to 10,000 feet, where a little barostat triggered a sequence of events which separated him from the seat and automatically opened his 'chute. The authorities were not pleased, but we celebrated his escape in style."

The aircraft crashed 18 miles east of Zerka. The uninjured pilot was picked up by the Station Anson flown by Grp Capt J.H. Giles, the Station Commander.

Later in the month a Canberra arrived at Amman from Cyprus, remaining for the weekend, which allowed bomber affiliation sorties to be flown. Several new pilots arrived during mid 1955, including Flt Lt D.G. Slade, Flg Offs M.J. Waterhouse, T.S. Syme and T.L. Lecky-Thompson, thereby bringing the Squadron up to establishment once again. In early June the Squadron participated in a three-day exercise with Sabres of 20 Squadron from 2ATAF, the latter operating temporarily from Cyprus. Squadron pilots were not over-impressed with their opponents, neither were groundcrews when Grp Capt Giles belly-landed a Squadron Venom at Amman on the 13th. Another exercise ended the month when Sabres of 71 Squadron, also a 2ATAF unit operating from Cyprus, carried out rat and terrier sorties against the Squadron's Venoms, the Squadron's diarist noting:

"Both sides learned many lessons — good co-operation."

Exercises continued throughout July, simulated ground attacks being carried out in conjunction with Army units in North Ma'an and RAF Regiment units at Aqaba, before flying to Nicosia on the 26th for APC, the air party comprising 17 Venoms and three Vampire T11s. Exercises included successful interceptions of Canberras. Soon after the Squadron's return from Cyprus, Amman was visited by six Hunter F1s piloted by members of the Day Fighter Leaders School, three of whom were Korean war veterans and led by Wg Cdr Scott-Vos, a former CO of 249. The following day, two sections of Venoms, each section containing a DFLS pilot, fired rockets at a target which was obliterated, and later eight Venoms engaged four Hunters at high level "and more than held their own." The Hunters departed for Habbaniya on the 20th, Wg Cdr Scott-Vos congratulating the Squadron on its performance. At the end of the month sorties were flown in conjunction with Arab Legion forces, 249 receiving a congratulatory message from the exercise commander.

At the beginning of September the Venoms carried out 20 dive-bombing sorties, the Squadron's first attempt to release bombs in this fashion using the Venom, when varied results were achieved. A number of new pilots had joined in recent weeks including Flg Offs D.E. Williams, D.D. Moyes, and J.A. Anderson, the latter posted from a unit in Kenya. The new pilots were urgently required to replace some of the Squadron stalwarts who departed at this time, including Flg Off Kjestrup, who was posted to Habbaniya, tour-expired, while Flg Offs Cock and Fletcher were also posted from the Squadron, the former cruelly struck down with polio which ended his flying career, the latter with a perforated ear drum; both were returned to the UK.

News trickled in of a clash between Egyptian Vampires and Israeli Meteors over the Sinai, when two of the former were shot down, intensifying the threat of a further major conflict between the hostile nations, both of which had been under British influence until recent times. Throughout the last quarter of 1955 and the early months of 1956, training continued unabated at Amman with high- and low-level sorties being flown, including dive-bombing, rocket-firing and air-to-ground gunnery on the local range. A new rocket range was sited during the month due to the existing one throwing up a lot of ricochets. One departure, albeit temporarily, was that of Flt Lt Dallison who returned to the UK to attend a DFLS course. At this time the Squadron received a new pilot — Plt Off P.J. Purnell — and acquired a Tiger Moth, courtesy of the Royal Jordanian Air Force, many of the pilots enjoying the change of mount, spending off-duty hours cavorting under Jordan's clear blue skies. A number of the Squadron's non-flying personnel were also given the opportunity of flights in the biplane, at least two — Cpl Bowtell and LAC Thomas — going solo.

February saw three incidents, two of which involved the ever-present problem of bird strikes. The first involved Flg Off Syme on 6 February and occurred whilst he was flying a dusk sortie in a low-level battle formation. Although the aircraft's tail fin was dented, he was able to land safely. Just over a week later, on 14 February, Flt Lt Slade experienced a more serious collision while on a low-level strike against a previously constructed target in the desert. Unable to avoid a flock of birds, the Venom's cockpit canopy was shattered and the nose damaged. Slade suffered slight facial abrasions, only his bonedome saving him from more serious injury. The other incident involved Flg Off Williams who experienced a canopy blow-out when flying at 40,000 feet in WR380/E, the Squadron's original FB4. However, he was able to return to base and landed safely. Two more pilots departed during the month, Flt Lt Birnie, B Flight commander, ostensibly on compassionate leave to the UK, where he was absorbed into the Home Establishment, while Flg Off Broughton also returned to the UK, tour-expired; he was later killed in a Canberra accident.

SAC Ray Crompton, an Armament Mechanic (Guns), arrived at Amman in March. Having initially worked in the Station Armoury, he was attached to the Technical Wing Armoury on second-line servicing for 249:

"On one occasion another armourer and myself accompanied the Station Armament Officer
on a demolition exercise, with a truck load of time-expired ammo, pyrotechnics, rocket motors

and some 250lb and 500lb bombs. We drove into the desert to a weapons range which had a few shot-up armoured cars lying around. As we drove across the range we spotted a Venom from 249 Squadron circling. The pilot must have thought a moving target would make a nice change and carried out a dummy cannon attack on us. We retaliated with panic, rude gestures and foul language. After stopping the truck and switching off the engine, we dug a fairly deep hole and put the explosives in it. Then, after taping some slabs of gun-cotton onto the bombs, primed and fused the charge, lit the fuse and ran to the truck. The SAO jumped behind the wheel and the engine refused to start, so we leaped out again and managed to dive behind one of the armoured cars before the lot went up. It was a strange sensation; you seem to stay still and the ground drops and then comes up and hits you. I could hear the shrapnel hitting the other side of the armoured car."

Flg Off Williams experienced a bird strike on 16 March, which caused damage to the jet intake although he was able to land safely. Three replacement pilots arrived during the month, Flg Off P. Warden, an Australian who had been serving with the MEAF Communication Squadron at Amman, and two pilots direct from the UK, Plt Offs B. Clayton and G. Garner. In the opposite direction went tour-expired Flg Off Smith.

Another new pilot arrived at the start of April, Plt Off R.N. Waite. The month saw exercises in conjunction with a detachment of the 10th Hussars at Ma'an, the targets being gun emplacements, tanks and the railway station at Ma'an. Later, a detachment went over to the new airfield at Mafraq and flew from there all day to give the groundcrews experience on first-line servicing and to carry out a practical trial of the refuelling facilities there. On 20 April, newly promoted Flt Lt Syme was obliged to abort a sortie when flying WR443/Y owing to a faulty canopy seal. At the end of the month four Venoms flew to Malta via Abu Sueir and El Adem to participate in a weekend exercise.

On 10 May a total of 22 high-level battle formation sorties were flown, the sections being trailed by a higher flying 'bouncer' whose purpose was to strike unnoticed whenever the opportunity arose, but throughout the morning the 'bouncer' was able to claim only one 'kill'. Detachments continued to operate from Mafraq, while four aircraft briefly visited Habbaniya. The second half of the month saw exercises which comprised strikes against units of the 21 LAA Squadron at Qasr al-Tuba. On 24 May a combined sortie was flown with six Venoms of 73 Squadron which had arrived at Amman specially for the exercise, followed by 15 sorties using 1,000lb bombs. The month ended with a Ceremonial Parade celebrating the Queen's Birthday, when the salute was taken by the British Ambassador.

There were further personnel changes during the month including the departure of Sqn Ldr Gough, the Squadron's CO for the past two years. Flt Lt Tetley also departed, while Flt Lt L.W.M. Dodds had arrived to take command of A Flight and Flg Off A.J. Hilliard as a replacement pilot. With the departure of Sqn Ldr Gough, Flt Lt Dallison, recently returned from the DFLS course in the UK, assumed temporary command of the Squadron until the arrival from the UK of the new CO, Sqn Ldr J.R. Maitland, holder of the US DFC won in the skies of Korea and one of the DFLS Hunter pilots who had visited the Squadron the previous year. Sqn Ldr Maitland had left England on 1 June in his own private aircraft, Proctor G-AKYB, and flew via France, Italy, Sicily, Malta, Libya and Egypt, arriving at Amman on the 18th:

"I set off in my own Proctor. I knew the Middle East well, having served there on Spitfires [with 32 Squadron] in what seemed more troubled times at the end of the British mandate in Palestine. The RAF made it very easy to operate your own aircraft, Jordan was a lovely country and I looked forward to flying down at weekends to the blue seas of the Gulf of Aqaba. All went well until, on arrival at Mersa Matruh in western Egypt, there was a choice of going to Cairo West or Abu Sueir in the Canal Zone. I chose the latter, having been stationed there during the British occupation.

On arrival I was greatly surprised to find the place teaming with MiG-15 fighters, with gun positions being dug all around the perimeter track. A whole wing [of MiGs] had arrived the previous day. It was my intention to complete the long journey that day via Aqaba. Taxiing out to the enormous runway built by the RAF, I was suddenly ordered to stop. No reason was given but it was soon obvious. A staff car and a three-ton truck drove in front of me. A small man in khaki shirt and slacks leapt out and gesticulated wildly at me to get out of the aircraft . . . and pointed a large, black automatic pistol at me. As I switched off and got out a troop of slightly puzzled but hostile-looking soldiers jumped down from the truck and pointed their rifles my way. I was taken to the top of the control tower where I had only just filed my flight plan and there was subjected to violent abuse. The little man was obnoxious and extremely menacing."

Sqn Ldr Maitland was held at Mersa Matruh for three days under suspicion of being a spy. On the third day he was visited by an Egyptian Air Force officer, whom he believed to be a MiG squadron commander, and a number of Egyptian pilots:

"They were charming and we immediately got into fervent discussions on the relative merits of the MiG and the Sabre jet which I had flown against it in Korea. [The little man] appeared suddenly, broke up the discussion and gave myself and the senior Egyptian a tremendous dressing down. It was funny at the time. After three boring days the [British] Air Attaché in Cairo got me out."

Shortly before the new CO's arrival at Amman, the Squadron lost another Venom when WR380/E was abandoned after engine flame-out when flying at 4,000 feet. Flg Off Lecky-Thompson ejected six miles north-east of the airfield, as remembered by SAC Crompton:

"The pilot ejected and a Sycamore picked him up. In keeping with RAF tradition he bought a crate of beer for the Armourers and Safety Equipment bods."

In conjunction with 73 Squadron at Cyprus, 249 carried out a series of live strikes against a prepared target when 26 sorties were flown. Rocketry and gunnery were adjudged to be fairly good. A few days later six Venoms flew a sweep to Akrotiri and engaged 208 Squadron Meteor FR9s which attempted to intercept. While two Venoms acted as bait the remaining four bounced the Meteors from height and claimed six 'shot down.' At the beginning of July, the Squadron was involved in a desert tank exercise and four pilots were sent to observe from the ground the effectiveness of strikes. Pilots were told there would be no simulated fighter attack or AA and that they were to attack and film as many vehicles as possible. A good deal of film was subsequently obtained from which it was determined that a considerable number of vehicles would have been destroyed. However, as both 'sides' and the umpires' cars were attacked indiscriminately, the umpires decided that the course of the land battle had not been diverted by air attack, much to the chagrin of the pilots concerned. But it was not all work and no play, as SAC Crompton recalled:

"We worked from 7am to 1pm and had some pleasant trips during our off-duty hours, to Jerusalem, Bethlehem, Jerash and if you could afford it, fly down to Cairo or up to Beirut and Damascus. Of course, Amman itself was a fascinating city and I enjoyed every minute of it. Then, if you were broke, there was always the open-air swimming pool on camp. About 40 miles from Amman was an emergency landing strip called Dawson's Field, near which was a village and an Arab Legion fort on a hill overlooking the remains of a Roman Baths and a large swamp area. The Baths had virtually become just a water hole, but there was good duck shooting to be had in the swamp, providing you kept an eye out for snakes. We used to stay in an old building in which survival rations were stored. There was one Arab villager who used to come down to the water hole and fill up an old oil drum on the back of a cart pulled by a donkey. One morning when he was carrying out his daily chore, the lads were out in the swamp shooting. A friend was on the other side of the water hole when he spotted a duck, flushed out of the swamp, coming towards us. He fired, missed the duck, but hit the Arab, the donkey and the water drum. The donkey took off with water pouring out of the holes in the drum, while the Arab leaped around shouting insults before chasing after the donkey. The Arab came back later; he was not badly hurt and it cost us some packets of hardtack biscuits and a couple of tins of cheese to get rid of him. Unfortunately, our leisure hours came to an end when President Nasser nationalized the Suez Canal in July and the anti-British feeling in Amman developed into rioting. We were then confined to camp."

Dawson's Field came into its own again on 21 August when Flg Off Gronert's aircraft suffered a flame-out; he carried out a successful forced-landing on the bed of the dried-up salt lake. A party of three under Sgt Dodd was rushed to the scene and had the Venom repaired in quick time, under difficult conditions.

The Squadron was suddenly ordered to move to Cyprus at the end of August. Trouble was brewing.

Chapter Fifteen

BACK TO WAR – SUEZ AND OMAN

1956 – 1957

"When strafing Egyptian vehicles I buzzed them first to allow the occupants to escape. I had no arguments with the Egyptians."

Sqn Ldr Jock Maitland, Commanding Officer 249 Squadron

Thus, on 27 August 1956, 249 moved, lock, stock and barrel, to Cyprus. Led by the CO, 15 Venom FB4s and the two Vampire T11s flew to Akrotiri, there to join another Venom unit, 6 Squadron, which had arrived from Habbaniya in April; one unserviceable aircraft had been left behind by 249 at Amman. To make room for the new arrivals at Akrotiri, 208 Squadron moved its Meteor FR9s to Malta. Of their new surroundings, Flg Off Gronert recalled:

"Akrotiri was far from being ready to accommodate the Squadron. The Squadron offices were in tents, the Officers' Mess and the Sergeants' Mess shared a hangar, and the living accommodation was in the married quarters, as yet unoccupied. At the same time as the build up was going on there was also the EOKA* terrorist threat, and there were several incidents in and around the camp. Two of the Squadron members, living in Larnaca, witnessed a shooting and gave chase firing a couple of rounds from their Smith & Wesson .38s."

Flt Lt Slade added:

"Pete Warden and Andy Anderson were credited with one damaged on their way to work one day."

Once settled in at the new base, training continued with a keener sense of urgency, including air-to-ground and air-to-air firing, 45° dive-bombing and R/p firing on the Larnaca Range. Results were not generally good. Detachments of Hunter F5s arrived from the UK and, on occasions, these attempted mock interceptions of the Squadron's Venoms. Detachments of Canberra jet bombers also arrived, followed by more Venoms at the beginning of October, 8 Squadron flying in from Habbaniya, fuelling suspicions that something important was about to happen. Rumour was rife. Some would have it that the squadrons would soon be called into action against the Israelis, whose aggressive actions were upsetting the Jordanians who, in turn, threatened to call British forces to their aid, under the terms of the Anglo-Jordan Treaty. Others suggested Egypt would be the likely target since President Nasser had nationalised the Suez Canal. Gronert continued:

"It was fairly common knowledge what was going on with the build up but no one talked very much about it. The [Venom] squadrons were each augmented by three extra pilots from the

---

* EOKA (Ethniks Organosis Kypriou Agonistou), a Greek Cypriot terrorist organisation, emerged in 1955 and commenced bombing British military and government property and assassinating British military and civilian personnel. In February 1956 two airmen were murdered while on duty at AHQ and another at Nicosia air base. Aircraft were also targeted and a Skyways Hermes transport was blown up at the civil airport.

UK*. They were all Venom pilots but of the night-fighter version. They were all impressed by the enhanced performance of the Mark 4. We had a feeling of frustration at the massive build up. It was generally thought that we were ready operationally from the time we had arrived in Cyprus, and that the powers that be were going for the overkill. We had no doubts about our ability to achieve complete air supremacy in a couple of days.

During October the [Venom] Wing was flying a large number of Alert Patrol sorties, with security tightened up considerably. Escape and evasion techniques and procedures were taken more seriously than previously. Escape kits were issued with button magnetic compasses, saw blades, knives, maps and the usual paraphernalia stitched into flying suits and underwear. We were also given a pile of 'goolie chits' which valued us at about a fiver each! We also had a sealed rubber bag reputed to contain five gold sovereigns; they must have been there because they were very insistent on them being returned afterwards. Apart from the standard water bag which was integral in the ejector seat, we all took another couple of bottles. Together with our Smith & Wesson .38s strapped to our waists, it was with some difficulty we managed to fit into the cockpit."

Towards the end of the month detachments of Armée de l'Air F-84F fighter-bombers and RF-84F reconnaissance jets began arriving at Cyprus, these being based at both Akrotiri and Nicosia. Gronert also remembered the arrival of the French pilots at Akrotiri:

"I do not recall the squadron number but they were a PR squadron flying the RF-84F. The three [Venom] squadrons gave them a good welcome with an invitation to a hooley in the Officers' Mess, which went down very well with everyone until it was discovered that most of the French pilots had the equivalent rank of Corporal, but we didn't care. We got on very well with them."

Flg Off Lecky-Thompson added:

"We struck up a very good liaison with the French at Akrotiri and, by some magical means, we found ourselves a plentiful supply of red wine and spare petrol to run our Squadron cars."

The balloon finally went up on 29 October, when Israeli forces launched a surprise attack against Egyptian military targets in the Sinai Peninsula, with paratroopers landing near the vital Mitla Pass. Fighting was fierce and, in the air, Israeli Mystères, Ouragans and Meteors clashed with Egyptian MiG-15s, Vampires and Meteors. Despite public denials of any form of collusion between Britain, France and Israel, secret meetings between representatives of all three governments had produced a plan by which an Anglo-French force would seize control of the Suez Canal, at the same time allowing Israel to occupy Egyptian territory in Sinai, thereby creating a buffer zone, and to take control of the neighbouring Gaza Strip, from where Palestinian terrorists frequently infiltrated into Israel.

On the evening of 30 October, according to plan and with Israeli forces making significant advances towards the Canal, Britain and France demanded that both Egypt and Israel stop fighting. The ultimatum to the Egyptian Government stated:

"The Governments of the United Kingdom and France have taken note of the outbreak of hostilities between Israel and Egypt. This event threatens to disrupt the freedom of navigation through the Suez Canal on which the economic life of many nations depends.

The Governments of the United Kingdom and France are resolved to do all in their power to bring about the early cessation of hostilities and to safeguard the free passage of the Canal. They accordingly request the Government of Egypt:
(a) to stop all warlike action on land, sea and air forthwith.
(b) to withdraw all Egyptian military forces from the neighbourhood of the Suez Canal.

---

* 249's three additional pilots were Flt Lt A. Webster, Flg Off K.E. Bridge and Flg Off D.A. Watts.

(c) to accept the temporary occupation by Anglo-French forces of key positions at Port Said, Ismailia and Suez.

A communication has been addressed to the Government of Israel, requesting them to cease hostilities and to withdraw their forces to a distance ten miles east of the Canal.

The Governments of the United Kingdom and France request an answer to this communication within twelve hours. If at the expiration of that time one or both Governments have not undertaken to comply with the above requirement, United Kingdom and French forces will intervene in whatever strength may be necessary to secure compliance."

Egypt, as expected, rejected the demand since she was not only defending her own territory, but was as yet doing so very effectively. However, by rejecting the demand the Egyptians had inadvertently accepted the bait, enabling Israeli forces to continue their air and ground attacks despite the call to end the fighting.

From their bases in Cyprus and Malta, RAF Valiant and Canberra bombers were despatched to raid Egyptian Air Force bases on the night of 31 October/1 November while, off the Egyptian coast a mighty Anglo-French naval armada, which included five aircraft carriers of which two were French, plus two helicopter support carriers, manoeuvred into position to continue the aerial assault with the coming of daylight. The Fleet's Sea Hawk and Sea Venom fighter-bombers were to operate against airfields west of the 32° line of longitude — Cairo West, Cairo International, Almaza, Inchas, Bilbeis (home of the EAF's Flying Training School) and Dekheila — while the Venoms and F-84Fs were tasked to attack airfields to the east of the line: Abu Sueir, Deversoir, Fayid, Kabrit, Kasfareet and Shallufa. The latest photographs of the airfields taken by PR Canberras and RF-84Fs revealed the strength of the EAF to comprise at least 110 MiGs, 14 Meteors (F4s, F8s and NF13s), 44 Vampire FB52s and T55s, and 48 Il-28 Russian-built jet bombers, dispersed as follows:

Abu Sueir	35 MiG-15s
Fayid	9 Meteors, 12 Vampires
Kabrit	31 MiG-15s
Kasfareet	2 Vampires, 1 Meteor
Inchas	20 MiG-15s
Almaza	24 MiG-15s, 4 Meteors, 21 Vampires, 10 Il-28s
Cairo West	9 Vampires, 16 Il-28s
Luxor	22 Il-28s

However, only 50 per cent of these were operational and ready for action since only a limited number of pilots and support personnel had yet been trained to fly and maintain these aircraft. Despite the superiority of the MiG over any aircraft available to the British and French, a French assessment of the EAF's capabilities provided some comfort for the anxious Anglo-French air commanders*:

"Pilots of MiG-15s, Vampires and Meteors were well trained in the use of rockets and bombs against ground targets and naval targets. But there was no air-support organisation. The lack of a system to detect enemy aircraft and to control Egyptian fighters, and the lack of Egyptian experience in this field, meant that the EAF's effectiveness here was low. Nevertheless, training in the Soviet Union had improved the capability. Because all training on the Il-28 in the Soviet bloc had been done in daytime, the operational standards of these squadrons was low, particularly at night."

Meanwhile at Akrotiri, with the approach of dawn, rocket-armed Venoms and F-84Fs stood by ready for take-off, rumours of MiG activity over Egypt causing a certain amout of concern. Flg Off Gronert:

---

* The RAF's Hunter F5s at Akrotiri, with a performance to match the MiG, lacked sufficient range to operate over Egypt and were used mainly in a defensive role.

"It is difficult to recall my feelings before the first sortie. I suppose it was a mixture of anticipation, apprehension and a fear of the unknown."

While Flg Off Williams commented:

"At 23 years of age I was thoroughly excited by the whole operation. Few postwar fighter pilots have the opportunity to put into practice their extensive and expensive training so I viewed this opportunity as wonderful good fortune. Not exactly the accepted manner in which to go to war but I knew no fear and was quite oblivious to any risk involved."

Another Venom pilot wrote:

"I suppose for any young man, contemplating battle for the first time must be more or less traumatic. On the one hand is the desire to put into practice all that one has striven to learn — for, after all, that is the whole purpose of military training. On the other hand there is the healthy fear of failure or even worse. Our main concern had to be how the Egyptian Air Force would react to any raids over and against their territory. We knew the EAF had MiG-15s, either flown by themselves or their Russian advisers. We knew the Venom was much slower than the MiG and that the standard of flying would be an unknown quantity, depending on which pilots flew against us. The Venom was quite slow but very manoeuvrable. We would be able to out-turn them comfortably but at some stage would have to set off back for Cyprus, or run out of fuel somewhere along the route. They would then be able to easily catch us. A low-level dash right on the deck, weaving irregularly, seemed likely to be the best defence, presenting a difficult target. If they stayed to dogfight, our manoeuvrability would give us a good chance to shoot them down."

Early-morning Canberra and RF-84F reconnaissance flights had already been intercepted by MiGs, and a Valiant had been attacked by an EAF Meteor night-fighter during the night, although no serious damage had been inflicted. Nonetheless, these early reports of MiG activity did nothing to allay the fears of those about to be thrust into the unknown . . .

First off, at 0520, were a pair of Venoms led by Flt Lt Slade in WR506/W, followed 15 minutes later by a second pair including WR533/F flown by Flg Off Moyes, their task to frustrate any possible attack on the aircraft preparing for the morning's operations. No Egyptian aircraft were seen although there was a scare at 0600 when the crew of a returning PR Canberra called up to report they were being pursued by a MiG. Sirens were sounded at Cyprus and defences put on alert, but 15 minutes later radar operators were able to explain that the Canberra was in fact being 'pursued' by a returning French RF-84F.

Meanwhile, the first wave of Venoms had already been launched, 6 Squadron pilots briefed to attack the EAF bases at Kasfareet and Kabrit, followed closely by 8 Squadron heading for Abu Sueir and Fayid; half an hour later, F-84Fs were despatched to the same aerodromes to continue the attacks. With the safe return to Akrotiri of the first wave of Venoms and F-84Fs, whose jubilant pilots claimed 20 MiGs, three Meteors and a Vampire destroyed or damaged without meeting any aerial opposition and only relatively light and inaccurate flak, three more sections of French fighter-bombers were sent off, followed 30 minutes later by two sections each of four of Venoms from 249.

The F-84Fs visited Abu Sueir, al-Firdan, Deversoir and Fayid, destroying a Meteor and a Vampire at the latter base. 249's Venoms followed close behind, giving the Egyptians little respite. Sqn Ldr Maitland (WR499/V) led his section to Kabrit and Kasfareet, while Flt Lt Dallison (WR529/A) and his section went first to Kabrit and then Abu Sueir. Flying with Dallison's section was Flg Off Gronert in WR504/Z:

"On 249 Squadron we had developed a system for rocket firing which gave more time for target identification and longer tracking time, thus enabling much greater accuracy. This also gave us a longer time flying at altitude, a significant factor due to the distance between Cyprus and Egypt. It involved flying from 30,000 feet and maintaining Mach 0.7 until 300 knots was reached, and this speed was maintained to the target.

> I was in a formation of four led by Flt Lt Doug Dallison. His No2 was [Flt Lt] Mick Waterhouse with myself as No3 and [Flg Off] Bill Barker as No4. It was a very experienced section and we were first off with our target being Kabrit, which was a MiG-15 base. Our long dive worked out very well and we all had a good strike on aircraft parked neatly in lines on the dispersal area. Following our rocket attack we flew on to Abu Sueir where we attacked further MiGs and motor transport targets. It appeared that the Egyptian Air Force was taken completely by surprise and at that time made no attempt to hide or disperse its aircraft, though some that survived were very skilfully hidden in sunken blister hangars, particularly at Abu Sueir.

> I recall the debriefing officer wanting to know our mission number but no one could remember it. We didn't want to be bothered with trifles like that, we wanted to tell about the MiGs we had shot up and so on."

The Squadron claimed a total of six MiGs destroyed as a result of this first operation, Gronert alone claiming one at Kabrit and a second at Abu Sueir. The MiGs were probably from 20 Squadron EAF or the Fighter OTU. Two more sections of Venoms, four aircraft each from 6 and 8 Squadrons, followed in 249's wake and by the time they returned, at 0930, a total of 58 sorties had been flown by the Venoms and F-84Fs, and it was assessed that up to 30 MiGs plus four Meteors and two Vampires had been destroyed or disabled. As yet no Egyptian aircraft had been encountered in the air, although further to the west a number of MiGs had been seen by Fleet Air Arm Sea Hawks attacking Almaza, although these did not engage. The British and French pilots were unaware that President Nasser had ordered his air commanders not to contest the air assault. The EAF possessed only 120 pilots fully trained for combat, and another 250 to 260 still in training. He argued the folly of sending these to fight against the Anglo-French air forces, when they would be required to fight the Israelis:

> "We are going to be in a state of war with Israel for years, and we shall need all the pilots we can get. Planes can be replaced overnight, but it takes years to train a pilot."

Nasser had obviously made a wise but painful decision, but the accusation of a lack of *esprit de corps* among its pilots was deeply resented by the EAF. Many pilots wanted to fight back despite Nasser's orders and some did and a number of MiGs flown away from the blitzed bases were able to operate, with the help of ground personnel, from the Cairo to Suez highway during the ensuing few days.

Following the initial strikes, RF-84Fs were sent to photograph the damage inflicted on various airfields. One pilot reported seeing 17 MiGs and five unidentified aircraft at Kabrit, of which only three appeared to have suffered damage. At Kasfareet a single Vampire was sighted, while Fayid revealed the wrecks of three Vampires and a Meteor; three other Vampires on the airfield appeared undamaged. Returning Venom pilots had also reported seeing a dozen apparently undamaged aircraft at Abu Sueir. Clearly further strikes were necessary.

Having refuelled and rearmed, sections of Venoms and F-84Fs began taking off for a second series of airfield attacks, 249 despatching two sections just before midday, the pilots briefed to attack Fayid and Kasfareet. Led respectively by Flt Lt Syme (WR531/R) and Flt Lt Slade (WR506/W), the two sections attacked a hangar with rockets, leaving it in flames before destroying a Meteor by cannon fire, and a second damaged. Flg Off Lecky-Thompson's aircraft (WR533/F) sustained some damage during the attack:

> "After firing the rockets I got a hole in the port pylon tank from some ground fire and had to abort, returning before the fuel ran out."

Following the strike against Fayid, the Venoms flew to Kasfareet where a hangar was strafed. On this strike WR504/Z suffered damage to its port pylon and tip tanks. Nevertheless, the pilot was able to return to Akrotiri safely. A Venom from one of the other squadrons also returned in a damaged condition, as witnessed by SAC Brian Cooper, an RAF Medic at Akrotiri, who wrote in his journal:

"At 1130 I observed a Venom fighter approaching RAF Akrotiri which seemed to be in difficulty. On closer examination, I observed a wing tank missing, leaving a jagged edge at the wingtip. The aircraft made a safe landing."

Although a number of Venoms had suffered from ground fire, as yet none had been lost, nor had any of the F-84Fs several of which similarly returned with battle damage. By 1330, an additional 62 sorties had been flown by Akrotiri's fighter-bombers, with the tally of aircraft destroyed or damaged on the ground having risen to an estimated 50 to 60, mainly MiGs.

The airfield strikes continued unabated and unchallenged throughout the afternoon, all three Venom squadrons despatching sections at 1330 with 249 leading the way. At 1410, the section of which Flg Off Williams (WR492/U) was a member, arrived over Abu Sueir and commenced its attack. Williams claimed a Meteor F8 destroyed and a second Meteor was seen to be burning. A Vampire was also destroyed before the section headed for Kasfareet where it inflicted damage on the control tower. An hour later, three more sections from 249 repeated the attacks on Fayid, Kasfareet and Abu Sueir. Sqn Ldr Maitland (WR506/W) led a rocket strike against hangars and other buildings at Fayid, while Flt Lt Syme (WR489/D) claimed damage to a long-nose Meteor — obviously a NF13 of 10 Squadron EAF — during a rocket attack. His section then flew to Kabrit where Syme strafed a MiG and a Fury despite the attention of Egyptian AA gunners. Meanwhile, Flt Lt Dallison's section struck at Abu Sueir and then Fayid, as noted by Flg Off Gronert (WR504/Z):

"My second sortie was similar to the first except that I was not so apprehensive; this is what we had trained to do and we set about it in a professional way. This time the targets were Abu Sueir for our rockets, and Fayid afterwards with our 20mm cannon.

On our return the feeling was one of great exhilaration and relief that everything had gone so well; debriefing was a mad affair with everyone wanting to talk at once. We were asked on our return about damage to the runways and infrastructure at the various airfields, but it was obvious that the damage and disruption caused was miniscule. For all the damage inflicted by the bomber force, they might just as well have stayed at home."

It had become apparent by now that the night bomber raid by Canberras and Valiants had not achieved the desired results. During his attack on Fayid, Gronert claimed a Meteor destroyed. Flg Off Moyes participated in this attack and subsequently claimed a Vampire destroyed by cannon fire, plus a hangar damaged during the rocket strike. However, his aircraft (WR527/C) suffered flak damage when a piece of shrapnel penetrated the port fin although he was able to fly back to Akrotiri and land safely:

"I remember being apprehensive on the way in, doing as much damage as quickly as possible, then breathing a sigh of relief as we coasted out."

Meanwhile, Flt Lt Waterhouse and Flg Off Lecky-Thompson (WR492/U) visited Fayid, Kasfareet and Kabrit in quick succession:

"Mick [Waterhouse] and I found aircraft partly dug in and camouflaged around the perimeter track of the airfields and we had a field day. We had a mutual agreement with the other squadrons that we would leave a few undamaged so that when we went in — 249 was planned to deploy in Egypt — we would be able to have fun flying the MiG-15s!"

Nonetheless, the pair claimed six MiGs and a Vampire T55 destroyed by cannon fire, although Lecky-Thompson noted that his salvo of four rockets aimed at some parked Vampires missed the target. With the safe return of Akrotiri's strike force, a final tally of the day's claims was made. A total of 65 sorties had been flown during the afternoon, resulting in 54 additional claims for Egyptian aircraft destroyed or damaged on the ground, taking the total for the day to an estimated 130, achieved for no loss save minor damage to a dozen Venoms and three F-84Fs, much of it caused by debris. The three Venom squadrons had flown 104 sorties and jointly claimed 59 aircraft destroyed, the vast majority of which were MiGs; in addition, claims were submitted for 11 probables and 37 damaged. 249's share was estimated to be about a dozen MiGs, two or three Meteors, two Vampires and a Sea Fury.

Despite the assault on Egyptian airfields and the near-annihilation of the Egyptian Air Force, some form of retaliation against the air bases at Cyprus was anticipated, as witnessed by the entry in SAC Cooper's journal:

> "The time is now 0200 and we are still waiting for the air raid that we expected tonight. Let's hope that dawn brings us good news of operations carried out [during the night]."

There was no Egyptian strike against Cyprus but, with the onset of darkness, Canberras and Valiants from Cyprus and Malta carried out further raids on Cairo West, Fayid, Kasfareet and Luxor, followed by a daylight Canberra raid aimed at destroying the Cairo Radio Station. Although the latter was not particularly successful, the station was nevertheless off the air for a period of time. Venoms and F-84Fs were again very active, the first strikes leaving Akrotiri at 0515, the base a hive of activity:

> "Akrotiri base, shared by French and British, was the scene of fabulous activity. Every two minutes four aircraft took off in pairs, wing to wing, coming back in to land an hour and a quarter later. As they touched down, others took off. It needs no great effort of imagination to appreciate the effect of such a continuous bludgeoning. The Egyptian aircrews and ground staff, already stunned by the thunderous crash of the first attack, had not time to leave their shelters and reach the runways before another wave of fighter-bombers was upon them."

The CO (WR504/Z) led one strike against Fayid and Abu Sueir, strafing a number of MiGs seen on the ground. Fayid was also the target for the section led by Flt Lt Slade (WR506/W), where a Meteor F8 was damaged and a Vampire claimed destroyed, the latter by Flg Off Moyes (WR398/H). A later strike led by Flt Lt Dallison (WR529/A) flew to Kabrit where Flg Off Williams (WR504/Z) damaged a MiG. Flg Off Lecky-Thompson (WR527/C) also claimed a MiG damaged but then had to abort and return to Akrotiri. Meanwhile, Flg Off Gronert (WR533/F) claimed two MiGs and a Proctor:

> "We were enjoying things now. There was no resistance from the ground, they [the anti-aircraft defences] had all been silenced during the first day. We were starting to diversify our targets now. The first sortie [against Kabrit and Abu Sueir] was similar to the first day, but our second was an armed recce between Deversoir, Geneifa and Fayid."

At Fayid a number of Egyptian military vehicles were seen, Gronert personally destroying a tank and a petrol bowser. Flt Lt Slade's section visited Abu Sueir where a number of MiGs and a Vampire trainer were strafed, Flg Off Moyes claiming two destroyed although his aircraft (WR489/D) was hit; a bullet passed through the port aileron and a piece of shrapnel penetrated the fuselage and engine:

> "Except for attacking a Vampire [on the earlier sortie], where I had first crack, all my attacks were as No4 in the formation. Here I attacked any target that seemed whole, or I took the fourth in line. Some were hidden on shallow Nissen hut type of shelters. Being No4 was a vulnerable position. They [the Egyptian gunners] heard No1, saw No2, aimed at No3, and fired at No4! And No4 always used more fuel than any other position."

All told, the section claimed two MiGs destroyed plus three damaged, and strafed four hangars which it was believed housed more MiGs. Of the morning's attacks, Flg Off Garner wrote:

> "Twenty more sorties were made against the same targets as yesterday's operations. Once again considerable damage was done to Egyptian aircraft and installations without loss to ourselves. No enemy air opposition was encountered and anti-aircraft fire was reported to be light and inaccurate."

Although 249 had not met any hostile aircraft in the air, two pilots from one of the other Venom units had been intercepted over the Mediterranean by two swept-wing fighters. Supposing their assailants to be MiGs, the Venoms had just gained favourable firing positions when it was realised they were F9F-8 Cougars of the US Navy, operating from one of the two US Sixth Fleet carriers in the area. The Americans, opposed to the Anglo-French venture, were making a nuisance of themselves, even complaints from the RN Task Force Commander to his counterpart made little difference and further misidentifications occurred. Two Hunters were vectored on to what was believed to be a flight of four MiGs flying in the direction of the Suez Canal. The lead Hunter closed to within 1,000 yards of one of the jets before the pilot realised his target was in fact a US Navy FJ-3 Fury from one of the American carriers. But EAF fighters were about and, further to the west, a Royal Navy Sea Hawk narrowly missed intercepting two Egyptian Vampires, while during an attack on Kabrit a Sea Venom caught an EAF Harvard just as it was taking off. With rumours and imaginations running wild, some of the Venom pilots obviously indulged in a spot of line-shooting at the expense of the ground staff, as the following entry in SAC Cooper's journal would suggest:

"This evening, pilots have been telling us of their experiences over Egypt. One pilot of a Canberra jet bomber told us that while flying over enemy occupied territory he was intercepted by MiG-15s; they began firing at him and hit him twice in the tail. He immediately put his aircraft into full throttle and pulled the joystick thus placing his aircraft into a vertical climb and the MiGs just went plain sailing underneath him, after which Venom fighter aircraft attacked them from the air, assisted by French Thunderstreaks [F-84Fs], resulting in the shooting down of two MiG-15s. Another pilot, who was in a Venom fighter, said that whilst over an Egyptian airfield, two MiGs were taking off along the runway. He followed behind them and placed himself between them as they became airborne. He then put his kite into a loop and placed himself a little further away from the two enemy aircraft. He opened fire with his 20mm shells and fetched both aircraft down."

While the first part of the account is undoubtedly correct, since a PR Canberra had been intercepted and damaged by a MiG, the references to Venoms and F-84Fs shooting down MiGs was total fabrication. Whether the story-tellers were from 249 is not clear.

The air assault was about to change direction. By mid-morning, the Anglo-French air commanders, having concurred that the Egyptian Air Force had been effectively destroyed, ordered strikes to be switched away from the airfields and, instead, be directed against the Egyptian Army's main tank and transport depot at Huckstep Camp near Almaza, where reconnaissance photographs showed over 1,000 vehicles tightly parked. 6 Squadron carried out the first strike, the pilots returning to tell of vehicles left in flames, tanks damaged and buildings destroyed. A dozen rocket-armed F-84Fs arrived as the 6 Squadron Venoms completed their attacks, followed by three sections from 249 led by the CO (WR497/B). Another section was led by Flt Lt Syme in WR499/V whose aircraft suffered flak damage during the attack, causing a hydraulic failure although he was able to land safely at Akrotiri on return from the raid. WR506/W also sustained minor damage when debris or shrapnel struck its port wing leading edge. Of the attack, Syme commented:

"Our own attacks were not particularly accurate because we came in from 40,000 feet at high speed and high angles of attack."

As the strikes against Huckstep continued throughout the afternoon, 249 was instructed to send two sections to keep an eye on the airfields. One section flew to Almaza where the military barracks was rocketed and strafed, while the other section visited Shallufa and included Flg Off Lecky-Thompson (WR527/C):

"Had a very aggressive AA group trying to get us. I remember being the closest and so I immediately dropped down as low as I could (below 50 feet above ground level) and went under the flak, straight at them until, at about 500 yards, I opened up with four 20mm cannon and thankfully silenced them. I then realised how frightened I had been!"

During the course of the morning sorties against the airfields, the Squadron had claimed a further four MiGs, a Meteor, a Vampire and a Proctor, raising its tally for the two days to 23, including 16 MiGs. A number of vehicles and tanks at Huckstep had also been destroyed or damaged. Although none of the Venoms or F-84Fs had been lost during the two days of intensive operations, several had suffered minor damage from flak and debris. Ground personnel of all squadrons worked round the clock to keep the aircraft serviced, as recalled by 249's Cpl Bob Byrne:

> "When the conflict began the squadrons were operating dawn and dusk strikes in their ground-attack role. Several aircraft were damaged, mostly by debris from the low-level attacks. Hence work had to be carried out on the dispersal with arc lights, to change engines, fuel tanks that had been pierced, plus other structural reports on the airframes by the best means we had. In the rush to get aircraft back in service there were inevitable accidents. One night we were ground testing a new engine fitted to an aircraft while the armourers were loading up the ammunition bays, which were immediately above the air intakes. Unfortunately, due to the haste, we did not fit the engine debris guards and a whole ammunition belt got sucked into the engine air intake and wrecked the new engine. As I recall, there were no inquests — we just got on with installing the replacement and having the aircraft ready for dawn, come what may."

Fears of Egyptian retaliation against Cyprus remained, as SAC Cooper recorded:

> "At 0400 this morning, all electricity was switched off at RAF Akrotiri. The first thoughts that ran through everyone's mind was that we were about to be attacked by Egypt. At 0420 the electricity was resumed and the atmosphere once again became normal. A report stated that an unknown and unaccounted for aircraft was seen on Akrotiri's radar screen. Hunter jet fighters intercepted it and it turned out to be an aircraft of the French Air Force."

With the EAF in no position to launch an attack against Cyprus, only bad weather in the central Mediterranean prevented the full quota of planned sorties by Malta-based Valiants and Canberras, although one raid against Huckstep Camp was made before the weather deteriorated. However, Canberras from Cyprus were able to make an attack on Luxor airbase in southern Egypt, to where a number of Il-28 jet bombers had withdrawn, in addition to two smaller raids against Huckstep Camp.

Next morning (3 November) the air strikes continued, although operations were switched away from airfield attacks to armed reconnaissances over specified areas. Flt Lt Syme (WR533/F) led one sortie to the Deversoir/Geneifa area where he rocketed and strafed a petrol bowser, a tank transporter and two lorries. Flg Off Lecky-Thompson (WR507/S) also rocketed a tank transporter before he and Flt Lt Waterhouse strafed three bowsers and three trucks. After lunch, sections of Venoms continued to hunt for military vehicles in the Canal Zone, the strafing of airfields now considered to be of secondary importance. Flg Off Williams (WR507/S) was in the section which flew to Shallufa, where a mobile power unit was strafed, while Flg Off Gronert (WR492/U) noted:

> "We carried out only one sortie [each] today. Army intelligence had reported a build up of armour at Almaza so we were to go and sort it out. We employed our usual system of the long approach to attack and shortly after breaking cloud at 20,000 feet we found that we were being fired at by what appeared to be radar-controlled anti-aircraft guns. We pressed on down to the target only to find that any armoured vehicles which might have been there had since disappeared. We fired our rockets into the barracks and flew at below the level of the house tops with guns still firing at us. They didn't hit us but they must have given a lot of work to the local builders!"

Akrotiri's Station Commander, Grp Capt J.C. Macdonald DFC AFC, flew one of the 15 sorties carried out by the Squadron during the day, the final mission being a strike against Abu Sueir when two MiGs were destroyed and two others damaged. The Akrotiri Wing had suffered its first loss during an early morning armed recce, when a Venom of 8 Squadron crashed during a low-level sortie between al-Qantara and Ismailia, killing the pilot.

Four Squadron Venoms led by Flt Lt Slade (WR520/T) followed a section from 6 Squadron, early on the morning of 4 November, to strike at Abu Sueir, where several MiGs were strafed; four were claimed by Flg Off Moyes (WR507/S). Fayid was then visited where two petrol bowsers, trucks and hangars were also strafed. Huckstep Camp was on the receiving end of further attacks by both RAF and French fighter-bombers during the early afternoon. A section led by Flt Lt Syme (WR531/R) claimed damage to a tank and three or four trucks, but the leader suffered cannon stoppage. Light but accurate anti-aircraft fire from the northerly limit of the depot hit WR443/Y in the starboard wing and port tip tank. The day's final sorties were armed reconnaissances over the Port Said area where military vehicles were strafed, including half-tracks and jeeps, Flg Off Williams (WR497/B) attacking a three-ton truck. The CO (WR499/V) then led the Venoms in attacks against anti-aircraft guns sited around the port. The other two Venoms of his section, WR531/R and WR375, both suffered minor flak damage, the latter returning with a small hole in the cockpit canopy. Neither pilot was hurt.

British and French paratroopers were dropped over Gamil airfield and south of Port Said on the morning of 5 November, the drop preceded by a softening up of the defences by sections of Venoms. 249 sent two sections, one led by Sqn Ldr Maitland (WR499/V), the other by Flt Lt Dallison. Flying one of the Venoms was Flg Off Gronert:

"We took off before dawn and arrived in the target area at first light. There were a couple of smallish guns there, which were taken out without any trouble, and we did a sweep along the beach. I had not had the opportunity to fire my rockets due to the fact that there were no targets in the vicinity, so I brought them home with me. When we arrived back at base the groundcrew found that my aircraft [WR497/B] had been hit by small-arms fire, and they gave me a piece of shrapnel taken from near my right foot. They also found that the electric cable to my rockets had been severed by a bullet, so I could not have fired the rockets even if I had wanted to. Bill Barker, my No2, told me later that he had noticed an Egyptian soldier firing what appeared to be a Bren gun from the hip, on the shore near Port Said. I would have been very cross had he shot me down."

During one of these sorties Venom WR492/U suffered shrapnel damage, as Flg Off Williams remembered:

"R/p and 20mm attacks on gun installations at Port Said. Five HAA and LAA positions silenced. The underside of the Venom was damaged by shrapnel which penetrated the lower engine cowl, piercing one of the burner cans. This produced a certain amount of heat and consequent fire hazard, all of which I was blissfully unaware of."

Other sections were also despatched on armed reconnaissances and attacked military vehicles, Flt Slade (WR420/T) noting that a number were destroyed including a tank and two bowsers, while Flg Off Lecky-Thompson (WR533/F) recalled:

"The locals had got used to us only firing if they had abandoned their vehicles, so they were very stubborn and only when we took off the front wheels of the transports did they stop and run. I also remember going for the tanks at very low level — 20 feet or so — so that we could go at the tracks from very close range. These early dawn (and dusk) strikes showed where the ricochet damage was flying; it was like a peacock array of feathers, the flashes curving up and away, whilst those that went horizontally had gone to earth before we got to the target; thus the safest escape route was to dip a wing and go down the side of the target, rather than pull up."

During the sortie Lecky-Thompson claimed the destruction by cannon fire of an armoured troop carrier, two three-ton lorries and a Land Rover, and also damaged a tank, a scout car and a second Land Rover. Apart from the damage to Gronert's aircraft, two more Venoms returned to Akrotiri with minor damage from the morning's sorties: WR507/S with a hole in its engine cowling and WR412 with a damaged aileron.

With the paratroop drop having been successfully carried out and the ground fighting progressing favourably, Venoms and F-84s returned over the battle areas in support of the troops. One of the French fighter-bombers was hit by flak but the pilot was able to eject safely. 249 undertook a further 15 sorties between midday and dusk, one section led by Flt Lt Syme (WR504/Z):

> "Armed recce of French dropping zone. Nothing there. Recced road south of port. No2 hacked jeep."

One of the Venoms, WR533/F, took a hit in its rear fuselage which holed the rear spar. As a consequence it was withdrawn from operations. Others damaged during the day were repaired overnight and made ready for the morrow.

Gamil airfield had fallen to the paratroops by midday on the 5th and by mid-afternoon the defenders of Port Said had clearly had enough; by 1630 surrender terms and conditions were being discussed, although these were later rejected by Cairo and fighting resumed that night. However, on the political front the Soviets began making dire threats to the British, French and Israeli governments. Already under pressure from the Americans, the Allies had no option but to agree to a ceasefire, as from midnight on 6 November, but this did not stop them from going ahead with their planned seaborne invasion on the morning of the 6th.

The pilots had only just turned in for the night when they were suddenly awakened, as SAC Cooper's journal recorded:

> "At 0215, a tannoy by the RAF police at Akrotiri broadcast a message calling out all 249 Squadron and all armament sections to report to their places of duty. Now everyone is guessing, is it going to be another attack on Egypt, are we expecting an air raid? We will have to wait and see."

On assembling at the Wing Operations briefing room, pilots from all three Venom squadrons were informed that they were to suppress a number of troublesome guns in concrete emplacements, most on the West Mole breakwater running north from Port Said. Thirty-two Venoms were to take part in the strike and these began taking-off into the stormy darkness above Akrotiri, leaving behind Flg Off Lecky-Thompson whose aircraft failed to start. Once airborne, the Venoms formed up in sections for the series of attacks which were to be controlled by the CO of 6 Squadron (the senior Venom squadron commander). However, following take-off, he discovered that his radio was unserviceable and it fell to Sqn Ldr Maitland (WR499/V) to take over the role of Master Bomber. One pilot recalled:

> "By now the weather was breaking, with rain and thunderstorms. Take-off, with wave after wave of aircraft taking off into the pitch darkness in the rain, with lightning flashes here and there, was exciting and demanding . . ."

Over the sea the leading section was approached by an unidentified aircraft, as Sqn Ldr Maitland recalled:

> "In the very early morning the flight I was leading was shadowed by a jet of some sort. It was too dark to identify but if it was hostile, as presumably it was, that was the only Egyptian aircraft any of us [in 249] saw airborne during the entire campaign."

Shortly afterwards in the lightening sky, Flg Off Jim Budd, a former Squadron pilot now serving with 6 Squadron, who had joined up in the darkness with a 249 section, attempted to intercept another or the same aircraft, which was definitely identified as a MiG-15. The Egyptian jet easily escaped, passing close to another 6 Squadron Venom, both pilots claiming that the MiG bore

Russian markings rather than the green and white roundel of the EAF. Flg Off Gronert commented:

> "It was rumoured that the Russians would be drawn into the conflict especially as there were unofficial reports that several of the pilots with the Egyptians had been killed."

Nonetheless, a handful of EAF MiGs were operating from a road in the Delta area, and one of these strafed British troops on Gamil airfield at dawn.

Heavy cloud over Port Said made any chance of a co-ordinated attack on the gun emplacements difficult. The Venoms instead struck in sections and fired their rockets into an area soon covered by smoke and dust. A section from 6 Squadron went in first; some of the following pilots were unable to see the designated target so searched for military vehicles instead, as Flt Lt Syme (WR443/Y) noted:

> "Abortive strike against mole at Port Said. Recced on road to Ismailia. Rocketed trucks in Army camp. Flak and tracer."

Flg Off Williams reflected:

> "Fleeting impressions of the operation — taking off heavily loaded into an early dawn. The first sight of the Egyptian coastline. Hunting for targets. Sweeping low over the tenement buildings of Port Said looking for gun emplacements. Flak that puffed so innocently lethal alongside you. Pouring 20mm cannon into ground targets and seeing the devastating effect."

The strike against the gun emplacements achieved some success but not all the guns were disabled. It was estimated that only 50 per cent of the rockets fired hit the breakwater although the seaborne landings went ahead unhindered by the West Mole guns. Sqn Ldr Maitland observed:

> "While over the west area of the place where the British troops were fighting, I saw several dumps and buildings on fire. One was very big, sending a long column of smoke into the sky."

Following the dawn strike, the Venoms were required to fly only a few operational sorties throughout the remainder of the day. Flg Offs Gronert (WR492/U) and Barker carried out an armed reconnaissance between Tel al-Kebir and Ismailia:

> "We had orders to attack any target that could be considered military. In the event we found plenty of targets, each of us taking turns at attacking them while the other gave cover. I had some spectacular cine film of that sortie, particularly the attack on a tank where the rockets were seen to hit and the cupola was tossed spinning into the air. On the way back we saw a lot of aerial activity on our track and wondered what it was. As it turned out, it was the US Sixth Fleet being awkward. We had very frosty relations with the Sixth Fleet, which was positioned to the north of the Suez Canal. Aircraft from their carriers had been operating in the area of the eastern Mediterranean in considerable numbers. We had decided amongst ourselves that we were not going to let them interfere with us and, if necessary, we would take any action considered necessary to maintain our security.
>
> I instructed Bill to carry on [back to base] as his fuel state was at a stage where you wonder how good a glider pilot you are. I climbed above all this and kept watch over everything going on and when they [the American fighters] started to interfere, I made as to attack even though the situation was that while I was comparatively flush with fuel, I had no ammunition. While they did threaten, they did not actually interfere, so we left them behind and landed without further incident."

By the end of the day the F-84Fs had logged 33 sorties, the Venoms an additional 50. None of Akrotiri's aircraft had been lost but a PR Canberra from Nicosia was shot down over the Syria/

Lebanon border by a Syrian Meteor F8; one member of the crew was killed and the other two captured. Further to the west the Fleet Air Arm suffered two Sea Hawks shot down during the day's operations, making its total losses three Sea Hawks (one lost in an accident), two Wyverns and a Whirlwind. The French Navy's Aeronavale losses were two Corsairs, one in an accident.

As ordered by the politicians, the fighting ceased at midnight by which time British forces had advanced as far as al-Cap, a small village a few miles short of their objective, al-Qantara. Having consolidated their positions, the Anglo-British force was to await the arrival of United Nations Emergency Force troops before beginning to withdraw but, by 22 December 1956, the last of the occupying force had departed. Israeli forces were also compelled to pull out of the Sinai but delayed their move until March 1957. Before the withdrawal however, four 249 pilots paid a visit to Gamil airfield, as recalled by Flg Off Gronert:

> "Following the cessation of hostilities, our section of four [Flt Lts Dallison, Waterhouse and Flg Off Barker being the others] managed to arrange a visit to Gamil airfield. We flew over in a Valetta and spent a couple of nights there. We met the people we would have been working with had things gone ahead as planned [249 was to have been temporarily based at Gamil had the capture of the Canal succeeded]. Half the Squadron equipment had been on the high seas when operations ceased, along with some of the groundcrews. The Group Captain in charge of the airfield and the Wing Commander Flying had been seconded from 2ATAF Germany. I don't know how good they would have been operationally, but the two days there were spent either drunk or getting towards that state! We had a good look round Port Said and apart from one or two areas, it looked very much as it always looked."

Initial British estimates of the number of EAF aircraft damaged or destroyed by air attack were 229 destroyed, 24 probably destroyed and 239 damaged by Venoms and F-84Fs from Akrotiri, by aircraft of the Fleet, and during bombing attacks. Those claimed destroyed included 104 MiG-15s and MiG-17s, 11 Meteors of various Marks, 30 Vampires, 26 Il-28s plus 63 trainers and support aircraft. This estimate appears to be high given the fact that around 40 aircraft had flown out of Egypt to safety, while PR analysis revealed only 105 aircraft destroyed including 62 MiGs, although this figure excluded trainers destroyed at Bilbeis Flying School. The Venoms were credited with 101:12:66 of which 249's share was 30 destroyed — 23 MiGs, three Vampires, two Meteors, one Sea Fury and one Proctor — plus six probables and 15 damaged; in return, 11 of the Squadron's aircraft had suffered flak, shrapnel or debris damage during the course of the 134 sorties flown, when 430 rockets were launched and 25,947 rounds of 20mm were fired. Despite the successes achieved, many considered the Venom obsolete, including the AOC Levant:

> "It should be noted that although the EAF, equipped with a fair number of high-performance fighters, was completely neutralised by a force containing a high percentage of fighters of inferior performance, no firm conclusion can be drawn from this because of the imponderable factor of the morale and general willingness to fight of EAF. The Venom has many short-comings; it is no longer good enough to use obsolete fighters in this role."

The Secretary to the Chief of Staff Committee was somewhat kinder in his appraisal:

> "The Venoms' 20mm guns were not as good as the 30mm of the Hunters, but nevertheless the Venoms did their stuff extremely well. The Venoms were all right, but were getting long in the tooth."

Notwithstanding this, Flt Lt Slade was full of praise for the nimble aircraft:

> "The Venom was a fine aircraft with twice the thrust of the Vampire and could maintain Mach 0.8 above 50,000 feet. Squadron practice interceptions started at 48,000 feet and were often up to 52,000 feet before 'combat' started."

But he was critical of the lack of organisation:

> "The RAF effort was badly organised and handled. Nothing of the ground-attack skill gained in 1941 to 1945 seemed to have been formally retained. For example, no one could remember the sighting picture for the 25lb rocket. Co-ordination of the RAF and Naval air operations was non-existent; no common frequencies for rescue; no post-strike photographs available for follow-on missions. There was no indoctrination of the forces involved, many of whom were National Servicemen, who could see quite plainly that [Prime Minister] Eden was lying when he denied co-operation with the Israelis. Two wings of French F-84Fs and Mystères had been refuelled in Squadron dispersals at Akrotiri en route to Israel in the week before operations commenced."

For the Egyptian Air Force the conflict had been a disaster. Five days and nights of intensive air strikes had destroyed most of its aircraft and caused serious damage to its airfields and installations. However, the EAF had suffered fewer than 200 casualties of whom about 25 were fatal, including five fighter pilots killed in action against the Israelis. But, as President Nasser had wisely stated, aircraft were replaceable overnight, pilots and aircrew were not. Over the next few days, the 40-odd MiGs and Il-28s which had fled the country to Saudi Arabia and Syria began returning; in March 1957 three Romanian ships arrived with 15 crated MiG-17s, ten disassembled Il-28s and other military equipment; by June of the same year, the EAF could boast of 100 MiGs and 40 Il-28s. Moscow was indeed generous. Despite the success of the Anglo-French/Israeli attacks they did not, however, bring about the fall of the Egyptian Government and similarly failed to establish international control over the Suez Canal. Indeed, the Sinai-Suez War strengthened Nasser's position in Egypt and the Arab World, where he was seen as having fought against three invaders and of scoring a diplomatic victory. By way of contrast, British Prime Minister Eden, a sick man, resigned.

During this period the Squadron remained at readiness in case of a renewal of hostilities. At the same time, EOKA terrorists stepped up their activities against British military and civilian personnel living on the island. On 10 November terrorists managed to infiltrate Nicosia air base and plant a time bomb on a 1 Squadron Hunter, which was damaged beyond repair. There were many shootings. In one two-week period during November, the blackest month in the emergency, no fewer than 21 Britons and 17 Cypriots were killed. All told in November 416 acts of violence were recorded and 693 persons were held in detention. Against this background, 249 continued operating from Akrotiri, where training continued. Cpl Byrne remembered:

> "In order to expedite turn-round times, all trades would descend on an aircraft when the need arose. On one occasion at Akrotiri, an aircraft was being prepared for a ground-attack practice sortie and everyone was working to get it ready. A Corporal armourer was fitting 100lb practice rockets to the port pylon as an electrician in the cockpit was testing a variety of circuits. By chance the rocket circuit was made and the rocket careered across the end of the runway into a dry lake area, causing the armourer severe burns and injuries to his arm and chest where he had been supporting the fins."

By the end of the year, with the last of the Anglo-French invasion forces gone, Nasser consolidated Egyptian control over the strategic waterway and nationalised most British and French property and companies. A section from 249 had provided cover for the evacuation of Anglo-French forces from Port Said, as did F-84Fs of EC1/3. The Squadron's diarist commented:

> "The Navy were over the area in strength and did not appreciate the Squadron low run over the town."

249 received a number of replacement pilots in the aftermath of Suez, Flg Offs Barker, Alcock and Gronert departing, tour-expired, as did Flt Lt Dallison, while Flt Lt Syme was posted to 8 Squadron at Khormaksar. New arrivals included Flt Lt M.F. Goodwin, Flt Lt S.B. Lambert and Flg Off Beck from 32 Squadron, Flg Off J. McCallum from 111 Squadron, Flg Off

R. Jackson from 73 Squadron, Flg Off E.C. Williamson from OCU Pembrey, plus Flg Off G. MacIntosh, Flg Off D.R. Elford and Plt Off J.A. Richards. However, both Lambert and Beck were shortly re-posted to 6 Squadron, together with Flg Off Anderson. The Squadron remained at Akrotiri until March 1957, having participated in a Wing flypast on 1 March, when it moved to El Adem in Libya. Another new arrival at this time was SAC Roy Jones, a radar mechanic:

"My arrival in Cyprus was at the time of the troubles, but I only had two weeks to wait before we were transferred to El Adem. In the meantime I had to rapidly retrain myself on the obsolete gear used in the Venom and Vampire, having discovered that I would be the Squadron's only radar mechanic after leaving Cyprus.

The radar on the Venom consisted of two strip aerials mounted under the aircraft body, just forward of the cockpit. The radar gear box was mounted in the body behind the cockpit. The radar equipment was a very basic homing device. At this time not all the Middle East was covered by homing beacons and when flying from Kenya to Aden, for example, pilots had the Eastleigh beacon, then one in Ethiopia and finally Aden. As the radar beam range was, I believe, 200 miles, one flew over areas just by compass reading and trusted that you were not too far off the nearest homing beacon.

To service the radar gear box, it had to be withdrawn as one stood in front of the engine air intake. Unfortunately, the radar equipment would tend to go faulty just as the aircraft was about to taxi out for take-off. Flying time was limited and the pilot would want to get away. Therefore, you would find yourself standing on tip-toe with your body pressed over the engine air intake, trying to change the faulty equipment, with the pilot wanting you to speed up by slightly increasing the revs. Therefore you would be kept in place by the suction on your midrift! The exchange of words between pilot and mechanic would be drowned by the noise of the engine, but both knew them to be 'choice'. It was all part of life, as was the use of ground staff for target practice. Walking around the airfield, one always kept a look-out for low-flying aircraft.

Upon arrival at El Adem I drew the short straw and was put on night guard duty, guarding a Comet parked on the far side of the airfield. This was my first guard duty abroad. At about 1.30 in the morning, I heard an explosion in the surrounding desert, followed by another. My rife, complete with five rounds, was ready for action — but then nothing. I waited in a state of panic for a further 30 minutes before the guard arrived to relieve me. It was then I was told that the airfield was still surrounded by WWII minefields. The explosions could have been caused by an Arab or a camel stepping on a mine; or sometimes the mines went off following years of high daytime and freezing nightime temperatures.

We had a problem with drinking water. The Squadron was living in tents — our tent had its own live-in chameleon which kept the fly population down — and around the camp were water containers, which were filled by water bowsers from Tobruk. Unfortunately, one day a petrol bowser was used to transport drinking water, resulting in contaminated water throughout the camp. It was while at El Adem that the Salvation Army did so well with newspaper and magazine sales. Due to the non-availability of toilet rolls, the printed word was much in demand — but not necessarily for reading!"

At the end of the month a detachment flew to Malta for armament training. Sqn Ldr Maitland took another detachment to Maritza (Rhodes) and Crete on 20 April, returning to El Adem four days later where WR506/W belly-landed after its pilot had forgotten to lower the undercarriage. Between 6-9 May the Squadron took part in Operation Medflex Epic, operating from Takali with Meteors of 208 Squadron in the defence of Malta, before returning to El Adem. Many of the junior technicians who serviced and carried out first and second line repairs on the Squadron's aircraft were National Servicemen. The CO was very praiseworthy of their efforts, and told a visiting journalist:

"After a short training course these young men come to us for practical training and experience. They really are first class. Led by Regular senior NCOs and Warrant Officers, we absolutely depend on them."

On 8 July the Squadron was on the move once again, this time returning to RAF Eastleigh in Kenya, its home during the immediate postwar years. Staging via Habbaniya, Sharjah, Khormaksar and Hargeisa, the first four aircraft reached Eastleigh four days later. The others followed, Flg Off Waite being obliged to make a wheels-up landing at Nicosia en route due to undercarriage problems. A few days after arrival at Eastleigh, half the Squadron was detached to Sharjah in Trucial Oman to help quell a local uprising. Of these frequent moves, Cpl Byrne remembered:

> "From July through to November the Squadron spent periods in Aden, Sharjah and Nairobi. During these times we operated and serviced our Venoms in sandstorms and from the most basic airstrips with ourselves living in hangars, tents — in fact anything that had a roof on."

The moves inspired one Squadron member to compose a special song, usually sung with great gusto to the tune of the Eton Boat Song. The reference to 'pig' was the Valetta used to move the crews and kits but this duty was often undertaken by a Hastings or a Shackleton:

> "We're a gypsy squadron, moving in sunshine or rain;
> Soon as we hit a station, we're posted out again.
> All over MEAF, the bastards have made us roam;
> We've been all over MEAF, ain't we got no bleeding home?
>
> Ask how's our flying target, we must admit it's not big;
> How the hell can the pilots fly Venoms, with the groundcrew aloft in a Pig?
> If they'd build us an airborne airfield, we'd all have a bloody good do.
> We've more flying hours in than our pilots, if only Air Headquarters knew.
>
> Just a gypsy squadron we know, that we're here today;
> But where will we be tomorrow, where are we going to stay?
> Too late to change now, we're getting too set in our ways;
> Too late to change now, I'll be home before too many days.
>
> And when I'm back in Blighty, I'll be thinking of you
> Little band of gypsies, scattered all over the blue.
> All the days I'm living, for the wanderers life I'll pine;
> And if I turn a civvy gypsy, I'll blame it on 249."

Trucial Oman (formerly the Sultanate of Muscat and Oman), at the south-eastern corner of the Arabian Peninsula, had a long association with Britain dating back to 1835 but since WWII it had taken on a greater importance due to the oil potential of the region. In 1952, when the Saudis first took an active interest in the area, the Sultan called for British help. Detachments of RAF aircraft were flown to Sharjah and Masirah, but these could not prevent Saudis from entering Omani territory since force could not be used, as it was believed that support for the infiltrators was provided by the Arabian-American Oil Company (ARAMCO). By 1955 the anti-government Imam Ghalib-bin-Ali openly colluded with the Saudis, an action which caused the Sultan to despatch forces to his base at Nizwa. The Imam's brother escaped to Saudi Arabia where he formed the Omani Liberation Army (OLA), possibly with funds provided by ARAMCO. By June 1957 elements of the OLA had moved into central Oman and the Sultan again sought British help. As a result, detachments of Venoms from both 8 and 249 Squadrons were sent to Sharjah, as was a flight of Meteor FR9s from Malta, while two Shackletons of 37 Squadron from Malta were sent to nearby Masirah landing ground, their task to drop leaflets on rebel positions prior to cannon and rocket attacks by flights of Venoms.

Having reconnoitred the new theatre of operations from the comfort of a Shackleton, Sqn Ldr Maitland led the first operation on 28 July when he and Flt Lt Waterhouse carried out a closer inspection of the area over which they were to operate. The next morning (29 July) two sections of Venoms — the CO (WR531/R) leading Flt Lt Slade and Flg Off Clayton, with

Flt Lt Warden (Flight Commander), Flt Lt Waterhouse and Flg Off Jackson following a few minutes later — executed a strike against a fortified tower at Birkat al Mauz. Strikes, interdictions and armed reconnaissances followed on a daily basis, as the CO's logbook entries testify. Targets included desert forts and watch towers:

28/7 Venom WR531/R	Recce Nizwa area — Fort 1.40		
29/7 Venom WR531/R	R/p strike Birkat al Mauz — tower 1.45		
30/7 Venom WR531/R	Interdiction — M/T 1.40		
31/7 Venom WR506/W	R/p strike Baklam — castle 1.30		
1/8 Venom	Firq camp r/p strike 1.35 — huts		
1/8 Venom	Nizwa tower 1.30 — castle		
3/8 Venom	Interdiction 1.40 — tented camp		
4/8 Venom WR444/E	„ 1.35		
5/8 Venom WR439/V	„ 1.40		
6/8 Venom WR506/W	„ 1.35		
7/8 Venom WR531/R	„ 1.40		
8/8 Venom WR489/D	Close support with ACT* 1.25		
8/8 Venom WR506/W	„ 1.55		
9/8 Venom WR489/D	„ 1.45		
10/8 Venom WR504/Z	„ 1.50 R/p tower east of Firq		
10/8 Venom WR506/W	„ 1.45		
11/8 Venom WR489/D	„ 1.30 R/p tower west of Nizwa		
11/8 Venom WR489/D	„ 1.35 Tribesmen in wadi east of Firq		
12/8 Venom WR443/Y	„ 1.30		

Within a month of the incursion, OLA forces had occupied many villages in the Jebel Kaur area. It was to this area that the Venoms were sent and after a period of softening up from the air, ground forces moved in and occupied both Firq and Nizwa. Following the capture of these strongholds, the OLA withdrew to Jebel Akhdar where they presented less of a threat to the Sultan. By the time Sqn Ldr Maitland returned to Eastleigh in mid August the Squadron had logged almost 200 operational sorties against the Imam rebels, inclusive of operations flown on 13, 14 and 15 August as recorded by Flg Off Moyes:

13/8 Venom WR439/V	Firq rebel concentration in hill. Ricochet hit tail cone.
14/8 Venom WR560	Strike Gumbrah 1.30
15/8 Venom WR436	Ops — 8 R/p & 20mm 1.30

On 21 August a section of four Venoms overflew Muscat 'showing the flag', only to be called into action for one final strike five days later when Flt Lt Dodds with Flg Offs Lecky-Thompson, Purnell and Moyes carried out an R/p and cannon attack against rebel forces north of Birkat. Meanwhile, the Sultan's Army began an offensive against the OLA at Jebel Akhdar although the rebels were able to take the initiative and threatened to capture Tanuf, necessitating further operations by the Venoms. The CO had returned to Sharjah with two replacement pilots to relieve those who had been there for over a month, where he learned of the death of Flg Off Dave Elford who had been killed on 9 September when WR381 hit the ground and blew up during a practice rocket attack. Back on operations, Sqn Ldr Maitland recorded in his logbook:

18/9 Venom WR529/A	Recce Nizwa area 1.30	
25/9 Venom X	Cabrank Firq 1.45 Ops against rebel tribesmen	
26/9 Venom WR531/R	Cabrank Tanuf 1.35 „	
27/9 Venom WR398/H	„ 1.40 „	

---

* ACT — Air Contact Team; British forward air controllers working with the Sultan's Armed Forces responsible for calling in fighter strikes.

By 1 October, when the detachment was recalled to Eastleigh, the Squadron had flown a total of 242 operational sorties in support of the Sultan's forces. One aircraft had been lost in an accident and several suffered minor damage from ricochets. On arrival at Eastleigh rumours of the imminent disbandment of the Squadron as a day-fighter/ground-attack squadron were confirmed and, on 15 October 1957, 249 ceased to exist in that role. Ironically, the Squadron had just been awarded the Lloyd Trophy for the best all-round fighter squadron in the Middle East.

While the Squadron's peacetime fighter pilots, when called upon to go to war, had followed the fine examples set by their predecessors in WWII, thereby further enhancing the illustrious reputation of 249, the final word should go to one of the Squadron's stalwart groundcrew NCOs, Cpl Byrne:

"What should not be forgotten are the atrocious conditions the mobile groundcrews had to work under. Often as not we never had the luxury of a hangar — for the most part we had to work outside in remote dispersal areas where there was no cover from the relentless sun and frequent sand storms. The lower part of the Venom engine, guns and ammunition feed were barely above the ground which made maintainability a nightmare — sand got into everything — its a wonder anything functioned and in many respects this says a lot for British engineering. Most of the time we lived in tents or redundant hangarage. At Sharjah there was no proper airfield — just a strip of sand as a runway with the outer periphery marked out with old 50-gallon oil drums. Many who were there at the time will remember the antiquated water purifier that couldn't cope when 249 arrived, hence we had to resort to canned fruit juice in lieu of tea. Keeping the aircraft serviceable in these conditions was, to say the least, most difficult. Often we had to work around the clock. There were times aircraft became unserviceable or damaged and we had no spares — the rest of the Squadron moved on, leaving an NCO and relevant tradesmen behind to repair the aircraft as soon as possible, and then catch up by scrounging lifts on any routing aircraft."

Chapter Sixteen

BY CANBERRA TO DISBANDMENT

1957 – 1969

"It is very sad to me, with such a long association with the Middle/Near East area of operations, the running elephant will no longer be seen in Mediterranean skies . . ."

Air Marshal Sir Edward Gordon Jones KCB CBE DSO OBE DFC,
AOC-in-C NEAF, 24 February 1969

In 1957 the Air Ministry began re-equipping its MEAF fighter-bomber squadrons with the Canberra B2 light-bomber, having taken note of the criticism levelled against the obsolete Venom, although this time it was not simply a question of pilots and groundcrews converting to new aircraft as before, but a complete replacement of crews and aircraft; in effect, when the Squadron disbanded as a fighter/ground-attack unit it was immediately re-formed in its light-bomber role. 249's new Commanding Officer, Sqn Ldr R.J.W. Motley, wrote:

"On 6 August 1957, the Squadron commenced a separate re-equipment with Canberra B2 aircraft at RAF Coningsby, Lincolnshire with the intention of moving to the Middle East Air Force to operate in the light-bomber role. This second edition of the Squadron moved to Akrotiri, Cyprus on 16 October 1957. The Venom element formally disbanded on 31 October and were succeeded by the Canberra element."

The eight Canberras arrived at Akrotiri on 16 October, six in the first flight shortly followed by the remaining two:

WJ628	Sqn Ldr R.J.W. Motley; Flt Lt P.C. Stevens; Flg Off R.G. Sims
WJ564	Flg Off A.K. McLean; Flg Off S.W. Gravell
WH647	Flg Off D.D. Wyman; Flg Off J.A. Hawkins
WH655	Flg Off C. Westwood; Flt Lt A.J. Mayo
WK113	Flt Lt R.H. Gidman; Flt Lt J.M. Greenland
WJ626	Flg Off F. Newton; Flg Off R.F. Parrott
WH650	Flt Lt M.A. Noble; Flt Lt J.A. Wainwright
WH638	Flg Off E. Bates; Plt Off G.T. Gitsham

On arrival the Squadron discovered that the dispersal area allocated for its use was occupied by a Valiant detachment and would remain so until 6 November when the V-bombers departed for the UK. Of the groundcrews posted to the Squadron, one-third were old hands from the original 249, one-third came from other Canberra units at Cyprus, while the remaining third were posted direct from the UK. Of the total, only half were Canberra-trained. Akrotiri still lacked permanent buildings and, until these were built in the early 1960s, most RAF personnel remained accommodated in tents. The Squadron was particularly unlucky and had been allocated a piece of rocky ground on which to erect its tents, borrowing a pneumatic drill from the Royal Engineers to help in the task.

One of the Squadron's first tasks was to send a Canberra to Eastleigh for the purpose of collecting the Squadron Silver and other properties, Flt Lts Noble and Wainwright departing in WH650 on 18 November, staging through El Adem and Khartoum. The crew returned four days later with the hoard, plus a highly decorated aircraft courtesy of ground staff at Eastleigh who had been let loose with paintbrush and stencil, the Canberra's fuselage being adorned with numerous mini 'elephants' as recalled by SAC Jones:

"The instruction had been from Sqn Ldr Maitland that the 'elephant' should not be forgotten. That was the last we saw of the colourful Canberra." *

For the remainder of the year and into the early months of 1958 however, the Squadron suffered a number of problems with its aircraft, as typified by its state of serviceability in mid-January when WJ628 was shown as having been unserviceable since its arrival at Akrotiri in October; WH650, WH655, WH638 and WJ564 had been unserviceable for three days awaiting double oelo leg changes, while WK113 was troubled by a tailplane actuator fault, leaving just two aircraft available for training purposes. With most of its aircraft thus grounded, groundcrews were able to smarten their charges by painting the Station Crest (a flamingo) on each side of the tail fin, plus an adaptation of the Squadron's earlier markings — an elephant inset in a stylised Ashanti spear — on each wingtip tank.

New crews arrived for the Squadron during the early part of 1958 to replace those tour-expired, including those commanded by Flg Offs M.A. Hicks and T.E. Gill. With aircraft serviceability having been restored, detachments were sent at regular intervals to the El Adem bombing ranges where, on 29 August, Flt Lt Noble was obliged to carry out a wheels-up landing at night in WH655 when its undercarriage jammed; he and his navigator were unhurt but the aircraft suffered Category 3 damage to its airframe and also required a replacement starboard engine, but before long was cleared for duty although it did not return to the Squadron. The following month a replacement, WD995, arrived from Malta.

Despite the considerable forces now available to combat the EOKA terrorists, violence continued and saw mass demonstrations by Turkish Cypriots culminating in a clash with British troops resulting in the deaths of seven of the demonstrators. A chilling reminder of the frosty relations with the Soviet bloc was given to the Squadron in a MEAF memo at this time, which suggested that Cyprus would be a prime target in time of war:

"In the event of war it is expected the enemy will have a large, efficient and balanced force capable of striking at RAF Akrotiri by air, land and sea. The station would be a target for the employment of all types of modern weapons, including nuclear missiles. Paratroops could be dropped on or near the airfield by day or night. In the event of local uprisings and internal strife, sabotage and attacks by armed bands, with little or no warning, is to be expected."

Consequently, Squadron ground staff were organised into defence flights with specific duties should the need arise, but all were vigilant at this time anyway due to the ongoing EOKA situation. September saw an increase in assassinations and bombings following a brief cessation of violence, including a bomb explosion in a RAF canteen which killed two airmen and injured others. On 2 October, one of a pair of 249 Canberras which had just taken off for El Adem was recalled when it was feared that a bomb had been placed aboard. In the event, the aircraft was thoroughly searched and nothing was found. However, a solution to the crises was eventually forthcoming and hostilities came to an end in February 1959. Britain granted Cyprus independence† but retained sovereignty over two areas round Akrotiri and the Army base at Dhekelia, and the right to use military sites elsewhere on the island.

The Squadron suffered another landing accident, on 27 February 1959, at El Adem when the nose wheel of WJ628 became detached from the stub axle causing Category 2 damage. Flg Off Hicks and his navigator were unhurt. At this time, Sqn Ldr Motley wrote:

"In addition to the Squadron's primary operational role, it is in support of the Baghdad Pact countries along with 6, 32 and 73 Squadrons. Frequent flights are made to the Baghdad Pact

---

* However, some 20 years later at a BP Company Staff Conference, Roy Jones met Geoff Gitsham "who happened to have been a member of the new 249 Squadron and had helped to clean off our work . . . it cost me a round of drinks, even after 20 years."
† Cyprus became an Independent Republic on 21 September 1960 and six months later joined the Commonwealth.

countries, ie Pakistan, Iran (Persia) and Turkey [Iraq having left in 1959], where the aircrew associate with their national air forces, their personnel and officials."

In mid-1959, the Squadron was advised that it was to have a new role, that of target marking, and that it was to be re-equipped with the Canberra B6, as recalled by Flt Lt Jerry Turner, who had arrived in October of that year:

"At that time the Squadron was equipped with Canberra B2s and was commanded by Sqn Ldr Ray Motley. The following month saw the replacement of the B2s with B6s from 139 Squadron [a target marking squadron] at RAF Binbrook, together with half 139 Squadron personnel. The new CO was Sqn Ldr Doug Barfoot and our role changed from light-bomber to pathfinder."

Sqn Ldr Barfoot, the new CO, recalled:

"Once again 249's role departed from the routine. Not unusually, our tactical Air Force in the Med lagged behind the operational needs of the troublesome area; not only in supporting CENTO [Central Treaty Organisation, which superceded the Baghdad Pact] but national interests. Oil, its wealth and its control, sought-after by ambitious national leaders, further highlighted the need to update the capability of the Strike Wing. More suitable aircraft were a long way ahead; the updating of the Canberra to include nuclear and some tactical capability had to be speeded up. To determine which Canberra B2 squadron should be the first to re-equip with the B6, fore-runner of the B15/16, the Wing ran a squadron operational efficiency contest. Having been adjudged the winner, 249's euphoria was soon dampened by the realisation that the Squadron would take on yet another role — target marking, and that five crews including the CO and a flight commander from 139 Squadron, the last remnant of the Pathfinder Force, would replace an equal number of 249 Squadron crews."

Flg Off Bryan Montgomery, Flt Lt Turner's navigator, added:

"When the ex-139 Squadron personnel arrived to join us, there was a bit of an identity crisis and for a short while we were referred to as 12349 Squadron! However, this soon sorted itself out."

The CO continued:

"The demanding task of multi-role training was taken up: keenly, at gathering pace, the challenge of LABS*, rocketry, dive-bombing and the close team work of target marking, under limited light flares, was a welcome change from the routine of the immediate past. In addition, the cohesion of a mobile squadron, with its own aircraft and servicing crews, raised capabilities and *esprit de corps*. The operating capabilty of the Squadron improved progressively but instrumentation, navigation and weapons would have limited effectiveness under actual operations. We came to a high state of alert several times; once fully armed at cockpit readiness for night attack."

The Squadron began conducting trials and was soon able to carry out exercises in its new role in conjuction with the other Canberra units at Akrotiri, as recalled by Flt Lt Turner:

"The pathfinder role involved shallow dive-bombing and we very quickly learnt the new

---

* Low Altitude Bombing System (LABS) involved a high-speed, low-level approach to the target area, followed by a sharp pull-up into a loop, in the course of which a Red Beard tactical atomic bomb would be released (in time of war) to follow a trajectory to the target. The delivery aircraft meanwhile half-rolled out of the loop and dived to low level, clearing the target area in sufficient time to escape damage from the explosion.

technique both on the range at Akrotiri and at El Adem in Libya. The Squadron was still in tented accommodation at the dispersal and the aircraft had no hangars. They were painted silver with yellow tip tanks; previously the B2s had yellow tip tanks with an assengai and a shield with the elephant thereon. We used to fly the aircraft (each of us) about three sorties a week of two to three hours duration. Occasionally we did a five-hour cross-country around the Med, west of Crete, and back, and about every three months each crew would do a Lone-Ranger to RRAF Thornhill (now Gwelo) in Southern Rhodesia [now Zimbabwe], or Tehran, Ankara, Karachi, Aden or Kenya. We did several CENTO exercises to Peshawar in Pakistan, where we operated against the F-86 Sabre fighters of Turkey and Pakistan. Occasionally RAF Akrotiri was host to a fighter squadron, or a Canberra B(I)8 squadron from the UK, Aden or 2ATAF in West Germany. We would then try to attack Cyprus, with the fighter force defending. We finally moved into permanent (non-airconditioned) accommodation sometime in 1961, but the Canberras were always left out in the open."

Bryan Montgomery, added:

"In early 1961, [Flg Off] Hamish Harvey was posted into the Squadron. Shortly after, our crew was to do a Lone Ranger to Thornhill. We were to stage through Nairobi, and Hamish told us to be sure to say hello to a relative (I think it was an uncle) who was in the Kenyan Police. We called him up when we landed, and he turned out to be a high-ranking member of the force. On our way back from Thornhill, our aircraft unfortunately went u/s at Nairobi. We again contacted Hamish's uncle, who very kindly showed us around the local game-park and sites of Nairobi. All too soon our aircraft was repaired and we had to go back to Akrotiri."

In March 1961, the Near East Air Force (NEAF) was formed with its HQ on Cyprus (replacing the MEAF), and was soon called into action in July when Iraq, which had left the Baghdad Pact in 1959 and had not joined CENTO, threatened neighbouring Kuwait, which it claimed as part of its territory. Britain had an agreement with oil-rich Kuwait and two squadrons of Hunter FGA9s were despatched to nearby Bahrein while two 2ATAF Canberra squadrons were sent to Sharjah. Meanwhile, Akrotiri-based Canberras were also allocated targets in Iraq should hostilities break out, as recalled by Flt Lt Turner:

"At some stage in 1961, Iraq made threatening noises to Kuwait and we were down to two-hour cockpit readiness, with weapons we had never seen before in our bomb bays, and escape/survival packs for evading Iraqi capture, in our nav bags. Very exciting times, I seem to remember. In December 1961 the first of our B6s was returned to the UK to be replaced with the refurbished B16, strengthened for the LABS manoeuvre at low-level. Throughout my tour, all crews had nuclear targets to study and prepare for in the event of war with the Soviet Union. Each month a B6 would depart for the UK to be replaced by another B16 until all the Squadron aircraft had been replaced. Sadly, I left the Squadron in February 1962, so never had experience of the Canberra in the low-level LABS role. We were, in my opinion, the best of the Akrotiri Canberra squadrons: we always won the sporting competitions and the bombing tournaments. Morale was extremely high."

The Canberra B16 was very similar to the B6, having been updated with modified navigation equipment and weaponry; this included the Blue Shadow sideways-looking radar system and wing-mounted rocket pods capable of housing 72 2-inch rocket projectiles. The new radar system was not appreciated by the majority of crews, as confirmed by navigator Flt Lt K.G. Logan:

"The main problem was that you were looking at things that you were already going past and unless it was a very distinctive piece of coast it was often hard to determine what you were looking at. Some towns showed up but generally the results were considered so poor that most navs didn't spend too much time using the equipment."

Flg Off Montgomery added, with a touch of humour:

"One of its characteristics was that it only looked to starboard — consequently for it to be of any use to us we had to fly anti-clockwise round the Med! Even now the southern coast of Crete is imprinted in my mind! We never did work out what we would have done if we had to attack somewhere where all the salient points had been on our port side."

At the end of the year (1961) with the Kuwait crisis unresolved, the Squadron was ordered to send two aircraft, WJ774 captained by Flt Lt P.J. Wilson, and WJ782 commanded by Master Plt C.E. Saunders, to Embakasi (Nairobi Civil Airport) on standby as part of Operation Solamos, ready to fly to Bahrein should the need arise. They were joined early in the new year by the Squadron's B6 (WT374) flown by Wg Cdr G.J.C. Hogan DFC AFC, Akrotiri's Wing Commander Flying. However, the Kuwaiti Crisis did not develop into a shooting war and the detachment had returned to Cyprus by 16 January 1962. 249, along with others, returned to its training role, occasionally highlighted by Lone Ranger detachments and escort duties to flights of Hunters and Javelins staging through the Near East. Flg Off Montgomery recalled one of the off-duty pastimes:

"While they were not flying, some of the aircrew indulged in a pastime known as 'Splinge'. It was played on a volley-ball court just outside the crew room, and was loosely based on that game, but with very loose and wide interpretation of the rules, with net-pulling and lifting allowed, if not actively encouraged! No one knew the origin of the name, and we think it was peculiar to 249. Since Jerry [Turner] was well over six feet tall, and Dick Byfield (our other crew member) was also quite tall, we soon became the unofficial top crew — I contributed the weight!"

By April 1963 the Squadron had received its full complement of eight Canberra B16s. Training included the usual exercises carried out in conjunction with RN vessels operating in the Mediterranean, when crews were able to launch their R/ps at targets towed by obliging naval craft. Sqn Ldr Barfoot's period of command was coming to an end:

"One of the most rewarding highlights, in my recollection of my time in command, was the Squadron's second successive win of the Sassoon Trophy, competing against representative crews from all theatres operating Canberras. This success was followed by winning the inter-squadron sports event. Frequent detachments and Lone Rangers throughout the theatre: Malta, Tehran, Iran, NW Frontier and East Africa etc, combined with the holiday atmosphere of Cyprus at peace, added to the enjoyment for all Squadron members and their families. Undoubtedly, for many, the halcyon days of their service career. It was a privilege and honour to be part of the history of 249."

Sqn Ldr J. Ewan arrived in June 1963 to take over command of 249 vice Sqn Ldr Barfoot who was tour-expired. A number of new crews arrived about this time including Flg Off Barry Dove, a navigator:

"I arrived on the Squadron in August 1963 in the days when air trooping was done by British Eagle and the Britannia landed at Nicosia. There followed a very long ride (at least three hours) in an RAF 39-seater coach to Akrotiri, via all the hirings in Limassol to drop off families, before I was deposited in the car park behind SHQ where my baggage had been dropped off from a three-ton lorry. A phone call to the Squadron brought someone to take me to the Squadron and thence to the Officers' Mess.

The CO was Sqn Ldr Jamie Ewan and the Squadron had not had any new crews for some time. I think three new crews arrived in the summer of '63 and we came from a UK which was on the brink of the swinging sixties (the Beatles had had their first No1 and That Was The Week That Was was all the rage on Saturday night TV). I mention this because the swinging sixties had not quite reached Cyprus so we were looked upon with some suspicion by the old hands, particularly when [Flg Off] John Richards turned up at a Squadron function wearing a Beatles-style jacket without a collar!"

In February 1964, six Canberras were detached to RAF Sharjah to exercise airfield facilities and to familiarise air and groundcrews with operational conditions at that base. Flt Lt D.J. Foster with a crew composed of three navigators was the first to depart Akrotiri, on 10 February, followed next day by the remaining five aircraft led by Sqn Ldr Ewan. The ground party was transported by a Hastings. The following month saw a four aircraft detachment to RAF El Adem, again led by the CO. Flg Off Dove, who had teamed up with Flt Lt MacGregor, recalled testing the new Swedish Lepus flare, which was later adopted for use with the Squadron and was also used by RAF and RN Buccaneers:

"The WWII 4.5-inch flares were delivered straight and level from about 10,000 feet and coloured markers from a 30-degree dive attack which was known as Shallow Dive-Bombing! Due to the age and unreliability of the flare, the RAF was looking for something new. We were to test for the first time the Swedish flare at El Adem and flew only at night over several days. As far as I can remember the trial was a success although I do not recall that the Squadron was so equipped in my time. The Lepus was much brighter than the 4.5-inch (one million candlepower comes to mind) and gave a few nasty moments to the pilot of the marker aircraft. On at least one occasion, when under cloud cover, the Lepus on the end of its parachute started to gently oscillate, giving the pilot the sensation that the horizon was swinging from side to side! The flare casings were collected from the range each day for examination."

But it was not all work and no play, as suggested by another of Dove's recollections:

"I remember an occasion when, unusually, we had to spend the night on the Squadron as part of an exercise. Early next morning the CO decided that the aircrew should start the day with some PT rather than a lie-in. We were assembled with the exception of Flg Off Peter Harding and his crew (Flg Off Steve Saunders and Flt Lt Simon Wright) who had locked themselves in an office and refused to come out. The rest of us started to run around the Squadron dispersal which would not have been too bad had not the CO had us in formation, eg line astern, vic, etc, and to further add to our embarrassment kept calling formation changes! Word soon spread around the rest of the Wing, who were greatly amused by the spectacle, which took some living down. Peter Harding and his crew claimed that they were so sound asleep that they had not heard the CO hammering on the office door!"

This dispersal manoeuvre consolidated the nickname 'Biggles' on the CO! However, a change in command was imminent and, in August 1964, Sqn Ldr Ewan was succeeded by Sqn Ldr J.M.D. Sutton. For some time it had been felt at the Ministry of Defence that more of a fighter/ ground-attack mentality was required on the Akrotiri Wing rather than a 'bomber' approach and, as a result, the decision was taken to post in COs who had a fighter background*. Unfortunately, the same policy had not been applied to the staff of HQNEAF, whose members were almost wholly V-bomber orientated. This led to differences in outlook and some friction. Sqn Ldr Sutton recalled:

"Although the Wing still retained the traditional Canberra medium- bombing role, much more emphasis was to be placed upon attacks in formations with rockets and bombs at low-level. Nevertheless, 249 retained the commitment of identifying and marking targets at night for the remaining Canberra squadrons to bomb from medium-level. This was practised at El Adem range, some 500 miles away. Target marking was a fairly exciting affair involving two crews — during my time, my own and that of Flg Off David Coldicutt. We would orbit the target area at about 5,000 feet, trying to avoid each other while at the same time searching for the target under the hopelessly inadequate light given by the WWII 4.5-inch flares. Whoever saw the target first would immediately go into a 30-degree dive and lay the first marker. Other markers were then laid in different colours until one was actually on the target. Despite the

---

* Sqn Ldr Sutton's previous four tours had all been on fighters, one of them as a member of the Day Fighter Leaders School. The new COs of both 6 and 73 Squadrons were also former fighter pilots.

lack of a useable sight for this manoeuvre it was remarkable how accurate one could become with just a little practice.

The Wing also had a nuclear role for which we would practice the LABS toss manoeuvre. There were two types of toss: the forward throw and the more vertical over-the-shoulder release which was used when one had passed the pull-up point for forward-throw release. The change from forward to over-the-shoulder was by a pilot-operated switch. One of the practice venues was Episcopi Bay. From time to time a 28lb practice bomb from one of the squadrons would land in the orange plantation, positioned a couple of miles or so beyond the bay target. The reason, of course, was that the pilot had forgotten to change the setting when realising he had passed the point of pull-up for a forward-throw release."

The new CO led a detachment of five Canberras to RAF Idris at the beginning of September for LABS and low-level training but, as he describes, the detachment ended prematurely:

"Training had gone well and we held a Squadron party at the end of the first week. Like everyone else I had gone to bed quite late and it seemed had no sooner gone to sleep when I was awakened by the Duty Officer with a 'flash' signal from Headquarters. It was in code which meant going to the building being used by the Squadron and getting the code books from the safe. Rather stupidly I dressed in what was quickest to hand — the slacks and rather colourful shirt worn at the party — and rushed out without taking any form of identity. I was in the middle of opening the safe when accosted by an armed Libyan guard who spoke no English. That took just a little sorting out. The decoded signal ordered an immediate recall so I then roused the NCO in charge of our groundcrew and told him to prepare the aircraft for take-off at first light. It was immediately obvious that he wondered whether to take me seriously or not. After all, here was a new CO he hardly knew, dressed in a happy-hour shirt, having had a good party . . .!

We took off at first light and back at base learned that the 'Confrontation' with Indonesia, as it was called, required reinforcements to the Far East, and Akrotiri was involved in providing them."

Since December 1962 British forces had been actively involved in ground operations against Indonesian incursions into the neighbouring Crown Colonies of Sabah (North Borneo) and Sarawak, and the British Protectorate of Brunei. Anti-British President Sukarno of Indonesia had declared an unhealthy interest in these territories following the British proposal to incorporate them into a federation with Malaya and Singapore. Britain had airlifted troops to the area in response to an Indonesian-inspired revolt which broke out in Brunei, and detachments of Shackletons, Hunters, Javelins and Canberras were sent in support and these operated from Labuan, an island off the west coast of Sabah, and from Kuching in Sarawak, very close to the border with Indonesian Borneo. An Air Defence Identification Zone (ADIZ) was established along Borneo's Malaysian/Indonesian border in 1963 and was regularly patrolled by Hunters and Javelins based at Labuan.

"The Rules of Engagement applying to interceptions were amended to give pilots the authority to engage and destroy Indonesian aircraft overflying the ADIZ without first obtaining authority from the ground after a sighting. Some indication of the seriousness with which the threat [of invasion] was regarded was the order issued to 65(SAM) Squadron to bring one of its missile sections to immediate operational readiness and prepare to defend Singapore. Yet another deterrent to Indonesian air strikes was the presence of a number of V-bombers [Victors of 57 Squadron] at Tengah. On 29 March 1965, Indonesian anti-aircraft guns on the Riau island to the south began to fire indiscriminately on aircraft approaching and leaving Singapore. In addition Indonesia placed a total ban on flying over two of her islands, namely Bintan and Batam, with a threat to shoot down without warning any aircraft ignoring the ban." *

* See *Eastward* by Air Chief Marshal Sir David Lee GBE CB.

During a sortie in September 1964, two Indonesian Air Force C-130s penetrated Malaysian airspace and dropped almost 100 paratroopers and their equipment over Johore as part of a large-scale incursion by regular forces; one of the C-130s was lost during its return flight, apparently when trying to evade a pursuing RAF Javelin, while most of the paratroopers were wiped out by rocket attacks carried out by RAF Hunters, the survivors being mopped up by the Army. On another occasion a Javelin encountered an Indonesian C-130 head-on, the aircraft passing within a 100 feet of each other. The Javelin pilot reported that he was able to discern the clearly shocked faces of the crew. However, by the time the Javelin turned to engage, the C-130 had fled back across the border.

The Indonesians were known to have squadrons of Soviet-built MiG-17 and MiG-19 fighters, plus Il-28 and Tu-16 jet bombers. One of the latter was intercepted by a Javelin on the edge of the ADIZ, but it was not engaged. On another occasion a Hunter engaged a MiG-17 in an encounter in which neither pilot fired, but attempted to outfly each other. The RAF pilot considered he would have emerged the victor following a rolling pull-out from a high speed dive which the Indonesian pilot was apparently unable to perform without losing control. Although the Indonesians did use WWII-vintage B-25s and B-26s for low-level raids on villages close to the border, these intruders always managed to scurry back across the border before patrolling Hunters or Javelins could be called in.

It was into this scenario that detachments of Canberras from Bomber Command, 2ATAF and the NEAF were sent on a rotational basis. In May 1965 it was 249's turn to provide reinforcements, and Sqn Ldr Sutton took six aircraft on a seven-week detachment to Kuantan in Malaysia. To provide support for the detachment, three Britannias of RAF Transport Command conveyed a total of 87 air/ground personnel, plus equipment and spares. The Canberras, including two spare aircraft which were to remain at Masirah as back up, departed Akrotiri on 28 May and when they landed at Masirah all but one reported problems; however, six departed for Gan the following morning and all had reached RAAF Butterworth by 0618 on 30 May, including one flown by Flt Lt Joyce of 73 Squadron attached for the operation due to illness among the Squadron's pilots; the aircraft and captains were:

XH570 Sqn Ldr J.M.D. Sutton   WJ783 Flt Lt A.J. Baker
WT373 Flg Off R.R. Wood   WT303 Flg Off J.F. Fisher
WJ773 Flg Off D.A. Coldicutt   WJ780 Flt Lt R.L. Joyce

249's arrival allowed the Canberras of 16 Squadron to return to the 2ATAF. It was now the turn of the Squadron's crews to benefit from the opportunity to operate in a potentially hostile environment under warlike conditions. Sqn Ldr Sutton:

"Kuantan airfield consisted of a 2,000-yard jungle strip, surrounded by 200-foot-high trees — which concentrated the mind wonderfully when night flying — and an air-traffic building. All other accommodation was in tents which was excellent for communication; one simply stood outside and shouted. We took great care about our salt and fluid intake and, reasonably acclimatised from Cyprus, had no bother at all with the hot and humid conditions. The area had its own charm in other ways, too. One night I was rung by one of the guards on duty at the aircraft dispersal area. 'There is a tiger here', he said 'What should I do about it?' Fortunately the problem soon solved itself.

Although somewhat cut off in the jungle we were soon welcomed by the small, mainly planter, community in the local area and social life became surprisingly full. To return hospitality we decided to hold what perhaps could be described as a mini summer ball, but since it had to be held in tents with duckboard floors, activities were somewhat restricted, especially those of ladies wearing high heels."

Having acclimatised and reconnoitred the area, the detachment carried out exercises with the RAF Hunters and Javelins and RNZAF Canberras from Tengah in Singapore, and also with the RAAF Sabre squadrons based at Butterworth, as the CO remembered:

"We were pleased to find that we could easily out-turn any fighter but, of course, lacked any air-to-air armament."

Six of the Squadron's aircraft participated in Exercise Bush Ranger which commenced 22 June and lasted three days. The purpose of the exercise was to simulate war operations over North Borneo and, as some of the targets were close to the Indonesian border, it was considered prudent to descend early to ensure accurate navigation and thereby avoid antagonizing the Indonesians. Canberras operating in East Borneo refuelled at Labuan or Kuching, while those operating over West Borneo were supposed to return direct to Kuantan after completing their mission but most landed at Kuching. Three of the Squadron's six aircraft developed faults during the three days of operations: one returned with a faulty booster pump, the second with an unserviceable compass, and the third with unserviceable UHF, VHF and intercom. Sqn Ldr Sutton recalled:

"I remember one such exercise involved taking off for Borneo at about 0430, which meant laying our own flarepath with paraffin goose necks. The order from FEAF Headquarters — who were difficult to contact with the communications we had — had unhelpfully omitted to indicate the time zone they were referring to. Had it been Zulu we should have been getting airborne over seven hours too early, but after all the hassle associated with such an early departure, I was relieved to find that we had guessed correctly and the intended time was local."

While at Kuantan the Squadron received a new crew captained by Flt Lt Sulaiman-bin-Sujak, a Malaysian, of whose arrival the Squadron diarist recorded:

"It is a custom that a special welcome be afforded to new crews. Accordingly, Sulaiman and crew found themselves armed, kitted in jungle green and within five minutes of arrival despatched into the jungle supposedly to join up with the remainder of the Squadron and search for terrorists."

In July, while still detached to Kuantan, there followed a two-day exercise codenamed Scots Mist, when the Squadron flew six sorties using live rocket projectiles, firing at tank hulks, an enjoyable and rewarding experience for the crews although on one occasion they had difficulty in making contact with the FACs since two other controllers and two Meteors were transmitting at the same time as the Squadron's Canberras were running in to the target. On 15 July, Flt Lt Smith (who had arrived with a replacement crew) participated in a trial with Javelins from Tengah to test the capabilities of air-to-air missiles: the Canberra released a number of 4.5-inch flares at which missiles were launched. The trial was deemed successful. The detachment participated in two further exercises in late July: Exercise Kangaroo Tail called for two aircraft to simulate bombing and R/p attacks on the deployed Brigade Maintenance Area of the 28th Commonwealth Brigade, but a repeat attack the following day was cancelled owing to bad weather at Kuantan. Then, on 2 and 3 August during Exercise Gunex 3, four aircraft supported the Army in a simulated attack against RAAF Butterworth, and next day one aircraft tested the airfield defences. These sorties included co-ordinated strikes with Hunters of 20 Squadron and surface-to-air missile calibration trials.

There occurred one incident which might have involved the Squadron in an engagement with the Indonesians, as recalled by the CO:

"FEAF Headquarters seemed to plan for every conceivable operation except the one in which we very nearly became engaged. Suddenly they realised that two ships of the Royal Navy were approaching an area where they could be at risk from Indonesian fast patrol boats fitted with Styx anti-ship missiles. Late one afternoon from FEAF Headquarters came the cry: 'You are the night-marker squadron. Fit flares and rockets and devise tactics to meet such a threat which might have to be countered this evening.' Although it seemed that hurriedly cobbled together Rules of Engagement would restrict us to retaliation only, we nevertheless did our best to work out tactics which we thought would allow for patrol-boat manoeuvrability and, of course, we would have been helped by the phosphorescent wake in such waters. We got quite keen as the prospect of action approached, and were beginning to feel quite operational when issued with revolvers and a supply of Maria Theresa dollars which were supposed to solve all our problems should we have to bale out. In the event the threat did not materialise and we felt quite deflated when stood down."

Within days the detachment was advised of its imminent return to Cyprus, crews having gained much from the experience. They were to be relieved at Kuantan by 6 Squadron from Akrotiri.

"At Akrotiri the Squadron had developed quite a reputation for playing jokes on newly arrived visitors and this was successfully continued for those new crews who joined us at Kuantan. When we were due to return to Cyprus, the Headquarters there decided that we should leave our 249 aircraft at Kuantan for use by 6 Squadron, and we in turn would use theirs back at base. As it happened, all in-theatre transport aircraft had been grounded and 6 Squadron arrived at Singapore only to be told that they would have to complete the journey [to Kuantan] by road, which meant a rather uncomfortable eight or nine hours by bus or truck. Not unreasonably, they assumed this was all part of an arrival spoof by 249 and it was only with the greatest difficulty that they were eventually persuaded to board the vehicles."

Flt Lt Sulaiman-bin-Sujak travelled with the Squadron back to Akrotiri but there, on 30 September, he prematurely retired from the RAF and transferred to the newly formed Royal Malaysian Air Force, becoming its Chief of Air Staff a few years later.

By 1966, 249 was the sole remaining marker squadron in the RAF, the introduction of new targeting systems and weaponry making its role practically redundant. Sqn Ldr Sutton was due to hand over command of the Squadron on 8 October, his last act as Commanding Officer being to organise and preside over the presentation of the Royal Standard to the Squadron by, fittingly, Air Chief Marshal Sir John Grandy KCB KBE DSO, the Squadron's Battle of Britain CO and currently C-in-C Far East Command; of the occasion, Sqn Ldr Sutton recalled:

"The Standard Presentation is very much a squadron affair and consequently the squadron is given considerable say in how such a ceremony is to be organised. We were determined to celebrate in style and were wondering how to raise sufficient funds when one of the groundcrew — sadly I do not remember who — suggested that we run a charter flight from UK to Cyprus. He should have been promoted on the spot because the idea took off and was very successful. It happened to be the very time of the World Cup in the UK and we had no difficulty in filling 130-odd Britannia seats by family and friends out to Cyprus, and a similar number of football supporters on the return flight, repeating the process a fortnight later. There were times when I wondered whether I was running a squadron or an airline booking office but it was worth it. We netted over £1,000 — a great deal of money in 1966 — and were able to entertain royally at an all-ranks lunch and then have a ball in the evening."

Among the distinguished guests was Mrs Muriel Nicolson, widow of Wg Cdr J.B. Nicolson VC DFC, who had been flown to Cyprus for the occasion together with their son James. Another guest was the new Squadron Commander-designate, Sqn Ldr T.A. Hastings. The CO continued:

"It was a wonderful end to a most interesting tour and I handed the Squadron to Alan Hastings the next day. In doing so I was conscious that I had been more fortunate than Alan was likely to be. Although we had all fought hard to prevent it, a system of centralised servicing was eventually forced upon us by the Headquarters. Although I only had a few weeks' experience of it, it was already clear that, just as we had predicted, both flying hours and morale would be much reduced."

The new CO was also a former fighter pilot and had trained on F-86s in the USA, flown Sabres and Hunter F4s with the 2ATAF, Vampires as a QFI at RAF College, Cranwell, Hunters with the CFS, and Hunter GA11s and T8s plus Scimitars while seconded to the Royal Navy. He had been appointed to take command of 28 Squadron at Hong Kong but, before he could take up the post, the Squadron changed from Hunter FGA9s to Whirlwind helicopters, and he was duly re-posted, this time to 249.

The versatility of the Squadron's role remained impressive, namely: LABS nuclear-strike, reconnaissance, night-marker and night-strike; 'pop-up' bombing, medium-level bombing, shallow dive-bombing, and rocket-projectile. 'Pop-up' bombing required the target to be approached at low-level (i.e. 50 feet AGL at 420 knots) before a short climb to higher-level flight (i.e. 1,000 feet AGL at 420 knots) to allow the bombs to be dropped accurately, followed by a dive escape, but, as Sqn Ldr Hastings, commented:

> "Against un-alerted defences it would be fine — against alerted defences it would, or could, be suicide!"

A number of exercises were carried out, as recalled by the new CO:

> "Adex and Cypex were air defence exercises in which 249 Squadron simulated attacks against Cyprus. Shabaz were air defence exercises versus the F-86s of the Iranian Air Force for which 249 Squadron was based in Tehran (May 1967, November 1967 and again in May 1968). The Shabaz exercises produced some amusement when the Iranians accused the Canberras (the attacking force) of flying in excess of Mach 1.0 as a reason for the failure of their F-86s (the defending force) to intercept!"

Other events of note in the overall period were the introduction of night formation take-offs, attacks against splash targets towed by the Royal Navy to the south of Cyprus, and, at long last, the advent of the new Lepus flare for 249's night-marker work. The crews continued to fly Lone Rangers to various destinations. This involved single crews departing on Saturday and returning Sunday/Monday, and included flights to the UK, Malta, Gibraltar, Ankara, Tehran, Sharjah and Masirah. In addition, the Squadron as an entity was detached to Hal Far (Malta) in October 1966, and to Sharjah in February 1967; Sqn Ldr Hastings recalled:

> "During the February 1967 detachment, Flt Lt Ian Henderson (Flight Commander) and myself took a Canberra each and made the first ever Canberra landings on the coral strip at Salalah. These sorties proved the inadvisability of landing on such strips as every tyre on both aircraft had to be changed on return to Sharjah because of excessive cuts and slashes."

An amusing incident occurred when the Squadron attended a party held by Flg Off Brian Parsons to celebrate the christening of his first child. This was held just outside Limassol, as remembered by the CO:

> "After much champagne etc had been drunk (it was a Sunday), a corporal came puffing up to me with a written order to scramble the Squadron to Malta immediately. I looked at the boys and realised that this would be an act of lunacy as all were relying on their wives or girlfriends to get them in their cars to drive them home! So, for the first time in my life, I had to declare the Squadron non-operational until the next morning. In the meantime, 6 Squadron were deployed in our place — I never did find out what HQ thought of this!"

Six aircraft from all four squadrons of the Akrotiri Wing, led by Sqn Ldr Hastings, were detached to RAF Wyton in September 1967, there to participate in Exercise Unison with UK-based Canberras. It was only partially successful for the Wing detachment:

> "One observer did not screw in the 'safety break' multi-pin plug properly [which activated the armament circuits] and another navigator mis-selected bomb switches. Not a happy moment!"

However, the CO was much happier with the result of a navigation competition held the following month, in which the four squadrons of the Akrotiri Wing participated, when 249 emerged triumphant. This was followed by a fire-power demonstration on the Episcopi range for the benefit of visiting CENTO staff officers, in which the air aspects were planned and briefed by Sqn Ldr Hastings. In February 1968, the Squadron was again detached to Sharjah where it participated in a 50th anniversary of the RAF flypast on 30 March:

"A 249 Squadron formation flew by the tower, synchronising its arrival in sequence with Army helicopters, a Shackleton and an Andover. You can imagine the furrowed brows of the navigators in planning to accommodate the speed differences!"

In mid-1968 the runway at Akrotiri was closed for repair. Accordingly, the then current central servicing ground force was split into four and each squadron of the Wing was allocated its own personnel. Morale and serviceability soared and very few sorties were lost in the next four months or so even though the squadrons spent much time away from Cyprus. 249 initially went to Luqa, in July, where an amazing incident occurred on 26 August 1968. The CO was returning from Gibraltar and saw (from the air) a Canberra (WT369) seemingly parked, slightly askew and left wing low, in the dispersal area. When he landed he was told of the circumstances of this flight, as he recalled:

"Flt Lt Graham Chilvers had taxied out of dispersal and flown his sortie. On landing his left main undercarriage failed and collapsed. Initially he applied power to attempt to get airborne but he was too late and the aircraft fizzed across the grass area and came to rest exactly in the spot where it had started. The awaiting groundcrew ran for their lives, as did Chilvers and his crew once the entrance hatch had been jettisoned!"

The Squadron spent September 1968 at Nicosia, October back at Luqa and November at Sharjah. During the detachment to Sharjah, three pairs of Canberras went to Tengah via Gan in rotation on Lone Ranger exercises. They were looked after by 45 Squadron in Tengah and while there flew low-level sorties over Malaysia. These were Indian Summer times for the Akrotiri squadrons and saw them reach higher peaks of efficiency as well as causing incredulity amongst the advocates of centralised servicing. But the end was in sight for Akrotiri's Canberra squadrons.

It had been the intention to re-equip two of Akrotiri's squadrons with the TSR2 low-level, nuclear-strike bomber, and for the others to change to the fighter/ground-attack, but with the cancellation of the TSR2 programme it was decided instead to re-equip Akrotiri's Strike Wing with two squadrons of Vulcan B2s from the UK. The end came suddenly and, on 10 January 1969, a disbandment flypast by the Canberras was held. Sqn Ldr Hastings received a message from Air Chief Marshal Sir John Grandy KCB KBE DSO, then Chief of the Air Staff:

"My thoughts are with you on the occasion of the disbandment of 249 Squadron and the dispersal of the NEAF Strike Wing. I send you, and all members of the Squadron, sincere congratulations on your fine contribution to the achievements of this force. I have warm memories of both the Squadron Standard Presentation Day and my visit to the Squadron last year.

During your long service in NEAF you have well upheld the Squadron's tradition by adding to them and providing another excellent chapter in the proud history of 249. The disbandment of the Squadron is a sad day for you and for me. We have to adapt to changing circumstances. 249 has reached the highest in many roles in many theatres, both in war and peace, and the Squadron's stirring achievements will live, not only in the memories of those who served *Pugnis et Calibus*, but in the history of the Royal Air Force. I send best wishes to all members of 249 Squadron past and present — well done."

The CO immediately despatched the following message to Sir John:

"Your heartening message greatly appreciated by all members of 249 Squadron. I can assure you that, despite the disappointment of losing our fine Squadron, my ground and air crews will put the same efforts into their new tasks as they gave to 249, RAF Akrotiri and the Near East Air Force. The high standards set with 249 over the past years will give them the inspiration to seek similar standards of efficiency and morale with their new units. Nevertheless, if ever 249 re-form, the Royal Air Force will have an immediate pool of eager volunteers anxious to serve once more with *Might and Main* and hoping to see Lady Grandy and yourself at the ceremony. The Squadron sends best wishes to you both."

First to depart Akrotiri was 6 Squadron which began re-equipping with Phantoms at RAF Coningsby in mid-January; next, it was the turn of 32 Squadron, which disbanded on 3 February, followed by 249 on 24 February. The following message was received from Air Marshal Sir Edward Gordon Jones KCB CBE DSO OBE DFC, AOC-in-C Near East Air Forces:

"Today marks the end of an era with the disbandment of your illustrious Squadron. It is very sad to me, after such a long association with the Middle/Near East area of operations, the running elephant will no longer be seen in Mediterranean skies. The long and distinguished history of 249 is one of which I know you are all justly proud and I share that pride. Latterly you have distinguished yourselves as the specialist marker squadron of [the] Strike Wing, in addition to your other roles. In saying goodbye I would like to express the fervent hope that the famous Number 249 will be resurrected at some time in the future so that it may once more take its rightful place alongside other first-class squadrons of the Royal Air Force. Please give my warmest good wishes to all your officers and airmen and their families and congratulate them on a job very well done."

Sqn Ldr Hastings responded with:

"Your kind thoughts expressed on the occasion of the Squadron's disbandment have been much appreciated by all officers and airmen. We share with you hopes for our resurrection and the opportunity to give further service to the Royal Air Force and the Command with which we have been long associated. The Squadron sends best wishes to you and all at HQ NEAF."

A representative of the British Aircraft Corporation presented a solid silver model of a Canberra to the Station to commemorate the occasion. Thus, on that mild February day in 1969, 249 Squadron slipped quietly into the annals of the history of the Royal Air Force. Gone but not forgotten . . .

Pugnis et Calcibus

Gone but not forgotten . . .

Many members who had served with 249 Squadron sought to maintain their previous connections, enjoying occasional *ad hoc* gatherings until 1983, when ex-members of all ranks and trades who could be traced formalised an Association under the Patronage of Marshal of the Royal Air Force Sir John Grandy GCB GCVO KBE DSO. Wg Cdr Laddie Lucas CBE DSO DFC accepted the role of Chairman, while Sqn Ldr D.P.F. McCaig MBE AFC became Hon Sec/Treasurer. In 1995, Air Marshal Sir John Sutton KCB accepted the Presidency of the Association, with Wg Cdr Lucas as Vice-President.

Sqn Ldr Mac McCaig:

"The aim of the Association is to give practical form to the friendship and goodwill experienced through service with 249 Squadron, for all ranks and trades. This has been achieved with reunion gatherings on special or historic occasions, such as the presentation of a new Squadron badge to the RAF Club; and anniversary dates commemorating the RAF Battle Honours, Fighter Squadrons of Malta, the Battle of Britain, VE Day, VJ Day, and then, on 12 September 1997, the Grub Street publication of the Squadron's authorised history — *249 at War* by Brian Cull."

Appendix I

ROLL OF HONOUR

ENGLAND

16/7/40	Sgt A.D.W. MAIN		KinFA	Hurricane I	P2995
16/8/40	Plt Off M.A. KING		KinA	Hurricane I	P3616
7/9/40	Plt Off R.D.S. FLEMING		KinA	Hurricane I	R4114
18/9/40	Flg Off D.G. PARNALL		KinA	Hurricane I	V6685
27/9/40	Plt Off P.R.F. BURTON	(SA)	KinA	Hurricane I	V6683
	Plt Off J.R.B. MEAKER DFC	(Eire)	KinA	Hurricane I	P3834
10/10/40	Sgt E.A. BAYLEY		KinA	Hurricane I	V7537
30/10/40	Flg Off W.H. MILLINGTON DFC	(A)	KinA	Hurricane I	V7536
7/4/41	Plt Off R.E.N. WYNN		KinFA	Hurricane II	Z2663

MALTA

12/6/41	Plt Off R.H.McK. MUNRO	(Rh)	KinA	Hurricane I	Z4043
18/6/41	Sgt A. LIVINGSTON		KinA	Hurricane I	Z4048
17/7/41	Sgt M. GUEST		KinA	Hurricane II	Z2818
4/9/41	Plt Off G.V. SMITH		KinA	Hurricane II	Z3056
	Sgt J.C. KIMBERLEY		KinA	Hurricane II	Z3521
20/12/41	Flg Off B.M. CAVAN		KinA	Hurricane II	Z2418
	Sgt H. MOREN		KinA	Hurricane II	BV162
22/12/41	Flg Off R.H. MATTHEWS		KinA	Hurricane II	BV156
29/12/41	Flt Lt S. BRANDT		KinA	Hurricane II	BD834
	Flt Sgt R.W. LAWSON		KinA	Hurricane II	BE344
4/2/42	Plt Off J.G.K. HULBERT		KinA	Hurricane II	Z4003
	Sgt H.J. McDOWALL		KinA	Hurricane II	Z4016
9/2/42	Plt Off J.R.A. STUART		KinFA	Hurricane II	Z3526
24/2/42	Plt Off D.A. TEDFORD	(US)	KinA	Hurricane II	BG771
10/3/42	Plt Off K.N.L. MURRAY RAAF	(A)	DofW	Spitfire Vc	AB343
17/3/42	Flt Sgt I.M. CORMACK		KinA	Spitfire Vc	AB330
18/3/42	Plt Off H.M. FOX		KinA	Spitfire Vc	AB334
20/3/42	Plt Off D.C. LEGGO	(Rh)	KinA	Spitfire Vc	AB337
21/3/42	Flg Off J.C.M. BOOTH		Killed on ground (bomb)		
	Plt Off J.J. GUERIN RAAF	(A)	Killed on ground (bomb)		
4/5/42	Flt Lt N.C. MACQUEEN DFC		KinA	Spitfire Vc	BR226
9/5/42	Plt Off H.A. MILBURN		KinA	Spitfire Vc	BP845
14/5/42	Flt Sgt H.J. FOX RCAF	(US)	KinA	Spitfire Vc	BP878
17/5/42	Plt Off P.A. NASH DFC		KinA	Spitfire Vc	BP951
26/6/42	Flt Sgt M.E. TOMKINS		KinA	Spitfire Vc	BR382
2/7/42	Plt Off H. KELLY	(US)	KinA	Spitfire Vc	BR184
8/7/42	Flg Off J. SMITH		KinA	Spitfire Vc	BR233
	Plt Off J.C. GILBERT		KinA	Spitfire Vc	BR227
11/7/42	Plt Off C.B. RAMSAY RCAF	(C)	KinA	Spitfire Vc	BR111
12/7/42	Plt Off O.W.H. BERKELEY–HILL		KinA	Spitfire Vc	BR324
22/7/42	Plt Off J.H.R. PARADIS RCAF	(C)	KinA	Spitfire Vc	BR128
25/8/42	Flg Off R.P. ROUND RNZAF	(NZ)	KinA	Spitfire Vc	BP976
	Flt Sgt B. BUTLER RCAF	(C)	KinFA	Spitfire Vc	EN695
15/9/42	Flt Sgt B.C. PETERS		KinA	Spitfire Vc	BP867
4/10/42	Flt Sgt M. IRVING GASS		KinA	Spitfire Vc	EP700
	Flt Sgt G.A. HOGARTH RCAF	(C)	DofW	Spitfire Vc	BR379
15/10/42	Wt Off E.T. HISKENS RAAF	(A)	KinA	Spitfire Vc	EP340
16/10/42	Wt Off P. CARTER RCAF	(C)	KinA	Spitfire Vc	EP338
15/11/42	Sgt J.E. ROBERTS		KinFA	Spitfire Vc	EP199
6/1/43	Flg Off J.A.N. DAWKINS		KinA	Spitfire Vc	AB465
26/2/43	Plt Off A. NOTLEY		KinA	Spitfire Vc	AR559
11/3/43	Sqn Ldr M.G. MacLEOD RCAF	(C)	KinA	Spitfire Vc	EP519
20/3/43	Flg Off W.J. LOCKE RCAF	(C)	KinA	Spitfire Vc	BR345
9/4/43	Wt Off W.L. YAHOLNITSKY RCAF	(C)	KinFA	Spitfire Vc	BR131

BALKANS

17/11/43	Flt Sgt J.D. SHEERAN		KinA	Spitfire Vc	EF638
19/11/43	Flt Sgt K.L. DALE RCAF	(C)	KinA	Spitfire Vc	BP978

27/11/43	Flg Off A.J. SYKES RNZAF	(NZ)	KinA	Spitfire Vc	JL346
30/3/44	Lt M. McCARDLE SAAF	(SA)	KinA	Spitfire Vc	JK532
	Wt Off P.V. WADDELL RAAF	(A)	KinA	Spitfire Vc	AR596
6/4/44	Flt Sgt J.G. BELEC		KinA	Spitfire Vc	EF607
23/6/44	Flt Lt C.F. JACOBSEN RNZAF	(NZ)	Killed*	Spitfire Vc	ES299
4/7/44	Sgt R. PENNY		KinA	Spitfire Vc	LZ873
8/7/44	Flt Sgt R.W. TAYLOR		KinFA	Spitfire Vc	JK929
10/8/44	Flt Lt O.B. ANDREWS		KinA	Spitfire Vc	MA332
	Lt R. BRIGGS DFC SAAF	(SA)	KinA	Spitfire Vc	JK660
22/9/44	Flt Lt A.E. DRYDEN RNZAF	(NZ)	KinA	Mustang III	KH468
27/9/44	Flt Sgt E. RAY RAAF	(A)	KinA	Mustang III	KH476
19/10/44	Wt Off C.J.V. DAVEY		KinA	Mustang III	KH428
24/10/44	Lt H.K. RACHMANN SAAF	(SA)	KinA	Mustang III	HB941
30/10/44	Sgt H.G. PALLETT		KinA	Mustang III	KH437
2/2/45	Lt R.V. JACOBS SAAF	(SA)	KinA	Mustang III	FB308
1/3/45	Flt Lt J.R. MUIR DFC		KinA	Mustang III	HB851
16/3/45	Lt P.E. HILL SAAF	(SA)	KinA	Mustang III	HB859
29/4/45	Sgt E. RAMSBOTHAM		KinA	Spitfire IX	MH980

* Flt Lt C.F. Jacobsen RNZAF was shot down on 23/6/44 and was killed as a POW on an undetermined date.

PRISONERS OF WAR

10/2/41	Plt Off W.L. DAVIS			Hurricane I	V7171
29/11/42	Sgt W.D. WENDT RCAF*	(US)		Spitfire Vc	BR293
8/2/43	Flg Off G. NEWBERRY			Spitfire Vc	BR373
20/3/43	Flt Sgt K. BROWNE			Spitfire Vc	BP869
30/4/43	Flt Sgt D.E. CRUSE			Spitfire Vc	EP188
13/6/43	Sgt B.W. SHEEHAN RNZAF	(NZ)		Spitfire Vc	ER811
17/12/43	Flt Sgt W. DOCHERTY			Spitfire Vc	ES306
16/7/44	Flt Lt D. SINCLAIR DFC RCAF	(C)		Spitfire Vc	LZ822
2/12/44	Sgt F.J. WEED			Mustang III	KH472
26/2/45	Flg Off D.P.F. McCAIG	(Fiji)		Mustang III	HB912

* Sgt W.D. Wendt RCAF later escaped from captivity and reached safety, but was killed later in the war.

GROUND PERSONNEL KILLED ON ACTIVE SERVICE (possibly incomplete)

29/10/40	AC1 T.H. SAUNDERS, RAF North Weald
19/1/42	Cpl J. SMALL, RAF Takali
5/2/42	LAC A. ROBINSON, RAF Takali
1/3/42	AC1 G. WRIGHT, RAF Takali
13/3/42	LAC G. WHITE, RAF Takali

POST WWII – MIDDLE EAST

24/8/48	P2 C. PETERS	KinFA Iraq	Tempest F6	NX209
11/9/48	P1 A.McH. ROLLO	Died (illness) Iraq		
16/1/49	Flt Lt M.P. FISHER DFC	Died (illness) Iraq		
10/2/50	P2 R. WATSON	KinFA Iraq	Tempest F6	NX252
3/8/50	P3 C. FIRMIN	KinFA Cyprus	Vampire FB5	VV553
8/12/50	Plt Off W.L. BULL	KinFA Egypt	Vampire FB5	VV622
7/9/51	Sgt S. ZAGROBA	KinFA Iran	Vampire FB5	VX989
24/8/54	Flg Off L.C. WALTERS	KinFA Jordan	Vampire FB9	WR192
23/3/55	Plt Off D.L. SHELCOTT	KinFA Jordan	Venom FB1	WR472
9/9/57	Flg Off D.R. ELFORD	KinFA Oman	Venom FB4	WR381

Appendix II
COMBAT CLAIMS

(NB: The claims shown are those actually credited to 249 Squadron.)

ENGLAND (Hurricanes)

Date	Aircraft	Pilot	Claim
8/7/40:	P3615 GN-D	Flg Off D.G. Parnall	
	P3055 GN-N	Plt Off H.J.S. Beazley	½ Ju88
	P2995 GN-	Sgt A.D.W. Main	
		2 pilots/41 Sqn	
15/8/40:	P3123 GN-	Plt Off J.R.B. Meaker	Bf110
	P3055 GN-N	Flt Lt R.A. Barton	Bf110
			Bf110 damaged
	P3615 GN-D	Flg Off D.G. Parnall	
	P3855 GN-P	Plt Off H.J.S. Beazley	Bf110
	P3866 GN-	Sgt H.J. Davidson	
	P3656	Sqn Ldr E.B. King	Ju88 damaged
16/8/40:	P3576 GN-A	Flt Lt J.B. Nicolson	Bf110 probable
24/8/40:	P3055 GN-N	Flt Lt R.A. Barton	Bf109
	P3866 GN-	Plt Off R.E.N. Wynn	
2/9/40:	V6625 US-K	Flt Lt R.A. Barton	Do17
	P5206 US-L	Plt Off J.R.B. Meaker	
	R4229 US-J	Sqn Ldr J. Grandy	Do17 probable
	P2863 US-	Sgt J.M. Bentley Beard	
	P3384 US-	Plt Off P.R.F. Burton	Do17 probable
	P2988 US-	Plt Off H.J.S. Beazley	Bf110 probable
	V6559 US-	Flt Lt D.G. Parnall	Bf110 damaged
	V6559 US-	Flt Lt D.G. Parnall	Bf110
	P5206 US-L	Plt Off J.R.B. Meaker	Bf110
	P3579 US-Y	Sgt H.J. Davidson; pilot/72 Sqn	½ Bf110
	V6610 US-	Plt Off R.G.A. Barclay	Bf110 damaged
5/9/40:	V6635 US-	Plt Off H.J.S. Beazley	Bf109 probable
	P3667 US-	Sgt H.J. Davidson	Bf109 probable
	P2863 US-	Sgt R. Smithson	Do17 probable
			Do17 damaged
	V6614 US-	Sgt W.L. Davis	Do17 probable
	P3594 US-O	Flg Off P.H.V. Wells	Do17 damaged
			Bf109 damaged
	P5206 US-L	Plt Off J.R.B. Meaker	Do17 damaged
6/9/40:	R4229 GN-J	Sqn Ldr J. Grandy	
	V6635 GN-	Plt Off H.J.S. Beazley	Ju88
	V6534 GN-	?Sgt H.J. Davidson	
	V6614 GN-	?Sgt W.L. Davis	Ju88 probable
	V6610 GN-	?Plt Off P.R.F. Burton	Ju88 damaged
	P5206 GN-L	Plt Off J.R.B. Meaker	2 Bf109
	V7313 GN-F	Sgt J.M. Bentley Beard	Bf109
	V6559 GN-	?Flt Lt D.G. Parnall	Bf109 probable
	V6635 GN-	?Plt Off H.J.S. Beazley	Bf109 probable
	P3594 GN-O	Flg Off P.H.V. Wells	Bf110
	P3579 GN-Y	Plt Off R.D.S. Fleming	Bf110 probable
7/9/40:	V6610 GN-	Plt Off R.G.A. Barclay	Bf109
			Do17 damaged
	V7313 GN-F	Plt Off T.F. Neil	Bf109
	R4230 GN-	Sgt F.W.G. Killingback	Do17
			Bf109 probable
	V6559 GN-	Flt Lt D.G. Parnall	½ He111
	V6534 GN-	Sgt H.J. Davidson	Do17
			Bf109 damaged
	V6628 GN-	Plt Off H.J.S. Beazley	½ Do17
	P3594 GN-O	Flg Off P.H.V. Wells	He111 probable
11/9/40:	V7313 GN-F	Plt Off T.F. Neil	He111
	V6682 GN-	Sgt W.L. Davis	He111 probable
	V6559 GN-	Flt Lt D.G. Parnall	
	V6534 GN-	Plt Off W.B. Pattullo	He111
	P3579 GN-Y	Flt Lt R.A. Barton	He111 damaged
15/9/40:	V6656 GN-	Plt Off J.R.B. Meaker	Do17

	V6683 GN-	Plt Off R.G.A. Barclay	Do17 probable
	P3834 GN-	Sgt W.R. Evans	Do17 damaged
	V6656 GN-	Plt Off J.R.B. Meaker	Do17
			Bf109 damaged
	V6693 GN-	Flt Lt R.A. Barton	Do17 probable
	V6656 GN-	Plt Off J.R.B. Meaker ⎱	Do17 probable
	V6693 GN-	Flt Lt R.A. Barton ⎰	
	V6635 GN-	Plt Off H.J.S. Beazley	Do17
	V6680 GN-	Plt Off J.T. Crossey	Do17 probable
	P3615 US-G	Sgt G.C.C. Palliser	½ Do17
	V6683 GN-	Plt Off R.G.A. Barclay	Do17
			Do17 probable
			Do17 damaged
	V6622 GN-C	Plt Off T.F. Neil	1½ Do17
	V6617 GN-R	Plt Off A.G. Lewis	He111
			½ He111 probable
	V6566 GN-	Flg Off K.T. Lofts	½ He111
	V6559 GN-	Flt Lt D.G. Parnall	He111 probable
			Bf109 damaged
18/9/40:	V6617 GN-R	Plt Off A.G. Lewis	Bf109
	P3834 GN-	Sgt J.M. Bentley Beard	Bf110
	V6622 GN-C	Plt Off R.G.A. Barclay	½ He111
	V6693 GN-	Flt Lt R.A. Barton	He111 damaged
	V7313 GN-F	Plt Off T.F. Neil	He111 damaged
19/9/40:	V6622 GN-C	Plt Off R.G.A. Barclay ⎱	Ju88
	V6559 GN-	Flg Off H.J.S. Beazley ⎰	
26/9/40:	V6622 GN-C	Flg Off H.J.S. Beazley ⎫	
	V6683 GN-	Plt Off P.R.F. Burton ⎬	Do17 damaged
	V6614 GN-	Sgt G.C.C. Palliser ⎭	
27/9/40:	V6729 GN-T	Flt Lt R.A. Barton	Bf110
	P3615 GN-G	Sgt J.M. Bentley Beard	Bf110
			Bf110 probable
	V6617 GN-R	Plt Off A.G. Lewis	2 Bf110
			Bf110 probable
	V6566 GN-	Flg Off K.T. Lofts	Bf110
	V7713 GN-F	Plt Off T.F. Neil	Bf110
	V6614 GN-	Sgt G.C.C. Palliser ⎱	Bf110
	V6693 GN-	Plt Off P.A. Worrall ⎰	
	V6614 GN-	Sgt G.C.C. Palliser	Bf110 probable
	V6635 GN-	Plt Off J.R.B. Meaker ⎱	Bf110
	V6594 GN-	Sgt H.J. Davidson ⎰	
	V6559 GN-	Flg Off H.J.S. Beazley ⎱	
	V7713 GN-F	Plt Off T.F. Neil ⎰	Bf110 probable
	V6683 GN-	Plt Off P.R.F. Burton	Bf110 by collision
	V6617 GN-R	Plt Off A.G. Lewis	Bf109
			Bf109 probable
	V6622 GN-C	Plt Off R.G.A. Barclay	Bf109
	V6693 GN-	Plt Off P.A. Worrall	Bf109 damaged
	V6617 GN-R	Plt Off A.G. Lewis	2 Bf109, Ju88
	V6614 GN-	Plt Off W.H. Millington	Ju88
	V7313 GN-F	Plt Off T.F. Neil	Ju88
	V6622 GN-C	Plt Off R.G.A. Barclay	Ju88
			2 Ju88 damaged
	V6614 GN-	Plt Off W.H. Millington ⎫	
	V7313 GN-F	Plt Off T.F. Neil ⎬	Ju88
	P5206 GN-L	Sgt J.P. Mills ⎭	
	V6594 GN-	Sgt H.J. Davidson ⎱	½ Ju88
	P5206 GN-L	Sgt J.P. Mills; pilot/229 Sqn ⎰	
	P3615 GN-G	Sgt J.M. Bentley Beard	2 Bf109
			Do17 damaged
28/9/40:	P3615 GN-G	Sgt J.M. Bentley Beard	Bf109
6/10/40:	V6854 GN-W	Plt Off T.F. Neil	Do17 damaged
7/10/40:	V6692 GN-	Plt Off W.H. Millington	Bf109 probable
12/10/40:	P3615 GN-D	Sgt J.M. Bentley Beard	Bf109 damaged
15/10/40:	V7600 GN-	Plt Off R.G.A. Barclay	Bf109 probable
16/10/40:	V6878 GN-	Flt Lt K.T. Lofts ⎱	Do17 probable
	V6565 GN-	Sgt H. Bouquillard ⎰	

25/10/40:	V6854 GN-W	Flg Off T.F. Neil	Bf109 probable
	P3579 GN-Y	Plt Off P.A. Worrall	Bf109
	P3463 GN-L	Plt Off W.H. Millington	Bf109 probable
27/10/40:	V6854 GN-W	Flg Off T.F. Neil	Do17 probable
28/10/40:	V6854 GN-W	Flg Off T.F. Neil ⎫	
	V7677 GN-N	Plt Off W.H. Millington ⎪	Ju88
	V7600 GN-	Plt Off W.W. McConnell ⎬	
	V6561 GN-A	Plt Off A.R.F. Thompson ⎭	
29/10/40:	V7538 GN-T	Flt Lt R.A. Barton	Bf109
			2 Bf109 damaged
	P3463 GN-L	Sgt M.K. Maciejowski	Bf109
	V6692 GN-	Sgt G.A. Stroud	Bf109 probable
			Bf109 damaged
	V7677 GN-N	Plt Off W.H. Millington	Bf109 probable
	V6534 GN-	Sgt H.J. Davidson	Bf109 probable
30/10/40:	V6561 GN-A	Plt Off A.R.F. Thompson	Bf109
			Bf109 damaged
7/11/40:	V7676 GN-J	Flg Off T.F. Neil	2 Bf109, Ju87
	V6534 GN-	Sgt M.K. Maciejowski	Bf109
	V7677 GN-	Sgt G.C.C. Palliser	Bf109
	V7538 GN-T	Flt Lt R.A. Barton	Bf109 probable
	V6692 GN-	Plt Off R.G.A. Barclay	2 Bf109 probable
	P3463 GN-L	Flg Off P.H.V. Wells	Bf109 probable
	V6958 GN-H	Plt Off A.R.F. Thompson	Ju87 damaged
8/11/40:	V7677 GN-N	Plt Off P.A. Worrall	Bf109 probable
11/11/40:	P3579 GN-Y	Flt Lt R.A. Barton	FW58 (claimed as Ju86)
	V6534 GN-	Flg Off R.G.A. Barclay ⎫	
	V6693 GN-	Flg Off P.H.V. Wells ⎬	He59
14/11/40:	V6534 GN-	Flg Off R.G.A. Barclay ⎪	
	V6565 GN-	Sgt R.F. Smythe; pilot/46 Sqn ⎭	½ Bf109
21/11/40	V6614 GN-	Plt Off A.R.F. Thompson ⎫	
	V6728 GN-Z	Sgt G.C.C. Palliser ⎬	Do17 damaged
28/11/40:	V6855 GN-	Sgt M.K. Maciejowski	Bf109 probable
5/12/40:	V6614 GN-	Sgt M.K. Maciejowski	Bf109
10/1/41:	V6615 GN-B	Sgt M.K. Maciejowski	Bf109
4/2/41:	V7538 GN-T	Flt Lt R.A. Barton	Bf110
	V7538 GN-T	Flt Lt R.A. Barton ⎫	
	V6635 GN-	Sgt G.C.C. Palliser ⎬	Bf110
10/2/41:	V6565 GN-	Sgt G.C.C. Palliser	Bf109
	R4198 GN-	Sgt S. Brzeski	Bf109
	V6614 GN-	Sgt M.K. Maciejowski	Bf109
13/4/41:	Z2648 GN-	Plt Off F.E. Fayolle	Bf110 damaged

MALTA (Hurricanes)

3/6/41: night	Z4043	Sqn Ldr R.A. Barton	SM79
8/6/41: night	Z3063	Sqn Ldr R.A. Barton	BR20M
		Flg Off H.J.S. Beazley ⎫	
	Z4028	Plt Off G.C.C. Palliser ⎬	BR20M probable
9/6/41:		Sgt A. Livingston ⎫	
	Z4087	Sgt D.C.H. Rex ⎬	SM79
		Flg Off E.J.F. Harrington	SM79 damaged
		Sgt R.W. Lawson	SM79 damaged
12/6/41:	Z2397	Flt Lt T.F. Neil	MC200
			(claimed as Bf109)
		Sgt A. Livingston	MC200 probable
		Flt Sgt F.A. Etchells	Z506B
18/6/41:	Z4041	Plt Off G.C.C. Palliser ⎫	MC200
	Z4070	Sgt F.G. Sheppard RAAF ⎬	
		Plt Off R.H. Matthews	MC200 probable
8-9/7/41: night		Flg Off E. Cassidy	SM79
17/7/41:	Z3262	Sqn Ldr R.A. Barton	MC200
		Plt Off P.G. Leggett	MC200
		Flg Off C.C.H. Davis	MC200 damaged
25/7/41:	Z3492	Sqn Ldr R.A. Barton	MC200
		Plt Off F.C. Hill	MC200
		Plt Off R.H. Matthews	MC200
	Z2481	Flt Lt D.W.A. Stones; 5 pilots/185 Sqn	½ Z1007bis

17/8/41:		Plt Off J.K.H. Hulbert ⎫ Sgt D.C.H. Rex ⎭	SM84 (claimed as Ca312 floatplane)
4/9/41:		Sgt D. Owen	MC200
		Sgt J.G. Parker	MC200
	Z2794	Sqn Ldr R.A. Barton	MC200 probable
			MC200 damaged
		Plt Off R.H. Matthews	MC200 damaged
	Z3056	Plt Off G.V. Smith ⎫	
	Z3521	Sgt J.C. Kimberley ⎭	Z506B damaged
19/10/41:	Z3155 GN-	Sqn Ldr R.A. Barton ⎫	
	Z4005 GN-	Plt Off G.C.C. Palliser ⎭	SM81
22/10/41:	unknown pilot		MC202 damaged
22/11/41:	Z3764 GN-	Sqn Ldr R.A. Barton	MC202
	GN-	Flg Off C.C.H. Davis	MC202
	GN-	Flg Off C.C.H. Davis ⎫	
	BV156 GN-	Sgt A.T. Branch ⎭	MC202 probable
19/12/41:	GN-	Sqn Ldr E.B. Mortimer-Rose	Ju88
	GN-	Sgt A.G. Cairns ⎫	
	GN-	Sgt D.C. Skeet-Smith ⎭	Ju88 damaged
20/12/41:	Z3562 GN-	Plt Off G.C.C. Palliser	Ju88
			Bf109 damaged
	GN-	Flg Off J.T. Crossey	MC202 probable
	GN-	Sgt H.J. McDowall	MC202 probable
	Z2418 GN-	?Plt Off B.M. Cavan	Ju88 damaged
	BV162 GN-	?Sgt H. Moren	Ju88 damaged
	GN-	?Sgt R. Rist	Ju88 damaged
21/12/41:	GN-	Flg Off C.C.H. Davis	MC202 probable
	GN-	Flt Lt H.J.S. Beazley	Bf109 damaged
	GN-	Flt Sgt F.A. Etchells	Bf109 damaged
22/12/41:	BV156 GN-	Plt Off R.H. Matthews	Bf109
24/12/41:	GN-	Sqn Ldr E.B. Mortimer-Rose ⎫	
	Z2904 GN-	Plt Off G.C.C. Palliser ⎭	Ju88
	GN-	Flg Off J.T. Crossey ⎫	
	GN-	Flt Sgt F.A. Etchells ⎬	Ju88
	Z2904 GN-	Plt Off G.C.C. Palliser ⎭	
	Z2526 GN-D	Plt Off H.H. Moon ⎫	
		Sgt R.W. Lawson ⎭	Bf110 probable
26/12/41:	GN-	Sgt R. Rist; 3 pilots/126 Sqn	½ Ju88
	GN-	Flg Off C.C.H. Davis ⎫	
	GN-	Plt Off D.A. Tedford ⎭	Bf109 damaged
29/12/41:	GN-	Plt Off J.R.A. Stuart	Bf109
30/12/41:	GN-	Sgt D.C.H. Rex	Ju88
	GN-	Sgt H.J. McDowall	Ju88 damaged
3/1/42:	GN-	Plt Off J.K.H. Hulbert; pilot/126 Sqn	½ Ju88 probable
19/1/42:	GN-	Flt Sgt F.A. Etchells; 2 pilots/126 Sqn	½ Ju88 damaged
	Z3757 GN-	Sgt A.T. Branch	Bf109 damaged
22/1/42:	GN-	Flt Lt C.C.H. Davis ⎫	
	GN-	Plt Off D.A. Tedford; pilot/126 Sqn ⎭	½ Ju88 damaged
23/1/42:	GN-	Flt Sgt F.A. Etchells	Ju88 damaged
24/1/42:	BD789 GN-G	Plt Off H.H. Moon; pilot/185 Sqn	½ Ju88
4/2/42:	GN-	Flt Lt C.C.H. Davis ⎫	
	GN-	Sqn Ldr H.J.S. Beazley ⎬	Ju88 probable
	GN-	Plt Off D.A. Tedford ⎭	
22/2/42:	Z3761 GN-M	Plt Off H.H. Moon ⎫	
	BE583 GN-	Sgt A.T. Branch ⎬	Ju88 damaged
	GN-	Sgt A.G. Cairns ⎭	
	GN-	Sqn Ldr P.S. Turner	Bf109 damaged
	GN-	Plt Off D.A. Tedford	Bf109 damaged

MALTA (Spitfires)

10/3/42:	AB262 GN-B	Flt Lt P.W.E. Heppell	Bf109
	AB335 GN-F	Plt Off P.A. Nash	Bf109 probable
	AB346 GN-K	Plt Off J.A. Plagis	Bf109 probable
	AB343 GN-D	Flg Off W.R. Daddo-Langlois	Bf109 damaged
	GN-	Flt Lt N.C. Macqueen	Ju88 damaged
	AB262 GN-B	Flg Off G.A.F. Buchanan	Ju88 damaged
11/3/42:	AB262 GN-B	Sqn Ldr S.B. Grant	Bf109 probable
	AB335 GN-F	Flt Lt W.C. Connell RCAF	Bf109 damaged

14/3/42:	GN-	Flt Lt N.C. Macqueen	Bf109
	GN-L	Flt Lt P.B. Lucas	Bf109 damaged
			Bf109 damaged
15/3/42:	GN-	Flt Lt P.W.E. Heppell	Bf109 damaged
	GN-	Plt Off J.G. West RNZAF ⎱	Ju88 damaged
	GN-	Sgt J.L. Tayleur ⎰	
	AB346 GN-K	Flt Lt W.C. Connell RCAF	Ju88
17/3/42:	AB346 GN-K	Sgt V.P. Brennan RAAF	Bf109
	GN-	Sqn Ldr S.B. Grant	Bf109 damaged
	AB335 GN-F	Plt Off J.A. Plagis	Bf109 damaged
18/3/42:	GN-	Wg Cdr P.S. Turner ⎱	Bf109 damaged
	GN-	Flt Lt R.W. McNair RCAF ⎰	
	GN-	Flt Lt N.C. Macqueen	Bf109
	GN-	Flt Lt R.W. McNair RCAF	Bf109 damaged
	GN-	Sgt J. Berchamps	Bf109 damaged
	AB336 GN-	Plt Off R.H. Sergeant	Bf109 damaged
			Bf109 probable
	GN-	Flg Off N.W. Lee	Ju88 damaged
20/3/42:	GN-	Flt Lt R.W. McNair RCAF	Bf109
22/3/42:	GN-	Flt Lt N.C. Macqueen	Bf109
23/3/42:	GN-	Flt Lt N.C. Macqueen ⎱	½ Ju88
	GN-	Plt Off R.H. Sergeant; 2 pilots/185 Sqn ⎰	
	BP846 GN-	Plt Off J.A. Plagis	Ju88 damaged
24/3/42:	GN-	Flg Off G.A.F. Buchanan	Bf109 damaged
25/3/42:	GN-	Sqn Ldr S.B. Grant	Ju87, Bf109
	BP850 GN-	Plt Off J.A. Plagis	Ju87
			Ju87 damaged
	GN-	Flg Off N.W. Lee	Ju87 damaged
	AB264 GN-H	Plt Off P.A. Nash	Ju87
26/3/42:	AB335 GN-F	Sgt V.P. Brennan RAAF ⎱	Ju88
	AB344 GN-M	Flt Lt W.C. Connell RCAF ⎰	
	GN-	Flt Lt R.W. McNair RCAF ⎰	
	GN-	Flt Lt R.W. McNair RCAF	Ju87
	GN-L	Flt Lt W.C. Connell RCAF ⎱	Ju88
	GN-	Flg Off G.A.F. Buchanan	
	GN-	Flt Lt R.W. McNair RCAF ⎰	
	GN-	Flt Lt R.W. McNair RCAF	Ju88 damaged
28/3/42:	GN-	Sqn Ldr S.B. Grant ⎱	Ju88 probable
	GN-	Flg Off N.W. Lee	
	AB346 GN-K	Plt Off J.A. Plagis	
	AB264 GN-H	Plt Off P.A. Nash ⎰	
30/3/42:	GN-	Flt Lt N.C. Macqueen ⎱	Ju88 probable
	GN-A	Flg Off W.R. Daddo-Langlois ⎰	
1/4/42:	AB335 GN-F	Plt Off J.A. Plagis	Bf109
	GN-Z	Plt Off P.A. Nash	Ju88
	AB335 GN-F	Plt Off J.A. Plagis	Ju88
			½ Ju88 probable
	GN-	Sqn Ldr S.B. Grant	Ju88 damaged
	AB335 GN-F	Plt Off J.A. Plagis	Bf109
	GN-	Sgt R.B. Hesselyn RNZAF	Bf109
	GN-	Sqn Ldr S.B. Grant	Bf109 damaged
	GN-	Flg Off G.A.F. Buchanan	Bf109 damaged
	AB335 GN-F	Plt Off J.A. Plagis	Ju87
	BP844 GN-W	Plt Off P.A. Nash	Ju87
	GN-	Sgt R.B. Hesselyn RNZAF	Ju87
	GN-	Sqn Ldr S.B. Grant	Ju87 probable
			Ju87 damaged
	GN-	Flg Off G.A.F. Buchanan	Ju87 probable
4/4/42:	GN-	Flt Lt N.C. Macqueen	Ju88
	AB264 GN-H	Plt Off R.H. Sergeant	Ju88 damaged
	BP849 GN-U	Flg Off W.R. Daddo-Langlois	Ju88 damaged
8/4/42:	GN-	Plt Off J.G. West RNZAF	Bf109
			Ju88 damaged
	AB346 GN-K	Flt Lt P.W.E. Heppell	Ju88
	GN-	Plt Off D.W. Kelly	Ju88 damaged
	AB346 GN-K	Flt Lt P.W.E. Heppell ⎱	½ Ju88 probable
	GN-	Flg Off R. West; pilot/185 Sqn ⎰	
	GN-	Flg Off R. West	Bf109

Date	Code	Pilot	Claim
10/4/42:	GN-	Plt Off D.W. Kelly	Ju88
	GN-	Flt Lt N.C. Macqueen	Ju88
	GN-	Flg Off G.A.F. Buchanan	Bf109
	GN-	Flg Off N.W. Lee	Ju88 probable
			Ju88 damaged
	GN-X	Plt Off P.A. Nash	Ju87 probable
14/4/42:	AB342 GN-	Plt Off D.W. Kelly	Bf109 damaged
	GN-	Flt Lt N.C. Macqueen ⎱	Bf109, Bf109
	AB340 GN-	Plt Off R.H. Sergeant ⎰	damaged
20/4/42:		Sgt J.L. Tayleur	Ju87 probable
		Flt Lt R.W. McNair RCAF	Bf109
	GN-C	Flg Off W.R. Daddo-Langlois	Bf109
		Flt Lt R.W. McNair RCAF	Ju88 damaged
			Bf109 probable
		Flg Off R. West	Ju87
	1-L*	Plt Off R.H. Sergeant	Ju88 damaged
	2-W		Ju88
		Sgt R.B. Hesselyn RNZAF	Ju88 damaged
			Bf109
		Flg Off G.A.F. Buchanan	Ju88 damaged
		Flt Lt N.C. Macqueen	Bf109
	2-W	Sgt V.P. Brennan RAAF	Ju88
		Flt Lt P.B. Lucas	Bf109, Ju88
21/4/42:		Sqn Ldr S.B. Grant ⎱	Bf109 damaged
	AB263	Plt Off J.A. Plagis ⎰	Ju88
	AB263	Plt Off J.A. Plagis	Bf109 probable
			Bf109 damaged
		Sgt R.B. Hesselyn RNZAF	Ju87, Bf109,
			Bf109 damaged
		Flg Off G.A.F. Buchanan	Ju87, Ju88,
			Ju88 damaged
		Flt Lt N.C. Macqueen	Bf109
			Ju88 damaged
	2-W	Sgt V.P. Brennan RAAF	Ju88 probable
	BR190 2-A	Plt Off L.W. Watts	Bf109 damaged
22/4/42:	AB332 GN-N	Flt Lt R.W. McNair RCAF	Ju88
		Flg Off R. West	2 Ju88 damaged
	2-W	Sgt V.P. Brennan RAAF	Ju88 damaged
25/4/42:	2-E	Sgt V.P. Brennan RAAF	Bf109, Ju88
		Flt Lt R.W. McNair RCAF	Ju88, Ju87
			2 Bf109 damaged
26/4/42:		Sgt R.B. Hesselyn RNZAF	Ju87
			Bf109 damaged
1/5/42:		Flt Lt N.C. Macqueen ⎱	
	2-R	Plt Off L.W. Watts ⎰	Bf109
	2-R	Plt Off L.W. Watts	Bf109 damaged
2/5/42:		Flg Off G.A.F. Buchanan	Bf109 damaged
3/5/42:	BR184 2-C	Plt Off P.A. Nash	Bf109
		Plt Off H.A. Milburn	Bf109 damaged
	AB332 GN-N	Plt Off L.W. Watts	Bf109 damaged
4/5/42:	BR190 2-A	Sgt V.P. Brennan RAAF	Bf109
		Sgt R.B. Hesselyn RNZAF	Bf109 damaged
9/5/42:	BR109 C-30†	Plt Off P.A. Nash	Bf109
			Bf109 probable
		Flg Off G.A.F. Buchanan	Bf109 probable
	BR108 C-20	Plt Off P.A. Nash	Bf109 damaged
			Ju87 probable
10/5/42:	3-N†	Plt Off J.A. Plagis	Ju87
			Bf109 damaged
	BR108 C-20	Plt Off P.A. Nash	2 Ju87

* The Spitfires which arrived from the USS *Wasp* on 20 April 1942 carried an unusual form of coding, 601 Squadron's aircraft bearing the number '1' forward of the fuselage roundel on the starboard side, and a letter aft (1-A, 1-B etc), whilst 603 Squadron machines were marked with the number '2' and individual letter (2-A, 2-B etc). In the apparent rush to get the job done in time, it would appear that some machines were marked the opposite way round — letter fore, number aft. Some of these aircraft were flown in action by pilots of 249 Squadron.

† As with the previous delivery of Spitfires, those arriving in May 1942 also carried unusual codes — 'C' plus a number, '3' plus a letter, and '4' plus a letter. With little time available for repainting, these Spitfires went into action carrying such non-standard markings.

		Sgt V.P. Brennan RAAF	Ju87
			Ju87 damaged
		Flt Lt N.W. Lee	Ju87 probable
		Flg Off G.A.F. Buchanan	Ju87 damaged
			Ju88 probable
		Sqn Ldr S.B. Grant	Ju88
	4-N	Plt Off L.W. Watts	Bf109
		Sgt R.B. Hesselyn RNZAF	Bf109
		Plt Off E.L. Hetherington	Bf109 probable
		Flt Lt R. West	Bf109 damaged
11/5/42:	3-N	Plt Off J.A. Plagis	Bf109
		Sgt V.P. Brennan RAAF	Bf109
			Bf109 damaged
	BR107 C-22	Plt Off P.A. Nash	Bf109
		Plt Off C.B. McLean RCAF	Bf109 damaged
		Flt Sgt J.W. Williams RCAF	Ju88 probable
12/5/42:		Sgt R.B. Hesselyn RNZAF	Bf109
			Bf109 probable
		Flt Lt R. West	Ju88 probable
		Flt Lt R. West	
		Plt Off O.M. Linton RCAF }	Ju88 damaged
13/5/42:		Sgt R.B. Hesselyn RNZAF	2 Bf109
14/5/42:		Flt Lt R. West	Ju88
		Sgt R.B. Hesselyn RNZAF	Ju88
		Flt Lt R. West	
		Plt Off O.M. Linton RCAF }	Ju88 damaged
		Flt Sgt J.W. Williams RCAF	Bf109 damaged
		Flg Off G.A.F. Buchanan	Bf109 probable
	BP878	Flt Sgt H.J. Fox RCAF	Bf109
15/5/42:		Flt Lt N.W. Lee	S84 damaged
		Plt Off L.A. Verrall RNZAF	MC202
		Sgt J.C. Gray	2 Bf109 damaged
16/5/42:		Flg Off G.A.F. Buchanan	Re2001
		Sgt C.G.S. De Nancrede RCAF	Bf109 damaged
	BR176 C-25	Plt Off J.A. Plagis }	Bf109
	BR195	Plt Off P.A. Nash }	
17/5/42:		Flg Off G.A.F. Buchanan	Ju88
	BP951	Plt Off P.A. Nash	Bf109
		Plt Off L.A. Verrall RNZAF	Bf109
			Bf109 damaged
	BR176 C-25	Plt Off J.A. Plagis	Re2001 damaged
18/5/42:		Sgt J.C. Gilbert	Re2001
	BR176 C-25	Sgt V.P. Brennan RAAF	Re2001
		Sgt J.C. Gilbert	Bf109
		Sgt J.C. Gray	Bf109 probable
22/5/42:		Flt Lt R.W. McNair RCAF	Bf109
25/5/42:		Flt Lt R. West	Re2001
	BR176 C-25	Sgt V.P. Brennan RAAF	Re2001 damaged
		Flt Lt R.W. McNair RCAF	Bf109 damaged
		Sgt C.G.S. De Nancrede RCAF	Bf109 damaged
		Flt Lt N.W. Lee; pilot/126 Sqn	½ S84 damaged
6/6/42:	BR109 C-30	Flt Lt P.B. Lucas }	Ju88
	BR246 C-40	Plt Off F.E. Jones RCAF }	
	BR111 C-18	Plt Off O.M. Linton RCAF }	Ju88
	BR377 C-41	Flt Sgt B. Butler RCAF }	
	BR352 GN-W	Wt Off C.B. Ramsay RCAF	Re2001
	BR119 C-1	Sgt J.C. Gilbert	Re2001
	BR175 C-51	Sgt J.C. Gray	Bf109 damaged
	BR176 C-25	Plt Off L.W. Watts }	Z1007 damaged
	BR119 C-1	Sgt J.C. Gilbert }	
	BR107 C-22	Flg Off W.R. Daddo-Langlois	Re2001
	BR246 C-40	Plt Off F.E. Jones RCAF	Re2001
	BR111 C-18	Plt Off O.M. Linton RCAF	Re2001 damaged
	BR377 C-41	Flt Sgt B. Butler RCAF	Re2001 damaged
	BR175 C-51	Sgt J.C. Gray	Re2001 damaged
	BR109 C-30	Flt Lt P.B. Lucas	Bf109 damaged

Date	Serial/Code	Pilot	Result
10/6/42:	BR309 T-W*	Sgt J.C. Gray	MC202
	BR175 C-25	Wt Off C.B. Ramsay RCAF	Bf109 probable
	BR108 C-20	Flt Lt P.B. Lucas ⎱	Do24 damaged
	BR111 C-18	Plt Off O.M. Linton RCAF ⎰	
	BR176 C-25	Sqn Ldr S.B. Grant	Re2001
	BR165 C-23	Flt Sgt J.W. Williams RCAF	Re2001 damaged
	BR107 C-22	Flt Lt R.W. McNair RCAF	Bf109
12/6/42:	BR176 C-25	Sgt G.F. Beurling	Bf109 damaged
	BR254 X-G†	Wt Off J.D. Rae RNZAF	Bf109 damaged
15/6/42:	BR107 C-22	Flt Sgt J.W. Williams RCAF	Bf109 damaged
	BR251 C-26	Flg Off J. Smith	Z1007 damaged
	BR377 C-41	Flt Lt P.B. Lucas ⎱	Ju88
	BR254 X-G	Plt Off L.W. Watts ⎰	
	BR119 C-1	Plt Off F.E. Jones RCAF	Ju88
	BR111 C-18	Plt Off O.M. Linton RCAF	Ju88 damaged
	BR377 C-41	Flt Lt P.B. Lucas	Ju88 damaged
23/6/42:		Plt Off C.H. Lattimer RNZAF	SM84 damaged
		Sgt C.L. Baxter RAAF	Re2001 damaged
25/6/42:	EP117 T-A	Plt Off O.W.H. Berkeley-Hill	Bf109 probable
	BR108 T-W	Plt Off C.H. Lattimer RNZAF	Bf109
			Bf109 probable
27/6/42:	BR377 T-K	Wt Off J.D. Rae RNZAF	MC202
			MC202 probable
	BR184 T-C	Flt Sgt R.G. Middlemiss RCAF	MC202
			MC202 damaged
	BR295 T-H	Plt Off L.A. Verrall RNZAF	MC202
2/7/42:	BR379 T-V	Flt Sgt T. Parks RCAF	Bf109
	BR324 T-R	Sqn Ldr P.B. Lucas	Bf109 probable
	BR254 T-G	Plt Off J.F. McElroy RCAF	Bf109 damaged
	BR246 T-J	Sgt C.G.S. De Nancrede RCAF ⎱	½ Z1007 damaged
		3 pilots/603 Sqn ⎰	
	BR246 T-J	Sgt C.G.S. De Nancrede RCAF	Z1007 damaged
			Bf109 damaged
	BR251 T-E	Wt Off C.B. Ramsay RCAF	Bf109 damaged
	BR347 T-Z	Plt Off O.M. Linton RCAF ⎱	2 Ju88 damaged
	BR111 T-M	Plt Off B.W. Spradley RCAF; pilot/185 Sqn ⎰	
	BR295 T-H	Flt Sgt R.G. Middlemiss RCAF	Bf109
	BR170 T-B	Flt Lt W.R. Daddo-Langlois	Ju88
	BR324 T-R	Sqn Ldr P.B. Lucas	Bf109 damaged
	BR379 T-V	Flt Sgt T. Parks RCAF	Bf109 damaged
4/7/42:	BR324 T-R	Sqn Ldr P.B. Lucas	Z1007
	BR233 T-Q	Plt Off J.D. Rae RNZAF	Z1007
	BR170 T-B	Flt Lt W.R. Daddo-Langlois ⎱	Z1007
	BR295 T-H	Flt Sgt R.G. Middlemiss RCAF ⎰	
	BR111 T-M	Plt Off J.F. McElroy RCAF	Re2001 probable
	BR254 T-G	Flt Sgt L.G.C. de l'Ara	Re2001 damaged
6/7/42:	BR379 T-V	Flt Lt N.W. Lee ⎱	
	BR295 T-H	Flg Off J. Smith ⎰	3 Z1007 damaged
	BR111 T-M	Plt Off C.B. McLean RCAF	
	BR323 T-S	Sgt G.F. Beurling	
	BR379 T-V	Flt Lt N.W. Lee	MC202
	BR323 T-S	Sgt G.F. Beurling	2 MC202, Bf109
7/7/42:	AB562 X-R‡	Plt Off V.P. Brennan RAAF	Bf109
			Bf109 damaged
	BR324 T-R	Plt Off O.M. Linton RCAF	Bf109
	BR301 UF-S‡	Plt Off J.F. McElroy RCAF	MC202
	BR165 T-Y	Flt Sgt T. Parks RCAF	Ju88 damaged
	BR323 T-S	Plt Off J.D. Rae RNZAF	Bf109
	BP990 4-O	Sgt C.G.S. De Nancrede RCAF	Ju88 damaged
	BR347 T-Z	Flg Off E.L. Hetherington	Ju88 damaged

* BR309 was probably an incorrect recording of the serial number; this aircraft apparently did not go to Malta. Should possibly be BR109 although the code letters T-W were allocated to BR108, or perhaps BR379 although its code letters were T-V.

† BR254 X-G was a 603 Squadron aircraft; it was transferred to 249 Squadron and became T-G.

‡ AB562 X-R was an aircraft of 603 Squadron; BR301 UF-S was originally allocated to 601 Squadron.

Date	Aircraft		Pilot	Claim
8/7/42:	AB562	X-R	Plt Off R.B. Hesselyn RNZAF	Bf109
	BR128	3-W	Sgt G.F. Beurling	Bf109
	BR111	T-M	Plt Off J.W. Williams RCAF	Bf109 damaged
	AB562	X-R	Plt Off R.B. Hesselyn RNZAF	Ju88
				Ju88 damaged
	BR111	T-M	Plt Off J.W. Williams RCAF	Ju88
				Ju88 damaged
	BR324	T-R	Plt Off O.W.H. Berkeley-Hill	Ju88 damaged
	BR128	3-W	Sgt G.F. Beurling	Ju88 damaged
				Bf109 probable
	BR323	T-S	Plt Off C.B. McLean RCAF	Bf109 damaged
9/7/42:	BR301	UF-S	Plt Off J.F. McElroy RCAF ⎫	Ju88
	BR323	T-S	Plt Off J.D. Rae RNZAF ⎬	
	BR323	T-S	Plt Off J.D. Rae RNZAF	MC202 probable
	BR128	3-W	Plt Off J.R.H. Paradis RCAF	Ju88 damaged
	BR324	T-R	Plt Off F.E. Jones RCAF	Bf109 damaged
10/7/42:	BR128	3-W	Plt Off C.H. Lattimer RNZAF	MC202
				Bf109 damaged
	BR323	T-S	Sgt G.F. Beurling	Bf109, MC202
	BR324	T-R	Plt Off J.W. Williams RCAF	Bf109
	BR301	UF-S	Flt Sgt B. Butler RCAF	Bf109 damaged
11/7/42:	BR379	T-V	Sqn Ldr P.B. Lucas	Ju88 damaged
	BR301	UF-S	Plt Off A.S. Yates RAAF ⎫	Bf109
	BR111	T-M	Wt Off C.B. Ramsay RCAF ⎬	
	BR565	T-U	Flt Lt W.R. Daddo-Langlois	Bf109
	BR324	T-R	Plt Off F.E. Jones RCAF	Bf109
				Bf109 damaged
	BR110	X-C*	Plt Off J.R.H. Paradis RCAF	Bf109 damaged
	BR107	C-22	Flt Sgt T. Parks RCAF	Bf109 damaged
12/7/42:	BR565	T-U	Sgt G.F. Beurling	Re2001
	BR379	T-V	Flg Off E.L. Hetherington	Re2001
	BR565	T-U	Sgt G.F. Beurling	2 Re2001
13/7/42:	BR323	T-S	Plt Off J.D. Rae RNZAF	Re2001
				2 Re2001 damaged
	BR301	UF-S	Plt Off J.F. McElroy RCAF	Bf109
				Bf109 damaged
14/7/42:	BR301	UF-S	Plt Off J.W. Williams RCAF	Bf109 damaged
23/7/42:	BR301	UF-S	Sqn Ldr R.A. Mitchell	Ju88
	EP135	T-Z	Sgt G.F. Beurling	Re2001
				Ju88 damaged
	BR373	T-N	Flt Lt E.L. Hetherington	Ju88 damaged
	BR373	T-N	Flt Lt L.W. Watts ⎫	Bf109 probable
	BP976	T-C	Plt Off J.F. McElroy RCAF ⎬	
	BP976	T-C	Plt Off J.F. McElroy RCAF	Bf109 damaged
	EP135	T-Z	Plt Off R.P. Round RNZAF	Bf109 damaged
27/7/42:	BR301	UF-S	Sgt G.F. Beurling	2 MC202, Bf109
				Bf109 damaged
	EP196	T-M	Sgt H.G. Brydon RCAF	Bf109
	BP976	T-C	Plt Off J.W. Williams RCAF	Bf109
	BR301	UF-S	Sgt G.F. Beurling	Bf109,
				Bf109 damaged
	BP976	T-C	Plt Off J.W. Williams RCAF	Bf109
	BR301	UF-S	Plt Off J.D. Rae RNZAF	Bf109 probable
				Re2001 damaged
28/7/42:	BR373	T-N	Sqn Ldr R.A. Mitchell	Ju88 probable
	BR301	UF-S	Plt Off J.D. Rae RNZAF ⎫	Ju88 probable
	EP196	T-M	Sgt M. Irving Gass ⎬	
	BR301	UF-S	Plt Off J.D. Rae RNZAF	Ju88 damaged
	BP975	T-T	Plt Off A.S. Yates RAAF	Ju88 damaged
	BR131	T-O	Flt Sgt T. Parks RCAF	Bf109 probable
	BP869	T-K	Sgt V.H. Wynn RCAF	Bf109 damaged
	EP135	T-Z	Plt Off J.F. McElroy RCAF	Bf109 damaged
				Re2001 damaged
29/7/42:	BR301	UF-S	Sgt G.F. Beurling	Bf109
	BR131	T-O	Sgt A.E. Budd	Bf109

* BR110 X-C was an aircraft of 603 Squadron.

Date	Aircraft	Pilot	Claim
8/8/42:	BP975 T-T	Plt Off G.F. Beurling	Bf109
	BP867 T-E	Plt Off F.E. Jones RCAF	Bf109
	BR131 T-O	Sgt A.E. Budd	Bf109 damaged
13/8/42:	EP448 T-F	Flt Lt L.W. Watts	BR20 damaged
	EP448 T-F	Plt Off F.E. Jones RCAF ⎤	
	EP135 T-Z	Plt Off G.F. Beurling ⎬	Ju88
	BR565 T-U	Sgt V.H. Wynn RCAF ⎦	
14/8/42:	EP706 T-L	Flt Sgt E.T. Hiskens RAAF	Bf109 damaged
2/9/42:	BR529 T-D	Wg Cdr A.H. Donaldson ⎤	
	EP338 T-A	Flt Lt E.L. Hetherington ⎬	MC202
	BR373 T-N	Plt Off J.G.W. Farmer ⎦	
5/9/42:	BP867 T-E	Plt Off J.W. Williams RCAF	Bf109 damaged
	AR488 T-S	Plt Off K.C.M. Giddings	Bf109 damaged
16/9/42:	BR373 T-N	Flt Lt E.L. Hetherington	Bf109 damaged
25/9/42:	EP706 T-L	Plt Off G.F. Beurling	2 Bf109
			Bf109 damaged
2/10/42:	BR565 T-T	Flt Sgt L.G.C. de l'Ara	MC202 damaged
10/10/42:	EP706 T-L	Sqn Ldr M.M. Stephens	Bf109 damaged
	EP706 T-L	Plt Off G.F. Beurling	2 Bf109
	BR373 T-N	Plt Off J.G. Sanderson RAAF	Bf109
	EP708 T-U	Flg Off J.F. McElroy RCAF	Bf109
			Bf109 damaged
	EP706 T-L	Sqn Ldr M.M. Stephens	Bf109 probable
	EP199 T-K	Sgt A.B. Stead RNZAF	Bf109 probable
	BR498 PPH*	Wg Cdr P.P. Hanks	Bf109 damaged
	AR466 T-R	Sqn Ldr E.N. Woods	Bf109 damaged
12/10/42:	AR466 T-R	Sqn Ldr E.N. Woods	Ju88 probable
			Bf109 damaged
			Ju88 damaged
			Bf109
	EP199 T-K	Sgt A.B. Stead RNZAF	2 Bf109 damaged
	AB377 T-E	Sqn Ldr M.M. Stephens	Bf109
	AR488 T-S	Flg Off J.F. McElroy RCAF	Bf109, Ju88
	AB388 T-E	Sqn Ldr M.M. Stephens ⎤	Bf109
	EP199 T-K	Sgt A.B. Stead RNZAF ⎦	
	EP135 T-Z	Flt Sgt E.T. Hiskens RAAF	Bf109 probable
			Ju88
	EP338 T-A	Flt Sgt L.G.C. de l'Ara	Ju88 probable
			Ju88 damaged
	EP135 T-Z	Plt Off J.G. Sanderson RAAF	Bf109 damaged
	EP706 T-L	Plt Off J.L. Lowry RCAF	Ju88 damaged
	EP340 T-M	Plt Off J.G. Sanderson RAAF	Bf109 probable
	EP199 T-K	Plt Off A.S. Yates RAAF	Bf109 damaged
	EP338 T-A	Flt Sgt L.G.C. de l'Ara ⎤	Ju88 probable
	EP135 T-Z	Flt Sgt E.T. Hiskens RAAF ⎦	
13/10/42:	BR173 T-D	Plt Off G.F. Beurling	2 Bf109, Ju88
	AR488 T-S	Plt Off R. Seed	Bf109
			Ju88 probable
	AR466 T-R	Flt Lt E.L. Hetherington	Ju88 damaged
	EP338 T-A	Plt Off K.C.M. Giddings	Ju88 damaged
	EP135 T-Z	Sgt W.S. Shewell RCAF	Ju88 damaged
	EP338 T-A	Sqn Ldr M.M. Stephens	Ju88
	BR254 T-E	Sgt A.B. Stead RNZAF	Ju88 damaged
	AR466 T-R	Sqn Ldr E.N. Woods	2 Bf109
	EP135 T-Z	Flt Sgt E.T. Hiskens RAAF	MC202
	EP340 T-M	Flg Off J.F. McElroy RCAF	MC202 (claimed as Re2001)
	EP338 T-A	Sqn Ldr M.M. Stephens ⎤	MC202
	BR565 T-T	Flt Sgt L.G.C. de l'Ara ⎦	
14/10/42:	AR466 T-R	Sqn Ldr E.N. Woods	Ju88 probable
	BR565 T-T	Flt Sgt L.G.C. de l'Ara	2 Ju88 damaged
	AR466 T-R	Flt Lt E.L. Hetherington	Ju88 probable
	EP338 T-A	Plt Off K.C.M. Giddings	Bf109
			Ju88 damaged

* BR498 PPH was Wg Cdr Hanks' personal aircraft; Wing Leaders were allowed to personalise their aircraft in this fashion.

Date	Aircraft	Pilot	Claim
	BR254 T-E	Sgt H.G. Brydon RCAF	Ju88 damaged
	BR373 T-N	Sgt V.H. Wynn RCAF	Bf109 probable
	EP340 T-M	Plt Off J.W. Williams RCAF	2 Bf109 damaged
	BR173 T-D	Plt Off G.F. Beurling	2 Bf109, Ju88
15/10/42:	BR373 T-N	Sgt V.H. Wynn RCAF	Bf109
	EP135 T-Z	Plt Off V.K. Moody RCAF	Ju88
	EP340 T-M	Plt Off J.W. Williams RCAF	Ju88 probable
			Bf109 damaged
	BP966 T-V	Plt Off K.C.M. Giddings	Ju88 damaged
	AR466 T-R	Sqn Ldr E.N. Woods	Ju88 damaged
			Bf109
	EP338 T-A	Sgt A.B. Stead RNZAF	Bf109 probable
	EP448 T-F	Plt Off J.G. Sanderson RAAF	Ju88 probable
	BR373 T-N	Flg Off J.F. McElroy RCAF	Ju88
			Ju88 damaged
	BP869 T-E	Flt Sgt P. Carter RCAF	Ju88 damaged
	EP338 T-A	Sgt A.B. Stead RNZAF ⎫	
	EP448 T-F	Plt Off A.S. Yates RAAF ⎭	Ju88 probable
16/10/42:	BR565 T-T	Flt Sgt L.G.C. de l'Ara	Ju88
	AR466 T-R	Sqn Ldr E.N. Woods	Ju88 damaged
	EP448 T-F	Flg Off J.F. McElroy RCAF	Ju88 damaged
	EP201 V-F*	Plt Off J.L. Lowry RCAF	Bf109
	BR565 T-T	Flt Lt E.L. Hetherington	Ju88 damaged
	EP459 X-P*	Plt Off A.E. Budd	Ju88 damaged
	AR488 T-S	Plt Off J.W. Williams RCAF	Ju88
	BP869 T-E	Sgt V.H. Wynn RCAF	Ju88 probable
	EP488 T-F	Plt Off J.G. Sanderson RAAF	Bf109
17/10/42:	AR488 T-S	Plt Off K.C.M. Giddings	Ju88, Bf109
	BP866 T-Q	Plt Off R. Seed	Ju88 probable
	BR565 T-T	Flt Lt E.L. Hetherington	Bf109
	EP201 V-F	Plt Off A.E. Budd	Bf109 probable
19/10/42:	EP201 V-F	Flt Sgt L.G.C. de l'Ara ⎫	
	EP520 T-V	Sgt A.B. Stead RNZAF ⎬	Ju88
	EP199 T-K	Plt Off J.G. Sanderson RAAF ⎭	
22/10/42:	EP708 T-U	Flt Lt J.F. McElroy RCAF ⎫	
	EP201 V-F	Plt Off J.L. Lowry RCAF ⎭	Bf109
	EP199 T-K	Plt Off J.G. Sanderson RAAF	MC202
	BR529 T-D	Sqn Ldr E.N. Woods	Bf109 damaged
	EP520 T-V	Sgt A.B. Stead RNZAF	Bf109 damaged
			MC202 damaged
24/10/42:	BR565 T-T	Plt Off K.C.M. Giddings	MC202
			MC202 probable
	EP520 T-V	Plt Off J.W. Williams RCAF	Bf109
27/10/42:	BR529 T-D	Sqn Ldr E.N. Woods	Bf109 damaged
	AR466 T-R	Plt Off V.K. Moody RCAF	Bf109 damaged
	EP708 T-U	Flt Lt J.F. McElroy RCAF	Bf109 damaged
25/11/42:	EP708 T-U	Flt Lt R. Seed	Bf109 damaged
11/12/42:	ER622 T-P	Wg Cdr S.B. Grant	Ju52
	ER728 T-S	Flt Lt R. Seed	Ju52
			Ju52 damaged
	AR559 T-W	Sqn Ldr E.N. Woods	Bf110
	ER833 T-F	Flg Off J.J. Lynch	Bf110
			Ju52 probable
	ER728 T-S	Flt Lt R. Seed ⎫	
	BR373 T-N	Plt Off W.J. Cleverly ⎭	Bf110
	ER622 T-P	Wg Cdr S.B. Grant ⎫	
	EP132 T-J	Plt Off W.J. Locke RCAF ⎭	Bf110
	AR559 T-W	Sqn Ldr E.N. Woods ⎫	
	BS166 T-E	Flt Sgt J.C. Hughes RCAF ⎬	Ju88
	AB535 T-Z	Flt Sgt M.J. Costello RNZAF ⎭	
	AB535 T-Z	Flt Sgt M.J. Costello RNZAF	Ju52 damaged
13/12/42:	EP833 T-F	Flg Off J.J. Lynch ⎫	
	AB535 T-Z	Plt Off A.B. Stead RNZAF ⎭	Ju88 damaged

---

* EP201 V-F was a 1435 Squadron aircraft; EP459 X-P was a 229 Squadron aircraft. When 229 Squadron was resurrected from the disbanded 603 Squadron it took over the latter's letter 'X' code marking.

14/12/42:	EP140 T-M	Flg Off J.J. Lynch	
	BR373 T-N	Plt Off A.B. Stead RNZAF	Ju88
	EP201 T-L	Sgt W.J.B. Stark	
	AR559 T-W	Sqn Ldr E.N. Woods	
	EP708 T-U	Flt Lt R. Seed; pilot/272 Sqn	½ Ju88
17/12/42:	EP343 T-V	Flg Off J.J. Lynch	
	BR131 T-O	Flt Sgt M.J. Costello RNZAF; pilot/272 Sqn	½ Ju88
	EP343 T-V	Flg Off J.J. Lynch	
	EP140 T-M	Plt Off W.J. Locke RCAF; pilot/272 Sqn	½ Ju88
19/12/42:	EP728 T-S	Sqn Ldr E.N. Woods	Do24
	EP186 T-K	Plt Off W.J. Locke RCAF	
	BR373 T-N	Flt Sgt J.C. Hughes RCAF; pilot/272 Sqn	½ Ju88
24/12/42:	EP833 T-F	Plt Off J.G. Sanderson RAAF; unknown pilot	Bf110
7/2/43:	BR373 T-N	Flt Lt J.J. Lynch	
	EP519 T-C	Plt Off I.F. Kennedy RCAF	Ju52
3/3/43:	EP833 T-F	Plt Off B.J. Oliver RNZAF	
	EP343 T-V	Plt Off I.F. Kennedy RCAF	Ju88
	EP706 T-U	Sgt W.J.B. Stark	
20/3/43:	EP712 T-C	Flg Off D.A.S. Colvin	
	EP201 T-D	Flt Sgt J.C. Hughes RCAF	Bf109 damaged
25/3/43:	EP343 T-V	Flg Off I.F. Kennedy RCAF	
	BR110 T-A	Flt Sgt E.D. Kelly RCAF	Ju88
7/4/43:	EP829 T-N	Flt Lt J.J. Lynch	Ju88
16/4/43:	EP712 T-C	Flg Off I.F. Kennedy RCAF	
	BR565 T-T	Plt Off M.J. Costello RNZAF	Ju88
	EP188 T-Y	Plt Off B.J. Oliver RNZAF	
22/4/43:	AB535 T-Z	Flg Off I.F. Kennedy RCAF	2 Ju52
	EP829 T-N	Sqn Ldr J.J. Lynch	2 Ju52
25/4/43:	EP829 T-N	Sqn Ldr J.J. Lynch	Ca313
28/4/43:	EP829 T-N	Sqn Ldr J.J. Lynch	Ju52
	AB535 T-Z	Flg Off A.F. Osborne	
	EP829 T-N	Sqn Ldr J.J. Lynch	Ju52
10/5/43:	JK465 X*	Sqn Ldr J.J. Lynch	Z506B
			RS14 (claimed as Z506B)
			Ju52
			Me210 damaged
	AB535 T-Z	Flg Off H.C. Holmes	Z506B
21/5/43:	EP833 T-F	Sgt R. Keating	FW190 damaged
13/6/43:	ER811 T-J	Sgt B.W. Sheehan RNZAF	MC202
			MC202 damaged
	JK879 T-B	Plt Off D.E. Nicholson	Bf109 probable
29/6/43:	EP928 T-S	Flg Off J. Beatson RAAF	Bf109 damaged
13/7/43:	JK465 X	Sqn Ldr J.J. Lynch	FW190
22/8/43:	MA500 T-Z	Flt Lt K.L.B. Debenham	Ju88
27/8/43:	EN256 T-B	Flg Off K. MacBain RCAF	Ju88

BALKANS (Spitfires)

17/11/43:	EN256 GN-B	Flt Sgt K.L. Dale RCAF	Bf109
1/12/43:	JK366 GN-H	Flg Off J.W. Brooks RCAF pilot/82nd FS USAF	½ Ju52
2/12/43:	JK817 GN-Z	Flt Lt D.A.S. Colvin	
	JK625 GN-K	Flg Off K. MacBain RCAF	Bf109
4/12/43:	MA701 ENW†	Wg Cdr E.N. Woods	Ju87
	JK465 GN-X	Flt Lt J. Beatson RAAF	
	ES306 GN-T	Flt Sgt C.F. Jacobsen RNZAF	Ju52
27/4/44:	GN-S	Flt Lt J. Beatson RAAF	Fi156
26/5/44:	EF720 GN-	Sqn Ldr D.A.S. Colvin	
	JK678 GN-	Lt R.T. Whittingham SAAF	Hs126
	JK101 GN-U	Flg Off D. Sinclair RCAF	Hs126
	JK450 GN-	Flg Off J.H. Hingston	Hs126
	EF720 GN-	Sqn Ldr D.A.S. Colvin	
	JK678 GN-	Lt R.T. Whittingham SAAF	
	ES299 GN-	Flt Lt P. Quine	Hs126
	JL220 GN-	Wt Off A.G. Bowen	

---

* Apparently JK465 originally carried simply 'X' as its code but 'GN' was added at a later date.
† MA701 ENW was Wg Cdr Woods' personal aircraft.

30/6/44:   JK725 GN-   Lt R. Briggs SAAF   Ju52

BALKANS (Mustangs)
31/10/44:   KH427 GN-V   Flt Lt P.F. Noble RCAF ⎫
                    KH575 GN-Z   Flg Off J. Dickerson   ⎬   Fi156
                                                              ⎭

AIR-TO-GROUND CLAIMS:
18/2/41:   Sgt S. Brzeski   Bf109
19/1/42:   Sqn Ldr H.J.S. Beazley ⎫
                                       Flt Sgt F.A. Etchells ⎬   2 Ju88 probable
                                       2 pilots 126 Sqn   ⎭
8/4/42:   Flg Off R. West ⎫
                                       Plt Off H. Kelly ⎬   Do24 (on water)
27/8/42:   Plt Off R. Seed   Ju88
                                       Sqn Ldr E.N. Woods   MC202
                                       Plt Off J.W. Williams RCAF   Ju87 probable
                                       Sgt H.G. Brydon RCAF   Ju88 probable
                                       Sgt W.S. Shewell RCAF   Bf109 probable
                                       Flt Lt E.L. Hetherington   Bf109 damaged
8/6/44:   Lt R. Briggs SAAF   Hs126
21/9/44:   Flg Off T.H. Ashworth   Ju52
                                       Sgt A.W. Manning   Ju52
22/9/44:   Sqn Ldr J. te Kloot RAAF   2 Ju52
23/9/44:   Sqn Ldr J. te Kloot RAAF   3 Ju52
                                       2/Lt A.J. Malherbe SAAF   2 Ju52
27/9/44:   Flt Sgt C.N.V. Davey   FW190
                                       Flg Off D.P.F. McCaig   2 FW190 probable
28/9/44:   Sqn Ldr J. te Kloot RAAF   Ju52, He111,
                                                                                Italian aircraft,
                                                                                Gotha 242 damaged

                                       Flt Lt P.F. Noble RCAF   Ju52 damaged, Go242
                                                                                damaged, u/i aircraft
                                                                                damaged

15/2/45:   Sqn Ldr C.E. Edmondson RAAF ⎫
                                       Lt W. Shields SAAF   ⎪
                                       Flt Sgt A.W. Gordon   ⎪
                                       Flt Sgt D.A. Gardiner   ⎬   3 Ju52 damaged
                                       Flt Sgt P.C. Jones   ⎪
                                       Flt Sgt E.J. Clarke   ⎭

22/3/45:   Flt Lt T.H. Ashworth   ⎫
                                                                  ⎬   Ju88 probable,
                                       Wt Off R.N. Wheeler RAAF   ⎭   Bf109 damaged

24/3/45:   Flg Off E. Geddes   FW190, Ju88
                                       Lt A.J. Malherbe SAAF   FW190, u/i aircraft
                                                                               damaged

SCORE SHEET

	Destroyed	Probably Destroyed	Damaged
Aircraft (in the air)	328½	109	242
Aircraft (on the ground)	21	8	10
Locomotives	137	43	144
M/T	663	–	1079
Railway wagons	135	–	1091

In March 1953, the Under Secretary of State for Air, the Rt Hon George Ward MP made the following written statement to a question by the Rt Hon P.B. Lucas MP (Wg Cdr Laddie Lucas DSO DFC), who commanded the Squadron for a brief period in 1942:

"Mr Lucas had asked for the numbers of the three fighter squadrons which achieved the highest totals of enemy aircraft destroyed in all theatres and for the individual total of 249 Squadron.
It is sometimes possible to assess with some accuracy, after examination of enemy records, the number of aircraft destroyed in a particular campaign. I regret, however, that it is not possible to give official figures, as distinct from claims, for the total number of aircraft destroyed by any particular squadron or by any particular pilot. 249 Squadron claim to have destroyed 244 [sic] enemy aircraft during the war. This is one of the highest claims."

The above listing of 249 Squadron's claims would suggest the figure quoted of 244 was somewhat of an underestimate, and would appear to refer only to its Malta claims. In fact, 249 emerged as the top-scoring RAF fighter squadron of WWII.

To the above totals must be added the Squadron's air-to-ground claims during the 1956 Suez War: 30 destroyed, six probables and 15 damaged.

APPENDIX III

Officers Commanding 249 Squadron, 1918 – 1969

WWI

Maj E.V.S. WILBERFORCE	18/8/18 — 8/18
Maj J.E.B. MACLEAN	8/18 — 10/19

WWII

Sqn Ldr J. GRANDY	5/40 — 12/40
Sqn Ldr R.A. BARTON DFC	12/40 — 7/41
Flt Lt T.F. NEIL DFC+ (temp)	8/41 — 8/41
Sqn Ldr R.A. BARTON DFC+	8/41 — 12/41
Sqn Ldr E.B. MORTIMER – ROSE DFC+	12/41 — 12/41
Sqn Ldr H.J.S. BEAZLEY	12/41 — 2/42
Sqn Ldr P.S. TURNER DFC	2/42 — 3/42
Sqn Ldr S.B. GRANT DFC	3/42 — 6/42
Sqn Ldr P.B. LUCAS DFC	6/42 — 7/42
Sqn Ldr R.A. MITCHELL DFC	7/42 — 8/42
Sqn Ldr E.N. WOODS DFC	8/42 — 12/42
Sqn Ldr M.G. MACLEOD RCAF	1/43 — 3/43
Sqn Ldr J.J. LYNCH DFC+	3/43 — 7/43
Sqn Ldr E.N. WOODS DFC+	7/43 — 12/43
Sqn Ldr D.A.S. COLVIN DFC	12/43 — 5/44
Sqn Ldr J. te KLOOT DSO RAAF	6/44 — 11/44
Sqn Ldr C.E. EDMONDSON DSO RAAF	12/44 — 6/45
Flt Lt T.H.E.B. ASHWORTH DFC (temp)	6/45 — 8/45

POSTWAR

Wg Cdr H.J.D. MATSON AFC	8/45 — 4/46
Sqn Ldr D.C. DAVIES DSO DFC (Acting)	10/45 — 3/46
Sqn Ldr J.M.O. DYER DFC AFC (Acting)	3/46 — 4/46
Wg Cdr J.H. PLAYER DSO DFC	4/46 — 8/46
Sqn Ldr J.I. KILMARTIN DFC	12/46 — 11/47
Sqn Ldr P.F. STEIB DFC	12/47 — 10/48
Flt Lt R.P. FISHER DFC (temp)	10/48 — 1/49
Sqn Ldr J.R. BALDWIN DSO DFC (temp)	1/49 — 2/49
Sqn Ldr C. SCOTT – VOS DFC	2/49 — 10/50
Sqn Ldr R.J. BOULDING	10/50 — 4/53
Sqn Ldr J.R. GIBBONS AFC	4/53 — 6/54
Sqn Ldr E.C. GOUGH	6/54 — 5/56
Flt Lt D.M. DALLISON (temp)	5/56 — 6/56
Sqn Ldr J.R. MAITLAND DFC(US)	6/56 — 10/57
Sqn Ldr R.J.W MOTLEY	10/57 — 11/59
Sqn Ldr D.B. BARFOOT	11/59 — 6/63
Sqn Ldr J. EWAN	6/63 — 8/64
Sqn Ldr J.M.D. SUTTON	8/64 — 10/66
Sqn Ldr T.A. HASTINGS	10/66 — 2/69

Appendix IV

AWARDS

ENGLAND 1940 — 1941

VC	Flt Lt J.B. Nicolson (11/40)
DFC	Flg Off T.F. Neil (10/40), Plt Off J.R.B. Meaker (10/40), Flg Off R.G.A. Barclay (10/40), Sqn Ldr R.A. Barton (10/40), Flt Lt K.T. Lofts (10/40)
Bar to DFC	Flg Off A.G. Lewis DFC (10/40), Flg Off T.F. Neil DFC (11/40)
DFM	Sgt J.M Bentley Beard (10/40)

MALTA 1941 — 1943

DSO	Plt Off G.F. Beurling DFC DFM and Bar (10/42)
DFC	Flt Lt G.C.C. Palliser (1/42), Plt Off J.A. Plagis (4/42), Sqn Ldr S.B. Grant DFC (5/42), Flt Lt N.C. Macqueen (5/42), Flt Lt R.W. McNair RCAF (5/42), Plt Off V.P. Brennan DFM RAAF (5/42), Plt Off P.A. Nash (5/42), Flg Off G.A.F. Buchanan (7/42), Sqn Ldr P.B. Lucas (7/42), Plt Off R. West (7/42), Plt Off G.F. Beurling, DFM and Bar (9/42), Flt Lt N.W. Lee (9/42), Plt Off J.W. Williams RCAF (9/42), Flt Lt E.L. Hetherington (10/42), Flt Lt F.E. Jones RCAF (10/42), Flt Lt J.F. McElroy RCAF (10/42), Sqn Ldr R.A. Mitchell (12/42), Plt Off J.D. Rae RNZAF (12/42), Flt Lt R. Seed (2/43), Sqn Ldr J.J. Lynch (6/43), Flg Off I.F. Kennedy RCAF (6/43)
Bar to DFC	Sqn Ldr R.A. Barton DFC (10/41), Flt Lt J.A. Plagis DFC (6/42), Flt Lt R. West DFC (7/42), Sqn Ldr E.N. Woods DFC (10/42), Sqn Ldr J.J. Lynch DFC (7/43)
DFM	Sgt R.B. Hesselyn RNZAF (5/42), Sgt V.P. Brennan RAAF (8/42), Sgt G.F. Beurling (7/42), Flt Sgt L.G.C. de l'Ara (10/42)
Bar to DFM	Sgt R.B. Hesselyn DFM RNZAF (5/42), Sgt G.F. Beurling DFM (7/42)

BALKANS 1943 — 1945

DSO	Sqn Ldr J te Kloot RAAF (12/44), Sqn Ldr C.E. Edmondson RAAF (8/45)
DFC	Sqn Ldr D.A.S. Colvin (5/44), Flt Lt J. Beatson RAAF (7/44), Flt Lt K. McBain RCAF (9/44), Wt Off J.S. Simmons (9/44), Flt Lt D. Sinclair RCAF (10/44), Capt R.T. Whittingham SAAF (10/44), Wt Off E. Davison (1/45), Flg Off G.C. Nichols (5/45), Lt R. Briggs SAAF (6/45, deceased), Flt Lt T.H.E.B. Ashworth (8/45), Flt Lt J.R. Muir (10/45, deceased)
DFM	Flt Sgt W.M. Monkman RCAF (3/45), Flt Sgt T.D. Finlay (8/45), Sgt A.W. Manning (2/46)

NB: Decorations were awarded to several former 249 pilots after they had left the Squadron, which invariably reflected their earlier service with 249; these included Sqn Ldr J. Grandy (DSO), Sqn Ldr H.J.S. Beazley (DFC); Sqn Ldr P.H.V. Wells (DSO), Sqn Ldr A.R.F. Thompson (DFC), Sqn Ldr E. Cassidy (DFC), and Sgt M.K. Maciejowski (DFM). Postwar, Sqn Ldr T.S. Syme, who served with 249 as a Flight Commander at the time of Suez (1956), was awarded the DFC in 1957 following further operations as CO of 8 Squadron.

Appendix V

SQUADRON BASES

August 1918	RNAS Dundee	March 1919	RNAS Killingholme

Disbanded 10/19

Re-formed

16 May 1940	RAF Church Fenton	30 June 1946	RAF Habbaniya, Iraq
18 May 1940	RAF Leconfield	29 March 1949	RAF Deversoir, Egypt
9 July 1940	RAF Church Fenton	28 June 1949	RAF Nicosia, Cyprus
14 July 1940	RAE Boscombe Down	8 August 1949	RAF Deversoir, Egypt
1 September 1940	RAF North Weald	July 1951	RAF Shaibah, Iraq
21 May 1941	RAF Takali, Malta	October 1951	RAF Deversoir, Egypt
23 November 1942	RAF Qrendi, Malta	October 1954	RAF Amman, Jordan
25 September 1943	RAF Hal Far, Malta	August 1956	RAF Akrotiri, Cyprus
22 October 1943	Grottaglie, Italy	March — October 1957	RAF El Adem, Libya
10 November 1943	Brindisi, Italy	(Venom element)	RAF Takali, Malta
10 December 1943	Grottaglie, Italy		RAF Eastleigh, Kenya
15 July 1944	Canne, Italy		RAF Sharjah, Trucial Oman
18 April 1945	Prkos, Yugoslavia		
16 May 1945	Biferno, Italy	6 August 1957	
30 June 1945	Brindisi, Italy	(Canberra element)	RAF Coningsby
6 October 1945	RAF Eastleigh, Kenya	16 October 1957	RAF Akrotiri, Cyprus

Disbanded 24/2/69

Appendix VI

Aircraft flown by 249 Squadron included:

SCOTLAND 1918 – 1919
Short S184 including N1276, N1661, N1831
Sopwith Baby including N1197

ENGLAND 1940 – 1941
Spitfire Is delivered 18-20 May 1940 were P9311, P9332 (GN-D), P9335-9336, P9380-9381, P9423-9424, P9468, P9491, P9493-9494, P9505-9508, P9510-9513

Hurricane Is delivered June-August 1940 included L1595, L1715, L1832, L1998, L2067, N2351, N2386, N2434, N2597, P2910 (GN-J), P2995, P3055, P3057, P3088 (GN-C), P3123, P3154 (GN-H), P3421, P3576 (GN-A), P3615 (GN-D), P3616 (GN-F), P3656, P3660, P3855, P3862, P3866, P3868, P3870, P3902, V6625

Hurricane Is handed over to 56 Sqn on 1 September 1940 believed to have included L1595, L1832, L1998, N2386, N2434, N2597, P2910 (GN-J), P3055 (GN-N), P3123, P3154, P3421, P3660, P3855 (GN-P), P3866, P3868, P3870, P3902, V6625 (which included GN-M, GN-O, GN-V, GN-W)

Hurricane Is inherited from 56 Sqn on 1 September 1940 believed to have included N2440 (US-N/GN-N), P2863, P2988, P3384, P3579 (US-Y/GN-Y), P3594 (US-O), P3667, P5206, R4114, R4229 (US-J), R4230, V6534, V6561, V6574, V6610, V6615, V6625 (US-K), V7352

Hurricane Is received September 1940 onwards included P3834, P3868, P3870, V6559, V6566, V6582, V6614, V6617 (GN-R), V6622, V6635, V6680, V6682, V6683, V6685, V6692, V6693, V6694, V6728 (GN-Z), V6729 (GN-U), V6798, V7313 (GN-F), V7409, V7507 (GN-B), V7536, V7537, V7538 (GN-T), V7600, V7627, V7676 (GN-J), V7677 (GN-N)

Hurricane IIs received March 1941 onwards included Z2349 (GN-O); Z2388, Z2389, Z2409 (GN-L), Z2410, Z2411, Z2450, Z2521, Z2522, Z2577, Z2578, Z2579, Z2638 (GN-W), Z2639 (GN-P), Z2640 (GN-C), Z2663 (GN-O), Z2684, Z2685, Z2695, Z2744 (GN-I), Z2892, Z2893, Z2912, Z3026, Z3027, Z3081, Z3084, Z3097, Z3148, Z3170, Z3174, Z3176, Z3239

MALTA 1941-1942
Hurricane Is/IIs (recorded as having been flown by 249 pilots at Malta, 1941/1942) included V6629, V7103, V7732, V7747, V7797, Z2349, Z2388, Z2395, Z2397, Z2411, Z2414, Z2418, Z2455, Z2481, Z2491, Z2522, Z2526 (GN-D), Z2527, Z2578, Z2639, Z2663, Z2665, Z2678 (GN-E), Z2680, Z2684, Z2698, Z2794, Z2818, Z2825, Z2829, Z2904, Z2941, Z2961, Z2981, Z3033, Z3056, Z3063, Z3148, Z3155, Z3176, Z3262, Z3452 (GN-B), Z3453, Z3462, Z3492, Z3495, Z3498, Z3505, Z3521, Z3526, Z3562, Z3570, Z3580, Z3730, Z3757, Z3746, Z3761 (GN-M), Z3993 (GN-T), Z4002 (GN-M), Z4003 (GN-S), Z4005, Z4016, Z4025, Z4028, Z4041, Z4043, Z4048, Z4058, Z4060, Z4068, Z4070, Z4087, Z4315, Z4354, Z4380, Z4385, Z4389, Z4428, Z4502, Z4507, Z4941, Z5140 (GN-A), Z5149 (GN-C), BD703, BD789 (GN-G), BD834, BE344, BE583, BG771, BP612 (GN-H), BP615, BP618 (element of doubt regarding latter three), BV156, BV162, BV163, BV171, BV173, BV174

MALTA 1942 — 1943
Spitfire Vs (initial delivery, 7/3/42) were AB262 (GN-B), AB264 (GN-H), AB329, AB330, AB331, AB332 (GN-N), AB334 (GN-J), AB335 (GN-F), AB336, AB337, AB338, AB341 (GN-E), AB343, AB344 (GN-M), AB346 (GN-K)

Spitfire Vs (recorded as having been flown by 249 pilots at Malta, 1942/1943) subsequent deliveries included AB263, AB333, AB340, AB342, AB347, AB348, AB377 (T-E), AB388 (T-E), AB418, AB419, AB420, AB451 (GN-T), AB454, AB465 (T-R), AB535 (T-Z), AB562 (X-R), AR464, AR466 (T-R), AR488 (T-S), AR559 (T-W), BP844 (GN-W), BP845, BP846, BP849 (GN-U), BP850, BP866 (T-Q), BP867 (T-E), BP869 (T-K), BP874, BP878, BP951, BP955, BP961 (T-G), BP963, BP966 (T-V), BP969, BP974, BP975 (T-T), BP976 (T-C), BP978 (T-O/GN-O), BP983, BP990 (4-O), BR106, BR107 (C-22), BR108 (C-20/T-W), BR109 (C-30), BR110 (X-C/T-A), BR111 (C-18/T-M), BR112, BR118 (T-W/GN-W), BR119 (C-1/T-B), BR128 (3-W), BR130, BR131 (T-O), BR135, BR136, BR163, BR165 (C-23/T-Y), BR166, BR170 (T-B), BR173 (T-D), BR175 (C-51), BR176 (C-25), BR177 (T-E), BR184 (2-C/T-C), BR190 (2-A), BR194, BR195, BR198, BR199, BR203, BR226, BR227 (T-T), BR233 (T-Q), BR246 (C-40/T-J), BR251 (C-26/T-E), BR254 (X-G/T-G/T-E), BR293, BR290 (T-I), BR292 (T-M), BR295 (T-H), BR300, BR301 (UF-S), BR312, BR316, BR317, BR323 (T-S), BR324 (T-R), BR327, BR328, BR345, BR347 (T-Z), BR352 (GN-W), BR356, BR364, BR367, BR373 (T-N), BR377 (C-41/T-K), BR379 (T-V), BR380 (T-N/GN-N), BR382, BR463, BR529 (T-D), BR565 (T-U/T-T), BS166 (T-E), EF539 (T-F), EF646 (T-F), EN695, EN954, EN972, EN973 (T-T), EN976, EP117 (T-A), EP122, EP132 (T-J), EP135 (T-Z), EP136 (T-P), EP140 (T-M), EP186 (T-K), EP188 (T-Y), EP194 (T-H), EP196 (T-M), EP199 (T-K), EP201 (V-F/T-L/T-D), EP207, EP257, EP332, EP338 (T-A), EP340 (T-M), EP343 (T-V), EP374, EP448 (T-F), EP458 (X-P), EP517, EP519 (T-C), EP520 (T-V), EP557 (T-R), EP566 (T-V), EP622 (T-P), EP652, EP700 (T-Q), EP706 (T-L), EP708 (T-U), EP712 (T-C), EP728 (T-K/GN-K), EP829 (T-N), EP833 (T-F), EP835 (T-Z), EP928 (T-S), ER549 (T-U/GN-U), ER591 (T-M/GN-M), ER622 (T-P), ER728 (T-S), ER774

(T-T/GN-T), ER811 (T-J), ER819 (T-M), ER833 (T-F), ER878 (T-H/GN-H), JK465 (X/GN-X), JK803 (T-A), JK889, JK879 (T-B), JL346 (T-K/GN-K)

MALTA/BALKANS 1943 — 1944
Spitfire IXs included EN186, EN201, EN256 (GN-B), EN306 (GN-A), EN350 (GN-D), EN392 (GN-V), EN456 (GN-P), LZ811 (GN-P), MA500 (GN-Z)

BALKANS 1943 — 1944
Spitfire Vs included AR596 (GN-D), BP978 (GN-O), BR118 (GN-W), BR201, BR380 (GN-N), EF567, EF607, EF608, EF638 (GN-K), EF720, EP728 (GN-K), EP795, EP828 (GN-O), EP879, EP972, ER226, ER466, E539, ER549 (GN-U), ER565, ER591 (GN-M), ER596, ER673 (GN-F), ER774 (GN-T), ER783 (GN-L), ER874, ER878 (GN-H), ER889, ER928, ES257, ES284, ES299, ES306 GN-T), ES311, JG593, JK101 (GN-U), JK214, JK266, JK366 (GN-H), JK450, JK465 (GN-IX), JK532, JK564, JK625 (GN-K), JK660, JK678, JK723 (GN-V), JK725, JK817 (GN-Z), JK929, JL220, JL328, JL346 (GN-F), JL368, LZ822, LZ873, MA332, MA900

BALKANS 1944 — 1945
Mustang IIICs included FB306 (GN-C), FB308 (GN-E), FB309, FB327 (GN-S), FB328 (GN-X), FB330, HB851, HB859, HB869 (GN-W), HB883, HB884, HB892, HB896 (GN-Z), HB907 (GN-G), HB911, HB912 (GN-A), HB921 (GN-C), HB924 (GN-D), HB926, HB927, HB928 (GN-A), HB933 (GN-X), HB937, HB941, HB946, HB851, HB952 (GN-F), KH422, KH424 (GN-V), KH425, KH427 (GN-V), KH428, KH437, KH462, KH465, KH467, KH468, KH472 (GN-E), KH476, KH512 (GN-U), KH520 (GN-B), KH530, KH532, KH538, KH543, KH549, KH561 (GN-B), KH575 (GN-Z), KH594 (GN-Y), KH619 (GN-H), KH640 (GN-T)

BALKANS 1945
Spitfire IXs were EN145 (GN-C), EN461, EN513 (GN-B), EN530, JF953 (GN-G), JG123 (GN-A), MA485, MA533 (GN-F), MH894 (GN-T), MH899 (GN-W), MH956 (GN-X), MH980, MJ719 (GN-D), MJ730 (GN-Y), MK444 (GN-H), MK478, MT714, PT681; MH550 (GN-A) arrived to replace JG123 (GN-A)

Mustang IVDs were KH682 (GN-B), KH718 (GN-W), KH757 (GN-Z), KH762 (GN-H), KH811 (GN-E), KH835, KH870 (GN-X), KM144, KM231, KM247 (GN-F), KM258 (GN-A), KM268 (GN-D), KM293 (GN-T)

POSTWAR 1945 — 1969
Baltimore B5s (ex-500 Squadron) included FW367 (GN-P), FW609, FW718 (GN-F), FW739 (GN-Y), FW820 (GN-D), FW838 (GN-R), FW848 (GN-U), FW849 (GN-Q), FW865 (GN-J), FW866, FW880 (GN-T)

Mosquito FB26s included KA161, KA248, KA294, KA308, KA322, KA356, KA370 (GN-Q), KA372, KA378, KA417 (GN-C)

Tempest F6s included NX120 (GN-T), NX125 (GN-X), NX126 (GN-A), NX132 (GN-B), NX135 (GN-W), NX139 (GN-D), NX141 (GN-?), NX142 (GN-G), NX143 (GN-P), NX150 (GN-H), NX153 (GN-?), NX170 (GN-K), NX171 (GN-H), NX172 (GN-G), NX182 (GN-Q), NX200 (GN-F), NX203 (GN-D), NX208 (GN-N), NX209 (GN-E?), NX232 (GN-S), NX233 (GN-W), NX241 (GN-A), NX245 (GN-J), NX252 (GN-Q), NX263 (GN-M), NX268 (GN-?), NX281 (GN-F), NX284 (GN-C), NX285 (GN-B), SN232 (GN-N)

Harvard T2 FS741

Vampire FB5s included VV221/Y, VV435/A, VV536/B, VV552/T, VV553, VV608/D, VV622/P, VV658/V, VV691/O, VX473/B, VX989/R, VX990/M, VZ105/S, VZ118/C, VZ123/N, VZ180/K, VZ213/G, VZ268/S, VZ276/J, VZ343/W, VZ345/O, VZ304/X, WA102/O, WA104/T, WA108, WA132/Y, WA142/A

Meteor T7s included WA596, WA611, WA627, WF882, WG941, WG945, WG949

Vampire FB9s included WG889/T, WL496, WL501, WL606/C, WL612, WP991, WR102/V, WR104/W, WR122/H, WR126/A, WR155, WR192
Venom FB1s included WE459, WK392/R, WL931/B, WR126/A, WR287/S, WR296/A, WR301, WR303/B, WR307, WR319/Y, WR336, WR340/E, WR343, WR345/V, WR348/D, WR356/U, WR358/G, WR368/F, WR373/C, WR472/E, WR495

Vampire T11s included WE229, WZ552, XE886, XE946, XE991, XE996

Venom FB4s included WR358, WR375, WR380/E, WR381, WR398/H, WR399, WR412, WR420, WR436, WR439/V, WR443/Y, WR444/E, WR489/D, WR492/U, WR497/B, WR499/V, WR504/Z, WR506/W, WR507/S, WR520/T, WR527/C, WR529/A, WR531/R, WR533/F, WR541/A, WR542, WR547, WR560

Canberra B2s included WH638, WH647, WH650, WH655, WH872, WJ564, WJ626, WJ628, WK104, WK113, WD995 (replacement for WH655 which crash-landed 8/58)

Canberra B6s included WJ773, WJ780, WJ783, WT303, WT369, WT370, WT374, joined later by XH570 (all ex-139 Sqn); WJ777, WJ781

Canberra B15s (Akrotiri Wing) flown by 249 included WH948, WH956, WH964, WH970, WH971, WH972, WH983, WH984, WJ762, WT213

Canberra B16s (Akrotiri Wing) flown by 249 included WJ773, WJ774, WJ778, WJ780, WJ782, WJ783, WT302, WT303, WT306, WT369, WT372, WT373, WT374, XH570

Canberra T4s (Akrotiri Wing) flown by 249 included WH637, WJ566, WJ863, WJ872, WJ881

APPENDIX VII

Song popular with airmen based at RAF Sharjah in the mid-1950s, including those of 249 Squadron

RAF SHARJAH

Just below the border line
Sharjah is the spot
Where we are doomed to spend our time
In the land that God forgot

With prickly heat and scorpions
And black-faced natives too
Bang in the middle of nowhere
Four thousand miles from you

We airmen of the Air Force
Earn our measley pay
Guarding shieks with millions
For a few rupees a day

Living with our millions
And waiting to see our gals
Hoping that whilst we're away
They haven't wed our pals

These sweltering months at Sharjah
Are months we wish had gone
And when our tour is over
By jove we won't sign on

And when our time is over
We shall hear St Peter yell
"Come on boys of Sharjah
You've had your share of hell."

SELECT BIBLIOGRAPHY

Primary Souces

249 Squadron Operations Record Books (F540s) PRO Air 27 series; Combat Reports PRO Air 50/96.

Published Sources

Aces High: Christopher Shores & Clive Williams
Action Stations 4: Bruce Barrymore Halpenny
A Few of the Few: Dennis Newton
After the Battle: Then and Now: (edited by Winston G. Ramsey)
Air Wars and Aircraft: Victor Flintham
Battle of Britain Day: 15 September 1940: Dr Alfred Price
Battle of Britain: The Forgotten Months: John Foreman
Battle over Sussex: Pat Burgess & Andy Saunders
Black Crosses off my Wingtip: Sqn Ldr I.F. Kennedy DFC
British Combat Aircraft in Action Since 1945: David Oliver
Eastward: Air Chief Marshal Sir David Lee GBE CB
Flight from the Middle East: Air Chief Marshal Sir David Lee GBE CB
Fighter Pilot: The Diary of George Barclay (edited by Humphrey Wynn)
Fighters over Tunisia: Christopher Shores, Hans Ring and William Hess
Five Lives: Laddie Lucas
Flames over Malta: Richard Mifsud
Gun Button to Fire: Wg Cdr T.F. Neil DFC AFC
Malta Spitfire: George Beurling & Leslie Roberts
Malta: The Hurricane Years 1940-41: Christopher Shores and Brian Cull with Nicola Malizia
Malta: The Spitfire Year 1942: Christopher Shores and Brian Cull with Nicola Malizia
Malta: The Thorn in Rommel's Side: Laddie Lucas
Nicolson VC: Peter D. Mason
Men of the Battle of Britain: Kenneth G. Wynn
Onwards to Malta: Wg Cdr T.F. Neil DFC AFC
Operation Bograt: Donald Stones
Out of the Blue: Laddie Lucas
Spitfires over Israel: Brian Cull & Shlomo Aloni with David Nicolle
Spitfires over Malta: Paul Brennan & Ray Hesslyn
The Air Battle for Malta: Lord James Douglas-Hamilton
The Blitz: Then and Now, Vol 1 & 2: (edited by Winston G. Ramsey)
The Luftwaffe War Diaries: Cajus Bekker
Together We Fly: S.M-M
What if the Heavens Fall: Eric Clayton
Wings Aflame: Doug Stokes
Wings in the Sun: Air Chief Marshal Sir David Lee GBE CB
Wings of War: Laddie Lucas
Wings over Suez: Brian Cull with David Nicolle and Shlomo Aloni
1941: The Turning Point, Parts 1 & 2: John Foreman

Air-Britain RAF Aircraft Serial Registers series

Unpublished manuscripts

A Fringe of Winged Fear: Sqn Ldr D.P.F. Mac McCaig MBE AFC
A History of 249 Squadron: Flg Off W.H.A. Spy Boulton
An Ordinary Marching Airman: Terry Gladwell
Untitled Ms: Leighton Fletcher

Other souces include

Extracts from Bill Metcalf's diary (courtesy of NWMA Malta); Brian Cooper's journal (RAF Akrotiri, 1956); various logbooks.

INDEX

249 SQUADRON PERSONNEL

(Ranks shown are those held while serving with the Squadron, or when otherwise mentioned in the narrative.)

OTHERS

GERMAN PERSONNEL

ITALIAN PERSONNEL